TV in the USA

TV in the USA

A HISTORY OF ICONS, IDOLS, AND IDEAS

Volume 2: 1970s–1980s

VINCENT LOBRUTTO

GREENWOOD™

An Imprint of ABC-CLIO, LLC
Santa Barbara, California • Denver, Colorado

Library of Congress Cataloging-in-Publication Data

Names: LoBrutto, Vincent, author.
Title: TV in the USA : a history of icons, idols, and ideas / Vincent LoBrutto.
Description: Santa Barbara, California : Greenwood, 2018. | Includes bibliographical references and index.
Identifiers: LCCN 2017016821 (print) | LCCN 2017039414 (ebook) | ISBN 9781440829734 (ebook) | ISBN 9781440829727 (set : alk. paper) | ISBN 9781440848452 (volume 1 : alk. paper) | ISBN 9781440848469 (volume 2 : alk. paper) | ISBN 9781440848476 (volume 3 : alk. paper)
Subjects: LCSH: Television programs—United States—History—20th century. | Television programs—United States—History—21st century.
Classification: LCC PN1992.3.U5 (ebook) | LCC PN1992.3.U5 L68 2018 (print) | DDC 791.450973—dc23
LC record available at https://lccn.loc.gov/2017016821

ISBN: 978-1-4408-2972-7 (set)
978-1-4408-4845-2 (vol. 1)
978-1-4408-4846-9 (vol. 2)
978-1-4408-4847-6 (vol. 3)
978-1-4408-2973-4 (ebook)

22 21 20 19 18 1 2 3 4 5

This book is also available as an eBook.

Greenwood
An Imprint of ABC-CLIO, LLC

ABC-CLIO, LLC
130 Cremona Drive, P.O. Box 1911
Santa Barbara, California 93116-1911
www.abc-clio.com

This book is printed on acid-free paper ♾

Manufactured in the United States of America

Contents

Guide to Related Topics

ACTION

The A Team (Vol. 2: The 1970s–1980s)
The Avengers (Vol. 1: The 1950s–1960s)
Baywatch (Vol. 2: The 1970s–1980s)
Blindspot (Vol. 3: The 1990s–Present)
Buffy the Vampire Slayer (Vol. 3: The 1990s–Present)
Criminal Minds (Vol. 3: The 1990s–Present)
Dark Angel (Vol. 3: The 1990s–Present)
The Fugitive (Vol. 1: The 1950s–1960s)
Hawaii Five-0 (Vol. 1: The 1950s–1960s)
Hawaii Five-0 (Vol. 3: The 1990s–Present)
Miami Vice (Vol. 2: The 1970s–1980s)
Mission Impossible (Vol. 1: The 1950s–1960s)
NCIS (Vol. 3: The 1990s–Present)
The Pretender (Vol. 3: The 1990s–Present)

ACTION/ADVENTURE

The A Team (Vol. 2: The 1970s–1980s)
The Adventures of Superman (Vol. 1: The 1950s–1960s)
Alias (Vol. 3: The 1990s–Present)
Angel (Vol. 3: The 1990s–Present)
Batman (Vol. 1: The 1950s–1960s)
The Bionic Woman (Vol. 1: The 1950s–1960s)
Black Sails (Vol. 3: The 1990s–Present)
Flipper (Vol. 1: The 1950s–1960s)
Hawaiian Eye (Vol. 1: The 1950s–1960s)
Hercules: The Legendary Journeys (Vol. 3: The 1990s–Present)
Highlander: The Series (Vol. 3: The 1990s–Present)
I Spy (Vol. 1: The 1950s–1960s)
The Incredible Hulk (Vol. 2: The 1970s–1980s)
Kung Fu (Vol. 2: The 1970s–1980s)
La Femme Nikita (Vol. 3: The 1990s–Present)
Lost (Vol. 3: The 1990s–Present)
MacGyver (Vol. 2: The 1970s–1980s)
Run for Your Life (Vol. 1: The 1950s–1960s)
Sea Hunt (Vol. 1: The 1950s–1960s)
The Six Million Dollar Man (Vol. 2: The 1970s–1980s)
Sky King (Vol. 1: The 1950s–1960s)
Stargate SG-1 (Vol. 3: The 1990s–Present)
Star Trek (Vol. 1: The 1950s–1960s)
Star Trek: Deep Space Nine (Vol. 3: The 1990s–Present)
Star Trek: The Next Generation (Vol. 2: The 1970s–1980s)
Star Trek: Voyager (Vol. 3: The 1990s–Present)
Supertrain (Vol. 2: The 1970s–1980s)
Tarzan (Vol. 1: The 1950s–1960s)
Then Came Bronson (Vol. 1: The 1950s–1960s)
The Wild Wild West (Vol. 1: The 1950s–1960s)
Wonder Woman (Vol. 2: The 1970s–1980s)
Xena: Warrior Princess (Vol. 3: The 1990s–Present)
The Young Indiana Jones Chronicles (Vol. 3: The 1990s–Present)
Zorro (Vol. 1: The 1950s–1960s)

ANIMALS

Animal Planet (Vol. 3: The 1990s–Present)
Flipper (Vol. 1: The 1950s–1960s)
Lassie (Vol. 1: The 1950s–1960s)
Mutual of Omaha's Wild Kingdom (Vol. 1: The 1950s–1960s)
Those Amazing Animals (Vol. 2: The 1970s–1980s)
Training Dogs the Woodhouse Way (Vol. 2: The 1970s–1980s)

ANIMATED

The Adventures of Jimmy Neutron: Boy Genius (Vol. 3: The 1990s–Present)
Bob's Burgers (Vol. 3: The 1990s–Present)
Cartoon Network (Vol. 3: The 1990s–Present)
Colonel Bleep (Vol. 1: The 1950s–1960s)
The Critic (Vol. 3: The 1990s–Present)
Dilbert (Vol. 3: The 1990s–Present)
Dr. Katz: Professional Therapist (Vol. 3: The 1990s–Present)
Family Guy (Vol. 3: The 1990s–Present)
Fat Albert and the Cosby Kids (Vol. 2: The 1970s–1980s)
The Flintstones (Vol. 1: The 1950s–1960s)
Futurama (Vol. 3: The 1990s–Present)
The Jetsons (Vol. 1: The 1950s–1960s)
King of the Hill (Vol. 3: The 1990s–Present)
Mr. Magoo (Vol. 1: The 1950s–1960s)
Pokémon (Vol. 3: The 1990s–Present)
The Ren & Stimpy Show (Vol. 3: The 1990s–Present)
Rocky and His Friends (Vol. 1: The 1950s–1960s)
Rugrats (Vol. 3: The 1990s–Present)
The Simpsons (Vol. 2: The 1970s–1980s)
South Park (Vol. 3: The 1990s–Present)
SpongeBob Squarepants (Vol. 3: The 1990s–Present)
Top Cat (Vol. 1: The 1950s–1960s)

ANIMATED ADULT

Cartoon Network (Vol. 3: The 1990s–Present)
The Critic (Vol. 3: The 1990s–Present)
Dr. Katz: Professional Therapist (Vol. 3: The 1990s–Present)
Family Guy (Vol. 3: The 1990s–Present)
King of the Hill (Vol. 3: The 1990s–Present)
South Park (Vol. 3: The 1990s–Present)

ANIMATED SITCOMS

Bob's Burgers (Vol. 3: The 1990s–Present)
Cartoon Network (Vol. 3: The 1990s–Present)
Crusader Rabbit (Vol. 1: The 1950s–1960s)

ANTHOLOGY

ABC Afterschool Specials (Vol. 2: The 1970s–1980s)
Alfred Hitchcock Presents/The Alfred Hitchcock Hour (Vol. 1: The 1950s–1960s)
Alive from Off Center (Vol. 2: The 1970s–1980s)
Amazing Stories (Vol. 2: The 1970s–1980s)
American Crime (Vol. 3: The 1990s–Present)
American Horror Story (Vol. 3: The 1990s–Present)
Faerie Tale Theatre (Vol. 2: The 1970s–1980s)
Night Gallery (Vol. 2: The 1970s–1980s)
The Outer Limits (Vol. 1: The 1950s–1960s)
Playhouse 90 (Vol. 1: The 1950s–1960s)
Police Story (Vol. 2: The 1970s–1980s)
Ray Bradbury Theater (Vol. 2: The 1970s–1980s)
Route 66 (Vol. 1: The 1950s–1960s)
Serling, Rod (Vol. 1: The 1950s–1960s)
Tales from the Crypt (Vol. 2: The 1970s–1980s)
Tales from the Darkside (Vol. 2: The 1970s–1980s)
Thriller (Vol. 1: The 1950s–1960s)
True Detective (Vol. 3: The 1990s–Present)
The Twilight Zone (Vol. 1: The 1950s–1960s)

ANTHOLOGY DRAMA

The Outer Limits (Vol. 1: The 1950s–1960s)
Playhouse 90 (Vol. 1: The 1950s–1960s)
Police Story (Vol. 2: The 1970s–1980s)
Route 66 (Vol. 1: The 1950s–1960s)
Serling, Rod (Vol. 1: The 1950s–1960s)
Thriller (Vol. 1: The 1950s–1960s)
True Detective (Vol. 3: The 1990s–Present)
The Twilight Zone (Vol. 1: The 1950s–1960s)

THE ARTS

Art and Television (Vol. 1: The 1950s–1960s)
Book Beat (Vol. 1: The 1950s–1960s)
The Joy of Painting (Vol. 2: The 1970s–1980s)
PBS (Public Broadcasting Service) (Vol. 2: The 1970s–1980s)
Sneak Previews (Vol. 2: The 1970s–1980s)

BLACK COMEDY

Arrested Development (Vol. 3: The 1990s–Present)
Celebrity Deathmatch (Vol. 3: The 1990s–Present)
Childrens Hospital (Vol. 3: The 1990s–Present)
Curb Your Enthusiasm (Vol. 3: The 1990s–Present)

BLAXPLOITATION

Get Christie Love! (Vol. 2: The 1970s–1980s)

CHILDREN'S AND ADOLESCENT

ABC Afterschool Specials (Vol. 2: The 1970s–1980s)
The Adventures of Jimmy Neutron: Boy Genius (Vol. 3: The 1990s–Present)
The All New Mickey Mouse Club (Vol. 2: The 1970s–1980s)
Captain Kangaroo (Vol. 1: The 1950s–1960s)
Ding Dong School (Vol. 1: The 1950s–1960s)
The Electric Company (Vol. 2: The 1970s–1980s)
Faerie Tale Theatre (Vol. 2: The 1970s–1980s)
Fat Albert and the Cosby Kids (Vol. 2: The 1970s–1980s)
Flipper (Vol. 1: The 1950s–1960s)
The Gumby Show (Vol. 1: The 1950s–1960s)
Howdy Doody (Vol. 1: The 1950s–1960s)
Kukla, Fran and Ollie (Vol. 1: The 1950s–1960s)
Lassie (Vol. 1: The 1950s–1960s)
The Mickey Mouse Club (Vol. 1: The 1950s–1960s)
Mister Rogers' Neighborhood (Vol. 1: The 1950s–1960s)
Pee-Wee's Playhouse (Vol. 2: The 1970s–1980s)
The Pinky Lee Show (Vol. 1: The 1950s–1960s)
Sesame Street (Vol. 1: The 1950s–1960s)
The Shari Lewis Show (Vol. 1: The 1950s–1960s)
SpongeBob Squarepants (Vol. 3: The 1990s–Present)
The Soupy Sales Show (Vol. 1: The 1950s–1960s)
Watch Mr. Wizard (Vol. 1: The 1950s–1960s)
Winky-Dink and You (Vol. 1: The 1950s–1960s)
Zorro (Vol. 1: The 1950s–1960s)

CITATIONS AND AWARDS

Peabody Award (Vol. 1: The 1950s–1960s)

CLAYMATION

Celebrity Deathmatch (Vol. 3: The 1990s–Present)
Davey and Goliath (Vol. 1: The 1950s–1960s)
The Gumby Show (Vol. 1: The 1950s–1960s)

COMEDY

Ally McBeal (Vol. 3: The 1990s–Present)
Amos 'n' Andy (Vol. 1: The 1950s–1960s)
Batman (Vol. 1: The 1950s–1960s)
The Bob and Ray Show (Vol. 1: The 1950s–1960s)
Candid Camera (Vol. 1: The 1950s–1960s)
Car 54 Where Are You? (Vol. 1: The 1950s–1960s)
The Colbert Report (Vol. 3: The 1990s–Present)
Curb Your Enthusiasm (Vol. 3: The 1990s–Present)
Da Ali G Show (Vol. 3: The 1990s–Present)
The Daily Show with Jon Stewart (Vol. 3: The 1990s–Present)
Dilbert (Vol. 3: The 1990s–Present)
Family Guy (Vol. 3: The 1990s–Present)
Fernwood 2-Night (Vol. 2: The 1970s–1980s)
The Flying Nun (Vol. 1: The 1950s–1960s)
Fractured Flickers (Vol. 1: The 1950s–1960s)
George Lopez (Vol. 3: The 1990s–Present)
Get Smart (Vol. 1: The 1950s–1960s)
Gilligan's Island (Vol. 1: The 1950s–1960s)
The Hathaways (Vol. 1: The 1950s–1960s)
In Living Color (Vol. 3: The 1990s–Present)
It's Garry Shandling's Show (Vol. 2: The 1970s–1980s)
The Jack Benny Program (Vol. 1: The 1950s–1960s)
The Jerry Lewis Show (Vol. 1: The 1950s–1960s)
King of the Hill (Vol. 3: The 1990s–Present)
Last Comic Standing (Vol. 3: The 1990s–Present)
MADtv (Vol. 3: The 1990s–Present)
Malcolm in the Middle (Vol. 3: The 1990s–Present)
The Man Show (Vol. 3: The 1990s–Present)
Michael Nesmith in Television Parts (Vol. 2: The 1970s–1980s)
Modern Family (Vol. 3: The 1990s–Present)
The Monkees (Vol. 1: The 1950s–1960s)
Morton & Hayes (Vol. 3: The 1990s–Present)
My Favorite Martian (Vol. 1: The 1950s–1960s)
My Name Is Earl (Vol. 3: The 1990s–Present)
Mystery Science Theater 3000 (Vol. 2: The 1970s–1980s)
New Girl (Vol. 3: The 1990s–Present)
The Office (Vol. 3: The 1990s–Present)
Police Academy: The Series (Vol. 3: The 1990s–Present)
Police Squad! (Vol. 2: The 1970s–1980s)
Portlandia (Vol. 3: The 1990s–Present)
The Red Skelton Show (Vol. 1: The 1950s–1960s)

Rowan & Martin's Laugh-In (Vol. 1: The 1950s–1960s)
Saturday Night Live (Vol. 2: The 1970s–1980s)
Scrubs (Vol. 3: The 1990s–Present)
The Smothers Brothers Comedy Hour (Vol. 1: The 1950s–1960s)
The Sonny and Cher Comedy Hour (Vol. 2: The 1970s–1980s)
The Spike Jones Show (Vol. 1: The 1950s–1960s)
Talk Soup (Vol. 3: The 1990s–Present)
That Was the Week That Was (Vol. 1: The 1950s–1960s)
3rd Rock from the Sun (Vol. 3: The 1990s–Present)
30 Rock (Vol. 3: The 1990s–Present)
The Tracey Ullman Show (Vol. 2: The 1970s–1980s)
You'll Never Get Rich (Vol. 1: The 1950s–1960s)

COMEDY SKETCH SHOWS

Chappelle's Show (Vol. 3: The 1990s–Present)
Fridays (Vol. 2: The 1970s–1980s)
In Living Color (Vol. 3: The 1990s–Present)
MADtv (Vol. 3: The 1990s–Present)
Portlandia (Vol. 3: The 1990s–Present)
Rowan & Martin's Laugh-In (Vol. 1: The 1950s–1960s)
Saturday Night Live (Vol. 2: The 1970s–1980s)
Second City T.V. (Vol. 2: The 1970s–1980s)
Super Dave (Vol. 2: The 1970s–1980s)
The Tracey Ullman Show (Vol. 2: The 1970s–1980s)

COMMERCIALS

Commercials of the Era (Vol. 1: The 1950s–1960s)

COOKING

Child, Julia (Vol. 1: The 1950s–1960s)
Food Network (Vol. 3: The 1990s–Present)
The Frugal Gourmet (Vol. 2: The 1970s–1980s)
The Galloping Gourmet (Vol. 1: The 1950s–1960s)

COOKING COMPETITION

Food Network (Vol. 3: The 1990s–Present)
Hell's Kitchen (Vol. 3: The 1990s–Present)

COURT

Court TV (Vol. 3: The 1990s–Present)
Divorce Court (Vol. 1: The 1950s–1960s)
Night Court (Vol. 2: The 1970s–1980s)
The People's Court (Vol. 2: The 1970s–1980s)

CRIME

American Crime (Vol. 3: The 1990s–Present)
America's Most Wanted (Vol. 2: The 1970s–1980s)
Blindspot (Vol. 3: The 1990s–Present)
Boardwalk Empire (Vol. 3: The 1990s–Present)
Bones (Vol. 3: The 1990s–Present)
Breaking Bad (Vol. 3: The 1990s–Present)
Charlie's Angels (Vol. 2: The 1970s–1980s)
Commander in Chief (Vol. 3: The 1990s–Present)
Criminal Minds (Vol. 3: The 1990s–Present)
Crossing Jordan (Vol. 3: The 1990s–Present)
CSI: Crime Scene Investigation (Vol. 3: The 1990s–Present)
Damages (Vol. 3: The 1990s–Present)
Dexter (Vol. 3: The 1990s–Present)
Diagnosis Murder (Vol. 3: The 1990s–Present)
Dragnet (Vol. 1: The 1950s–1960s)
Hannibal (Vol. 3: The 1990s–Present)
Homeland (Vol. 3: The 1990s–Present)
Homicide: Life on the Streets (Vol. 3: The 1990s–Present)
Honey West (Vol. 1: The 1950s–1960s)
Ironside (Vol. 1: The 1950s–1960s)
Justified (Vol. 3: The 1990s–Present)
The Magician (Vol. 2: The 1970s–1980s)
McCloud (Vol. 2: The 1970s–1980s)
Miami Vice (Vol. 2: The 1970s–1980s)
The Mod Squad (Vol. 1: The 1950s–1960s)
The Night Stalker (Vol. 2: The 1970s–1980s)
Prison Break (Vol. 3: The 1990s–Present)
Profiler (Vol. 3: The 1990s–Present)
Sherlock (Vol. 3: The 1990s–Present)
The Shield (Vol. 3: The 1990s–Present)
The Six Million Dollar Man (Vol. 2: The 1970s–1980s)
Sons of Anarchy (Vol. 3: The 1990s–Present)
The Sopranos (Vol. 3: The 1990s–Present)
True Detective (Vol. 3: The 1990s–Present)
24 (Vol. 3: The 1990s–Present)

The Untouchables (Vol. 1: The 1950s–1960s)
The Wire (Vol. 3: The 1990s–Present)
Wiseguy (Vol. 2: The 1970s–1980s)

DANCE COMPETITION

America's Got Talent (Vol. 3: The 1990s–Present)
Dance Fever (Vol. 2: The 1970s–1980s)
Dancing with the Stars (Vol. 3: The 1990s–Present)
So You Think You Can Dance (Vol. 3: The 1990s–Present)

DAYTIME TALK AND VARIETY

Geraldo (Vol. 2: The 1970s–1980s)
Live with Regis and Kathie Lee (Vol. 2: The 1970s–1980s)
The Oprah Winfrey Show (Vol. 2: The 1970s–1980s)
The Rosie O'Donnell Show (Vol. 3: The 1990s–Present)

DETECTIVE SHOWS

Alien Nation (Vol. 2: The 1970s–1980s)
Baretta (Vol. 2: The 1970s–1980s)
Charlie Chan (Vol. 1: The 1950s–1960s)
Columbo (Vol. 2: The 1970s–1980s)
Dragnet (Vol. 1: The 1950s–1960s)
Hawaiian Eye (Vol. 1: The 1950s–1960s)
Johnny Staccato (Vol. 1: The 1950s–1960s)
Moonlighting (Vol. 2: The 1970s–1980s)
Monk (Vol. 3: The 1990s–Present)
77 Sunset Strip (Vol. 1: The 1950s–1960s)
The Streets of San Francisco (Vol. 2: The 1970s–1980s)

DOCUMENTARIES

Behind the Music (Vol. 3: The 1990s–Present)
Biography (Vol. 1: The 1950s–1960s)
E! True Hollywood Story (Vol. 3: The 1990s–Present)
In Search Of . . . (Vol. 2: The 1970s–1980s)
Joseph Campbell and the Power of Myth (Vol. 2: The 1970s–1980s)
P.O.V. (Vol. 2: The 1970s–1980s)
See It Now (Vol. 1: The 1950s–1960s)
This Is Your Life (Vol. 1: The 1950s–1960s)
The Twentieth Century (Vol. 1: The 1950s–1960s)
Victory at Sea (Vol. 1: The 1950s–1960s)
Vietnam: A Television History (Vol. 2: The 1970s–1980s)

DRAMA

The Affair (Vol. 3: The 1990s–Present)
The Agency (Vol. 3: The 1990s–Present)
Alfred Hitchcock Presents/The Alfred Hitchcock Hour (Vol. 1: The 1950s–1960s)
Ally McBeal (Vol. 3: The 1990s–Present)
American Crime (Vol. 3: The 1990s–Present)
The Americans (Vol. 3: The 1990s–Present)
Baywatch (Vol. 2: The 1970s–1980s)
Beauty and the Beast (Vol. 2: The 1970s–1980s)
Behind the Candelabra (Vol. 3: The 1990s–Present)
Believe (Vol. 3: The 1990s–Present)
The Bionic Woman (Vol. 1: The 1950s–1960s)
Bitten (Vol. 3: The 1990s–Present)
Blindspot (Vol. 3: The 1990s–Present)
Bones (Vol. 3: The 1990s–Present)
Boston Public (Vol. 3: The 1990s–Present)
Breaking Bad (Vol. 3: The 1990s–Present)
Brooklyn Bridge (Vol. 3: The 1990s–Present)
Charlie Chan (Vol. 1: The 1950s–1960s)
Charlie's Angels (Vol. 2: The 1970s–1980s)
China Beach (Vol. 2: The 1970s–1980s)
CHiPs (Vol. 2: The 1970s–1980s)
The Closer (Vol. 3: The 1990s–Present)
Crime Story (Vol. 2: The 1970s–1980s)
Dark Angel (Vol. 3: The 1990s–Present)
Family (Vol. 2: The 1970s–1980s)
Fantasy Island (Vol. 2: The 1970s–1980s)
Felicity (Vol. 3: The 1990s–Present)
Friday Night Lights (Vol. 3: The 1990s–Present)
The Fugitive (Vol. 1: The 1950s–1960s)
Game of Thrones (Vol. 3: The 1990s–Present)
Hannibal (Vol. 3: The 1990s–Present)
Heroes (Vol. 3: The 1990s–Present)
Highlander: The Series (Vol. 3: The 1990s–Present)
House (Vol. 3: The 1990s–Present)
House of Cards (Vol. 3: The 1990s–Present)
The Incredible Hulk (Vol. 2: The 1970s–1980s)
Kojak (Vol. 2: The 1970s–1980s)
Las Vegas (Vol. 3: The 1990s–Present)
Little House on the Prairie (Vol. 2: The 1970s–1980s)

Mad Men (Vol. 3: The 1990s–Present)
The Magician (Vol. 2: The 1970s–1980s)
Max Headroom (Vol. 2: The 1970s–1980s)
McCloud (Vol. 2: The 1970s–1980s)
The Mentalist (Vol. 3: The 1990s–Present)
The Millionaire (Vol. 1: The 1950s–1960s)
The Mod Squad (Vol. 1: The 1950s–1960s)
NCIS (Vol. 3: The 1990s–Present)
Night Gallery (Vol. 2: The 1970s–1980s)
NYPD Blue (Vol. 3: The 1990s–Present)
The Paper Chase (Vol. 2: The 1970s–1980s)
Picket Fences (Vol. 3: The 1990s–Present)
Prison Break (Vol. 3: The 1990s–Present)
The Psychiatrist (Vol. 2: The 1970s–1980s)
Run for Your Life (Vol. 1: The 1950s–1960s)
Sex and the City (Vol. 3: The 1990s–Present)
The Shield (Vol. 3: The 1990s–Present)
Sisters (Vol. 3: The 1990s–Present)
Six Feet Under (Vol. 3: The 1990s–Present)
The Six Million Dollar Man (Vol. 2: The 1970s–1980s)
Skag (Vol. 2: The 1970s–1980s)
The Sopranos (Vol. 3: The 1990s–Present)
Supertrain (Vol. 2: The 1970s–1980s)
Then Came Bronson (Vol. 1: The 1950s–1960s)
thirtysomething (Vol. 2: The 1970s–1980s)
The Untouchables (Vol. 1: The 1950s–1960s)
The Waltons (Vol. 2: The 1970s–1980s)
The West Wing (Vol. 3: The 1990s–Present)
The White Shadow (Vol. 2: The 1970s–1980s)
The Wire (Vol. 3: The 1990s–Present)

DRAMEDY

Ally McBeal (Vol. 3: The 1990s–Present)
The Big C (Vol. 3: The 1990s–Present)
The Commish (Vol. 3: The 1990s–Present)
Diagnosis Murder (Vol. 3: The 1990s–Present)
Doogie Howser, M.D. (Vol. 2: The 1970s–1980s)
Eight Is Enough (Vol. 2: The 1970s–1980s)
Enlightened (Vol. 3: The 1990s–Present)
Gilmore Girls (Vol. 3: The 1990s–Present)
Girls (Vol. 3: The 1990s–Present)
Glee (Vol. 3: The 1990s–Present)
The Goldbergs (Vol. 1: The 1950s–1960s)
Louie (Vol. 3: The 1990s–Present)
*M*A*S*H* (Vol. 2: The 1970s–1980s)
Monk (Vol. 3: The 1990s–Present)
Northern Exposure (Vol. 3: The 1990s–Present)
Orange Is the New Black (Vol. 3: The 1990s–Present)
Oz (Vol. 3: The 1990s–Present)
Rescue Me (Vol. 3: The 1990s–Present)
Room 222 (Vol. 1: The 1950s–1960s)
Scrubs (Vol. 3: The 1990s–Present)
Tremé (Vol. 3: The 1990s–Present)
United States (Vol. 2: The 1970s–1980s)

EDUCATIONAL

Ding Dong School (Vol. 1: The 1950s–1960s)
Meeting of Minds (Vol. 2: The 1970s–1980s)
Mister Rogers' Neighborhood (Vol. 1: The 1950s–1960s)
PBS (Public Broadcasting Service) (Vol. 2: The 1970s–1980s)
Sesame Street (Vol. 1: The 1950s–1960s)
Watch Mr. Wizard (Vol. 1: The 1950s–1960s)
You Are There (Vol. 1: The 1950s–1960s)

ENTERTAINMENT NEWS

Access Hollywood (Vol. 3: The 1990s–Present)
Entertainment Tonight (Vol. 2: The 1970s–1980s)
Extra: The Entertainment Magazine (Vol. 3: The 1990s–Present)
Talk Soup (Vol. 3: The 1990s–Present)

ESPIONAGE

The Agency (Vol. 3: The 1990s–Present)
Alias (Vol. 3: The 1990s–Present)
The Americans (Vol. 3: The 1990s–Present)
The Avengers (Vol. 1: The 1950s–1960s)
Get Smart (Vol. 1: The 1950s–1960s)
The Girl from U.N.C.L.E. (Vol. 1: The 1950s–1960s)
Homeland (Vol. 3: The 1990s–Present)
I Spy (Vol. 1: The 1950s–1960s)
The Man from U.N.C.L.E (Vol. 1: The 1950s–1960s)
Mission Impossible (Vol. 1: The 1950s–1960s)
The Prisoner (Vol. 1: The 1950s–1960s)
The Saint (Vol. 1: The 1950s–1960s)
24 (Vol. 3: The 1990s–Present)

EXERCISE

Body by Jake (Vol. 2: The 1970s–1980s)
The Jack LaLanne Show (Vol. 1: The 1950s–1960s)
The Richard Simmons Show (Vol. 2: The 1970s–1980s)

EXPERIMENTAL TELEVISION

Alive from Off Center (Vol. 2: The 1970s–1980s)
Art and Television (Vol. 1: The 1950s–1960s)
Max Headroom (Vol. 2: The 1970s–1980s)

FAMILY DRAMA

Family (Vol. 2: The 1970s–1980s)
Gilmore Girls (Vol. 3: The 1990s–Present)
Highway to Heaven (Vol. 2: The 1970s–1980s)
Parenthood (Vol. 3: The 1990s–Present)
Party of Five (Vol. 3: The 1990s–Present)
Sisters (Vol. 3: The 1990s–Present)

FAMILY SITCOMS

The Adventures of Ozzie and Harriet (Vol. 1: The 1950s–1960s)
The Cosby Show (Vol. 2: The 1970s–1980s)
The Donna Reed Show (Vol. 1: The 1950s–1960s)
Family Affair (Vol. 1: The 1950s–1960s)
Father Knows Best (Vol. 1: The 1950s–1960s)
Full House (Vol. 2: The 1970s–1980s)
Happy Days (Vol. 2: The 1970s–1980s)
The Jeffersons (Vol. 2: The 1970s–1980s)
Leave It to Beaver (Vol. 1: The 1950s–1960s)
Malcolm in the Middle (Vol. 3: The 1990s–Present)
Modern Family (Vol. 3: The 1990s–Present)
My Three Sons (Vol. 1: The 1950s–1960s)
Webster (Vol. 2: The 1970s–1980s)
The Wonder Years (Vol. 2: The 1970s–1980s)

FANTASY

Amazing Stories (Vol. 2: The 1970s–1980s)
Angel (Vol. 3: The 1990s–Present)
Beauty and the Beast (Vol. 2: The 1970s–1980s)
Believe (Vol. 3: The 1990s–Present)
Bewitched (Vol. 1: The 1950s–1960s)
Bitten (Vol. 3: The 1990s–Present)
Buffy the Vampire Slayer (Vol. 3: The 1990s–Present)
Faerie Tale Theatre (Vol. 2: The 1970s–1980s)
Game of Thrones (Vol. 3: The 1990s–Present)
Hercules: The Legendary Journeys (Vol. 3: The 1990s–Present)
Highlander: The Series (Vol. 3: The 1990s–Present)
Highway to Heaven (Vol. 2: The 1970s–1980s)
Night Gallery (Vol. 2: The 1970s–1980s)
The Outer Limits (Vol. 1: The 1950s–1960s)
Resurrection (Vol. 3: The 1990s–Present)
Topper (Vol. 1: The 1950s–1960s)
The Twilight Zone (Vol. 1: The 1950s–1960s)
Xena: Warrior Princess (Vol. 3: The 1990s–Present)

FINANCIAL PROGRAMMING

Adam Smith's Money World (Vol. 2: The 1970s–1980s)
Wall $treet Week with Louis Rukeyser (Vol. 2: The 1970s–1980s)

GAME SHOWS

Are You Smarter Than a Fifth Grader? (Vol. 3: The 1990s–Present)
The Chair (Vol. 3: The 1990s–Present)
The Dating Game (Vol. 1: The 1950s–1960s)
Deal or No Deal (Vol. 3: The 1990s–Present)
Family Feud (Vol. 2: The 1970s–1980s)
Game Show Network (Vol. 3: The 1990s–Present)
The Gong Show (Vol. 2: The 1970s–1980s)
The Hollywood Squares (Vol. 1: The 1950s–1960s)
I've Got a Secret (Vol. 1: The 1950s–1960s)
Jeopardy! (Vol. 1: The 1950s–1960s)
The Krypton Factor (Vol. 2: The 1970s–1980s)
Let's Make a Deal (Vol. 1: The 1950s–1960s)
The Newlywed Game (Vol. 1: The 1950s–1960s)
1 vs. 100 (Vol. 3: The 1990s–Present)
The Price Is Right (Vol. 1: The 1950s–1960s)
Queen for a Day (Vol. 1: The 1950s–1960s)
Supermarket Sweep (Vol. 1: The 1950s–1960s)
$10,000 Pyramid (Vol. 2: The 1970s–1980s)
To Tell the Truth (Vol. 1: The 1950s–1960s)
Twenty-One (Vol. 1: The 1950s–1960s)
What's My Line? (Vol. 1: The 1950s–1960s)
Who Wants to Be a Millionaire? (Vol. 3: The 1990s–Present)

Win Ben Stein's Money (Vol. 3: The 1990s–Present)
You Bet Your Life (Vol. 1: The 1950s–1960s)

HOME IMPROVEMENT

American Dream Builders (Vol. 3: The 1990s–Present)
HGTV (Home and Garden Television) (Vol. 3: The 1990s–Present)
This Old House (Vol. 2: The 1970s–1980s)

HORROR

Amazing Stories (Vol. 2: The 1970s–1980s)
American Horror Story (Vol. 3: The 1990s–Present)
Angel (Vol. 3: The 1990s–Present)
Bitten (Vol. 3: The 1990s–Present)
Buffy the Vampire Slayer (Vol. 3: The 1990s–Present)
Dark Shadows (Vol. 1: The 1950s–1960s)
Hannibal (Vol. 3: The 1990s–Present)
Night Gallery (Vol. 2: The 1970s–1980s)
The Night Stalker (Vol. 2: The 1970s–1980s)
The Outer Limits (Vol. 1: The 1950s–1960s)
Tales from the Crypt (Vol. 2: The 1970s–1980s)
Tales from the Darkside (Vol. 2: The 1970s–1980s)
Thriller (Vol. 1: The 1950s–1960s)
Twin Peaks (Vol. 3: The 1990s–Present)
The Walking Dead (Vol. 3: The 1990s–Present)
The X-Files (Vol. 3: The 1990s–Present)

HORROR/COMEDY

The Addams Family (Vol. 1: The 1950s–1960s)
The Munsters (Vol. 1: The 1950s–1960s)

HUMAN INTEREST

You Asked for It (Vol. 1: The 1950s–1960s)

INFLUENTIAL INDIVIDUALS

Allen, Steve (Vol. 1: The 1950s–1960s)
Arledge, Roone (Vol. 1: The 1950s–1960s)
Ball, Lucille (Vol. 1: The 1950s–1960s)
Barris, Chuck (Vol. 1: The 1950s–1960s)
Berle, Milton (Vol. 1: The 1950s–1960s)
Brothers, Dr. Joyce (Vol. 1: The 1950s–1960s)
Burns, George (Vol. 1: The 1950s–1960s)
Caesar, Sid (Vol. 1: The 1950s–1960s)
Cannell, Stephen J. (Vol. 2: The 1970s–1980s)
Child, Julia (Vol. 1: The 1950s–1960s)
Clark, Dick (Vol. 1: The 1950s–1960s)
Coe, Fred (Vol. 1: The 1950s–1960s)
Cronkite, Walter (Vol. 1: The 1950s–1960s)
Disney, Walt (Vol. 1: The 1950s–1960s)
Falwell, Jerry (Vol. 2: The 1970s–1980s)
Gleason, Jackie (Vol. 1: The 1950s–1960s)
Godfrey, Arthur (Vol. 1: The 1950s–1960s)
Goldenson, Leonard (Vol. 1: The 1950s–1960s)
Goodson, Mark, and Bill Todman (Vol. 1: The 1950s–1960s)
Hope, Bob (Vol. 1: The 1950s–1960s)
Kovacs, Ernie (Vol. 1: The 1950s–1960s)
Lear, Norman (Vol. 2: The 1970s–1980s)
Leno, Jay (Vol. 3: The 1990s–Present)
Letterman, David (Vol. 3: The 1990s–Present)
McLuhan, Marshall (Vol. 1: The 1950s–1960s)
Miner, Worthington (Vol. 1: The 1950s–1960s)
Moore, Garry (Vol. 1: The 1950s–1960s)
Murrow, Edward R. (Vol. 1: The 1950s–1960s)
Paley, William S. (Vol. 1: The 1950s–1960s)
Sarnoff, David (Vol. 1: The 1950s–1960s)
Serling, Rod (Vol. 1: The 1950s–1960s)
Silverman, Fred (Vol. 2: The 1970s–1980s)
Spelling, Aaron (Vol. 1: The 1950s–1960s)
Walters, Barbara (Vol. 2: The 1970s–1980s)
Ward, Jay (Vol. 1: The 1950s–1960s)
Weaver, Sylvester "Pat" (Vol. 1: The 1950s–1960s)
Webb, Jack (Vol. 1: The 1950s–1960s)
Westheimer, Dr. Ruth (Vol. 2: The 1970s–1980s)
Winchell, Walter (Vol. 1: The 1950s–1960s)
Wiseman, Frederick (Vol. 2: The 1970s–1980s)

LATE NIGHT TALK

ABC News Nightline (Vol. 2: The 1970s–1980s)
The Arsenio Hall Show (Vol. 2: The 1970s–1980s)
Jimmy Kimmel Live! (Vol. 3: The 1990s–Present)
Last Call with Carson Daly (Vol. 3: The 1990s–Present)
The Late Late Show with Craig Ferguson (Vol. 3: The 1990s–Present)
Late Night with Conan O'Brien (Vol. 3: The 1990s–Present)

The Late Show Starring Joan Rivers (Vol. 2: The 1970s–1980s)
Leno, Jay (Vol. 3: The 1990s–Present)
Letterman, David (Vol. 3: The 1990s–Present)
The Tonight Show (Vol. 1: The 1950s–1960s)

LEGAL DRAMA

Ally McBeal (Vol. 3: The 1990s–Present)
Boston Legal (Vol. 3: The 1990s–Present)
Damages (Vol. 3: The 1990s–Present)
The Defenders (Vol. 1: The 1950s–1960s)
The Good Wife (Vol. 3: The 1990s–Present)
Judging Amy (Vol. 3: The 1990s–Present)
L.A. Law (Vol. 2: The 1970s–1980s)
Law & Order (Vol. 3: The 1990s–Present)
Owen Marshall: Counselor at Law (Vol. 2: The 1970s–1980s)
Perry Mason (Vol. 1: The 1950s–1960s)
The Practice (Vol. 3: The 1990s–Present)
Rectify (Vol. 3: The 1990s–Present)

LITERATURE AND THEATER

Joseph Campbell and the Power of Myth (Vol. 2: The 1970s–1980s)
The Life and Adventures of Nicholas Nickleby (Vol. 2: The 1970s–1980s)
Masterpiece Theatre (Vol. 2: The 1970s–1980s)
PBS (Public Broadcasting Service) (Vol. 2: The 1970s–1980s)
Roots (Vol. 2: The 1970s–1980s)
Sherlock (Vol. 3: The 1990s–Present)
War and Remembrance (Vol. 2: The 1970s–1980s)
The Winds of War (Vol. 2: The 1970s–1980s)

MARTIAL ARTS

Kung Fu (Vol. 2: The 1970s–1980s)
Mortal Kombat: Conquest: Defenders of the Realm (Vol. 3: The 1990s–Present)

MEDICAL DRAMA

Ben Casey (Vol. 1: The 1950s–1960s)
Chicago Hope (Vol. 3: The 1990s–Present)
Crossing Jordan (Vol. 3: The 1990s–Present)
Diagnosis Murder (Vol. 3: The 1990s–Present)
Doogie Howser, M.D. (Vol. 2: The 1970s–1980s)
Dr. Kildare (Vol. 1: The 1950s–1960s)
Dr. Quinn, Medicine Woman (Vol. 3: The 1990s–Present)
ER (Vol. 3: The 1990s–Present)
General Hospital (Vol. 1: The 1950s–1960s)
Grey's Anatomy (Vol. 3: The 1990s–Present)
House (Vol. 3: The 1990s–Present)
Medic (Vol. 1: The 1950s–1960s)
Nip/Tuck (Vol. 3: The 1990s–Present)
The Psychiatrist (Vol. 2: The 1970s–1980s)
Quincy, M.E. (Vol. 2: The 1970s–1980s)
Scrubs (Vol. 3: The 1990s–Present)
St. Elsewhere (Vol. 2: The 1970s–1980s)

MINISERIES

Masada (Vol. 2: The 1970s–1980s)
North and South (Vol. 2: The 1970s–1980s)
Rich Man, Poor Man (Vol. 2: The 1970s–1980s)
Roots (Vol. 2: The 1970s–1980s)
Shōgun (Vol. 2: The 1970s–1980s)
Tanner '88 (Vol. 2: The 1970s–1980s)
The Thorn Birds (Vol. 2: The 1970s–1980s)
War and Remembrance (Vol. 2: The 1970s–1980s)
The Winds of War (Vol. 2: The 1970s–1980s)

MOCKUMENTARY

Tanner '88 (Vol. 2: The 1970s–1980s)

MORNING NEWS/TALK

Good Morning America (Vol. 2: The 1970s–1980s)
The Today Show (Vol. 1: The 1950s–1960s)

MUSIC

American Bandstand (Vol. 1: The 1950s–1960s)
Country Music (Vol. 1: The 1950s–1960s)
Don Kirshner's Rock Concert (Vol. 2: The 1970s–1980s)
Fuse (Vol. 3: The 1990s–Present)
Great American Country (Vol. 3: The 1990s–Present)
Hullabaloo (Vol. 1: The 1950s–1960s)
The Liberace Show (Vol. 1: The 1950s–1960s)
The Midnight Special (Vol. 2: The 1970s–1980s)
The Monkees (Vol. 1: The 1950s–1960s)

MTV (Vol. 2: The 1970s–1980s)
Nashville Star (Vol. 3: The 1990s–Present)
The Partridge Family (Vol. 2: The 1970s–1980s)
Rainbow Quest (Vol. 1: The 1950s–1960s)
Shindig (Vol. 1: The 1950s–1960s)
Sing Along with Mitch (Vol. 1: The 1950s–1960s)
Solid Gold (Vol. 2: The 1970s–1980s)
Soul Train (Vol. 2: The 1970s–1980s)
The Spike Jones Show (Vol. 1: The 1950s–1960s)
VH1 Storytellers (Vol. 3: The 1990s–Present)
Where the Action Is (Vol. 1: The 1950s–1960s)
Your Hit Parade (Vol. 1: The 1950s–1960s)

MUSIC PERFORMANCE

American Bandstand (Vol. 1: The 1950s–1960s)
Don Kirshner's Rock Concert (Vol. 2: The 1970s–1980s)
Fuse (Vol. 3: The 1990s–Present)
Great American Country (Vol. 3: The 1990s–Present)
Hullabaloo (Vol. 1: The 1950s–1960s)
The Liberace Show (Vol. 1: The 1950s–1960s)
The Midnight Special (Vol. 2: The 1970s–1980s)
The Monkees (Vol. 1: The 1950s–1960s)
The Partridge Family (Vol. 2: The 1970s–1980s)
Shindig (Vol. 1: The 1950s–1960s)
Sing Along with Mitch (Vol. 1: The 1950s–1960s)
Solid Gold (Vol. 2: The 1970s–1980s)
Soul Train (Vol. 2: The 1970s–1980s)
The Spike Jones Show (Vol. 1: The 1950s–1960s)
VH1 Storytellers (Vol. 3: The 1990s–Present)
Where the Action Is (Vol. 1: The 1950s–1960s)
Your Hit Parade (Vol. 1: The 1950s–1960s)

MUSICALS

Cop Rock (Vol. 3: The 1990s–Present)
Glee (Vol. 3: The 1990s–Present)

MYSTERY

The Affair (Vol. 3: The 1990s–Present)
Alfred Hitchcock Presents/The Alfred Hitchcock Hour (Vol. 1: The 1950s–1960s)
Charlie Chan (Vol. 1: The 1950s–1960s)
CSI: Crime Scene Investigation (Vol. 3: The 1990s–Present)
Damages (Vol. 3: The 1990s–Present)
Desperate Housewives (Vol. 3: The 1990s–Present)
Dexter (Vol. 3: The 1990s–Present)
Diagnosis Murder (Vol. 3: The 1990s–Present)
Lost (Vol. 3: The 1990s–Present)
The Mentalist (Vol. 3: The 1990s–Present)
Monk (Vol. 3: The 1990s–Present)
Murder, She Wrote (Vol. 2: The 1970s–1980s)
The Saint (Vol. 1: The 1950s–1960s)
Twin Peaks (Vol. 3: The 1990s–Present)
The X-Files (Vol. 3: The 1990s–Present)

NETWORKS

ABC (American Broadcasting Company) (Vol. 1: The 1950s–1960s)
Animal Planet (Vol. 3: The 1990s–Present)
Bloomberg (Vol. 3: The 1990s–Present)
Cartoon Network (Vol. 3: The 1990s–Present)
CBS (Columbia Broadcasting System) (Vol. 1: The 1950s–1960s)
CNN (Cable News Network) (Vol. 2: The 1970s–1980s)
Court TV (Vol. 3: The 1990s–Present)
DuMont (Vol. 1: The 1950s–1960s)
Encore (Vol. 3: The 1990s–Present)
ESPN (Vol. 2: The 1970s–1980s)
Food Network (Vol. 3: The 1990s–Present)
Fox Broadcasting Company (Vol. 2: The 1970s–1980s)
Fuel TV (Vol. 3: The 1990s–Present)
Fuse (Vol. 3: The 1990s–Present)
Game Show Network (Vol. 3: The 1990s–Present)
Golf Channel (Vol. 3: The 1990s–Present)
Great American Country (Vol. 3: The 1990s–Present)
HBO (Home Box Office) (Vol. 2: The 1970s–1980s)
HGTV (Home and Garden Television) (Vol. 3: The 1990s–Present)
The History Channel (Vol. 3: The 1990s–Present)
Independent Film Channel (Vol. 3: The 1990s–Present)
MSNBC (Vol. 3: The 1990s–Present)
MTV (Vol. 2: The 1970s–1980s)
NBC (National Broadcasting Company) (Vol. 1: The 1950s–1960s)
Oxygen (Vol. 3: The 1990s–Present)

PBS (Public Broadcasting Service) (Vol. 2: The 1970s–1980s)
Showtime (Vol. 2: The 1970s–1980s)
Soapnet (Vol. 3: The 1990s–Present)
Sundance Channel (Vol. 3: The 1990s–Present)
Syfy Channel (Vol. 3: The 1990s–Present)
Turner Classic Movies (Vol. 3: The 1990s–Present)
TV Land (Vol. 3: The 1990s–Present)
WE tv (Vol. 3: The 1990s–Present)

NEWS

ABC News Nightline (Vol. 2: The 1970s–1980s)
Bloomberg (Vol. 3: The 1990s–Present)
Both Sides with Jesse Jackson (Vol. 3: The 1990s–Present)
CNN (Cable News Network) (Vol. 2: The 1970s–1980s)
Cronkite, Walter (Vol. 1: The 1950s–1960s)
Crossfire (Vol. 2: The 1970s–1980s)
Eye to Eye with Connie Chung (Vol. 3: The 1990s–Present)
Frontline (Vol. 2: The 1970s–1980s)
Hardball with Chris Matthews (Vol. 3: The 1990s–Present)
Meet the Press (Vol. 1: The 1950s–1960s)
MSNBC (Vol. 3: The 1990s–Present)
PBS (Public Broadcasting Service) (Vol. 2: The 1970s–1980s)
The 700 Club (Vol. 1: The 1950s–1960s)
60 Minutes (Vol. 1: The 1950s–1960s)
The Today Show (Vol. 1: The 1950s–1960s)
This Week with David Brinkley (Vol. 2: The 1970s–1980s)
Walters, Barbara (Vol. 2: The 1970s–1980s)
Washington Week in Review (Vol. 1: The 1950s–1960s)

NEWS MAGAZINES

A Current Affair (Vol. 2: The 1970s–1980s)
Dateline NBC (Vol. 3: The 1990s–Present)
Eye to Eye with Connie Chung (Vol. 3: The 1990s–Present)
Geraldo at Large (Vol. 3: The 1990s–Present)
Hour Magazine (Vol. 2: The 1970s–1980s)
Inside Edition (Vol. 2: The 1970s–1980s)
The Insider (Vol. 3: The 1990s–Present)
Monitor (*First Camera*) (Vol. 2: The 1970s–1980s)
See It Now (Vol. 1: The 1950s–1960s)
60 Minutes (Vol. 1: The 1950s–1960s)
20/20 (Vol. 2: The 1970s–1980s)
West 57th (Vol. 2: The 1970s–1980s)

NEWS SATIRE

The Colbert Report (Vol. 3: The 1990s–Present)
The Daily Show with Jon Stewart (Vol. 3: The 1990s–Present)

NEWSWORTHY EVENTS

Army/McCarthy Hearings (Vol. 1: The 1950s–1960s)
Coronation of Queen Elizabeth II (Vol. 1: The 1950s–1960s)
George Wallace Shooting (Vol. 2: The 1970s–1980s)
Kennedy, John F., Assassination (Vol. 1: The 1950s–1960s)
Kennedy, John F., Inauguration (Vol. 1: The 1950s–1960s)
Kennedy, Robert, Assassination (Vol. 1: The 1950s–1960s)
King, Martin Luther, Jr., Assassination (Vol. 1: The 1950s–1960s)
1972 Munich Olympics (Vol. 2: The 1970s–1980s)
Watergate Scandal (Vol. 2: The 1970s–1980s)

NIGHTTIME SOAP OPERAS

Melrose Place (Vol. 3: The 1990s–Present)
Peyton Place (Vol. 3: The 1990s–Present)

PARODY

Celebrity Deathmatch (Vol. 3: The 1990s–Present)
Childrens Hospital (Vol. 3: The 1990s–Present)
Police Academy: The Series (Vol. 3: The 1990s–Present)

PERIOD DRAMA

The Americans (Vol. 3: The 1990s–Present)
Boardwalk Empire (Vol. 3: The 1990s–Present)
Downton Abbey (Vol. 3: The 1990s–Present)
Mad Men (Vol. 3: The 1990s–Present)

POLICE DRAMA

Cop Rock (Vol. 3: The 1990s–Present)
Hill Street Blues (Vol. 2: The 1970s–1980s)
Ironside (Vol. 1: The 1950s–1960s)
The Shield (Vol. 3: The 1990s–Present)
T.J. Hooker (Vol. 2: The 1970s–1980s)

POLICE PROCEDURALS

Bones (Vol. 3: The 1990s–Present)
Cagney & Lacey (Vol. 2: The 1970s–1980s)
Chicago P.D. (Vol. 3: The 1990s–Present)
The Closer (Vol. 3: The 1990s–Present)
Cold Case (Vol. 3: The 1990s–Present)
Criminal Minds (Vol. 3: The 1990s–Present)
Dragnet (Vol. 1: The 1950s–1960s)
Hawaii Five-0 (Vol. 1: The 1950s–1960s)
Hawaii Five-0 (Vol. 3: The 1990s–Present)
Hill Street Blues (Vol. 2: The 1970s–1980s)
Homicide: Life on the Street (Vol. 3: The 1990s–Present)
Honey West (Vol. 1: The 1950s–1960s)
The Mentalist (Vol. 3: The 1990s–Present)
Monk (Vol. 3: The 1990s–Present)
NYPD Blue (Vol. 3: The 1990s–Present)
Police Story (Vol. 2: The 1970s–1980s)
Police Woman (Vol. 2: The 1970s–1980s)

POLITICAL COMMENTARY

Crossfire (Vol. 2: The 1970s–1980s)
The McLaughlin Group (Vol. 2: The 1970s–1980s)
Politically Incorrect (Vol. 3: The 1990s–Present)
Rush Limbaugh: The Television Show (Vol. 3: The 1990s–Present)
That Was the Week That Was (Vol. 1: The 1950s–1960s)

POLITICAL DRAMA

Commander in Chief (Vol. 3: The 1990s–Present)
Homeland (Vol. 3: The 1990s–Present)
House of Cards (Vol. 3: The 1990s–Present)
Tanner '88 (Vol. 2: The 1970s–1980s)
The West Wing (Vol. 3: The 1990s–Present)

POLITICAL SATIRE

Tanner '88 (Vol. 2: The 1970s–1980s)
That Was the Week That Was (Vol. 1: The 1950s–1960s)

PRIVATE DETECTIVE PROGRAMS

Johnny Staccato (Vol. 1: The 1950s–1960s)
Monk (Vol. 3: The 1990s–Present)
Sherlock (Vol. 3: The 1990s–Present)

PSYCHIC SHOWS

Crossing Over with John Edward (Vol. 3: The 1990s–Present)

PSYCHOLOGICAL DRAMA

American Horror Story (Vol. 3: The 1990s–Present)
Damages (Vol. 3: The 1990s–Present)
Dexter (Vol. 3: The 1990s–Present)
Hannibal (Vol. 3: The 1990s–Present)
Heroes (Vol. 3: The 1990s–Present)
Homeland (Vol. 3: The 1990s–Present)
Lost (Vol. 3: The 1990s–Present)
Nip/Tuck (Vol. 3: The 1990s–Present)
Oz (Vol. 3: The 1990s–Present)
The Prisoner (Vol. 1: The 1950s–1960s)
The Psychiatrist (Vol. 2: The 1970s–1980s)
The Twilight Zone (Vol. 1: The 1950s–1960s)
Twin Peaks (Vol. 3: The 1990s–Present)

REALITY COMPETITION

The Amazing Race (Vol. 3: The 1990s–Present)
America's Next Top Model (Vol. 3: The 1990s–Present)
American Dream Builders (Vol. 3: The 1990s–Present)
American Idol (Vol. 3: The 1990s–Present)
American Inventor (Vol. 3: The 1990s–Present)
The Apprentice (Vol. 3: The 1990s–Present)
The Biggest Loser (Vol. 3: The 1990s–Present)
Dancing with the Stars (Vol. 3: The 1990s–Present)
Last Comic Standing (Vol. 3: The 1990s–Present)
Nashville Star (Vol. 3: The 1990s–Present)
Project Runway (Vol. 3: The 1990s–Present)

Queer Eye for the Straight Guy (Vol. 3: The 1990s–Present)

REALITY SHOWS

The Amazing Race (Vol. 3: The 1990s–Present)
America's Funniest Home Videos (Vol. 3: The 1990s–Present)
America's Most Wanted (Vol. 2: The 1970s–1980s)
America's Next Top Model (Vol. 3: The 1990s–Present)
American Chopper (Vol. 3: The 1990s–Present)
American Dream Builders (Vol. 3: The 1990s–Present)
American Inventor (Vol. 3: The 1990s–Present)
Amish in the City (Vol. 3: The 1990s–Present)
The Andy Dick Show (Vol. 3: The 1990s–Present)
The Anna Nicole Show (Vol. 3: The 1990s–Present)
The Apprentice (Vol. 3: The 1990s–Present)
The Bachelor (Vol. 3: The 1990s–Present)
Big Brother (Vol. 3: The 1990s–Present)
Bridezillas (Vol. 3: The 1990s–Present)
Candid Camera (Vol. 1: The 1950s–1960s)
Crossing Over with John Edward (Vol. 3: The 1990s–Present)
Divorce Court (Vol. 1: The 1950s–1960s)
Extreme Makeover (Vol. 3: The 1990s–Present)
Fear Factor (Vol. 3: The 1990s–Present)
Growing Up Gotti (Vol. 3: The 1990s–Present)
Jackass (Vol. 3: The 1990s–Present)
Kathy Griffin: My Life on the D-List (Vol. 3: The 1990s–Present)
Last Comic Standing (Vol. 3: The 1990s–Present)
Lifestyles of the Rich and Famous (Vol. 2: The 1970s–1980s)
The Mole (Vol. 3: The 1990s–Present)
Nashville Star (Vol. 3: The 1990s–Present)
The Osbournes (Vol. 3: The 1990s–Present)
Project Runway (Vol. 3: The 1990s–Present)
Punk'd (Vol. 3: The 1990s–Present)
Queen for a Day (Vol. 1: The 1950s–1960s)
The Real Housewives of Orange County (Vol. 3: The 1990s–Present)
The Real World (Vol. 3: The 1990s–Present)
Ripley's Believe It or Not (Vol. 2: The 1970s–1980s)
The Simple Life (Vol. 3: The 1990s–Present)
Supernanny (Vol. 3: The 1990s–Present)
The Surreal Life (Vol. 3: The 1990s–Present)
Survivor (Vol. 3: The 1990s–Present)
That's Incredible! (Vol. 2: The 1970s–1980s)
This Is Your Life (Vol. 1: The 1950s–1960s)
Unsolved Mysteries (Vol. 2: The 1970s–1980s)
Wahlburgers (Vol. 3: The 1990s–Present)
Wife Swap (Vol. 3: The 1990s–Present)

RELIGIOUS PROGRAMMING

Davey and Goliath (Vol. 1: The 1950s–1960s)
Falwell, Jerry (Vol. 2: The 1970s–1980s)
The 700 Club (Vol. 1: The 1950s–1960s)

RURAL SITCOMS

The Andy Griffith Show (Vol. 1: The 1950s–1960s)
The Beverly Hillbillies (Vol. 1: The 1950s–1960s)
The Dukes of Hazzard (Vol. 2: The 1970s–1980s)
Green Acres (Vol. 1: The 1950s–1960s)
Hee Haw (Vol. 1: The 1950s–1960s)
Lassie (Vol. 1: The 1950s–1960s)
Mister Ed (Vol. 1: The 1950s–1960s)
The Real McCoys (Vol. 1: The 1950s–1960s)

SATIRE

Celebrity Deathmatch (Vol. 3: The 1990s–Present)
Childrens Hospital (Vol. 3: The 1990s–Present)
The Colbert Report (Vol. 3: The 1990s–Present)
Da Ali G Show (Vol. 3: The 1990s–Present)
The Daily Show with Jon Stewart (Vol. 3: The 1990s–Present)
Get Smart (Vol. 1: The 1950s–1960s)
Louie (Vol. 3: The 1990s–Present)
Mary Hartman, Mary Hartman (Vol. 2: The 1970s–1980s)
Portlandia (Vol. 3: The 1990s–Present)
Rocky and His Friends (Vol. 1: The 1950s–1960s)
The Simpsons (Vol. 2: The 1970s–1980s)
South Park (Vol. 3: The 1990s–Present)

SCIENCE FICTION

Alf (Vol. 2: The 1970s–1980s)
Alien Nation (Vol. 2: The 1970s–1980s)
Amazing Stories (Vol. 2: The 1970s–1980s)

Babylon 5 (Vol. 3: The 1990s–Present)
Battlestar Galactica (Vol. 2: The 1970s–1980s)
Believe (Vol. 3: The 1990s–Present)
Dark Angel (Vol. 3: The 1990s–Present)
Futurama (Vol. 3: The 1990s–Present)
Heroes (Vol. 3: The 1990s–Present)
The Invaders (Vol. 1: The 1950s–1960s)
Lost (Vol. 3: The 1990s–Present)
Lost in Space (Vol. 1: The 1950s–1960s)
The Man from Atlantis (Vol. 2: The 1970s–1980s)
The Man in the High Castle (Vol. 3: The 1990s–Present)
Max Headroom (Vol. 2: The 1970s–1980s)
Mystery Science Theater 3000 (Vol. 2: The 1970s–1980s)
The Outer Limits (Vol. 1: The 1950s–1960s)
The Prisoner (Vol. 1: The 1950s–1960s)
Quantum Leap (Vol. 2: The 1970s–1980s)
Resurrection (Vol. 3: The 1990s–Present)
The Six Million Dollar Man (Vol. 2: The 1970s–1980s)
Star Trek (Vol. 1: The 1950s–1960s)
Star Trek: Deep Space Nine (Vol. 3: The 1990s–Present)
Star Trek: The Next Generation (Vol. 2: The 1970s–1980s)
Star Trek: Voyager (Vol. 3: The 1990s–Present)
Stargate SG-1 (Vol. 3: The 1990s–Present)
Starman (Vol. 2: The 1970s–1980s)
Syfy Channel (Vol. 3: The 1990s–Present)
The Twilight Zone (Vol. 1: The 1950s–1960s)
V (Vol. 2: The 1970s–1980s)
War of the Worlds (Vol. 2: The 1970s–1980s)
The Wild, Wild West (Vol. 1: The 1950s–1960s)
The X-Files (Vol. 3: The 1990s–Present)

SITCOMS

According to Jim (Vol. 3: The 1990s–Present)
The Addams Family (Vol. 1: The 1950s–1960s)
Alf (Vol. 2: The 1970s–1980s)
Alice (Vol. 2: The 1970s–1980s)
All in the Family (Vol. 2: The 1970s–1980s)
The Andy Griffith Show (Vol. 1: The 1950s–1960s)
Arrested Development (Vol. 3: The 1990s–Present)
Benson (Vol. 2: The 1970s–1980s)
Beulah (Vol. 1: The 1950s–1960s)
Bewitched (Vol. 1: The 1950s–1960s)
The Bill Cosby Show (Vol. 1: The 1950s–1960s)
Blossom (Vol. 3: The 1990s–Present)
Bob (Vol. 3: The 1990s–Present)
The Bob Newhart Show (Vol. 2: The 1970s–1980s)
Buffalo Bill (Vol. 2: The 1970s–1980s)
Cheers (Vol. 2: The 1970s–1980s)
Chico and the Man (Vol. 2: The 1970s–1980s)
Childrens Hospital (Vol. 3: The 1990s–Present)
Community (Vol. 3: The 1990s–Present)
The Cosby Show (Vol. 2: The 1970s–1980s)
Dave's World (Vol. 3: The 1990s–Present)
Dharma & Greg (Vol. 3: The 1990s–Present)
The Dick Van Dyke Show (Vol. 1: The 1950s–1960s)
Diff'rent Strokes (Vol. 2: The 1970s–1980s)
Ellen (Vol. 3: The 1990s–Present)
Evening Shade (Vol. 3: The 1990s–Present)
Everybody Loves Raymond (Vol. 3: The 1990s–Present)
Family Ties (Vol. 2: The 1970s–1980s)
The Farmer's Daughter (Vol. 1: The 1950s–1960s)
Frasier (Vol. 3: The 1990s–Present)
The Fresh Prince of Bel Air (Vol. 3: The 1990s–Present)
Friends (Vol. 3: The 1990s–Present)
George Lopez (Vol. 3: The 1990s–Present)
Gilligan's Island (Vol. 1: The 1950s–1960s)
The Golden Girls (Vol. 2: The 1970s–1980s)
Good Times (Vol. 2: The 1970s–1980s)
Growing Up Fisher (Vol. 3: The 1990s–Present)
Happy Days (Vol. 2: The 1970s–1980s)
Hazel (Vol. 1: The 1950s–1960s)
Hogan's Heroes (Vol. 1: The 1950s–1960s)
Home Improvement (Vol. 3: The 1990s–Present)
Hope & Faith (Vol. 3: The 1990s–Present)
How I Met Your Mother (Vol. 3: The 1990s–Present)
I Dream of Jeannie (Vol. 1: The 1950s–1960s)
I Love Lucy (Vol. 1: The 1950s–1960s)
The Jeffersons (Vol. 2: The 1970s–1980s)
Julia (Vol. 1: The 1950s–1960s)
The King of Queens (Vol. 3: The 1990s–Present)
Laverne and Shirley (Vol. 2: The 1970s–1980s)
The Life of Riley (Vol. 1: The 1950s–1960s)
The Love Boat (Vol. 2: The 1970s–1980s)
Mad About You (Vol. 3: The 1990s–Present)
Make Room for Daddy (Vol. 1: The 1950s–1960s)

Malcom in the Middle (Vol. 3: The 1990s–Present)
The Many Loves of Dobie Gillis (Vol. 1: The 1950s–1960s)
Married . . . with Children (Vol. 2: The 1970s–1980s)
The Mary Tyler Moore Show (Vol. 2: The 1970s–1980s)
Maude (Vol. 2: The 1970s–1980s)
Mister Ed (Vol. 1: The 1950s–1960s)
Modern Family (Vol. 3: The 1990s–Present)
Mork & Mindy (Vol. 2: The 1970s–1980s)
The Munsters (Vol. 1: The 1950s–1960s)
Murphy Brown (Vol. 2: The 1970s–1980s)
The New Adventures of the Old Christine (Vol. 3: The 1990s–Present)
New Girl (Vol. 3: The 1990s–Present)
Newhart (Vol. 2: The 1970s–1980s)
Night Court (Vol. 2: The 1970s–1980s)
The Odd Couple (Vol. 2: The 1970s–1980s)
The Office (Vol. 3: The 1990s–Present)
Our Miss Brooks (Vol. 1: The 1950s–1960s)
Parks and Recreation (Vol. 3: The 1990s–Present)
The Partridge Family (Vol. 2: The 1970s–1980s)
The Patty Duke Show (Vol. 1: The 1950s–1960s)
The Real McCoys (Vol. 1: The 1950s–1960s)
Reba (Vol. 3: The 1990s–Present)
Roseanne (Vol. 2: The 1970s–1980s)
The Sarah Silverman Program (Vol. 3: The 1990s–Present)
Seinfeld (Vol. 2: The 1970s–1980s)
Soap (Vol. 2: The 1970s–1980s)
Spin City (Vol. 3: The 1990s–Present)
Tammy (Vol. 1: The 1950s–1960s)
Taxi (Vol. 2: The 1970s–1980s)
That '70s Show (Vol. 3: The 1990s–Present)
That '80s Show (Vol. 3: The 1990s–Present)
That Girl (Vol. 1: The 1950s–1960s)
3rd Rock from the Sun (Vol. 3: The 1990s–Present)
30 Rock (Vol. 3: The 1990s–Present)
Three's Company (Vol. 2: The 1970s–1980s)
Topper (Vol. 1: The 1950s–1960s)
Welcome Back Kotter (Vol. 2: The 1970s–1980s)
Who's the Boss? (Vol. 2: The 1970s–1980s)
Will & Grace (Vol. 3: The 1990s–Present)
Wings (Vol. 3: The 1990s–Present)
WKRP in Cincinnati (Vol. 2: The 1970s–1980s)

SOAP OPERAS

As the World Turns (Vol. 1: The 1950s–1960s)
Beverly Hills 90210 (Vol. 3: The 1990s–Present)
Dark Shadows (Vol. 1: The 1950s–1960s)
Days of Our Lives (Vol. 1: The 1950s–1960s)
General Hospital (Vol. 1: The 1950s–1960s)
The Guiding Light (Vol. 1: The 1950s–1960s)
Mary Hartman, Mary Hartman (Vol. 2: The 1970s–1980s)
Search for Tomorrow (Vol. 1: The 1950s–1960s)
Soapnet (Vol. 3: The 1990s–Present)

SPECULATIVE FICTION

The Outer Limits (Vol. 1: The 1950s–1960s)
The Twilight Zone (Vol. 1: The 1950s–1960s)
Twin Peaks (Vol. 3: The 1990s–Present)
The X-Files (Vol. 3: The 1990s–Present)

SPORTS

The Battle of the Sexes: Billie Jean King vs. Bobby Riggs (Vol. 2: The 1970s–1980s)
Bowling (Vol. 1: The 1950s–1960s)
Boxing (Vol. 1: The 1950s–1960s)
ESPN (Vol. 2: The 1970s–1980s)
Football (Vol. 1: The 1950s–1960s)
Friday Night Lights (Vol. 3: The 1990s–Present)
Fuel TV (Vol. 3: The 1990s–Present)
The George Michael Sports Machine (Vol. 2: The 1970s–1980s)
Golf Channel (Vol. 3: The 1990s–Present)
NFL Monday Night Football (Vol. 2: The 1970s–1980s)
1977 World Series (Vol. 2: The 1970s–1980s)
1972 Munich Olympics (Vol. 2: The 1970s–1980s)
The Ultimate Fighter (Vol. 3: The 1990s–Present)
The White Shadow (Vol. 2: The 1970s–1980s)
The World Series (Vol. 1: The 1950s–1960s)

STANDARDS AND PRACTICES

The Code of Practices for Television Broadcasters (Vol. 1: The 1950s–1960s)
Family Hour (Vol. 2: The 1970s–1980s)

FCC (Federal Communications Commission) (Vol. 1: The 1950s–1960s)
Nudity on Television (Vol. 2: The 1970s–1980s)

SUPERHEROES

The Adventures of Superman (Vol. 1: The 1950s–1960s)
Batman (Vol. 1: The 1950s–1960s)
The Bionic Woman (Vol. 1: The 1950s–1960s)
Heroes (Vol. 3: The 1990s–Present)
The Incredible Hulk (Vol. 2: The 1970s–1980s)
Wonder Woman (Vol. 2: The 1970s–1980s)

SUPERNATURAL DRAMA

Angel (Vol. 3: The 1990s–Present)
Buffy the Vampire Slayer (Vol. 3: The 1990s–Present)
Lost (Vol. 3: The 1990s–Present)
Resurrection (Vol. 3: The 1990s–Present)
Touched by an Angel (Vol. 3: The 1990s–Present)
The X-Files (Vol. 3: The 1990s–Present)

TABLOIDS

E! True Hollywood Story (Vol. 3: The 1990s–Present)
Hard Copy (Vol. 2: The 1970s–1980s)
Hollywood Babylon (Vol. 3: The 1990s–Present)

TALENT SHOWS

America's Got Talent (Vol. 3: The 1990s–Present)
American Idol (Vol. 3: The 1990s–Present)
Star Search (Vol. 2: The 1970s–1980s)
Ted Mack & the Original Amateur Hour (Vol. 1: The 1950s–1960s)

TALK SHOWS

The Arsenio Hall Show (Vol. 2: The 1970s–1980s)
The Colbert Report (Vol. 3: The 1990s–Present)
The Daily Show with Jon Stewart (Vol. 3: The 1990s–Present)
The Dick Cavett Show (Vol. 1: The 1950s–1960s)
Geraldo (Vol. 2: The 1970s–1980s)
Hour Magazine (Vol. 2: The 1970s–1980s)
The Howard Stern Show (Vol. 3: The 1990s–Present)
The Jerry Lewis Show (Vol. 1: The 1950s–1960s)
Jimmy Kimmel Live! (Vol. 3: The 1990s–Present)
The Joe Franklin Show (Vol. 1: The 1950s–1960s)
The Larry King Show (*Larry King Live*) (Vol. 2: The 1970s–1980s)
The Late Late Show with Craig Ferguson (Vol. 3: The 1990s–Present)
Late Night with Conan O'Brien (Vol. 3: The 1990s–Present)
The Late Show Starring Joan Rivers (Vol. 2: The 1970s–1980s)
Leno, Jay (Vol. 3: The 1990s–Present)
Letterman, David (Vol. 3: The 1990s–Present)
The Morton Downey Jr. Show (Vol. 2: The 1970s–1980s)
Open End (*The David Susskind Show*) (Vol. 1: The 1950s–1960s)
The Oprah Winfrey Show (Vol. 2: The 1970s–1980s)
The Phil Donahue Show (Vol. 2: The 1970s–1980s)
Playboy after Dark (Vol. 1: The 1950s–1960s)
Playboy's Penthouse (Vol. 1: The 1950s–1960s)
The RuPaul Show (Vol. 3: The 1990s–Present)
Rush Limbaugh Show: The Television Show (Vol. 3: The 1990s–Present)
Sally Jessy Raphael (Vol. 2: The 1970s–1980s)
The 700 Club (Vol. 1: The 1950s–1960s)
Soul! (Vol. 2: The 1970s–1980s)
The Today Show (Vol. 1: The 1950s–1960s)
Tomorrow with Tom Snyder (*The Tomorrow Show*) (Vol. 2: The 1970s–1980s)
The Tonight Show (Vol. 1: The 1950s–1960s)

TECHNOLOGY

Satellite Television (Vol. 1: The 1950s–1960s)

TEEN DRAMA

Angel (Vol. 3: The 1990s–Present)
Beverly Hills 90210 (Vol. 3: The 1990s–Present)
Buffy the Vampire Slayer (Vol. 3: The 1990s–Present)
Dawson's Creek (Vol. 3: The 1990s–Present)
Felicity (Vol. 3: The 1990s–Present)
Glee (Vol. 3: The 1990s–Present)
Melrose Place (Vol. 3: The 1990s–Present)
The O.C. (*The Heights*) (Vol. 3: The 1990s–Present)
Party of Five (Vol. 3: The 1990s–Present)
Spelling, Aaron (Vol. 1: The 1950s–1960s)
21 Jump Street (Vol. 2: The 1970s–1980s)

TEEN SITCOMS

Hannah Montana (Vol. 3: The 1990s–Present)
Saved by the Bell (Vol. 2: The 1970s–1980s)

TELEVISION FORMATS

Made-for-Television Movies (Vol. 2: The 1970s–1980s)

THRILLERS

Alfred Hitchcock Presents/ The Alfred Hitchcock Hour (Vol. 1: The 1950s–1960s)
Blindspot (Vol. 3: The 1990s–Present)
Criminal Minds (Vol. 3: The 1990s–Present)
Dexter (Vol. 3: The 1990s–Present)
The Fugitive (Vol. 1: The 1950s–1960s)
Hannibal (Vol. 3: The 1990s–Present)
Heroes (Vol. 3: The 1990s–Present)
Homeland (Vol. 3: The 1990s–Present)
Lost (Vol. 3: The 1990s–Present)
The Man in the High Castle (Vol. 3: The 1990s–Present)
The Saint (Vol. 1: The 1950s–1960s)
Serling, Rod (Vol. 1: The 1950s–1960s)
Thriller (Vol. 1: The 1950s–1960s)
True Detective (Vol. 3: The 1990s–Present)
24 (Vol. 3: The 1990s–Present)

VARIETY

The Andy Williams Show (Vol. 1: The 1950s–1960s)
Caesar, Sid (Vol. 1: The 1950s–1960s)
The Carol Burnett Show (Vol. 1: The 1950s–1960s)
The Ed Sullivan Show (Vol. 1: The 1950s–1960s)
Hee Haw (Vol. 1: The 1950s–1960s)
The Hollywood Palace (Vol. 1: The 1950s–1960s)
Hootenanny (Vol. 1: The 1950s–1960s)
Hullabaloo (Vol. 1: The 1950s–1960s)
In Living Color (Vol. 3: The 1990s–Present)
The Jerry Lewis Show (Vol. 1: The 1950s–1960s)
The Lawrence Welk Show (Vol. 1: The 1950s–1960s)
Michael Nesmith in Television Parts (Vol. 2: The 1970s–1980s)
The Muppet Show (Vol. 2: The 1970s–1980s)
Night Gallery (Vol. 2: The 1970s–1980s)
Playboy after Dark (Vol. 1: The 1950s–1960s)
Playboy's Penthouse (Vol. 1: The 1950s–1960s)
The Red Skelton Show (Vol. 1: The 1950s–1960s)
The RuPaul Show (Vol. 3: The 1990s–Present)
Saturday Night Live (Vol. 2: The 1970s–1980s)
Shields and Yarnell (Vol. 2: The 1970s–1980s)
The Smothers Brothers Comedy Hour (Vol. 1: The 1950s–1960s)
The Sonny and Cher Comedy Hour (Vol. 2: The 1970s–1980s)
The Spike Jones Show (Vol. 1: The 1950s–1960s)
Super Dave (Vol. 2: The 1970s–1980s)
Texaco Star Theater (Vol. 1: The 1950s–1960s)
Variety Shows (Vol. 2: The 1970s–1980s)

WAR DRAMA

Combat! (Vol. 1: The 1950s–1960s)
North and South (Vol. 2: The 1970s–1980s)
The Rat Patrol (Vol. 1: The 1950s–1960s)
Twelve O'Clock High (Vol. 1: The 1950s–1960s)
War and Remembrance (Vol. 2: The 1970s–1980s)
The Winds of War (Vol. 2: The 1970s–1980s)

WESTERNS

The Big Valley (Vol. 1: The 1950s–1960s)
Bonanza (Vol. 1: The 1950s–1960s)
Deadwood (Vol. 3: The 1990s–Present)
Death Valley Days (Vol. 1: The 1950s–1960s)
Dr. Quinn, Medicine Woman (Vol. 3: The 1990s–Present)
Gunsmoke (Vol. 1: The 1950s–1960s)
Have Gun Will Travel (Vol. 1: The 1950s–1960s)
Kung Fu (Vol. 2: The 1970s–1980s)
The Lazarus Man (Vol. 3: The 1990s–Present)
Little House on the Prairie (Vol. 2: The 1970s–1980s)
The Lone Ranger (Vol. 1: The 1950s–1960s)
Rawhide (Vol. 1: The 1950s–1960s)
The Rifleman (Vol. 1: The 1950s–1960s)
The Roy Rogers Show (Vol. 1: The 1950s–1960s)
Sky King (Vol. 1: The 1950s–1960s)
Wagon Train (Vol. 1: The 1950s–1960s)
Wanted Dead or Alive (Vol. 1: The 1950s–1960s)
The Wild, Wild West (Vol. 1: The 1950s–1960s)
Zorro (Vol. 1: The 1950s–1960s)

List of Television Programs by Network

A & E

Growing Up Gotti (Vol. 3: The 1990s–Present)
Wahlburgers (Vol. 3: The 1990s–Present)

ABC (AMERICAN BROADCASTING COMPANY)

ABC Afterschool Specials (Vol. 2: The 1970s–1980s)
ABC News Nightline (Vol. 2: The 1970s–1980s)
According to Jim (Vol. 3: The 1990s–Present)
The Addams Family (Vol. 1: The 1950s–1960s)
The Adventures of Ozzie and Harriet (Vol. 1: The 1950s–1960s)
The Adventures of Superman (Vol. 1: The 1950s–1960s)
Alias (Vol. 3: The 1990s–Present)
America's Funniest Home Videos (Vol. 3: The 1990s–Present)
American Bandstand (Vol. 1: The 1950s–1960s)
American Crime (Vol. 3: The 1990s–Present)
American Inventor (Vol. 3: The 1990s–Present)
The Andy Williams Show (Vol. 1: The 1950s–1960s)
The Avengers (Vol. 1: The 1950s–1960s)
The Bachelor (Vol. 3: The 1990s–Present)
Baretta (Vol. 2: The 1970s–1980s)
Batman (Vol. 1: The 1950s–1960s)
Battlestar Galactica (Vol. 2: The 1970s–1980s)
Ben Casey (Vol. 1: The 1950s–1960s)
Benson (Vol. 2: The 1970s–1980s)
Beulah (Vol. 1: The 1950s–1960s)
Bewitched (Vol. 1: The 1950s–1960s)
The Big Valley (Vol. 1: The 1950s–1960s)
The Bionic Woman (Vol. 1: The 1950s–1960s)
Boston Legal (Vol. 3: The 1990s–Present)
Candid Camera (Vol. 1: The 1950s–1960s)
The Chair (Vol. 3: The 1990s–Present)
Charlie's Angels (Vol. 2: The 1970s–1980s)
China Beach (Vol. 2: The 1970s–1980s)
Columbo (Vol. 2: The 1970s–1980s)
Combat! (Vol. 1: The 1950s–1960s)
Commander In Chief (Vol. 3: The 1990s–Present)
The Commish (Vol. 3: The 1990s–Present)
Cop Rock (Vol. 3: The 1990s–Present)
The Critic (Vol. 3: The 1990s–Present)
Dancing with the Stars (Vol. 3: The 1990s–Present)
Dark Shadows (Vol. 1: The 1950s–1960s)
The Dating Game (Vol. 1: The 1950s–1960s)
Desperate Housewives (Vol. 3: The 1990s–Present)
Dharma & Greg (Vol. 3: The 1990s–Present)
The Dick Cavett Show (Vol. 1: The 1950s–1960s)
Diff'rent Strokes (Vol. 2: The 1970s–1980s)
The Donna Reed Show (Vol. 1: The 1950s–1960s)
Doogie Howser, M.D. (Vol. 2: The 1970s–1980s)
Dragnet (Vol. 1: The 1950s–1960s)
Eight Is Enough (Vol. 2: The 1970s–1980s)
Ellen (Vol. 3: The 1990s–Present)
Extreme Makeover (Vol. 3: The 1990s–Present)
Family (Vol. 2: The 1970s–1980s)
Family Feud (Vol. 2: The 1970s–1980s)
Fantasy Island (Vol. 2: The 1970s–1980s)
The Farmer's Daughter (Vol. 1: The 1950s–1960s)
The Flintstones (Vol. 1: The 1950s–1960s)
The Flying Nun (Vol. 1: The 1950s–1960s)
Fridays (Vol. 2: The 1970s–1980s)
The Fugitive (Vol. 1: The 1950s–1960s)
Full House (Vol. 2: The 1970s–1980s)
General Hospital (Vol. 1: The 1950s–1960s)
George Lopez (Vol. 3: The 1990s–Present)
Get Christie Love! (Vol. 2: The 1970s–1980s)
Good Morning America (Vol. 2: The 1970s–1980s)

Grey's Anatomy (Vol. 3: The 1990s–Present)
Happy Days (Vol. 2: The 1970s–1980s)
The Hathaways (Vol. 1: The 1950s–1960s)
Hawaiian Eye (Vol. 1: The 1950s–1960s)
The Hollywood Palace (Vol. 1: The 1950s–1960s)
Home Improvement (Vol. 3: The 1990s–Present)
Honey West (Vol. 1: The 1950s–1960s)
Hootenanny (Vol. 1: The 1950s–1960s)
Hope & Faith (Vol. 3: The 1990s–Present)
The Invaders (Vol. 1: The 1950s–1960s)
The Jack LaLanne Show (Vol. 1: The 1950s–1960s)
The Jerry Lewis Show (Vol. 1: The 1950s–1960s)
The Jetsons (Vol. 1: The 1950s–1960s)
Jimmy Kimmel Live (Vol. 3: The 1990s–Present)
The Krypton Factor (Vol. 2: The 1970s–1980s)
Kukla, Fran and Ollie (Vol. 1: The 1950s–1960s)
Kung Fu (Vol. 2: The 1970s–1980s)
Laverne and Shirley (Vol. 2: The 1970s–1980s)
The Lawrence Welk Show (Vol. 1: The 1950s–1960s)
Leave It to Beaver (Vol. 1: The 1950s–1960s)
Let's Make a Deal (Vol. 1: The 1950s–1960s)
The Life of Riley (Vol. 1: The 1950s–1960s)
Live with Regis and Kathie Lee (Vol. 2: The 1970s–1980s)
The Lone Ranger (Vol. 1: The 1950s–1960s)
Lost (Vol. 3: The 1990s–Present)
The Love Boat (Vol. 2: The 1970s–1980s)
MacGyver (Vol. 2: The 1970s–1980s)
Make Room for Daddy (Vol. 1: The 1950s–1960s)
Masada (Vol. 2: The 1970s–1980s)
Max Headroom (Vol. 2: The 1970s–1980s)
The Mickey Mouse Club (Vol. 1: The 1950s–1960s)
Mission Impossible (Vol. 1: The 1950s–1960s)
The Mod Squad (Vol. 1: The 1950s–1960s)
Modern Family (Vol. 3: The 1990s–Present)
The Mole (Vol. 3: The 1990s–Present)
Moonlighting (Vol. 2: The 1970s–1980s)
Mork & Mindy (Vol. 2: The 1970s–1980s)
My Three Sons (Vol. 1: The 1950s–1960s)
The Newlywed Game (Vol. 1: The 1950s–1960s)
NFL Monday Night Football (Vol. 2: The 1970s–1980s)
The Night Stalker (Vol. 2: The 1970s–1980s)
North and South (Vol. 2: The 1970s–1980s)
NYPD Blue (Vol. 3: The 1990s–Present)
The Odd Couple (Vol. 2: The 1970s–1980s)
The Outer Limits (Vol. 1: The 1950s–1960s)
Owen Marshall: Counselor at Law (Vol. 2: The 1970s–1980s)
The Partridge Family (Vol. 2: The 1970s–1980s)
The Patty Duke Show (Vol. 1: The 1950s–1960s)
Peyton Place (Vol. 1: The 1950s–1960s)
Police Squad! (Vol. 2: The 1970s–1980s)
The Practice (Vol. 3: The 1990s–Present)
Queen for a Day (Vol. 1: The 1950s–1960s)
The Rat Patrol (Vol. 1: The 1950s–1960s)
The Real McCoys (Vol. 1: The 1950s–1960s)
Resurrection (Vol. 3: The 1990s–Present)
Rich Man, Poor Man (Vol. 2: The 1970s–1980s)
The Rifleman (Vol. 1: The 1950s–1960s)
Ripley's Believe It or Not (Vol. 2: The 1970s–1980s)
Rocky and His Friends (Vol. 1: The 1950s–1960s)
Room 222 (Vol. 1: The 1950s–1960s)
Roots (Vol. 2: The 1970s–1980s)
Roseanne (Vol. 2: The 1970s–1980s)
Scrubs (Vol. 3: The 1990s–Present)
Shindig! (Vol. 1: The 1950s–1960s)
77 Sunset Strip (Vol. 1: The 1950s–1960s)
The Six Million Dollar Man (Vol. 1: The 1950s–1960s)
Sky King (Vol. 1: The 1950s–1960s)
Soap (Vol. 2: The 1970s–1980s)
The Soupy Sales Show (Vol. 1: The 1950s–1960s)
Spin City (Vol. 3: The 1990s–Present)
Starman (Vol. 2: The 1970s–1980s)
The Streets of San Francisco (Vol. 2: The 1970s–1980s)
Supermarket Sweep (Vol. 1: The 1950s–1960s)
Supernanny (Vol. 3: The 1990s–Present)
Supertrain (Vol. 2: The 1970s–1980s)
T.J. Hooker (Vol. 2: The 1970s–1980s)
Tammy (Vol. 1: The 1950s–1960s)
Taxi (Vol. 2: The 1970s–1980s)
$10,000 Pyramid (Vol. 2: The 1970s–1980s)
That Girl (Vol. 1: The 1950s–1960s)
That's Incredible! (Vol. 2: The 1970s–1980s)
thirtysomething (Vol. 2: The 1970s–1980s)
This Week with David Brinkley (Vol. 2: The 1970s–1980s)
The Thorn Birds (Vol. 2: The 1970s–1980s)
Those Amazing Animals (Vol. 2: The 1970s–1980s)
Three's Company (Vol. 2: The 1970s–1980s)

Top Cat (Vol. 1: The 1950s–1960s)
Twelve O'Clock High (Vol. 1: The 1950s–1960s)
20/20 (Vol. 2: The 1970s–1980s)
Twin Peaks (Vol. 3: The 1990s–Present)
The Untouchables (Vol. 1: The 1950s–1960s)
V (Vol. 2: The 1970s–1980s)
War and Remembrance (Vol. 2: The 1970s–1980s)
Webster (Vol. 2: The 1970s–1980s)
Welcome Back Kotter (Vol. 2: The 1970s–1980s)
Where the Action Is (Vol. 1: The 1950s–1960s)
Who Wants to Be a Millionaire? (Vol. 3: The 1990s–Present)
Who's the Boss? (Vol. 2: The 1970s–1980s)
Wife Swap (Vol. 3: The 1990s–Present)
The Winds of War (Vol. 2: The 1970s–1980s)
Wonder Woman (Vol. 2: The 1970s–1980s)
The Wonder Years (Vol. 2: The 1970s–1980s)
The Young Indiana Jones Chronicles (Vol. 3: The 1990s–Present)
Zorro (Vol. 1: The 1950s–1960s)

AMAZON

The Man in the High Castle (Vol. 3: The 1990s–Present)

AMC

Breaking Bad (Vol. 3: The 1990s–Present)
Mad Men (Vol. 3: The 1990s–Present)
The Walking Dead (Vol. 3: The 1990s–Present)

BRAVO

Kathy Griffin: My Life on the D-List (Vol. 3: The 1990s–Present)
Project Runway (Vol. 3: The 1990s–Present)
Queer Eye for the Straight Guy (Vol. 3: The 1990s–Present)
The Real Housewives of Orange County (Vol. 3: The 1990s–Present)

CBS (COLUMBIA BROADCASTING SYSTEM)

The Agency (Vol. 3: The 1990s–Present)
Alfred Hitchcock Presents/ The Alfred Hitchcock Hour (Vol. 1: The 1950s–1960s)
Alice (Vol. 2: The 1970s–1980s)
All in the Family (Vol. 2: The 1970s–1980s)
The Amazing Race (Vol. 3: The 1990s–Present)
Amos 'n' Andy (Vol. 1: The 1950s–1960s)
The Andy Griffith Show (Vol. 1: The 1950s–1960s)
The Andy Williams Show (Vol. 1: The 1950s–1960s)
As the World Turns (Vol. 1: The 1950s–1960s)
Beauty and the Beast (Vol. 2: The 1970s–1980s)
The Beverly Hillbillies (Vol. 1: The 1950s–1960s)
Big Brother (Vol. 3: The 1990s–Present)
Bob (Vol. 3: The 1990s–Present)
The Bob Newhart Show (Vol. 2: The 1970s–1980s)
Brooklyn Bridge (Vol. 3: The 1990s–Present)
Cagney & Lacey (Vol. 2: The 1970s–1980s)
Candid Camera (Vol. 1: The 1950s–1960s)
Captain Kangaroo (Vol. 1: The 1950s–1960s)
The Carol Burnett Show (Vol. 1: The 1950s–1960s)
Chicago Hope (Vol. 3: The 1990s–Present)
Cold Case (Vol. 3: The 1990s–Present)
Criminal Minds (Vol. 3: The 1990s–Present)
CSI: Crime Scene Investigation (Vol. 3: The 1990s–Present)
Dave's World (Vol. 3: The 1990s–Present)
The Defenders (Vol. 1: The 1950s–1960s)
Diagnosis Murder (Vol. 3: The 1990s–Present)
The Dick Van Dyke Show (Vol. 1: The 1950s–1960s)
Dr. Quinn, Medicine Woman (Vol. 3: The 1990s–Present)
The Dukes of Hazzard (Vol. 2: The 1970s–1980s)
The Ed Sullivan Show (Vol. 1: The 1950s–1960s)
Evening Shade (Vol. 3: The 1990s–Present)
Everybody Loves Raymond (Vol. 3: The 1990s–Present)
Eye to Eye with Connie Chung (Vol. 3: The 1990s–Present)
Family Affair (Vol. 1: The 1950s–1960s)
Fat Albert and the Cosby Kids (Vol. 2: The 1970s–1980s)
Father Knows Best (Vol. 1: The 1950s–1960s)
The Galloping Gourmet (Vol. 1: The 1950s–1960s)
Get Smart (Vol. 1: The 1950s–1960s)
Gilligan's Island (Vol. 1: The 1950s–1960s)
Good Times (Vol. 2: The 1970s–1980s)
The Good Wife (Vol. 3: The 1990s–Present)
Green Acres (Vol. 1: The 1950s–1960s)
The Guiding Light (Vol. 1: The 1950s–1960s)

Gunsmoke (Vol. 1: The 1950s–1960s)
Have Gun Will Travel (Vol. 1: The 1950s–1960s)
Hawaii Five-0 (Vol. 1: The 1950s–1960s)
Hawaii Five-0 (Vol. 3: The 1990s–Present)
Hee Haw (Vol. 1: The 1950s–1960s)
Hogan's Heroes (Vol. 1: The 1950s–1960s)
How I Met Your Mother (Vol. 3: The 1990s–Present)
I Love Lucy (Vol. 1: The 1950s–1960s)
The Incredible Hulk (Vol. 2: The 1970s–1980s)
I've Got a Secret (Vol. 1: The 1950s–1960s)
The Jack Benny Program (Vol. 1: The 1950s–1960s)
The Jeffersons (Vol. 2: The 1970s–1980s)
Judging Amy (Vol. 3: The 1990s–Present)
The King of Queens (Vol. 3: The 1990s–Present)
Kojak (Vol. 2: The 1970s–1980s)
Lassie (Vol. 1: The 1950s–1960s)
The Late Late Show with Craig Ferguson (Vol. 3: The 1990s–Present)
Leave It to Beaver (Vol. 1: The 1950s–1960s)
Lost in Space (Vol. 1: The 1950s–1960s)
*M*A*S*H* (Vol. 2: The 1970s–1980s)
Make Room for Daddy (Vol. 1: The 1950s–1960s)
The Many Loves of Dobie Gillis (Vol. 1: The 1950s–1960s)
The Mary Tyler Moore Show (Vol. 2: The 1970s–1980s)
Maude (Vol. 2: The 1970s–1980s)
The Mentalist (Vol. 3: The 1990s–Present)
The Millionaire (Vol. 1: The 1950s–1960s)
Mission Impossible (Vol. 1: The 1950s–1960s)
Mister Ed (Vol. 1: The 1950s–1960s)
Morton & Hayes (Vol. 3: The 1990s–Present)
Mr. Magoo (Vol. 1: The 1950s–1960s)
The Munsters (Vol. 1: The 1950s–1960s)
The Muppet Show (Vol. 2: The 1970s–1980s)
Murder, She Wrote (Vol. 2: The 1970s–1980s)
Murphy Brown (Vol. 2: The 1970s–1980s)
My Favorite Martian (Vol. 1: The 1950s–1960s)
My Three Sons (Vol. 1: The 1950s–1960s)
NCIS (Vol. 3: The 1990s–Present)
The New Adventures of Old Christine (Vol. 3: The 1990s–Present)
Newhart (Vol. 2: The 1970s–1980s)
Northern Exposure (Vol. 3: The 1990s–Present)
Our Miss Brooks (Vol. 1: The 1950s–1960s)
The Paper Chase (Vol. 2: The 1970s–1980s)
Pee-Wee's Playhouse (Vol. 2: The 1970s–1980s)
Perry Mason (Vol. 1: The 1950s–1960s)
Picket Fences (Vol. 3: The 1990s–Present)
Playhouse 90 (Vol. 1: The 1950s–1960s)
The Price Is Right (Vol. 1: The 1950s–1960s)
Rawhide (Vol. 1: The 1950s–1960s)
The Real McCoys (Vol. 1: The 1950s–1960s)
Route 66 (Vol. 1: The 1950s–1960s)
The Saint (Vol. 1: The 1950s–1960s)
Search for Tomorrow (Vol. 1: The 1950s–1960s)
See It Now (Vol. 1: The 1950s–1960s)
Shields and Yarnell (Vol. 2: The 1970s–1980s)
60 Minutes (Vol. 1: The 1950s–1960s)
The Smothers Brothers Comedy Hour (Vol. 1: The 1950s–1960s)
Sonny and Cher Comedy Hour (Vol. 2: The 1970s–1980s)
Star Search (Vol. 2: The 1970s–1980s)
Survivor (Vol. 3: The 1990s–Present)
Ted Mack & the Original Amateur Hour (Vol. 1: The 1950s–1960s)
To Tell the Truth (Vol. 1: The 1950s–1960s)
$10,000 Pyramid (Vol. 2: The 1970s–1980s)
Topper (Vol. 1: The 1950s–1960s)
Touched by an Angel (Vol. 3: The 1990s–Present)
The Twentieth Century (Vol. 1: The 1950s–1960s)
The Twilight Zone (Vol. 1: The 1950s–1960s)
The Waltons (Vol. 2: The 1970s–1980s)
Wanted Dead or Alive (Vol. 1: The 1950s–1960s)
West 57th (Vol. 2: The 1970s–1980s)
What's My Line? (Vol. 1: The 1950s–1960s)
The White Shadow (Vol. 2: The 1970s–1980s)
The Wild, Wild West (Vol. 1: The 1950s–1960s)
Winky-Dink and You (Vol. 1: The 1950s–1960s)
Wiseguy (Vol. 2: The 1970s–1980s)
WKRP in Cincinnati (Vol. 2: The 1970s–1980s)
You Are There (Vol. 1: The 1950s–1960s)
You'll Never Get Rich (Vol. 1: The 1950s–1960s)
Your Hit Parade (Vol. 1: The 1950s–1960s)

CNN (CABLE NEWS NETWORK)

Both Sides with Jesse Jackson (Vol. 3: The 1990s–Present)
Crossfire (Vol. 2: The 1970s–1980s)
The Larry King Show (Larry King Live) (Vol. 2: The 1970s–1980s)

COMEDY CENTRAL

Chappelle's Show (Vol. 3: The 1990s–Present)
The Colbert Report (Vol. 3: The 1990s–Present)
The Daily Show with Jon Stewart (Vol. 3: The 1990s–Present)
Dr. Katz: Professional Therapist (Vol. 3: The 1990s–Present)
MADtv (Vol. 3: The 1990s–Present)
The Man Show (Vol. 3: The 1990s–Present)
Mystery Science Theater 3000 (Vol. 2: The 1970s–1980s)
Politically Incorrect (Vol. 3: The 1990s–Present)
The Sarah Silverman Program (Vol. 3: The 1990s–Present)
South Park (Vol. 3: The 1990s–Present)
Win Ben Stein's Money (Vol. 3: The 1990s–Present)

DISCOVERY

American Chopper (Vol. 3: The 1990s–Present)

DISNEY CHANNEL

The All New Mickey Mouse Club (Vol. 2: The 1970s–1980s)
Hannah Montana (Vol. 3: The 1990s–Present)

DUMONT

The Goldbergs (Vol. 1: The 1950s–1960s)
Ted Mack & the Original Amateur Hour (Vol. 1: The 1950s–1960s)
You Asked for It (Vol. 1: The 1950s–1960s)

E! ENTERTAINMENT TELEVISION

The Anna Nicole Show (Vol. 3: The 1990s–Present)
E! True Hollywood Story (Vol. 3: The 1990s–Present)
Talk Soup (Vol. 3: The 1990s–Present)

FOX BROADCASTING COMPANY

Alien Nation (Vol. 2: The 1970s–1980s)
Ally McBeal (Vol. 3: The 1990s–Present)
America's Most Wanted (Vol. 2: The 1970s–1980s)
American Idol (Vol. 3: The 1990s–Present)
Are You Smarter Than a Fifth Grader? (Vol. 3: The 1990s–Present)
Arrested Development (Vol. 3: The 1990s–Present)
Beverly Hills 90210 (Vol. 3: The 1990s–Present)
Bob's Burgers (Vol. 3: The 1990s–Present)
Bones (Vol. 3: The 1990s–Present)
Boston Public (Vol. 3: The 1990s–Present)
Dark Angel (Vol. 3: The 1990s–Present)
Family Guy (Vol. 3: The 1990s–Present)
Futurama (Vol. 3: The 1990s–Present)
Geraldo at Large (Vol. 3: The 1990s–Present)
Glee (Vol. 3: The 1990s–Present)
Hell's Kitchen (Vol. 3: The 1990s–Present)
House (Vol. 3: The 1990s–Present)
In Living Color (Vol. 3: The 1990s–Present)
King of the Hill (Vol. 3: The 1990s–Present)
The Late Show Starring Joan Rivers (Vol. 2: The 1970s–1980s)
MADtv (Vol. 3: The 1990s–Present)
Malcolm in the Middle (Vol. 3: The 1990s–Present)
Married . . . with Children (Vol. 2: The 1970s–1980s)
Melrose Place (Vol. 3: The 1990s–Present)
New Girl (Vol. 3: The 1990s–Present)
The O.C. (The Heights) (Vol. 3: The 1990s–Present)
Party of Five (Vol. 3: The 1990s–Present)
Prison Break (Vol. 3: The 1990s–Present)
The Simple Life (Vol. 3: The 1990s–Present)
The Simpsons (Vol. 2, The 1970s–1980s)
So You Think You Can Dance (Vol. 3: The 1990s–Present)
That '70s Show (Vol. 3: The 1990s–Present)
That '80s Show (Vol. 3: The 1990s–Present)
The Tracey Ullman Show (Vol. 2: The 1970s–1980s)
24 (Vol. 3: The 1990s–Present)
21 Jump Street (Vol. 2: The 1970s–1980s)
The X-Files (Vol. 3: The 1990s–Present)

FX

American Horror Story (Vol. 3: The 1990s–Present)
The Americans (Vol. 3: The 1990s–Present)
Damages (Vol. 3: The 1990s–Present)
Justified (Vol. 3: The 1990s–Present)
Louie (Vol. 3: The 1990s–Present)
Nip/Tuck (Vol. 3: The 1990s–Present)
Rescue Me (Vol. 3: The 1990s–Present)

The Shield (Vol. 3: The 1990s–Present)
Sons of Anarchy (Vol. 3: The 1990s–Present)

HBO (HOME BOX OFFICE)

Behind the Candelabra (Vol. 3: The 1990s–Present)
Boardwalk Empire (Vol. 3: The 1990s–Present)
Curb Your Enthusiasm (Vol. 3: The 1990s–Present)
Da Ali G Show (Vol. 3: The 1990s–Present)
Deadwood (Vol. 3: The 1990s–Present)
Enlightened (Vol. 3: The 1990s–Present)
Game of Thrones (Vol. 3: The 1990s–Present)
Girls (Vol. 3: The 1990s–Present)
Oz (Vol. 3: The 1990s–Present)
Ray Bradbury Theater (Vol. 2, The 1970s–1980s)
Sex and the City (Vol. 3: The 1990s–Present)
Six Feet Under (Vol. 3: The 1990s–Present)
The Sopranos (Vol. 3: The 1990s–Present)
Tales from the Crypt (Vol. 2, The 1970s–1980s)
Tanner '88 (Vol. 2, The 1970s–1980s)
Tremé (Vol. 3: The 1990s–Present)
True Detective (Vol. 3: The 1990s–Present)
The Wire (Vol. 3: The 1990s–Present)

INDEPENDENT FILM CHANNEL

Portlandia (Vol. 3: The 1990s–Present)

LOCAL AFFILIATES

The Morton Downey Jr. Show (Vol. 2: The 1970s–1980s)
Rainbow Quest (Vol. 1: The 1950s–1960s)

MSNBC

Hardball with Chris Matthews (Vol. 3: The 1990s–Present)

MTV

The Andy Dick Show (Vol. 3: The 1990s–Present)
Celebrity Deathmatch (Vol. 3: The 1990s–Present)
Jackass (Vol. 3: The 1990s–Present)
The Osbournes (Vol. 3: The 1990s–Present)
Punk'd (Vol. 3: The 1990s–Present)
The Real World (Vol. 3: The 1990s–Present)

NBC (NATIONAL BROADCASTING COMPANY)

The A Team (Vol. 2: The 1970s–1980s)
Access Hollywood (Vol. 3: The 1990s–Present)
Alf (Vol. 2: The 1970s–1980s)
Alfred Hitchcock Presents/The Alfred Hitchcock Hour (Vol. 1: The 1950s–1960s)
Amazing Stories (Vol. 2: The 1970s–1980s)
America's Got Talent (Vol. 3: The 1990s–Present)
American Dream Builders (Vol. 3: The 1990s–Present)
The Andy Williams Show (Vol. 1: The 1950s–1960s)
The Apprentice (Vol. 3: The 1990s–Present)
Baywatch (Vol. 2: The 1970s–1980s)
Believe (Vol. 3: The 1990s–Present)
The Biggest Loser (Vol. 3: The 1990s–Present)
The Bill Cosby Show (Vol. 1: The 1950s–1960s)
Blindspot (Vol. 3: The 1990s–Present)
Blossom (Vol. 3: The 1990s–Present)
The Bob and Ray Show (Vol. 1: The 1950s–1960s)
Bonanza (Vol. 1: The 1950s–1960s)
Buffalo Bill (Vol. 2: The 1970s–1980s)
Car 54 Where Are You? (Vol. 1: The 1950s–1960s)
Cheers (Vol. 2: The 1970s–1980s)
Chicago P.D. (Vol. 3: The 1990s–Present)
Chico and the Man (Vol. 2: The 1970s–1980s)
CHiPS (Vol. 2: The 1970s–1980s)
Columbo (Vol. 2: The 1970s–1980s)
Community (Vol. 3: The 1990s–Present)
The Cosby Show (Vol. 2: The 1970s–1980s)
Crime Story (Vol. 2: The 1970s–1980s)
Crossing Jordan (Vol. 3: The 1990s–Present)
Dateline NBC (Vol. 3: The 1990s–Present)
Days of Our Lives (Vol. 1: The 1950s–1960s)
Deal or No Deal (Vol. 3: The 1990s–Present)
Diff'rent Strokes (Vol. 2: The 1970s–1980s)
Ding Dong School (Vol. 1: The 1950s–1960s)
Dr. Kildare (Vol. 1: The 1950s–1960s)
Dragnet (Vol. 1: The 1950s–1960s)
ER (Vol. 3: The 1990s–Present)
Family Ties (Vol. 2: The 1970s–1980s)
Father Knows Best (Vol. 1: The 1950s–1960s)
Fear Factor (Vol. 3: The 1990s–Present)
Flipper (Vol. 1: The 1950s–1960s)
Frasier (Vol. 3: The 1990s–Present)

The Fresh Prince of Bel Air (Vol. 3: The 1990s–Present)
Friday Night Lights (Vol. 3: The 1990s–Present)
Friends (Vol. 3: The 1990s–Present)
The Girl from U.N.C.L.E. (Vol. 1: The 1950s–1960s)
The Goldbergs (Vol. 1: The 1950s–1960s)
The Golden Girls (Vol. 2: The 1970s–1980s)
The Gong Show (Vol. 2: The 1970s–1980s)
Growing Up Fisher (Vol. 3: The 1990s–Present)
The Gumby Show (Vol. 1: The 1950s–1960s)
Hannibal (Vol. 3: The 1990s–Present)
Hazel (Vol. 1: The 1950s–1960s)
Heroes (Vol. 3: The 1990s–Present)
Highway to Heaven (Vol. 2: The 1970s–1980s)
Hill Street Blues (Vol. 2: The 1970s–1980s)
Hollywood Squares (Vol. 1: The 1950s–1960s)
Homicide: Life on the Street (Vol. 3: The 1990s–Present)
Howdy Doody (Vol. 1: The 1950s–1960s)
Hullabaloo (Vol. 1: The 1950s–1960s)
I Dream of Jeannie (Vol. 1: The 1950s–1960s)
Ironside (Vol. 1: The 1950s–1960s)
I Spy (Vol. 1: The 1950s–1960s)
Jeopardy! (Vol. 1: The 1950s–1960s)
The Jerry Lewis Show (Vol. 1: The 1950s–1960s)
Johnny Staccato (Vol. 1: The 1950s–1960s)
Julia (Vol. 1: The 1950s–1960s)
Kukla, Fran and Ollie (Vol. 1: The 1950s–1960s)
L.A. Law (Vol. 2: The 1970s–1980s)
Las Vegas (Vol. 3: The 1990s–Present)
Last Call with Carson Daly (Vol. 3: The 1990s–Present)
Last Comic Standing (Vol. 3: The 1990s–Present)
Late Night with Conan O'Brien (Vol. 3: The 1990s–Present)
Law & Order (Vol. 3: The 1990s–Present)
Let's Make a Deal (Vol. 1: The 1950s–1960s)
The Liberace Show (Vol. 1: The 1950s–1960s)
The Life of Riley (Vol. 1: The 1950s–1960s)
Little House on the Prairie (Vol. 2: The 1970s–1980s)
Mad About You (Vol. 3: The 1990s–Present)
The Magician (Vol. 2: The 1970s–1980s)
The Man from Atlantis (Vol. 2: The 1970s–1980s)
The Man from U.N.C.L.E. (Vol. 1: The 1950s–1960s)
McCloud (Vol. 2: The 1970s–1980s)
Medic (Vol. 1: The 1950s–1960s)
Meet the Press (Vol. 1: The 1950s–1960s)
Miami Vice (Vol. 2: The 1970s–1980s)
Michael Nesmith in Television Parts (Vol. 2: The 1970s–1980s)
The Midnight Special (Vol. 2: The 1970s–1980s)
Monitor (First Camera) (Vol. 2: The 1970s–1980s)
The Monkees (Vol. 1: The 1950s–1960s)
Mr. Magoo (Vol. 1: The 1950s–1960s)
Mutual of Omaha's Wild Kingdom (Vol. 1: The 1950s–1960s)
My Name Is Earl (Vol. 3: The 1990s–Present)
Nashville Star (Vol. 3: The 1990s–Present)
Night Court (Vol. 2: The 1970s–1980s)
Night Gallery (Vol. 2: The 1970s–1980s)
The Office (Vol. 3: The 1990s–Present)
1 vs. 100 (Vol. 3: The 1990s–Present)
Parenthood (Vol. 3: The 1990s–Present)
Parks and Recreation (Vol. 3: The 1990s–Present)
The Pinky Lee Show (Vol. 1: The 1950s–1960s)
Police Story (Vol. 2: The 1970s–1980s)
Police Woman (Vol. 2: The 1970s–1980s)
The Pretender (Vol. 3: The 1990s–Present)
Profiler (Vol. 3: The 1990s–Present)
The Psychiatrist (Vol. 2: The 1970s–1980s)
Quantum Leap (Vol. 2: The 1970s–1980s)
Quincy, M.E. (Vol. 2: The 1970s–1980s)
The Red Skelton Show (Vol. 1: The 1950s–1960s)
The Rosie O'Donnell Show (Vol. 3: The 1990s–Present)
Rowan and Martin's Laugh-In (Vol. 1: The 1950s–1960s)
The Roy Rogers Show (Vol. 1: The 1950s–1960s)
Run for Your Life (Vol. 1: The 1950s–1960s)
The Saint (Vol. 1: The 1950s–1960s)
Saturday Night Live (Vol. 2: The 1970s–1980s)
Saved by the Bell (Vol. 2: The 1970s–1980s)
Scrubs (Vol. 3: The 1990s–Present)
Search for Tomorrow (Vol. 1: The 1950s–1960s)
Second City (Vol. 2: The 1970s–1980s)
Seinfeld (Vol. 2: The 1970s–1980s)
The Shari Lewis Show (Vol. 1: The 1950s–1960s)
Shōgun (Vol. 2: The 1970s–1980s)
Sing Along with Mitch (Vol. 1: The 1950s–1960s)
Sisters (Vol. 3: The 1990s–Present)
Skag (Vol. 2: The 1970s–1980s)

Sky King (Vol. 1: The 1950s–1960s)
The Spike Jones Show (Vol. 1: The 1950s–1960s)
St. Elsewhere (Vol. 2: The 1970s–1980s)
Star Trek (Vol. 1: The 1950s–1960s)
Tarzan (Vol. 1: The 1950s–1960s)
Taxi (Vol. 2: The 1970s–1980s)
Ted Mack and the Original Amateur Hour (Vol. 1: The 1950s–1960s)
Texaco Star Theater (Vol. 1: The 1950s–1960s)
That Was the Week That Was (Vol. 1: The 1950s–1960s)
Then Came Bronson (Vol. 1: The 1950s–1960s)
3rd Rock from the Sun (Vol. 3: The 1990s–Present)
30 Rock (Vol. 3: The 1990s–Present)
This is Your Life (Vol. 1: The 1950s–1960s)
Thriller (Vol. 1: The 1950s–1960s)
To Tell the Truth (Vol. 1: The 1950s–1960s)
The Today Show (Vol. 1: The 1950s–1960s)
Tomorrow with Tom Snyder (The Tomorrow Show) (Vol. 2: The 1970s–1980s)
The Tonight Show (Vol. 1: The 1950s–1960s)
Twenty-One (Vol. 1: The 1950s–1960s)
United States (Vol. 2: The 1970s–1980s)
Unsolved Mysteries (Vol. 2: The 1970s–1980s)
V (Vol. 2: The 1970s–1980s)
Victory at Sea (Vol. 1: The 1950s–1960s)
Wagon Train (Vol. 1: The 1950s–1960s)
Watch Mr. Wizard (Vol. 1: The 1950s–1960s)
The West Wing (Vol. 3: The 1990s–Present)
Will & Grace (Vol. 3: The 1990s–Present)
Wings (Vol. 3: The 1990s–Present)
You Bet Your Life (Vol. 1: The 1950s–1960s)
Your Hit Parade (Vol. 1: The 1950s–1960s)

NETFLIX

House of Cards (Vol. 3: The 1990s–Present)
Orange Is the New Black (Vol. 3: The 1990s–Present)

NICKELODEON

The Adventures of Jimmy Neutron: Boy Genius (Vol. 3: The 1990s–Present)
The Ren & Stimpy Show (Vol. 3: The 1990s–Present)
Rugrats (Vol. 3: The 1990s–Present)
SpongeBob Squarepants (Vol. 3: The 1990s–Present)

PBS (PUBLIC BROADCASTING SERVICE)

Adam Smith's Money World (Vol. 2: The 1970s–1980s)
Alive from off Center (Vol. 2: The 1970s–1980s)
Book Beat (Vol. 1: The 1950s–1960s)
Downton Abbey (Vol. 3: The 1990s–Present)
The Electric Company (Vol. 2: The 1970s–1980s)
Frontline (Vol. 2: The 1970s–1980s)
The Frugal Gourmet (Vol. 2: The 1970s–1980s)
Joseph Campbell and the Power of Myth (Vol. 2: The 1970s–1980s)
The Joy of Painting (Vol. 2: The 1970s–1980s)
The Life and Adventures of Nicholas Nickleby (Vol. 2: The 1970s–1980s)
Masterpiece Theatre (Vol. 2: The 1970s–1980s)
The McLaughlin Group (Vol. 2: The 1970s–1980s)
Meeting of Minds (Vol. 2: The 1970s–1980s)
Mister Rogers' Neighborhood (Vol. 1: The 1950s–1960s)
P.O.V. (Vol. 2: The 1970s–1980s)
Sesame Street (Vol. 1: The 1950s–1960s)
Sherlock (Vol. 3: The 1990s–Present)
Sneak Previews (Vol. 2: The 1970s–1980s)
Soul! (Vol. 2: The 1970s–1980s)
This Old House (Vol. 2: The 1970s–1980s)
Vietnam: A Television History (Vol. 2: The 1970s–1980s)
Wall $treet Week with Louis Rukeyser (Vol. 2: The 1970s–1980s)
Washington Week in Review (Vol. 1: The 1950s–1960s)

SHOWTIME

The Affair (Vol. 3: The 1990s–Present)
The Big C (Vol. 3: The 1990s–Present)
Dexter (Vol. 3: The 1990s–Present)
Faerie Tale Theatre (Vol. 2: The 1970s–1980s)
Homeland (Vol. 3: The 1990s–Present)
It's Garry Shandling's Show (Vol. 2: The 1970s–1980s)
The Paper Chase (Vol. 2: The 1970s–1980s)
Stargate SG-1 (Vol. 3: The 1990s–Present)
Super Dave (Vol. 2: The 1970s–1980s)

SPIKE

The Ultimate Fighter (Vol. 3: The 1990s–Present)

STARZ

Black Sails (Vol. 3: The 1990s–Present)

SUNDANCE CHANNEL

Rectify (Vol. 3: The 1990s–Present)

SYFY CHANNEL (PREVIOUSLY SCI FI)

Bitten (Vol. 3: The 1990s–Present)
Crossing Over with John Edward (Vol. 3: The 1990s–Present)
Stargate SG–1 (Vol. 3: The 1990s–Present)

SYNDICATION

A Current Affair (Vol. 2: The 1970s–1980s)
The Andy Williams Show (Vol. 1: The 1950s–1960s)
The Arsenio Hall Show (Vol. 2: The 1970s–1980s)
Baywatch (Vol. 2: The 1970s–1980s)
Biography (Vol. 1: The 1950s–1960s)
Body by Jake (Vol. 2: The 1970s–1980s)
Colonel Bleep (Vol. 1: The 1950s–1960s)
Crusader Rabbit (Vol. 1: The 1950s–1960s)
Dance Fever (Vol. 2: The 1970s–1980s)
Davey and Goliath (Vol. 1: The 1950s–1960s)
Death Valley Days (Vol. 1: The 1950s–1960s)
Divorce Court (Vol. 1: The 1950s–1960s)
Don Kirshner's Rock Concert (Vol. 2: The 1970s–1980s)
Entertainment Tonight (Vol. 2: The 1970s–1980s)
Extra: The Entertainment Magazine (Vol. 3: The 1990s–Present)
Fernwood 2-Night (Vol. 2: The 1970s–1980s)
Fractured Flickers (Vol. 1: The 1950s–1960s)
The George Michael Sports Machine (Vol. 2: The 1970s–1980s)
Geraldo (Vol. 2: The 1970s–1980s)
Hard Copy (Vol. 2: The 1970s–1980s)
Hercules: The Legendary Journeys (Vol. 3: The 1990s–Present)
Highlander: The Series (Vol. 3: The 1990s–Present)
Hollywood Babylon (Vol. 3: The 1990s–Present)
Hour Magazine (Vol. 2: The 1970s–1980s)
The Howard Stern Show (Vol. 3: The 1990s–Present)
In Search of (Vol. 2: The 1970s–1980s)
Inside Edition (Vol. 2: The 1970s–1980s)
The Insider (Vol. 3: The 1990s–Present)
Jeopardy! (Vol. 1: The 1950s–1960s)
The Joe Franklin Show (Vol. 1: The 1950s–1960s)
The Lawrence Welk Show (Vol. 1: The 1950s–1960s)
Let's Make a Deal (Vol. 1: The 1950s–1960s)
The Liberace Show (Vol. 1: The 1950s–1960s)
Lifestyles of the Rich and Famous (Vol. 2: The 1970s–1980s)
Mary Hartman, Mary Hartman (Vol. 2: The 1970s–1980s)
The McLaughlin Group (Vol. 2: The 1970s–1980s)
Mr. Magoo (Vol. 1: The 1950s–1960s)
The Morton Downey Jr. Show (Vol. 2: The 1970s–1980s)
Mutual of Omaha's Wild Kingdom (Vol. 1: The 1950s–1960s)
The Newlywed Game (Vol. 1: The 1950s–1960s)
Open End (The David Susskind Show) (Vol. 1: The 1950s–1960s)
The Oprah Winfrey Show (Vol. 2: The 1970s–1980s)
The People's Court (Vol. 2: The 1970s–1980s)
The Phil Donahue Show (Vol. 2: The 1970s–1980s)
Playboy after Dark (Vol. 1: The 1950s–1960s)
Playboy's Penthouse (Vol. 1: The 1950s–1960s)
Police Academy: The Series (Vol. 3: The 1990s–Present)
The Prisoner (Vol. 1: The 1950s–1960s)
The Richard Simmons Show (Vol. 2: The 1970s–1980s)
Rush Limbaugh: The Television Show (Vol. 3: The 1990s–Present)
Sally Jessy Raphael (Vol. 2: The 1970s–1980s)
Sea Hunt (Vol. 1: The 1950s–1960s)
The 700 Club (Vol. 1: The 1950s–1960s)
Solid Gold (Vol. 2: The 1970s–1980s)
Soul Train (Vol. 2: The 1970s–1980s)
Star Search (Vol. 2: The 1970s–1980s)
Star Trek: Deep Space Nine (Vol. 3: The 1990s–Present)

Star Trek: The Next Generation (Vol. 2: The 1970s–1980s)
Tales from the Darkside (Vol. 2: The 1970s–1980s)
Training Dogs the Woodhouse Way (Vol. 2: The 1970s–1980s)
War of the Worlds (Vol. 2: The 1970s–1980s)
Xena: Warrior Princess (Vol. 3: The 1990s–Present)

TNT

Babylon 5 (Vol. 3: The 1990s–Present)
The Closer (Vol. 3: The 1990s–Present)
The Lazarus Man (Vol. 3: The 1990s–Present)

UPN

America's Next Top Model (Vol. 3: The 1990s–Present)
Amish in the City (Vol. 3: The 1990s–Present)
Buffy the Vampire Slayer (Vol. 3: The 1990s–Present)
Dilbert (Vol. 3: The 1990s–Present)
Star Trek: Voyager (Vol. 3: The 1990s–Present)

USA

La Femme Nikita (Vol. 3: The 1990s–Present)
Monk (Vol. 3: The 1990s–Present)
Mortal Kombat: Conquest: Defenders of the Realm (Vol. 3: The 1990s–Present)
Nashville Star (Vol. 3: The 1990s–Present)

VH1

Behind the Music (Vol. 3: The 1990s–Present)
The RuPaul Show (Vol. 3: The 1990s–Present)
VH1 Storytellers (Vol. 3: The 1990s–Present)

WB

Angel (Vol. 3: The 1990s–Present)
Buffy the Vampire Slayer (Vol. 3: The 1990s–Present)
Childrens Hospital (Vol. 3: The 1990s–Present)
Dawson's Creek (Vol. 3: The 1990s–Present)
Felicity (Vol. 3: The 1990s–Present)
Gilmore Girls (Vol. 3: The 1990s–Present)
Pokémon (Vol. 3: The 1990s–Present)
Reba (Vol. 3: The 1990s–Present)
The Surreal Life (Vol. 3: The 1990s–Present)

WE TV

Bridezillas (Vol. 3: The 1990s–Present)

Preface

The purpose of this encyclopedia, *TV in the USA: A History of Icons, Idols, and Ideas*, is to inform students, teachers, scholars, and other interested readers about the history and scope of American television from its inception into the 21st century. Readers of this encyclopedia will gain knowledge about the content and technical aspects of the medium in order to understand its complex inner workings and programming decisions. Each of the three volumes contains valuable features and covers series and programs that best represent the era in which they were first broadcast. There is a keynote essay, a detailed commentary on the history of television, covering the development of the hardware, trends, and major events, for the decades of the 1950s and 1960s in the first volume, the 1970s and 1980s in the second volume, and the 1990s to the present in the third volume.

Entries were chosen applying a multitude of criteria and are organized in an A to Z alphabetical structure in each volume. These entries describe people who made a substantial contribution to the development of television in artistic, business, and entertainment areas, including scientists, inventors, and creators of networks and other media outlets.

Iconic and extremely popular programs of the 1950s and 1960s such as *I Love Lucy*, *Gunsmoke*, *Texaco Star Theatre* starring Milton Berle, *The Andy Griffith Show*, *The Twilight Zone*, *Perry Mason*, *The Red Skelton Show*, and *The Tonight Show* starring Johnny Carson are featured and described for their significance in Volume 1. In Volume 2, iconic programs that began in the 1970s and 1980s such as *M*A*S*H*, *All in the Family*, *Happy Days*, *Cheers*, *Saturday Night Live*, *The Mary Tyler Moore Show*, and *Seinfeld* are presented and discussed for their importance. Volume 3 identifies iconic shows spanning the 1990s through 2015, such as *Hill Street Blues*, *Friends*, *Law and Order*, *The X-Files*, *The Sopranos*, *Modern Family*, and *Breaking Bad*, which are presented and described in detail. Other types of entries include biographical profiles of prominent figures in television and programs that best represent the cutting edge of the medium, studied for their influence, legacy, and the historical significance of the landmark programs and their creators. The cultural significance and thematic importance of fictional programs and their ability to demonstrate the narrative and aesthetic nature of the television medium is evaluated. Entries stress information, detail, and the art, craft, and commerce of television. Decade by decade in the three volumes, the broadcasting of newsworthy events of national and international significance is discussed. These events include the assassination of President John F. Kennedy, live coverage of the Vietnam War, the Watergate hearings, and the terrorist attack on the Israeli weightlifting team at the Munich Olympics.

In *TV in the USA: A History of Icons, Idols, and Ideas* each entry includes, as applicable, air dates and network or cable on which the show appeared, genre, premise, story lines, featured and continuing casts and recurring guest stars, ratings and awards, reasons for cancellation and the significance of the entry in the history of television. Birth and death dates of individuals identified with the show are noted. Genres include Westerns, sitcoms, game shows, police procedurals, teen dramas, music and variety shows, science and speculative fiction, legal dramas, medical dramas, nighttime soap operas, regional programs, public broadcasting, adult animated programs, documentaries, miniseries, anthologies, docudramas, award shows, reality shows, sports programming, children's programming, cartoons, limited series, spin-offs and remakes, and the advent of cable outlets. Entries also include informational programming such as current events, breaking news, political commentaries, and daily news programs. The differences between network and cable programming are examined. Topic-specific essays address movements, trends, and television's relationship to the society and culture. Sidebars provide additional specific information that offers more detail about an entry subject. All these features interact to give a broad scope about television at a specific point in time. Every entry concludes with further resources for future study and cross-referencing of related programs in other volumes. The volumes are arranged to allow the reader access to the encyclopedia's various aspects, and there are tables of contents listing every element.

TV in the USA: A History of Icons, Idols, and Ideas is an overview of a medium that transformed the way the world is viewed and contributes to the achievement of common ground by connecting diverse groups in American society.

Introduction: The Evolution of Television from Color TV to Satellite Broadcasts

With the dawning of the 1970s, home use of television after three decades was about to change in every way. What was once a stand-alone device was about to experience the communication possibilities of interacting with outside content and with new technology. Satellite television allowed signals from communications satellites to connect with a dish on Earth and deliver television to the user's TV—in some cases into areas where TV was not available due to prior technological insufficiencies. In the 1980s satellite television would become a major breakthrough in broadcasting. It was a delivery agent that seemed right out of the future as depicted on the animated television show *The Jetsons*. The amount of growth of U.S. television was increasing in leaps and bounds. The social, political, and cultural impact of television had been enormous. The emergence of television forever changed the media and cultural landscape of America. In the 1970s and 1980s, it continued to be a source of news, information, drama, reality, and comedy, and with a new decade came a reinvention of content to suit the times and reflect them in every way possible.

By the 1970s, the television set itself had changed. On the market was every size imaginable, the shape was evolving, and the choices available to the public could suit their apartment, home, and lifestyle. The Zenith Space Command model came with a remote control. Prior to this, the user had to get up or reach over and physically change the channel. The remote was good for the elderly and others who had difficulty getting up, but largely it allowed the viewer to not just change the channel, but to do what later became known as "surfing," to sit in one spot and use the remote control to see what's going on from channel to channel, going back as often as wanted until resting on a particular channel or show. This would revolutionize television and the relationship between network or station and the home watcher.

Panasonic made a portable flip-top TV with radio. Looking right out of the space age in a science fiction film was the Orbitel that looked like a silver eye on a triangle stand. TVs were no longer in the traditional mode; there were tabletop and desktop models. Small was big again with Sony, who made it clear in their advertising that their product was expensive but the quality was so good, many professional control rooms used the Sony small screen as a monitor. Competition became fierce among the manufacturers, which were primarily Sylvania, Hitachi, Magnavox, Sanyo, Sansui, Sony, and Toshiba, showing the advent of Japanese manufacturers.

Along with these new models and types of televisions available to consumers, color TV became widespread throughout the United States in the 1970s. Although color TV had a long history as an experimental television concept and an attempt at turning black-and-white images into living color, it finally came into being in the mid- to later part of the 1960s, and it emerged as a major appliance of the 1970s. Already in 1970, 39 percent of households in the United States owned a color television set. By 1978, 56.9 million households owned a color television, or 78 percent (Buffalo History Museum). Sets could be adjusted by viewers in terms of color and brightness. Color TV launched a never-ending dialogue about what was good color. Some programs gave their shows naturalistic color, others used it as an artistic tool. At home there were arguments about when the color was adjusted right. There was a factory setting, but everyone sees or perceives color in their own way. Just adjusting the brightness impacted the tone and hue of the color. Discussions of black-and-white programs as an art form didn't happen as they did in the motion picture community. NBC and its peacock logo remained the leaders in color television. Audiences seemed to favor NBC over CBS and ABC partly because NBC had a Disney show, *Disney's Wonderful World of Color* (1954–2008), which produced shows in vivid color.

In the 1980s, sets continued to evolve and Japanese manufacturer Sony Corporation dominated the market. Although Sony products were more expensive than most others, consumers seeking top-of-the-line products bought Sony. However, consumers looking for more affordable options could buy Panasonic, General Electric, Zenith, Samsung, Casio, JVC, Sylvania, and Toshiba. As the American family dynamic began to change, more sets were sold in the 1980s, when families rarely watched television at the same time as they did in the 1950s and 1960s.

New technology, such as high definition, emerged in 1981, with NHK demonstrating the technology by packing 1,125 lines of resolution into a set. The results were remarkable; however, they were far from the standards of high definition set in the 21st century. Many also saw improved sound as the last frontier for television. In 1982, the Dolby Corporation developed home theater options for consumers, allowing for a more immersive television experience at home. After research, inspection, and demonstration, stereo broadcasts were approved, allowing concert-quality presentation in the home.

Network and Programming Changes in the 1970s

A new decade brings changes in the kinds of programs being broadcast. The 1970s gave birth to a genre many moviegoers and television viewers were waiting for. When the movies adapted a bestselling or classic novel to the screen, they had two to two and a half hours at the most to adapt a 300-, 400-, 500-, or more page book. Characters became compressed, scenes were cut. The television movie had the same problem and commercials ate into the time slot. However, the miniseries adapted a novel by keeping more material intact, literally filming more of the original novel than ever before. They originally were considered television events and shown for a number of hours each night over a week to as long as three weeks. *QB VII* was a legal drama concerning war crimes during World War II. It began airing on ABC on April 29, 1974; in total, it ran for six and a half hours. The miniseries based on the bestselling book written by Leon Uris (1924–2003) captured the public's attention, so more miniseries were put into production by all three networks.

One of the important events in television's history was the miniseries *Roots* by Alex Haley (1921–1992), largely the story of his family going back to the time of slavery and depicting how blacks were treated and struggled in the land they were brought to; 130 million people watched *Roots*. It aired over eight consecutive nights on ABC in January 1977. The audience cut through all demographics and backgrounds. It was reported that the streets were virtually empty as the serial drama unfolded night after night. The form as well as the content was responsible for the mega-success of *Roots* as audiences were fixed on every detail, character, and story line. The seventies would be the decade of the miniseries and change television forever.

Also during the 1970s, staple programs like the sitcom underwent dramatic changes, featuring more complex characters and touching on topics and themes that were previously taboo for television in the 1950s and 1960s. One of the controversial sitcoms was *All in the Family* (1971–1979), which centered on Archie Bunker, played with gusto by Carroll O'Connor (1924–2001). This character was a bigot who didn't like anyone and let his family know about it all the time. The show took on themes such as abortion, which had never been presented in a comedy; its dramatic moments made it a dramedy. The language was offensive and funny at the same time. Norman Lear (1922–) created the show to expose a part of America other shows hadn't. Laughing at Archie empowered the viewer and exposed the bigot.

Sanford and Son (1972–1977) was about an African American junkman and his son. Fred Sanford, played by Red Foxx (1922–1991), a prominent comedian, was proud living in a ghetto of his own making. He was loud, always spoke his mind, was insulting, and was constantly going after his son Lamont, played by Demond Wilson (1946–), who tried constantly to calm his father down and begged him for a better life. *The Bob Newhart Show* (1972–1978) featured the dry-humored comedian playing Robert Hartley, a psychologist with a practice in Chicago. The group therapy sessions were a significant aspect of the show. The majority of the patients were neurotic, which was fodder for humor. Instead of being in bad taste, this allowed viewers to see themselves and others in their circle, and to see the humanity and absurdity in this kind of behavior.

Another innovation of programming during the decade was the rise of cable networks, notably, the Home Box Office (HBO) network. Prior to this period, all television programming on the traditional networks was free, but HBO was introduced in 1972 as the first paid subscription television network. HBO's rise would begin in 1965 when cable pioneer Charles Dolan won a franchise to create and build a cable TV system named Sterling Information Services in lower Manhattan in New York City. Later it became Sterling Manhattan Cable, and eventually it became Time Warner Cable. Sterling Information Services was the first urban cable system in the United States. Dolan came up with the idea of laying cable underground to deliver content. Time Life Inc. bought 20 percent of Dolan's company, and for six years, the company lost money due to the cost of laying the cables. By 1971, the company had only 400 subscribers.

However, Dolan would solve this problem by envisioning a cable service where individual consumers would subscribe to the channel, which he initially called the Green Channel. However, with the backing of Time Life, HBO was founded on

November 8, 1972. The new service featured programs such as *HBO World Championship Boxing* in 1973, the hit variety show *Standing Room Only* in 1976, and a stellar documentary program beginning in 1979 with Dick Cavett (1936–) hosting the program *Time Was*. HBO also featured miniseries such as *The Seekers*, which aired in 1979.

HBO's success ushered in the rise of competition, with the Showtime network launching on July 1, 1976. They converted 10,000 subscribers of the former Channel One franchise on the Times-Mirror Cable systems in Escondido, Long Beach, and Palos Verdes, California. Showtime's first program was called *Celebration*, a lively concert featuring the rock band Pink Floyd, Rod Stewart, and the mega-group ABBA. By the end of Showtime's opening year, they had 55,000 subscribers nationwide. Showtime went national after being uplinked by satellite, quickly making the network a strong competitor to HBO.

Emergence of the Videocassette

The advancement of television's place in society and pop culture soon gave rise to new forms of the medium, especially allowing consumers to experience their favorite television programs and films on cassettes. The first home videocassette machine, called the U-Matic system, launched in 1971 (there was a prototype in 1969), made commercially available by the Sony Corporation. The cartridges were a bit larger than what would be distributed in the near future. The cassette was loaded with three-quarter-inch videotape and played up to 60 minutes, later up to 80 minutes. Sony introduced the VP-1100 cassette player and the VO-1600 videocassette player designed to play the new U-Matic tapes. It was simple to use and quickly made obsolete other systems that were on the market. U-Matic equipment was widely used in television newsrooms, schools, and businesses. Unfortunately the high cost, $1,395 in 1971 for a combination TV/VCR, equivalent to $8,000 in 2014 dollars, made it nearly impossible for the average consumer.

In October 1970 the Phillips Company created a videocassette format for a TV station. It was made available to consumers in 1972 and called the VCR but was referred to as the N1502 because of the model number of the first unit. It used square cassettes and half-inch tape mounted on coaxial reels, allowing a 60-minute recording time. It was first made available in the United Kingdom, but again it was too expensive for the average user. In 1972 the Avco Cartrivision system, which was a combination of a television set and VCR from Cartridge Television Inc. and sold for $1,350, was the first videocassette recorder that could use prerecorded major motion pictures, as well as tapes on sports, travel, art, and how-to subjects. Like the Phillips VCR format it had two reels of half-inch videotape mounted on top of each other and could record up to 114 minutes by way of video compression that recorded only every third video field and played it back three times.

By 1975 significant improvements had been made on the VCR and major companies were involved in its development: Matsushita Electric, Panasonic, RCA, VCR, JVC, Sony, and Toshiba. By 1979 the videocassette recorder was on its way to being a major mass-market consumer product. Standardization of format had not yet taken place as there were three different systems available. The major players were Sony with its Betamax, marketed in 1975, and JVC's VHS (Video Home System), out in the marketplace in 1977. The Betamax had an external timer and could only record one hour at a high quality, or two hours at a lower speed and lesser image quality. The VHS had a two-hour recording time and more hours at a slower speed and lesser quality. A T-120 tape was used as opposed to a Beta tape for Sony's machine. The Betamax was also considerably more expensive than the VHS machine.

Another contender was the Phillips Video 2000, which operated with a different kind of cassette. It was put on the market later than the two front-runners in 1979, didn't sell well, and was out of the picture in 1985. Minor contenders were Sanyo's V-Cord in 1974, VX put out by Panasonic in 1975, and Compact Video Cassette brought out by Funai and Technicolor in 1980. In the late 1970s tapes of Hollywood movies were available for sale and rent. Those with foresight about what kinds of tapes would be available predicted that there would be tapes available on almost any subject of interest. They were especially excited about what they thought was a growing how-to market that would let consumers buy tapes to learn how to fix their car, cook, do home improvement projects; they felt this market was limitless. These ideas did eventually become reality but decades after they were promised. At the very beginning of the market in the late 1970s the number-one selling and rental tapes were in the adult film area. Movies picked up strongly to the extent that the motion picture industry was very worried.

Satellite Television in the 1980s

Although the technology would not become widely available until the 1980s, satellite television had its roots in the decades prior. The world's first commercial satellite, called Intelsat-1 and nicknamed "Early Bird," was launched into orbit on April 5, 1965. The first national network of television satellites, called Orbita, was created by the Soviet Union in October 1967. The first commercial North American satellite to carry television signals was Canada's geostationary Anik, launched on November 9, 1972. ATS6, the world's first experimental educational and direct broadcast satellite to carry television transmission, was launched on May 30, 1974.

The satellite industry began in the United States from the cable television business with communication satellites deployed to distribute television programming to master facilities. HBO, Turner Broadcasting System (TBS), and the Christian Broadcasting Network (CBN), later renamed the Family Channel, became the first television services to utilize satellite television to deliver programming. In 1976, the first person to receive C-band satellite signals with a home-grown system was Taylor Howard, an American scientist and engineer in San Andreas, California. In 1978, the Public Broadcasting Service (PBS), a nonprofit public entity, began to distribute its television programming by satellite.

On October 18, 1979, the Federal Communications Commission (FCC) allowed citizens to have home satellite dishes without a federal government license. The first home satellite TV station for sale was featured at $36,500, with a dish nearly 20 feet in diameter and operated by remote control. These early systems were not particularly popular because of the price and size. However, by 1985, the size of the dishes was greatly reduced and as sales increased, the prices fell. Satellite systems allowed consumers who could not receive a good conventional broadcast signal to receive programming in their home without monthly fees. In October 1984, Congress passed the Cable Communications Policy Act of 1984, which gave those using particular systems the right to a free signal unless they were scrambled and required a fee. In 1986, scrambling came into practice, which made it difficult, if not impossible, for other stations or channels to be picked up.

Rise of Cable TV Networks

Satellite broadcasting allowed networks to reach a nationwide audience, which fueled the rise of cable networks that would soon come to dominate the television landscape. The 1980s were a boom for cable TV networks, with the Entertainment and Sports Programming Network (ESPN) emerging in 1979 and Ted Turner's (1938–) Cable News Network (CNN) debuting in 1980. ESPN debuted with its flagship program *SportsCenter*, offering highlights and recaps of the day's sporting events. The network aimed to broadcast sports content 24 hours a day. Likewise, CNN did the same with news content for around-the-clock coverage. This had a major impact on how news would be delivered in the future. News events that were typically covered for a few minutes on a network's nightly news broadcast could be covered in depth on CNN with extensive camera coverage and a wide range of information and commentary. Eventually, CNN could cover a major event all day and night without viewers having to wait for the scheduled evening news on the traditional networks.

Other cable networks soon arrived, such as Bravo Media LLC on December 1, 1980; Cinemax on August 1, 1980; the Weather Channel on May 2, 1982; Black Entertainment Television (BET) on January 25, 1980; the Discovery Channel on June 17, 1985; Arts & Entertainment, or A&E, on February 1, 1984; and American Movie Classics (AMC) on October 1, 1984. These networks catered to specific audiences or devoted their programming to specific topics and genres. BET, for instance, showcased music videos and reruns of sitcoms, all focused on appealing to African Americans and offering them a channel and content devoted to their culture. Other networks focused on delivering specific information, such as the Weather Channel broadcasting weather-related programming like forecasts, news and analysis, and weather-related documentaries. For educational programming, the Discovery Channel focused on wildlife and nature documentary series, as well as science and historical programs. A&E launched as a counterpart to PBS, with the signature show being *Biography*, a one-hour documentary series with limited commercials.

Delivering motion pictures was a major focus for many cable networks in the 1980s. Bravo delivered independent films, while AMC broadcast major motion picture classics. By 1989, AMC had 39 million subscribers. Already in the game, HBO and Showtime also ran films, but not more than in a long block. Cinemax debuted in 1980 and delivered movies on a 24-hour basis. On-air spokesman and actor Robert Culp (1930–2010) stated that Cinemax would feature movies and nothing else. The network focused on films released between 1950 and 1970 (whereas AMC focused on films released prior to 1950). To compete, HBO began playing R-rated films, and in a counter-move, Cinemax launched *Friday after Dark* in 1984, which showed adult films.

Videotape Rental and Purchases

While the videocassette was in its infancy in the 1970s, the 1980s saw a major format competition between Betamax from Sony and the VHS format supported by JVC, Matsushita, Panasonic, Hitachi, Mitsubishi, and Sharp. While Sony was known for its high-end products, VHS was supported by far more corporations, and it would eventually become the standard videotape format. After 41 years, Sony ceased Betamax production in 2015.

Videotape rentals and purchases grew in the 1980s, with dedicated stores offering consumers the chance to rent their favorite films or television programs for a set period of time, or purchase them outright. Entrepreneurs saw the financial opportunities in establishing video rental stores across the country as purchasing tapes was often more costly for consumers. Quickly, the country was flooded with video stores, with the first opened in December 1977 in Los Angeles, California by George Atkinson. He offered 50 titles from Magnetic Video. In the 1980s, these private stores led to the creation of chains such as West Coast Video, Blockbuster Video, and Rogers Video. A customer would usually join a chain for a fee, then pay a few dollars to rent a title. The infamous phrase "Be kind, please rewind" entered American pop culture as consumers were asked to rewind the tapes before returning them to the rental store.

The advancing technology for television in the home, as well as the video rental stores, created serious competition with the motion picture industry. In 1987, rental revenues surpassed box office receipts as films were released for rent after their motion picture release, leading many consumers to wait to watch films for a cheaper price in their own home. Also, with so many video rental stores, consumers opted to watch videotapes as opposed to conventional television programming. This competition between television networks, video rentals, and conventional cinemas saw cable networks push the envelope of content, language, and material that could be shown on television in order to attract more viewers. Television in the 1980s was encouraged, some say forced, to create more mature programming that could compete with the mature content in major motion pictures and on videotape. New forms like the miniseries and later the reality program would be a strong tool against the competition.

Television continued its evolution in the 1970s and 1980s, expanding the options for viewers at home while improving picture size, quality, and sound. The advent of new and sophisticated cable networks, as well as satellite delivery systems, opened a door for entrepreneurs and companies to present unlimited shows to millions of viewers.

The 1970s

ABC Afterschool Specials (1972–1997)

These very significant shows were developed and produced for young people to watch when they returned home from junior high school or high school. As with many programs in the earlier years of television, they were shot on film. Although *ABC Afterschool Specials* were intended to entertain young people, they also taught students lessons they didn't necessarily learn in school, exploring topics such as divorce, drug use, gender roles, and even death. Others like "A Home Run for Love," which aired in 1978 concerned a friendship between a young Caucasian boy and an elderly African American gentleman. Many of the dramas were based on young adult novels and in the first season of 1972–1973, an episode introduced Shakespeare to young people.

The Producer

The force behind *ABC Afterschool Specials* was producer Martin Tahse (1930–2014), who began in theater producing road tours of plays such as *Funny Girl, The Miracle Worker,* and *A Funny Thing Happened on the Way to the Forum* before they found their way to Broadway. In children's television programming Tahse produced the last 13 episodes of *Kukla, Fran and Ollie.*

Martin Tahse was responsible for over 20 *Afterschool Specials* that investigated the problems of teens and others. They accomplished teachable moments while striving for authenticity and refused to end with a parent solving the issue at large. In 2006 Tahse said, "The kid had to resolve the problem by him- or herself."

One of Tahse's motivations was that he was the child of an alcoholic parent. He was serious and passionate about the shows he produced for *ABC Afterschool Specials,* and the young viewers felt the same way and learned greatly from watching the shows. Some critics found the shows preachy, while others mocked them.

Martin Tahse was the winner of two daytime Emmy awards. In 1978 he won the Emmy award for Outstanding Children's Informational Special for "Very Good Friends" (aka "Beat the Turtle Drum"). In 1981 Martin Tahse won the Outstanding Children's Entertainment Special award for "A Matter of Time."

Of all the *ABC Afterschool Specials* that aired during the 1970s, two stand out as classic examples of the form. "Me and My Dad's Wife" (1975) starred Kristy McNichol (1962–), who was one of the stars of the ABC television drama *Family* (1976–1980), playing "Buddy," the youngest girl, and who also was featured in the movies *Little Darlings* (1980), *White Dog* (1982), and *Dream Lover* (1986). McNichol was one of many young actors who got their start from this anthology series. This story concerned divorce. McNichol played Nina Beckwith, a girl who lived with her mother while her father remarried and was stepfather to two boys, one her age and one much younger. The father and his new wife, who was a teacher, moved back to town to be closer to his daughter, and on the first day of school her stepmother turned up as Nina's teacher. Nina had deep issues accepting her father's remarriage and especially to the woman who was her math teacher. The kids organized a psychological plot to get the teacher to quit by remaining silent one day and copying all her movements the next. They succeeded. Her father picked up Nina for a ride and told her that his new wife was planning on transferring to another school. He informed Nina that his wife was ill in bed with a bug and wanted to drive to their house first to check on her. Nina immediately bonded with her young stepbrother. When her father started to bring up a tray of food for his wife, Nina asked to do it. In the bedroom Nina and her stepmother finally came to a warm understanding, and the stepmother promised to return to Nina's class. The acting was more than serviceable and the direction and production values, although low budget, were effective and served the story well. There were fewer shots than many night-time TV shows, in part to deal with the low budgets the producers and directors were given.

"A Special Gift" aired in 1979. Three ballet companies, the Joffrey and a New York and a San Francisco troupe, and a choreographer were involved in the production. A good-looking teenage boy with long layered blond hair was on the basketball team; he also worked after school at a hardware store and, without anyone's knowledge except his sister, took ballet lessons. The point of this story was whether society could accept gender roles that might be different from those conventionally accepted. A friend found out first, then others, because the boy was selected for a special production of *Nutcracker* and his photo wound up in the local paper. The boy lived on a farm and his dad loved him but was dead set against the boy dancing. When some of his schoolmates found out as well as his best friend, they called him nasty names, insinuating that he was gay. The only person who mattered to the boy in terms of acceptance was his dad, who drove him to the theater for a dress rehearsal. The boy asked his dad to come in but the dad refused. He drove off as the viewers saw the dance in progress; he then drove back and saw how brilliant a young dancer his son was, and then the father was able to accept him. This episode was especially entertaining because of all the excellent dance sequences as well as delivering an important message. "A Special Gift" won a Peabody Award. This hallowed organization celebrated *Afterschool Specials* because they "took a story in which a reasonable young boy faces the first great dilemma of his life and brought it to life in such a way that no viewer was spared the agony of helping him make the choice."

ABC Afterschool Specials enjoyed a long run from October 14, 1972 to July 1, 1997. The series presented dramatic shows, some in a documentary format. *Afterschool Specials* were broadcast on occasional afternoons.

A Start for Cast and Crew

Some of the actors who later became "names" and who were featured on the anthology series are Jodie Foster in the 1973–1974 season; Rob Lowe and Scott Baio in the 1980–1981 season; Ben Affleck in the 1986–1987 season; and Vince Vaughan in the 1990–1991 season. Some of the adult actors working in the series included Beau Bridges, Cloris Leachman, and Lindsay Crouse. Music stars included Davy Jones of the Monkees, Michael Jackson, and Carole King (1942–). Oprah Winfrey also hosted some panel discussions in the 1991–1994 seasons of the program.

It was not only actors who got a start and career boost from *ABC Afterschool Specials*; many specialists behind the scenes developed their trade in cinematography, production design, editing, sound, and music. The show supported writers in two ways; many of the shows were based on books that were optioned and, of course, then a teleplay writer was employed to write the scenario that guided the actors and crew.

ABC Afterschool Specials are remembered fondly by those who were raised on them. More than milk and cookies or homework was waiting for them when they arrived home—a television show made for them.

Further Resources

Colker, David. 2015. "Martin Tahse Dies at 84; TV Producer of 'ABC Afterschool Specials.'" *Los Angeles Times*. http://www.latimes.com/local/obituaries/la-me-martin-tahse-20140720-story.html

de Rosnay, Tatiana. *Sarah's Key*. 2006. New York: St. Martin's Griffin.

Merrill, Jean. 2006. *The Toothpaste Millionaires*. Boston: Houghton.

Ross, Sharon Marie, and Louise Ellen Stein, eds. 2008. *Teen Television: Essays on Programming and Fandom*. Jefferson, NC: McFarland.

Alice (CBS, 1976–1982, 1983–1985)

Alice was based on the feature film *Alice Doesn't Live Here Anymore* released in 1974. The creators of the

TV show were able to develop the series in less than two years. The creator of *Alice* was Robert Getchell (1936–), who wrote the original screenplay for the film as a first effort and was nominated for an Academy Award. Getchell also wrote the teleplay for the series, also acclaimed. Warner Bros. was the studio of record for the film and television show.

The Story

Alice follows Alice Hyatt, played by Linda Lavin (1937–), a recently widowed woman who settles in Phoenix, Arizona with her 12-year-old son Tommy, portrayed by Philip McKeon (1964–). Alice had been a saloon singer in the past and would like to be one again, but settles on working as a waitress, a new profession for her, at Mel's Diner, which is owned and operated by a man who barks but has a tender heart. The story lines revolve primarily around Alice's relationship with Tommy and her day-to-day activities at Mel's, which at best are hectic. Everyone there is funny, especially the senior waitress, Flo, played by Polly Holliday (1937–), who is famous for saying "Kiss my grits" at least once an episode. The verbal comedic exchanges are sharp one-liners shooting around the room from Mel to Flo and Alice, while a third waitress, Vera, played by Beth Howland (1941–), provides plenty of physical comedy. She is high-strung, always hyper and nervous—constantly crashing into people and dropping food trays. Mel was played by Vic Tabak (1930–1990) in both versions. Tabak's physical, vocal, and acting style is the same in both movie and series, playing the pivotal character with a gruff, sandpaper voice but with a good heart. Flo was played by Diane Ladd (1935–) in the movie and by Polly Holliday in the TV show for four years; then Ladd came on as a new waitress, Belle Dupree, for one season.

The musical theme for *Alice* made the perfect connection to Alice and her goals and dreams. "There's a New Girl in Town" was written by the mega-hit duo Alan Bergman (1925–) and Marilyn Bergman (1929–) and David Shire (1937–) and is sung over the opening credits by Linda Lavin.

Sexually suggestive themes abound for the characters. Flo is always bragging about her prowess with men, bending over them at a table to get bigger tips and counseling Alice to show more cleavage by repeating Flo's tricks. Alice has an adolescent son, Tommy. In her mid-thirties, men are always hitting on her. She has many dates, which usually go wrong. They often begin in the diner and end up in the small apartment where she and Tommy live. One time a man too young for Alice pretends to be a Hollywood agent as a sexual maneuver. Another date was set up by Mel whose friend was a hunky former pro football player now acting in Italian Westerns. Everything goes smoothly until one night it seems the moment for a kiss or more when the handsome, kind, and sensitive man reveals he is gay. This turns out to be a life lesson about stereotypes, especially for Tommy, who is surprised because friends gave him the impression that gay men spoke and moved in a particular manner not at all evident in this man. Alice and Tommy become friends with the ex-football pro turned actor.

There were poignant episodes as well. In episode 3 of season 1, called "A Piece of the Rock," Alice learns that her departed husband left an insurance policy she was not aware of. She finds out it is only for $1,500 and, to make matters worse, the beneficiary is another woman. Alice tracks her down in a sleazy motel, at first thinking the woman is a young floozy, but in fact she is a senior citizen. As the story unfolds, it is revealed that Alice's husband, a long-distance trucker, frequently stopped at the motel and talked to the lady about Alice's singing and the fact that she didn't have a piano. The woman, named Bubbles, encouraged him to buy his wife a piano and lent him $1,500. The policy was his way to pay her back.

The major difference between *Alice Doesn't Live Here Anymore* and the modern sitcom *Alice* is that Alice and Tommy don't arrive at Mel's Diner until midway through the feature film. It was a clever and effective way to mine the material and focus on the feminist aspects of the story, handling them with comedic writing and performing.

It was now the 1970s and the women's movement began to influence the portrayals of female characters on television. Women were shown as capable, strong, and often employed, but, of course, still vulnerable. Shows like *That Girl* (1966–1971) and *The Mary Tyler Moore Show* (1970–1977) paved the way for a new era in the presentation of women. In coming decades this evolved further, but *Alice* made its impact by depicting a working single parent with humor and purpose.

Alice was a hit. It ran for nine seasons and 202 episodes were broadcast.

See also: *The Mary Tyler Moore Show*; *Vol. 1, The 1950s–1960s: That Girl.*

Further Resources

Getchell, Robert. 1975. *Alice Doesn't Live Here Anymore.* New York: Grand Central Publishing.

Taylor, Candacy A. 2009. *Counter Culture: The American Coffee Shop.* Ithaca, NY: ILR Press.

All in the Family (CBS, 1971–1979)

The 1970s were known as a decade in which the American situation comedy became controversial and unafraid to take on whatever socially relevant issues confronted the country. *All in the Family* aired on the CBS network from 1971 to 1979 and for the last four seasons as *Archie Bunker's Place*, a spin-off and continuation of the show. For five years it was the top-rated show in the United States and won four consecutive Emmy awards for Outstanding Comedy Series. It's an important and influential program that is considered by viewers, many critics, and culture-watchers as possibly the greatest sitcom of the 1970s.

> Archie Bunker excitedly runs into his house telling his family he had the great entertainer Sammy Davis Jr. in his cab and that they had a nice friendly chat. Archie is the sort of bigot who dislikes and demeans blacks, but makes an exception for what he believes is "a credit to his race" type like Mr. Davis. Archie tells his family they will get to meet Sammy Davis because the entertainer left a suitcase in the back of his cab. On the phone, Davis tells Archie that he'll pick up the suitcase in person because he's going to the airport. At the end of the episode, Davis and Bunker pose for a picture, and at the last second Davis quickly turns his head and kisses Archie on the cheek. This is a seminal moment in the history of television.

Themes

The story lines and many issues, especially bigotry, are centered on Archie Bunker, the head of the family living in the borough of Queens, New York. Archie Bunker rules the roost, mainly from "his chair," which is positioned dead center in their modest middle-class living room. Legions of fans laughed at Archie Bunker's rantings and prejudices.

The entire cast of *All in the Family* was very good, but two were brilliant. Archie Bunker, a dock worker, spoke loudly and with conviction against African Americans, Jews, hippies, and other minorities and ethnic groups. During the height of the women's movement Archie believed men were superior and that women should stay home and do men's bidding. Bunker was played by Carroll O'Connor (1924–2000), an actor who could scream and yell one minute and reveal a tender side in the next. His interpretation of a blue-collar bigot trying to cope with a changing society was quintessential.

Bunker's wife Edith was portrayed by stage actress Jean Stapleton (1923–2013), who made the bold decision to play a woman labeled by her TV husband as a "dingbat." She acted daffy at times and spoke with a high, screechy voice. In reality Edith was not dumb; she had a pure heart and in her mind knew Archie was wrong about most cultural and social issues. Stapleton's finesse in her role as Edith allowed audiences to see the wisdom in her character and her deep love for her family.

Their daughter Gloria was played by Sally Struthers (1947–). Here we have the dumb blonde of the 1950s and 1960s transformed in modern times to an independent thinker who loved and supported her hippie husband, Mike Stivic, played with grace and humor by Carl Reiner's son Rob Reiner (1947–). Archie called his son-in-law "meathead" incessantly. Gloria and Mike had Aquarian ideas that carried over from the sixties. They were a chorus against inequity and hatred and were defenders of freedom and justice. Archie, as the opening musical theme song announces, believes that the best days of America are behind them, but Mike and Gloria are there to tell the viewers that the old days may have had some good qualities, but that the country is moving on and

Just one of the many argumentative exchanges between Archie Bunker, played by Carroll O'Connor, and his wife Edith Bunker, played by Jean Stapleton, on *All in the Family*. The enormously popular show introduced social commentary to the sitcom genre. (Bettmann/Getty Images)

changing. The show's essence came down to a battle of the generations—conservative Archie Bunker vs. liberal Mike Stivic.

The show's theme song, "Those Were the Days," was written by Lee Adams and Charles Strouse. The show began with Archie and Edith sitting at the piano with Edith facing the camera and singing. The lyrics spoke of the 1940s and 1950s when big band music reigned and men and women were in traditional gender roles.

The main set for *All in the Family* is the Bunkers' living room decorated in a recognizable middle-class American style. It is simply furnished and has a stairway that leads to the second floor; there are decorative plates on the wall and everything is designed to support the king's throne known as Archie's chair.

All in the Family was videotaped in front of a live studio audience at the CBS television center in Hollywood, California. It was not a continuous experience for the audience. The production stopped when an actor missed a line or for some technical problem requiring a break; then they would roll tape again until they completed the episode. The actual sounds of laughter and applause from the live audience were transferred to the final edited tape, and more sounds were added, a technique known as sweetening.

The genesis of *All in the Family* began when producers Norman Lear (1922–) and Alan (Bud) Yorkin

(1926–2015) gathered the U.S. rights to a hit BBC comedy series, *Till Death Us Do Part*. Norman Lear developed two pilots based on its concept for ABC. Mickey Rooney (1920–2014) was actually Lear's first choice to play Archie, but he went ahead with O'Connor. It was called *Those Were the Days* and ABC turned it down. Luckily, president of CBS Robert Wood was looking for more urban shows to appeal to a then-changing viewership. He even cancelled popular shows like *Green Acres* and *The Red Skelton Show* to make room for a new lineup. Wood thought Lear's show was what he was looking for, but it was a risk, so he made a 13-episode commitment as a mid-season replacement. Aspects of the show could be seen as unacceptable such as Mike and Gloria's active sex life and Archie's constant burping and the flushing of toilets. Even worse was the language, which included the N-word and all sorts of sub-par vocabulary not heard on television before. Over the course of its long run, the show tackled taboo subjects such as abortion, rape, race relations, homosexuality, Vietnam, and child custody, issues not commonly investigated on a sitcom.

Audience test results were below average, but with little advertising support on TV or in print, CBS put *All in the Family* into the marketplace on January 12, 1971. The first response was lukewarm and the first episode received a poor 15 percent audience share. It was sluggish for months until it built a following by strong word of mouth. By the end of the season it earned three Emmy awards including Outstanding Comedy Series. The show eventually spawned a group of spin-offs including *Maude, The Jeffersons,* and *Gloria.*

Controversial Stories

It was a challenge to write, act, and produce the show's tough themes. The creators found a way to treat mental illness with a comic touch. In "Edith Flips Her Wig," Mrs. Bunker is convinced she is a kleptomaniac. She was arrested after leaving a local store with a wig and a necklace. Mike and Gloria want her to see a psychiatrist and, of course, Archie doesn't. Even though she is not Catholic, she talks to a priest, who helps solve her problem. Meanwhile Archie talks to the department store manager and makes antisemitic remarks about Jewish-owned stores. The manager throws Archie out of the office, calls Edith, and clears her of all charges but makes it known he never wants Archie in his store again.

The Vietnam War and draft resisters living in Canada were a hot-button issue. In the 1970s many were still there. For a season 7 Christmas show and the episode "The Draft Dodger," the issues were dealt with straight on. An old friend of Mike's shows up at the house. Mike can't understand why this young man would risk coming to the States. The family prepares Christmas Eve dinner. Archie has invited an old friend who is alone and whose son was killed in Vietnam. The table conversation eventually turns serious and everyone learns there is a draft dodger in their home. Archie immediately goes ballistic, a tour-de-force by O'Connor. He wants the boy to leave, but wants to hear from his friend first. The man says his son was against the war and died; the resister is alive and he believes his son would have liked him, and further, he likes him and wants to continue the dinner. But Archie is not always a man of his word. Edith pulls him aside and makes him promise not to make a scene; he starts to calm down, saying he's trying to work it out. Archie goes back to the table with Edith and announces to everyone that after dinner he's still going to work things out. Lessons have been learned by all.

The legacy of *All in the Family* is that everyone involved with the production believed in what they were doing—this was not controversy for controversy's sake. *All in the Family* was committed to being a show with a comedic approach to its time from the point of view of a blue-collar everyman in conflict with the turbulent times in which he lived.

See also: *The Jeffersons*; Lear, Norman; *Maude*.

Further Resources

Kerr, Lawrence, and Rob Reiner. 2014. *156 Success Facts—Everything You Need to Know about Rob Reiner.* Amazon Digital Services.

McChrohan, Donna. 1988. *Archie and Edith, Mike and Gloria: The Tumultuous History of All in the Family.* New York: Workman.

O'Connor, Carroll. 1999. *I Think I'm Outta Here.* New York: Pocket Books.

America 2-Night

See *Fernwood 2-Night*

Baretta (ABC, 1975–1978)

The story of how *Baretta* became a television series goes back to the hour-long crime show *Toma,* which ran from October 4, 1973 to September 6, 1974 and starred Tony Musante (1936–2013) as a real-life Newark Police Department detective, David Toma. The character was a master of disguise and used unorthodox methods to catch bad guys. Musante surprised the network, which cleared the series for a second season, by abruptly leaving the show. ABC then became interested in Robert Blake (1933–), a former child actor who attracted attention with roles featuring characters who were on the other side of what is consider normal by society. The decision was made to scrap *Toma* but to create a one-hour crime show about a maverick cop who also was a master of disguise. They named the character Tony Baretta.

Blake brought some of himself to Baretta's character as well as traits that would make him interesting to watch. Baretta always wears a cap pulled down over his forehead. He lives in a rundown hotel in a shabby room with a Murphy bed in the wall. California is his beat and he knows his surroundings like the back of his hand. Baretta dresses down, looking more like a street person than a detective. He is a diminutive type who is tough as nails; even the biggest thug has little chance in a fight with him. He is a rebel on the force, constantly fighting with his boss; he always has an unconventional plan to catch hoods. His constant companion is a pet cockatoo named Fred, who wises off at him. Baretta has a reliable streetwise informant named Rooster, played by Michael D. Roberts (1947–), who dressed the part of a street person and wore colorful 1970s fashion appropriate to his low place in society.

The show was created by Stephen J. Cannell (1941–2010), who would become a TV mogul best known for his speed in writing a series episode. The theme song was written by Dave Grusin (1934–) and Morgan Ames. The instrumental was played over shots of Baretta, some live action in color and some in black-and-white using the photomation technique in which a still image is made to move by panning the camera. Eventually Sammy Davis Jr. (1925–1990) recorded "Keep Your Eyes on the Sparrow," which was played over the opening and became indelibly associated with the Baretta series and with the Tony Baretta character and Robert Blake, the actor.

A main subject on the show is drugs, substance abuse, selling drugs in large quantities, and its association with murder. In one episode Baretta's girlfriend is murdered while he looks on, in another a childhood friend is killed and Baretta tries to protect his pregnant widow from the same fate and from her drug habit. Crime czars are targeted by Baretta as are drug dens and houses of ill repute, all controlled by mob figures. Tony Baretta is a one-man force, a funky shopworn figure determined to rid his part of California of crime.

See also: *Columbo*; *Kojak*; *Police Story.*

Further Resources

Armstrong, Lois. 1977. "Baretta's Blake. Money's Cold Comfort Now to Robert Blake, Sleeping with a Stranger Called Success." *People Magazine*. September 19.

Blake, Robert. 2012. *Tales of a Rascal: What I Did for Love*. Black Rainbow Productions.

Kane, Bob. 1990. *Batman: Batman and Me*. Eclipse Books.

Battle of the Sexes: Billie Jean King vs. Bobby Riggs (1973)

The modern women's movement emerged and flourished during the 1970s. It was a time when women fought for equal jobs, equal pay, and liberation from the old images and roles women held in society. Male-female relationships were a major point of discussion across the country; male-dominated society and women's desire for change was a major topic of conversation. In this vein, the "Battle of the Sexes" was a tennis match that was a glorified publicity stunt between former Wimbledon men's tennis champion Bobby Riggs and women's Wimbledon champion Billie Jean King, to prove whether men and women were equal on the tennis court and in everyday society.

A Tennis Match for the Ages in the Works

Bobby Riggs (1918–1995) was a tennis pro who had won Wimbledon. He also was a character who thrived on attention and gambling. Riggs decided he would exploit the battle of the sexes and asked Billie Jean King (1943–), a champion on the women's tennis circuit, to play him in a match. King quickly declined the offer.

Riggs next approached the number-one player in the world, Margaret Court (1942–), for a match. Court accepted the challenge. They played on May 13, 1973 and the results were disastrous for Court, who lost 6–2, 6–1. The win bolstered Riggs's boasting that no woman could beat a man at tennis. He became a huge celebrity. Riggs had been a top champ in the 1940s; now he was in his sixties and admittedly not as fast or agile as he once was, but he still won. He was on the covers of *Sports Illustrated* and *Time* magazines.

Now that he had the national spotlight, Riggs began to taunt all the major women tennis players. At this time Billie Jean King became interested in the challenge, hoping that this overhyped "Battle of the Sexes" would help bring attention to the women's tour, women's tennis, and sports in general. She was paid a lucrative undisclosed sum to participate but later learned, to her chagrin, that Riggs was paid more money, emphasizing that women were being paid less for doing the same job as a man. The prize for the winner was $100,000.

Before the match Bobby Riggs pulled publicity stunts like charging people to watch him sit in a chair and blast tennis balls into a mounted poster of Billie Jean King to humiliate her. He showed up everywhere he could to boast and usually had his arms around a group of young women. He made chauvinistic comments for the press, suggesting that women should stay home and tend to their husbands. All of it had a circus-like atmosphere.

ABC Sports secured the rights to televise the match live with Howard Cosell (1918–1995), their top man, to call the match, which was held in Texas at the Astrodome. This was not so much planned as a big, important tennis match; rather, it was a spectacle. King entered the stadium as if she were Cleopatra, sitting in a chair held by four bare-chested men. Riggs, who had a lot of bets down on the game, entered in a rickshaw drawn by a group of scantily dressed female models. They exchanged gifts: Riggs gave his female opponent a very large lollipop and King in return gave Riggs a pig—as in chauvinist pig. The tone was giddy; everyone in the stands and presumably at home was having a great time. The viewers were estimated at 50 million. The players took to the court. Some said that King played like a man. Riggs ran himself all over the court, missing main points by hitting the ball right into the net, sometimes the lower part of the net. The results were that King triumphantly won in three straight sets, 6–4, 6–3, and 6–3. It was a win for women's tennis, proving that women are as good and as strong as the men's tour. "The Battle of the Sexes" was a strong push forward for the women's movement, going well beyond tennis into the sociopolitical arena.

History is a double-edged sword; what millions saw during the King/Riggs match was a woman beating a man at tennis building steam for the women's movement. Later inconclusive but persistent rumors suggested that Riggs threw the game, deliberately losing a match he could have won as he did with Margaret Court, caving to the will of a group of mafia kingpins who offered to drop his considerable gambling debt if he threw the game.

The event and the broadcast remain a 1970s moment. The whole world was watching a woman hit a tennis ball over a net for gender equality. Riggs was a great tennis player who became a trickster, a gambler, and a man willing to humiliate women to gain publicity and a buck. A more respectable male tennis player could have been on the other side of the challenge, but the 1970s were a time of bombast, excess, and enormous social and political changes. Television was there, supported by an ABC Sports mega-telecast that pulled out all the stops, employing the definitive 1970s sports broadcaster Howard Cosell as the ringmaster. It couldn't have taken place at a better time, place, or with a more perfect cast of characters. It was like an event taking place in a coliseum in ancient Rome.

See also: ESPN; 1972 Munich Olympics.

Further Resources

King, Billie Jean, and Christine Brennan. 2008. *Pressure Is a Privilege: Lessons I've Learned from Life and the Battle of the Sexes.* New York: LifeTime Media.

Riggs, Bobby. 1973. *Court Hustler*. Philadelphia: J. P. Lippincott.

Battlestar Galactica (ABC, 1978–1979)

The science fiction genre has been around since the beginning. On television in the 1950s there was *Captain Video and His Video Rangers* (1949–1955), *Tom Corbett, Space Cadet* (1950–1955), *Space Patrol* (1950–1955), *Rod Brown of the Rocket Rangers* (1953–1954), *Captain Z-Ro* (1951–1956), and *Tales of Tomorrow* (1951–1953). In the 1960s there was *Lost in Space* (1965–1968) and the seminal *Star Trek* (1966–1969).

Creation

Glen A. Larson (1937–2014) was the creator of *Battlestar Galactica,* which ran on ABC. It was influenced by science fiction television that came before, especially the iconic *Star Trek,* but science fiction motion pictures of the 1970s released prior to 1978 are reflected brightly in this action-packed and somewhat socially conscious show. *Battlestar Galactica* had much to offer, great characters and the overarching concept of searching for Earth from another galaxy. The massive space battles and amazing aerodynamic crafts were especially attractive to youngsters.

The show was narrated by Lorne Greene (1915–1987) of *Bonanza* fame, who played Commander Adama. Some of the other major characters in the large cast included Richard Hatch (1945–2017) as Captain Apollo; Dirk Benedict (1945–) portrayed Lt. Starbuck. Lt. Boomer was played by Herb Jefferson Jr. (1946–), Maren Jensen was Athena (1956–), and Flight Sgt. Jolly was portrayed by Tony Swartz (1943–).

Battlestar Galactica begins in the seventh millennium CE at the end of an endless and bloody war conducted by a race of robots named Cylons and defended by the 12 colony worlds of humanity where the viewer finds a possible hope for peace. The ship is the only surviving craft for the good guys to fight the bad guys. This, however, turns out to be a ruse because the Cylons again ruthlessly attack as a team of quickly assembled troops with good on their side try to fight them back in hopes that they can find a 13th colony they identity as—Earth.

Battlestar Galactica had a solid beginning audience, but later episodes were considered by the viewers to be more like recycled Westerns than cutting-edge sci-fi TV. The fan base that existed was outraged after the network felt burdened by a show that cost one million dollars an episode and cancelled *Battlestar Galactica* after just one single season.

A mammoth write-in campaign was underway. Glen Larson and the network executives trimmed down the budget. They also asked Larson to create what has to be considered a spin-off or a retool named *Galactica 1980.* Numerous changes were made to the characters. There was an Earth landing, but not without the Cylons forcing everyone but two men to flee.

Sadly, *Galactica 1980* was a dismal failure and heavily disliked by the fans who tried to save *Battlestar Galactica* in the first place. *Galactica 1980* did not even receive a full season to show what it could do—it was cancelled after 10 episodes.

The original *Battlestar Galactica* was a spectacle of sight and sound. The visual effects by John Dykstra, who was also the man in that department for *Star Wars,* were unprecedented for television. The exterior space scenes were overwhelming in size and presence. There were constant bombs in the air and explosions galore. The sound by the nine-man sonic crew was spectacular and like motion pictures, proved that TV as well was all about picture and sound. There seems to be an influence from *Star Wars* master sound designer Ben Burtt (1948–). The music was composed by Stu Phillips (1929–) and performed with precision and emotion by the prestigious Los Angeles Philharmonic. Weapons included zapping guns and buzzing lasers.

Controversy concerning similarities between *Battlestar Galactica* and *Star Wars* (1977) came down to two high-stakes lawsuits. Twentieth Century-Fox sued Universal, stating there were as many as 38 instances in which Larson and Universal must have copied *Star Wars.* Universal in turn sued Fox, saying *Star Wars* copied *Silent Running,* released by Universal in 1972. Both suits were summarily dismissed by the court.

The acting on *Battlestar Galactica* and *Galactica 1980* is over-the-top the way people perceive acting in a day or nighttime soap opera. The costumes are colorful, the music is broad and at times overreaching.

Some audience members and critics find religious, spiritual, and philosophic tones in the characters and narrative of *Battlestar Galactica,* but they are not as pronounced at those on *Star Trek,* a show whose foundation is built on higher meaning and learning life lessons. *Battlestar Galactica* is an epic science fiction show with plenty of action.

Not all the stories on the Galactica shows concern warring platforms. One such episode, "Murder on the Rising Star," from season One, episode 16 from the original series, broadcast on February 19, 1979, was actually a murder mystery, concerning aggressive play during a game that is a futuristic cross between hockey and basketball. A man is killed, a key member of the flying staff is accused and arrested, and a plan for a trial is established. While waiting for the trial there is an escape, a search for the real killer, lots of red herrings, and of course justice at the end for the real killer and the wrongly accused. A lesson about the dangers of too much aggression, hatred, and violence is brought to bear as well.

For its short run *Battlestar Galactica* was cutting-edge television in terms of sound, image, and a grand, sweeping story.

See also: *Star Trek: The Next Generation*; *Vol. 1, The 1950s–1960s: Star Trek*; *Vol. 3, The 1990s–Present: Stargate SG-1*; *Star Trek: Deep Space Nine*; SyFy Channel

Further Resources

Battlestargalactica.com

Bennett, Linda. 2004. *My Father's Voice: The Biography of Lorne Greene*. Lincoln, NE: iUniverse.

Ruditis, Paul. 2015. *Battlestar Galactica Vault.* New York. Sterling.

Benson (ABC, 1979–1986)

Benson was a spin-off from the landmark sitcom *Soap* (1977–1981). It ran from 1979 to 1986 on ABC. Over the years ABC moved it to different days of the week and times to air. *Benson* is Benson Dubois, played by the charming and debonair Robert Guillaume (1927–2017). The actor began on the stage in musicals where his most famous accomplishment was succeeding Michael Crawford in the demanding lead role of *The Phantom of the Opera* in the Los Angeles production. In television Robert Guillaume made guest appearances on many shows including *Good Times* (1974–1979), *The Jeffersons* (1975–1985), *Sanford and Son* (1972–1977), *Saved by the Bell: The College Years* (1993–1994), *The Fresh Prince of Bel-Air* (1990–1996), and *A Different World* (1987–1993). He also starred in the highly acclaimed *Sports Night* in 1998–2000.

> Every network television series has a director who works with the writers, the actor, and the crew. Most professionals in the field report that comedy is much more difficult to direct successfully. The names of film directors are better known to the public that those who work in television, but there is one television director who in the 1970s dominated the field of directing sitcoms—Jay Sandrich (1932–). His resume in that decade is overwhelmingly impressive. Sandrich directed most of the run of *The Mary Tyler Moore Show* and the controversial *Soap*. He directed a range of episodes for *WKRP in Cincinnati, The Betty White Show, Welcome Back Kotter, Phyllis, Ball Four, Rhoda, Laverne and Shirley, The Bob Newhart Show, Julia, Nanny and the Professor,* and *Here's Lucy*. A humble man, Sandrich loved to work with actors and the writers. Crews respected him because he had a good balance between being laid back and having a firm hand on the production. He prided himself on his ability to read a script and he learned to move the actors and the camera will follow. Sandrich felt that if the viewer was aware of an angle or shot or the movement of a camera, then he was doing something wrong. What made him such a great director was that the viewer got into the episode he directed and just enjoyed the story.

The Story

On *Soap* Robert Guillaume played the butler in a very daffy household where one of the characters, Jessica Tate, played by Katherine Helmond (1929–), turns out to be the cousin of Governor James Gating of an unnamed state, played by James Noble (1922–2016). The governor has just been elected when the series begins and he asks his cousin Jessica if he can borrow Benson for a week or so to help with the transition. When the week is up, Benson has distinguished himself performing more than his butler duties. He saves the governor's neck by coming up with a plan to solve a delicate conservation problem concerning beavers and real estate. Benson is asked to stay and he does.

The creator of the show is Susan Harris (1940–), also responsible for *Soap*. Harris is a prolific comedy writer who first started writing for *Then Came Bronson* (1969–1970). In the tradition of the times, *Benson* was another show that was videotaped in front of a live audience.

The role of a butler as played by an African American male serving a wealthy white family has a racial-profiling history, especially in countless motion pictures. There was concern about the character of Benson being perceived as a negative stereotype and whether it would be chancy, if not improper, and possibly racist. The black butler was an age-old stereotype.

Susan Harris set out to do what Norman Lear (1922–) had done on so many breakthrough television shows, which was to challenge the audience's cultural perceptions.

Benson DuBois is a black butler but he shatters the conventional image in myriad ways. He is youngish, very well dressed, smart and witty. This is the heart of Benson's character—he always has a one-liner to return in any circumstance. He makes jokes about being black, but they are rarely at his own expense and usually reveal foolishness on the governor's part. The governor and the other characters try but are no match for Benson's skilled wit.

It is important that Benson, working for a very upwardly mobile family, has stature and is literate, composed, and dignified. Casting a stage actor was astute on Harris's part. Robert Guillaume moves well and has a deep resonant voice enhanced by singing in important musicals. Without singing in this role, Guillaume still brings a musicality, rhythm, and pace to every line.

Working at the governor's mansion, Benson is at odds with a tall and dominant German housekeeper, Gretchen Krause, played to the hilt by Inga Swenson. They butt heads constantly over any situation that concerns the caretaking of the mansion. She is an attractive older woman, but Benson regularly makes jokes about her looks and height as part of their competition. Jokes and mockery about Gretchen's German ancestry generate another controversial aspect of *Benson*. Gretchen talks about her nationality, makes jokes in a self-effacing way, and Benson wisecracks with countless remarks about German heritage. This type of repartee was enjoyable to some of the viewing public during this decade; however, questions about societal acceptability deepened in the eras to come.

The show was shot and edited in the conventional sitcom method of its day. The sets, mainly the mansion and its many rooms, look real but there is just enough artifice to make it clear this is not a realistic drama, but indeed a comedy. *Benson* was not shot in an actual mansion. The impressive exteriors were shot at the Bundy house, a 1914 building in Pasadena, California named after Harlow E. Bundy, who invented the time clock.

The director of the pilot and many other episodes was Jay Sandrich (1932–), one of the top sitcom directors of the era. Seasoned sitcom watchers felt assured in his capable hands, knowing he had the expertise to oversee the staging, acting, and storytelling aspects.

In one episode Rene Auberjonois (1940–) is introduced as Pete Downey, a key aide to the governor and part of his inner circle. This actor would go on to do much television work and receive an Emmy nomination for his work on *Benson*. He was known to viewers who were familiar with 1970s Robert Altman movies. He appeared in *M*A*S*H, Brewster McCloud, McCabe and Mrs. Miller,* and *Images*.

An Episode to Remember

An especially memorable episode concerns Benson and Krause when they are asked to go out in the dead of night to a convenience store to pick up specialty sandwiches for a critical meeting. The store is held up by two men and Krause and Benson are tied back to back; hours go by because of a police standoff, and finally the governor makes the difficult and dangerous decision to allow a SWAT team to charge the place in a daring rescue. The duo was very afraid but also infused humor into the situation. In the resolve, everyone is safe.

Jessica Tate is introduced during season 1, in episode 8 when she comes to visit her cousin. She meets a European baron, a man of some age and wealth, and they conduct a whirlwind romance mainly in a bedroom at the mansion. There is public outcry and the angry governor tells his cousin to leave. Later Benson is called to a hotel room where the baron and Jessica are staying only to learn he has expired. Death is only funny in a sitcom, and there is an extended routine with the dead baron propped up on some sort of wheeled device being pushed around by Benson while Jessica is in hysterics over the possibility they will get caught.

Benson was a drawing room comedy—1970s sitcom style.

See also: *Soap*.

Further Resources

Bryant, Natricece. 2009. *African American Television Sitcom Stereotypes: The Stereotypical Connotations Used in African American Television*. Buchanan, NY: VDM Verlag.

Guillaume, Robert, and David Ritz. 2002. *Guillaume: A Life*. Jackson: University of Missouri Press.

Leonard, David J., and Lisa A. Guerrero, eds. 2013. *African Americans on Television: Race-ing for Ratings*. Santa Barbara, CA: ABC-CLIO.

The Bionic Woman (ABC 1976–1977; NBC 1977–1978)

The backstory of Jamie Sommers sets up the circumstances for *The Bionic Woman*. Jamie had great promise and success on professional tennis courts around the world. Her parents were political science professors, but unbeknownst to Jamie they were undercover agents for the U.S. government. They were killed in an accident, most likely murdered. Jamie grew up under the prudent care of her legal guardians who had a son, Steve Austin, who became Jamie's sweetheart. He joined the Air Force and became an astronaut in the U.S. space program. Jamie studied at Carnegie Tech, majoring in education, and planned to become a schoolteacher until tennis called her. Eventually she was ranked among the top five women players. During a visit home her relationship with Steve grows stronger until tragedy strikes and Jamie is severely injured in a skydiving accident—her right arm crushed beyond repair. She also suffers damage to her right ear. Steve gets his boss, Oscar Goldman, an intelligence man, involved, and pleads with Goldman to authorize a bionic replacement.

Steve Austin had had the same experimental government operation two years before, making him a bionic man. Jamie became the bionic woman and was on call to the OSI, a government agency that did undercover work. She resigned, however, having suffered brain damage and memory loss. Another operation partially resolved this, but her love for Steve does not seem recoverable.

Background

That is the premise of *The Bionic Woman,* which ran on ABC from January 14, 1976 to May 1977, then switched to NBC, continuing its run from September 10, 1977, to September 2, 1978. This was a spin-off from *The Six Million Dollar Man,* which starred Lee Majors (1939–) as Steve Austin. *The Bionic Woman* is based on the novel *Cyborg,* written by Martin Caidin, published in 1971.

The bionic woman was played by Lindsay Wagner (1949–), who was able to run full out convincingly and move through various situations that, through the use of slow-motion photography, seemed believable. She was a warm and sensitive girl-next-door except that because of her mission Jamie was ready to use her astounding powers of strength and speed at any time necessary.

Lindsay Wagner had been a model, appeared as a hostess on *Playboy after Dark* (1969–1970), and was a contestant on *The Dating Game* (1965–2000.) In 1971 she signed a contract with Universal Studios and was a contract player on many projects and shows like *The F.B.I.* (1965–1974), *Night Gallery* (1970–1973), *Marcus Welby, M.D.* (1969–1976), and *Owen Marshall: Counselor at Law* (1971–1974) and was in two episodes of *The Rockford Files* (1974–1980). She also acted in the film *The Paper Chase* (1973). In 1975 her contract was extended and she played the role of Jamie Sommers on *The Six Million Dollar Man* (1973–1978) where her character as the bionic woman was born.

This was supposed to be Lindsay Wagner's final role under her current contract, but the public literally demanded to see more of her, so in January 1976 the run of *The Bionic Woman* began.

Jamie's operative contact was Oscar Goldman, played by Richard Anderson (1926–2017), who appeared in both bionic shows. He had a long career in series television and appeared in two legendary films, *Paths of Glory* (1957) directed by Stanley Kubrick and *Seconds* (1966) directed by John Frankenheimer.

Women in 1970s Television

Television in the 1970s presented challenges to women's images and the concept of female empowerment in the medium. There is a certain kind of eroticism watching the slow-motion sequences in *The Bionic Woman,* yet her feats of great strength, also in slow motion, are a testament to the heights a woman could achieve. It was one purpose of the show to have Jamie act as a role model for female youngsters.

The slow-motion moments of the show were accompanied by what sounds like digital sound, a very effective combination to convince the viewers Jamie truly is bionic.

Jamie had a bionic ear, so at times there are extreme close-ups of her ear as we hear an amplification of some far-off sounds or dialogues. Another interesting touch is the almost subliminal use of music, which sounds like drums beating as if they were accompanying a jungle sequence.

The first episode of the first season lays out the story. The main title sequence each week repeats the story as a capsule for those new to the show. There is a clever use of early computer readouts; letter by letter they explain what a narrator would have done in the early period, especially in the 1960s.

There is a human aspect to each story, which covers a government assignment. In one Jamie investigates animals being killed and becomes very close to a girl who works at an animal shelter where lions and game are trained for eventual stardom in a circus or television show. The mystery is whether the star lion, named Neil, is the culprit or if there is a cougar on the loose hunting game. A local rancher gets more and more agitated as the animals he uses for food sales are killed. He wants to kill Neil. Ultimately, Lindsay saves the day by proving the cougar is the predator. She rescues Neil from a bar after he has been caged by the rancher and his neighbors.

The science behind the shows may not be realistic, but *The Six Million Dollar Man* and *The Bionic Woman* were ahead of their time in the use of technology.

See also: *The Six Million Dollar Man*; *Wonder Woman*.

Further Resources

Cohen, Joel H. 1976. *The Six Million Dollar Man and The Bionic Woman: Lee Majors and Lindsay Wagner.* New York: Scholastic Books Services.

Johnson, Frank E., MD, ed. 2005. *The Bionic Human: Health Promotion for People with Implanted Prosthetic Devices*. New York: Humana Press.

Lottman, Eileen. 1977. *Bionic Woman: Extracurricular Activities*. New York: Berkley Publishing Group.

The Bob Newhart Show (1972–1978)

In 1972 Bob Newhart returned to television with *The Bob Newhart Show* on which he played a Chicago psychologist, Bob Hartley. It was an ensemble comedy distributed by Mary Tyler Moore's company, MTM, which had great success in the 1970s. Bob's wife Emily was a third-grade teacher played by Suzanne Pleshette (1937–2008), who displayed great comic gifts and had perfect chemistry with Newhart, who basically played the same character he played in his stand-up comedy routines: button-down, very dry style, honed on sharp one-liners and as many phone routines as they could get into the episodes. Newhart felt the reason the show worked was because the large cast of zany characters were so quirky that any outrageous things he would say wouldn't sound outrageous but just funny. There were a large group of patients with various neuroses who provided a lot of the comedy. Each is a well-drawn character but never really offensive to those who really suffer from such ailments. It is clear to the audience that these people have a sense of humor and insight into themselves. The star of all the patients was Elliot Carlin (Jack Riley), who had every possible neurosis and issue imaginable and was a character who stood out from the crowd. He constantly clashed with other

The Bob Newhart Show starred the famous comedian as a psychologist with some very wacky patients. (CBS Photo Archive/Getty Images)

patients in group therapy session; he was always looking for attention and was Bob's biggest challenge. The popularity of Elliot Carlin resulted in almost constant appearances. Also part of the ensemble were Peter Bonerz (1938–) as orthodontist Jerry Robinson, Bob's officemate; and Bill Daily (1927–) as Howard Borden, Bob's neighbor across the hall in the apartment building where Bob and Emily lived. Borden was a navigator who worked for the airlines and constantly entered the Hartley apartment unannounced. Marcia Wallace (1942–2013) was the snappy receptionist, Carol Kester, who worked for both Dr. Hartley and Dr. Robinson. After six seasons *The Bob Newhart Show* left the airwaves of its own volition.

See also: *Newhart*; *Vol. 1, The 1950s – 1960s: The Bob Newhart Show*; *Vol. 3, The 1990s–Present: Bob.*

Further Resources

Green, Joey. 1996. *Hi Bob! A Self-Help Guide to the Bob Newhart Show.* New York: St. Martin's Press.

Newhart, Bob. 2007. *I Shouldn't Even Be Doing This: And Other Things That Strike Me As Funny.* New York: Hyperion.

Charlie's Angels (ABC, 1976–1981)

Mega-creator and producer Aaron Spelling (1923–2006) dreamed up this show concerning three beautiful women, each different in personality and in height, body type, and hair color. They are policewomen turned crime-fighting private investigators who work for Charles Townsend's agency. Charlie is basically a filtered phone voice coming out of an audio speaker, played by John Forsythe (1918–2010). The show racked up 115 episodes running from September 1976 to August 1981 and during these years had a total of six actresses playing the trio of angels.

From 1976 to 1979 Kate Jackson (1948–) played Sabrina Duncan. Ms. Jackson had dark hair and was slim and pretty. She had been on *The Rookies* (1972–

1976), which was put together by Spelling and Leonard Goldberg (1934–). Partly responsible for the creation of the series, Jackson came up with the name "Harry's Angels," inspired by another series, *Harry O*. Jackson was one of the original three and was known as the smart one. In 1979 she was forced to turn down a role in the film *Kramer vs. Kramer* because of scheduling conflicts and then left after three years to pursue an acting career in film.

The most famous, sexy, and beautiful of the original women was Farrah Fawcett (1947–2009), who played Jill Monroe from 1976 to 1977. Known at the time as Farrah Fawcett-Majors, she was married at the time to Lee Majors, star of *The Six Million Dollar Man* series. She had also appeared in a group of films including *Logan's Run,* released in 1976. She had done TV guest spots on shows such as *Marcus Welby, M.D.* (1969–1976) and posed for a swimsuit poster that was on the wall of practically every high school and college male in America. Fawcett's hairstyle, a blonde center-parted mane that had top wings and cascading layers, took the country by storm, forcing practically every hairdresser in the country to execute it on female clients of all shapes, sizes, and hair colors. Ms. Fawcett was a merchandising bonanza. In 1977 after only one year she left for stardom on the silver screen. She was sued for breach of contract and settled out of court, promising to make six guest appearances on the show over a two-year period. With the exception of the telefilm *The Burning Bed,* broadcast in 1984, her film career was less than stellar.

Rounding out the original three was the glamorous Jaclyn Smith (1945–) playing Kelly for the five-year run. She had auditioned poorly and the producers were looking for a redhead, but Spelling and Goldberg fell in love with Jaclyn Smith and gave her the role. Early on her TV roles included commercials, *The Rookies, Get Christie Love!* (1974), and impressive modeling for Max Factor print ads.

That could have been it for the entire run but it wasn't. In 1977 a new angel, number four, the blonde and beautiful Cheryl Ladd (1951–), wife of actor David Ladd, and a woman who could look good in a bathing suit like Farrah Fawcett, agreed to replace her if her character could be funny and not infallible. Spelling suggested her character be Jill Munroe's (Farrah's character) kid sister. This move literally saved the series. Before joining the series, Ladd voiced the singing parts for Melody on the animated show *Josie and the Pussycats* (1970–1971).

The fifth angel, the willowy and sophisticated Shelley Hack (1947–), replaced the Kate Jackson part in 1979. She had been Revlon's "Charlie" perfume girl. During her tenure the ratings were not impressive and she was let go.

In 1980 the search was on again and Tanya Roberts (1955–) came on board. She had previously done a guest shot on the television show *Vega$*. Roberts, who played Julie Rogers from 1980 to 1981, was the sixth and final angel.

Plots

Story ideas for *Charlie's Angels* included a foiled plot to murder a young woman who returns home to receive a large inheritance. Two of the angels have impersonated her. The man who dominated the woman's mother murdered her father by strangling him and throwing him in a swamp. As always the case is closed with positive results.

Another episode takes place at a flight attendant school where all three angels come to the aid of a young woman who has been psychologically manipulated and is being forced to crash a real plane. In the resolve the angels land the plane and all is right with the world again.

Once of the big myths about this television show was that you never see Charlie and only hear his voice. This proves untrue; at times, after delivering orders to the angels and his sidekick, Bosley, Charlie would be on the phone and when the cut is complete, viewers can see a poolside scene with a man passing a phone handpiece to a beautiful blonde assistant. You don't really see his face but the implication is clear.

A plea for female empowerment would be pushing it, although the angels start each episode with a tease of them as former police officers at a time when women were barely in the rank and file and held petty jobs. As P.I.s they knew how to wield a gun and fire on target and could fight the male bad guys, usually martial arts style. The important themes were not really there except the good gals go against the bad guys each week and always succeed for Charlie. Although many objected to it, there was much action and entertainment and in this respect *Charlie's Angels* delivered in total.

The other significant character is Bosley, played with wit and bravado by David Doylė (1929–1997), who was Charlie's visible right-hand man and went out in the field when the angels were on a mission. If not groundbreaking in terms of gender, *Charlie's Angels* was the first show to earn $1,000,000 per minute for advertising—a major accomplishment.

See also: *Baywatch*; *Cagney and Lacey*.

Further Resources

Charles River Editors. 2014. *Farrah Fawcett: American Legends*.

Charlie's Angels. http://www.charliesangels.com.

Pingel, Mike. 2006. *Angelic Heaven—A Fan's Guide to Charlie's Angels*. Henderson, NV: JM Media Group.

Chico and the Man (NBC, 1974–1978)

This situation comedy was broadcast on NBC from 1974 until 1978. It starred Jack Albertson (1907–1981) as Ed Brown, "The Man" of the title, a white senior citizen who ran a decrepit automobile repair garage located in an East L.A. barrio, where customers could gas up and have their cars fixed. Ed Brown is the last W.A.S.P. in the neighborhood. His mechanic, Francisco "Chico" Rodriguez, played by Freddie Prinze (1954–1977). was a street-wise Mexican or Chicano.

Controversy

Ed Brown's character led to considerable controversy and viewer complaints for using almost every ethnic slur in the book when referring to Chico and his people. This name-calling was part of a trend in 1970s sitcoms. One of the main sources of this kind of provocative TV was Norman Lear, especially with *All in the Family* (1971–1979) and *Maude* (1972–1978).

A good part of the problem with this show was that there were few Chicanos in the cast; further, very few Mexican Americans were involved in any aspect of television production even though a large Chicano community was available in Los Angeles where the show was produced. The creator and executive producer of *Chico and the Man* was James Komack (1924–1997), who, like Norman Lear, dealt with negative reactions by listening to the feedback and tweaking a bit. Basically Komack stayed the course.

In an astute act, the production hired blind Puerto Rican musician and singer Jose Feliciano (1945–) to write the theme and background music. Feliciano is best known for his stirring cover of the Doors' classic "Light My Fire" on which he croons passionately and plays a dynamic guitar. He also created a perennial Christmas standard using the Spanish phrase for "Merry Christmas," "Feliz Navidad." The theme for *Chico and the Man* had an interesting slant. The lyrics were in the third person, conveying to Chico that he is a good man and to be tolerant and show the way, perhaps helping Ed Brown overcome his prejudices.

In one episode Ed Brown disrespects a Latino man who has been his long-time friend. Chico intervenes and learns that an interracial marriage between their children was the sore spot that caused a nine-year split between the men—they finally make up and all is well.

When a building inspector visits the garage he finds abominable conditions; he tells Brown he'll give him 25 hours to fix up the place. Ed and Chico run a garage sale to raise money but it turns into a circus because two older ladies bid and rebid, sell and resell

> Freddie Prinze worked the comedy clubs in New York and broke into television in 1973 on one of the last episodes of *The Jack Paar Tonight Show*. On *The Tonight Show with Johnny Carson* (1962–1992) he performed, was the first young comic to sit next to Carson at the desk, and guest hosted on several occasions. He landed the role of his career on *Chico and the Man* (1974–1978). During the run of the show on January 28, 1977, Prinze succumbed to his battle with drugs and depression and shot himself. He died the next day at 22 years old. The producers of *Chico and the Man* considered shutting down the series, but decided instead to write Chico out of the story line and replace him with another character. The death of Freddie Prinze brought attention in Hollywood to fame, vices, and dealing with mental health issues that were hidden from the public by a skilled comic performer.

until Brown ends up at the short end of the stick. Nevertheless, the building inspector is kept at arm's length and the place is at least decent.

At the beginning of an episode Brown complains he can't see well as he holds a newspaper up to his face. There is a car accident and Ed is a witness but is challenged by one of the drivers. At the garage an obnoxious woman is hounding him about body work for her car. A neighborhood policeman tells Brown he is farsighted while they both stand in the alley next to his car shop. This episode's theme in the *Chico and the Man* universe is about friendship. Other themes addressed are racial harmony, prejudice, aging, and the condition of neighborhoods in California and the country.

Chico sometimes speaks Spanish on the show. Sometimes it is one or two lines like "Dios mio," which translates to "Oh, my God," but often Chico is involved in a lengthy conversation with another Spanish-speaking person. The decision to forgo subtitles might be considered a curious one; on the other hand, it can be deemed as part of the show's structure.

At the time Freddie Prinze was working the comedy club circuit with his stand-up routine. He spoke unaccented English, which confirms that Chico's accent was a decision for the character. *Chico and the Man* was filmed in front of a live studio audience and sweetened later in postproduction. The live and home audience would laugh at these Spanish-speaking moments because they knew they were supposed to be funny. Often someone on the show, usually Ed Brown, asks what was said and Chico repeats it in English.

Chico and the Man represented an important demographic—the country's Hispanic community. It is another 1970s attempt at the inclusion of minorities in television.

See also: *All in the Family*; Lear, Norman; *Maude*; *Vol. 1, The 1950s–1960s: I Love Lucy*.

Further Resources

Pruetzel, Matia, 1978. *The Freddie Prinze Story*. Graham, TX: Master's Press.

Vinson, Peggy. 2014. *Jack Albertson: 147 Success Facts—Everything You Need to Know About Jack Albertson*. Brisbane, QLD, Australia: Emereo.

CHiPs (NBC, 1977–1983)

This television show was in an almost unique category—the motorcycle genre. With the exception of *Then Came Bronson*, there wasn't any programming with this premise. Motion pictures had many instances of men on motorcycles, most famously, *The Wild One* (1953), *The Wild Angels* (1966), *Easy Rider* (1969), but *CHiPS* wasn't about drifters finding themselves and America or about motorcycle gangs—this show told the story of the California Highway Patrol and delighted young people and adult viewers.

CHiPS ran on NBC from September 15, 1977 to July 17, 1983. There was a large cast with character changes during the seasons. The three principals at the show's inception were Larry Wilcox (1947–) as Officer Jon Baker, Erik Estrada (1949–) as Officer Frank "Ponch" Poncherello, and Robert Pine (1941–) as Sgt. Joe Getraer, who was the boss of these first motorcycle "cops." These guys fought crime from lowly parking tickets to major scams or heists. Sometimes the cops rode together and sometimes one was in front, one was behind. The great majority of the show took place on the road in heavy traffic. Wilcox had a walkie-talkie and was the lead person talking to headquarters, advising on a situation or requesting help such as ambulances, police cars, or other vehicles or services.

The Glendale Freeway was used for driving sequences in the first season. Crashes were performed and photographed on highways still under construction. The two leads did most of their own driving and stunts although there was some doubles work. It is reported that Wilcox came out relatively unscathed with no major injuries while throughout the series Estrada constantly suffered minor injuries, plenty of falls and scrapes.

There was very little real violence on *CHiPS*. There were a lot of human interest stories and enough humor to offset the dramatic aspects. Each one-hour episode had several segments, different exploits that were juggled back and forth. It was a unique police show, not so much cops and robbers as life on a California highway, which was Ponch and Jon's world.

How do you inject romance in a show where two guys are on the road most of the time? Poncherello was the ladies' man of the two. He would pick up women on the road by riding alongside a car, checking them out, and then making future plans. In one episode a billboard of a woman caught Ponch's eye; he was crazy for her and literally saw her everywhere on posters or billboards. He let everyone at the precinct know he was crazy about her. The head sergeant told him they were related. One thing led to another and a date was set. Unbeknownst to Ponch, not only was the sergeant there, but practically all the guys in the division were hidden to see his reaction. The episode's lighthearted payoff came when the girl was revealed as a preteen who obviously photographed well. In the end, a good time was had by all, except maybe Poncherello.

Further Resources

Estrada, Erik, and Davin Seay. 1997. *Erik Estrada: My Road from Harlem to Hollywood*. New York: William Morrow.

http://larrywilcox.net.

Olsen, Marilyn. 2001. *America's State Troopers and Highway Patrolmen*. Paducah, KY: Turner.

Columbo featured Peter Falk as Inspector Columbo, seen here with guest star Mel Ferrer. As a rumpled, dogged police detective who would often repeatedly question witnesses and suspects until he eventually solved the case, Falk's charm and personal style made him a fan favorite. (Ullstein bild via Getty Images)

Columbo (NBC, 1968–1978; ABC, 1985–2003)

This very popular detective series featured a character with one name—Columbo, who was always disheveled on the job, appeared to be slow-witted, asked countless questions, and was constantly apologizing while he relentlessly probed for answers to each episode's homicide. He was a lieutenant for the L.A.P.D. What is unique and practically unprecedented in the "whodunit" genre is that the killer was revealed in the first 20 minutes before Columbo appeared on the scene. The audience then watched Columbo's detailed, pressing, relentless, and dogged process of interrogation and deduction that revealed the guilty party. Columbo became one of America's most famous and beloved detectives.

Columbo began as a made-for-TV movie, *Prescription Murder,* that aired in 1968 in which the Columbo character was born in full form. Then the show became part of *The NBC Mystery Movie*, a rotation of programs that was an innovation for the network. Some of the other shows included *McCloud* (1970–1977), *McMillan and Wife* (1971–1977), and *Quincy, M.E.* (1976–1983). The episodes usually were in a two-hour format.

Peter Falk (1927–2011) and Ben Gazzara (*Run for Your Life*) along with the director's wife and muse Gena Rowlands are indelibly associated with the work of maverick actor and director John Cassavetes (*Johnny Staccato*). Falk first worked with the man considered the father of the independent film movement on *Husbands* (1970), and then in Cassavetes's masterwork *A Woman under the Influence* to which Falk contributed a considerable amount of money from his *Columbo* earnings to ensure the film would be made. He also was in the director's *Opening Night* (1977) and *Big Trouble* (1986).

Columbo had many great actors on the show as actors or directors and these were colleagues he worked

> Before he became a television star with *Columbo,* Peter Falk had performed on the stage, in movies, and on TV. Falk first appeared on the stage at Camp High Point in upstate New York—the play was *The Pirates of Penzance.* In the early 1950s while working in Hartford, Connecticut, Peter Falk joined the Mark Twain Masquers, a community theater group, and performed in plays that included *The Caine Mutiny Court-martial, The Crucible,* and *The Country Girl.* On January 3, 1956 Falk made his first New York stage appearance in an Off-Broadway production, *Don Juan* by Moliére, which closed that day after the only performance. That May he had more of a career booster in a revival of *The Iceman Cometh* with Jason Robards (1922–2000) at the Circle in the Square where he played the bartender. In 1956 Falk made his Broadway debut in *Diary of a Scoundrel* by Alexander Ostrovsky. At the end of the year he returned to Broadway as an English soldier in George Bernard Shaw's *Saint Joan.* Peter Falk then played small roles in the movies, *Wind Across the Everglades* (1958), *The Bloody Brood* (1959), and *Pretty Boy Floyd* (1960). His career headed toward stardom when he played a real-life hood in *Murder Inc.,* released in 1960, about a gang that terrorized New York City in the 1930s, a part for which he received critical acclaim. Throughout the 1960s he appeared in many movies including *Pocketful of Miracles* (1961), *It's a Mad, Mad, Mad, Mad World* (1963), and *The Great Race* (1965).

with from the Cassavetes community including actors John Finnegan (1926–2012), Val Avery (1924–2009), Fred Draper (1923–1999), and Timothy Carey (1929–1994). John Cassavetes (1929–1989) appeared as an actor and also directed. Ben Gazzara (1930–2012) directed two episodes, and Gena Rowlands (1930–) appeared as an actress alongside her old friend.

Falk was not the first choice for the role of Columbo. It was originally offered to popular crooner and actor Bing Crosby (1903–1977), but he declined because he decided not to come out of retirement. Lee J. Cobb (1911–1976) was also approached, but he had other commitments. Falk's interpretation was that the character was like "a guy with a mind like Einstein who sounds like the boxboy at Food Giant."

One of the most distinctive aspects of the Columbo character was the way he dressed and how the rumpled, disheveled look came about. Prior to production, wardrobe laid out the usual sort of ensemble worn by such characters and Falk knew it was the wrong way to go. He remembered the raincoat in his closet—revisited it and knew immediately it was perfect. Ironically, this became the *Columbo* trademark. Falk picked one of the suits that had been shown to him, a blue and white seersucker, and instructed the wardrobe person to dye it drab brown. The rest of the ensemble came together. Falk also told the creative team he would wear the same outfit for each show. He also insisted on no makeup, tousled hair, and a look as if he had forgotten to shave.

Columbo was the brainchild of the very successful team of television writers and producers Richard Levinson (1934–1987), and William Link (1933–). Just some of their accomplishments include *Mannix* (1967–1975), *Ellery Queen* (1975–1976), *Murder, She Wrote* (1984–1996), and many television movies such as *That Certain Summer* (1972), *The Execution of Private Slovik* (1974), and feature films like *The Hindenburg* (1975).

The murder cases vary as they do in the life of real detectives. On *Columbo* the stress was on finding unique situations in which to put the master sleuth. One concerned the secret formula for a magic-like skin cream. A chemist who said he would turn over the formula's details, which he said were in his head, is murdered. Another case involved ESP and a magician who murders another magician using a guillotine trick that turns deadly.

Audiences in the 1970s and earlier decades couldn't get enough mystery in their television viewing. *Columbo* proved beyond a shadow of a doubt that audiences are more interested in the process of solving a crime than the particular crime itself. Every question, every answer, and counter-question ran on incessantly so Columbo had to apologize when the person being grilled complained or turned to leave only to have a series of even more questions stop them in their tracks. By the end of the episode almost everyone but Columbo was exhausted, but the case was finally solved due to meticulous deduction.

See also: *McCloud*; *Murder, She Wrote*; *Quincy, M.E.*

Further Resources

Dawidziak, Mark. 1989. *The Columbo Phile: A Casebook.* New York: Mysterious Press.

Falk, Peter. 2006. *Just One More Thing: Stories from My Life*. New York: Carroll & Graf.

Kessler, Felix. 2011. "Peter Falk, Television's Rumpled Detective Columbo, Dies at 83." *Bloomberg Business*. June 24.

Link, William. 2010. *The Columbo Collection*. Norfolk, VA: Crippen & Landru.

Dance Fever (Syndication, 1979–1987)

This dance show, which was consistent with the period, featured dances by professionals and amateurs and also included a contest. The show ran from 1979 to 1987, and the original host was disco master Deney Terrio, born Denis George Mahan Terrio (1950–), who is best known as the dance coach for John Travolta (1954–) in the iconic motion picture *Saturday Night Fever* (1977). Terrio choreographed the film. *Dance Fever* was a half-hour show and was broadcast out of Los Angeles. The format of the show featured Terrio dancing to disco music with two women known as "Motion." The contest segment involved three couples dancing one at a time in front of a panel of three judges. Freeman King (1943–2002) was the video disc jockey. A rock act also performed each week. The initial prize for the amateur dancers was $25,000. The top-rated teams were eligible for the Grand Prix finals, which were held every year and had a grand prize of $50,000.

Dance Fever was flashy, with pulsating lights and spectacular dance routines right out of *Saturday Night Fever*. As disco began to disappear from the scene, the show presented other forms of contemporary dancing. Terrio left *Dance Fever* in 1985 and was replaced by actor Adrian Zmed (1954–).

One particular episode opened with a rousing dance routine by Terrio and Flo Solder and Janice Ricard, who comprised "Motion." Audience members were all around. The special guests were the Temptations. The panel of judges were Olympic medal winner in skating Linda Fratianne (1960–), actor Lyle Waggoner (1935–) of *The Carol Burnett Show* fame, and nutsy funnyman Rip Taylor (1934–). There were four couples competing and the scoring system was 1 to 100. The highest scorer got a base amount of money, which increased as they won more competitions. The routines ran around a minute and a half and were danced on a runway with audience members on each side cheering them on. The music consisted of cover versions of top hits of the day.

Toward the end of the show "Motion" and the three judges would line up for a dance lesson from Deney Terrio.

Dance Fever came out of the tradition of *American Bandstand* (1950–1989); all along the way the dances moved with the times. Disco hit big in the 1970s, not always to the delight of hard rock fans, but it did capture plenty of young people and many of all ages.

See also: *Vol. 1, The 1950s–1960s: American Bandstand*.

Further Resources

"Dance Fever." Retroland.com. http://www.retroland.com/dance-fever/

Miller, Chuck. 2012. "'Dance Fever,' with Deney Terrio!!" *Times Union*. December 13. http://blog.timesunion.com/chuckmiller/dance-fever-with-deney-terrio/16619/

Diff'rent Strokes (NBC, 1978–1985; ABC, 1986)

This poignant half-hour comedy was developed by Norman Lear's Tandem Productions especially with

> What happened to the young stars of *Diff'rent Strokes* when the show went off the air? Todd Bridges suffered a serious addiction to crack cocaine during his twenties. In 1988, he was arrested for the attempted murder of a drug dealer; eventually a witness came forward and he was acquitted. He managed to eventually get off drugs and worked as an actor and director. Gary Coleman twice tried to commit suicide by pills. In 1999 he filed for bankruptcy. He was twice arrested for disorderly conduct in disputes with his wife. On May 26, 2010, due to a possible seizure, Gary Coleman fell down a flight of steps, which caused his death at the age of 42. Dana Plato fell into poverty after the show and became addicted to prescription drugs. Her death on May 6, 1999 was ruled a suicide as she had overdosed on painkillers.

little Gary Coleman (1968–2010) in mind. The premise involves a Caucasian Park Avenue millionaire widower, Phillip Drummond, played by Conrad Bain (1923–2013), who has a teenaged daughter, Kimberly, played by Dana Plato (1964–1999), and adopts two African American boys. Drummond is keeping a promise to their deceased mother, his longtime housekeeper, that he would take care of the boys. Arnold Jackson, age eight, is played by Coleman and his older brother Willis Jackson, 13, is played by Todd Bridges (1965–). Coleman, who had already had a sterling guest spot on another Lear/Tandem show, *Good Times*, was unusually short because he suffered from a congenital kidney condition and his illness kept his height at around 4' 8". The boys were from Harlem and had a poor background; now they were part of a wealthy family and had a swanky Park Avenue address.

The opening show of season one lays out the basics and offers possibilities for typical sitcom humor, but because this is a Norman Lear production, social issues will be explored. Because of the long run of *Diff'rent Strokes,* the joys and struggles of growing up are also part of the narratives. Right at the start there is tension. Arnold loves everything about his new situation, but Willis doesn't. He is sullen and isn't moved by Mr. Drummond's commitment. Willis has a constant flow of arguments about living the rich life, but eventually sees the benefits of being part of a new and different family, setting the stage for all the shows to come.

The Drummonds' current housekeeper, Mrs. Edna Garrett, was played by Charlotte Rae (1926–) from 1978 to 1979 until she got her own spin-off, *The Facts of Life* (1979–1988); then other actors followed.

Some of the sensitive subjects on *Diff'rent Strokes*, not particularly well presented on television at the time, included busing, child molestation, smoking, lung cancer, and drug use. The most memorable line of the show comes from Arnold addressing his brother, "Whatchoo talkin' bout, Willis?" spoken at least once per episode. Although Willis and Arnold were African American and some of their culture is on the show, the family maintains the predominately white rich lifestyle of Mr. Drummond.

Diff'rent Strokes was part of a 1970s renaissance of shows featuring blacks not born out of *Amos 'n' Andy* (1951–1953) and *Beulah* (1950–1953), but instead out of change that had emerged in the United States.

See also: *The Cosby Show*; *Fat Albert and the Cosby Kids*; *Good Times*; *The Jeffersons*; Lear, Norman; *Roots*; *Vol.1, The 1950s–1960s: Amos 'n' Andy*; *Beulah*; *The Bill Cosby Show*.

Further Resources

The Coleman Family and Bill Davidson. 1982. *Gary Coleman: A Gift of Life*. New York: Berkeley Books.

Ross, Shavar. 1971. *On the Set of Diff'rent Strokes: How I Beat Out 250 Kids for the Role of Dudley.* Las Vegas, NV: CreateSpace Independent Publishing Platform.

Don Kirshner's Rock Concert (Syndication, 1973–1981)

This breakthrough music program was exactly what the title implies—each week Don Kirshner (1934–2011) delivered a real rock concert. Unlike other shows that had rock acts in their studio, *Don Kirshner's Rock Concert* traveled to concerts all over the country. It presented literally every genre of rock music during its broadcast years of 1973 to 1982. This fertile period, now known as classic rock, was at the time rock 'n' roll, which included heavy metal, blues, art rock, folk rock, and punk rock. The roster of acts presented by Don Kirshner read like an encyclopedia of modern rock music. A sampling includes the Steve Miller Band, Black Sabbath, Kiss, Devo, Bad Company, the Eagles, Cheap Trick, REO Speedwagon, Johnny Winter, Linda Ronstadt, Nitty Gritty Dirt Band, the Ramones, New York Dolls, and Led Zeppelin. Kirshner either did a voice-over intro to the night's proceedings or he was on camera. Kirshner was the brunt of some kidding and imitation by Paul Shaffer (1949–), later known as the bandleader of the *David Letterman Show*. Kirshner looked into the camera with a blank expression and spoke in a steady monotone. His hair was a comb-over on the top and longish on the sides, the whole effect being rather flat and close to his head. What made him unique and different from Dick Clark (1929–2012) is that he would start his intro with the name of the band and proceed in detail to list every possible person connected with the act including the manager, producer, and sometimes the technical people who worked with the recording of material.

In the end *Don Kirshner's Rock Concert* was a late-night joy. It aired every Saturday night at 11:30 and ran most often for 90 minutes, which means it continued into Sunday morning. Rock lovers got the best seat in the house without the crowds and watched the greatest rock 'n' roll bands on the planet.

See also: *The Midnight Special.*

Further Resources

Perl, Sheri. 2014. *The Economics of a Rock Concert.* New York. Crabtree Publishing.

Podolsky, Rich. 2012. *Don Kirshner: The Man with the Golden Ear: How He Changed the Face of Rock and Roll.* Milwaukee, WI: Hal Leonard Books.

The Dukes of Hazzard (CBS, 1979–1985)

Feature-length motion pictures such as *Bullitt* released in 1968 have long car chases, but this one-hour weekly television series, *The Dukes of Hazzard,* had more long and multiple car chases, crashes, and movie car effects than practically any series before it. This rural adventure series was separate from those like *The Beverly Hillbillies* (1962–1971), *Green Acres* (1965–1971), and *The Andy Griffith Show* (1960–1968). It saluted the South, going as far as hav-

The Dukes of Hazzard was a country comedy that featured low humor and lots of car chases. Pictured here is John Schneider as Bo Duke, Tom Wopat as Luke Duke, Ben Jones as Cooter Davenport, and the 1969 Dodge Charger known as the "General Lee." (Fotos International/Hulton Archive/Getty Images)

ing a Confederate flag on the top of a car whose horn plays "Dixie."

As the simple title suggests, the show is about three Dukes who live in Hazzard County. Luke Duke is played by dark-haired Tom Wopat (1951–), blonde-haired Bo Duke is portrayed by John Schneider (1960–), and Daisy Duke is played by Catherine Bach (1954–), who played a sexy, curvaceous, and pretty character, sporting long light brown hair. The basic plot concerned outwitting lawmen and local officials, usually by applying lightning-fast car speeds to accomplish the task. The slapstick action seemed to be aimed at children and teens, but for a show to be as successful as *The Dukes of Hazzard*, it needed a wider audience. There was an appeal to female preteens and teenagers and even grown women. The Duke boys, who were both handsome and with different physical characteristics, had broad appeal. One was dark, handsome, and spunky; the other was blonde, handsome, and shy. Boys, teenage boys, and men could certainly be attracted to Catherine Bach, who showed off her figure in a bikini or a tank top and short shorts (leading to the style name of "Daisy Dukes" for short shorts) or skin-tight jeans.

Other characters included Denver Pyle (1920–1997) as Uncle Jesse, who provided country wisdom to his family. Pyle, ironically, was in *Bonnie and Clyde* (1967) and played the sheriff who brought down one of the most dangerous criminal teams of their time, even participating as one of the gunman. There were car chases in that film and the famous banjo and guitar musical style played on the soundtrack by Lester Flatt (1914–1979) and Earl Scruggs is echoed on *The Dukes of Hazzard*.

Sorrell Booke (1930–1994) is the large-bellied Jefferson Davis "Boss" Hogg who is at the root of trouble almost every week. He wore all white including his wide Southern gentleman hat. The dimwitted Sheriff Roscoe Coltrane, played by James Best (1926–2015), is outsmarted by Bo, Duke, and Daisy at every turn, along with his trusty dog Flash, who was anything but.

The theme song, "Good Ol' Boys," was written and performed by Waylon Jennings (1937–2002), who was also the show's narrator and topped the country music charts for a time. Long associated with the rockabilly and outlaw rock movements, Jennings was perfect for the series, which likely attracted a Southern demographic.

In addition to the song and underscore music, the sound sold the believability of the car maneuvers—elevating the excitement with loud booms when the car jumps, skidding sounds, and all sorts of crash noises. Slow-motion photography was used to emphasize action moments, and freeze frames were employed either to fade to black, then to a commercial, or to stop the action so the narrator could speak. It was also used at the end of an episode so the tail credits could roll over them.

There were fisticuffs at times during the show, most often by the men, but Daisy Duke seemed to be some sort of jujitsu expert, taking out an opponent with a swift kick and/or a well-placed hand chop. She worked as a waitress, so this skill was needed when a customer got too frisky.

The car driven by the boys was considered the real star of *The Dukes of Hazzard*. The 1969 Dodge Charger named "General Lee" was integral to the show each week. Usually three General Lees were utilized per episode because of the wear and tear produced while speed driving and especially due to the high jumps and big loud landings.

Burt Reynolds (1936–) is mentioned in at least one episode. His *Smokey and the Bandit* feature film was released in 1977 and was a huge box office hit, and was probably an inspiration for *The Dukes of Hazzard*'s production team.

One storyline involved Boss Hogg's twin brother, who dressed all in black, and a tussle over who inherited a beloved relative's estate. In another episode Hogg is at it again hoarding slot machines. The boys want the money to go to an orphanage and it does, after Hogg and the sheriff are once again fooled and outsmarted.

The Dukes of Hazzard was fun, without any real message—a show for good ole boys and good ole gals.

See also: *Vol. 1: 1950s–1960s: The Andy Griffith Show*; *The Beverly Hillbillies*; *Green Acres*.

Further Resources

Bates, Billy Rae. 2006. *Them Dukes! Them Dukes! A Guide to TV's The Dukes of Hazzard*. Charleston, SC: BookSurge Publishing.

Hofstede, David. 2005. *The Dukes of Hazzard: The Unofficial Companion*. New York: St. Martin's Griffin.

Eight Is Enough (ABC, 1977–1981)

This one-hour dramedy is based on the autobiography of Tom Braden (1917–2009), a Washington columnist, and is set in Sacramento, California. Dick Van Patten (1928–2015) plays Tom Bradford, a columnist for the Sacramento *Register*. Originally Diana Hyland (1936–1977) was cast to co-star as his wife, Joan Bradford. Tragically, Hyland died of breast cancer in 1977 at age 41. She only appeared in the first four episodes of the premiere season. The series pressed on with Tom as a widower with eight children, seven still at home and one living in his own apartment. In the fall of 1977 a children's tutor, Abby Abbott, played by Betty Buckley (1946–), and a widow (her husband died in Vietnam, we're told), entered the show; she and Tom were married on November 9, 1977.

When Diana Hyland died, there were four episodes in which Joan was explained as being away. When the show returned in the fall it was established that Tom's wife had died and that he was a widower. The challenge for the writers and actors was to make that dramatic emotional transition from being a natural family to one with a stepmother. There was resentment and struggle, but Abby was strong and won them all over.

Joan Bradford gave birth to all eight children. They are David (Grant Goodeve, 1952–), Mary (Lani O'Grady, 1954–2001), Joannie (Laurie Walters, 1947–), Susan (Susan Richardson, 1952–), Nancy (Dianne Kay, 1954–), Tommy (Willie Aames, 1960–), Elizabeth (Connie Newton, 1959–), and Nicholas (Adam Rich, 1968–).

The Bradfords lived in a very large house, which must have been an expensive piece of property; the interior is homey but not overdecorated. Even in 1977 dollars with a wife who didn't work, at least not into several episodes of season 1, it wasn't totally plausible that Tom could support his family on a reporter's salary, but the creators and all the principals communicated the family's reality and finances were not an explicit issue on the show. When Abby became the mom, Buckley was 30, the oldest boy was 23, and the actress playing Joanie was actually six months older than Buckley. This was a family show about family problems and day-to-day occurrences. The family audience related to the show and saw themselves reflected in the Bradford family's circumstances.

In the pilot, the oldest son, David, later played by Grant Goodeve, was actually played by Mark Hamill (1951–), the actor who became famous for playing Luke Skywalker in *Star Wars* (1977) and subsequent sequels.

Over the seasons *Eight Is Enough* experienced a slow decline. In the last season the show couldn't make it into the top 30. It was cancelled and no wrap-up or true ending occurred—just life goes on.

See also: *Family Ties*.

Further Resources

Braden, Thomas Wardell. 1975. *Eight Is Enough*. New York: Random House.

Van Patten, Dick, and Robert Baer. 2009. *Eighty Is Not Enough: One Man's Journey through American Entertainment*. Beverly Hills, CA: Phoenix Books.

The Electric Company (PBS, 1971–1976)

The Children's Television Work, the organization responsible for *Sesame Street*, a fun learning show for young children developed and aired in the 1960s, developed and produced *The Electric Company* for PBS to target older children in the 7- to 10-year-old age range. While it was in its initial development, influences that helped shape *The Electric Company* included the music of Motown, Broadway musicals, and the inventive staging and New Wave comedy of *Laugh-In* (1968–1973).

Regular performers on the show included Bill Cosby (1937–), Rita Moreno (1931–), and Morgan Freeman (1937–), who played characters (some actors played more than one) designed to entertain children while teaching.

For *Electric Company's* first six years it was documented as the most popular instructional television show and would go on to win an Emmy for Outstanding Children's Series in 1977. The goal was to teach children at home basic reading and grammar

Seen here is comedian Bill Cosby in 1971 rehearsing with a group of children on the set of *The Electric Company*. This series was produced by the Children's Television Workshop. (Bettmann/Getty Images)

skills using animation, clever skits, songs, and blackout segments.

Some elements seen on *The Electric Company* included black-and-white movies played at high speed, psychedelic colors and shapes, word development, diverse groups of children together, many different styles and approaches to animation, all nationalities and races represented, letter and word play, news of the day, a police officer and other recognizable authority figures, kids singing, and montages.

See also: PBS (Public Broadcasting Service); *Vol. 1, The 1950s–1960s: Sesame Street.*

Further Resources

Mumford, Thad, Michaela Muntean, and Peter Bramley. 1978. *Make Your Own TV Show (The Electric Company).* New York: Grosset & Dunlap.

Preiss, Bryon. 1973. *The Electric Company Joke Book.* Racine, WI: Western.

ESPN (1979–)

Upon its founding in 1979, the Entertainment and Sports Programming Network (ESPN) shook up the TV sports landscape. Eventually known solely by the initials ESPN, it was a 24-hour sports cable network, debuting with its landmark program *SportsCenter* on September 7, 1979. Founded by Bill Rasmussen, Scott Rasmussen, and Ed Eagan, the channel soon came to dominate sports on television in the late 1990s and 2000s. It expanded from *SportsCenter* to showing live games of major sports, as well as new sports talk shows, documentaries, and eventually branching out into numerous affiliate channels such as ESPN2, ESPNU, and more.

ESPN's debut broadcast of *SportsCenter* featured anchors Lee Leonard and George Grande, who announced and narrated prerecorded sports highlights for a half-hour. Due to the dominance of the four major networks (ABC, CBS, NBC, Fox) in the sports field, ESPN struggled financially in the early 1980s, until Anheuser-Busch invested $1 million in the company, followed by an additional $5 million in 1981.

Collegiate sports were crucial to ESPN's early success. The network secured a contract with the National Collegiate Athletic Association (NCAA) to air the organization's Division I Men's Basketball Tournament, first airing on ESPN in March 1980. The success of the broadcasts launched the tournament into a cultural event known as "March Madness," and the network also launched the television careers of numerous former college players and coaches who joined the broadcasts for play-by-play or color commentary. In the 1980s, ESPN gained its foothold in broadcasting the major professional sports of the time (basketball, baseball, football) by negotiating a deal with the National Basketball Association (NBA) from 1982 to 1984. Following the conclusion of the deal in 1984, ABC purchased ESPN, and the company negotiated a new deal with the NBA for $2.4 billion, allowing ESPN to broadcast NBA games for six years.

ESPN began broadcasting hockey games of the National Hockey League (NHL) in 1980 and continued until 1982. The league returned to ESPN from 1986 to 1989, and then again from 1992 to 2004. Continuing its rise, ESPN soon gained rights to the National Football League (NFL) in 1987, but with a caveat, that ESPN agree to simultaneously broadcast games on local stations in the areas of each team. The network's debut NFL program was *ESPN Sunday Night Football*, which continued for 19 years until NBC obtained the Sunday night games, and ESPN moved to broadcasting NFL games on *Monday Night Football* in 2006.

Acquiring yet another professional sport was on ESPN's radar in the 1990s as the network secured the rights to Major League Baseball (MLB) in 1990, which it continues to broadcast to the present day. ESPN was again purchased by a larger corporation in 1996, when the Walt Disney Company purchased Capital Cities/ABC for $19 billion.

Having the financial backing of major corporations and the success of airing the four major professional sports, ESPN began expanding with new networks and programming. ESPN Radio debuted in 1992, and the following year, ESPN2 launched, broadcasting more youth-oriented programming, beginning with *SportsNite* with Keith Olbermann and Suzy Kolber. ESPN2 also featured a late-night talk show with host Jim Rome. Expanding yet again, ESPN added ESPNews to its channel lineup in 1996. This channel focused on the more hard news aspects of sports and press conferences. Its next expansion came through an acquisition of the Classic Sports Network in 1997, which the company then christened as ESPN Classic, broadcasting sports games and documentaries of years past. A channel focusing on collegiate sports, ESPNU, launched in 2005.

Talk Shows and Documentaries

To supplement the hours of the day when live sports are not scheduled, ESPN began developing talk shows and other programs to fill morning, daytime, and nighttime slots. Some of the most notable programs are *Baseball Tonight* (1990–), *Monday Night Countdown* (1993–), a preview to the Monday night NFL game, *Outside the Lines* (1990–), *Pardon the Interruption* (2001–), *First Take* (2007–), and many more.

In 2007, ESPN began developing a documentary series from then-ESPN.com columnist Bill Simmons and Connor Schell. The 30-minute sports documentaries were slated to celebrate ESPN's 30th anniversary and highlighted the biggest sports stories of the past 30 years that ESPN had been on the air. The first set of documentaries, "Volume I," aired in 2009 and featured stories on NHL Hall of Famer Wayne Gretzky's 1988 trade from the Edmonton Oilers to the Los Angeles Kings, titled "King's Ransom." Another feature, "The U," looked at the evolution of the Miami University football program in the 1980s and its racial and cultural impact on sports and society.

The series expanded to include four additional series, with Volume III premiering in 2015. The documentary series won a Peabody award in 2010 and a 2014 Emmy award for Outstanding Short-Format Nonfiction Program. Most notably, in 2016, the five-part *O.J.: Made in America*, directed by Ezra Edelman, received an Academy Award for Best Documentary Feature. The program detailed the life of former NFL player O.J. Simpson, his career in college and the NFL, as well as the 1995 murder trial in which he was acquitted of charges of murdering his ex-wife Nicole Simpson Brown and her friend Ron Goldman.

Continuing to the present, ESPN remains the most dominant network in sports. The network broadcasts live games for the NBA, NFL, MLB, and Major League Soccer (MLS), although since severing ties with the NHL in 2004, it has not returned to showing professional hockey. Collegiate sports remain a mainstay of the network's many splinter channels, and the network continues to be a constant source of news and information for sports enthusiasts around the world. Despite its prestigious spot as the top sports network, ESPN has suffered in recent years as cord-cutting and streaming services provide more sports possibilities to consumers looking to shed traditional cable packages.

See also: *NFL Monday Night Football*

Further Resources

"ESPN's Layoffs Spell Trouble for Live Sports." 2017. *Business Insider*. March 7. http://www.businessinsider.com/espns-layoffs-spell-trouble-for-live-sports-2017-3

Fabrikant, Geraldine. 1995. "The Media Business: The Merger; Walt Disney to Acquire ABC in $19 Billion Deal to Build a Giant for Entertainment." *The New York Times*. August 1. http://www.nytimes.com/1995/08/01/business/media-business-merger-walt-disney-acquire-abc-19-billion-deal-build-giant-for.html?pagewanted=all

Scott, A. O. 2016. "Review: 'O.J.: Made in America,' an Unflinching Take on His Rise and Fall." *The New York Times*. May 19. https://www.nytimes.com/2016/05/20/movies/oj-made-in-america-review.html?smid=pl-share

Thompson, Derek. 2013. "The Global Dominance of ESPN." *The Atlantic*. September. https://www.theatlantic.com/magazine/archive/2013/09/the-most -valuable-network/309433/

Falwell, Jerry (1933–2007)

During the 1970s televangelism soared in popularity. Worshipers sat in front of their television sets as if they were in a church pew and experienced everything they could have in an actual brick and mortar church.

Televangelism started before the 1970s and was born out of radio when preachers broadcast their sermons across the airwaves. Later many established their congregations through television. Telepreachers of this era include Pat Robertson (1930–) and Oral Roberts (1918–2009), but there was one man who dominated the 1970s. He may have been the most influential TV preacher of all time because of his power to deliver religion to the masses while merging politics and his views on personal and cultural matters.

The Rise of Jerry Falwell

Jerry Falwell's background is incongruous with the world of religion. His father had been a bootlegger and was agnostic. His grandfather was a dedicated atheist. On April 12, 1958 Jerry Falwell married the former Macel Pate (1933–2015). They were both born and raised in Lynchburg, Virginia. God spoke to Jerry and Macel, she reported later, and told them to create a ministry. Jerry Falwell founded what has become known as Liberty Christian Academy. During the 1950s and 1960s Falwell spoke harshly against the Reverend Martin Luther King Jr. and racial desegregation. In 1971 Jerry Falwell co-founded the Moral Majority, an organization that became the centerpiece of Christian fundamentalism. It embraced strong conservative views on the media, abortion, and the Equal Rights Amendment.

During this period *The Old Time Gospel Hour* (1956–) was hosted by Falwell and was often taped at one of his revival meetings. Falwell, who was a Baptist, preached in the old tradition. He had a well-groomed appearance and spoke in a controlled manner with great conviction about the Bible and his views concerning the direction of the country during the 1970s.

Falwell made viewers part of his churchly home, cultivating the ministry as if the audience was part of a congregation at their neighborhood house of worship. There was plenty of inspirational gospel music to move the brethren. Falwell understood the electronic medium of television and was able to use it to make the transition.

Falwell believed he influenced his viewers by telling them God loved them and Jesus Christ loved them. He delivered this message with conviction and intensity. Bible teaching was an essential segment of *The Old-Time Gospel Hour*. The complex book was used to support Falwell and his church's beliefs.

Falwell liked to tell stories about worshippers he'd met in his travels. He related a story of a congregant who claimed he was going to commit suicide until he heard Falwell talk about establishing a personal relationship with God. This was a theme he used to conclude most of his shows. Falwell preached eternity and salvation.

Until the end of his days Jerry Falwell grew his brand, visiting talk shows and involving himself with people in the public eye like Ellen DeGeneres, whom he challenged about her lesbianism, and Larry Flint, whom he chastised for spreading pornography. He was unabashed and said what he felt was right and wrong. Falwell was a devout student of the Bible and quoted it chapter and verse to prove his point about America being a decadent society getting worse. He was as much a politician and arbiter of cultural morality as a small-town preacher. His powerful beliefs influenced politicians, many of whom believed in his conservative philosophy.

Falwell had an unflappable personality. He could vehemently attack issues he considered immoral on the one hand and present himself as a gentle, accepting, smiling churchman on the other. His legacy is the ingrained power of Christian conservatism in American society, which became a powerful force and strong inspiration to the next generation.

See also: *Vol. 1, The 1950s–1960s: The 700 Club*.

Further Resources

Falwell, Jerry. 1996. *Falwell: An Autobiography*. New York: Tab Books.

Winters, Michael Sean. 2012. *God's Right Hand: How Jerry Falwell Made God a Republican and Baptized the American Right*. New York: HarperCollins.

Family (ABC, 1976–1980)

This generically named program aired on ABC and was a landmark in the family drama genre because its concept embraced a reasonable definition of family. Its focus was the nature of family itself. The stories were told in a straightforward and honest manner, avoiding the overdramatized, over-the-top stylization of this genre in the 1950s and 1960s. The story concerned a family of five living in Pasadena, California. The mother was played by Sada Thompson (1927–2001). Kate Lawrence was a strong and sensitive woman. James Broderick (1927–1982), father of Matthew, played Douglas Lawrence, a lawyer. Two actresses played their spoiled daughter, Nancy Maitland, who had divorced and lived in her parents' guest house with her young son while she attended law school. In the spring of 1976 Elaine Heilveil (1948–) played the part of Nancy, and beginning in fall 1978 through 1980 the role was played by Meredith Baxter Birney (1947–). Gary Frank (1950–) played their son, who quit school to be a writer. Buddy, the youngest daughter, was portrayed by Kristy McNichol (1962–). Her true name was Letitia and she was a young teenager honestly trying to find her way through adolescence.

> James Broderick (1927–1982), who played the father in the aptly titled *Family*, was an emotional and believable actor. Some of his best roles include the complex father figure of a New England commune in *Alice's Restaurant* (1969), the subway motorman in *The Taking of Pelham 1, 2, 3* (1974), a lead FBI agent in *Dog Day Afternoon* (1975), and Joe in the television movie based on the play *The Shadow Box* (1980) directed by Paul Newman. He died of cancer in 1982 at 55 years old. He also is the father of actor Matthew Broderick (1962–), who named his son after his dad.

Family had excellent lineage. Jay Preston Allen (1922–2006), who wrote noted screenplays and teleplays for films like *Cabaret* (1972) and *The Prime of Miss Brodie* for television in 1978, was the creator. The executive producers included a giant in theater and film, Michael Nichols (1931–2014), whose extensive credits in film include *The Graduate* (1967), *Silkwood* (1983), and *The Birdcage* (1996). The producers were television legends Aaron Spelling (1923–2006) and Leonard Goldberg (1934–).

Family garnered a strong and faithful audience and did well during award season. It was intelligently written and acted with intensity and honesty. Family interaction and especially the parental role drove the narrative. Home viewers identified with members of this family and could see themselves mirrored in the one-hour drama. The subject each week was middle-class life. *Family* held its own in a strong and very large field of cop and detective shows. Even though the family drama genre seemed to be fading, *Family* kept it alive by reflecting an honest depiction of current domestic life in America.

Further Resources

Katz, Susan. 1979. *Kristi and Jimmy McNichol: An Unauthorized Biography*. New York: Grosset & Dunlap.

Wiseman, Dennis G. 2009. *The American Family: Understanding Its Changing Dynamics and Place in Society*. Springfield, IL: Charles C. Thomas.

Family Feud (ABC, 1976–1985; CBS, 1988–1992; Syndication, 1977–1985, 1988–1995, 1999–present)

This durable game show must have its roots in the old American story of the Hatfields and the McCoys when two neighboring families of five relatives and maybe a friend battled against each other. *Family Feud* selected two families to go against each other, not with fists or guns, but by guessing what an in-studio, off-camera group of 100 said in a survey about a particular item, action, or topic. The setup was a central board that contained the survey answers in percentage order of importance. Responses were revealed when flipped over and signaled by a loud gong bell. On the air, two families appeared behind a long table for each family with large oval signage stating their family name.

A host is always key on a game show. This show was launched with Richard Dawson (1932–2012), who was well known for playing Peter Newkirk in the controversial television show *Hogan's Heroes* (1965–1971). His job as host included talking to the family members during the game, joking and cajoling, and basically entertaining everyone there and at home until they gave him an answer. Comments and facial expressions were constants. Then famously he would point up to the board and yell, "The survey says!" A board would flip only if a team member had given that answer. If not, an angry buzzer and a large red X would show up. As in baseball, three strikes and you were

Richard Dawson, shown here in the late seventies, was the first of many hosts of the popular game show *The Family Feud*. Each show featured two families competing for a cash prize by trying to guess the most popular answers to survey questions. (AP Photo/HO)

out. There were points assigned for each right answer and the highest point total won the round.

In the game's next round Richard Dawson called over a comparable member from each team to a stand in front of a large buzzer. A question was asked and the first to bang the buzzer and answer correctly could decide either to play or pass, the latter being a popular strategy because the team in control forced the other family to get it right. If they felt confident they were good enough to do it, then they said "play."

After the rounds were complete, one family had a winning score. The winner of the day picked two family members for a lightning round. One was in a silent booth while the other answered a series of questions in a short time period. If the family members finished with a prescribed number of points, they won the big money of the day.

The most memorable aspect of Richard Dawson's presence on the *Family Feud* was that he kissed each and every woman in both families. Audiences adored Richard Dawson for his wit and his kissability.

This show, created by Mark Goodson (1915–1992) and Bill Todman (1916–1979) of Goodson-Todman Productions, has lasting power because of the classic nature of the game and its simplicity. Hosts change, families change, but home viewers don't change; they still like a good tussle among "neighbors."

Ray Combs (1956–1996) took over hosting duties in 1988, when the series aired on CBS and in syndication. The daytime version of the show was cancelled in 1993. Goodson-Todman Productions asked Dawson to return as host of the syndicated program for the 1994–1995 season. The show left syndication following that season, but not for long. A return to syndication in 1999 brought host Louie Anderson, a comedian and television actor. He hosted the show until 2002 when Richard Karn was selected. Karn himself was subsequently replaced with John O'Hurley in 2006. Comedian Steve Harvey (1957–) took on the hosting duties from 2010 to the present.

Despite the turnover in hosts, *Family Feud* has changed little in gameplay over the years. More recently, the show has broached more intimate topics with innuendos and more outright sexual questions and answers than the more subtle winks in the game's early days.

See also: $10,000 Pyramid; *Vol. 1, The 1950s–1960s: Jeopardy!*

Further Resources

Imagination International. 2008. *Family Feud Quiz Book.* Australia: Imagination Entertainment.

Rea, Louis M., and Richard A. Parker. 2005. *Designing and Conducting Survey Research: A Comprehensive Guide.* San Francisco, CA: Jossey-Bass.

Family Hour

In 1975 the Federal Communications Commissions (FCC) established a policy in the United States that each and every television network had a responsibility to provide family-friendly programing from 8 p.m. to 9 p.m., the first hour of their prime-time scheduling. After a court action that ended in 1977, the rule was overturned. Some viewers continued to believe there should be shows appropriate to children available during the 8 to 9 evening hour, when kids were most likely to be watching network television.

The family hour concept came about in 1974 where there was extensive criticism concerning the growing amounts of sex and violence on network television. Although there were many programs found offensive, the television movie *Born Innocent*, which aired in 1974, contained a rape scene; promotions for the telefilm were even shown during the day and included brief moments of the violent sex scene. Many blamed the real-life rape of a young girl on the TV movie. This led to a case before the California Supreme Court.

In January 1975 FCC chairman Richard E. Wiley appeared before both the House and Senate Communications and Commerce committees stating that all three networks, CBS, NBC, and ABC, had agreed to a family viewing hour in response to criticism that there was too much sex and violence during the early hours of prime-time television. The broadcasters took the issue further, telling local stations to also air family programing from 7 p.m. to 8 p.m., an hour that affiliates were given to do with as they wished.

CBS had been number one in the ratings since the mid-1950s and they were concerned about the other networks coming on board with the family hour programming idea. CBS stated they would only commit to the policy if the other two networks did because they didn't want their ratings to drop if they were the sole network to do this. By the end of 1974 all three major executives representing the three networks agreed and promised to put it into gear for the fall 1975 season.

The family hour did have a negative impact on some shows. *All in the Family* (1971–1979) had been the number-one show since 1971. It was moved by the network, CBS, to 9 p.m. on Mondays after playing earlier on Saturdays for five seasons. Producer Norman Lear (1922–) complained that his First Amendment rights had been violated and launched a lawsuit with the support of many industry guilds including the Writer's Guild of America (WGA). The case was won by Lear and his supporters.

In 1976 Judge Warren J. Ferguson from the U.S. District Court ruled against the family viewing policy, declaring it null and void starting with the fall 1977 season. The judge felt the idea had merit but the FCC had erred by not holding public hearings on the issue, rendering it without merit. The National Association of Broadcasters mandate that told affiliates they had to run family programming in the hour before prime time was also overturned.

There were numerous studies that tried to prove that violence on TV was harmful to young people, but nothing was conclusive. Even more extreme were murder trials in which the defense argued that their client committed murder after having seen a violent television show. There is no conclusive proof that the family hour prevented violence or really shielded young people from early exposure to the birds and the bees. Many critics and TV scholars and a large segment of the viewership felt that television, like contemporary movies, reflected the world outside the living room where most children were watching, some would say, too much television.

See also: *All in the Family*, Lear, Norman; Nudity on Television; *Vol. 1, The 1950s–1960s:* FCC (Federal Communications Commission).

Further Resources

Lemish, Dafna. 2007. *Children and Television: A Global Perspective*. Malden, ME: Blackwell.

Winn, Marie. 2002. *The Plug-In Drug: Television, Computers, and Family Life*. New York: Penguin Group.

Fantasy Island (ABC, 1978–1984)

There were two made-for-TV movies entitled *Fantasy Island,* one in 1977 and the other in 1978, the year it became a series. The story takes place at a beautiful tropical resort where people pay a fee to realize their life fantasy. Every week a plane lands on the beach carrying a small group who arrive to fulfill their dreams. The island is run by a man named Roarke, played by Ricardo Montalbán (1920–2009), and his little people assistant Tattoo, portrayed by Hervé Villechaize (1923–1993), famous for spotting the plane from a tower and saying "The plane, the plane!" in his high-toned voice. In the opening the two men are wearing a full white ensemble with a black bowtie as Roarke tells Tattoo the background of the arrivals so the audience knows their dream. The concept of *Fantasy Island* is that what people think they want isn't always really what they want or what is good for them. Roarke and his large team at the resort supply the truth of a thing, even though others are playing out the fantasy. As the desires unfold, life lessons are learned.

On the ABC show *Fantasy Island*, the mysterious Mr. Roarke, played by Ricardo Montalbán, is served a delectable drink by his sidekick, played by Christopher Hewitt. Each episode featured visitors to the island who would be granted fulfillment of their greatest fantasies, albeit at a steep price, and with unexpected results. (AP Photo/Wally Fong)

Examples of fantasies included a woman who wanted to be a superstar actress and live happily ever after and marry her boyfriend. An older gentleman has just remarried. In his past he was part of a gang of robbers. Documentation about the man's past is flown to the island along with a threat unless he pays hush money. The old gang is also on the island and they attempt to steal back the papers. A race car driver wants to recreate a crash that haunts him in his nightmares, a plumber wants to be a king, and a career gambler wants to win every game he plays. None of these implausible fantasies play out the way the chooser intends. Instead the participants are offered more meaningful insights that help them improve their actual lives.

Mystery Man

Roarke is a mysterious figure who always dresses in white. Based on information contained in the episodes throughout the series' run, certain facts can be extracted. The man in white is addressed by the guests as Mr. Roarke, but is that his first or last name? Intimates refer to him simply as Roarke, suggesting the theory that he may have only one name. He is a gentleman with impeccable manners and speaks with an accent. This leads us to believe he is of Hispanic origin. He is the sole owner and proprietor of the island and resort, thus he appears to be very wealthy. He also gets fees from the guests in undisclosed amounts. He once remarked that his guests were so mortal and there is a hint he may be immortal. Roarke's age is unknown. Although critics dubbed *Fantasy Island* escapist entertainment, Roarke has a very strong moral code and the whole purpose of buying fantasies is to teach people to be happy with what they have.

At times the situations had a touch of danger or a twist of fate. Sometimes Roarke was in control of the outcome but not invariably; this was a bit of a shock to the audience, who expected things to always work out. The enigma around Roarke is never revealed.

Aaron Spelling (1923–2006) and Leonard Goldberg (1934–) were the executive producers of *Fantasy Island,* which was an anthology series with several connections to *The Love Boat* (1977–1987)—multiple story lines, people on a quest, a single location, and interaction with the person in charge.

Fantasy Island relied on many guest stars for each one-hour episode. Some of the actors who landed on *Fantasy Island* included Loni Anderson (1945–), Macdonald Carey (1913–1994), Broderick Crawford (1911–1986), Kim Darby (1947–), Susan Lucci (1946–), Michele Pfeiffer (1958–), and Vic Taybak (1930–1990). Actors who were known for movies and television were a big draw. The island and the resort were physically beautiful. There was a constant flow of pretty island ladies putting rings of flowers around guests, other islanders taking care of the visitors' needs; the resort was in paradise.

Every episode a new batch of fantasy seekers came to the island; by the end of the episode they were a bit wiser than when they first arrived. As Roarke said goodbye to each person at the end of their experience, he made sure he told them what lessons they had learned. In later episodes Roarke seemed steeped in the supernatural, giving his presence and his interactions with the guests an even deeper spiritual meaning, but without foreboding.

Fantasy Island ran on Saturday nights back to back with *The Love Boat,* which gave Aaron Spelling the potential for winning the night's ratings on a consistent basis. The shows were alike in interior ways, but very different in their exterior presentation. Viewers of both shows went on a cruise and later ended up on a magical island.

See also: *The Love Boat*; *Vol. 1, The 1950s–1960s:* Spelling, Aaron.

Further Resources

Montalbán, Ricardo, and Bob Thomas. 1980. *Reflections: A Life in Two Worlds*. New York: Doubleday.

Spelling, Aaron, and Jefferson Graham. 2002. *Aaron Spelling: A Prime-Time Life*. New York: St. Martin's Press.

Fat Albert and the Cosby Kids (CBS, 1972–1985)

From 1972 to 1985 *Fat Albert and the Cosby Kids* was a pioneering animated program that aired on CBS that presented situations and stories that emphasized values while still being entertaining and very amusing to its young audience. The episodes followed the kids into school, home, and the junkyard where they hung out and provided situations that involved social contact. *Fat Albert and the Cosby Kids* were responsible for inspiring NBC and ABC to add values-oriented programming to the Saturday-morning lineups.

Fat Albert and the Cosby Kids began as a series of specials; *Hey, Hey, Hey—It's Fat Albert* (1969), which was created, as the series would be, in the Filmation style, which was very limited animation but the characters with Cosby's input became a fun bunch of kids with plenty of energy and movement in their design. Among the voice actors Cosby played two parts, Fat Albert and Bill, who was based on his younger brother. All the characters were based on Bill Cosby's youthful memories growing up in a housing project in Philadelphia. *Weird Harold,* a second special, aired in 1973. There have also been Easter, Halloween, and Christmas specials featuring Albert and the kids. *Fat Albert and the Cosby Kids* ran 12 years before going into syndication. In its last five years it was known as *The New Fat Albert Show*. As the show developed new characters were added and Cosby did additional voices. Many of Bill Cosby's classic routines from his stand-up days were used to create episodes. Cosby also starred in wraparound segments in live action, which were used at the beginning and end of an episode as well as bits that came in during the show to comment on the animated action. Although the characters were black, they and their stories were crafted to appeal to a wide audience, continuing Cosby's belief in a color-blind world. A CBS study found that middle-class and lower-class white children were better absorbing the messages in the show than lower-class black children. As *Fat Albert and the Cosby Kids* progressed, it moved away from issues like being teased for wearing glasses to bigotry, protecting your own body, and social diseases.

Further Resources

Cosby, Bill, and George Booth. 2011. *I Didn't Ask to Be Born (But I'm Glad I Was).* New York: Hachette Group.

Whitaker, Mark. 2014. *Cosby: His Life and Times.* New York: Simon & Schuster.

Fernwood 2-Night (Syndication, 1977)

Fernwood 2-Night was a spin-off of the Norman Lear soap opera parody, *Mary Hartman, Mary Hartman* (1976–1977). In that show Martin Mull (1943–) played Garth Gimble, a wife beater who died tragically when impaled on a fake Christmas tree in his closet. For *Fernwood 2-Night* Garth's identical twin brother, a self–created showbiz star from Miami, comes to Fernwood after running into a problem in Florida and stages a career comeback by heading his own talk show.

Fernwood 2-Night was hilarious at every turn—brilliantly written and performed. The format was a totally down-market late-night show like *The Tonight Show.* The show was produced by Alan Thicke (1947–2016). The team of 13 writers included Thicke, Lear, Tom Moore, Jeremy Stevens, and Judith Kahan.

The Production

The production was mounted in the 1970s and the costumes and dećor highlight all those fashion statements that decades later serve as a sort of museum of bad taste. Barth wears Hawaiian shirts or pastel colors with the collar open. The furniture was tacky and overcrowded.

The announcer and co-host of *Fernwood 2-Night* is Jerry Hubbard, played by Fred Willard (1939–). The role was designed to parody the kind of second banana who supports his host like Ed McMahon's relationship to Johnny Carson.

The house band, "Happy Kyne and the Mirth-Makers," were a shadow of what the big boys had: Happy was the bandleader, there was a bass player, an accordion player, a guitar, and drums. Happy was played by working actor and real film composer Frank De Vol (1911–1999). Because of his nerdish looks, De Vol was perfect for the role of Happy. The inside joke for those in the know was that Frank De Vol had a prestigious career in music, especially in Hollywood where he scored movies that included *Kiss Me Deadly* (1955), *Whatever Happened to Baby Jane* (1962), and *Krakatoa, East of Java* (1969). The guitarist was no third-string man; he was Tommy Tedesco (1930–1997), a master session man.

The viewers were told the show was broadcast from the studios of Channel 2 in Fernwood, Ohio. Like an actual talk show, *Fernwood 2-Night* had guests. In most cases those who were booked on the fake show were locals who had an interesting job or something to say. Others were oddballs with crazy inventions or inane philosophies. Barth Gimble was an impatient interviewer when he didn't like the guest, squirming in his chair or making faces to the camera so the viewers could feel the pulse of his celebrity psyche. The material written for the host, co-host, and guests was raunchy at times and often in bad taste, which made the parody aspects caustic, sarcastic, and sardonic.

Some of the episodes included Barth pitching a get-rich-quick scheme to build a wax museum that would showcase replicas of local citizens. Fernwood teacher and poet Martin Worth recites "The Ballad of Watergate" backed by Happy Kyne on the violin. Barth announces the upcoming Barth Gimble Pro Am Golf Tournament will not happen; instead his late twin brother will be honored at the Garth Gimble Memorial Tennis Classic.

Fernwood 2-Night did a modest summer run in 1977, but Norman Lear believed in the concept and in 1978 introduced *America 2-Tonight* in which Barth and Jerry had moved to Alta Coma, California and relocated the show in hopes that it would boost viewership if they could book appearances with major stars, and they did: Charlton Heston, Robin Williams, George Gobel, and Elke Sommer appeared. This gave the show a strange reality because the celebrities had material written for them, not like their ordinary banter on a real talk show. They were also in the company of the usual weird, wacky, and borderline appropriate guests, similar to the original show.

In its own strange way *Fernwood 2-Night* influenced talk shows in the future such as *The David Letterman Show* (1993–2015).

See also: *All in the Family*; Lear, Norman; *Vol. 1, The 1950s–1960s: The Tonight Show.*

Further Resources

Mull, Martin, and Allen Rucker. 1986. *A Paler Shade of White: The History of White People in America.* New York: Perigee.

Reilly, Sue. 1977. "With 'Fernwood 2-Night' Norman Lear Mulls Over the Idiocy of TV Talk." *People Magazine.* July 18.

George Wallace Shooting (May 15, 1972)

George Wallace (1919–1988) was the four-term governor of Alabama. A strict segregationist, he was a controversial figure because of his views against busing and his generally negative attitude toward the civil rights movement of the 1960s. He ran for president of the United States a total of four times, three as a Democrat and the last time on the Independent Party ticket. His fiery anti-Washington rhetoric and divisive opinions on race relations in America made him a national figure as a demagogue and kept him in the limelight over the decades.

A Fateful Day

His third bid for the presidency began on December 13, 1972 when he entered the field of Democrats that included Senator George McGovern (1922–2012), Hubert Humphrey (1911–1978), and others. On May 15, 1972, Wallace was at a podium giving a campaign speech to a crowd in Maryland, near Washington, D.C. He took off his jacket and stepped down into the crowd for a meet and greet; there was a swirl of people around him and the mood was joyous and supportive.

There was an ABC crew there and cameraman Charlie Jones was close and had a clear composition of the event. Suddenly, as the footage revealed, a young man with blond hair thrust forward as if he wanted to shake the governor's hand. He had a gun and more than four shots were fired; Wallace was hit in the legs, arm, and chest. During the confusion, the camera was knocked up in the air for a short interval and Jones quickly moved through the crowd toward the fallen Wallace. The jostling of the camera brought an eerie sense of reality and horror to the assassination attempt. The assailant was apprehended and was also injured, and brought away by a phalanx of police officers. Governor Wallace was brought to Holy Cross Hospital in Maryland where doctors determined he was in critical, but stable condition.

The ABC News on-air coverage was delivered by both Howard K. Smith (1914–2002) and Harry Reasoner (1923–1991). It was explained that the unusual format was necessary to carry this volatile event. The two anchors took turns reporting the events. In both camera shots there was an anchor and background still photos of Governor Wallace. Because there was no conclusive information, the two anchors made it clear they would continue their investigation and report back in the near future.

Wallace survived the attack and continued his political career. He was paralyzed from the waist down and suffered constant pain. He became a born-again Christian and begged forgiveness for his racist views. The man who shot Wallace, Arthur Bremer (1950–), was a troubled young man. He was 21 years old at the time and was struggling terribly to hold a job. He decided he was going to prove his manhood by killing either Richard Nixon or George Wallace. He was tried and found guilty and sentenced to 63 years in a Maryland prison. Later, on appeal, the sentence was reduced to 53 years.

Bremer kept a diary of his inner thoughts and plans. Portions were published under the title *An Assassin's Diary*. The book influenced screenwriter Paul Schrader (1946–) when he wrote *Taxi Driver* (1976), directed by Martin Scorsese (1942–), which among many other elements featured a deranged man who attempted to assassinate a presidential candidate.

The shooting of Wallace was not on live TV, but a news cameraman was there to film it and it was broadcast a little while later. During the 1970s the role of network news became much more important. The assassination of President John F. Kennedy (1917–1963) was a tragic lesson but one that showed the major networks that they could cover almost any event for news. As a result, the pool of reporters in the field was extensive for what should have been a routine campaign stop for Wallace.

See also: *Vol. 1, The 1950s–1960s:* Kennedy, President John F., Assassination; Kennedy, Robert F., Assassination; King, Martin Luther, Jr., Assassination.

Further Resources

Carlson, Jody. 1981. *George C. Wallace and the Politics of the Powerless: The Wallace Campaigns for the Presidency 1964–1976*. New Brunswick, NJ: Transaction Books.

Wallace, George C. 1976. *Stand Up for America*. New York: Doubleday.

Get Christie Love! (1974–1975)

Blaxploitation was a genre movement in 1970s motion pictures. These films were exploitation movies that had previously starred and been peopled with Caucasian actors. Now they showed black heroic figures or other action types, creating a new platform for African American actors who became stars in their own right.

African American actress Teresa Graves (1948–2002), who had appeared on *Rowan and Martin's Laugh-In* (1968–1973), played the lead role in *Get Christie Love!*, television's first African American policewoman on probably the only blaxploitation television show. Following the blaxploitation movie model Teresa Graves fit the bill to a T. She was a beautiful, thin, shapely, and sexy African American woman sporting an Afro hairstyle and wearing brightly colored slacks and at times a midriff-revealing top. Although she carried a standard pistol, Christie Love threw the rule book away and had a take-no-prisoners approach, using her body and everything she had around her to put down the bad guys.

Get Christie Love! was originally a 1974 made-for-television movie starring Graves as an undercover detective. In the TV movie Christie helps bring down a drug ring. The movie was based on the crime/thriller novel *The Ledger* written by Dorothy Uhnak (1930–2006). *Get Christie Love!* was a one-hour program with the supporting team of Charlies Cioffi (1935–) as boss Lieutenant Matt Reardon of the Special Investigations Unit of the Los Angeles Police Department, Dennis Rucker (1946–) as Lieutenant Steve Belmont, and Andy Romano (1941–). By January of the first season changes were made including replacing producer Andy Mason with *Battlestar Galactica* creator Glen A. Larson (1937–2014).

Christie Love specialized in undercover work. She was very trendy and used hip phrases like "You're under arrest, sugah!" The show may have been on the outer edges of programming in the seventies, but time would reveal its influence when considering 21st-century shows like *Scandal* (2012–).

Further Resources

Goldman, Adria Y., VanNatta S. Ford, Alexa A. Harris, and Natasha R. Howard, eds. and contributors. 2014. *Black*

Women and Popular Culture: The Conversation Continues. Lanham, MD: Lexington Books.

Sims, Yvonne D. 2006. *Women of Blaxploitation: How the Black Action Film Heroine Changed American Popular Culture*. Jefferson, NC: McFarland.

The Gong Show (NBC, 1976–1978)

Chuck Barris (1929–2017) hosted *The Gong Show* and reinvented the game show genre. The program totally turned the form of the amateur entertainment show upside down. Barris's soft curly hair was his version of an Afro. He wore a tux and popularized a shuffle he devised that moved him forward and back in delight and to the pleasure of the audience. Regular performers who worked in between the competitive acts were "The Unknown Comic," a comedian who made very poor jokes and was well dressed but had a large brown paper bag over his head, and Gene Gene the Dancing Machine, a stagehand who was asked to warm up the audience prior to air and then was put on the show as a popular segment that pleased the panel, the host, the audience, and the viewers. Gene Gene came out casually dressed with a cap on his head and did an infectious soft tap routine while the band vamped a showbiz/Vegas–type number.

Television Chaos

Barris would give Gene Gene a big introduction bordering on hysteria and they would dance in place wildly while the man did his work. The intercutting between Barris and Gene Gene was so often fast that the act the viewers thought they were seeing was both men dancing at the same time. Over the run of *The Gong Show* there were always three celebrity judges, who at any time could be singer Jaye P. Morgan, comedian Arte Johnson (1929–), and Jamie Farr (1934–) of *M*A*S*H* fame. The judges would create hysterical mayhem, with Jaye P. Morgan going from man to man fake mussing them up. They were a critical part of the show's humor and chaos. Others sat in at times such as film critic Rex Reed (1938–) and actress and singer Michele Lee (1942–).

Chuck Barris wore an endless array of silly hats during the show and didn't always keep his tux jacket on. On the stage backdrop would be a word or phrase connected to the act. For Gene Gene it would read "Stuff" and the audience (and probably off camera-staff) would lovingly throw stuffed animals and other soft items at him. "We'll be back with more stuff" was commonly Barris's line to go into commercials.

The Gong Show had trouble with the censors. Barris showed them outrageous acts in advance that he assumed they would censor, so he could slip other risqué material on the air. One of the most notorious acts ever on the show was "Have You Got a Nickel?" The act consisted of two 17-year-old girls. They came out dressed in cut-off shorts, each wielding a long Popsicle, and the act consisted on them sitting down and licking the ice pops in such a highly suggestive manner that there could be no question of the intent. Somehow for the first feed or two the Popsicle act actually aired, but finally the censors caught on and cut it from any other airings.

The unpredictable Jaye P. Morgan flashed her naked breasts on more than one occasion in response to an act, and eventually she was asked to leave the show.

Originally ABC was convinced to purchase *The Gong Show,* which was pitched as a talent show with the best and worst performing talent. They put it in nighttime syndication for fall 1976, not really knowing that Barris's idea of a good act would be outrageous, bad, silly, or worse. The studio audience reaction was strong and Gary Owens (1934–2015), the over-pompous announcer from *Rowan and Martin's Laugh-In* (1968–1973), was the host. The original panelists came mainly from that hit show as well: Arte Johnson (1929–), Joanne Worley (1937–), Richard Dawson (1932–2012), and an actress on *Maude,* Adrienne Barbeau (1945–). Next to the judges was a hostess; those who played this role included Sivi Aberg (1944–), a Swedish-born model who worked on a Chuck Barris show before; actress Marlena Clark (1949–); pornographic movie actress Carol Connors (1952–); and Barris's then teenage daughter.

History

The first filmed episode was so successful that NBC was interested in running the show in the daytime. NBC was having trouble finding an audience for their game shows and requested a different host. Barris went through a lot of possibilities and eventually settled on John Barbour (1933–), but Barris was not happy with the results and there wasn't enough time to find a replacement, so he took on the job himself. The NBC show aired first and audiences really responded to Barris, although he was the most unlikely of hosts. He ultimately took over the nighttime hosting duties as well.

A very large gong and a striker were behind the celebrity judging panel. If any of the three disliked the act on stage, after they were given a big build-up by the host, they could strike the gong, which was followed by the band playing what sounded like crying, "wah wah wah . . ." The performer stopped the act and Barris, often surprised, pointed them in the direction of the backstage, and their television dreams were over. The aesthetic was that the bad acts thought they were good or certainly the kind of entertainment the show would like. If they made it to the end of their perform ance, the judges then scored them from 1 to 10 on a card and usually made short funny, obtuse, or salacious remarks. The contestant with the highest score won the grand prize, which Barris established costing $516.32 so it never would become too important. Professionals weren't allowed to compete for the grand prize but were paid union scale, which was $516. The nighttime edition went up to $712.05, then $1,000 for the pros.

The Gong Show taped on Saturdays and Sundays. Three hundred performers auditioned per week and 65 acts made it to the show for each weekend taping. Barris and his staff combed the ranks of practically every bit actor in town and put most of them on the show at one time or another. Five shows were taped on the weekend and snacks and drinks were served; drunkenness commonly hit the celebrities well into the day.

The acts were far from standard fare of the genre. A demented-looking dentist drills a patient's teeth, flipping the dreaded tool on and off to the rhythm of "Stars and Stripes Forever." A morbidly obese man tap dances to *Swan Lake* and is joined later by his equally large wife squeezed into a tutu, who puts her head into a teacup and spins around while playing "Old Folks at Home" on a mandolin. An Elvis impersonator performs the King's classic "Hound Dog" but his voice is flat and monotone. Some of the ongoing gags from the original run included a musician who announces he's going to play a musical instrument, then drops it on the floor right on cue. Scarlett and Rhett were comedians whose every joke was dirty, causing an "Oops" sign to flash. One of the celebrities who performed in a segment without judging and gong-proof was Alice Cooper (1948–).

Other acts included a magician trying to get his pigeons to dance, teenaged girls in prom dresses singing "People" while dancing in a conga line, a comic who did impressions of noted actors doing Shakespeare, a woman with a dog that could imitate barnyard animals, and Professor Flamo who sang out in pain when lowering various body parts into burning candles. One episode was actually dedicated to singing the song "Feelings," which every performer sang. At times there was a fight among the judges for the gong mallet; sometimes two or all three gonged an act they really hated. In the early shows some contestants were gonged within seconds of beginning their act, so Barris made it a rule that a contestant couldn't be gonged until 45 seconds had gone by.

There were many camera cuts to celebrity reaction during the performance, which mostly was negative but could be positive and could show enjoyment as well. A successful un-gonged performance could run as long as two and a half minutes. Eventually, due to pressure practically everywhere, the network, the sponsors, and the viewers.

The Gong Show, having gotten racier and in even worse taste than when it started, was cancelled July 21, 1978. *The Gong Show* went on to be successful in syndication over the years.

See also: *Vol. 3, The 1990s–Present: America's Got Talent.*

Further Resources

Bowles, Jerry G. 1977. *The Gong Show Book*. New York: Grosset & Dunlap.

Stein, Joel. 2003. "Chuck Barris: Lying to Tell the Truth." *Time*. January 7. http://content.time.com/time/magazine/article/0,9171,404266,00.html

Times Union.com. 2010. "The Gong Show: The Greatest TV Game Show." August 31. http://blog.timesunion.com/chuckmiller/the-gong-show-the-greatest-tv-game-show-of-all-time/2868

Good Morning America (ABC, 1975–)

The ABC network wanted to compete with the highly rated morning program *Today* (1952–). On January 6, 1975 they launched *A.M. America* with hosts Bill Beutel (1930–2006) and Stephanie Edwards (1943–). Peter Jennings (1938–2005) delivered the news. The format was derived from *Ralph's Story* (1964–1970), which ran on the network's KABC-TV in Los Angeles. It included feature stories, events, news, and interviews with celebrities. The show did not catch on. By May Edwards quit the show and Beutel left a few months later. On November 3, the Monday following the last broadcast of *A.M. America*, *Good Morning America* premiered—a second chance at giving NBC's *Today* a run for its money.

Good Morning America was also in a two-hour slot and it had practically the same format as *Today*, but the NBC show that dominated morning television was staged in a newsroom, which sent the message to viewers that they were watching something directly from the NBC newsroom facility. In contrast to *Today*, the creators of *Good Morning America* designed a set that was a virtual living room to mirror the homes from which the viewers were watching. The set was casual, comfortable, and inviting.

The male host was a familiar face to TV watchers, David Hartman (1935–), who had been a regular cast member of both *The Virginian* (1962–1971) and *The Bold Ones* (1969–1973). On camera Hartman was folksy, a tall man with a good voice who could establish a relationship with the viewers. Nancy Dussault (1936–), who had an impressive resume as a theater actress, was the co-host.

The producers brought in contributors to give the show entertainment, variety, and depth. They included Erma Bombeck (1927–1996), a humorist who talked about home life, former New York mayor John Lindsay (1921–2000), top-notch Hollywood gossip columnist Rona Barrett (1936–), hard-hitting investigative journalist Geraldo Rivera (1943–), and medical journalist Dr. Timothy Johnson (1936–).

Movie and television series stars would appear to promote their shows—others were just invited as guests. Throughout the decade *Good Morning America* tried hard to live up to its name, cheerfully greeting its viewers upon rising and helping them through the early morning hours. The show helped workers get off to work and provided entertainment, news, and a warm atmosphere for those who stayed home.

See also: *Vol. 1, The 1950s–1960s: The Today Show.*

Further Resources

Lunden, Joan. 1986. *Good Morning, I'm Joan Lunden.* New York: Putnam Publishing Group.

Stelter, Brian. 2014. *Top of the Morning: Inside the Cutthroat World of Morning TV.* New York: Grand Central Publishing.

Good Times (CBS, 1974–1979)

The African American–themed *Good Times* holds the distinction of being the first ever spin-off of a spin-off. First there was *All in the Family* from which the program generated *Maude,* and from *Maude* came the spin-off *Good Times*. The show was set in Chicago and highlighted the travails and adventures of a middle-class family comprised of mother Florida Evans, who was the maid on *Maude*, played by Esther Rolle (1920–1998); father James Evans, portrayed by John Amos (1939–); and J.J., standing for James Junior, the eldest son, an artist who expressed himself with his work and looked everywhere for money. J.J.'s witty and snappy humorous remarks made him the center of the show, especially for his oft-said line, "Dyn-o-mite!" J.J. was played effortlessly by Jimmie Walker (1947–); BernNadette Stanis (1953–) played their youngest daughter, teenager Thelma; and Michael was the younger son,

> It has taken television some time to present characters and families that represent the African American communities across America rather than perpetuate long-worn stereotypes. By the 1970s, the industry was making shows, primarily sitcoms, for a newly discovered demographic. This major slate includes *What's Happening!!* (1976–1979), *Diff'rent Strokes* (1978–1985), *Julia* (1968–1971), *Good Times* (1974–1979), *Fat Albert and the Cosby Kids* (1972–1985), *The Jeffersons* (1975–1985), *Sanford and Son* (1972–1977), and *The Bill Cosby Show* (1969–1971).

Good Times was part of a wave of African American sitcoms that were popular in the 1970s. Cast members shown here are (left to right) John Amos, Esther Rolle, Jimmy Walker, Ralph Carter, and Ja'net DuBois. (CBS Photo Archive/Getty Images)

very serious and politically astute. He was portrayed by Ralph Carter (1961–). The family's friend and neighbor Willona Woods was played by Ja'net DuBois (1945–), and the regular cast was rounded out by the strongly disliked janitor Mr. Bookman, played by Johnny Brown (1937–).

The Evans family is depicted as experiencing the pressures of middle-class black urban society during the difficult period of the mid-seventies. James Evans is dissatisfied and resents the federal government and depressing events such as Watergate, the Vietnam War, rapidly growing unemployment, and a miserable economy. He is vocal about his ghetto surroundings and his difficulties supporting his family.

Serious themes investigated on *Good Times,* a family sitcom created by Eric Monte and Michael Evans who also developed *The Jeffersons* (1975–1985), were evictions, gangs, and racial discrimination. Norman Lear developed the show and it is very much in the Lear tradition. *Good Times* produced sitcom episodes that were funny but politically and socially relevant. J.J. commanded much of the attention during the episodes; he was funny, making one-liners as fast as he could and usually positioned himself in the center of the camera frame.

Both John Amos and Esther Rolle left the series before it ended in 1979, Amos at the end of the 1975–1976 season and Rolle when production began for the 1977–1978 season. It is believed they both felt that Jimmie Walker's J.J. had taken over the show and was the main reason viewers tuned in. Rolle especially didn't like the outsized portrayal of a young black man that Walker seemed to relish and make larger every week. Rolle and Amos were both written out of future scripts. The three children stayed in Chicago and took care of themselves, with an assist from Willona. Janet Jackson (1966–) was brought in as Penny, a battered child adopted by Willona.

At the end of the run ratings were plummeting and CBS pulled *Good Times* from the schedule during December 1978. They did, however, bring it back in spring 1979. After a spate of reruns, the last original show allowed everyone to succeed in what they wanted. Thelma was pregnant with her first child, her husband Keith finally got his football contract as a running back, J.J developed a comic strip and sold it for a lot of money, and Willona got promoted to head buyer at the clothing boutique where she worked.

See also: *All in the Family*; *The Jeffersons*; Lear, Norman; *Maude*.

Further Resources

Campbell, Sean. 2006. *The Sitcoms of Norman Lear*. Jefferson, NC:

Walker, Jimmie, and Sal Manna. 2012. *Dyn–o– mite! Good Times, Bad Times—A Memoir*. New York: Da Capo Press.

Happy Days (ABC, 1974–1984)

This show aired during the 1970s but was set in the 1950s. It tapped into a nostalgia craze that made people remember the good old days while living in a decade filled with negativity. *Happy Days* became a trajectory for ABC with the network landing on the top of the heap as the series gained in popularity. The show's ratings were midrange at best for the first year and a half on the air, but by season three *Happy Days* landed in Nielsen's top 10, and one year later it was the number one television show in the country.

> *Happy Days* is responsible for a phrase common to declining television series: "jumping the shark." This phrase, which describes a desperate gimmick used to keep viewers' attention, refers to the season five premiere episode of *Happy Days*, in which Fonzie responds to a challenge by water skiing and jumping over a shark. After that episode, Fonzie, who had originally been a side character, became the focus of the series. Despite the original popularity of the episode, a "jump the shark" moment is when a defining moment has occurred and "it's all downhill from here."

The Road to Success

The creator of *Happy Days* was Garry Marshall (1934–2016), a veteran comedy writer and sitcom producer. The journey of the show began when in 1971 Marshall produced a pilot for ABC called *New Family in Town*. The network was not interested in this series but on February 25, 1972 they played the pilot as a segment of *Love, American Style*. The story concerned a 1950s family buying their first television sets and featured Ron Howard (1954–), Marion Ross (1928–), Harold Gould (1923–2010), and Susan Neher (1959–).

During this period George Lucas (1944–) saw the pilot because he was interested in actor Ron Howard for his film about the 1950s, *American Graffiti*. The film was released in 1973 and was a mega-hit in all age demographics. Now ABC was interested in having Garry Marshall develop the pilot into a series, which he named *Happy Days*.

Happy Days was set in the late 1950s and took place in Milwaukee. The Cunningham family was the focus of the story lines. Ron Howard played Richie Cunningham, a teenager who fretted over girls; Tom Bosley (1927–2010) portrayed his father, Howard, who owned a local hardware store; Marion Ross played Marion Cunningham, wife and mother; and Erin Moran (1960–2017) played Richie's little sister Joanie.

Richie's three closest friends included Warren "Potsie" Webber played by Anson Williams (1949–), his best friend who is with him on many adventures, some including girls. Potsie is fun-loving and very buoyant. Donnie Most (1953–) portrayed Ralph Malph, a know-it-all big mouth who may be a friend of Richie but sometimes when he seemed against him, it is hard to believe it. Arthur "Fonzie" (or "The Fonz") Fonzarelli, played by Henry Winkler (1945–), was mysterious, a bit of a loner, sort of a James Dean type but a funny young man who represented the 1950s hipster. Fonzie wore a black leather jacket, rode a motorcycle, and purported to be an expert on cars and girls. He was originally meant to be a minor character, but he immediately became an icon to the viewers, who couldn't get enough of him, so his appearances increased. The ABC network executives were against the Fonz wearing a black leather jacket because they felt he would come across as menacing, so he wore a plain cloth jacket reminiscent of James Dean's character in the movie *Rebel Without a Cause*.

The local hangout was that very 1950s establishment, the drive-in, a place viewers either remembered or wished still existed. "Arnold's" was first owned by Arnold (Mitsuko Takahashi), played by Pat Morita (1942–2005). Misty Rowe (1950–) played Wendy, a waitress. This was the place where Richie and his friends devoured burgers and shakes in a car with a tray of food hooked to a partly rolled-down window.

The show begins with a 45 RPM record playing the sprightly *Happy Days* theme written by Norman Gimbel (1927–) and Charles Fox (1940–) on a vintage jukebox. Other music used in the show includes recordings by Bill Haley and the Comets ("Rock Around the Clock") as well as records by Fats Domino, Connie Francis, Johnny Ray, and Kay Starr.

Happy Days had story lines not unlike real 1950s sitcoms like *The Adventures of Ozzie and Harriet* and *Leave It to Beaver*; interactions with parents, the travails of dating, hanging out at the drive-in, the car culture of the era, and life on the road. *Happy Days* was very successful because it was a comfortable show. It was not meant to be a highly accurate and detailed show about the fifties, but deliberately a sketch of a time that is saturated with the idea of the good old days.

The seventies was a decade of spin-offs and Garry Marshall created spin-offs to *Happy Days*. They are *Laverne and Shirley* (1976–1983), *Mork & Mindy* (1978–1982), *Joanie Loves Chachi* (1982–1983), *Blansky's Beauties* (which ran only during 1977), and animated versions of some of the shows.

There was a certain artificiality to *Happy Days*, which made it feel generic. This was its greatest strength because the viewers didn't want details that might not have allowed them to relate to all the elements of the show. The title is perfect. *Happy Days* ensured the viewer would indeed have a happy day.

See also: *Laverne and Shirley*; *Mork & Mindy*; *Vol. 1, The 1950s–1960s: The Adventures of Ozzie and Harriet*; *Leave It to Beaver*.

Further Resources

Gray, Beverly. 2003. *Ron Howard: From Mayberry to the Moon and Beyond*. Nashville, TN: Rutledge Hill Press.

Marshall, Garry. 2012. *My Happy Days in Hollywood: A Memoir*. New York: Crown, Archetype.

HBO (Home Box Office) (1972)

Home Box Office (HBO) was one of the first cable television networks and is still dominant in the industry due to its successful mix of sporting events and groundbreaking original programming, a departure from its original diet of recent film releases.

HBO's origin is a complex story. It begins in 1965 when a cable pioneer named Charles Dolan (1926–) created Teleglide, a cable TV system that he sold to New York hotels that allowed visitors to watch a television program that detailed the city and its attractions via closed-circuit TV. Dolan then won a franchise to create and build a cable TV system in lower Manhattan. Dolan named the new venture Sterling Information Services; later it became Sterling Manhattan Cable and eventually was called Time Warner Cable. Sterling Information Services was the first urban cable system in the United States. To make this happen Sterling came up with the modern method of providing cable. He ruled out stringing cable on telephone pole wires, or using microwave antennas. He came up with the idea to lay cable underground below the New York streets. Time Life Inc. bought 20 percent of Charles Dolan's company.

For six years the company lost money mainly because of the cost of laying the cables. In 1971 the company only had 400 subscribers. While on vacation Dolan pondered the problem of profitability and came up with the idea of a cable television service he called the Green Channel. He convinced Time Life to back him on this pay television service. A direct mail campaign had a wildly positive response; homeowners around the country said they would sign up for such a service. The working title for the service became Home Box Office and as time went by the concept stuck.

Early HBO programming included *HBO World Championship Boxing*, which began January 22, 1973.

In the 1950s boxing was a major television sport. Several shows carried the best bouts and marquee names in the sport fought hard while commentators informed viewers as to the blow-by-blow action. These programs were telecast during the black-and-white broadcasting era.

HBO presented their fights in color and had flamboyant commentators like Jim Lampley (1949–), who was good looking and knew how to go for controversy when there was any hint of it. The real star of the show was Larry Merchant (1934–), a sportswriter who really knew all the details within details about boxing. Merchant had a way of antagonizing fighters with his cutting opening remarks and more so as an after-fight interviewer. Merchant asked questions that were so provocative, the home viewer often thought there would be another fight with Larry Merchant on the other end. One of the major fights featured on the show was "The Rumble in the Jungle" in 1973 when Muhammad Ali won back his title from George Foreman. The program was a good draw, pulling fight fans away from the network offerings. *HBO World Championship Boxing* continues to air on HBO.

In June 19, 1976 HBO premiered *Standing Room Only* (SRO). This variety show featured magicians, burlesque, ventriloquists, singers, and various other popular acts. A long list of entertainers who worked the show includes Linda Ronstadt, George Burns, Bette Midler, Olivia Newton-John, and Neil Sedaka. This show ran on HBO until 1982. *On Location* was a stand-up comedy show that premiered in 1976 and featured, among others, George Carlin, Billy Crystal, Phyllis Diller, Buddy Hackett, and Redd Foxx. It ended its run in 1985.

Over the years HBO built a stellar documentary department. On November 11, 1979 Dick Cavett (1936–) began hosting *Time Was*, a nonfiction program that examined one decade each time out, covering the 1920s to the 1970s.

The Seekers was a miniseries that ran July 8–9 in 1979. This drama written by John Jakes (1932–) is the third part of *The Kent Chronicles,* also known as the Bicentennial Series. It blends fictional characters with historical ones. It concerns the settlement in America of the sons and grandchildren of Philip Kent. The large cast includes Martin Milner (1931–2015) as Philip Kent, Edie Adams (1927–2008) as Flora Cato, and Vic Morrow (1929–1982) as Leland Pell.

Over time the network branched out, creating the sister channel Cinemax and a 24-hour comedy network, Comedy Central, among other ventures. In the 1990s, the network began venturing into original programming. With such shows as *Oz, The Larry Sanders Show*, *The Sopranos*, and *Deadwood,* HBO blazed new paths with series that were not subject to the constraints of broadcast television. Cable shows were able to address sensitive subject matter and were not constrained by broadcast standards. Such shows as *Sex and the City, Deadwood*, and *Game of Thrones* pushed the boundaries.

HBO arguably found its greatest hit with the fantasy series *Game of Thrones* (2011–), which has received 38 Emmy awards and numerous Golden Globe nominations. The show has become one of HBO's most-watched programs of all time, and averaged over 23 million viewers per episode in season six (Dockterman 2016). Based on the "A Song of Ice and Fire" novels written by George R. R. Martin (1948–), the series is slated to end in 2018.

Although HBO is still dominant in the number of subscribers it has, compared to other networks, many other stations, including Showtime and such basic cable networks as AMC, have provided strong competition for the cutting-edge programming that was pioneered by the network. Early on HBO saw the importance of competition; the cable station could do what the networks were doing but without commercials. HBO developed in-depth material that pushed the envelope of television programming. It continues to produce quality and entertaining programming.

See also: *Ray Bradbury Theater*; *Tales from the Crypt*; *Tanner '88*; *Vol. 3, The 1990s–Present: Boardwalk Empire*; *Deadwood*; *Enlightened*; *Game of Thrones*; *Girls*; *Oz*; *Sex and the City*; *Six Feet Under*; *True Detective*; *The Wire*.

Further Resources

Dockterman, Eliana. 2016. "*Game of Thrones* Finale Ratings Record Proves It's the Last Consensus Show on TV." *Time*. June 28. http://time.com/4385886/game-of-thrones-final-record-ratings/

Leverette, Mark, and Brian L. Ott. 2008. *It's Not TV: Watching HBO in the Post-Television Era*. New York: Routledge.
Mesce, Bill. 2015. *Inside the Rise of HBO: A Personal History of the Company That Transformed Television*. Jefferson, NC: McFarland.

In Search Of . . . (Syndication, 1976–1982)

This 30-minute documentary series narrated and hosted by *Star Trek*'s Leonard Nimoy (1931–2015) that explored unexplained phenomena was an Alan Landsburg (1933–2014) production. Landsburg had been involved in producing over 50 movies of the week and logged in over 2,000 hours of television production during his long career. His experience in nonfiction TV also included *Biography* (1961–1963), National Geographic specials, and *The World of Jacques Cousteau* (1968–1975), and he produced *Alaska Wilderness Lake,* a 1971 documentary that was nominated for an Academy Award.

Utilizing intriguing graphics, moving and duplicating typography, the main title sequence of *In Search Of* presents the subjects covered over the course of the series: extraterrestrials, magic/witchcraft, the missing, myths, and lost civilizations phenomena. There is music, the kind that would accompany a show like *The Twilight Zone* or *The Outer Limits*.

A voice-over note performed by Leonard Nimoy explains the program and makes a statement concerning the show's intentions. The voice says, "This series presents information based in part on theory and conjecture. The producer's purpose is to suggest some possible explanations."

Examples of specific shows whose focus falls under the topic headings are those on the lost city of Atlantis, the Loch Ness monster, Bigfoot, Amelia Earhart, Dracula, and even the end of the world.

One particular episode, called "The Easter Island Massacre," concerned itself with tall and long statues of a man's head with different expressions that were made out of volcanic rock by people from an ancient civilization. These heads were considered gods with extraordinary powers when the "eye" was chiseled open. It was determined that a warring tribe attacked the people and their gods and killed them all, destroying all but a few of the statues, which still existed as of the show's original airing.

After a presentation of facts as they are known, Leonard Nimoy, who had been narrating and was on camera at times, delves into the show's goal, to suggest possible reasons for this spectacular, spiritual, and unfortunately deadly event.

In Search Of was in syndication only; it was never a network program or locally broadcast. The show was expertly crafted. Crews were sent to document the events being investigated. Then they would conduct interviews to bring the story alive.

The editing was adroit and moved the documentary material at a pace that is surprisingly modern. The music is expressive and interpretive. There are sound effects when necessary and the cinematography is direct, well composed, and structured in a storytelling style similar to that of a fictional show.

Leonard Nimoy spoke with authority, looking serious when on camera. The studio host shots are staged simply but at times with still pictures mounted on boards and hung alongside and behind Mr. Nimoy. He often started the show speaking over images but ended on camera for a wrap-up and final word representing the voice of the producers.

The intended audience for *In Search Of* was those interested in strange and unusual events and situations, unexplained phenomena, science, science fiction, and history. *In Search Of* was an unusual show that was a fine example of the documentary television craft and one that may have sent its viewers to the library to learn more and to continue searching.

See also: *Vol. 1, The 1950s–1960s: Biography.*

Further Resources

Bainton, Roy. 2013. *The Mammoth Book of Unexplained Phenomena*. London: Constable & Robinson.
Landsburg, Alan. 1977. *In Search of Phenomena* 4. New York: Bantam Books.

The Incredible Hulk (CBS, 1978–1982)

This series is based on the Marvel Comics character, the Hulk. The origin of this character concerns Robert Bruce Banner, who as a child absorbed much rage and anger from the behavior of his alcoholic father, Dr. Brian Banner, but also received tender loving care from his mother. His father was a physicist working to make atomic power an energy source, and he was concerned that he genetically passed on mutated genes to his son. The boy grew up with great intelligence and the father grew more convinced the boy had the altered genes. In a rage Brian killed his wife and was committed to a mental institution.

This horrific event left Bruce unable to get close to people, but he did become a doctor in the same field as his father. Eventually he became the Hulk, a giant man with a heavily muscled body who transforms from Bruce when he becomes angry. During these transitions, he expresses violence and when he reverts to Bruce Banner he is calm.

The television series took the basic story but made some changes. In the TV show Robert Bruce Banner is a doctor and scientist who survives a car accident in which his wife dies. He is mentally tormented by the death of his wife and that he couldn't save her. He conducts a gamma experiment to see if people confronted by danger can develop superhuman strength to save others. He leaves his lab in frustration one night after he is not able to achieve his goal. While driving home he gets a flat tire and injures himself while changing it; in his rage he transforms and the Hulk is born.

The cast includes Bill Bixby (1934–1993) as Dr. Robert Bruce Banner and Lou Ferrigno (1951–) as the Hulk. Bixby, an accomplished actor and director, was best known for *My Favorite Martian* (1963–1966) and *The Courtship of Eddie's Father* (1969–1972). Ferrigno began weight training at age 13; his role model was Steve Reeves (1926–2000) and the character Reeves played in films, Hercules. After high school Lou Ferrigno won the body-building titles Mr. America and Mr. Universe before becoming famous for participating in the documentary *Pumping Iron* (1975) in which he lost the Mr. Olympia title to Arnold Schwarzenegger (1947–). Ferrigno still needed to earn money; first he got a $10 an hour job as a sheet metal worker in Brooklyn, New York. He was there for three years. For a brief time he was a defensive lineman for the Toronto Argonauts. He was big but had never played football before and was cut from the team after two games. In 1977 producers were looking for an actor to play the Hulk. Ferrigno's amazing physique was perfect and with the support of the production he learned to act and became a central part of the show as audiences waited to see him after the opening dramatic scenes.

In the show Ferrigno wore a black mop-top wig and green body makeup. The transition begins with Bill Bixby—it was all in the eyes as the actor grimaces and yells as his eyeballs are hit by a strong light that initiates the conversion from human to monstrous being. The uncontrolled anger of the Hulk initiated by his human counterpart was an enthralling theme for a show that kids and adults found exciting.

Banner is on the run like Richard Kimble in *The Fugitive* (1963–1967) and Paul Bryan in *Run for Your Life* (1965–1968), but for different reasons. Law enforcement is looking for a big green man who they believe murdered the doctor. Each week he tries to keep the lowest profile possible, avoiding people and relationships while going from menial job to menial job, well beneath his true profession. In some of the week by week episodes people he encounters catch on to his identity by witnessing the highly experienced doctor ply his trade as part of the circumstances. Bruce Banner will find himself in an instance where he resolves issues for others by righteous rage, which turns him into the Hulk. Invariably, the result is a positive resolution for people he has just met.

Because the Hulk originated in comic books, children and teenagers were a natural audience for this series. Bill Bixby's compelling acting and Lou Ferrigno's massive, sculpted physique attracted a wider audience of adult males and females.

See also: *Vol. 1: 1950s–1960s: The Fugitive; Run for Your Life*.

Further Resources

Disney Book Group. 2011. *The Incredible Hulk: An Origin Story*. New York: Marvel Press.

Ferrigno, Lou. 2003. *My Incredible Life as the Hulk*. California: Lou Ferrigno Enterprises.

The Jeffersons (CBS, 1975–1985)

On *All in the Family* the Bunkers had a black couple as neighbors in Queens, New York. George Jefferson was

The Jeffersons was a spinoff of *All in the Family* that ran from 1975 to 1985, and portrayed an African American couple who moved up in economic status. Pictured here is Sherman Hemsley as George Jefferson, Franklin Cover as Tom Willis, Roxie Roker as Helen Willis, and Isabel Sanford as Louise Jefferson. (CBS Photo Archive/Getty Images)

played by Sherman Helmsley (1938–2012) and Louise Jefferson, his wife, was portrayed by Isabel Sanford (1917–2004). Their popularity created another comedic seventies spin-off. George ran a dry cleaning store, which expanded into a chain of stores and made the Jeffersons very rich. They said goodbye to their neighbors and to the borough of Queens and headed to the East Side of Manhattan and a luxury apartment building.

Other characters on *The Jeffersons* include their son Lionel, played by Damon Evans (1949–); Harry Bentley, an eccentric neighbor who is a translator at the UN, played by Paul Benedict (1938–2008); Marla Gibbs (1931–) as Florence Johnson, their maid; and the first racially mixed married couple to appear on prime-time television, Caucasian Tom Willis, played by Franklin Cover (1928–2006), and his African American wife, Helen, portrayed by Roxie Roker (1929–1995).

The comedy comes from many places. Harry Bentley seems to speak with some sort of British accent and almost always says the opposite of what he should say; he is constantly misunderstanding situations. George struts most of the time when he isn't walking as if he owns the universe. His one-liners are sharp and either have a bigoted nature or address money, lots of money. Marla Gibbs as the sassy maid may be the funniest; her shoot-from-the-hip dialogue gets the most laughs on the soundtrack. They can be wisecracks, lightning-fast retorts, and denigrations of everyone and everything.

The theme song, "Movin' on Up" by Jeff Barry (1938–) and Ja'net DuBois (1945–), tells the story of the Jeffersons' rise from Queens to New York City and is performed as a gospel song with a strong lead female vocal by DuBois, backed by a choir who sing and clap a steady beat.

This is a Norman Lear show so the sitcom elements combine comedy with serious themes. A major focus on *The Jeffersons* is race and the approach is direct and controversial. The "N" word is frequently used and one episode even took on the Ku Klux Klan.

How George handles his wealth and life among the rich is a good part of the comic story line. His circumstances, dialogue, and actions are more than amusing, and his physicality and dance-like moves contribute to the show's humor.

Audiences liked spin-offs because they already knew the characters on some level and the expansion of their adventures was something to look forward to. This is another show where black characters are in roles that are 180 degrees from early depictions like *Amos 'n' Andy* (1951–1953) and *Beulah* (1950–1953). The country was changing and shows like *The Jeffersons* reflected its new direction.

See also: *All in the Family*; Lear, Norman; *Vol. 1, The 1950s–1960s: Amos 'n' Andy*; *Beulah*.

Further Resources

Acham, Christine. 2004. *Revolution Televised: Prime Time and the Struggle for Black Power*. Minneapolis: University of Minnesota Press.

WSJ Staff. 2012. "Seven Lessons on 'Movin On Up' from 'The Jeffersons' and Sherman Hemsley." Deaths. July 25. http://blogs.wsj.com/speakeasy/2012/07/25/seven-lessons-on-movin-on-up-from-the-jeffersons-and-sherman-hemsley/

Kojak (CBS, 1973–1978)

Telly Savalas (1922–1994) was an accomplished film actor who appeared in *The Birdman of Alcatraz* (1962), *The Greatest Story Ever Told* (1965), *Dirty Dozen* (1967), and *Mackenna's Gold* (1969). Like actor Yul Brynner, Savalas had a clean dome. Viewers of his movies and later television watchers found him distinctive, cool, and even sexy. The creator of *Kojak* was Abby Mann (1927–2008). Mann was a screenwriter who had written *Judgement at Nuremberg*. He was also the executive producer of *Kojak* and wrote many of the teleplays for the series.

The lead character, Theo Kojak, is a New York City police lieutenant assigned to the south side of Manhattan. Although Savalas was an actor and not a police lieutenant, his performance is so indelible, it is nearly impossible to separate one from the other. Kojak is always on top of things, sharp, imperturbable, and an impeccable dresser. He either shows his sleek, bald head or wears a dark fedora; he smokes a cigarette or slurps on a lollipop. His voice is low in register and the cadence of his speech is just short of machine gun speed, but every word is understandable.

Kojak is a good leader. He is hands-on planning every step of a stake-out, raid, or arrest. He is a New York guy with a decidedly distinctive New York accent. The show's location work gives it the grit associated with parts of that great city. Kojak was never promoted past lieutenant because he is an honest cop and a solitary man who doesn't always play ball with his superiors. He is suited for his tough beat, which he knows like the back of his hand. He was known to stretch the law to make a case stick.

Telly Savalas was respected by police all over the country for his realistic portrayal of a police lieutenant. This veracity is supported by shooting in New York and the believable production design for interior scenes.

Many TV shows, especially in the 1970s, have classic tag lines. Kojak's was "Who loves you, baby?" Not a classically handsome man, Kojak had a little black book filled with names and was rarely without a date when he wanted one.

The supporting cast on *Kojak* included the lieutenant's right-hand man, Detective Bobby Crocker, played by Kevin Dobson (1943–), and his perpetually weary boss, Captain Frank McNeil, portrayed by Dan Frazer (1921–2011).

Kojak was a one-hour police drama and it made good use of its time. The stories were well written with plenty of back and forth complications. One episode deals with a drug kingpin who hates Kojak and whom the lieutenant fervently wants put behind bars forever. Plans are calculated, some are pulled off, and some go awry, but in the end the criminal is busted, not in a Hollywood manner, but just the way it would read right off the police ledgers.

Kojak had a perfect tempo, dialogue scenes, moved nicely and action scenes were both logical and unexpected. Perhaps it's Kojak's lollipop habit, but this show was more than a cop show about one figure, it was about a man and a city and the day-to-day grunt work of catching the bad guys.

See also: *Columbo*.

Further Resources

Daly, Marsha. 1975. *Telly Savalas*. New York: Berkley Publishing.

Miller, Victor B. 1975. *Girl in the River (Kojak)*. New York: Pocket Books.

Kung Fu (ABC, 1972–1975)

This show was classified as a Western at a time when that once popular genre was on the wane. Although martial arts films were flourishing on the big screen, *Kung Fu* was the only show in the genre on television. The show's title, *Kung Fu,* directly relates to that particular martial art form.

Breaking New Ground

Kung Fu was a unique and complex show; scenes take place either at a temple in China or in the byways and towns of the old West. The producers chose to title the show based on the China segment, but let *TV Guide* and others know it was a Western.

There never has been a television series like *Kung Fu.* The main character was training as a Shaolin monk in philosophy and to protect himself from those who mean harm. He witnessed the murder of his mentor and retaliated by striking the killer dead, although he had been trained not to take a life. There was a wanted poster for his capture, and he wandered through the West encountering bad guys, good guys, and women to whom he is taught to show interest only when it is reciprocal.

The style of the show looked as if it fit into the American New Wave cinema, a movement begun in the late 1960s that dominated the 1970s, in which young filmmakers attempted to create a new American cinema that opposed old Hollywood in content and aesthetics. In *Kung Fu* there was constant intercutting between the past and present, representing the East and West. Voice-over was used as a storytelling strategy. Techniques such as flash-cutting, which restructures conventional narrative filmmaking, long lensing, and shooting into the sun to cause the elements of the lens to show a jewel-like imagery were employed. These visible metaphors were inventive for television in the 1970s. Zoom and long lenses were utilized, one for movement and the other for perspective. *The Wild Bunch,* directed by Sam Peckinpah (1925–1984) and released in 1969, was a landmark Western that revolutionized the use of slow-motion photography. It was this last technique that was most frequently adapted to *Kung Fu* and was used to detail the martial arts fighting sequences.

David Carradine (1936–2009) played the loner Kwai Chang Caine, who found himself endlessly on the move and hunted by the law. Carradine was a member of the distinguished acting family led by his father, John Carradine (1906–1988), who played Shakespeare on the stage, had a long movie career in horror films and westerns, and was part of the stock company of two legendary Hollywood directors, Cecil B. DeMille (1881–1959) and John Ford (1894–1973). The family is rounded by Keith Carradine (1949–), who worked with Ridley Scott (1937–), Robert Altman (1925–2006), and many other fine directors. Casting for Caine as a teenager was easy for the producers who selected Keith for the part. Radames Pera (1960–) played the part of Caine as a boy. The youngest Carradine is Robert (1954–), who has a long string of credits including the 1972 film *The Cowboys* staring John Wayne (1907–1979.) He was also on *Kung Fu* as Sunny Jim, the deaf companion of Serenity Johnson, an old blind preacher played by John Carradine. The Asian actors include Keye Luke (1904–1991) and Philip Ahn (1905–1978.)

For the part of Caine, Buddhist David Carradine first shaved his head but then let his hair grow back, allowing steady viewers of this cult show to watch the progression of his locks as it grew to shoulder length. Carradine did not know anything about martial arts before the show began production, so he was given lessons and as the episodes progressed he became quite adroit throwing kicks, chopping his opponent with his arms and hands, and throwing a bad guy who would fly through the air flipping around until he landed in a cloud of dirt.

The name Caine is a biblical reference to Cain who murdered his brother and was marked and sent off. Kwai Chang Caine had the image of the dragon and tiger branded on his forearms showing he was wanted for murder. The $10,000 bounty was a curse that followed him wherever he went once he was banished from the temple.

Kung Fu had strong production values but kept a modest budget because it could use the old Western sets from Warner Brothers. The Buddhist temple was achieved by redressing the castle of the 1967 movie *Camelot*.

Bruce Lee (1940–1973) initiated a lawsuit against the *Kung Fu* camp, claiming he was once attached to the show but was dropped by the studio, which apparently didn't think an Asian actor could play the lead. The choice of David Carradine, who wasn't a major star, was interesting, because he had changed his lifestyle to include unusual philosophies. He lived in a curious ramshackle house, which made him a person of interest in certain quarters.

Caine didn't believe in killing and was a vegetarian. He lived life the way it was taught to him at the temple. A major attraction of the show, especially for the growing numbers of Americans interested in anything Zen, were the bits of wisdom that came from the Chinese master and were absorbed by the student: "What happens in a man's life is already written," "As we prize peace and quiet above victory, there is a simple and preferred method . . . run away," "Fear is the enemy. Trust is the armor," "To hate is like drinking salt water. The thirst grows worse," and "In every loss there is a gain. As in every gain there is a loss."

Further Resources

Carradine, David. 1995. *Endless Highway*. North Clarendon, VT: Journey Editions.

Pilato, Herbie J. 1993. *Kung Fu Book of Caine*. North Clarendon, VT: Tuttle.

Laverne and Shirley (ABC, 1976–1983)

Laverne and Shirley is a spin–off of *Happy Days* and one of the most successful spin–offs of the 1970s. It sat in the number two slot in the ratings above its predecessor on more than one occasion. Like *Happy Days*, *Laverne and Shirley* was also set in Milwaukee in the late 1950s. It featured two young women who worked in a Shotz beer brewery, a comic reference to Schlitz beer, which was one of many popular beers during the 1950s. They worked on the assembly line in the plant's bottle cap division. Laverne DeFazio was played by Penny Marshall (1943–) who is the sister of the show's co-creator, Garry Marshall (1934–2016). She had a dry sense of humor, was down-to-earth, always explained her foibles, had a hot temper, and was afraid of getting injured, which often happened. Shirley Feeney was portrayed by Cindy Williams (1947–). Williams had a leading role as Ron Howard's girlfriend in *American Graffiti* (1973). Shirley was naïve and believing, and was sucked into every sad story she heard from friends. The local hangout was a pizzeria.

Laverne and Shirley were middle-class, not moneyed, and were not educated; they were young women with plenty of spunk. Laverne's father, Frank DeFazio, played by Phil Foster (1913–1985), owned a bowling joint. The ladies had two male friends who worked as drivers at the brewery. "Squiggy," Andrew Squigman, was played by David L. Lander (1947–) and Lenny Kowznovski was portrayed by Michael McKean (1947–). They were offbeat, sported super 1950s hairstyles, were close pals, were not particularly bright, talked funny, and were always causing trouble even though they were both good-hearted. The show's theme song, "Making Our Dreams Come True," was created by hit makers Norman Gimbel (1927–) and Charles Fox (1940–) and sung by Cyndi Grecco. The song speaks to these two 20-something women and their determination to never give up and take on whatever life throws at them. It also conveys the solid, unbreakable nature of their friendship.

Like *Happy Days*, *Laverne and Shirley* took place during a 1950s that was stylized in sitcoms. The show's artificiality sent the message that this is what the decade should have been. At the same time *Laverne and Shirley* shed some light on a tough decade, the 1970s, that weathered the Nixon Watergate scandal, the trial of Charles Manson, and economic depression.

It has been said that hair, makeup, and costumes are 50 percent responsible for creating a character; the rest is what the actor brings to the role. Laverne was a

1950s sweater girl, she wore her sweaters to show off her assets and accentuated the positive by having a large cursive-style letter "L" just off her front shoulder. Her hair was short and teased in the back, the color brown with lighter streaks. Shirley dressed conservatively with a high-neck blouse. Her hair was black, parted in the middle, also short but combed downward and kept flat to the head. As for the rest, the men and women looked and dressed like copies of a fifties catalogue from the Eisenhower decade.

Although the comedy could be silly, *Laverne and Shirley* was just about first in a prime-time sitcom to advocate independence for women. This was an important message for viewers in the 1970s, demonstrating that even in the 1950s there were young women of independent spirit.

See also: *Happy Days*.

Further Resources

Breingan, Judy. 2012. *Penny Marshall: Her Extraordinary Journey from the Bronx to Hollywood.* P.M.I.; 1.0 edition.

Williams, Cindy. 2012. *Shirley, I Just! A Storied Life*. Lanham, MD: Taylor Trade Publishing.

Television writer, producer, and creator Norman Lear began changing the face of the sitcom in the 1970s, with comedies that addressed some of the more controversial issues of the day. Some of the shows that Lear produced include *All in the Family, Sanford and Son, One Day at a Time, The Jeffersons*, and *Maude*. (AP Photo)

Lear, Norman (1922–)

Born in New Haven, Connecticut, Norman Lear first teamed with Ed Simmons (1919–1998) to write comedy and pursued major comedians like Danny Thomas (1912–1991), trying to convince them they could write just the right kind of comedy for their acts. Eventually it worked and Danny Thomas bought a routine they had written.

David Susskind (1920–1987) recognized their talent and signed them to write for *The Four Star Review,* a musical, comedy, variety series. Unfortunately, the show only lasted through the 1950–1951 season. Their next assignment was *The Colgate Comedy Hour* (1950–1955). Even though it went up against *The Ed Sullivan Show* (1948–1971), it was successful and ran five years. Dean Martin (1917–1995) and Jerry Lewis (1926–) were at the height of their fame as a comedy duo and made rotating regular appearances on the program with Lear and Simmons writing all their material. Later, Lear began writing on his own and in 1959 he and Bud Yorkin (1926–2015) created Tandem Productions. They produced several feature films on which Lear took various production roles, writer, executive producer, and the director of *Cold Turkey* (1971). In 1970 Lear and Yorkin made their move into television. During a visit to England Lear saw the comedy show *Till Death Do Us Part* (1965–1975). It was an inspiration for a pilot he developed, which was commissioned by ABC. He called the show *All in the Family* (1971–1979.) When it was complete that network rejected it. Lear took it to CBS, which had just hired a new president, Robert Wood, who bought the show because he wanted to change the network's direction from shows like *The Beverly Hillbillies. All in the Family* aired on January 12, 1971. The show became a big, controversial hit due to the themes and language tackled on the show. The main character,

Archie Bunker, played by Carroll O'Connor (1924–2002), was a lovable bigot who had something to say (usually negative) about everything in his and the larger world. The majority of the audience laughed at him, but some agreed with him while others protested the language and the raw approach to sensitive subjects. Lear clearly had liberal views and found a way to express them and make people laugh at the same time.

In 1972 he brought *Maude* (1972–1978) to television, which featured a lead character played by Bea Arthur (1922–2009) with decidedly liberal views. The most controversial episode dealt with abortion, which brought discussion, division, and dialogue to the issue. Lear and Yorkin also brought two African American–themed shows to television, *Good Times* (1974–1979) and *The Jeffersons* (1975–1985). Lear started a cult following with a show he intended to air in the daytime, *Mary Hartman, Mary Hartman* (1976–1977), a satire on soap operas, but he had no takers, so he put it into syndication where it was aired nightly, usually at a late hour. Surprisingly, even though it was an outrageous satire on soap opera, its loyal fans got deeply involved with Mary and the other wacky characters, just as if it were a regular soap opera. Lear's point of view was to show the worst aspects of everyday society.

Norman Lear became deeply involved in politics and supporting free speech and went on to develop and produce TV that contained messages that mattered to him.

See also: *All in the Family*; *Good Times*; *The Jeffersons*; *Mary Hartman, Mary Hartman*; *Maude*.

Further Resources

Gordon, Peggy. 2014. *Norman Lear: 180 Success Facts—Everything You Need to Know about Norman Lear*. Brisbane, Australia: Emereo.

Lear, Norman. 2014. *Even This I Get to Experience*. New York: Penguin Press.

Little House on the Prairie (NBC, 1974–1982)

Michael Landon (1936–1991) of *Bonanza* (1959–1973) fame, was the star, executive producer, and frequent teleplay writer and director of this Western/family series based on the "Little House" series of books written by Laura Ingalls Wilder (1867–1957).

Family Viewing

Little House on the Prairie was a show parents watched with their children. Mothers especially watched the

Mary Ingalls, played by Melissa Sue Anderson, is escorted by her father Charles Ingalls, played by Michael Landon, during Mary's wedding to Adam on *Little House on the Prairie*. This family show stressed good values and hard work. (AP Photo/Huynh)

> Laura Ingalls Wilder was a columnist and editor of the *Missouri Realist* at the beginning of the 20th century. After the stock market crash, Wilder hoped to publish her story for income. The first book in this series, originally titled *When Grandma Was a Little Girl*, was published in 1932 by Harper & Brothers as *Little House in the Big Woods*. The original series, an eight-volume record of pioneering life in the 19th century, is based on Wilder's family's experiences on the American frontier. The books have been translated into 40 languages.

program with their daughters because they identified with the mother on the show, Caroline Quiner Ingalls, played by Karen Grassle (1942–), and her daughters, particularly Laura, played by Melissa Gilbert (1964–), who narrated the show and was a featured character. There was an expansive general audience with many others watching this show and it turned into a major hit.

In motion pictures some critics believe in the auteur system, a way of measuring and listing film directors who took total possession over their films and had themes that recurred in their work. There are only a handful of individuals who might fit in this category in television. Michael Landon was an auteur who started as an actor. The man with the rock 'n' roll haircut who sported long locks had just about total control over *Little House on the Prairie*. He was a commanding actor as the farmer Charles Ingalls and before, during, and after shooting Michael Landon was the man everyone listened to during production.

The story line of *Little House on the Prairie* depicts the Ingalls family and their trials and tribulations as settlers in the old West. The pilot, like a feature film, ran for 96 minutes and aired on March 30, 1974. At the outset the Ingalls are preparing to leave their larger family. A wagon is packed with all their belongings. Caroline is upset and Charles talks to her as they walk away from the family home to the wagon that will transport them to a different life. Charles tells her there is nothing left for them in the East and that he has great things in mind. They will have their own place where the children can grow up and have a new way of living.

The trip is rougher than Charles imagined, including having to ford a wide stream. Once they arrive at their destination, far from their original home, they put down stakes and Charles and a neighbor, Isaiah Edwards, portrayed by Victor French (1934–1989), build a cabin for the family. In their new locale, there are many difficulties. Wolves are waiting to attack the house and family, Charles must travel a long distance to get to town, there is no way to attend church, and Charles must convince Caroline that the children don't need a church because on the land they are close to God. The most feared aspect for white settlers on the prairie is the threat from hostile Indian tribes. A tremendous line fire imperils their barn; Charles organizes a bucket brigade, but then a miracle happens as the skies open up and a downpour douses the flames. After these incidents, Charles decides this is not their final destination and they move on. The wagon is loaded again and with Isaiah looking on, the show's pilot fades to black as the Ingalls travel on.

The show's first four seasons take place in Walnut Grove, Minnesota in the late 1870s. After the 1977–1978 season the Ingalls leave for Winnetka, South Dakota. The plot lines trace the growing family, the joys and difficulties of life on a farm back when America was younger.

The production values and the depiction of the surroundings and stories were so authentic they made viewers feel that Michael Landon had found a time machine and had produced the show in its actual era.

Family shows and Westerns were more prominent in the 1950s and 1960s, but *Little House on the Prairie* supplied a tenderness and historical detail that brought viewers back week after week to listen to Laura explain the inner aspects of her family's lives. The series struck a particularly heartwarming chord with the television audience.

See also: *Vol. 1, The 1950s–1960s: Bonanza*; *Wagon Train*.

Further Resources

Wilder, Laura Ingalls, and Pamela Smith Hill. 2014. *Pioneer Girl: The Annotated Autobiography.* Pierre, SD: South Dakota Historical Society Press.

Wilson, Cheryl Landon. 1992. *I Promised My Dad: An Intimate Portrait of Michael Landon.* New York: Simon & Schuster.

The Love Boat (ABC, 1977–1987)

The unique storytelling structure of *The Love Boat* followed that of *Love American Style* (1969–1974), which used a vignette-style format with one story after another. *The Love Boat* was more complex. Each week a cruise designed to bring people together sailed across the sea, arrived at its destinations, and docked at its final port.

The crew of the *Pacific Princess* included Captain Merrill Stubing, played by Gavin MacLeod (1931–). The rest of the crew was comprised of Burt "Gopher" Smith, the yeoman purser played by Fred Grandy (1948–); Dr. Adam "Doc" Bricker, portrayed by Bernie Kopell (1933–); Isaac Washington, the bartender, played by Ted Lange (1948–); and the cruise director, Julie McCoy, portrayed by Lauren Tewes (1953–). In the credits the crew is introduced with the word "Your," which allows viewers to feel as if they are coming on board and taking the cruise along with those on the screen. The large number of guest stars included Marion Ross, Bert Convy, Ted Knight, Milton Berle, Sonny Bono, Betty White, and Suzanne Somers.

On every episode the crew would greet the passengers, who would play out comedic situations in their lives embracing a love theme. The show was designed to include a long string of guest stars. There were often up to three or four stories integrated and intercut with the flow of the voyage. The show and its writers and editors were skillful and knew just what story to segment on screen at the right time. The stories moved along sequentially.

Each story had its own writer and its own director. The set and the camerawork were constant, so *The Love Boat* always looked like one show. Shots of the ship, ports of call, on the seas, and other necessities were also integrated and convinced the home viewer that this was a real cruise.

The theme song for *The Love Boat* was popular, memorable, and fans enjoyed listening to it every week. The music was by Charles Fox (1940–), composer and hit maker. The lyrics were written by Paul Williams (1940–), who worked as an actor in addition to penning many hit songs. The singer was the debonair crooner Jack Jones (1938–), who told of love's many qualities in a swing/disco tempo.

The show was part of the Aaron Spelling empire. It was actually produced and photographed on two cruise ships, *The Pacific Princess* and *The Island Princess*. Actual paying passengers were encouraged to be extras on the show as background to stars who appeared in one of the stories each week.

The Love Boat received very poor and dismissive reviews, but Spelling knew the people at home would like it and despite critical disdain, the show had a long successful run.

See also: *Vol. 1, The 1950s–1960s:* Spelling, Aaron.

Further Resources

MacLeod, Gavin, and Mark Dagostino. 2013. *This Is Your Captain Speaking: My Fantastic Voyage through Hollywood, Faith, and Life* (eBook). Thomas Nelson.

Murray, Sheila Farrell. 2012. *The Love Boat Lady: The Authorized Real Life Story of Geraldine Saunders.* Glendale, CA: Auld Shamrock Press.

Made-for-Television Movies

In the early days of television during the 1940s and 1950s, broadcasters scrambled to get material to air. One of the solutions was to license classic Hollywood movies. Viewers were able to see films they hadn't seen before or revisit a favorite.

The films were structured for commercial breaks and in many cases scenes or parts of scenes had to be deleted to keep the time slot from going over. Regardless, motion pictures on television were very popular. Networks and stations created shows that would be programmed at a particular day and time slot. One was *The Late Show* (1951–1976), broadcast on WCBS channel 2 out of New York. There was an engaging opening and musical theme and a loyal audience. One of the most unique movie showcases also aired in New York—*The Million Dollar Movie* (1955–1966), a show that influenced the young Martin Scorsese (1942–) in his passion for the movies who went on to direct *Mean Streets* (1973), *Taxi Driver* (1976), and *Raging Bull* (1980). *The Million Dollar Movie* was perfect for filmmakers and film buffs because it was on every night and each selected film was broadcast two times in one night, allowing the viewer deeper study and analysis. Classic Hollywood films such as *Citizen Kane* (1941) and the original *King Kong* (1933) were shown on *The Million Dollar Movie. The Late Show* had a tick-tock sounding theme over a shot of an apartment building at night with some of the lights going out, and *The Million Dollar Movie* used Tara's theme from *Gone with the Wind* (1939) over shots of New York City.

The Birth of the Made-for-Television Movie

As time went by and many movies from the Hollywood studio vaults were exhausted for a first-run showing, executives at the networks and the local station managers agreed that television shows should have their own movies written, produced, shot, acted, and edited. This resulted in the made-for-television movie. The actual term "made-for-television movie" was coined and began to be used officially in the early 1960s. The first known example of the TV movie was *Talk Faster Mister* delivered by RKO and broadcast on WABD in New York in 1944.

In 1957 *The Pied Piper of Hamelin* was another made-for-television movie. The family musical was based on the poem by Robert Browning (1812–1889) and starred Van Johnson.

In 1961 *NBC Saturday Night at the Movies* appeared across the country. This was a platform to show Hollywood movies but on a grand scale. The early shows that presented motion pictures did so on beat-up black-and-white 16 mm prints, sometimes with footage missing, as the local stations did. Now in all their splendor some of the best products Hollywood had to offer were broadcast from clean 35 mm prints, many in full color. This practice lasted from 1954 to 1972. Some of the films broadcast during this time included *How to Marry a Millionaire* (1953), *The Day the Earth Stood Still* (1951), *Lust for Life* (1956), *The Diary of Anne Frank* (1959), and *The Asphalt Jungle* (1950).

Among all three networks home audiences had a major studio release to watch every day of the week including the weekends. The one issue was that the movie studios had a rule that their films could only be broadcast on television 12 years after their first theatrical release date.

For the 1963–1964 season the made-for-television *The Killers* (1964), based on the Ernest Hemingway short story featuring Ronald Reagan (1911–2004) before he became governor of California and president of the United States, directed by Don Siegel (1912–1991), was screened privately by executives, then deemed too violent. It then was released into movie theaters across the country.

In the 1960s many considered *See How They Run* (1964) as the first made-for-television movie. The story centers on three children stalked by mobsters who believe they have evidence proving the mobsters murdered their father. It starred John Forsythe (1918–2010). The second made-for-television movie was also directed by Don Siegel, who apparently toned down the violence with the Western *The Hanged Man,* airing in 1964.

By the 1970s the made-for-television movie came into its own and thrived. The networks went up against the big studios and gave them real competition, making their own movies. In most cases these were films the studios wouldn't make and in other cases they were timely topics that could get to television quicker than Hollywood, adaptations, and original stories. Just some of the many, many movies produced and aired during the 1970s included *All Quiet on the Western Front* (1979), *The Amazing Howard Hughes* (1977), *The Autobiography of Miss Jane Pittman* (1974), *The Boy in the Plastic Bubble* (1976), *Brian's Song* (1970), *Duel* (1971), which was eventually released in theaters, making it the first feature film by Steven Spielberg (1946–), *Friendly Fire* (1974), *Helter Skelter* (1976), *The Missiles of October* (1974), and *Sybil* (1970).

The made-for-television movie also allowed the major networks to move into controversial topics, some even too hot for the studios. *Born Innocent* aired in 1974 starring Linda Blair (1959–) as a runaway who goes to juvenile prison where she is raped by lesbians. There was such an outrage that the rape sequence was pulled from the film after its premiere airing—later a California court ruled that the film was not obscene. The young actress was also in *Sarah T: Portrait of a Teenage Alcoholic,* which attempted to deal with the issue facing youth struggling with alcohol abuse; it was aired in 1975. Broadcast in 1977 *Dawn: Portrait of a Teenage Runaway* starred Eve Plumb (1958–), who had been on *The Brady Bunch.* This telefilm explored the young life of a girl unhappy with her home life who takes to the streets. When she can't get a job she becomes a prostitute and learns that life at home was better; a sequel, *The Other Side of Dawn,* followed the well-rated original.

Race relations was explored in the 1970 TV movie *My Sweet Charlie* staring Patty Duke (1946–2016) and Al Freedman Jr. (1934–2012). The compelling story brought together a white pregnant young woman and a black lawyer who were both on the run and both needed each other to survive.

That Certain Summer, broadcast in 1972, focused on a teenager who had to deal with his father's homosexuality. The film might be timid by future standards but it did clearly portray a man in love with another man. It starred Hal Holbrook (1925–) and Martin Sheen (1940–).

Another use of the made-for-television format is for a network to air a pilot for a show as a TV movie. At times they have also made telefilms that ran during a series run or afterward. The networks have done an excellent job finding myriad uses of the made-for-television format. Many telefilms would be transferred to home video and sold to the public. Later the same happened when the DVD format was created. In the 21st century TV movies can be watched in several ways on the Internet.

Whether made-for-television movies are as good as Hollywood releases is an open argument. It was the 1970s that set the standard for made-for-television movies and during the decade television outlets pushed the envelope about what could be shown, what could be said, and how to show and say it. The wide spectrum from family fare to controversial subjects made 1970s television movies vital, memorable, and historically important.

Further Resources

Karol, Michael. 2005. *The ABC Movie of the Week Companion: A Loving Tribute to the Classic Series.* Lincoln, NE: iUniverse.

Marill, Alvin H. 2005. *Movies Made for Television: 1964–2004.* Lanham, MD: Scarecrow Press.

The Magician (NBC, 1973–1974)

In the 1970s actor Bill Bixby (1934–1993) starred in three very different television series, the comedy *The Courtship of Eddie's Father* (1969–1972), the superhero series *The Incredible Hulk* (1978–1982), and in between those, *The Magician* (1973–1974), a unique drama that combined two favorite TV genres: magic and the crime drama.

NBC borrowed from the movies to promote their star, billboarding up front in the credits "Bill Bixby *is* The Magician," a salute to Paul Newman (1925–2008) movies in which the actor was identified directly with characters he played. Magic on television took the form mainly of professional magicians performing on variety and other shows. The fictional magic crime drama had few if any precedents or competition.

On *The Magician* Bixby played a wealthy nightclub magician and escape artist, Anthony Blake, who applied his magic skills to solving crimes. Earlier in his life he had been in prison for a crime he didn't commit. This left him with a strong sense of personal freedom and he used his craft to help people in danger and sought to prevent crimes. Many of the tricks shown in rehearsals, during the act itself, and while tracking down criminals were part of magic's repertoire—employing a deck of cards or a chamber in which a woman disappears. The audience was pleased to watch a skillful magician perform a trick no matter how often they'd seen it. Combining that experience with a crime drama was the show's main attraction.

A key to the authenticity of *The Magician* was watching Bill Bixby perform the tricks by himself. Prior to shooting the series, master magician Mark Wilson was brought on to teach Bixby how to act like a magician, perform the tricks, indulge in the patter, and master the showmanship.

Another exciting aspect of the show was that the audience never knew what Blake was going to do while in pursuit of the crime, so the element of surprise was present throughout an episode.

Shows like *The Magician* that try to break new ground in network television needed to build an audience slowly and with support from the network. In 1974, during the show's second season, the day was changed; this can be a death knell for an evolving show, and it was the case for *The Magician.* A nonviolent crime drama was needed in a decade of violent shows, but it just wasn't given the chance.

Further Resources

Jay, Joshua. 2008. *Magic: The Complete Course.* New York: Workman Publishing.

Steinmeyer, Jim. 2004. *Hiding the Elephant: How Magicians Invented the Impossible and Learned to Disappear.* New York: Carroll & Graf.

The Man from Atlantis (NBC, 1977–1978)

The network executives at NBC must have decided that three would be the charm for a television series about a man with superhuman powers. The first attempt, *The Invisible Man* (1975–1976) starring David McCallum (1933–) of *The Man from U.N.C.L.E* (1964–1968) fame, was about an invisible scientist working for a think tank. It ran only 13 episodes. Next NBC tried *Gemini Man,* which was only able to sustain a pilot and 11 episodes. The objective was to fill *The Invisible Man* slot. *Gemini Man* featured Ben Murphy (1942–), who was known for the series *Alias Smith and Jones* (1971–1973). Here he plays a secret agent who rides a motorcycle and wears a black leather jacket. He is exposed to radiation and is turned visible by his agency and given new assignments. Even though it was based on H. G. Wells's science fiction classic *The Invisible Man*, it flopped.

The great white hope became *The Man from Atlantis,* starring Patrick Duffy (1949–) as Mark Harris, who claimed to be a survivor from the lost continent of Atlantis. He has webbed hands and feet and can breathe under water effortlessly. Harris was employed by the Foundation for Oceanic Research. Mark Harris had superhuman strength and hyperacute control over his five senses. His one limitation is that he can only survive for around 12 hours on land; then he has to return to the sea to breathe properly.

Harris is found nearly unconscious by Dr. Elizabeth Merrill, played by Belinda J. Montgomery (1950–), who was able to bring him back to good health. He joins her at the research facility and they explore the ocean floor using a special unit called the "Cetacean," a unique submersible vehicle. They confront extraterrestrial life and evil scientists.

> According to classical Greek–era philosopher Plato (427–347 BCE), Atlantis was an ancient island that sank deep into the sea. The tale was largely forgotten in the Middle Ages and was revived during the Enlightenment when Francis Bacon (1561–1626) used it as an example of utopia in *The New Atlantis,* written in 1626. It has been portrayed as a very advanced society with technology surpassing even that of the present and as a pinnacle of culture and enlightenment.

Although *The Man from Atlantis* had an intriguing lead character and like *Sea Hunt* (1958–1961) probed the bottom of the sea, it too failed to gather and build an audience. After just 13 episodes it was gone. Patrick Duffy, the lead in *The Man from Atlantis*, may not have been that well known when he appeared as a survivor of Atlantis, but his next role made him a household name. He was Bobby Ewing in the hit nighttime soap *Dallas* (1978–1991).

Science fiction had been popular on television during the decades of the 1950s and the 1960s, but it was less so during the 1970s. The uniqueness of *The Man from Atlantis* and Patrick Duffy's good looks and shirt-off physique should have helped the show, as it did on *Dallas*. Maybe if it had been given more time and a little tweaking, *The Man from Atlantis* might have made a decent showing, but the world of network television unfortunately gave few chances.

Further Resources

Santos, Arysio. 2011. *Atlantis: The Lost Continent Finally Found*. Miami, FL: Atlantis Publications.

Woodley, Richard. 1977. *Man from Atlantis*. New York: Dell.

Mary Hartman, Mary Hartman (Syndication, 1976–1977)

This syndicated half-hour show, which ran nightly, was developed by Norman Lear to parody and satirize the many daytime soap operas that ran on all three networks, ABC, CBS, and NBC at the time. It was set in the fictional town of Fernwood, Ohio and debuted with a mass murder and climaxed with the nervous breakdown of the show's heroine, Mary Hartman, who was played by Louise Lasser (1939–), who had been married to Woody Allen from 1966 to 1970.

The Players and the Characters

Mary Hartman had red hair that she wore in pigtails with low bangs just above her eyebrows. She wore gingham dresses. For Mary Hartman the faux-reality of television was as vibrant and alive as the world in which she lived. Mary tried to remain calm while her daughter Heather, played by Claudia Lamb, was held hostage by the mass murderer who killed a local family and their goats and chickens. Mary's unfaithful husband and Heather's father Tom was played by Greg Mullavey (1939–). Tom worked on an assembly line and was born with an inability to properly express emotions. Dody Goodman (1914–2008) portrayed Mary's addlepated mother who was daffy and not always aware of what was going on. Philip Burns (1931–2012) played Mary's father, who worked at the plant with his son-in-law, Tom. Debra Lee Scott (1953–2005), who played Mary's younger sister Cathy, was considered a maneater because she sexually devoured as many men as she could. "The Fernwood Flasher" was Mary's grandfather, Raymond Larkin, played by Victor Kilian (1891–1979). Sergeant Foley of the local Fernwood police was played by Bruce Solomon (1944–), who after much effort convinced Mary to have an affair with him. Mary's best friend was Loretta Haggers, an aspiring country and western singer played by Mary Kay Place. Her husband Charlie was portrayed by Graham Jarvis (1930–), who also worked with Tom. Sparky Marcus (1967–) portrayed eight-year-old child evangelist Jimmy Joe Jeeter, who was electrocuted when a TV set fell into his bathtub filled with water. His father, the devious Merle, was played by Dabney Coleman (1932–). Martin Mull (1943–) played the wife-assaulter Garth Gimble, who died by impaling himself on a Christmas tree. Later he would appear as the host of the talk show *Fernwood 2-Night* as Garth's twin brother Bart.

Although regular viewers at first laughed at some of the dialogue, characters, and especially the over-the-top story line, when they became regular viewers they began to believe in the world of *Mary Hartman, Mary Hartman*. They got sucked into the proceedings just as they would with a regular daytime soap.

The happenings were similar to the real thing, a bored housewife, a philandering husband, parent/child and older sister/younger sister tensions, but everything was a bit twisted and more outrageous in its presentation. Mary spent a lot of time in her kitchen but became obsessed with the waxy buildup on her floor and turned to TV commercials for everyday answers rather than her family and friends. The pacing of the show was deliberate and at many times slow. Pauses made it seem that something was supposed to happen or that a real commercial was looming, but nothing occurred.

Mary Hartman, Mary Hartman was a laboratory for exciting if quirky actors who were largely new to the medium. The sets looked like soap opera sets but were overdressed with bright colors and patterns that clashed.

Although *Mary Hartman, Mary Hartman* had a steady audience, after 325 episodes the star of the show, Louise Lasser, decided to leave. During the summer hiatus the faux talk show *Fernwood 2-Night* appeared and in its own way was just as bizarre in taking on an established television genre as *Mary Hartman, Mary Hartman*. From 1977 to 1978 *Fernwood Forever* appeared with most of the *Mary Hartman, Mary Hartman* cast sans Lasser.

At first glance it would seem as if Norman Lear had developed a show without social themes, but *Mary Hartman, Mary Hartman* might have taken on the largest theme of all: American life, morality, sexuality, madness, infidelity, and living in a world that seems detached from reality. The soap opera was a revered form, first on radio, then on TV. Soap operas started as an appeal to housewives and women at home, eventually spreading in interest to college kids and general audiences. To make fun of a hallowed institution like the soap opera may have been Norman Lear's greatest triumph.

See also: *Fernwood 2-Night*; Lear, Norman.

Further Resources

Copeland, Mary Ann. 1991. *Soap Opera History*. Bdd Promotional Book Co.

Lockwood, Daniel. 1976. *The Mary Hartman Story*. Whirlwind Book Company.

The Mary Tyler Moore Show (CBS, 1970–1977)

By 1970 when *The Mary Tyler Moore Show* aired on CBS, Mary Tyler Moore (1936–2017) was famous nationwide for playing Laura Petrie, the wife of the actor in the title of *The Dick Van Dyke Show* (1961–1966). A native New Yorker, she was in Hotpoint Appliances commercials; only her legs were shown and her voice was heard as she played a receptionist to *Richard Diamond, Private Detective* (1957–1960). She then appeared on a number of TV series including *Johnny Staccato* (1959–1960), *Bachelor Father* (1957–1962), *77 Sunset Strip* (1958–1964), and *Hawaiian Eye* (1959–1963).

A Formidable Actress

Mary Tyler Moore had more than proved she was a good actress and a first-class comedienne. Playing Laura Petrie she demonstrated she could stand up to the male characters, especially her TV husband Rob. She was intelligent, vulnerable, had great vocal abilities including a classic crying routine that usually started with "Oh Rob," and had impeccable comic timing. On that show she was a very attractive contemporary woman with snug-fitting capri pants and a double flip hairdo. For the time of the show she was liberated, certainly more so than the women on competing shows.

After such an audacious run on *The Dick Van Dyke Show* Mary Tyler Moore wanted her own show, one with her name in the title. So in 1969 her then husband Grant Tinker and Moore created MTM Productions.

The Mary Tyler Moore Show was a breakthrough in programming that showed women in the workplace with meaningful jobs. Pictured in the newsroom of WJM-TV in Minneapolis are Ted Knight (left) as Ted Baxter, Edward Asner as Lou Grant, and Mary Tyler Moore as Mary Richards. (Bettmann/Getty Images)

> In 1969 Mary Tyler Moore (1936–2017) and her then-husband Grant Tinker formed an independent production company, MTM Enterprises, to produce *The Mary Tyler Moore Show* (1970–1977) for CBS. The letters were her initials and the logo had a cat over MTM. Just in the 1970s alone the company productions were numerous: *The Bob Newhart Show* (1972–1978), *Paul Sand in Friends and Lovers* (1974–1975), *The Texas Wheelers* (1974–1975), *Rhoda* (1974–1978), *The Bob Crane Show* (1975), *The Lorenzo and Henrietta Music Show* (1976), *Doc* (1975–1976), *Three for the Road* (1975), *Phyllis* (1975–1977), and *The Tony Randall Show* (1976–1978).

The name of the company simply bore her initials. The show became enormously popular and was considered to support the women's liberation movement that started in earnest in 1970. The program was called *The Mary Tyler Moore Show*.

A Show for the Ages

In this iconic sitcom Mary Tyler Moore played Mary Richards, a single, 30-something woman who settles in Minneapolis after breaking up with her boyfriend. She attains a job as an associate producer of the evening news at the lowest-rated television station in the area, WJM-TV Channel 12. Mary was often in the center of chaos caused by various situations and especially by the wacky staff. The initial staff was comprised of Mary's often bad-tempered but ultimately caring boss and producer of the news program, Lou Grant, played by Edward Asner (1929–); Gavin MacLeod (1931–) as Murray Slaughter, the news writer who always had a quick retort; Ted Knight (1923–1986) playing anchorman Ted Baxter, who had a deep resonant voice and a lot of vanity, but lacked intellectual abilities. At home, Valerie Harper (1938–) played Rhoda Morgenstern, Mary's upstairs neighbor who was a window dresser, and Cloris Leachman (1926–) played Phyllis Lindstrom, Mary's high-strung landlady. In 1974 Betty White (1922–) joined the newsroom as the hilarious Sue Ann Nivens, a man-hungry "Happy Homemaker." The stable of characters was so impressive that Lou Grant, Rhoda, and Phyllis were all eventually spun off.

James L. Brooks (1940–), who would go on to be very successful in television and as a motion picture director, was executive producer of *The Mary Tyler Moore Show* along with Allan Burns (1935–).

The show's opening had a famous last shot (before introducing the other characters). The title song "Love Is All Around," written by Reg Presley, speaks to Mary and how she will have a successful future. There are a series of shots showing Mary conducting normal daily activities. The final shot of the opening montage is Mary facing the camera and throwing her hat up into the air. The hat does not fall to the ground but stops near the top of the frame via a freeze frame, which also captures her big, natural smile. In the end the most important aspect of this moment is not the hat but Mary's demonstration of independence.

The Mary Tyler Moore Show wasn't distinctly a satire or parody of the media or television news; rather it is a glimpse into a local news station similar to outlets all over the country. It was a way of investigating local celebrity, teamwork, male/female relationships, a perception of the news, and, above all, the found independence of Mary Richards.

The main set is a bare-bones local news station. The designers did a good overall job of simplifying the area so the actors can be featured. The one aspect of the set that viewers could relate to and recognize immediately is a row of clocks hung on a back wall that are set to the time zones across the country and world.

A Very Funny Episode

One of the show's many guest stars was German-born actor Eric Braeden (1941–), known for his work as a Nazi officer on *The Rat Patrol* (1966–1968). On *The Mary Tyler Moore Show* his guest shot was as an overbearing, critical, and nasty professor and writer named Karl Heller who is invited by a station head to be a "Critic-at-Large." He would sit next to Ted Baxter and talk about anything he wanted to criticize. He verbally takes apart Ted Baxter, local restaurants, and anything else he chooses. The phones ring off the hook with negative messages from viewers but that only prompts the top brass to give the insulting high-hatted elitist more air time to spew his bile. He is attracted to

Mary and takes her out for a disastrous meal at a local French restaurant where he insists the shrimp were first frozen and gets into a war of words with the staff over whether their bottle of wine is bad. Eventually he goes too far and is fired; in retaliation he is hit in the face with a cream pie by Sue Ann Nivens and Ted Baxter.

Like all good sitcoms, *The Mary Tyler Moore Show* had a wide demographic reach. Word of mouth spread quickly, and in a prestige Saturday night slot the ratings were strong and solid.

See also: *Vol. 1, The 1950s–1960s: The Dick Van Dyke Show.*

Further Resources

Armstrong, Jennifer Keishin. 2013. *Mary and Lou and Rhoda and Ted: And All the Brilliant Minds Who Made the Mary Tyler Moore Show.* New York: Simon & Schuster.

Moore, Mary Tyler. 2010. *Growing Up Again: Life, Loves, and Oh Yeah, Diabetes.* New York: St. Martin's Press.

*M*A*S*H* (CBS, 1972–1983)

First there was the book, *MASH: A Novel about Three Army Doctors* written by Richard Hooker (1924–1997), based on the author's Korean War (1950–1953) experience of a former army surgeon, H. Richard Hornberger. The book published in 1968 while the Vietnam War (1955–1975) was raging.

Film director Robert Altman (1925–2006), who had worked extensively in television, mounted a large cast and crew in an adaption of the novel with the shorter title *M*A*S*H.* The film was released in 1970 to critical acclaim and strong box office. This black comedy/satire of the MASH unit where the injured and severely wounded were operated on resonated with the 1960s counterculture.

*M*A*S*H* was created by Larry Gelbart (1928–2009), who also was a writer, producer, and director on the series. The executive producer was Gene Reynolds (1923–), who had a long career as an actor and also was a producer on *My Three Sons* (1960–1972) and *Hogan's Heroes* (1965–1971). The latter gave him direct experience with the war genre.

To cast the series, the producers retained a few members from the film cast: Gary Burghoff (1943–) again played Radar, and G. Wood (1919–2000) reprised Brigadier General Hammond. Timothy Brown (1937–), who played Judson in the motion picture, was given the part of Spearchucker Jones in the series.

The rest of the large cast of the *M*A*S*H* television series included Alan Alda (1926–) as Captain Benjamin Franklin (Hawkeye) Pierce; Wayne Rogers (1933–) played Captain John F. X. (Trapper John) McIntire; McLean Stevenson (1927–1996) played Lieutenant Colonel Henry Blake; Loretta Swit (1937–) portrayed Major Margaret (Hot Lips) Houlihan; Larry Linville (1939–2000) played Major Frank Burns; and Jamie Farr (1934–) played the cross-dressing Corporal Klinger.

A critical feature of this 1970s sitcom was that although it was outrageous and hilarious, it constantly dealt with serious themes of death and war. There was plenty of wisecracking during operations and on the base there was constant wheeling and dealing, harassment of the brass, and of the one woman with some power, nevertheless the calamity of war was always a counterpoint.

The theme song in the movie, "Suicide Is Painless," had music by Johnny Mandel (1925–) and lyrics by Mike Altman, the director's 14-year-old son. As the title reveals, the song's lyrics were controversial, suggesting the possibility that suicide was a viable choice for the characters. The television team made a wise decision to avoid problems that might have affected the ratings by orchestrating an instrumental version of the song sans lyrics.

The end of *M*A*S*H* came on February 28, 1983 when the 256th and final episode aired on CBS. Named "Goodbye, Farewell and Amen," it was written by a team of writers including Alan Alda, who directed the two-and-a-half-hour episode. From 1983 to 2010 it was the most watched television broadcast in television history when it was topped in total viewership but not ratings by Super Bowl XLIV. The story followed the end of the Korean War and the last days of the MASH unit. The dismantling of the unit and its effect on individual characters is investigated as they throw a farewell party. Over 105 million viewers watched that

This popular television adaptation of the hit movie *M*A*S*H* aired its final episode on Feburary 28, 1983, after 11 extremely successful seasons. The two-and-a-half-hour-long series finale was, until 2010, the most-watched television broadcast in American history. The cast pictured (left to right) are Loretta Swit, Mike Farrell, Jamie Farr, Harry Morgan, Alan Alda, and William Christopher. (AP Photo)

night and the total audience numbered 121.6 million. It is considered one of the most watched finales on network television and is warmly remembered by those who watched it.

*M*A*S*H* tapped into audience feelings about war and loss. Viewers reveled in the satiric approach to such a serious subject. In the end audiences loved *M*A*S*H* for the same basic reasons that always apply to good television. It was honest. It had strong story lines and unforgettable characters. That's always a good reason for anyone to turn on a TV set.

See also: *China Beach.*

Further Resources

Hooker, Richard. 1968. *MASH: A Novel about Three Army Doctors*. New York: HarperCollins.

Kalter, Suzy. 1988. *The Complete Book of M*A*S*H*. New York: Harry N. Abrams.

Masterpiece Theatre (PBS, 1971–2008)

The prehistory of *Masterpiece Theatre* began in 1967 when the broadcasting outlet National Educational Television (NET) in the United States, the precursor of the Public Broadcasting Service (PBS), aired *The Forsyte Saga,* a British Broadcasting Corporation (BBC) adaptation of a series of novels called *The Forsyte Saga* written by John Galsworthy (1847–1933). The story concerned a poor family who became rich and found their new wealth hard to deal with. The success of the broadcast led Stanford Calderwood, then president of WGBH, a Boston television station, to look into whether the BBC would let them purchase shows for their station.

Ideas for how to structure the proposed series came from Frank Gillard (1909–1998), a BBC executive in England, and Christopher Sarson in America. Eventually Calderwood met with Herb Schmertz of the Mobil Corporation. Funding for the venture was attained and at a meeting in England titles were selected for the first group of shows to run.

The Beginning

Season one began on January 10, 1971. The host was Alistair Cooke (1908–2004), a British journalist, television personality, and broadcaster. Alistair Cooke was a regal-looking gentleman, impeccably dressed and groomed with a compelling voice and the ability to draw an audience to him. The show's opening was an ever-moving camera passing over great leather-bound books, vintage photographs, sculptures and paintings. The musical theme seemed fit for a king or queen. It is "Rondeau," composed by Jean-Joseph Mouret, and was a rousing trumpet voluntary—Alistair Cooke's name, along with the show's title appeared on a white open book page.

Next Mr. Cooke was seated in a large room with a table, a candle on a pedestal, books, maps, and other items necessary for him to introduce the book that had been staged and filmed and would be presented over a period of weeks.

Some of the presentations of the 1970s included an adaptation of *Cold Comfort Farm*, a comic novel written by British writer Stella Gibbons (1902–1989). The story concerned a woman who had lost both of her parents and found she couldn't support herself, so she went to live with relatives who owned a farm. They took her in because they felt they must atone for wrongdoings never specified.

The Gambler, based on the novel by Fyodor Dostoyevsky, is the dark story of a man who was destroyed by what would now be called a gambling addiction. His game was roulette and it threatened to ruin his life.

Jude the Obscure was adapted from the novel by Thomas Hardy (1840–1928). Dealing with issues of class, this story followed a working-class young man who aspired to be a scholar.

The Spoils of Poynton was a Henry James (1843–1916) novel also adapted for *Masterpiece Theatre*. It was the story of a widow and her son struggling over the furniture in their house, told from the point of view of a young woman in love with the son, but who understood the woman's anguish.

Masterpiece Theatre also broadcast series that were written for *Masterpiece Theatre* and that were equal in stature to the great books. These included a series on the beginnings of the Churchill family and the six wives of Henry VIII.

Americans greatly enjoyed the series. PBS was founded on the principle of alternative programming that countered the networks. *Masterpiece Theatre* fits into the idea that television drama and long-form storytelling should be literate, intelligent, and uplifting both as entertainment and for its rich content.

The writing was crisp and smart, the visuals looked like fine filmed theater. Using motion picture feature film techniques, an episode of *Masterpiece Theatre* came alive on the home screen.

Through word of mouth the audience grew and others tuned in for a specific series of particular interest. Young people saw great novels come to life and understood them better beyond the written page. Hosts have changed and new material has been introduced, but the original intention of *Masterpiece Theatre,* renamed *Masterpiece* in 2008, continues to thrive. Some of the most popular programs on *Masterpiece* in the 2000s have originated from the BBC, including the Sherlock Holmes adaptation *Sherlock* (2010–), the historical drama *Downton Abbey* (2011–2015), and the historical drama about Queen Victoria (1819–1901) entitled *Victoria* (2017–).

See also: *Vol. 3, The 1990s–Present: Downton Abbey*; *Sherlock.*

Further Resources

Eaton, Rebecca. 2013 *Making Masterpiece: 25 Years Behind the Scenes at Masterpiece Theatre and Mystery! at PBS*. New York: Viking.

Graves, Robert. 1989. *I, Claudius. From the Autobiography of Tiberius Claudius Born 10 B.C. Murdered and Defiled A.D. 54*. New York: Vintage.

Maude (CBS, 1972–1978)

Maude was the first spin-off created from *All in the Family*, the megahit from the mind of Norman Lear (1922–). The premise was that arch-conservative and bigoted Archie Bunker had a cousin, Maude, played by Bea Arthur (1922–2009), who was an outspoken woman, a political liberal, and an upper-class individual who did not live in Queens, New York, like her in-every-way-opposite male cousin, Archie. Maude lived in Tuckahoe, a suburb of Westchester County. She was married to her fourth husband, Walter Findlay, played by Bill Macy (1922–), owner of Findlay's Friendly Appliances. Maude's divorced daughter Carol, portrayed by Adrianne Barbeau (1945–), and Carol's nine-year-old son Phillip, played by Brian Morrison (1961–), lived with them.

Maude

Maude was very tall with thick layered salt and pepper hair. She spoke in a commanding, low-pitched voice.

Maude was the first spin-off from *All in the Family*, and featured Bea Arthur as the title character, pictured here with Bill Macy as her husband Walter. The character of Maude was an outspoken and politically liberal female, which was unique for 1970s network television. (CBS via Getty Images)

The message of *Maude* was in the character herself. She strove to be a strong, if at times demanding, woman and was Norman Lear's entry into the women's movement.

Relationships between Maude and the other characters reflected her strong-minded independence. Ironically, she always had a female housekeeper, three during the run of the show. The first housekeeper was a black woman named Florida Evans played by Esther Rolle (1920–1998) who fared the best, but left in 1974 to star in her own show, *Good Times* (1974–1979). Maude's other relationships with her housekeepers were full of friction.

Divorce was one of the show's topics since both mother and daughter had experienced it. Carol's father was Maude's second husband. Politics and social issues were a great part of the comedic discourse, and the seventies was a good time for raw material with three presidents, financial difficulties for the country, and the rights of gays, women, and blacks all gaining steam.

Lear and his team dug deep into topical issues on *Maude* with some critics and viewers asking if they were proper for a sitcom. The self-centered and demanding lead character generated the most controversial topics: she got directly involved in politics, had a face lift, experienced menopause, and had an abortion, this last topic prompting major viewer reaction.

Walter had his stake in issues. He had a treacherous bout with alcoholism and had a nervous breakdown. These button-pushing topics generated top ratings for *Maude* for several seasons.

Whether it was just happenstance or an intentional part of the casting process, Adrianne Barbeau attracted more than her share of attention with her voluptuous figure. Nevertheless her Carol was vulnerable, defiant at times, troubled at others, and had to deal with a formidable mother as well as raise her son as a single parent.

During the run of the show there was considerable gossip about whether Bea Arthur was a lesbian or bisexual. This speculation may have been based on the inherent open-mindedness of Maude's character, but there is nothing in reality to suggest her orientation. She had been married with children and grandchildren. In a possible ironic twist she left in her will a donation of $300,000 to New York's Ali Forney Center, which supported homeless lesbian, gay, and transgender young people.

Maude was a landmark program of the 1970s. It featured a strong woman in the lead role and it more than pushed the envelope with issues that especially confronted women at the time. As with all experiments involving comedy and political/social issues taken on by Norman Lear, in the end *Maude* was a very funny sitcom that made good points.

See also: *All in the Family*; Lear, Norman.

Further Resources

Beal, Lewis. 1992. "Maude's Abortion Fades into History." *Chicago Tribune*. November 13. http://articles.chicagotribune.com/1992-11-13/features/9204130017_1_mothers-as-donna-reed-messy-family-life-maude-findlay

Murray, Noel. 2015. "10 Episodes That Show How 'Maude' Debated American Culture in the '70s."

McCloud (NBC, 1970–1977)

This Western-inspired crime series appeared in 1970 as one segment in NBC's *Four-in-One* rotation format. In the fall of 1971 *McCloud* grew from a one-hour show to 90 minutes and was featured as one part of *The NBC Mystery Movie* airing on Wednesday evening. The following year in 1972 the show was moved to Sunday night as a segment of *The NBC Sunday Mystery Movie* where it remained for the next five years, sometimes in a two-hour format, other times in a 90-minute running time.

Cast and Story Line

Dennis Weaver (1924–2006) was famous for appearing in 290 episodes of *Gunsmoke* (1955–1975) as Chester, Marshal Dillon's deputy from 1955 to 1964. He later became Sam McCloud, also a deputy marshal from Taos, New Mexico, sent to New York City to learn big-city crime-fighting techniques.

The cast was rounded out with J. D. Cannon (1922–2005) as Chief of Detectives Peter B. Clifford, Terry Carter (1928–) as Sergeant Joe Broadhurst, Ken

Lynch (1910–1990) as the gravel-voiced Sergeant Grover, and Diana Muldaur (1938–) as Chris Coughlin, McCloud's female friend. Glen A. Larson (1937–2014), the brain behind *Battlestar Galactica,* was the executive producer for Universal Television.

Actually Sam McCloud arrived in New York originally because he was on the trail of an escaped prisoner. The New York Police Department found it difficult to deal with McCloud's literally take-no-prisoners method of strong-arm tactics. The tough cowboy cop did get his man and was given a temporary assignment in Manhattan's 27th Precinct under Chief Clifford. McCloud was informed that he was there to learn their big-city police methods, but he most often took crime and criminal situations into his own hands, which aggravated and frustrated the chief no end. When McCloud was assigned a case, he usually cajoled Sergeant Broadhurst and more often than not solved the case, although this association with McCloud did little good with their superior, Chief Clifford.

The charm and distinction of the show is the stark contrast between McCloud, who wore a classic cowboy hat and a sheepskin jacket and spoke with a Western accent, and the New York City police and their big-city mentality. Sam McCloud combined the big-city and country ways of law enforcement to catch crooks. He had an uncanny sense for uncovering subtle clues and the smallest details. New York City at the dawn of the decade was rampant with crime and practically bankrupt. It also was filthy and far from the glimmering metropolis it had been in previous eras.

Chris Coughlin, McCloud's lady friend, was not in every episode, but her through line is that she is writing a book on the fugitive McCloud was pursuing during the series pilot.

Guest stars on *McCloud* included Milton Berle (1908–2002), Roddy McDowell (1928–1998), Della Reese (1931–), and Danny Thomas (1912–1991).

The other shows in the *Four-in-One* rotation with *McCloud* were *San Francisco Airport* (1970–1971), *Night Gallery* (1970–1973), and *The Psychiatrist* (1970–1971). Next it was grouped in the *NBC Mystery Movie* lineup with *Columbo* (1968–2003) and *McMillan and Wife* (1971–1977), where *McCloud* stayed for the rest of its on-air life.

In the 1950s and 1960s, the networks sought radio and movie stars to front TV series, banking on the name recognition and reputation of the performer. To a great extent this tactic worked. By the 1970s television had developed its own stars with names and reputation. Dennis Weaver was a beloved character on *Gunsmoke* playing the marshal's deputy, Chester, walking with a sliding limp and calling out his boss's name in a distinctive high-voiced manner that stretched out like his gait. Playing a character with the same lawman credentials and sticking to the cowboy persona, Weaver gave NBC a sure hit in a business where hardly anything is for sure.

See also: *Columbo*; *Night Gallery*; *The Psychiatrist.*

Further Resources

Weaver, Dennis. 2001. *All the World's a Stage*. Charlottesville, VA: Hampton Road.

Wilson, David. 1974. *The Killing*. Award Books.

Meeting of Minds (PBS, 1977–1981)

Steve Allen (1921–2000) can be identified as the inventor of the talk show with the original *The Tonight Show* back in the 1950s. That show had all the elements still utilized by modern-day practitioners of the form and craft such as the monologue, joking with the sidekick, having a great band, and interviewing celebrity guests. An exceedingly inventive man with high standards, Allen was filled with so many ideas for books, songs, and television shows that he kept a tape recorder on his bedside table. If he woke in the middle of the night with a new thought, he would record it and go back to sleep. In the morning he listened to his dictation. In the 1970s Allen became disillusioned with the quality of television fare. He knew he could do better, especially in terms of the talk show, which he thought had become stale, unimaginative, and even lacking class. Allen conceived an idea for a talk show for which there was no precedent. The concept was a revelation. He would host and interview guests, but the roster was not current celebrities but great historical figures who had made astounding accomplishments in the arts, politics, and history. He called the show *Meeting of Minds*.

Conception

The notion first came to Allen in the late 1950s. He was doing the weekly *The Steve Allen Show*. The time machine concept was to be a segment of that show, but his sponsor, the Chrysler Corporation, rejected the proposal and plans for a talk show where Allen would talk to figures from the past were benched.

The Public Broadcasting Service (PBS), which put forth educational and informational programs, took on Allen's radical talk show idea, and it was produced at the local station, KCET, located in Hollywood, California. The show was meticulously scripted. When possible the words of the historical guests were used. They included Plato, Socrates, Aristotle, Thomas Aquinas, Martin Luther, Cleopatra, Marie Antoinette, Florence Nightingale, Thomas Paine, Francis Bacon, Thomas Jefferson, Voltaire, Karl Marx, Charles Darwin, Catherine II, and Oliver Cromwell.

Some of the actors portraying these notables had name recognition, but many did not. The most well-known thespian on *Meeting of Minds* was Jayne Meadows (1919–2015), who was married to Steve Allen and played many of the female figures. She appeared on the show more often than any other actor. Once she even played someone other than a historic figure when she was the "Dark Lady" of one of Shakespeare's sonnets while an actor playing the bard appeared on the show.

Other well-known actors included Harris Yulin (1937–) as Leonardo Da Vinci, Katherine Helmond (1929–) as Emily Dickinson, and Roscoe Lee Browne (1922–2007) as Frederick Douglass.

Steve Allen was the host of this unusual program. He was dressed in a classic black tuxedo and held a hand mike, which he used to introduce and interview everyone. At times several interviewees sat around a table and had group discussions.

Steve Allen and everyone on camera worked from a prepared script presumably memorized in advance. The actors knew their lines as if it were a play; each script was meticulously written. If necessary, the actors took on a specific accent. They were all in detailed period clothes. Some seemed to know each other even though they were from different parts of the world. An off-screen audience or vocal sound track reacted to the proceedings as another aspect of the talk show format. Paganini played his violin for musical entertainment.

Steve Allen gave a more formal introduction as each subject entered. Each subject was identified visually with titles below them indicating their name, year of birth, and year of death. The research for the show was detailed, accurate, and far reaching. Historical eras and events were presented and explored. Images of locations, paintings, sculptures, and people came on screen to support the discussion that continued while the images stayed forefront.

The discussions ranged from past, to present, even to the future. The audience tuned in to learn about history, people, and events. They were entertained, engaged, and either liked or disliked a guest just as if it were a traditional television talk show.

Ownership of an idea in television is tricky at best. Often someone comes up with a revolutionary idea and then someone else comes along and does it better. Sometimes the first player is not from the United States. Sometimes even though the second TV show maker was aware of a predecessor, they had forgotten about it or paid it little to no mind.

Three years before *Meeting of Minds* the series *Witness to Yesterday,* created by Arthur Voronka, aired on Canadian television. For a 1976 episode Steve Allen appeared on the program portraying George Gershwin. *Meeting of Minds* was lauded by critics and won an Emmy award, and four Emmy nominations. Steve Allen was the personal winner of the prestigious Peabody Award.

See also: PBS (Public Broadcasting Service); *Vol. 1, The 1950s–1960s:* Allen, Steve/*The Steve Allen Show*.

Further Resources

Alba, Ben. 2005. *Inventing Late Night: Steve Allen and the Original Tonight Show*. Amherst, NY: Prometheus Books.

Allen, Steve. 1989. *Meeting of Minds: The Complete Scripts, with Illustrations of the Amazingly Successful PBS TV Series—Series 1*. Buffalo, NY: Prometheus Books.

The Midnight Special (NBC, 1973–1981)

This 90-minute show broadcast by NBC broke new ground in television programming by being first to provide late-night presentations as a regularly scheduled effort. It just happened to be rock and roll music. *The Midnight Special* aired on Friday from 1:00 a.m. until 2:00 a.m. Helen Reddy (1941–), a dominant female singer of the 1970s best known for co-writing and singing the feminist anthem "I Am Woman" released in December 1972, was the regular host of *The Midnight Special* from 1975 to 1977.

The producer was Burt Sugarman (1939–), who had on his resume game and variety shows, television series, and feature films. Sugarman told NBC they could capitalize on the large audience that watched *The Tonight Show with Johnny Carson* (1962–1992) because none of the networks had programming after 1:00 a.m.; they would just sign off after the last program aired. NBC rejected Sugarman's proposal, so he bought air time from the network and convinced the automobile company Chevrolet to be the show's sponsor. The ratings were high so NBC reconsidered and bought the program from Sugarman.

The announcer and frequent host was one of America's favorite disc jockeys, Wolfman Jack (1938–1995), born Robert Weston Smith. He had moderately long hair, a mustache, and a beard, which went with his moniker. To a DJ the voice is everything and Wolfman Jack had pipes that were beyond gravelly; his voice had a mysterious, almost otherworldly tone.

George Lucas paid homage to Wolfman Jack by giving him a perfect part, playing himself in *American Graffiti,* released in 1973, which put him on the map and positioned him to make a transition from radio to television. As announcer and often host on *The Midnight Special,* Wolfman Jack was informative, lively, enthusiastic, and gave rousing introductions to acts that played the music he loved.

Some of the many musical acts that appeared on *The Midnight Special* were Journey, the Bee Gees, Kiss, Genesis, Bread, K.C. and the Sunshine Band, the Four Seasons, REO Speedwagon, and Fleetwood Mac. At times Wolfman Jack interviewed a musical figure. For example, he interviewed Carl Wilson (1946–1998) of the Beach Boys on *The Midnight Special.*

The bands and acts really played their instruments and actually sang. This was a departure from many music shows in the 1950s and 1960s when lip-syncing over a recording was in vogue. The music on *The Midnight Special* was exciting and varied. The musical mix covered what is now known as classic rock, emerging groups of the 1970s, pop, folk, and even punk music.

Television politics can be brutal. The cancellation of *The Midnight Special* did not occur because of poor ratings. Producer Dick Ebersol (1947–) asked NBC to cancel Sugarman's show as part of a deal concerning Ebersol's taking over the then failing *Saturday Night Live* (1975–). The replacement show was *SCTV* (1981–1983).

See also: *Saturday Night Live.*

Further Resources

Hunter, B. R. 1997. *The Midnight Special, 1972–1981: Late Night's Original Rock & Roll Show.* New York: MTV.

Wolfman Jack. 2011. *Have Mercy! Confessions of the Original Rock 'n' Roll Animal.* New York: Warner Books.

Mork & Mindy (ABC, 1978–1982)

Sometimes when a new show does well in the ratings, the network (in this case, ABC) changes the time slot for the coming seasons. The thought behind this is that viewers who watched the show in its premiere time slot will follow the show to a new one. This also allows the network to put in another show in that former spot so it too will do well in the ratings. In the case of *Mork & Mindy* this methodology did not work.

The concept of *Mork & Mindy* was a sitcom in which an alien visits the Earth. Robin Williams (1951–2014) had little experience before achieving this role. He was simply known as a stand-up comic, but one who took on material, voices, movement, and interaction with the audience in such a zany and offbeat way that while the crowd laughed uproariously, they also wondered if he was just a little bit crazy. He was approached by the co-creator of the series, Garry Marshall, to take the part of Mork. The character of Mork could speak English but had manic behavior problems that expressed themselves through broad actions and speech patterns.

Story Line

Mork was ordered to Earth in a space capsule shaped like an egg by his boss, Orson, voiced off-screen by Ralph James (1924–1992), who regularly had Mork report on the primitive habits of earthlings. Mork from Ork didn't land in California, New York, or Chicago, three places well known for diversity, but instead in Boulder, Colorado. Once on terra firma Mork meets a young woman named Mindy, the other half of the show's title. Mork eventually persuades the pretty lady to allow him to room in her apartment, where they gradually fall in love as he studies Earth's civilization and human behavior. Mindy acts as a teacher and a provider of feedback. Pam Dawber (1951–), who played Mindy McConnell, was a Wilhelmina model and then transitioned to acting where she performed in commercials before being selected without an audition by co-creator Garry Marshall to play Mindy to Williams's Mork.

Mork's behavior speed-prancing around the room, making funny noises, moving and contorting his body is sometimes manic and sometimes shown in slow-motion movements. Upstaging was part of the role as were catchphrases that captured the country. People loved to repeat them to family and friends: "Na-oo, na-noo" (Orkan for hello) and "Shazbat!" (Drat).

Unfortunately, tinkering with its time slot created problems for the show and ratings plunged. To try to achieve a course correction the cast changed and changed again. In a desperate measure the creators of *Mork & Mindy* tried to come up with a guest star who could save the show. Eventually they hired a comedian and actor who was Robin Williams's idol and had perennially put audiences into hilarious fits—Jonathan Winters (1925–2003)—but the ploy didn't work. Mork and Mindy were married. Winters was hired as their boy Mearth, but on Ork children were hatched from very oversized eggs and arrived full-grown in body, but not in mind. The addition of Mearth on *Mork & Mindy* dropped it to a more than dismal 60th place in the ratings grid.

While it was running *Mork & Mindy* (which was a spin-off of sorts from *Happy Days* on which Mork appeared briefly) made everyone in the demographic laugh. Maybe if the time slot hadn't been moved at all and the show had stayed put, it would have maintained its initial good ratings. It did break one record: it lasted one season more than the last time a comedy contained a human and someone from another planet, *My Favorite Martian* (1963–1966).

See also: *Happy Days*; *Vol. 1, The 1950s–1960s: My Favorite Martian*; *Vol. 3, The 1990s–Present: 3rd Rock from the Sun*.

Further Resources

Church, Ralph. 1978. *Mork & Mindy*. New York: Pocket Books.

Herbert, Emily. 2014. *Robin Williams: When the Laughter Stops 1951–2014*. London: John Blake.

The Muppet Show (Syndication, 1976–1981)

When Jim Henson (1936–1990) created the Muppets in the mid-fifties he had no idea how popular they would become—lasting on television and in motion pictures past Mr. Henson's time on earth. In the second decade of the 21st century there is no end in sight for the Muppets.

After taking a class in puppetry and meeting Jane Nebel (1934–2013), the woman who would assist him and later become his wife, Henson broke new ground by combining the art of the marionette with the hand puppet, creating the name Muppet by combining letters from each method of entertaining with hand coverings and hand manipulation of strings.

Puppets and marionettes were most often used to entertain children, but the Muppets captured the hearts, minds, and funny bones of children of all ages—which started with the little ones and went into adulthood.

The Muppet Show was a half-hour variety extravaganza in the tradition of vaudeville and burlesque (without the striptease). It took place in a set created to look like a theater. The only real action in the audience occurred in the balcony, where Statler and Waldrof,

Kermit the Frog and singer/actress Julie Andrews meet on *The Muppet Show*, during a taping in London in November of 1977. The troupe of Jim Henson's unique puppet creations hosted a guest each week on this delightful series for children of all ages. (AP Photo)

two Muppets made to look like older gentleman, heckled, complained, interrupted, and harangued almost any acts the Muppets performed. There also was a backstage set where the star, Kermit the Frog, organized the acts, cued them, argued with them, and helped establish a joke theme that would occur while someone was on stage. There was a pit band of Muppets who played for the acts and at in-between times.

Each week there was a guest star who performed alone and with Kermit or one of the others in the gang. They included Florence Henderson (1934–2016), Jim Nabors (1930–), Julie Andrews (1934–), Steve Martin (1945–), and Loretta Lynn (1932–). The Muppets who put on the show included Kermit the Frog. Miss Piggy, Fozzie Bear, Gonzo, Animal, Sam the Eagle, Scooter, Mildred, Janice, and George the Janitor.

Memorable Guest Star

One of the most memorable moments on *The Muppet Show* was when drummer extraordinaire Buddy Rich (1917–1987) was a guest on the show. In the backstage area Buddy Rich talks to Kermit the frog, saying he heard someone challenged him to a drum battle. It turns out to be Animal, the out-of-control wild character who is kept in chains and plays a mean drum. Then in front of the red curtain Kermit introduces the two men and tells the audience they are about to see the drum battle of the century. Curtains part and Buddy

Rich is on one side with his drum kit and on the opposite side is Animal chained to his set. Rich is as good as he is known to be and Animal is a fighter. After several back and forths Rich declares himself the winner. Animal gets very mad and throws one of his drums at Buddy Rich. The drum lands over Buddy Rich's head, and we watch him struggle to get it off.

For the main body of the show we are watching as the house audience. The show consists of blackout sketches, songs, dances, and numbers that seem as if they are either from a Broadway musical or a regular variety show. The sketches are silly and seem familiar. There is a news segment and three levels of action, backstage, on stage, and in the balcony; sometimes they relate to each other. The theater is old as if it had been abandoned until rented by the Muppets.

A wide group of voice actors provided vocal variety for the characters, including Henson and Frank Oz (1944–), who in addition to being a loyal member of the stock company also directed the film *The Muppets Take Manhattan.*

The Muppet Show was family fare. Henson's brilliant idea was to bring an old-style theater variety show back to television. Regular viewers began to see the Muppets as real flesh and blood characters. Everyone had their favorites, Kermit, Miss Piggy, or Fozzie, but it was those two old cranks in the balcony that everyone wanted to hear, anticipating what insults they would offer next.

See also: *Vol. 1, The 1950s–1960s: Sesame Street.*

Further Resources

Jones, Brian J. 2013. *Jim Henson: The Biography.* New York: Ballantine Books.

Shemin, Craig. 2014. *Muppets Character Encyclopedia.* London: DK Publishing.

NFL Monday Night Football (ABC, 1970–2005; ESPN, 2006–present)

In 1977, Roone Arledge (1931–2002), president of sports for the ABC television network, created the innovative football program *NFL Monday Night Football.* The concept of *NFL Monday Night Football* was to televise a weekly NFL contest, along with informative description and analysis, plenty of repartee, and state-of-the-art television production techniques using the newest electronic tools and gadgets. The program's objective was to entertain, enlighten, and dazzle the home viewer who would watch an exciting game on the way to the Super Bowl. The high-rated show came over the television airways each week live at 9 p.m. Eastern Standard Time (EST). The initial audience was male, but more and more women became interested in the sport and watched the televised game.

The show opened inside a TV control room with plenty of chaotic camera movement and voices shouting phrases like the 10 to 1 countdown. The logo stating "NFL Monday Night Football" was prominent. The show's introduction was spoken in a clear, deep, well-enunciated and confident tone by Keith Jackson, the announcer and play-by-play reporter who did the voice-over and on-camera work as part of his dual position. Depending on the game, sometimes *NFL Monday Night Football* would begin with a wide shot of the field sans players or those along the sidelines there to watch the game. The game would be announced, identifying the location and the two teams.

Howard Cosell (1918–1995), the opinionated man viewers grew to love or hate, was the main color commentator. He wore a bright stiff blazer with the ABC logo in a circular patch on his coat. The same blazer was worn by the other screen broadcasters who stood in front of the camera or side by side with their fellow screen broadcasters.

Cosell was a near expert in an array of sports including boxing and baseball. His appearance was rigid and he more often appeared with a dead stare than a smile. His vocal ability was hesitant, droning, and relentless. He gave the impression that he knew everything. He seemed ever ready to pick a fight, challenge one of his experts, or overstay his welcome. Many of the fans at home and in the stands found Cosell arrogant, obnoxious, grating, and overbearing, yet the majority tuned in each week to get more of the same. Howard Cosell was a force to be reckoned with and the viewers knew he wasn't going anywhere soon, so they developed a love/hate relationship and yelled angry words of disagreement from their couches when he was on camera. Another color commentator was Don Meredith (1938–2010), whom Howard Cosell introduced as

"Dandy" Don Meredith. He was a former coach for the Dallas Cowboys. Meredith's delivery of football information and analysis was communicated in a folksy manner. He was known to sing a Willie Nelson song that signaled it was time to shut down and go home to bed.

Alex Karras (1935–2012) had been a defensive tackle for the Detroit Lions. His football commentaries were knowledgeable and his direct sense of humor was best displayed when he said on air that a bald player from the Oakland Raiders, who had not been to college, attended "the University of Mars." Fran Tarkenton (1940–) had played for the Minnesota Vikings and the New York Giants. He was a part-timer on *NFL Monday Night Football.*

Joining Howard Cosell and Keith Jackson for the play-by-play analysis was Frank Gifford (1930–2015), the movie-star-handsome former football player for the New York Giants who played both offense and defense. Gifford was smart about the game and able to drop a quip or two trying to deal with his fellow play-by-players.

Controlled Chaos

The coordination of who was going to say what or when was a quandary while watching *Monday Night Football*. Sometimes one or both of the flankers knew what Cosell was going to do because he would turn to the right or left and address one of the men specifically; nevertheless that didn't stop interruptions, arguments, disagreements, and out and out verbal fights. The beauty of the show was that no one in the booth was told to tell the on-camera talent what to do except perhaps where to stand. This was the genius of *NFL Monday Night Football.* Arledge selected the director and producer, Chet Forte (1935–1996), to inaugurate the innovative show because of his abilities to make football entertaining and a spectacle.

Split-screen technique was utilized to show two aspects of the game at once. Freeze frames or stills were employed to show a particular player or players. Players were identified during the game using superimposed spelled-out yellow letters, which appeared on the bottom third of the frame. The score was projected this way but covered more of the screen. The camerawork was far more inventive than previous telecasts of football had been, underlining the movement and tempo of the game. There were shots of spectators in the stands reacting and these were intercut during a game. Celebrities were brought into the broadcast area so Cosell or others could interview them and have them talk about the game. Hand microphones with the ABC circle attached to them were used by all. The coverage of the game employed more cameras than ever before.

In 1986, veteran sports broadcaster Al Michaels (1944–) was brought in for play-by-play duties, joining Gifford who continued providing additional commentary. Also in the late 1980s, the program debuted a theme song, with country music star Hank Williams Jr. performing "All My Rowdy Friends Are Here on Monday Night," a slight revision of his 1984 hit "All My Rowdy Friends Are Coming Over Tonight."

Michaels continued performing play-by-play for the Monday night game throughout the years, continuing until 2005. He was joined by numerous former players, coaches, and other personalities. Color commentators during the late 1980s and early 1990s included Hall of Fame quarterback Joe Namath (1985), former quarterback Joe Theismann (1997 and 2005), and former quarterback Boomer Esiason (1998–1999). In 2002, Hall of Fame former coach of the Oakland Raiders, John Madden, joined Michaels for a two-man booth, with Madden offering color commentary and analysis. Madden had been a prominent sports television broadcaster with CBS and Fox.

The broadcast of *Monday Night Football* moved to ESPN in 2006. The original broadcast team was Mike Tirico, Theismann, and Tony Kornheiser. The first ESPN broadcast for *Monday Night Football* was the preseason matchup between the Oakland Raiders and Minnesota Vikings on August 14, 2006. The program continues to air on ESPN.

See also: ESPN; *Vol. 1, The 1950s–1960s:* Football.

Further Resources

Arledge, Roone. 2004. *Roone: A Memoir*. New York: HarperCollins.

Cosell, Howard. 1973. *Cosell*. Chicago: Playboy Press.

Night Gallery (NBC, 1970–1973)

Night Gallery was an anthology series that covered the same ground as *The Twilight Zone* (1959–1964). It was first introduced during the 1970–1971 season on the NBC show *Four-in-One,* which had a unique format juggling four different series in one slot. The others were *McCloud* (1970–1977), *San Francisco International Airport* (1970), and *The Psychiatrist* (1970–1971).

NBC decided to go to a full series for *Night Gallery*. Rod Serling (1924–1975), who created *Night Gallery*, was to be the on-camera host and would write many of the teleplays. The concept of the show was to have Serling in a space that was mostly dark and had paintings on display. The paintings, created specifically for the show, created a provocative image. Serling would talk about the story as the painting made the viewers wonder what they were in the story for, the title was announced, and the story would begin. Every episode was in color. Like *The Twilight Zone* the casts were filled with name or semi-name actors. The stories were well crafted in every way and the show engaged a cult audience, but many were looking for another *Twilight Zone* and there was a factor missing that audiences didn't know about at the time. It was the critical tipping point for the series to live up to its predecessor. On *The Twilight Zone* Rod Serling had come off a long string of great live TV and anthology show teleplays. He had full control over his creation, *The Twilight Zone,* which aired on CBS.

All 100 paintings on display in the salon curated by Rod Serling in *Night Gallery* over the series' run were painted by hand on canvas in acrylic paint by Tom Wright. Some say the paintings were the soul of the show because they gave the viewer the first look of the strange and at times horrific world they were entering. Each picture frame was in the same style but not the same size or color. Wright would photograph each painting and send them to Serling, who would write his introductions based on what he saw. Tom Wright did tremendous research into the occult, in which he had a longtime interest. Wright also gave himself the challenge of trying to paint many of the works as if a different artist painted them.

On *Night Gallery* NBC took full advantage of the Rod Serling brand with one exception —they didn't give him artistic and creative control on *Night Gallery*, the vital necessary element for a show runner.

The first real look at *Night Gallery* was a TV movie in which three segments were featured. It aired on November 8, 1969 and one of the segments was directed by a young man who would become one of the most successful film directors in modern times—Steven Spielberg (1946–). The newcomer had a challenge—the great Joan Crawford (1904–1977) starred in the episode he directed. "Eyes" concerns a rich nasty woman, blind from birth, who does anything she can to get a young up-and-coming surgeon to give her sight. Things don't work out as she so meticulously planned.

Serling kept developing themes near and dear to him: the sanctity of every life, and ability for people to be who they are, the nature of evil, and the unexplained.

Color may have been a detriment for all those who watched *The Twilight Zone* and associated black-and-white photography with this kind of material. Some say Rod Serling's heart wasn't in *Night Gallery.* How do you follow up one of the most iconic TV shows of all time? Entering a new dimension is what drove Rod Serling to make television history more than once. *Night Gallery* (1970–1973) was a show designed to follow up on the great success of *The Twilight Zone* as an anthology show about strange happenings and moral tales. Serling had nothing to do with the production or the writing. He only lent his celebrity by appearing as a tour guide for brief introductions and conclusions.

See also: *Vol. 1, The 1950s–1960s:* Serling, Rod; *The Twilight Zone*.

Further Resources

Serling, Rod. 2014. *Night Gallery*. CreateSpace Independent Publishing Platform.

Skelton, Scott. 1998. *Rod Serling's Night Gallery: An After Hours Tour*. New York: Syracuse University Press.

The Night Stalker (ABC, 1974–1975)

Like many TV series during the 1970s, *The Night Stalker,* later known as *Kolchak: The Night Stalker,* could be classified as a cop show because the police were usually involved, but the lead character was actually a journalist who often interacted with cops. Its supernatural nature made it a combination horror/science fiction show. It might have been considered TV noir because bad things happened at night in a city, but Kolchak, the star character, didn't seem doomed and there rarely if ever was a femme fatale. It could be seen as a drama or a *Twilight Zone, Thriller,* or *The Outer Limits* kind of program. However it is categorized, it was an unusual program well ahead of its time.

The Concept

In this one-hour show Darren McGavin (1922–2006) played Carl Kolchak, a Chicago reporter who specialized in the hard-to-believe story but worked until he had proof and answers. His beat was murder but these seem unexplainable. He wrote for the Independent News Service where his unbelieving boss (until he saw hard evidence) was Tony Vincenzo, portrayed by Simon Oakland (1915–1983).

Reports came in about murders and the description of the crime and examination of the scene pointed not to normal flesh and blood criminals, but to one of many creatures: a swamp monster, a vampire, werewolf, zombies, or even an invisible force.

Carl Kolchak was a bit of a loner and a reporter always equipped with a standard-issue note pad and pencil or pen. He often wore a light sports jacket, close to white. His distinguishing sartorial item was a straw fedora that had a large reddish band around it. He usually didn't seem to eat or sleep much when hot on a case. His interviewing technique was brusque but direct. He hounded his boss, berated the police, and was an all-around relentless wise guy who didn't stop until he proved his point to naysayers, Vincenzo, and the police.

Carl Kolchak was created by novelist Jeff Rice in the unpublished book "The Kolchak Papers." It was optioned by ABC, which turned it into a TV movie, *The Night Stalker* (1972), featuring McGavin and Oakland in the parts they would continue to play. Ratings were very high. The novel was then published in a mass-market paperback edition in 1974 under the title *The Night Stalker* with the cover featuring a photo of McGavin. A second TV movie, *The Night Strangler* (1973), also was successful.

Surprisingly, when *The Night Stalker* moved to a series, it did poorly and only lasted one season, mainly due to the time slot it was given on Friday at 10 p.m. This cut out a younger audience and those who were out on the last night of the work week and not home to watch television.

In 1976 the network aired two movies, *The Demon and the Mummy* and *Crackle of Death*; both had some newly produced footage, but also material from the episodes already aired. They were patchy at best and Darren McGavin was asked to do a voice-over to make the stories more coherent.

The original *The Night Stalker* was a strange and captivating show. Some of the inventive story lines include a series of deaths of Jewish people by a creature who could get into their minds and lure them to death by making them see a person they knew, rather than the flesh-eating creature. The investigation turned up swastikas painted everywhere, especially in the alley where the murders took place. A gentleman from India is suspected until Kolchak investigates his restaurant and learns that the Nazi symbol is also a sign from this man's homeland and is meant to protect against evil spirits. The implied violence in this episode and others has a greater impact than on-screen violence in other shows. What is in the viewers' minds is far worse than what they can see.

Time slots shouldn't matter, but they did back in the 1970s before computers and the ability to tape or DVR a show was an option. Then viewers either had to be home most nights or schedule themselves appropriately. *The Night Stalker* was like a B horror movie except one didn't have to go to the local picture show—just turn on the set at the appropriate time and day.

See also: *Vol. 1, The 1950s–1960s: Thriller*; *The Twilight Zone.*

Further Resources

Dawidziak, Mark. 1997. *The Night Stalker Companion: A 25th Anniversary Tribute*. Beverly Hills, CA: Pomegranate Press.

Henderson, C. J. 2011. *Kolchak: The Night Stalker: A Black and Evil Truth*. Calumet City, IL: Moonstone.

1972 Munich Olympics

For the 20th Olympiad the bid from Germany was successful and the games were held in Munich in 1972. The German leaders and the German people wanted to show the world how much the country had changed for the better. However, the 1972 Olympic Games were marred by tragedy as 11 Israeli athletes were taken hostage and eventually killed by a Palestinian terrorist group known as Black September. The event was widely televised, igniting an international crisis.

The Journey to Tragedy Begins

ABC Sports was the network televising the games. The Olympics are a complex media event. Many units are needed to cover all the events with numerous reporters with knowledge of the particular sport. The host of the games was one of the best in the business—Jim McKay (1921–2008). In the 1950s he covered football for CBS and anchored the 1960 Summer Olympics held in Rome. He moved to ABC and was the host of the iconic *Wide World of Sports* for 37 years.

The Munich games were scheduled for August 26 through September 11. During the opening ceremonies doves were released to send a message of world peace. The events unfolded as planned. On September 5 the unthinkable happened. A group of men calling themselves Black September, a faction of the Palestine Liberation Organization (PLO), dressed as athletes and entered the Olympic village that housed the participants in the games. Black September entered the

A member of Black September, the Palestinian terrorist group that was holding members of the Israeli wrestling team hostage, appears wearing a hood on a balcony in the Olympic village in Munich, Germany, on September 5, 1972. The ABC television network broadcast the tragic events as they unfolded. (AP Photo)

quarters of the Israeli wrestling team by force and held the men hostage at gunpoint.

It was 4:30 in the morning. The ABC sports team was made aware of the takeover and mobilized their cameras and equipment to cover what was now a major news story. It would be the moment that sports and news became one and a challenge for the ABC professionals. Chris Schenkel (1923–2005) was the official ABC host but Roone Arledge (1931–2002), the man in charge of ABC Sports, put Jim McKay on the story because he knew that McKay had the most hard news background. McKay seamlessly made the transition and when viewers woke up anticipating more sporting events, they stared in horror at the images of gunmen holding the athletes hostage. McKay began reporting what he was seeing on camera and the information fed to him when he was off camera. His role now would be to talk over the footage of the live unfolding events and appear on camera in his light-colored ABC Sports jacket as a voice of calm and accuracy. Howard Cosell (1918–1995) and Peter Jennings (1938–2005) were brought in to present different aspects of the story. The reality sunk in. Jennings was a top reporter and Cosell was probably the most recognizable voice in all of sports telejournalism.

Long lenses captured men in the windows and elsewhere, the view similar to binoculars or the sniper scope of rescuers, but it was television. There were frightening, confusing images of guns and men in ski masks, but a sure-footed McKay explained everything using all his skills and the resources of ABC. The German police planned a rescue, but it failed. An arrangement was made. The Israeli athletes and their Black September captors were to be helicoptered to an airport. The plan was abandoned and the terrorists quickly realized the Germans had tried to dupe them.

Jim McKay sat behind the center of the anchor desk with Chris Schenkel next to him. McKay has just gotten updated information—his face turned even more serious. After looking directly into the camera—into the eyes of the viewers—he actually turned screen left, away from the camera, and in profile spoke to Chris Schenkel, saying, "I just got the final word. You know when I was a kid my father used to say, 'The greatest hopes and our worse fears are seldom realized.' The worst fears have been realized tonight."

At this point Jim McKay turned and looked straight into the camera lens. "They now said there were eleven hostages, two were killed in their rooms, nine were killed at the airport tonight. They're all gone."

Those three simple words said it all. Although the broadcast and the Olympics continued, it was Jim McKay speaking from his heart, probably hearing his father's voice saying that the worst has happened. Jim McKay's reportage immediately went into the annals of both sports and news reporting for television proving that the medium was not just radio with picture, it could be the voice of humanity and the image of a man who, along with his country and the world, shared an unspeakable tragedy in the Global Village. The communication transmitted by the television medium was as envisioned by philosopher/media man Marshall McLuhan (1911–1980).

In 1985 ABC anointed Roone Arledge president of both sports and news, affirming what was learned at the Munich Olympics in 1972—that life is not compartmentalized and the world is all one—for better or worse.

See also: *Vol. 1, The 1950s–1960s:* ABC (American Broadcasting Company); Arledge, Roone.

Further Resources

Large, David Clay. 2012. *Munich 1972: Tragedy, Terror, and Triumph at the Olympic Games*. Lanham, MD: Rowman and Littlefield.

Reeve, Simon. 2001. *One Day in September: The Full Story of the 1972 Munich Olympics Massacre and the Israeli Revenge Operation: Wrath of God*. New York: Arcade.

1977 World Series

In 1977 the World Series was scheduled from October 11 to 18 and featured the Los Angeles Dodgers from the National League against the New York Yankees of the American League. ABC billed it as an ABC Sports exclusive. The broadcasters were Howard Cosell, Keith Jackson (1928–), and former pitcher Tom Seaver (1944–) in the booth. The Series would become famous for the playing of Yankees right-fielder Reggie Jackson (1946–), earning him the nickname "Mr. October" due to his heroics, hitting three home runs in Game 6, the first player to do so since Babe Ruth (1895–1946).

The Tension Mounts

As Game 6 was about to begin, the Yankees led the Series three games to two. It was a must-win for the Dodgers or else the Yankees would win their first World Series since 1962. The game was played in Yankee Stadium and the excitement was electric. Over 56,000 fans were charged up and a bit rowdy.

The manager for the Dodgers was Tommy Lasorda (1927–) and the Yankee manager was the volatile and explosive Billy Martin (1928–1989). The Yankees were owned by George Steinbrenner (1930–2010), a controversial man in his own right with a hands-on approach to the team and a mania to win the World Series for the Bronx Bombers.

Both teams had future Hall of Famers. On the Yankee roster was slugger Reggie Jackson, who had had his share of strife prior to the game. Jackson had made a remark that he was the straw that stirs the drink, which implied he was the centerpiece of the team. In a game earlier in the season, Martin felt that Jackson was not making enough of an effort to play his best. This resulted in a physical fight in which both men had to be separated by the other players. Steinbrenner told Martin that if he didn't make Jackson, known as a great hitter, fourth in the lineup, known as the cleanup spot, a player who can bring men in with a stroke of the bat, he should leave the Yankees.

During Game 6, both teams played well and the Dodgers fought to the end. The Yankees had a good pitcher and in every position there was building momentum. In the third inning Reggie Jackson hit a smashing home run, estimated at 475 feet. In the fourth inning he was up again and blasted his second home run of the night, scoring two other players. In the fifth inning he was up once again and hit a three-run homer for his third home run. The crowd and the seasoned pros in the broadcast booth were stunned. They immediately reported that only one man had hit three home runs in a game and he did it twice—Ruth, in 1926 and 1928. Reggie Jackson won the MVP (Most Valuable Player) that year and became forever known as Mr. October. The field announcer told the fans to stay in their seats and not step on the field. As the end of the inning came closer there were rows of fans in the lower deck with their legs over the ledge ready to go. When the last out was called, a group of Yankees huddled and celebrated. Like a mass exodus, fans from everywhere filled the playing field.

Earlier Reggie Jackson, who played right field, saw paper and other junk being thrown on the field. At least one fan (off-camera) was reported by the booth as approaching Jackson and shaking his hand, as the player escorted him off the field. Jackson started to jog in and the booth thought he was coming in for the night, but, in reality, he came downfield to get a helmet for protection from the fans.

The call of "strike" that ended the game was a clarion call for Jackson. One of the ABC cameras stayed on Jackson as he tore through the crowded field as if he were a linebacker, zigging and zagging at top speed; the camera continued to follow Jackson and he had no choice but to knock aside two fans he couldn't get around. The shot ended with Jackson like lightning disappearing into the locker room.

For ABC Sports the 1977 World Series was a triumph. A player hitting three home runs in a single game is a rare accomplishment, made even more astonishing as it occurred during the sport's championship event. To date, only four players have hit three home runs in a single game during the World Series: Ruth, Jackson, Albert Pujols (St. Louis Cardinals, 2011), and Pablo Sandoval (San Francisco Giants, 2012). The network's coverage filled with cameras, graphics, and split-screen effects made it a memorable television event of the decade.

See also: *Vol. 1, The 1950s–1960s:* ABC (American Broadcasting Company); The World Series.

Further Resources

Jackson, Reggie, and Kevin Baker. 2013. *Becoming Mr. October: The Revealing Story of* Reggie Jackson *and the World Champion New York Yankees*. New York: Random House.

Pennington, Bill. 2015. *Billy Martin: Baseball's Flawed Genius*. Boston: Houghton Mifflin Harcourt.

Nudity on Television

Movie censors were long concerned with the impact of female nudity in films and were strict in controlling revealing images until the 1960s. Filmmakers reflected the tenor of the times and the sexual revolution that was going on outside the movie theater. The 1970s were going even further with male nudity and full frontal views. For television networks, sex sold but it had to be hidden with innuendo. This all changed on May 4, 1973 when actress Valerie Perrine (1943–) who was a former Las Vegas showgirl, became the first woman to bare her breasts on television. It happened on PBS in an adaption of the play *Steambath* in which people in the title location realize they are in the afterlife and that God is the Puerto Rican towel attendant. The nudity occurs when the Perrine character takes a shower. On October 20, 1976 Farrah Fawcett's naked breast accidentally popped out of her detective clothes on *Charlie's Angels.* Somehow this was not caught in postproduction before air. During the historic broadcast of *Roots* in 1977 native women of color were shown topless in the name of realism. There was controversy—there were those who felt nudity shouldn't be on network television, also some many were angry that it apparently was acceptable to display nudity with women of color, but not for Caucasian women. It was as if the *Roots* production was doing a television version of *National Geographic*, which printed photos of unclothed African and other indigenous women. Many women also criticized the fact that during this time, women, and rarely men, were shown without clothes, which was also true in movies. This would all change in the future, maybe to excess, in cable and subscription-based services

Further Resources

Faraci, Devin. 2012. "The Sad Story of Hollywood's First Naked Lady, Audrey Munson." Jan 19. http://birthmoviesdeath.com/2012/06/19/the-sad-story-of-hollywoods-first-naked-lady-audrey-munson

Friedman, Bruce Jay. 1971. *Steambath: A Play.* New York: Knopf.

The Odd Couple (ABC, 1970–1975)

On March 10, 1965, the Plymouth Theatre (which became the Eugene O'Neill Theatre shortly after) on Broadway experienced the premiere of a new play by Neil Simon (1927–), directed by Mike Nichols (1931–2014) and starring Walter Matthau (1920–2000) as Oscar Madison and Art Carney (1919–2003) as Felix Unger—it was *The Odd Couple.*

> Neil Simon (1927–) is best known as a playwright, but he also wrote for radio and television. He had been working as a mailroom clerk in the New York offices of Warner Brothers and got together with his brother Danny Simon (1918–2005), also a writer. They were tutored by the great Ace Goodman (1899–1982) and later wrote for *The Robert Q Lewis Show* (1950–1951) on radio when Sid Caesar (1922–2014) hired them to join his writing team for *Your Show of Shows* (1950–1954). Neil Simon began a streak of plays, *Come Blow Your Horn* (1961), *Little Me* (1962), and *Barefoot in the Park* (1963), then one of his all-time greatest hits, *The Odd Couple* in 1965, which served as the inspiration for the hit sitcom. Neil Simon went on to write over 25 more plays.

The play about a sloppy, well-known New York City sportswriter and a meticulous and obsessive photographer, Oscar and Felix, living together under one roof was a comic conflict that audiences loved and laughed long and hard at.

A movie followed with Matthau reprising his role and with Jack Lemmon (1925–2001) as Felix with a screenplay by Simon and directed by Gene Saks (1921–2015). Released to movie theaters nationwide, it too was a success and had audiences wanting more; so television listened.

The Odd Couple Come to Television

The co-executive producer of the television series *The Odd Couple,* Garry Marshall, had a challenge from the beginning in terms of casting. The choices were Martin Balsam (1919–1996) or Mickey Rooney (1920–2014) as Oscar and either Dean Martin (1917–1995) or Art Carney as Felix. There were two other actors to consider, Tony Randall (1920–2004) and Jack Klugman (1922–2012), who had been in different stage productions of the play. Tony Randall was officially hired first and he fought hard with the producers to have Mickey Rooney play Oscar Madison to his Felix

Jack Klugman (left) as Oscar Madison and Tony Randall as Felix Unger in the 1970s situation comedy *The Odd Couple*, about two very different men who, after divorcing their wives, end up sharing an apartment together. (CBS Photo Archive/Getty Images)

Unger, but Marshall did everything he could to lobby for Klugman and the rest is history—it was Klugman and Randall as Oscar and Felix.

The team of writers was committed to the concept of the play and had little trouble coming up with equally funny or in some cases funnier situations for Oscar and Felix.

The show's weekly opening depicted the situation, explained by a deep-voiced narrator who began by stating the exact day, November 13, but not the year, maybe 1970 when the TV series first aired. He went on to say that Felix Unger was told to leave his apartment and never return—that edict came from his wife. Felix, having really nowhere to go, heads to the apartment of his friend Oscar Madison, whom Felix remembered was also thrown out of his apartment by his wife. After some cajoling and begging Oscar decides to take Felix in—and establishes the show's premise: can two divorced men live together without killing each other?

Oscar Madison was sloppy in action and dress; he smokes a big, smelly cigar in the house. He constantly goes to sporting events for his job and likes to gamble. He likes women and keeps a black book containing all shapes and sizes. He is loud and not particularly sensitive; he is driven nuts by Felix but continues to love him.

Felix Unger is a toxic neatnik. He is obsessive, rarely stops talking, and is easily hurt. Felix constantly cleans the apartment right down to the bone. He is the house cook and prepares gourmet food although Oscar would prefer a hot dog slathered in mustard or a greasy cheeseburger. The two men argue all the time. Felix represents culture and high class and Oscar is a man of the New York City streets, but in the end Felix loves Oscar.

The cast also included Al Molinaro (1919–2015), a friend who was also Murray the cop; the Pigeon Sisters, Cecily and Gwen, played by Monica Evans and Carole Shelley (1939–); Elinor Donahue (1937–) as Dr. Nancy Cunningham, Felix's female friend; and Penny Marshall (1943–) (the co-executive producer's sister) played Myrna Turner, Oscar's secretary.

A typical episode involves Oscar coming home with four tickets to a hot Broadway play. Felix quickly gets a date but Oscar exhausts his little black book and has no luck. The three go to the theater. Oscar and Felix's date go inside while Felix tries to give the ticket away to a pretty young lady; there is a misunderstanding and Felix is arrested for the illegal sale of a theater ticket. Oscar comes out to see what's keeping his friend and then he is arrested as well. Back in the apartment Oscar is angry that they didn't settle the matter in night court but had a day court date set when Felix will act as their attorney. At the trial Felix annoys everyone, especially the judge. They are still found not guilty but because Felix humiliated Oscar in court, he wants the verdict turned around. The judge eventually fines him for contempt of court. Felix still won't stop talking and complaining and Oscar drags him out by the judge's order.

The series had a cut-and-dried logical ending. Felix gets married for the second time and leaves the apartment. Oscar now can be as sloppy as he wants to be, not have anyone inspecting him up and down and able to do what he wants when he wants to.

In 2015, CBS revived the *Odd Couple* product with a new sitcom starring Matthew Perry as Oscar Madison and Thomas Lennon as Felix Unger. In 2016, CBS renewed the show for a third season, appearing in October of that year, however, no additional episodes were ordered following that season.

Further Resources

Klugman, Jack, and Garry Marshall. 2013. *Tony and Me: A Story of Friendship*. West Linn, OR: Good Hill Press.

Leszczak, Bob. 2014. *The Odd Couple on Stage and Screen: A History with Cast and Crew Profiles and an Episode Guide*. Jefferson, NC: McFarland.

Owen Marshall: Counselor at Law (ABC, 1971–1974)

This legal drama was popular with television viewers because Owen Marshall, played by Arthur Hill (1922–2006), was a staid and solid defense lawyer who was passionate and understood how the pressing legal issues of the day impacted the small town in California where he maintained his practice.

For Owen Marshall, whether the issues were civil rights, murder, or desertion from the army during the Vietnam War, he treated the accused with a quiet but firm voice and was respected by everyone, opposition included.

There was a distinct connection between *Owen Marshall: Counselor at Law* and *Marcus Welby, M.D.* Both were practitioners in small towns and had a similar humanistic manner; in fact there were two joint episodes in which the lawyer defended someone connected to the doctor.

Owen Marshall was a widower, and his 12-year-old daughter Melissa was played by Christine Matchett (1957–). Frieda, his loyal law clerk, was portrayed by Joan Darling (1935–), who later had great success as a writer and director on shows like *Mary Hartman, Mary Hartman* (1976–1977) and *The Mary Tyler Moore Show* (1970–1977).

Over the course of its run, Owen Marshall had several young law clerks: Jess Brandon was played by Lee Majors (1939–), who was also in another ABC show, *The Six Million Dollar Man* (1973–1978). He was released and replaced by David Soul (1943–), who played Ted Warrick. Danny Paterno also was a partner during the final season, played by Reni Santoni (1939–).

Owen Marshall: Counselor at Law was such a realistic show that the legal community applauded it and it won several public service awards. It is rare to apply the word "folksy" to a law show, but Owen Marshall knew just about everyone in his environs and he was well liked. The show tackled issues of importance and Marshall was a serious man, but his manner put everyone at ease, a welcome quality for any television show.

See also: *Mary Hartman, Mary Hartman*; *The Mary Tyler Moore Show*; *The Six Million Dollar Man*.

Further Resources

Asimow, Michael, ed. 2009. *Lawyers in Your Living Room: Law on Television*. Chicago: American Bar Association.

The Paper Chase (CBS, 1978–1979; Showtime, 1983–1986)

This one-hour drama based on John Jay Osborn Jr.'s novel was first made into a motion picture of the same name, directed by James Bridges and released in 1975. The focus of attention was the feared Harvard law instructor Charles W. Kingsfield Jr. played by John Houseman (1902–1988), who badgered students to either learn or fail. Although there are many students, male and female, involved in the story and in Kingsfield's first-year contract law class, James T. Hart, played by Timothy Bottoms (1951–) was a focal point. In the television series Hart was portrayed by James Stephens (1951–).

Background of John Houseman

John Houseman was a formidable figure. He was a producer for Orson Welles (1915–1985) on many innovative and controversial stage productions with interpretations of Shakespeare such as the 1936 "Voodoo *Macbeth*" and on the radio with projects like *War of the Worlds* (1938), which caused panic when listeners really thought there was an invasion from outer space. He produced what is considered one of the greatest American movies ever made, *Citizen Kane* (1941).

After producing a large number of motion pictures for major studios including *The Blue Dahlia* (1946) and *Julius Caesar* (1953), Houseman was the founding director of the drama division at the Juilliard School, where he taught notable actors such as Kevin Kline (1947–) and Patti LuPone (1949–).

Barely having any acting experience outside of teaching at Juilliard, Houseman was asked to play Kingsfield in a film version of *The Paper Chase* and to reprise his role in the television series. Casting John Houseman in the first place was smart, even cagey. He wasn't very well known, but the role had made him a star, so the audience believed him because he looked the part. Houseman was an imposing man with razor-sharp diction. He was someone who looked as if he stood above everyone, a person with authority who could be condescending.

James Bridges (1936–1993), the director of *The Paper Chase* motion picture, helped to set up the TV series for many reasons but most importantly for John Houseman. Bridges had been Houseman's protégé and considered the older man a mentor. After the setup Bridges's involvement was minimal. The author of the book, John Jay Osborn Jr., who was one of the authors of the screenplay for the movie, wrote some teleplays for *The Paper Chase* TV series.

The tone of *The Paper Chase* on TV was equivalent to the movie with weekly stories about the educational and personal progress of the students, mostly James T. Hart. The show was unusual even for the 1970s, a law school drama that can be considered a subgenre of the legal drama, as if the audience was watching Owen Marshall or Perry Mason going to law school, up-scaled.

Showtime brought the show back in 1983, airing seasons 2 through 4 with both Houseman and Stephens. Hart finally graduated from law school at the end of the fourth season.

See also: Showtime; *Vol. 1, The 1950s–1960s: Perry Mason*.

Further Resources

Osborn, John Jay Jr. 1978. *The Paper Chase*. Malden, MA: Popular Library.

Houseman, John. 1972. *Run Through: A Memoir*. New York: Simon & Schuster.

The Partridge Family (ABC, 1970–1974)

This half-hour sitcom broadcast by ABC captured a young audience because it was about a widowed mother and her family of six who decide to hit the road as a rock and roll band. The mother, Shirley Partridge, was played by Shirley Jones (1934–). David Cassidy (1950–), her real-life stepson, played Keith; Susan Dey (1952–) was Laurie; Danny Bonaduce (1959–) played Danny; Jeremy Gelbwaks (1961–) (1970–1971) and Brian Forster (1960–) (1971–1974) played Chris;

The Partridge Family was a musical sitcom about a family that toured as a rock/pop band. Pictured here (from left to right) are cast members Shirley Jones, Danny Bonaduce, Brian Forster, Suzanne Crough, Susan Dey, and David Cassidy. (GAB Archive/Redferns)

Suzanne Crough (1963–2015) played Tracy; and Dave Madden (1931–2014) played their manager.

This series was inspired by the Cowsills, a rock band consisting of a mother and her six kids that was formed in 1965. They became extremely popular, making appearances on television shows and creating hit records like "The Rain, the Park, and Other Things," "Indian Lake," and their rendition of "Hair" from the Broadway show. There was an attempt to hire the Cowsills for the TV show but none of them were actors, so the casting shifted.

David Cassidy was a teen idol at the time, so his appearance brought countless teenage girls and others to their sets. There was a theme song, "When We're Singing," and plenty of music and typical sitcom hijinks usually centered on the family's sibling interactions and dealings with their mother. The show was an unusual combination of genres—musical performance and comedy.

The music of *The Partridge Family* was soft rock, which was palatable for many but not enough for those who preferred hard rock. It was also a family show sufficiently wholesome to please the majority of parents.

Further Resources

Cassidy, David, and Chip Deffaa. 1994. *C'mon Get Happy: Fear and Loathing on the Partridge Family Bus.* New York: Warner Books.

Jones, Shirley. 2014. *Shirley Jones: A Memoir.* New York: Gallery Books.

PBS (Public Broadcasting Service) (1970–)

The U.S. public broadcasting system comprises hundreds of local stations and several large national bureaucracies. The most recognizable symbol of this labyrinth is PBS, the logo of the Public Broadcasting Service, which appears on all nationally distributed public television programs, designed so that the letters P-B-S vaguely resemble the human brain. Since its creation in the late 1960s, PBS has positioned itself as the "oasis" of the vast wasteland—a home for televised art, intellectual culture, education, and quality information in a sea of mass cultural mediocrity. For almost as long, PBS has also been the principal target of politically charged disputes over public broadcasting's performance in the United States.

Public television arrived late in the United States. Whereas the United Kingdom, Canada, and many other Western democracies developed public service approaches to broadcasting that were overseen by tax-funded national broadcasting authorities, the United States took a "free-market" approach to radio and television. Not everyone supported this path: throughout the 1920s and into the 1930s, vocal educators, labor unions, and progressive reformers pressured the federal government to allocate a significant portion of the spectrum to nonprofit channels. The corporate sector's lobbying power, coupled with a distrust of "socialistic" activity in the American context, worked against this possibility, however. The 1934 Communications Act entrusted broadcasting entirely to the commercial market, presuming that private companies could turn a profit and serve the public interest as well.

In the 1950s and 1960s, fissures in the U.S. approach to broadcasting emerged. At this time, television culture was dominated by three networks (ABC, CBS, and NBC), and most programming was geared toward a huge mass audience. High-placed critics began to protest what they perceived as television's lowbrow homogeneity and worried that the nation's most popular medium did little to instruct or enlighten citizens. To correct these problems, the prestigious Ford Foundation invested considerable private resources in National Educational Television (NET), a small-scale alternative devoted to "respectable" culture such as operas, live plays, and British dramas and information such as documentaries and panel discussions. However, Ford's pockets were not bottomless and "educational" television remained a minor blip on the television landscape. Public investment was clearly needed to create a public alternative to market-driven commercial hegemony.

In the 1960s, the case for public television was advanced by many public figures, including former Federal Communications Commission (FCC) chairman Newton Minow and political columnist Walter Lippmann. In 1966, the philanthropic Carnegie Corporation of New York assembled a high-powered team of Ivy League intellectuals, renowned artists, university presidents, corporate executives, and other high-profile individuals to "look into" the issue; their report recommended "immediate federal action." The Public Broadcasting Act was swiftly passed by Congress and signed into law by President Lyndon Johnson in 1967, and programs carrying the PBS logo began to appear in late 1969. Defined as a "Chance for Better Television," PBS claimed a redemptive cultural identity and cultivated an aesthetic based more on pre-electronic media such as live drama and the printed word than on contemporary TV formats. Because PBS had been created to solve a range of perceived cultural problems without fundamentally altering the economic landscape of commercial television, it could not compete for the hearts and minds of TV viewers and maintain its legitimacy.

Children's programming was originally much more popular than adult PBS genres—largely because of *Sesame Street.* In 1969, Children's Television Workshop (CTW), the creators of *Sesame Street*, appropriated the look and style of popular television—including TV commercials—to "sell" cognitive and social skills to children. Contrary to prime-time PBS, which focused on small and usually upscale audiences, the goal was to reach as many kids as possible. CTW was concerned with poverty issues and *Sesame Street* received some of its funding from the Department of Health, Education, and Welfare to operate as a televised Head Start program for poor preschool children, which provided an impetus to bring "disadvantaged" child viewers, in particular, into the public television audience. Producers cleverly fused fast-paced visuals, humor, irony, storytelling, and celebrity guest stars to educational lessons, creating a brand of television "edutainment" that was spun off into *The Electric Company*, *Zoom*, and other shows. Children's programming continues to attract a cross-class, multicultural presence to PBS—but now as before, most kids tend to "drop out" of the public TV audience when they become adults.

PBS began offering more scripted programs in addition to educational programming in the 1970s with *Masterpiece Theatre*, although the programs at this time still focused on the arts. By the 2000s, the renamed *Masterpiece* housed many programs that provided entertainment, allowing PBS to diversify its programming content. Major hits like *Downton Abbey* and *Sherlock*, originally produced by the British Broadcasting Corporation (BBC), were released through PBS to U.S. audiences.

Laurie Ouellette

See also: *The Electric Company*; *Frontline*; *The Joy of Painting*; *Masterpiece Theatre*; *The McLaughlin Group*; *Sneak Previews*; *This Old House*; *Vietnam: A Television History*; *Vol. 1, The 1950s–1960s: Book Beat*; *Captain Kangaroo*; *Mister Rogers' Neighborhood*; *Sesame Street*; *Washington Week in Review*; *Vol. 3, The 1990s–Present: Downton Abbey*; *Sherlock*.

Further Resources

Ledbetter, James. 1998. *Made Possible By: The Death of Public Broadcasting in the United States*. London: Verso.

Lewis, Justin, and Toby Miller, eds. 2002. *Critical Cultural Policy: A Reader*. London: Blackwell.

Ouellette, Laurie. 2002. *Viewers Like You? How Public TV Failed the People*. New York: Columbia University Press.

The Phil Donahue Show (Syndication, 1970–1996)

Phil Donahue (1935–) began his career as a talk show host in 1967 when he worked in a local venue in Dayton, Ohio. The show was successful and by 1970 it was syndicated across the country. Stations carrying the show increased steadily over the decade of the 1970s. In 1977 Phil Donahue made a critical decision that greatly increased his visibility and popularity. He made Chicago the home base for his show. He became a brand when the show became known as *Donahue*. The show ran for a full hour and often had a single guest.

Throughout the seventies Phil Donahue's brown, fashionably long, slightly grey hair became notably longer and grey/stone white. The set was a stage with chairs and microphones and often foliage of some sort. There was a very lively in-studio audience. Donohue worked with a fixed mike when on stage so he and his guest could be hands free. When Phil Donohue stood up and went into the audience, he worked a hand mike.

The programing on *The Phil Donahue Show* embraced a wide range of personalities and celebrities. Guests during the 1970s included Christina Crawford (1939–), daughter of Hollywood superstar Joan Crawford, who wrote a best-selling book, "Mommie Dearest," published in 1978, which details the very bad behavior the actress demonstrated toward her child; a member of the American Nazi Party dressed in full uniform who was ready to march in Skokie, Illinois, home to many Holocaust survivors, some of whom were members of the studio audience; Johnny Carson (1925–2005), the famed late night show host; Ayn Rand (1905–1982), objectivist philosopher and writer best known for her novel *The Fountainhead*, published first in 1943; Betty Hutton (1921–2007), Hollywood movie star who fell on hard times and rose back; and David Duke (1950–), a grand wizard of the Ku Klux Klan (KKK).

Profile of a Maverick Interviewer

What distinguished Phil Donahue from the pack as an interviewer was a complex style that made the

President Jimmy Carter's wife, Rosalynn Carter, is interviewed by Phil Donahue in front of a studio audience at the WGN-TV studios in Chicago on May 16, 1979. The popular program featured a range of guests and Donahue was a perceptive and detailed interviewer. (AP Photo/Charles Knoblock)

subject comfortable at times, uncomfortable at times, and sometimes exposed. Donahue started with an introduction. Sometimes, usually for actors and other celebrities, there would be a generous opening, then the guest would walk out to thunderous applause as they approached the stage and sat down with the host. Donahue would then begin by detailing the person's accomplishments in a lengthy run of sentences that actually told the person what they had done. He would ask questions to clarify, to provoke, and would interrupt at times. Donahue sat at the edge of his chair—his hand moving constantly and expressively. The guests generally responded in an open and detailed manner because of Donahue's thorough examination. The audience would applaud during this portion of the show.

Phil Donahue's forte was working the audience with a hand mike. Taking their lead from the host, audience questions were sharp and direct. Phil Donahue seemed to fly through the audience going from one side to another. He seemed to come even further alive when he was in the pit with the audience.

Donahue always made it clear that he was a political liberal and supported liberal causes. He came across as a regular guy who was interested in furthering his understanding through communication. This man-of-the-people quality made Phil Donahue a superstar of daytime talk.

ABC-CLIO

See also: *Geraldo*; *The Oprah Winfrey Show*; *Sally Jessy Raphael.*

Further Resources

Donahue, Phil, and Company. 1980. *Donahue: My Own Story*. New York: Simon & Schuster.

Moll, James. 2001. "Phil Donahue: Talk Show Host." *The Archive of American Television*. May 9. http://www.emmytvlegends.org/interviews/people/phil-donahue

Police Story (NBC, 1973–1977)

Joseph Wambaugh (1937–), the creator of *Police Story*, was a policeman and then author of bestselling novels about the subject. Wambaugh joined the Los Angeles Police Department (LAPD) in 1960. He served as a patrolman and detective sergeant for 14 years. He attended California State University in Los Angeles and earned bachelor's and master's degrees. Wambaugh's first novel, *The New Centurions* (1971), focused on the stresses on police in Los Angeles. It was a *New York Times* bestseller and was made into a film in 1972. Further success followed. *Police Story*, an anthology series about the lives and work of LAPD police, was Wambaugh's idea. He was the creator and production consultant on the show. The result was an accurate and realistic television series about police work and their lives.

Each episode is by the book. The dialogue and actions are not overdramatized. Technical detail informs the audience about weapons, procedures, techniques, and strategies. The viewer can observe the step by step unfolding of a crime, its police resolution, and the aftermath.

The infrastructure of the department, the ranks, chain of command, the street men and those who make rules and judgments are examined in depth. The tedium of the job and the amount of waiting at a crime scene is convincing. The personal lives of the characters and their varied personalities are portrayed in full-bodied, convincing profiles. Personal problems that impact police such as drinking, high divorce rates, and psychological problems were depicted.

Each week was a new story and a new cast. Some actors who appeared on *Police Story* included Jan-Michael Vincent (1944–), James Farentino (1938–2012), Lloyd Bridges (1913–1998), Tony Lo Bianco (1936–), and Don Meredith (1938–2010).

Police Story was an important departure from prior cop/detective shows that were designed to entertain and featured colorful characters with bombastic action sequences. *Police Story* was authentic and educated the public about police work. Ultimately it gave viewers respect for a very difficult and necessary job.

See also: *Police Woman*.

Further Resources

Wambaugh, Joseph. 1977. *The Black Marble*. New York: Delacorte Press.

Wambaugh, Joseph. 1970. *The New Centurions*. New York: Dell.

Police Woman (NBC, 1974–1978)

Before television audiences saw Angie Dickinson (1931–), the capable and sexy blonde actress had been in many movies including *Rio Bravo* (1959), *The Killers* (1964), and *Point Blank* (1967). By the 1970s it was not unusual for popular movie stars to make the transition from the big to the small screen. Practically from the beginning of television, actresses had shifted from motion pictures to the television format. Lucille Ball, Ida Lupino, and Donna Reed are notable examples. Angie Dickinson had a presold audience from those who knew her on film. *Police Woman* was an adult show targeted for a mature audience. Women liked Dickinson because she had been in a variety of pictures with popular leading men. She had an appealing look, not overly glamorous, but a woman who could put herself together, then go out and take on the world. Men liked her for many of the same reasons; her image was that of a woman who could go shoulder to shoulder with a man.

It's difficult to classify *Police Woman* as a women's liberation show. It did have a woman in a job usually performed by a man—she was a policewoman, although she didn't wear the uniform often. At least at the beginning of the series, Sergeant "Pepper" Anderson, who was a divorcee, was asked to go undercover as either a prostitute, a B-girl, or someone a bad guy would hire to pretty-up his surroundings. So her costume usually was a very low-cut dress with some cleavage and lots of clothing changes, but Pepper played it fairly straight and avoided direct contact with the baddies, making arrests using the handgun in her purse.

The producers hired Angie Dickinson for her famous name and because she was sexy and commanded the camera's gaze. Many saw this as a breakthrough role for women.

The origin of *Police Woman* traces back to the anthology police series *Police Story* created by Joseph Wambaugh (1937–), a former police officer who became a best-selling author of novels about police, their jobs and lives. The show rotated characters and stories. *Police Woman* was in the rotation.

Her boss, Sergeant Bill Crowley, was played by Earl Holliman (1928–). The two spent a lot of time with each other and had great chemistry. His character was in an unusual situation for the times, a male cop supervising a female cop; he supported her, backed her up, and a sexual frisson buzzed through the show.

The locale was California—the Los Angeles Police Department. In the pilot, Dickinson's character, then called Lisa Beaumont, worked at a facility for troubled children, and it was established that her sister attended the program.

Police Woman could be considered just another cop show except that gender brought many issues into play. These included the crimes that were investigated, a woman's role in urban society, and the differences between a policeman undercover and a policewoman in the same circumstance. The show was well written and engaged the audience, who were pulled into the narrative each week while wondering if there were differences between male and female police officers.

See also: *Charlie's Angels.*

Further Resources

Trevor, Leslie. 1975. *Angie Dickinson Is Police Woman: #1 The Rape*. Award.

Trevor, Leslie. 1975. *Angie Dickinson as Police Woman: #3 Death of a Call Girl*. Award.

The Psychiatrist (NBC, 1970–1971)

From the beginning of television the fictional dramatic series had presented, in ancillary parts, the profession of psychiatrist as a character called in or visited to discuss psychological issues or mental illness. Their function was often to advise a family, law enforcement, or a governmental person or body about the condition and behavior of a loved one, a suspect, or political personage. The characterizations tended to be stereotypical, with qualities the audience, especially those not familiar with psychiatry, would expect to see. The role of the TV psychiatrist most often was to pass judgment on the person in question pertaining to the plot. The role of psychiatrist was part of a genre, usually a drama, a police/detective show, or a medical program.

New Ground Is Broken

The Psychiatrist created its own genre—the psychiatrist show. *The Psychiatrist* was a medical drama but up to 1979 it was the only television program to feature a professional psychiatrist as the main and principal character, a person at the center of each episode's story.

Jim Whitman, played by Roy Thinnes, best known at the time for his starring role in the cult show *The Invaders* (1967–1968), was a young psychiatrist associated with a Los Angeles, California institute examining mental issues and dedicated to serving the community in which it was based. Whitman did not practice the standard approach in treating emotionally troubled people, although he did conduct private and group therapy sessions. His older colleague, Dr. Bernard Altman, played by the legendary stage actor Luther Adler (1903–1984), represented the old school of psychiatry functioning in a new world of mental issues. Whitman was trying to break new ground in his field by spending enormous amounts of time with his patients, even seeing them outside the office, or whenever they needed him, day or night. He was committed to investigating his patients' inner selves at all costs.

The Psychiatrist first aired on NBC as part of what is known as a wheel series in which several different shows are rotated in the same time slot. The wheel series had an umbrella title under which the shows were shown. This one was called *Four-in-One* (1970–1971). Six episodes of four dramatic shows, *The Psychiatrist, McCloud* (1970–1977)*, San Francisco International Airport* (1970) and *Night Gallery* (1970–1973) were broadcast in order, then interspersed and rerun. A different series was aired each week. After *McCloud* was picked up for another wheel series, the *NBC Mystery Movie* (1971–1977), *Night Gallery* (1970–1973) was chosen to run as a stand-alone series, but *San Francisco International Airport* and *The Psychiatrist* were both cancelled. In the end *The Psychiatrist* had a two-hour pilot and six episodes.

Thinnes's character, Jim Whitman, was long and lean with blonde hair. Emotionally he was very complex with a turbulent inner life, pulled toward a woman in a mental hospital with whom he'd had a relationship. He is by turns focused, distracted, angry, gentle, reassuring, assertive, and even combative with his patients. He spends more time out of the office and facility than in one-on-one sessions and group therapy. The real world is very important to him and his major goal is to help people cope with that outer world in their individual ways.

Dr. Altman may be the old guard, but he is very much aware of how the world changed from his era to the sixties. He is concerned that the country is going to split apart. Jim embraces the new world and finds hope in it. He sees it as his role to keep it on track.

The psychological jargon, information, process, and purpose on *The Psychiatrist* may have been unorthodox, but from Jim Whitman's point of view he is finding new and exciting methodology. His approach outside the building is untraditional; the show is about reinventing the psychiatric wheel.

Some of the dialogue is a bit stiff and sounds as if it comes from the sixties, with terms like "I dig," "groovy," and "freaking out," but the scripts are intelligently written. Those who watched *The Psychiatrist* were viewing experimental drama investigating an aspect of a subject that was part of a brave new world.

The Psychiatrist is also notable because Steven Spielberg (1946–) directed two episodes, "The Private World of Martin Dalton," which aired on February 10, 1971, and "Par for the Course" airing on March 10, 1971. With *The Psychiatrist* network television once again proved it could offer shows with dramatic entertainment that probed innovative subject matter.

See also: *McCloud*; *Night Gallery*.

Further Resources

Huskinson, Lucy, and Terrie Waddell, eds. 2014. *Eavesdropping: The Psychotherapist in Film and Television*. London: Routledge.

Lieberman, Jeffrey A., M.D., and Ogi Ogas. 2015. *Shrinks: The Untold Story of Psychiatry*. New York: Hachette Book Group.

Quincy, M.E. (NBC, 1976–1983)

Quincy, as it was more popularly known, was a unique medical show because it was also a police or detective drama. This is because Quincy (it is unclear if his first name was ever mentioned) is a medical examiner in the Los Angeles County Coroner's office. The show began as one of the segments of *The Sunday Night Mystery Movie* (1971–1977) and was given a series go-ahead in 1977.

Jack Klugman played the lead role. The character usually had a first assessment when he conducted an autopsy, but then something gnaws at him and he suspects foul play, thus the transition between a medical show and the detective/cop genre.

Quincy was heavily influenced by the real-life medical examiner Thomas Noguchi (1927–), who had been the chief medical examiner–coroner for the county of Los Angeles from 1967 to 1988. He was very high profile because he handled the autopsies and deaths of many prominent celebrities. Noguchi also was known to make controversial statements and pronouncements.

Klugman made the character his own; he was impatient, quick to anger, a gentleman to the ladies, demanding, and on his own would follow what he knew was a crime to the end. One of the interesting points of the show is the mechanics of an autopsy and the medical issues concerning death.

Each week there were new cases and a new crime. The writers were encouraged to find a wide range of cases where the deaths were indeed suspicious. Quincy's great knowledge of forensic medicine constantly put him at odds with the police. Quincy would conduct his own investigation, ignoring law enforcement. The conflict between the two forces created tension and drama.

When an actor such as Jack Klugman has played another major part in a popular series as Klugman did with Oscar Madison in *The Odd Couple* (1970–1975), he can bring some of the DNA of the early character. Audiences liked Klugman and were quick to make the transition of roles. They knew the man with that wonderful gravelly voice who often barked words more than spoke them. What cemented the shows was that, although the characters were different, Klugman brought some recognizable qualities of Oscar to Quincy, the unrest and the jump to anger delivered with classic Klugman traits.

See also: *The Odd Couple*.

Further Resources

Rosin, James. 2009. *Quincy M.E. the Television Series*. Albany, GA: Bear Manor Media.

Timmermans, Stefan. 2006. *Postmortem: How Medical Examiners Explain Suspicious Deaths*. Chicago, IL: University of Chicago Press.

Rich Man, Poor Man (ABC, 1976)

One of the early miniseries, *Rich Man, Poor Man* was a 12-part adaptation of the novel of the same name that aired on ABC in 1976. The novel was written by Irwin Shaw (1913–1984). Born Irwin Gilber Shamforoff, he began his career at 21 writing radio scripts for the *Andy Gump* (1931–1937) and *Dick Tracy* (1934–1948) radio shows. He also wrote short stories for popular magazines. Shaw fought in World War II and saw a lot of action fighting in the European theater. Back home he translated his experiences into *The Young Lions,* published in 1948 and filmed in 1948. He continued to write successful novels. *Rich Man, Poor Man* was published in 1970 and badly trounced by the literary critics of the day. This miniseries was such a strong success it spawned *Rich Man, Poor Man: Book II*, which aired in 1976–1977. The original production ranked third in the seasonal Nielsen ratings and stacked up a whopping 23 Emmy nominations, winning four: Edward Asner, Outstanding Lead Actor for a Single Appearance in a Drama or Comedy Series; Fionnula Flanagan (1941–), Single Performance by a Supporting Actress in a Drama or Comedy Series; David Greene (1921–2003), Outstanding Directing in a Drama Series; and Alex North (1910–1991), Outstanding Music Composition for a Series.

The story follows the lives of the Jordache family from 1945 to 1965. Peter Strauss (1947–) played Rudy Jordache and Nick Nolte (1941–) played his brother Tom. Their father, Axel Jordache, was portrayed by Edward Asner (1929–), and the mother, Mary Jordache, was played by Dorothy McGuire (1918–2001). The love interest, Julie Prescott, was played by Susan Blakeley (1948–). The rest of the huge cast was made up of movie and television stars who played the various characters intersecting with the family's lives over the years.

Axel is German and was involved in World War I in his home country. He is an angry man and sings the praises of Germany on the evening World War II has ended. He is an American citizen who runs a small bakery. The sons are polar opposites. Rudy is gentle, smart, and responsible and wants to go to college, and Tom is burly, belligerent, always in trouble and fighting with others and his brother. The show's major theme, stated by Mary Jordache, is how two brothers can be so different. The story traces their polar opposite lives throughout their journeys.

Although not the first miniseries to air on network television, *Rich Man, Poor Man* struck a chord with the audience of the time. It is an immigrant story and it appeared one year after America's bicentennial. Baby boomers and their parents, the Greatest Generation, were ready for an examination of immigrants and how they lived their lives and were interested in the family dynamics. Even though Rudy and Tom didn't go as far as Cain and Abel, they represented the struggle between rich and poor relatives who share blood but not always heart.

See also: *North and South*; *Roots*.

Further Resources

Shaw, Irwin. 1970. *Rich Man, Poor Man*. New York: Open Road Integrated Media.

Shnayerson, Michael. 1989. *Irwin Shaw: A Biography*. New York: Putnam.

Roots (ABC, 1977)

Television history has witnessed many great achievements. Early on it established itself as a medium different from radio or motion pictures. From the beginning it could establish a genre or format and then evolve it into an even newer structure. This was the case with the miniseries, long-form television that grew out of the drama series and made-for-TV movies, which often took a popular book, then adapted it so the story would unfold in serial style over a specific period of time.

When *Roots* was publicly announced practically no one could have predicted that it would captivate an entire nation. There had been *QB VII* (1974), *Rich Man, Poor Man* (1976), and other miniseries but once it aired, historians, critics and those in the know crowned *Roots* as one of television's greatest achievements.

Seen here is actor LeVar Burton as Kunta Kinte in the landmark 1977 miniseries *Roots*. The nine-hour epic captured the hearts and minds of millions of Americans and firmly established the miniseries as a successful format for television. (Mondadori Portfolio via Getty Images)

The Book

This life-changing experience was based on the book *Roots: The Saga of an American Family,* written by African American writer Alex Haley (1922–1992). Haley was barely getting by as a freelance writer when in 1962 *Playboy* magazine gave him the assignment of interviewing innovative trumpeter Miles Davis. Pleased with the results, the magazine put Haley on a track of interviews of prominent African Americans including Martin Luther King, Sammy Davis Jr., Quincy Jones, and the controversial civil rights leader Malcolm X. This last interview led to a seminal book on civil rights when Malcolm X asked Haley to write what became *The Autobiography of Malcolm X: As Told to Alex Haley*, published in 1965. Haley was swamped with offers and assignments but chose to embark on a massive project in which he would research and document the journey of his ancestors from Africa to slavery. The book was a huge bestseller when it was published in 1976 and went on to win the Pulitzer Prize in 1977.

The 12-hour miniseries was a David L. Wolper (1928–2010) production. Wolper began with nonfiction TV and motion pictures. His projects had a swagger and expansiveness that made his name a brand.

As in the book, the TV series followed Haley's ancestors from Africa into slavery, creating a searing portrait of early American life and the tortured journey of blacks from Africa to America where their struggles still echo today.

It required one of the largest casts in recent history, pulling actors from television and motion pictures. Many were known, some were not, such as LeVar Burton (1957–), who was still in college and played the pivotal role of Kunta Kinte, a key ancestor of Alex Haley. Edward Asner played Captain Davies on whose ship Kunta Kinte and many others were kept captive during a long voyage so they could be sold as slaves. Ben Vereen (1946–), Louis Gossett Jr.. (1936–), Cicely Tyson (1924–), and other actors both Caucasian and African American held prominent roles. Opting for realism, *Roots* portrayed the African women in the background and those going about their chores on their tribal grounds naked from the waist up in a naturalistic style.

The style of *Roots* was like a massive feature film. The production design and cinematography put the viewer into the period. Also commendable was the lighting of the African American actors, long a challenge in movies to get the balance right so the skin tone looked realistic, especially when the actors in a scene were both Caucasian and African American. Once again television was able to do something that was considered a major challenge.

It seemed as if almost everyone in America sat in front of their TVs for over a week to learn about slavery and life in America during this historic period. One of the reasons for its success is the dramatic storytelling technique that made the times come alive. This miniseries hit ratings never before achieved—averaging a 44.9 rating and a 66 percent audience share for its run. People wanted to know more about their own family trees and family gatherings were held far and wide.

There was a sequel: *Roots: The Next Generations,* which aired in 1979, but it was not as successful as the original.

Roots stands like a giant achievement prefiguring what television could be in the 21st century. It created a high standard in television broadcasting. Its major accomplishment is its value as a mass teaching moment that educated its audience about a shameful chapter in the history of America. David L. Wolper understood that knowing where you've been informs the present and future. In 2016, a new and acclaimed version of *Roots* was broadcast in four episodes; among its producers were LeVar Burton and Mark Wolper, son of David Wolper.

See also: *North and South*; *Rich Man, Poor Man.*

Further Resources

Haley, Alex. 1976. *Roots: The Saga of an American Family.* New York: Dell.

Haley, Alex. 2007. *Alex Haley: The Man Who Traced America's Roots: His Life: His Works.* New York: Reader's Digest Association.

Saturday Night Live (NBC, 1975–)

For NBC the 11:30 time slot on Saturday night was problematic. It had been programmed with reruns of *The Tonight Show*, an idea that seemed to cater only to those who loved seeing episodes of that show again or for those hoping to catch a segment they had missed. Occasionally viewers who didn't watch the nightly show stumbled into it. The network wanted to claim that place in the television spectrum.

Three men set out to do a live comedy/variety show inspired by Sid Caesar, Steve Allen, and Ernie Kovacs. They were Lorne Michaels (1944–), Dick Ebersol (1947–), and Herb Schlosser, who was the president of NBC.

Sportscaster Howard Cosell decided to move into the variety show area, so ABC broadcast *Saturday Night Live with Howard Cosell* (1975–1976), preventing NBC from calling their show *Saturday Night Live.* Instead they came up with *NBC's Saturday Night.* Cosell's show only ran one season, so when season two arrived the title was changed to *Saturday Night Live*.

A Gathering of Young Comedians

The show was planned to have a comedy troupe, a stock company that performed comedy sketches, with recurring comic characters, a fake newscast, a celebrity host who would deliver a monologue in front of a live audience, then appear in skits with the bunch. A current rock or pop act would also perform in their own segment.

The comics chosen from what was dubbed "The Not Ready for Prime Time Players" were Chevy Chase (1943–), Dan Aykroyd (1952–), John Belushi (1940–1982), Jane Curtin (1947–), Garrett Morris (1937–), Laraine Newman (1952–), and Gilda Radner (1946–1989). Chase left the show in 1976 and was replaced by Bill Murray (1950–).

The first host was stand-up comic George Carlin. Others included Lili Tomlin, Rob Reiner, Candice Bergen, Jodie Foster, Paul Simon, Robert Kline, and Buck Henry. Host selection was tricky; they had to deliver a good and funny monologue standing in front of the house band. They also had to interact with the cast and be able to do cutting-edge skits. Milton Berle and Frank Zappa were said to be less than successful on the show. Successful hosts like Paul Simon (1941–) did multiple stints. Most variety shows had a single host, with the exception of *The Hollywood Palace* (1964–1970). The single host concept ensured a steady

The late-night sketch comedy show *Saturday Night Live*, which each week features a guest host and musical performances, has survived for over forty years and become an institution in popular culture. Seen here are Chevy Chase (right) as President Gerald Ford and host Buck Henry as his press secretary Ron Nessen on the live broadcast that aired on August 13, 1976. (AP Photo)

audience if the viewers liked them. SNL went the other way, banking on variety and unpredictability to build audience loyalty.

Musical guests were the other way to draw large audiences. Viewers looked forward to marquee acts such as Simon and Garfunkel, Tom Petty, Patti Smith, Elvis Costello, Blondie, and Randy Newman.

Early on the Muppets were part of the show as was Albert Brooks (1947–), who provided a short film segment. The sketches were the heart of the show; popular ones became recurring segments as the weeks moved on, but many were one-time mini productions. They included "The Coneheads," performed by Dan Aykroyd and Jane Curtin, alien characters with bald heads shaped like cones; and the Olympia coffee shop, which featured John Belushi and Dan Aykroyd repeating lines like "Cheeseburger, cheeseburger, cheeseburger" and "No Coke, Pepsi." Gilda Radner played the character Roseanne Roseannadanna, a reporter on the "Weekend Update" segment who had an odd, irritating way of speaking as she kept getting confused and turned normal words or phrases into inappropriate ones. The Frustrunk Brothers were played by Steve Martin and Dan Aykroyd. They were from Czechoslovakia, walked funny, talked funny, dressed in clothes with clashing patterns, and considered themselves swingers with the gals. "We're two wild and crazy guys" was their tag line. The Blues Brothers were Aykroyd and Belushi in black suits, black fedoras, black ties, dark sunglasses, and white shirts, singing and dancing their version of the Sam and Dave rhythm and blues act.

Lines like "I'm Chevy Chase, and you're not," spoken by Chase as he began the satiric news segment, helped to make *Saturday Night Live* an institution. People watched alone, with their families, friends, or in groups congregating at someone's house to watch the show. It was a Saturday night party atmosphere. *SNL* was an hour and a half of entertainment for a generation wanting something new, edgy, and dangerous. After four decades, the Saturday night tradition continues, with new and talented cast members constantly emerging.

In the 1980s and 1990s and into the 21st century a new batch of talented cast members emerged. These included Dana Carvey (1955–), who became known for his impersonation of George H. W. Bush and Ross Perot and for the sketch comedy of *Wayne's World*; Phil Hartman (1948–1998), who impersonated President Bill Clinton; Adam Sandler (1966–), who originated the hilarious "Hanukah Song" and went on to a prolific film career; *48 Hours* superstar Eddie Murphy (1961–), who memorialized a black interpretation of Mister Rogers; Julia Louis-Dreyfus (1961–), who became a top television sitcom star after her SNL run; and many performers who reinvented "Weekend Update," including Tina Fey (1970–) and Amy Poehler (1971–), both of whom breathed new life in the show and went on to enormous success, including co-hosting the Golden Globes. Jimmy Fallon (1974–) and Seth Myers (1973–) both became late night show hosts after their stints on *Saturday Night Live.* A breakout star who joined the cast in 2012 is Kate McKinnon (1984–), who has impersonated Hillary Clinton and Ellen DeGeneres. Alec Baldwin (1958–) continues to be a frequent host of the show and impersonates Donald J. Trump, and Melissa McCarthy (1970–) has become a frequent guest and part of the repertory as a sketch player.

See also: *Fridays*; *It's Garry Shandling's Show*; *The Midnight Special*; *Vol. 1, The 1950s–1960s:* Allen, Steve/*The Steve Allen Show*; Caesar, Sid; *The Hollywood Palace*; Kovacs, Ernie.

Further Resources

Miller, James Andrew, and Tom Shales. 2014. *Live from New York: The Complete Uncensored History of Saturday Night Live as Told by Its Stars, Writers and Guests.* New York: Little, Brown.

Tropiano, Stephen. 2013. *Saturday Night Live FAQ: Everything Left to Know About Television's Longest Running Comedy.* New York: Applause Theatre and Cinema Books.

Second City T.V. (NBC, 1977–1980)

This satiric videotaped program, later named *SCTV Television Network*, was a full half-hour each week presenting an alternate television station that was really a parody of television itself. Viewers tuned in to a nonstop program that made fun of the medium, its form, its content, and even its purpose. Toronto's Second City comedy troupe in Canada was the jumping-off point for this show, which was a sample of a day's television programming from a TV station in a fictitious town—Melonville.

The original cast members were at first unknown to American viewers, but as with *Saturday Night Live* they were launched to stardom and big roles in comedy motion pictures. They were John Candy (1950–1994), Joe Flaherty (1941–), Eugene Levy (1946–), Andrea Martin (1947–), Catherine O'Hara (1954–), Harold Ramis (1944–2014), and Dave Thomas (1949–).

The faux programming included commercials, PSAs, movies, series, the news, and "Dialing for Dollars," which was a rigged call-in show.

The humor skewered iconic TV shows like *Leave It to Beaver* (1957–1963), portraying Beaver as a man still living as a boy at home. An exercise show cleverly used the hit movie *The Exorcist* (1973) by featuring a young woman imitating the film's young actress, Linda Blair (1959–), in a bed that keeps tossing her as she talks about the good exercise she is getting in specific parts of the body. An animal show has a guest snake expert getting bitten repeatedly by poisonous snakes.

The performance level in every segment is high-energy—these are all talented comic actors. Commercial breaks are a card with the show's logo. The show's demographic was young teens and under 30s. For its time the material was cutting edge. For the baby boomers raised on television, *Second City T.V.* was an outlet for laughing at the establishment and at themselves as well.

See also: *Saturday Night Live.*

Further Resources

Knelman, Martin. 2014. *Laughing on the Outside: The Life of John Candy*. New York: St. Martin's Press.

Robbins, Jeff. 2007. *Second City Television: A History and Episode Guide*. Jefferson, NC: McFarland.

Shields and Yarnell (CBS, 1977–1978)

This 1970s variety show featured two mimes, one male, one female. The art of pantomime goes back to the ancient Greeks; an actor tells a story with his body, facial expressions, and movement, all without speaking. These performers are called mimes.

Robert Shields (1951–) was a street mime in California. When he was 18 he was performing at the Hollywood Wax Museum when he was discovered by the internationally renowned modern master of pantomime, Marcel Marceau (1923–2007), who offered the young man a full scholarship to his school for the silent art.

Lorene Yarnell (1944–2010), like Shields, was a native of Los Angeles. She was a tap dancer and an actress in shows like *Shindig!* (1964–1966) and *The Carol Burnett Show* (1967–1978). While performing in off-Broadway productions in San Francisco, Lorene Yarnell met Robert Shields and they married in 1972. She performed body acting in the Mel Brooks film *Spaceballs,* playing the character Dot Matrix, which was voiced by Joan Rivers (1933–2014).

CBS carried the half-hour show, which was unique in variety history because its hosts did not speak. They danced, they mime/danced, and they filled the show with sketches. One started with a shot of the Empire State Building. Next Lorene Yarnell is on a set built to look like the building's observation tower. She picks up what seems to be a large round object, although it is only an illusion created by the shape of her arms. She struggles to the precipice of the platform and drops it. Cut to the street. Robert Shields is walking in front of the building in mime style and is hit by the invisible object.

Their feature skit, which progressed over the course of the show, was playing the Clinkers. These two characters, presumably husband and wife, move in a style developed first by Robert Shields, in which the performers move like robots. This became very popular among viewers, especially young people.

Shields had exaggerated makeup and smoked a pipe; Yarnell often wore a housedress and flopping curlers in her hair. As they whirled around they bumped into each other, spilled milk and cereal all over the table, and then collapsed on it, bringing it and them to the ground. Speaking actors played supporting characters. There was a repairman who tells the wife not to throw things into the washing machine, which will clog it. Yarnell in turn silently throws the repairman's heavy tool kit right down the open center of the appliance.

Shields and Yarnell began as a summer replacement show. It did so well CBS brought it into their fall lineup; unfortunately it was scheduled against the enormously popular *Laverne and Shirley* and was gone in two months in 1978.

The marriage between Robert Shields and Lorene Yarnell ended in divorce during 1986. On July 29, 2010, Lorene Yarnell died of a cerebral aneurysm. Their legacy is the historic achievement of bringing a weekly pantomime show to American television.

Further Resources

Kipnis, Claude. 1988. *The Mime Book*. Englewood, CO: Meriwether.

Schubert, Leda, and Gerard DuBois. 2012. *Monsieur Marceau: Actor without Words*. New York: Roaring Brook Press.

Showtime (1976–)

Cable television was an exciting technological advancement for the medium. For many it meant getting a good clean, sharp picture in areas where broadcast television couldn't quite deliver. Others realized that cable could provide content the networks could not. Originally Showtime offered commercial-free programming. In the seventies it was the equivalent of the Wild West; there was much ground to settle and the opportunity to create programming that had a particular signature. There wasn't a lot out there, but there was a growing monolith that was gathering a lot of the market, Home Box Office (HBO).

Showtime launched their cable network on July 1, 1976 providing competition to HBO. They converted 10,000 subscribers from the former Channel One franchise on the Times-Mirror Cable systems in Escondido, Long Beach, and Palos Verdes, California. On July 8, the next week, Showtime was launched on Viacom Cablevision's system in Dublin, California, a channel that had been owned by Viacom.

The first program and television special delivered by Showtime was called *Celebration*, a lively concert featuring Pink Floyd, Rod Stewart, and the megagroup ABBA.

By the end of Showtime's flagship year it had 55,000 subscribers nationwide. It went national after being uplinked by satellite, which quickly made it a strong competitor to HBO and others.

The business of cable television is ever-changing. In 1979 Viacom sold 50 percent of its ownership in Showtime to the TelePrompTer Corporation.

See also: HBO (Home Box Office); *The Paper Chase*; *Vol. 3, The 1990s–2000s: Homeland.*

Further Resources

Showtime Networks Inc. Company Profile, Information, Business Description. History, Background Information on Showtime Networks Inc. Reference for Business. http://www.referenceforbusiness.com/history2/78/Showtime-Networks-Inc.html

Snowden, Jonathan. 2014. "The Real War: HBO and Showtime Battle for Boxing's Future." January 16. *Bleacher Report*. http://bleacherreport.com/articles/1903927-the-real-war-hbo-and-showtime-battle-for-boxings-future

Silverman, Fred (1937–)

During the 1970s Fred Silverman was an executive for all three television networks, CBS, NBC, and ABC, at different times. He was considered to be a programming genius, a man with the golden touch for identifying hit shows.

The Journey

Silverman received a master's degree from Ohio State University where he became interested in television. He landed a job at a local TV station, WGN-TV in Chicago, where he was in charge of children's programming. He then moved to New York City for a stint at their local station, WPIX. In 1963 at age 25 he was hired by CBS as an executive after they looked at his master's thesis, which analyzed 10 years of programming by the ABC network.

At the Tiffany Network he had his biggest responsibility yet—responsibility for all daytime network programming and then for all entertainment programming—in effect, making him in charge of everything that was scheduled.

In 1970 at CBS Fred Silverman was promoted from vice president of program planning to vice president of programs, which put him in total charge of the network's lineup. He was the instigator of what was seen as a purge of all the rural programs that took place in the country, the shows that had been seen as a low-end approach to television. He moved CBS into a more upscale schedule that attracted baby boomers with shows like *All in the Family* (1971–1979), *Kojak* (1973–1978), and *The Mary Tyler Moore Show* (1970–1977).

Silverman had the ability to perceive spin-offs from popular programs, thus creating *Maude* (1972–1978) and *The Jeffersons* (1975–1985) from *All in the Family* and *Rhoda* (1974–1978) from *The Mary Tyler Moore Show*. He also brought game shows back to the network. He ended the process of wiping videotapes clean and recording over them, instead preserving as much content as possible.

In 1975 Fred Silverman left CBS and became president of entertainment at ABC. That network had been in the doldrums for quite some time, and it looked to Silverman to turn things around. Silverman made a series of decisions that gave viewers more escapist fare with shows that included *The Love Boat* (1977–1986), *Fantasy Island* (1978–1984), and *Donny and Marie* (1976–1979). Silverman was a major proponent of "jiggle TV"—shows that featured curvaceous young women who seemed constantly in movement, such as *Charlie's Angels* (1976–1981) and *Three's Company* (1977–1984). He also revamped the morning schedule with *Good Morning America* (1975). Silverman expanded the soap operas *General Hospital* and *One Life to Live* from one half-hour daily to one hour daily. In game shows Silverman introduced *Family Feud* (1976–), which was very popular and would have a long, long life on TV. In long-form television *Rich Man, Poor Man* (1976) and especially *Roots* (1977) would command massive audiences and rating points. These programming changes on Fred Silverman's watch landed ABC in first place in the ratings wars.

Even with all these achievements Fred Silverman made another move, this time to NBC, where in 1978 he became president and CEO of the network. In his three years at NBC Silverman did not experience success. Silverman was a big advocate of *Supertrain* (1979), a show he considered *The Love Boat* on tracks. The costs for the show were unparalleled in modern television history. The show was disliked by critics and audiences from the outset. To make matters worse, Silverman pulled the show off the air and retooled it, throwing away more money. This failure put Silverman in a position of ridicule with industry insiders and the public. When the show was rebroadcast there were few viewers and it was cancelled with unaired episodes. The sitcom *Hello, Larry* (1979) and the variety shows *The Big Show* (1980) and *Pink Lady* (1980) were also disasters and lacked viewership.

He did have success at NBC with *Diff'rent Strokes* (1978–1986), *The Facts of Life* (1979–1980), and other shows. He realized the importance of a corporate logo and brought back the NBC peacock, which represented the network's early and continued commitment to color TV and quality programs that enhanced it.

In sports lingo one would say the Fred Silverman accomplished "the hat trick" by leading all three original networks. Television programming is part art, part science, and part metaphysics; some people have the instinct to know when a program will be successful. Fred Silverman possessed and applied a vision of what a major television network should be, and he used those skills in the service of three major corporations.

See also: *All in the Family*; *Charlie's Angels*; *Diff'rent Strokes*; *Good Morning America*; *The Jeffersons*; *Kojak*; *The Love Boat*; *The Mary Tyler Moore Show*; *Maude*; *Rich Man, Poor Man*; *Supertrain*; *Three's Company.*

Further Resources

Bedell, Sally. 1981. *Up the Tube: Prime-Time TV and the Silverman Years*. New York: Viking.

Gross, Lynn, Brian Gross, and Philippe Perebinossoff. 2005. *Programming for TV, Radio and the Internet: Strategy, Development and Evaluation.* Burlington, MA: Focal Press.

The Six Million Dollar Man (ABC, 1973–1978)

This show was a monthly feature on *The ABC Suspense Movie* and then became a weekly series in January 1974. Lee Majors (1939–) portrayed Steve Austin, an astronaut who had been badly injured in an accident and at the government cost of six million dollars, using bionic technology, he was completely rebuilt.

Lee Majors portrayed Colonel Steve Austin in the 1970s series *The Six Million Dollar Man.* The action program centered around the adventures of an astronaut whose damaged body is rebuilt using high-tech science after he is severely injured in an aviation accident. (Fotos International/ Getty Images)

To demonstrate the strength and power of a bionic person, the producers of *The Six Million Dollar Man* and *The Bionic Woman* slowed down the action so every leap, lift, jump, and feat of strength could be examined and watched with awe. These shows were photographed with a film camera shooting celluloid and edited on a Moviola, Kem, or Steenbeck editing machine before digital editing. Normal speed was 24 frames per second. When the camera is overcranked (an expression from the silent film days when cameras were hand-cranked), running at a speed considerably greater than the norm, slow motion is produced. The beauty of the bionic shows was that the camerawork was an integral aspect of the characters and stories.

The result was that he had great running speed and strength as well as enhanced vision. The Office of Strategic Information supported this work and had Steve Austin go on assignments for them. His main handler was Oscar Goldman, played by Richard Anderson (1926–2017), who kept a watchful eye on him, traveled to hot spots, and marveled at Austin's human robotic powers. Steve did have a mind of his own and didn't always do what he was told, but his commitments were in the interest of completing a mission.

Some of Steve Austin's adventures included saving a genius scientist who was kidnapped to Spain, rescuing a downed pilot who had information about UN violations; being launched again into space to save two stranded astronauts; being dispatched to the Himalayas to find secret documents in an old World War II plane uncovered during an earthquake; and stopping government conspirators who had put together an atom bomb.

The show's opening was packed with information. Images and narration explain what happened to Steve Austin and how he was put back together as well as his extraordinary capabilities. The title was over an iconic freeze frame of Steve charging ahead into the camera, his strength and intense determination powerfully displayed.

The main special effect used in *The Six Million Dollar Man* is slow motion. Although heavily used in motion pictures and considered by some to be a gimmick that takes the viewer out of the story, slow motion was perfect for demonstrating how Steve Austin could leap, jump, and run at great speeds and perform other feats that were impossible for an average man.

The Six Million Dollar Man was an enormously popular show. A clever spin-off was created with a love interest, a professional tennis player who injured herself and was turned into *The Bionic Woman* (1976–1978).

The Six Million Dollar Man was an adventure show, not really science fiction, which it would have been had it originated in the 1950s or 1960s. The 1970s was a more technological time with the mainstream audience capable of believing that a man could be part cyborg in service to his country.

See also: *The Bionic Woman*.

Further Resources

Anderson, Richard, and Alan Doshna. 2015. *Richard Anderson: At Last . . . A Memoir from the Golden Years of MGM and The Six Million Dollar Man to Now*. Albany, GA: Bear Manor Media.

Pilato, Herbie J. 2015. *The Bionic Book: The Six Million Dollar Man and the Bionic Woman Reconstructed*. Duncan, OK: Bear Manor Media.

Sneak Previews (PBS, 1975–1996)

Roger Ebert (1942–2013) was the film critic for the *Chicago Sun-Times*. Gene Siskel (1946–1999) was a film critic for the *Chicago Tribune*. They were competitors, not friends. Actually, their dislike for each other grew to herculean heights and they argued off camera, sometimes heatedly, just before they stepped into the theater where their television show *Sneak Previews* was filmed. They would eventually become the first millionaire film critics. They also brought their viewers back to Caesar's time using the thumbs up, thumbs down approach to rating movies. Two thumbs down was a death knell. Two thumbs up was a rave; one up, one down was a mixed review.

The concept of the show was to review movies that were about to be released to the public; as film critics they screened films in advance, so there was time to prepare a review. Both men were knowledgeable and had a good understanding of film history and a passion for movies.

One or the other would introduce a film, giving the title, director, actors, and the plot up to a certain point. Then a clip would be set up. The clip would run. They appeared to be in a real movie theater and a full shot captured Siskel and Ebert watching the chosen scene. After a while the clip would go full screen. The clips were on the lengthy side, which gave the viewer enough time to get a good sense of the film. Then back to the critics. They each would talk about how they felt about the film. Agreement was not a frequent occurrence and disagreement was the general order of the day. Siskel was dogged and pursued his point. Ebert had a bit of an air about him. He felt he knew more about movies than Siskel and most experts agreed. As the show's run progressed, the back and forth discussions sometimes changed to heated arguments with insults added. This became part of *Sneak Previews*' appeal.

Sitting in director's chairs Siskel and Ebert reviewed many important films including *Network,* (1976), *All the President's Men* (1976), and *Annie Hall* (1977).

Watching *Sneak Previews* was like reading two film reviews from different papers at the same time with two critics explaining, analyzing, discussing, and arguing all rolled into one. Of course, they gave their ratings not in stars but in thumbs.

The show, originally a local production, grew larger and larger; specials about the Oscars and other aspects of moviemaking were added. Then Siskel and Ebert left, other teams followed, the title changed, books were written, and a new nonfiction genre was formed and imitated.

Like most print film criticism in newspapers and magazines, Siskel and Ebert mainly discussed plot, acting, and directing, but it was rare that the crafts of moviemaking were discussed. The television film critic genre was born and it served a purpose beyond the newspapers and magazines themselves. It was entertaining and because it was a visual medium it engaged viewers more fully than print. Gene Siskel and Roger Ebert became stars if not superstars—celebrity was good for movies and in the end, although Ebert continued to gain celebrity, they went back to their respective newspapers and banged out a film review for the next edition. For TV stars they were newspapermen first.

See also: PBS (Public Broadcasting Service)

Further Resources

Ebert, Roger. 2012. *Life Itself: A Memoir*. New York: Grand Central Publishing.

Schoollmeyer, Josh. 2012. *Enemies: A Love Story: The Oral History of Siskel and Ebert*. Santa Monica, CA. Now and Then Reader.

Soap (ABC, 1977–1981)

Before this prime-time comedy serial, which like Norman Lear's groundbreaking *Mary Hartman, Mary Hartman* (1976–1977) used the traditional soap opera to delve into very unconventional subject matter, ABC ran seemingly endless, exaggerated, and more than excessive promotions for *Soap.* This enraged religious and ethnic groups who, based on only the promos, flooded the network with negative complaints and demands. The network at least had the good wisdom to let the angry barrage eventually die down. When it did, they ran the show.

Some of the commotion had come about because *Soap* dealt with incendiary subject matter such as impotence, transsexualism, extramarital affairs, and organized crime. The show's setting was Dunn's River, Connecticut and the premise has Shakespearean overtones as it is about two sisters, one wealthy, one not.

Two Sides

The large ensemble cast (like a daytime soap opera) includes on the rich side Katherine Helmond (1929–) as Jessica Tate, a socialite convicted of murder in the first season; Robert Mandan (1932–) as Chester Tate, who is a serial cheater on his wife; and Jennifer Salt (1944–), who plays their snobbish daughter Eunice. Another daughter, the promiscuous Corinne, was played by Diana Canova (1953–); their son Billy was portrayed by Jimmy Baio (1962–), the cousin of actor Scott Baio. Benson, the family cook with a mind of his own and a sharp tongue, was played by the African American actor Robert Guillaume (1927–2017).

On the not so rich side were Jessica's sister Mary Campbell, played by Cathryn Damon (1930–1987). Richard Mulligan (1932–2000) played her second husband, Burt Campbell. Mary's macho son Danny, who becomes involved in organized crime, was portrayed by Ted Wass (1952–). Billy Crystal (1948–) played Jodie Dallas, another son, who could be gay, straight, or bisexual and wanted to have gender-altering surgery. The Godfather was played by Richard Libertini (1933–); Katherine Reynolds portrayed Claire; Robert Urich (1946–2002) played Peter; and Grandpa, a veteran of World War II who was unaware the war was over, was played by Arthur Peterson (1912–1996).

Saunders, a new butler, was played by Roscoe Lee Browne (1922–2007), and Jay Johnston (1949–) played Chuck. Rod Roddy (1937–2003) was the announcer for this show that was created, produced, and written by Susan Harris (1940–).

Those who loyally watched as many daytime soap operas in a day as they could believed in the world and characters before them because the plot lines seemed to reflect life as it is really lived.

Soap began with a radio-style announcer letting the viewers know they were about to see a story of two sisters, one rich, one not. This element gave an old-style soap opera feel to this new and sometimes daring show, which sported an openly gay, sort of, major character. Ending the episode, which dangles with several cliffhangers, the announcer comes back positing a number of questions about the characters and the impending situations by starting each sentence with "Will . . . "

A parody or satire by nature takes a story and simply makes fun of it. Within the limits of what a network could put on the air and taking into consideration the approximately 32,000 cards and letters expressing outrage, the content on *Soap* as with daytime soaps was structured into what was believed to be a continuous story, and they still got away with what was not standard comedic fare on any network.

It turns out the off-screen narrator tells us that it wasn't Jessica who committed murder but Chester, who is convicted and goes to prison, only to escape. During his journey, which leads him way out West, he is aware that he has lost his memory and gets a job as a fry cook at a local eatery. Jessica falls in love with the detective she's hired to find Chester. When Chester returns she chooses him over the cop, but not before having an affair with a South American revolutionary named El Puerco. She later divorces Chester.

The other side also had its trials and travails. Benson the butler left (he would show up later in his own sitcom, but not until he rescued Billy from a religious cult named the Sunnies). Corinne married an ex-priest and after only six weeks had a baby possessed by Satan. Burt was kidnapped and cloned by aliens, Mary had sex with the clone, but didn't know who the father of the child was. Burt later became a sheriff and ran into a racketeer and his hooker, and on and on.

The sense of humor of the average viewer had changed radically since the 1950s and 1960s and Susan Harris and her team knew this. *Soap* was outrageous, insulting, and hard to believe at times, but that was just the attitude of those who didn't watch this nighttime comedy show; the rest were anxious and relieved to be able to laugh at subjects and situations that they had been holding in all these years.

See also: *Mary Hartman, Mary Hartman*; *Vol. 1, The 1950s–1960s: As the World Turns*; *Days of Our Lives*; *General Hospital.*

Further Resources

Berman, A. S. 2013. *Soap! The Inside Story of The Sitcom That Broke All the Rules*. Duncan, OK: Bear Manor Media.

Crystal, Billy. 2014. *Still Foolin' Em: Where I've Been, Where I'm Going and Where the Hell Are My Keys?* New York: St. Martin's Griffin.

Sonny and Cher Comedy Hour (CBS, 1971–1974)

Sonny Bono (1935–1998) and Cher (1946–) (Cherilyn Sarkisian) were married on October 27, 1964. They were both pop and rock singers and in 1965 went into a recording studio and made their signature hit record, "I Got You Babe," which told the world about their love and by extension the listener's feelings toward their mate, or girlfriend or boyfriend. The marital bond didn't last and they were divorced on June 26, 1975. They had one child, Chaz Bono (1969–). Cher went on to become a major singing superstar who also had a winning acting career. Sonny became the mayor of

The folk rock duo Sonny and Cher starred in their very popular variety show *The Sonny & Cher Comedy Hour* in the 1970s. They performed their hit records and engaged in comedy skits, bringing youth culture to television. (Michael Ochs Archives/Getty Images)

Palm Springs, California and held that office from 1988 to 1992. He later ran and won the congressional seat for California's 44th district beginning in 1995. Sadly, on January 5, 1998 while skiing near Lake Tahoe, California he slammed into a tree and died of his injuries.

On August 1, 1971 Sonny (whose birth name was Salvatore) and his then-wife Cher began their CBS summer show, *The Sonny and Cher Comedy Hour.* They had a great potential in a starting audience—all the fans of the Sonny and Cher music career. The audience could assume (rightly) that Sonny and Cher would sing on the show. What the fans didn't know when they first tuned in was that Sonny and Cher were a great comedy duo. Sonny was the straight man and fed his partner with great material. Cher was the queen of the one-liners, shooting back a witty or downright funny response as fast as Sonny could hurl them. Sonny couldn't stand still, turning his head and slowly twisting his body and flapping his arms and hands. Cher, thin and statuesque, was dressed in a Bob Mackie (1940–) sparkly gown and was stoic as she either looked away or quickly at Sonny while she shot out her retort. A subsection of America who would consider watching *The Sonny and Cher Comedy Show* were hippies. Sonny wore his hair in a medium-length shag with bangs, and Cher wore her jet-black, pin-straight hair long, parted in the middle and all the way down her back.

The show began with an announcer and a set filled with an enormous amount of strung circles. On each was a caricature of the duo in black with the background colored red. They came out singing a song and moving to the beat. Sonny made fun of his singing as it was widely known that it was Cher who had the great singing voice and not Sonny. Then came the monologue, which was the beginning of the comedy act. The focus on the jokes was usually aimed at Sonny and his intelligence or lack thereof. They had fun and the in-house audience loved it. Sonny also made self-effacing jokes, especially about being an Italian American.

Then there were comedy sketches. In one the guest host was Farrah Fawcett Majors (1947–2009), who played a mannequin in a store window alongside Cher. First they are stiff, then they come alive and talk about their jobs. Then they hear two workman approaching, one played by Sonny Bono. The workers approach the mannequins and rudely twist them into impossible shapes. They leave and come back to say that the dresses are on the wrong mannequins and announce that they are going to strip them. As they begin, there is a blackout and it is the end of the sketch.

In a Western sketch Cher plays women out of the past such as Calamity Jane. Then it switches to the Garden of Eden and she is Eve; she even plays Blanche DuBois from the play *A Streetcar Named Desire*. The male in these sketches is played by Burt Reynolds (1936–). An appearance is also made by Bobby Darin (1936–1973). In between these sketches there is a cut to Sonny playing piano and singing, dressed in honky-tonk style. Cher is on top of the piano in different positions dressed like a sassy Old West saloon gal. The song is a pro-woman song about how women overpower men.

At the end Sonny and Cher would come out with one of them carrying their young child, who would be asked to say good night.

The summer show was a big success and CBS told Sonny and Cher that they would take this show to series, which they did. Sonny and Cher are pop icons who helped define music, especially in the 1960s and the 1970s. Their all-around talents were a pleasant surprise to audiences who couldn't have imagined them as a new generation Abbott and Costello or Burns and Allen.

See also: *Vol. 1, 1950s–1960s:* Allen, Steve/*The Steve Allen Show*.

Further Resources

Bego, Mark, and Mary Wilson. 2012. *Cher: If You Believe*. Lanham, MD: Taylor Trade Publishing.

Braun, Thomas. 1978. *Sonny and Cher*. Mankato, MN: Creative Education.

Soul! (PBS, 1967–1973)

This unique and breakthrough variety show was targeted at African Americans. It was produced by WNET, an affiliate of the Public Broadcasting Service (PBS). Its purpose was to present, examine, and celebrate black culture in a myriad of ways, music, dance, literature, religion, and politics.

The host on the majority of the programs was Ellis Hailzip, an openly gay African American, who was intensely involved with the black arts movement, a controversial artistic branch of the Black Power movement that grew out of the assassination of Malcolm X (1925–1969).

The opening was a moving graphics presentation of the letters comprising the word "Soul" interwoven with a Warholesque portrait of a black woman with a large Afro haircut. The set was in New York, decorated with the word "Soul" and filled with a largely African American audience.

The announcer, Gerry Bledsoe, spoke off-camera in a deep, disc jockey–style voice and announced who was on the day's show. Bledsoe at times was the announcer and host when Ellis Hailzip wasn't there. Then Ellis Hailzip, also the weekly producer of *Soul!*, welcomed the home audience and started the proceedings. If it was a musical act, they would play; if it was a guest interview, it was conducted.

The guest list over the course of *Soul* was impressive in every way. They included the poet Nikki Giovanni (1943–), who was also a frequent guest host. Those from the music world included Stevie Wonder (1950–), Gladys Knight (1944–) and the Pips, Harry Belafonte (1927–), and Herbie Hancock (1940–). Distinguished actors on *Soul* included Sidney Poitier (1927–) and Cicely Tyson (1924–), and from the sporting world, Muhammad Ali (1942–2016). Politicians and activists Jesse Jackson (1941–) and Kathleen Cleaver (1945–) appeared.

A notable show featured the Honorable Minister Louis Farrakhan (1933–) from the Nation of Islam addressing a packed audience largely occupied by members of his sect, the women dressed in their traditional garb, which covered their heads but revealed their faces, and men in suits and ties. He was there to send a message about the importance of black culture and identity. He spoke about slavery and why black people should study their African heritage. He spoke often of the teachings of his leader, the Honorable Elijah Muhammad (1897–1975).

He sat down for a one-on-one interview with Ellis Hailzip and when that concluded the audience was told the Honorable Minister Louis Farrakhan wanted to address everyone with a final message. He stood and talked to black people who were in prisons and said that the crimes they had committed were sins of the white man. When he was finished he received rousing applause and those in the studio then rose and approached him as the credits ran out.

The musical shows were full-blown events staged in a concert setting. Also for the times, just after the psychedelic 1960s, visual effects were applied that multiplied images and changed colors to the beat and rhythm of the music.

Soul! presented its audience with an eclectic menu. It was an important show for displaying and celebrating black culture. Although it was intended for a black audience, other ethnicities tuned in and could experience the richness of this culture and perhaps learn lessons that could only bring everyone together.

See also: PBS (Public Broadcasting Service); *Soul Train*.

Further Resources

Guralnick, Peter. 1999. *Sweet Soul Music: Rhythm and Blues and the Southern Dream of Freedom.* Boston: Back Bay Books.

Handcock, Sibyl. 1983. *Famous Firsts of Black Americans.* Gretna, LA: Pelican.

Soul Train (Syndication, 1971–2006)

This show, produced and hosted by former announcer and disc jockey Don Cornelius (1936–2012), has been described as the African American version of the Dick Clark (1929–2012) music and dance show for young people—*American Bandstand* (1950–1989). *Soul Train* began as a local program in Chicago; then in 1971 Cornelius moved his show to Hollywood.

Soul Train, which eventually went into syndication around the country, was one hour long. Cornelius ran the show, telling the audience what musical star or act would be on that day. He would announce what song was about to be played so the kids, usually about 50 couples, could dance the latest styles or come up with original moves to make them stand out for the home viewers, who were predominately African American. After their intro by Cornelius, the musical guests either played live or lip-synched to their records.

There was a *Soul Train* scramble board. The way it worked was that Don Cornelius selected a couple who would move the magnetic letters around until they formed the name of a soul artist. They had 60 seconds to accomplish this; if they did, they went right back to the music in progress.

The most popular feature on *Soul Train* was when two lines were formed in the configuration of a railroad train track, with couples alternating on either side who would come out of an arch looking like a train tunnel, and they would dance down the line, trying to get as much attention as possible. Some moved to the groove of the music, others were flamboyant and a bit over the top but enjoyable. Sometimes the female would just dance normally and the male would go through every hypermove he knew, but the opposite also occurred during this segment; at times the man would hold the groove and the woman would outdance him so they got the spotlight and kept it.

Everyone including Don Cornelius sported Afro haircuts of various sizes, some quite large. Clothing was dressy seventies fashion. Here too some of the guys and gals looked within normal limits while others wore boas, long coats, and outrageous hats.

The opening was animated and depicted human-like trains chugging along to the *Soul Train* theme song. The main set had a large sign with lights spelling out Soul Train. Everywhere the eye could see there were track graphics, platforms, and every visual cue defining a train.

The music was rhythm and blues, soul music, and disco. The records were played full out and sometimes a whistle was blown by someone on the dance floor coming through.

Just some of the musical artists appearing on *Soul Train* were the Isley Brothers, the Delfonics, Earth, Wind, and Fire, the Four Tops, and the Fifth Dimension.

Throughout television history, those with vision looked at what shows were being broadcast and what demographics were being served and served well. Don Cornelius observed the dynamics of *American Bandstand* and used Dick Clark as a model to ride the Soul Train to success.

See also: *Vol. 1, The 1950s–1960s: American Bandstand.*

Further Resources

Lustgarden, Karen. 1978. *The Complete Guide to Disco Dancing*. New York: Warner Books.

Questlove. 2013. *Soul Train: The Music, the Dance, and Style of a Generation*. New York: Harper Design.

The Streets of San Francisco (ABC, 1972–1977)

One of the most pictorial and evocative locations for motion pictures and television is San Francisco, California. Many television police dramas of the 1950s and 1960s were shot on location in New York and Los Angeles, but the decision in the seventies to develop a fast-paced, action-packed police show with San Francisco as a backdrop was outstanding. In this city of steep hills and winding streets, driving can be treacherous with up and down bumps along the way. One of the most exciting car chases ever staged happens in Steve McQueen's (1930–1980) 1968 film *Bullitt,* set in San Francisco. It made sense that creator Quinn Martin (1922–1987) would place a cop show in San Francisco and put the city's name in the title to indicate that there was going to be a lot of exterior action.

The Streets of San Francisco was a one-hour show broadcast by ABC starring established movie star Karl Malden (1912–2009) as veteran detective lieutenant Mike Stone and relative newcomer Michael Douglas (1944–) as his young partner, Inspector Steve Keller. The casting had an interesting aspect in that Stone and Keller are almost like father and son in the series and Michael Douglas is the actual son of Hollywood giant Kirk Douglas (1917–), Malden's contemporary.

The Streets of San Francisco was a realistic cop show where modern methods were used to track down criminals. The stories were well written and had plenty of material that involved the complex relationship between the two leads, one seasoned, one cocky, but they both had something to learn from each other.

The show's location is further enhanced by prominently framing the Golden Gate Bridge in as many shots as possible. This iconic image with its unique orange glow gives atmosphere and character to the show. Actual official buildings were used for filming during the run of the production.

As the 1976–1977 season was about to begin, Michael Douglas left the show to concentrate on his growing movie career. The writers wrote out his character, having him leave to pursue a teaching career. He was replaced by Richard Hatch (1945–2017) as Inspector Dan Robbins.

Further Resources

Eliot, Marc. 2013. *Michael Douglas: A Biography*. New York: Three Rivers Press.

Malden, Karl. 1997. *When Do I Start? A Memoir with Carla Malden*. New York. Limelight.

Supertrain (ABC, 1979)

In 1978, programing wizard Fred Silverman left ABC to become president and CEO of the NBC television network. He had successes during his short tenure at ABC, but it was at NBC that he wholeheartedly supported a very expensive TV series, *Supertrain,* for which only nine episodes were produced. Among television critics, scholars, and historians, its legacy is that it was the biggest financial, creative, narrative, aesthetic, and physical production in modern television history. The show was *Supertrain*.

Supertrain was to television what *Heaven's Gate* (1980) was to motion pictures. The film brought down a movie studio because of its chaotic story, bloated production values, and less than stellar acting.

A Train Is Not a Ship

The concept of *Supertrain* was *The Love Boat* (1977–1987) on train tracks. Both were anthology shows, both had staff members who became involved in the lives and actions of the passengers. *The Love Boat* had at least three distinctly defined stories that ran over the course of the show in a parallel narrative method. *Supertrain* had one narrative with short side stories that were clearly connected to the principal plot.

The main set reportedly cost NBC $5,000,000. It was designed to look like a large luxury cruise liner. The train was purported to travel at more than 200 miles per hour. It was billed as a coast-to-coast trip. There were nine very large coach cars that had double decker windows. There was a swimming pool measuring 22 by 14 feet, also a bar and discotheque, a gym with a steam room, and a working medical center.

The train was powered by atomic energy and because it was so large, special extra-wide tracks were laid. For exterior shots a model of the Supertrain was built, often photographed with footage edited in to emphasize the power and speed of the Supertrain and to connect with the interior shots of the passengers engaged in the episodes' comings and goings.

It was a bold idea that the train was the star of the show. The interiors of the train were shot in a dark manner. Although the Supertrain was visually impressive, the design was a deliberate high-tech look that was absorbed quickly by the viewers and didn't have lasting excitement.

Less than a month after its premiere, while ratings continued to plummet, the decision was made to take the show off the air. Rather than accept failure, the decision was made by the NBC brass to retool the show mainly in terms of the cast and the teleplays. Dan Curtis (1927–2006), the driving force behind the cult classic horror soap opera *Dark Shadows* (1966–1971), was the creative power behind *Supertrain*. When asked by executives how to make the show successful, he told them to feed the project more money.

Supertrain was a drama, comedy, and adventure show—this made enjoying the stories difficult because at critical moments when the audience was on the edge of its seat, a joke would deflate the tension. None of the staff members were memorable or even likable like those on *The Love Boat*. The actors each week were not A stars but of B or C caliber.

NBC moved full out to publicize *Supertrain* as the next big thing. They even went so far as having the anchors and correspondents on the hit *The Today Show* (1952–) do many stories about the show.

After a month's hiatus *Supertrain* was back on the air, but it was too late and on July 28, 1979 *Supertrain* took its last trip.

In television there are no sure things; often a show that becomes a big hit almost didn't make air because an executive didn't like it. *Supertrain* could have been a big hit among youngsters because of the action, adventure, and pure size of the show. Adults should have enjoyed the drama and tension of a 36-hour trip from New York to Los Angeles with danger lurking and other emotional values, yet nothing clicked. *Jaws* (1975) had a lone shark as the star of the mega-hit movie. A train is not the same as a shark.

See also: *The Love Boat*.

Further Resources

Bedell, Sally. 1981. *Up the Tube: Prime Time-TV and the Silverman Years*. New York: Viking Adult.

Vranich, Joseph. 1991. *Supertrains: Solutions to America's Transportation Gridlock*. New York: St. Martin's Press.

Taxi (ABC, 1978–1982; NBC, 1982–1983)

Taxi was a sitcom placed in the Sunshine Cab Company located in New York City. The show was created by four veterans of *The Mary Tyler Moore Show* (1970-1977), including James L. Brooks (1940–), who would achieve more fame in television and become a top movie director.

Another workplace half-hour sitcom with an ensemble cast, *Taxi* featured Judd Hirsch (1935–) as Alex Reiger, a full-time, lifelong cab driver. Jeff Conaway (1950–2011) played a struggling actor, Bobby Wheeler,

Taxi was a popular sitcom about a taxi company and the various personalities who worked there. Pictured is Andy Kaufman (left) as Latka Gravas and Judd Hirsch as Alex Reiger in the episode "Paper Marriage," originally aired on October 31, 1978. (CBS via Getty Images)

a cabbie. Tony Danza (1951–) played Tony Banta, a struggling boxer and cab driver. Randall Carver (1946–) was John Burns, a naïve student who happens to land in the taxi business. Marilu Henner (1952–) played Elaine Nardo, an aspiring art dealer. Danny DeVito (1944–) was Louie DePalma, the cruel and sadistic dispatcher who taunted everyone through the fenced-in cage that separated him from everyone, and Andy Kaufman (1949–1984) was a cab mechanic named Latka. Added later was a most noteworthy character, "Reverend" Jim Ignatowski, a burned-out sixties type played to the hilt by Christopher Lloyd (1938–).

The clash of personalities kept *Taxi* full of funny situations and great one-liners. The characters were also a family of sorts. Most of the episodes took place in the taxi yard but the writers used locations to create scenes that would reveal more about the characters. The most unusual actor/comedian to appear in a network sitcom was Andy Kaufman, who literally defied categorization. He was really a performance artist who mimed to records and once had an audience gather in a theater only to load them on a bus and take them to a grammar school where they were fed milk and cookies. Latka was foreign, shy, spoke with a high-toned voice, and could barely be understood. He was perceived as possessing a demonic aura.

Louie was a favorite with his rants and raves, ordering everyone around like a dictator. Alex was the steady one who tried to look out for everyone. Still, they were a motley crew.

Taxi won 15 Emmys in five seasons but struggled in the ratings and eventually moved from ABC to NBC. There was even a deal in the works for Home Box Office to air the show, but that failed.

Taxi had the perfect combination for a successful show, a clever premise, good writing, excellent characters, and the actors to play them. Eventually it went into syndication and was available on DVD, but *Taxi* proved how difficult the game of network television was to play. This was a show that should have had a longer life.

See also: *Cheers*; *The Mary Tyler Moore Show*.

Further Resources

King, Susan. 2015. "Taxi: (TV Program) In 'Forever' and Beyond Judd Hirsch Has a Taste for History." *Los Angeles Times*. May 2. http://www.latimes.com/topic/entertainment/television/taxi-(tv-program)-ENTTV0000600-topic.html

Zmuda, Bob, and Lynne Margulies. 2014. *Andy Kaufman: The Truth, Finally*. Dallas, TX: Ben Bella Books.

The $10,000 Pyramid (CBS, 1973–1974; ABC, 1974–1976)

Looking practically the same as he had on *American Bandstand* (1952–1989) with his hair in the same parted-on-the-side style but just fashionably longer for the 1970s, Dick Clark was the first (and repeated through the decades) host of a game show that over time would increase the grand prize from $10,000, to $20,000, to $25,000, to $50,000, topping out at $100,000. The original show, *The $10,000 Pyramid,* was a great success in large part because of Dick Clark's cool, relaxed manner and smooth, resonant disc-jockey voice. He was a high-quality host who supported the clever game show by informing, instructing, and assisting the players as they moved through the phases.

The Setup

The set had a board on which two rows of topics were identified. There were two contestants teamed with celebrity players, who included Edward Asner (1929–), Sandy Duncan (1946–), Tony Randall (1920–2004), Rita Moreno (1931–), and Soupy Sales (1926–2009). They were asked to pick a topic like "Behind Bars." The team that went first had one clue giver and one receiver. There were seven clues and the giver offered the words such as "cell," "warden," "guard," and so on. The object was to get them all correct and move up the pyramid, but, if not, the team received the appropriate number of correct answers, which were identified in a box. Then the other team would pick a topic and proceed in the same fashion. This would go on until all the topics were used up. When the winner was declared Dick Clark escorted them to a back area where the lighting was lower. They were seated facing each other with the large $10,000 pyramid behind the receiver. This was a harder game because the contestant was going for the big money. The essence of the game was the same but where the first game allowed phrases and a nonstop approach including hand gestures, the segment for $10,000 only allowed one or two words at a time and the giver had to sit very still. The word turned on the board signaling the answer was right. If there was a problem getting the answer, "pass" could be called. If all topic segments of the pyramid were turned before the allotted 60 seconds, the contestant won $10,000.

To add excitement to the proceedings, the director of the show could get a side two-shot of the players as they moved up the pyramid board one correct answer at a time, and simultaneously below, show a split-screen of the board sections turning around as the right answer was recorded.

Dick Clark really knew the game and after a session was over he would suggest possible clues that might have helped the players. He commented about especially tough topics and gently joked about mistakes that had been made.

Bob Stewart (1920–2002) actually created *The $10,000 Pyramid*, but it is Dick Clark, who seemed to do everything in television, who will be forever associated with the game.

See also: *Vol. 1, The 1950s–1960s:* Clark, Dick.

Further Resources

Moll, James. 1999. "Dick Clark: Producer, Host, Executive." *Archive of American Television*. July 29. http://www.emmytvlegends.org/interviews/people/dick-clark

TV Tropes. "Series: Pyramid." http://tvtropes.org/pmwiki/pmwiki.php/Series/Pyramid

This Old House (PBS, 1979–)

Although he was not the host for the entire run of this home restoration/home building show, *This Old House* is synonymous with Bob Vila, who inspired decades of home-improvement enthusiasts, how-to shows, and even a comedy show, *Home Improvement* (1991–1999).

Bob Vila attended the University of Florida in his home state and later was in the Peace Corps where he was engaged in building houses in Panama. Still later he started a home remodeling business, which won a Better Homes and Gardens award. This led to him being approached to sign a contract to host a new home-restoration television series on PBS (Public Broadcasting Service) called *This Old House.* This launched Bob Vila into stardom and created a brand that included books and *This Old House* magazine.

The original concept was to restore houses of different styles. When one project was finished, the reno vating team moved on to the next. Some varieties of home styles were a modest city house, a stately home, a suburban ranch house, and a Greek revival farmhouse. Eventually the show, now retitled as *The All New This Old House,* actually built a house from scratch.

This Old House detailed the renovation of a home room by room and step by step. Sometimes the owners were involved, sometimes not. Bob Vila had a team of experts for each aspect of the remodeling. Some demolition was involved, such as ripping down sheetrock from the walls using the back end of a hammer, which Vila would engage in. There were plumbers, electricians, tile experts, and almost always on hand was master carpenter Norm Abram (1949–), who would eventually become a host on the show.

Viewers marveled at the documentary-like footage as the work was actually being done. Time cuts in the editing and other postproduction techniques were used to compress the long process into the show's one-hour time slot.

Although it wasn't a detailed how-to, step-by-step show, viewers were motivated to redo their own homes, bought new tools, researched various building techniques, and attempted to replicate what was accomplished on *This Old House*.

Bob Vila was a television superstar because he had name and face recognition and audiences related to him. His secret was that he explained things well and interviewed the workers so all the details of the project were clear. He always seemed in a hurry, talked fast, and, at times, had one foot out of the room. This was because he had to go to another part of the house to introduce the workers there and explain the nature of their tasks. Bob Vila was always on the run, covering a lot of ground each week. He often addressed the viewer directly by talking straight into the camera, which at times was hand-held to follow the action. *This Old House* presaged the how-to genre, which in the 21st century had its own cable channel—DIY.

See also: *Vol. 3, The 1990s–Present:* HGTV (Home and Garden Television); *Home Improvement.*

Further Resources

Vila, Bob. 1980. *This Old House: Restoring, Rehabilitating, and Renovating an Older House.* New York. Little, Brown.

Vila, Bob. 1981. *Bob Vila's This Old House.* New York: Plume.

Three's Company (ABC, 1977–1984)

Three's Company was a family sitcom with a twist: the family consisted of single roommates, two young women and a young man. Because of the landlord's rule against co-eds, the man pretends he is gay.

Three's Company is also a kind of sex farce with story lines about ongoing flirty relationships involving each of the roommates and their romantic entanglements. *Three's Company* is based on the British program *Man About the House* (1973–1976). The American show was set in Los Angeles. The half-hour sitcom starred John Ritter (1948–2003) as Jack Tripper, a self-employed chef; Joyce DeWitt (1949–) as the dark-haired, pretty, and sensible roommate Janet Wood, who is a florist; and Suzanne Somers (1946–) as Chrissy Snow, who is what the movies would call a dumb blonde and an extremely voluptuous one who is employed as a secretary. Stanley Roper, the landlord, was played by Norman Fell (1924–1998), and his sex-craved wife, Helen Roper, was played by Audra Lindley (1918–1991).

The episodes invariably included suggestive situations and repartee, as well as farcical circumstances. *Three's Company* is also what has been named by industry insiders as "jiggle TV." Simply put, this unofficial genre is defined by having female characters shake and shimmy so the top and bottom parts of their figures excite male viewers.

The Content

The comedy content of *Three's Company* is generated by male/female relationships between the roommates and other males and females who become characters in individual episodes. A side story, also sexual in nature, was the extent to which Stanley Roper would go to avoid having to make love to his wife, and Helen Roper's reaction to what she thinks goes on in the roommates' apartment—both characters have great one-liners about sex.

Jack, Janet, and Chrissy are put into a seemingly endless run of nonsensical situations involving sex. Double entendres pepper the dialogue for the slim but enjoyable stories.

Three's Company became an instant success, landing in the third most popular spot for the 1977–1978 season. Audiences enjoyed the three main characters, but it was Suzanne Somers who became a superstar and for many men followed in the tradition of Betty Grable, Marilyn Monroe, and Farrah Fawcett Majors—a sex goddess.

Unlike many 1970s comedies *Three's Company* had practically no serious aspects or political or social themes. Audiences needed a laugh without a message in addition to those comedies that made them laugh and think. *Three's Company* made them laugh and laugh.

See also: Silverman, Fred.

Further Resources

Mann, Chris. 1998. *Come and Knock on Our Door: A His and Hers Guide to "Three's Company."* New York: St. Martin's Press.

Somers, Suzanne. 2009. *Breakthrough: Eight Steps to Wellness.* New York: Crown.

Tomorrow with Tom Snyder (The Tomorrow Show) (NBC, 1973–1982)

Tom Snyder (1936–2007) began his career in radio as a reporter in several different markets across the United States. During the 1960s Snyder moved into television as a news anchorman, again in several markets, and then landed in New York, first at WNBC–TV, then WABC–TV.

In 1973 he and NBC embarked on a bold experiment. *The Tonight Show with Johnny Carson* (1962–1992) continued to dominate late night, but there was no talk show on the air after Carson for those who wanted to stay up later or those whose job shifts brought them home late with nothing to watch. *The Tomorrow Show* (as it came to be known) began at 1 a.m. and wasn't anything like the Carson show. After an opening title card, almost immediately the camera would be so close on Snyder there was little room for anything else in the frame. It revealed a man, usually smoking a cigarette, who had long, slightly gray hair and a gigantic comb-over. He had a good broadcaster's voice and communicated well with the viewers. He had a loud, rollicking "ho-ho-ho" kind of laugh, which showed how much he enjoyed himself.

There was no monologue to start the show. In a conversational tone that was most likely extemporaneous, Snyder would start talking about something in the news, something on his mind, or he'd pick a topic and run with it. He would look directly into the camera, then as if he'd studied the acting of Orson Welles, he would look off briefly and then reestablish direct eye contact with the viewer. At times he would talk about something a viewer sent him. He loved his viewers and told them they were the best audience because they cared, they listened, and they could laugh and then be deadly serious. Snyder would announce upcoming guests. Frequently, he spoke directly to his crew, whom he loved, while he was on the air.

One year very close to New Year's Eve, a particularly memorable letter was sent to Snyder. The writer said that some weeks back he had decided to end his life and had everything set to do so. For some reason the gentleman decided to turn on *The Tomorrow Show*. He had never watched it before. At the time,

Snyder happened to be telling a particularly emotional life–affirming story. It made the writer decide life was worth living and he halted his suicide plans. At this point, Snyder moved even closer to the camera lens and closer to his viewers. Tom Snyder's face turned angry. He believed in television and didn't like it when people said it wasn't meaningful. After a pause he said something like, "Now don't you tell me that television isn't important!" Then he went on with the show.

Tom Snyder loved broadcasting and adored old broadcasters, whom he invited as guests. They were his celebrities. Once he did a remote feed for an interview with Charles Manson (1934–). In the studio he conducted what is believed to be the last interview with John Lennon, who said he could just walk around and be a regular guy. When Lennon was murdered by a deranged fan, Snyder talked about it and then ran the entire interview.

When Snyder would toss to a commercial, he told the viewers precisely how long it would be before he'd be back—down to the second!

Later in the show's multiyear run, Snyder had rock groups on, but he never seemed to really know who they were, nevertheless, he enjoyed their company and it was great for the ratings as it attracted a younger demographic.

Tom Snyder was an innovator—with the help of NBC he invented late, late night TV, a staple of television in the 21st century. He also kept the tradition of quality broadcasting alive by preserving its history at the same time as he was making it.

See also: *Vol. 3, The 1990s–Present: Jimmy Kimmel Live!*; *The Late Late Show with Craig Ferguson.*

Further Resources

Chowka, Peter Barry. 2007. "Tom Snyder (1936–2007): A Personal Recollection." July 31. http://www.americanthinker.com/articles/2007/07/tom_snyder_19362007_a_personal.html

Horowicz, Michael. 2012. "A Fond Remembrance of Tom Snyder on the 5th Anniversary of His Death." July 26. http://www.tvweek.com/open-mic/2012/07/a-fond-rembrance-of-tom-snyder-on-the-5th-anniversary-of-his-death-a-larger-than-life-news-personality.

20/20 (ABC, 1978–)

In 1968 when the CBS News production *60 Minutes* began its run, it was described as a television news magazine. The format presented individual stories on different subjects featuring different reporters for each segment. This new television journal turned heads in the industry and the competing networks were quick to respond.

The show *20/20* was ABC's entry into the format. Unfortunately, it had a flatfooted start. The original hosts, Harold Hayes (1926–1989), a forward-thinking editor at *Esquire* magazine, and Robert Hughes (1938–2012), an Australian-born art critic, were both fired after the very first show. The situation improved when Hugh Downs (1921–) was brought in the next week. *20/20* became a co-hosted program when in 1979 Barbara Walters (1929–) joined the broadcast.

Hugh Downs had a big challenge. The audience that had tuned in the first week to see *20/20* watched a lopsided program with a blend of humorous features, investigative reports, and even definitions of polysyllabic words. Downs hit the ground running with quality investigative and background reports to spark viewer interest. It was a weekly show in the summer of 1978, moved to a monthly time slot in the fall, and eventually became a regular weekly show. Recurring contributors to *20/20* included Geraldo Rivera (1943–), Stone Phillips (1954–), and Sylvia Chase (1939–), among others.

The seasoned Barbara Walters was a top-notch interviewer who could talk to celebrities and political figures around the world. This was a move to out-guest the competition.

20/20 was the brainchild of Roone Arledge, who by 1978 was the president of sports and news. Competing with CBS's *60 Minutes* was formidable and Arledge did it by meeting the hit show on its own terms, offering news reports, investigative journalism, and celebrity interviews. The key was that the two shows ran on different nights so theoretically a viewer could watch both. Another strategy was to promote *20/20* heavily and have stories not covered by their competitor—stories with after network teasers the viewer was anxious to watch. Arledge understood there was room for more than one TV news magazine in the same way as there is more than one major print magazine on the rack.

See also: *A Current Affair*; *Entertainment Tonight*; *Hard Copy*; *Inside Edition*; *This Week with David Brinkley*; *Vol. 1, The 1950s–1960s: 60 Minutes*.

Further Resources

Downs, Hugh. 2012. *Yours Truly, Hugh Downs*. New Orleans, LA: Garrett County Press.

Jackson, Oprah. 2012. *Barbara Walters—Biography of a First Class Broadcast Journalist*. Amazon Digital Services.

Variety Shows

The genre of variety shows goes back to radio and its transference to early television. The format is simple, much like a talent show, with vaudeville or burlesque absent any profanity or female nudity.

On television there is a host or a pair or team of hosts who do an introductory monologue or routine, then for the rest of show, usually one hour of broadcast time, guests are introduced and perform their acts—singing, dancing, or being funny. The core of a variety show is the skit—a comic scene possibly with a theme related to the host and performed with the host and guests. The skit produces entertainment and merriment. Each week the host and format remains constant but the guest stars change.

The thought process behind a network's selection of variety show hosts on which to build a series is based largely on popularity. Name recognition or brand association can guarantee success or failure. Sometimes network wisdom moved in the direction of a household name, but other times the powers-that-be would go out on a limb and approach a cult personality, hoping they could discover new talent viewers would welcome into their homes.

The 1970s were no different from the 1950s or 1960s in that network chiefs, their staffs, and their programmers searched for just the right host to emcee a variety show. Variety shows were still very popular in the 1970s (unfortunately that would not last), and as always the Nielsen ratings were in their sights.

Big names were sought for popular shows that included *The Carol Burnett Show* (1967–1978), *Make Your Own Kind of Music* (1971) hosted by Richard Carpenter (1946–) and Karen Carpenter (1950–1983), *The Andy Williams Show* (1957–1976), *Glen Campbell Goodtime Hour* (1969–1972), *The Flip Wilson Show* (1970–1974), *The Sonny and Cher Comedy Hour* (1971–1974), *The Bobby Darin Show* (1973), *Sha Na Na* (1977–1981) hosted by Sha Na Na, a group of young men who dressed, groomed, acted, and sang as if they were in the 1950s and 1960s even though it was the 1970s, and *The Dean Martin Show* (1965–1974).

Some of these shows began before the 1970s and continued through the decade and beyond. Most were successful like *The Andy Williams Show* and some were not, such as the show hosted by the Carpenters. In an unfortunate turn of events, Bobby Darin died of chronic heart problems in 1973, the last year his show was produced.

The riskier names approached for their own variety show in the 1970s included Manhattan Transfer, whose self-named show ran for four weeks in the summer of 1975. This unique singing group selected tunes from the 1940s up to the present day with a distinctive harmonic style, but the show did not go to series. The syndicated *Bobby Goldsboro Show,* hosted by Bobby Goldsboro, a pop and country-western singer who had a number one hit with "Honey," did not make it past the year it began (1972). Dolly Parton's show, *Dolly,* ran for one season despite her popularity in the country-western world as a hit singer and performer. *The Rich Little Show* featured master impressionist and comedian Rich Little (1938–), but couldn't get out of 1976, the same year it had started. The most surprising selection for a variety show host was African American comedian Richard Pryor (1940–2005), because he was widely known for his very blue comedic material. NBC wanted to take advantage of his notoriety but made several misjudgments. They placed *The Richard Pryor Show* in the family hour when children would be watching. It was an hour-long show. They then put Pryor against two major sitcom hits on ABC, *Happy Days* and *Laverne and Shirley.* The star and the network entered into a heated dispute over censorship of a sketch in which the comedian appeared to be totally naked (he was really wearing a body stocking), and he explained to the viewers that he had given nothing up to get his own series. The network won and deleted the sketch. Pryor then put a halt to production. In total *The Richard Pryor Show* ran only from September 13, 1977 to October 1977.

Variety shows in the 1970s were plentiful and the music, the comedy, the sketches and dances all reflected the decade but in a more breezy way so audiences would not become depressed as they did when they watched the nightly news.

See also: *Saturday Night Live*; *The Sonny and Cher Comedy Hour*; *Vol. 1, The 1950s–1960s: The Andy Williams Show*; *The Carol Burnett Show*.

Further Resources

Cook, Kevin. 2013. *Flip: The Inside Story of TV's First Black Superstar*. New York: Viking.

Williams, Andy. 2008. *Andy Williams: Moon River and Me: A Memoir*. New York: Viking.

Wall $treet Week with Louis Rukeyser (PBS, 1970–2005)

Louis Rukeyser (1933–2006) was the son of financial journalist Merryle Stanley Rukeyser (1897–1989). Louis Rukeyser attended Princeton University in the Woodrow Wilson School of Public and International Affairs. He also was a part of the University Press Club.

Upon graduating Rukeyser reported for 11 years as a political and foreign correspondent for the *Baltimore Sun*, and in 1970 he began working on the popular show on the Public Broadcasting Service, *Wall $treet Week with Louis Rukeyser,* which was produced by Maryland Public Television (MPT), a PBS member station, at their facilities in Owings Mills, Maryland.

The basic format of *Wall $treet Week with Louis Rukeyser* was to begin with a commentary on the week's financial news delivered by Rukeyser, then a summary of market statistics. There was a panel discussion with financial analysts, usually three experts who opined about the stock market and gave specific stock recommendations.

Rukeyser moderated a mail segment in which the panelists would answer questions submitted by the viewers. The show had a serious tone because of its subject, but Rukeyser lightened the mood when he could, appealing to viewers to send more letters and delivering pun-filled comments.

Before the show's final segment, which was an interview with an important financial figure, Rukeyser would share his wisdom on a specific aspect of financial life such as mutual funds or a specific area of the stock market and investing.

Some significant guests included John Kenneth Galbraith (1908–2006), Alan Greenspan (1926–), and Malcolm Forbes (1919–1990).

The beauty of this long-running show is that it appealed not only to business people or Wall Street investors. It was an educational program and many who didn't know about finance and business tuned in for teaching moments. The show was the most watched PBS program for many years. *Wall $treet Week with Louis Rukeyser* was there to serve that important need.

See also: *Adam Smith's Money World*; PBS (Public Broadcasting Service).

Further Resources

Rukeyser, Louis. 1976. *How to Make Money on Wall Street*. St. Charles, MO: Main Street Books.

Rukeyser, Louis. 1997. *Louis Rukeyser's Book of Lists*. New York: Henry Holt.

Walters, Barbara (1929–)

Prior to the 1970s Barbara Walters had worked on the NBC *Today Show* (1952–) in different but not important capacities such as writing and producing stories that would interest women. She was an excellent interviewer, was popular with the viewers, and as a result was given more and more air time. Her life began to change in 1971 when host Hugh Downs left the show. Walters was not afforded the courtesy of input and NBC hired a capable broadcaster in Frank McGee (1921–1974). Although they worked together as she had with Hugh Downs, unlike Downs, McGee was unfriendly and even hostile, demanding control of the interview segment even if Walters was the interviewer. When McGee passed away, Walters had a clause added to her contract that she would have to become co-host on *Today,* which she did when Jim Hartz (1940–) was hired in 1974. Barbara Walters became the first woman in news or public affairs to have a co-host title. In 1976 she switched to ABC, the network that would continue to be her home, and joined the *ABC Nightly News* (1970–1978), triumphantly becoming the first woman to co-anchor a news program. The male broadcaster was Harry Reasoner (1923–1991). He was not happy to be co-hosting the show with anyone—especially a woman. Barbara Walters's dream had come true but speedily became a nightmare. Every night Reasoner barely acknowledged Walters and, at times, actually chided her on air. By all accounts, Harry Reasoner was openly mean to Barbara Walters and in 1978 the relationship was all over.

In 1976 Barbara Walters began hosting a special interview show several times a year. She would sit opposite actors and actresses, heads of state, the famous and the infamous, and demonstrate unique interview skills and a reputation as a tough questioner who could be relentless and could make her subject cry if she wanted to.

In 1979 she was happily reunited on the news/magazine program *20/20* with Hugh Downs. Special-interest stories were discussed by the co-hosts and an edited film package was presented for the stories covered each week.

As the 1970s drew to a close Barbara Walters would continue to be a dominant and iconic figure in news and entertainment, inventing new formats and continuing to create and execute specials that had mass audience appeal.

See also: *20/20*; *Vol. 1, The 1950s–1960s: The Today Show*.

Further Resources

Oppenheimer, Jerry. 1990. *Barbara Walters: An Unauthorized Biography*. New York: St. Martin's Press.

Walters, Barbara. 2009. *Audition: A Memoir*. New York: Vintage Books.

The Waltons (CBS, 1972–1981)

The very definition of family drama, *The Waltons* ran on CBS and was based largely on the experiences of the show's creator, Earl Hammer Jr. (1923–2016). It told stories of a large, close-knit family that lived in rural Virginia during the Great Depression in the 1930s. Hammer had written about his boyhood before and it was told in the feature film *Spencer's Mountain* released in 1963. He wrote a Christmas special titled *The Homecoming* that aired on December 19, 1971. In it he created the Walton family; the show was not intended as a series pilot but viewer reaction was strong, and CBS gave the go-ahead to develop a series around the Walton family. It required some retooling, which was no problem for Hammer.

The network, however, didn't give *The Waltons* much of a chance to succeed because in 1972 it was scheduled opposite the enormously popular *The Flip Wilson Show* on NBC. Despite that positioning, the show caught on and received good reviews and Emmys, and finished 20th in the ratings at the end of the first season.

The large cast included Richard Thomas (1951–) as John (John-Boy), the eldest child. Mary Elizabeth McDonough (1961–) portrayed Erin, one of his sisters. Ralph Waite (1928–2014) was John Walton, the patriarch of the family. Olivia Walton, his wife and mother of the large family, was portrayed by Michael Learned (1939–). Will Geer (1902–1978) appeared as Zeb Walton, the grandfather, and Ellen Corby (1911–1999) was the grandma, Esther Walton. There also was a supporting cast of townspeople, most notably Ike Goodsey, played by Joe Conley (1928–2013), who ran a general store in Walton's Mountain, as the town was named in the tradition of the locally historic family. In addition to selling candy, cheese, and sundries, he also could give a shave in the back of the store and help anyone, especially the Waltons, whenever he could. The family was poor, but they were filled with dignity.

The Waltons had exceptional production values. The period was represented with great accuracy; it made viewers feel as if they really were back in the 1930s. The costumes were especially exacting and looked like real clothes of that era.

The Waltons was a long-running CBS family drama that explored life in rural Virginia during the Great Depression. Pictured here celebrating around a Christmas tree in a 1977 episode are Eric Scott as Ben Walton, Mary Elizabeth McDonough as Erin Walton, David W. Harper as Jim-Bob Walton, Judy Norton Taylor as Mary Ellen Walton, Kami Cotler as Elizabeth Walton, Will Geer as Zeb Walton, Ralph Waite as John Walton, and Michael Learned as Olivia Walton. (CBS Photo Archive/Getty Images)

It also was a show with no sex or violence, which was a reprieve for family viewers who had a lot of the former with which to contend. This was a show the whole family could watch.

There was narration from John-Boy's perspective, a remembrance of the times depicted in each week's show. At times John-Boy was shown at his desk writing in his journal about his life and his family.

One of the points of interest of the show was that the loyal audience bonded with the family. Throughout the run of the series viewers watched the children grow up and saw the family evolve and deal with issues of the time and timeless ones concerning relationships and family.

The Waltons had a signature closing. It was a full shot of the house at night with voice-overs of the family saying good night. "Good night, John-Boy" moved into the American vernacular.

The message of *The Waltons* is the meaning and significance of family. Life was hard during the Depression, but the warmth and humanity of the Walton family charmed audiences who wanted to go back to a time when American families bonded together and when love was pure.

See also: *Little House on the Prairie*.

Further Resources

Hammer, Earl, and Ralph E. Giffin. 2002. *Goodnight John-Boy*. Nashville, TN: Cumberland House Publishing.

McDonough, Mary. 2012. *Lessons from the Mountains*. New York: Kensington Publishing.

Watergate Scandal

In 1972, Republican president Richard Nixon was running for reelection. After the primary process the Democratic Party chose George McGovern (1922–2012), a senator from South Dakota, to run against the president. McGovern originally selected Thomas Eagleton (1929–2004), a senator from Missouri, as his vice presidential running mate. More than two weeks after the nominating convention, it was revealed that Eagleton had been hospitalized and given electroshock therapy for nervous exhaustion and depression several times during the early to mid-1960s. At first McGovern remained constant in his support of Eagleton, but after pressure mounted the senator from Missouri resigned from the ticket. McGovern then selected John F. Kennedy's brother-in-law Sargent Shriver (1915–2001), then the U.S. ambassador to France, as his running mate. The campaign went poorly with George McGovern losing by a huge margin.

President Nixon apparently had no intention of losing the election. On June 17, 1972, five men were arrested for breaking and entering the offices of the Democratic National Committee in the Watergate Hotel in Washington, D.C. After an investigation a select committee was established to examine the facts of what was now called Watergate.

> On the March 27, 1970 episode of *The Merv Griffin Show,* host Merv Griffin had among his guests political radical and activist Abbie Hoffman. Hoffman was there for a debate with Tony Dolan of Young Americans for Freedom, a conservative group, concerning the Vietnam War, which began in the 1960s and was still raging at the dawn of the 1970s. At one point Hoffman took off his jacket and revealed he was wearing an American flag shirt. The screen went blank as a disclaimer explained that the producers of the show felt it was improper to allow this disrespect of the American flag on the air. This continued throughout the segment; the picture was on when Hoffman wasn't in the shot and off when he was. Co-host Virginia Graham remarked that it was terrible that young men were going to Canada to avoid the draft. Mark Frechette, who was currently starring in the movie *Zabriskie Point,* called her stupid and an old biddy. Tony Dolan got up, walked over to Frechette, and demanded he apologize. Frechette rose and knocked Dolan down to the floor with one punch. Merv Griffin came forward and ended the show by announcing the guests for the next show.

Illegal Activtity

Sam Ervin (1896–1985), a Democratic senator from North Carolina who considered himself an old country lawyer, was named committee chairman. The minority party had Howard Baker (1925–2014) as the ranking member. Five more men rounded out the panel, which had four Democrats and three Republicans.

It became clear that the president of the United States was specifically involved in illegal activities concerning his Committee to Re-elect the President, with the objective being to derail the McGovern campaign.

The decision was made to televise the committee hearings from May 17 to August 7, 1973 so the American people could see the proceedings on a very serious issue that concerned the president and some of his staff.

Sam Ervin immediately established himself as well informed, folksy, but cagey and very determined to get to the truth of the matter. He may not have been typical of Washington at the time but nothing distracted him from the job. He was rotund and a bit disheveled in his manner. Americans grew to love Irvin, a man they trusted. He asked strong questions and kept everyone on all sides in line.

Even though he was from the same party as the president, Howard Baker, a man who fit the image of a senator in the public's mind, became a hero for the way he interrogated witnesses he felt were not telling the truth.

On June 25, 1973 John Dean (1938–) began his testimony. He had served as White House counsel to President Nixon from July 1970 until April 1973. He had been deeply involved in events leading up to the burglary and afterward when the cover-up operation occurred. He pleaded guilty to a felony in exchange for his testimony at the Watergate hearing. He was telegenic, handsome, well groomed, and dressed in a light suit. His wife Maureen, an attractive blonde, had her hair pulled back tightly. In Hollywood terms John Dean was the key witness.

Blueprints of the Watergate Hotel were enlarged and put on an easel so witnesses could respond to logistical questions using a large pointer to indicate the area in question. The five men who were at the break-in were named and identified. These men were known only to a few before the hearings—after expansive television coverage, they were national figures of the criminal kind.

The hearings were so widely watched that a national dialogue was created. Although there are always two sides to a story, the pressure on President Nixon tightened. It was established that phones were wired.

The turning point of the hearings came on June 28, 1973. Nixon was becoming more of a focus. There was a sense that a cancer was growing on the presidency. Then Howard Baker asked a question that in many forms has echoed through the decades: "What did the president know and when did he know it?" Some of the president's supporters in the administration played ignorant or lied.

The coverage and direction of the hearings through the use of close-ups, full shots, and especially reaction shots made viewers feel they were in the room.

When Attorney General John Mitchell (1919–1988) testified, he seemed disingenuous and unaware of what was going on. When he tried to bolster Nixon's character, the camera made a slow zoom into his face so the viewers could look into his soul.

Witness after witness revealed knowledge about a particular aspect of this ever-growing scandal that became a major crime. On July 24, Nixon listened to the Watergate tapes recorded in the White House and stated he would not let others listen to them.

John Ehrlichman (1925–1999) was counsel and assistant to the president for domestic affairs. If anyone seemed to be in a Hollywood movie, it was Ehrlichman. He smiled inappropriately, didn't seem to want to be there, and did not appear to understand how to conduct himself. He seemed as if he had his own agenda and often talked over the person on the committee who was questioning him, then gave some sort of answer that he waved off and asked to have the question repeated. More and more viewers were wondering who the men were who surrounded the president of the United States.

H. R. Haldeman (1926–1993) was President Nixon's chief of staff. He asked to read a statement that made it more than clear that he and the president had no involvement in this Watergate affair.

The Watergate hearings were covered by television cameras gavel-to-gavel from day one until August 7. There were 319 hours of coverage amassed, the most coverage ever for a single event. NBC, CBS, and ABC devoted an average of five hours a day to broadcast the hearings for the first five days. On the sixth day the networks devised a rotation system, shifting responsibility to cover the hearings from one to the other every third day. Any of the three were welcome to cover more of the event than required by the agreement. This only happened once when all three networks chose to cover the more than 30 hours of testimony given by John Dean.

The Public Broadcasting Service (PBS) aired videotape of each day's proceedings and ran them in the evening. Many PBS managers were at first reluctant to run the hearings, but they did and ratings went up and more contributions came in to the stations.

At the conclusion of the first phase of the hearings ratings dropped a bit, but audience reaction moved in the direction of televising the coming aspect of this event to begin on September 24, 1973. The Ervin Committee continued with the Watergate hearing until February 1974 but there was hardly any coverage. Still, 85 percent of households watched some portion of the hearings.

On February 6 a new phase of the Watergate saga started. This one examined whether Richard Nixon should be impeached as president of the United States. There was a struggle to get the cameras in on this process; ultimately the networks agreed to broadcast the proceedings without commercial breaks.

The House Judiciary Committee began their televised public debate on the evening of July 24; the commercial networks used the rotation system again. They also chose to only air the nighttime sessions while PBS made the decision to air the morning and afternoon sessions as well. All totaled, the viewing public was able to watch all or part of 13 hours of coverage for each of the six days that the Judiciary Committee met for public deliberations.

After some time the full House and Senate allowed television coverage for the impeachment proceedings. The television personnel had to assure the political powers that the presence of TV cameras and lights would not interfere with the due process rights of the president. The proceedings came to a halt when Richard Nixon announced he would be stepping down as president of the United States.

On August 8, 1974, Richard Nixon addressed the nation from the Oval Office. It was the 37th time in his presidency that he had done so. A single camera from what appeared to be a fixed position started in a full shot revealing the president sitting behind his desk flanked on either side by a flag. He was holding a number of papers that contained his remarks. As he began the camera zoomed into a medium shot. After some general remarks he mentioned Watergate and that he wouldn't allow the misery it had brought to the country and his family to go on any longer. Then he said that he was resigning the presidency effective noon the next day, which was August 9.

He continued reading from the paper, looking up as often as he could. He talked about sadness. The camera zoomed back as he talked about the process of healing. He admitted that among the good decisions he had made as president, some were wrong. As he said he had no bitterness for those who opposed him, he appeared to pause and almost grimace. In a full shot he listed and annotated in great detail all the good things he had done for the country and the world during his presidency. He talked about peace and that he had made the world safer. Then it was over. The next day cameras would capture Richard Nixon's goodbye as he was about to board a helicopter taking his family to the plane that would take him home. With a big smile on his face he thrust his left arm across his body and straightened it out to a wave. Then he outstretched both arms and crossed them, his hands in peace signs. Then he turned and went into the helicopter.

Also televised was the swearing-in of the man who would follow Richard Nixon as president, Gerald Ford (1913–2006). The ceremony was held in the East Room of the White House. Supreme Court Justice Warren Burger (1907–1995) swore him in while Betty Ford (1918–2011), the new first lady, was at her husband's side.

Then the new president took to the podium and made his remarks. He talked about this extraordinary moment in history. He asked the country to pray for him. He made it clear that no secret promises had been made. He said he would be president to all the people. Then with candor and honesty his voice rose and he said, "My fellow Americans, our long national nightmare is over." He talked about the Constitution, the law, and the fact that the people rule. He talked about the wounds of Watergate and brotherly love and a higher power. He asked for prayers for Richard Nixon and his family, and for the country to pray for him. He closed with what the country needed to hear: "God helping me, I will not let you down!"

Television had been tested again, asked to cover a complex and historic political event—this one like no other. One for the ages.

See also: *Vol. 1, 1950s–1960s:* Army-McCarthy Hearings.

Further Resources

Bernstein, Carl, and Bob Woodward. 1976. *All the President's Men*. New York: Simon & Schuster.

Sheppard, Geoff. 2015. *The Real Watergate Scandal: Collusion, Conspiracy, and the Plot That Brought Nixon Down*. Washington, D.C.: Regnery History.

Welcome Back Kotter (ABC, 1975–1979)

This show is about a teacher who returns to James Buchanan High School in Brooklyn, New York where he had been a student. He is now teaching a rag-tag group called the Sweathogs. The main cast included teacher Gabe Kotter, who was played by Gabe Kaplan (1945–), a stand-up comedian who was the co-creator and one of the producers of the half-hour sitcom that aired on ABC. His wife, Julie Kotter, played by Marcia Straussman (1948–2014), was Gabe's best friend. She was concerned that her husband didn't always take his home life and classroom responsibilities seriously enough.

The vice principal who becomes the principal, Michael Woodman, played by John Sylvester White (1919–1988), didn't like the Sweathogs and considered them the bottom of the student food chain. He let the class know his opinion with a barrage of insults when he came into Kotter's classroom.

The actual unofficial star of the show was John Travolta (1954–), who was 25 years old when the show first aired. He played what most people called the most colorful character, Vinnie Barbarino. Barbarino was cocky and considered himself the leader of the Sweathogs. He sang out loud in class and was behind most of the stunts pulled against Mr. Kotter and Principal Woodman. He wore a shag haircut and was an all-around cut-up. This was John Travolta's first career exposure before he became a superstar in *Saturday Night Fever,* released in 1977.

Arnold Horshak was the class clown who had a laugh executed by taking air in forcibly while making a loud sound repeatedly. Horshak was played by Ron Palillo (1949–2012).

African American actor Lawrence Hilton-Jacobs (1953–) played Freddie Percy "Boom" Washington, a hip basketball-playing student. Most often he was considered the voice of reason among the Sweathogs, but he was not above joining in on the shenanigans from time to time.

Robert Hegyes (1951–2012), a student who was half Puerto Rican and half Jewish, was the tough guy of the Sweathogs troupe.

The theme song to *Welcome Back Kotter,* "Welcome Back," was composed and sung by Lovin' Spoonful front man John Sebastian (1944–) and was performed in the laid-back style of his successful solo career. It recalled bygone days and created a word picture of the dreams Kotter had as a student commenting on his realized dream as a teacher.

The main set was the classroom complete with American flag and a chalkboard. The show was filmed in front of a live audience and was very funny. The adolescent humor was balanced with the generally humorous adult life of Mr. Kotter. At times the show would begin at the Kotter home where he and his wife would chat in a comical manner and set up the show to follow. At the end they came back home and talked to wrap up the show.

See also: *Saved by the Bell.*

Further Resources

Kaplan, Gabe. 2007. *Kotter's Back: E-Mails from a Faded Celebrity to a Bewildered World.* New York: Simon Spotlight Entertainment.

Wensley, Clarkson. 1996. *John Travolta: Back in Character*. Woodstock, NY: Overlook Press.

The White Shadow (CBS, 1978–1981)

This show falls into the sports drama category. CBS along with all the major networks of the era were invested in actual sports, basketball being one of them. *The White Shadow* was about high school basketball, a fictional look at youngsters playing the game. The audience demographic was basketball and sports fans and drama enthusiasts who liked to see emotional depth regardless of topic or characters. Like all great TV shows *The White Shadow* was only tangentially about basketball. It was about perseverance, challenge, hope, race, intergenerational relationships, and learning to accept who you are and then do better.

The Narrative

The story concerned Ken Reeves, played by Ken Howard (1944–2016), a white professional basketball player for the Chicago Bulls who suffers a serious knee injury and must retire early. A former college classmate convinces Reeves to become a basketball coach at Carver High School, a mainly black and Hispanic institution in South Central Los Angeles, where the friend is now principal. It takes some prodding but he takes the jump. The team is in shambles and many of the players have been and continue to get in trouble with the law.

It takes some time but the coach gets the team on their feet; they win games and feel better about themselves. The beginning of the team/coach relationship was filled with lack of trust, stereotyping on both sides. Reeves learns that he has to do more than teach basketball. He visits the homes of his players and tries to get to the root of their problems. These players come from poor families with many struggles. *The White Shadow* is a significant show that places the students' conflicts in the real world and specifically in the world of urban high school life. The students dream of being important athletes one day or more importantly, successful, respected citizens.

The cast included Kevin Hooks (1958–) as Morris Thrope, Erik Kilpatrick as Curtis Jackson, Byron Stewart (1956–) as Warren Coolidge, Thomas Carter (1953–) as James Hayward, Nathan Cook as Milton Reese (1950–1988), Timothy Van Patten (1959–) as

Mario, Ken Michelman (1955–) as Abner Goldstein, and Ira Angustain (1958–) as Ricardo Gomez.

How to cope in a difficult world was a challenge and a lesson learned from the team and the coach. Ken Reeves learned that he was not just a coach but a teacher, a leader who got his team to win, but more importantly helped them make the transition from boys to men.

Most weeks *The White Shadow* had a feature that accomplished getting the themes of the show across but without dialogue. The scenes were so powerful and emotionally enjoyable that regular viewers waited for them religiously. In one scene the team is in the shower area, presumably after a practice or a game they may have won or lost. In the tradition of the 1950s and early 1960s, they begin to sing a capella. One of the boys starts to sing the oldies hit "Duke of Earl" written in 1962 by Bernice Williams and Earl Edwards and first sung definitively by Gene Chandler (1937–).

The lead singer pours his heart into his rendition of this classic song as the rest of the boys sing backup. The lyrics start with many repetitions of the title. Then "The Duke of Earl" sings to a woman he wants to be his duchess. "Duke of Earl" is about being invincible, about being someone, about love and protection, and empowerment, and because it is a group song it is ultimately about unity.

See also: *Vol. 3, The 1990s–Present: Friday Night Lights.*

Further Resources

Harnick, Chris. 2013. "Ken Howard on 'The White Shadow,' '30 Rock,' and More for 'Isn't That . . . ?'" October 13. *Huffpost TV.* http://www.huffingtonpost.com/2013/10/18/ken-howard-the-white-shadow-isnt-that_n_4098177.html

Kuchar, Bill. 2004. *Coaching High School Basketball: A Complete Guide to Building a Championship Team.* New York: McGraw-Hill.

Wiseman, Frederick (1930–)

Just one aspect (of many) that makes Frederick Wiseman unique as a documentary filmmaker is that he had received a bachelor's degree in law at the prestigious Yale Law School. In 1951 he achieved a bachelor's degree in the arts from Williams College. After a stint in the military and some time in Paris, Frederick Wiseman started teaching law at Boston University's Institute of Law and Medicine.

A Prestigious Documentary Film Career Begins

In June 1966 Frederick Wiseman filmed his first documentary, *Titicut Follies*, shot on location at the Massachusetts Correctional Institution, Bridgewater. The inmates were criminally insane. Wiseman filmed life there and also discovered that the guards were bullying the inmates. Before the film could be screened at the New York Film Festival, the government of Massachusetts tried to get an injunction to halt its release. At first a judge cleared the film, but then another banned it totally. The documentary community was now waiting to see what Frederick Wiseman would do next.

Wiseman announced that he was going to do a series of films about public institutions. His second film was *High School,* filmed in 1966 at Northeast High School in Philadelphia, Pennsylvania. This documentary reveals the strict discipline in the school whose mandate is to make the students respond to rules and order. The result is a look at the way students are stifled by the system.

Frederick Wiseman was confronted from the beginning with the extreme difficulties in marketing a documentary film. There have been some theatrical releases, often receiving lukewarm reception. There were screenings at film festivals that provided exposure, but didn't bring in revenue.

Wiseman was assertive about financing as well as distribution. The first five films, *Titicut Follies* (1967), *High School* (1968), *Law and Order* (1969), *Hospital* (1970), and *Basic Training* (1971), were bankrolled by a combination of grants from foundations, lab credits, and an assortment of friends who worked gratis. The most significant financing and distributing decision came in 1971 when Frederick Wiseman signed a contract with WNET public television for the first of two five-year, five-film contracts. Also in 1971 he formed his own production company, Zipporah Films, named after Wiseman's wife.

The terms agreed to by WNET Channel 13 and Frederick Wiseman were that half of the money for a particular film would be made available after the subject of the documentary was agreed upon, then the other half upon delivery of the finished film. Prior to this, WNET aired *High School* in October 1968 and *Law and Order*, a study of the breadth of functions the police serve and how negative elements affect their behavior, broadcast on March 2, 1969. *Hospital* was televised on February 10, 1970. It chronicled the daily activities of a large urban hospital and how economic strains and a lack of services affect the quality of health care delivered.

Basic Training, the first film under the WNET contract, aired on October 4, 1971. This documentary details the military's nine-week training cycle. *Essene,* aired on November 13, 1972, covers life in a Benedictine monastery and how the brethren deal with day-to-day issues in the same way as any other community. *Juvenile Court* was broadcast on October 1, 1973, documents various cases that come before a juvenile court, and shows the limits of the system. *Primate,* broadcast on December 5, 1973, examined the daily activities of a primate research center where the behavioral tendencies of various species, especially monkeys and apes, are examined. *Welfare* examines the complexities of the welfare system for both the caseworkers and the clients. It aired on September 24, 1975. *Meat,* which aired on November 13, 1976, was a documentary about the process of turning cattle and sheep into consumer products. *Canal Zone,* televised on October 8, 1977, focused on the life of those who live and work in the Panama Canal Zone. *Sinai Field Mission,* broadcast on October 17, 1978, is a documentary about the activities of diplomats and electronic technicians who operate the mission established to help facilitate the disengagement between Israel and Egypt after the 1973 war. The last Wiseman film completed in the 1970s was *Manoeuvre,* which followed a U.S. infantry tank company through NATO's annual fall maneuvers. It was completed in 1979 and aired on March 20, 1980. All the films had multiple showings on WNET and Wiseman continued to make documentaries throughout the decades.

Wiseman is often both the cameraman and editor on his films. He works in the style that the French called cinema vérité or American direct cinema. He films constantly on location and allows the documentary story to unfold by itself with direct sound and no narration.

His films are noted for long takes, which allow the action to unspool without manipulation. Wiseman comes back to the editing room with as many as 100 hours of material and then tries to find the truth of the subject by structuring scenes to best dramatize what actually happened. Frederick Wiseman's films are distinctive for their ability to let the viewer explore the content and be an observer as information is revealed. He is more contemplative than most other documentarians of his era, and the films take great concentration to watch because of their often long running times.

WNET's airing of Frederick Wiseman's documentaries again demonstrated the range of television programming. In the seventies there was an alternative to network sitcoms and medical dramas. There were those who wanted to watch nonfiction television in a form and style different from network news and even network documentaries. WNET embraced difficult subjects presented with a unique vision embodied by Frederick Wiseman.

Further Resources

Atkins, Thomas R. 1975. *Frederick Wiseman.* New York: Monarch Film Studies.

Benson, Thomas W., and Carolyn Anderson. 2002. *The Films of Frederick Wiseman.* Carbondale and Edwardsville: Southern Illinois University Press.

WKRP in Cincinnati (CBS, 1978–1982)

This half-hour sitcom about a local radio station and its comings and goings can be categorized as "jiggle TV" because the smart secretary Jennifer Marlowe, played by Loni Anderson (1945–), had a figure that fit the bill and wore tight tops. This aspect of the show actually pushed the envelope in that Jennifer Marlowe was flirty with men at the station and she at times would position herself, while talking to those in the room, so her assets were inches from a man. The character and actress become so popular Loni Anderson was considered the star of the show and had her own Farrah Fawcett Majors–type poster.

> *WKRP in Cincinnati* takes place in a rock 'n' roll radio station. Music plays very often during an episode. If the producers were to use actually recordings from name groups, the cost would be astronomical, so sound-alikes were used. If the sound-alike were too close to the original, the producer would have to pay not only for performance rights but the rights to the musical composition itself, so music was created that was similar in spirit but not in actuality. Audiences can easily be fooled, especially if the sound-alike is played in the background of a dialogue scene.

The rest of the cast included Gary Sandy (1945–) as Andy Travis, who transformed a dying station playing old-fashioned music and an out-of-touch staff into a budding Top 40 rock station. The station is owned by the mother of the station manager, Arthur Carlson, played by Gordon Jump (1932–2003), who fired a long line of program directors until Andy turned the station around, with the mother's consent. News, weather, and agricultural issues were handled by Les Nessman, portrayed by Richard Sanders (1940–). The conceited sales manager Herb Tarlek was played by Frank Bonner (1942–). Jan Smithers (1949–) portrayed the program assistant Bailey Quarters, who had been reduced to menial jobs like getting coffee for everyone until Andy arrived and took her seriously as a member of the staff. Howard Hesseman (1940–) as the DJ who had been known by countless on-air monikers practically steals the show as Johnny Caravella, now known as the rock and roll DJ Johnny Fever. Tim Reid (1944–) played Gordon Sims, an African American DJ brought in by Andy and known as Venus Flytrap, a flamboyant performer whose show had a whole mysterious concept to it. The mother was only occasionally seen on camera and she was played by the legendary film star Sylvia Sidney (1910–1999).

The set was bare-bones but very effective in evoking a small radio station. The music posed a bit of a problem in that real album cuts from major rock acts were pricey, so when music is played, and it is often instrumental, it sounds like a bunch of musicians playing guitars and drums in a jam session recorded on tape and pressed into vinyl.

Workplace sitcoms like *The Mary Tyler Moore Show, Taxi,* and *WKRP in Cincinnati* were popular in the 1970s. Audiences could relate to them because most of them worked in a place where there were colorful characters and the business had its own culture.

WKRP in Cincinnati was created by Hugh Wilson for MTM Enterprises, which was owned by Mary Tyler Moore. The show was taped in front of a live audience. The opening and other parts of the show featured location shots of Cincinnati to put the workplace into context.

The 1970s continued to be a time for what is now called classic rock. The show embraced the vibe of radio shows from that time, but from a small market that had its own quirks. In the end it was those wacky characters that audiences came back for, and television certainly has a long history of them.

See also: *Baywatch*; *The Mary Tyler Moore Show*; *Taxi*.

Further Resources

Anderson, Loni. 1997. *My Life in High Heels*. New York: Avon.

Kassell, Michael B. 1993. *America's Favorite Radio Station: WKRP in Cincinnati*. Madison: University of Wisconsin Press.

Wonder Woman (ABC, 1976–1977; CBS, 1977–1979)

The journey of Wonder Woman, a female superhero, began in the mind of talented William Moulton Marston (1893–1947), an American psychologist, lawyer, and inventor who created the comic book character Wonder Woman inspired by his wife and a woman who lived with them in a long-term relationship. Wonder Woman first appeared in the DC Comics title *All Star Comics* #8, which hit the stands in December 1941.

Wonder Woman is an Amazon warrior princess based on Greek mythology. She was known as Princess Diana of Themyscira in her homeland but in the outside world her secret identity was Diana Prince. She has a wide range of weapons including a tiara that could be used as a projectile, indestructible bracelets, and a lasso that seems endless when thrown to catch someone, save someone, or secure a building or object.

Wonder Woman Comes to Television

On television Wonder Woman first appeared in 1974 in the TV movie *Wonder Woman* starring the pretty blonde-haired Cathy Lee Crosby wearing a costume that had red, white, and blue—she was largely covered up except for a narrow area exposing the neck and neckline.

In November 1975 and subsequently in a series of specials, *The New Original Wonder Woman, Fausta, The Nazi Wonder Woman* (1976), and *Wonder Woman Meets Baroness Von Gunther* (1976), the superhero goddess was played by Lynda Carter, the woman who would be forever associated with the super-strong woman who could leap tall buildings, use all her weapons for the good of her country just after World War II, fling the strongest man or woman across a room, and was a role model for girls and women. Lynda Carter (1951–) was like the Wonder Woman of the comics come alive. A former Miss World, Lynda Carter was a tall 5 foot, 10 inches and was athletic, muscular, and well toned. Her hair was jet black and she had clear blue eyes.

She wore a costume from the 1940s time period, but it was very contemporary. Her top was red and gold and exposed as much cleavage as the censors allowed. Her shorts were a blue field dotted with white stars and were skin-tight. The show's patriotism is reflected in the weekly story lines that usually involved the military.

Major Steve Trevor of the U.S. Army, played by debonair Lyle Waggoner (1935–), a Carol Burnett regular, had crash-landed on the island where Wonder Woman lived. In a short time they fell in love and traveled to the United States where she acted as his personal secretary and was addressed as Yeoman Prince. Important to the story line is that Major Trevor never learned about her powers and was also perplexed when she would suddenly leave the premises when something critical was going on. Like Clark Kent she was off to turn into a superhero.

The process of transitioning from Diana Prince to Wonder Woman was simple but effective and only the audience would be there to see this television miracle. She would begin by spinning with her arms straight out as Diana, then via a superimposition Wonder Woman would appear spinning in the same body position, but in the opposite direction. Now whole, Wonder Woman would run off looking like a marathon athlete to the critical destination.

This transition visualization was used weekly, but not in excess. There are times where Yeoman Prince leaves a room or place, then a cut occurs and there she is as Wonder Woman, ready for action.

The Nazis are usually the bad guys in this show because of the World War II theme. On some occasions aliens were the subject of the narrative.

In the fall of 1977 CBS updated the show, placing it in the present. Debra Winger (1955–) occasionally appeared on the show as Drusilla, Diana's younger sister, who discovered that she also had superpowers, donned her own costume, and was called Wonder Girl.

The period was well established by the period cars and military vehicles and mainly the clothes. Like so many of the dramatic adventure shows or sitcoms of the 1970s, the settings were basic, not highly detailed or realistic looking as they were in feature films. Gradually, toward the end of the decade, this would evolve and the production design of shows began to equal their big-screen competition.

This action adventure show had a serious theme concerning the Nazis, but it wasn't explored deeply. The show was intended as entertainment and fun with a little sex appeal thrown in.

See also: *The Incredible Hulk*; *Vol. 1, The 1950s–1960s: The Adventures of Superman*; *Batman.*

Further Resources

Lepore, Jill. 2015. *The Secret History of Wonder Woman.* Toronto, Canada: Vintage Books.

Pingel, Mike. 2008. *The Q Guide to Wonder Woman: Stuff You Didn't Even Know You Wanted to Know . . . About Lynda Carter, the Iconic TV Show and One Amazing Costume.* Q Guides.

The 1980s

The A Team (NBC, 1983–1987)

This action/adventure series didn't always take itself seriously. The premise of hired hands stopping the bad guys was serious, but the characters and plot were often considered tongue-in-cheek. The A-Team was comprised of four Vietnam War veterans whose services were for hire if the price was right. They were also on the run from the U.S. Army, which suspected them of misappropriating funds after a raid on the Bank of Hanoi; they escaped the situation by breaking out of prison before trial when a guilty verdict could convict them.

The featured cast was George Peppard (1928–1994) as the leader of the team, Colonel John "Hannibal" Smith; Mr. T (Laurence Tureaud) (1952–) as B. A. Barracus, muscleman and crack mechanic, a striking man who wore strands of jewelry and sported a Mohawk haircut; Dirk Benedict (1945–) as Templeton "Face" Peck, a highly skilled imposter; and Dwight Schultz (1947–) as H. M. "Howlin" Mad Murdock, an off-centered pilot.

The series came into being when Brandon Tartikoff (1949–1997), head of entertainment for NBC, pitched an idea to Stephen J. Cannell (1941–2010). Cannell had been a writer, producer, and creator on many shows including *Columbo* (1968–2003), *The Rockford Files* (1974–1980), and *Baretta* (1975–1978). Network brass often asked for a show that was a combination of existing shows. Here Tartikoff asked Cannell for a show that was an eclectic mix of both movies and television series: *The Dirty Dozen* (1967), *Mission Impossible* (1966–1973), *The Magnificent Seven* (1960), *Mad Max* (1979), and *Hill Street Blues* (1981–1987).

Hannibal is most often smoking a cigar, wearing a white safari jacket and black leather gloves, and carrying a sidearm. To make sure potential clients are "clean" and not part of the military establishment pursuing them, he disguises himself as a dry cleaner. "Faceman" can partake of anything he wants for any given mission. He often uses his manly charm and has been known to exploit women during these conquests. Bosco Albert Barracus is a strongman whose B.A. initials mean Bad Attitude. He is the most outrageous of the characters in terms of physical looks and actions. His voice is a gritty rasp and he adopts comic book–like phrases such as calling Murdock a "crazy fool." The pilot Murdock is a precision ace whose mental illness caused by overexposure to action in Vietnam has him in and out of psychiatric settings.

Missions vary but at times the situations are topical. One episode entitled "The Children of Jamestown" clearly denotes the November 1978 murder of over 900 people in Guyana at the hands of fanatical Jim Jones in his cult retreat, Jonestown. *The A-Team* gets the details right and makes real life fit into their action/adventure format.

Overall *The A-Team* was harshly criticized for excessive violence. Posing as a show for kids and young people, it was rarely seriously considered by adult viewers. Despite its faults, it was considered an entertaining and fast-paced show.

See also: *Vol. 1, The 1950s–1960s: Mission Impossible.*

Further Resources

Boone, George. 2009. *George Peppard: 157 Success Facts—Everything You Need to Know About George Peppard.* Emereo Publishing. http://emereo.net/.

Mr. T. 1984. *Mr. T: The Man with the Gold: An Autobiography*. New York: St. Martin's Press.

ABC News Nightline (1980–) (2013–)

More commonly known as *Nightline,* this show began four days into the Iran hostage crisis in which radical Iranian students held 52 diplomats and U.S. citizens against their will. Roone Arledge (1931–2002), the president of ABC News, made the decision to go on air with a program updating the tense situation called *The Iran Crisis—America Held Hostage Day* . . . and the number of each day of the conflict became part of the title consecutively each night. Frank Reynolds (1933–1983) hosted the 20-minute reports each night. Not long after the show's creation, Reynolds exited as host. The show eventually expanded to a full half-hour. The new host was Ted Koppel (1940–), who at the time was ABC's State Department correspondent. Each night Koppel would update the country about what was going on in Iran and Washington. Through his understanding of the political and cultural issues, Koppel gave the story tremendous depth, and always, through his presentations, kept the content clean with a constant sense of the truth.

Ted Koppel, a skilled and determined interviewer, managed to elicit pertinent information from his guests. After 444 days the crisis ended in 1981with the hostages largely unharmed. Seeing a future for the show, it was renamed *Nightline.* Koppel had become one of the most visible members of the ABC News team and was respected by the viewing audience.

Standing in the control room of ABC's news program *Nightline* is anchorman Ted Koppel. The program began as a daily report of the Iran hostage crisis, and due to its popularity remained on the air after the crisis as a popular interview program focusing on the news events of the day. (AP Photo)

Nightline in the early years had a distinctive format. Each night the program would focus on a single topic. Koppel would begin with an introduction that pulled in the viewer. There was a videotape background piece on the topic. After a commercial break Koppel would usually conduct a live interview with someone directly linked to the night's theme.

In 1983 ABC expanded *Nightline* to one hour and the format was modified to embrace a number of topics. This restructuring didn't work, so *Nightline* went back to its original format. Originally *Nightline* was broadcast four nights a week, Monday through Thursday. This changed in 1982 when *Fridays* (1980–1982), ABC's answer to *Saturday Night Live,* was reslotted to follow *Nightline*.

Successful and Influential

Even though *Nightline* was up against a 15-minute segment of *The Tonight Show Starring Johnny Carson* (1962–1992), it maintained respectable ratings and inspired the other networks to launch their own late night news shows, *CBS Nightwatch* (1982–1992) and *NBC News Overnight* (1982–1983).

During the 1980s Ted Koppel and *Nightline* presented a wide range of guests, topics, and issues that were of current interest to the country. They included a 1982 interview with Yasser Arafat (1929–2004), who insisted he would not accept conditions concerning the U.S. recognizing the Palestine Liberation Organization (PLO). In 1984 Chief Justice Warren Burger (1907–1995) made his first live television appearance to honor the 40th anniversary of D-Day. In 1985 *Nightline* conducted its first on-remote broadcast from South Africa. In 1986 there were interviews with the first female president of the Philippines, Corazon Aquino (1933–2009), and the outgoing strongman, Ferdinand Marcos (1917–1989). In 1987 Colorado Democratic senator and presidential candidate Gary Hart (1936–) admitted he had cheated on his wife. Later a newspaper exposé led to his withdrawal from the race. Also that year *Nightline* broadcast for the first time in the Soviet Union. In 1988 they broadcast from Jerusalem. The show was always current on breaking news and would change the scheduling up to the last minute to cover news that was just occurring, like the night John Lennon (1940–1980) was shot and killed. In 1987 *Nightline* conducted its first town meeting. The subject was the AIDS epidemic—it ran four hours and 12 minutes, concluding at 3:47 a.m. Eastern Standard Time. Also in 1987 Koppel conducted controversial interviews with Jim Bakker (1940–) and Tammy Faye Bakker (1942–2007) after a sex scandal brought down their Praise the Lord (PTL) ministry. *Nightline* may have changed its time slot over the years, but it remains a vital aspect of the ABC News division.

Further Resources

Koppel, Ted. 1996. *Nightline: History in the Making and the Making of Television*. New York: Crown.

Koppel, Ted. 2001. *Off Camera: Private Thoughts Made Public*. New York: Vintage.

Adam Smith's Money World (PBS, 1984–1997)

In 1984, George Jerome Waldo Goodman (1930–2014) became the creator, anchor, and editor-in-chief of what was originally called *Adam Smith's Money World*. This weekly half-hour show presented stories and issues that were current and important for investors and the general public to understand.

The original Adam Smith (1723–1790) was a Scottish moral philosopher and pioneer of political economy. He is considered the founder of the classical free market economic theory. He felt that rational self-interest and competition could lead to economic prosperity. Goodman, an American author and broadcast commentator on economics, was assigned the pseudonym Adam Smith by Clay Felker, founder of *New York* magazine, in order to keep secret the articles he wrote about Wall Street. Goodman's gift was the ability to present complex financial ideas and processes in a lively way during a time when the public was turned off by a stodgy professorial approach.

Broadcast on PBS, *Adam Smith's Money World*, later changed in 1991 to *Adam Smith*, embraced many elements that made it both entertaining and informative. It had the qualities of a news program, a magazine, and even a documentary film. Goodman would be placed in front of an image appropriate for the episode at hand and he skillfully introduced the topic of the day. Throughout the show there were talking head interviews, setups where Goodman and the subject could be seen. Graphics and graphics with text livened up the well-paced show along with stock footage and setups such as a row of dominos collapsing to express the concepts put forth by Goodman's guests; his on-screen address to the camera and the narration, also voiced by Goodman, rounded out a total package of communication elucidating high-level economic and financial ideas. The show was an ideal example of PBS's signature—educational television that widened the perspective of their viewers. Where many news and financial shows were bland and tired, *Adam Smith's Money World* was textured and colorful and presented a wide spectrum of concepts. Sometimes a musical underscore was even used to enhance the entertainment factor.

Further Resources

Goodman, George Jerome Waldo. 1972. *Supermoney*. New York: Random House.

Smith, Adam. 1801. *An Inquiry into the Nature and Causes of the Wealth of Nations*. Basel: Printed and sold by James Decker.

Alf (NBC, 1986–1990)

Alf (short for Alien Life Form) was a small, fur-covered wisecracker from the planet Melmac, where he was known as Gordon Shumway, who crashed into the garage at the Tanner residence; they decided to take Alf into their family. Alf was played by a puppet. The family was comprised of Max Wright (1943–) as Willie Tanner, Anne Schedeen (1949–) as his wife, Andrea Elson (1969–) as their daughter, and Benji Gregory (1978–) as their son. John LaMotta (1939–) and Liz Sheridan (1929–) played their neighbors.

Alf was pint-sized, looked like a twisted version of an animal from space, and was 229 years old. At first glance it would seem that Alf was a Muppet, but he wasn't. The producers tried to keep secret the method for making Alf move. Michu Meszaros (1930–) was a little person who wore an Alf costume for walking scenes—a puppet was employed for stationary scenes. The voice of Alf was performed by Paul Fusco (1953–), who was the co-creator of the show with Tom Patchett. Alf liked to snack on cats, but the Tanners' cat always got out of the room when Alf was on the prowl.

Working with a puppet character made *Alf* more challenging than the average sitcom. The technical requirements for the show stretched the shooting of a half-hour episode to as much as 20 to 25 hours, at times under technically difficult conditions.

The viewers were unaware of the stress of the production, especially on the actors, and found *Alf* an enjoyable show, inventive and funny. As the star of the show Alf had the funniest lines and got into hilarious situations. From 1987 to August 1990 an animated rendition of *Alf* ran on NBC's Saturday morning lineup.

See also: *Vol. 3, The 1990s–Present: 3rd Rock from the Sun.*

Further Resources

Shellbach, Richard J. 1987. *Alf Sounds Off!* https://openlibrary.org/publishers/Checkerboard_Press Checkerboard Press

Shellbach, Richard J. 1987. *Alf Speaks Out!* https://openlibrary.org/publishers/Checkerboard_Press Checkerboard Press

Alien Nation (Fox, 1989–1990)

This series was based on the 1988 motion picture *Alien Nation,* which starred James Caan, Mandy Patinkin, and Terrence Stamp. The genre was a hybrid of science fiction, crime, and action and took place in the very near future when a race of aliens come to Earth and are integrated into human society.

The television series adopted the film's title and made it to air less than a year after the feature; it ran for only one year. The series was set in the near future in 1995, only six years from its premiere. The show's theme was an analogy of contemporary race relations issues. The refugees from another galaxy number as many as 300,000 and find their long assimilation process difficult because of the prejudice they encounter.

They were in a human form but had elongated stippled skulls and strange habits like a craving for sour milk and requiring three participants for sexual encounters.

The stories feature a Los Angeles cop, Mathew Sikes, played by Gary Graham (1950–) teamed with a partner from space, George San Francisco, played by Eric Pierpoint (1950–). Michele Scarbelli (1955–) played his wife, Susan.

George became the first of the "newcomer" breed to make detective in the L.A.P.D. He took an analytical approach to fighting crime, which was at odds with Matthew's more violent and visceral approach.

One of the most unique and odd episodes dealt with Susan Francisco's pregnancy. Susan carried the fetus for the first part of the term but George actually gave birth to their child.

Further Resources

Foster, Allan Dean. 1988. *Alien Nation*. New York: Warner Books.

Geraghty, Lincoln. 2009. *American Science Fiction and Television*. London: Bloomsbury Academic.

Alive from Off Center (PBS, 1985–1996)

This weekly half-hour program was a platform for avant-garde performance artists, video artists, and others working outside conventional art forms. The show's participants were given the freedom to present whatever they created specifically for the program or a representative work. Executive producer Melissa Ward sought not only to highlight creative young people working on the fringe of television, but to have them *make* television. The short videos were not in the style of music videos like those seen on MTV, but were highly personal works the artists generated for self-expression rather than to entertain an audience. The significance of *Alive from Off Center* was to create a venue where artists on the edge could deliver the kind of performance art ingrained in the American underground art scene.

The program presenters changed four times during its run. Susan Stamberg (1938–), a special correspondent for National Public Radio, was the host from 1985 to 1986. Experimental performance artist, violinist, and art/rock singer Laurie Anderson (1945–) was a memorable performer on the show and was a presenter in 1987. Ann Magnuson (1956–), actress, performance artist, and an intricate part of the downtown New York art scene in the 1980s, was a presenter in 1988, and William Wegman, a photographer known for his compositions of dogs in unusual settings, also anchored the show.

Alive from Off Center originated at the Minneapolis–St. Paul PBS affiliate KTCA TV. The show featured works in many forms including puppets. Some memorable episodes included one featuring actor, clown, performance artist, and new vaudevillian Bill Irwin (1950–). In the spirit of Ernie Kovacs, Buster Keaton, and Charlie Chaplin, Irwin goes in and out of an audition and gets trapped inside a television, watches a movie, walks through a ballet, dances with a ballerina, and ice skates. He plays a kid taking a bath to *Jaws* music, and he wakes up in bed next to a blonde.

Another show highlight was a video featuring Laurie Anderson playing two parts in the same sketch. The audience sees a woman resembling Anderson with spiky hair and a clone who is a diminutive male with combed-over straight hair and a mustache. He has been shaped and distorted electronically and his voice has been lowered by electronic manipulation. They talk about Hansel and Gretel and write a song that he sings. There is a miniature pagoda centered in a fishbowl. Then there is a sequence in which an off-camera director tells Laurie what he wants her to do.

These groundbreaking art forms were new to television and exposed avant-garde performance art to an audience who might never have experienced it. Importantly, it was an attempt to create a unique mode of television.

See also: PBS (Public Broadcasting Service); Vol. 1, 1950s–1960s: Kovacs, Ernie.

Further Resources

O'Pray, Michael. 2003. *Avant-Garde Film: Forms, Themes and Passions*. London: Wallflower.

Sitney, P. Adams. 2002. *Visionary Film: The American Avant-Garde, 1943–2000*. Oxford: Oxford University Press.

The All New Mickey Mouse Club (Disney Channel, 1989–1994)

When the Disney Corporation launched its own network, the Disney Channel, the original *The Mickey Mouse Show* was immediately made an essential aspect of their programming. The reruns did well with younger children, but executives at Disney felt the black-and-white program was dated and difficult for older kids and teens to relate to. The seventies reboot, *The New Mickey Mouse Club,* quickly became dated with its disco version of the theme song and those iconic hairstyles. Disney moved forward with a contemporary version of "the club." The Mickey Mouse ears that had been every kid's favorite headwear were put in storage and the new Mouseketeers wore high school–style jackets that became their uniform. The show was titled *The All New Mickey Mouse Club*, better known to young viewers as MMC with those three letters as a graphic part of the show's design.

Emerging Talent

Although previous renditions of the show produced talented young people who went on to fame in show business, *The All New Mickey Mouse Club* launched the careers of at least five performers: Britney Spears (1981–), Christina Aguilera (1980–), Justin Timberlake (1981–), Ryan Gosling (1980–), and Keri Russell (1976–).

For the first five seasons the show aired Monday through Friday at 5:30 p.m.; for season six it ran from Monday to Thursdays, and for the seventh and final season it aired only on Thursday, first at 7:00 p.m., and then at 7:30 p.m.

The All New Mickey Mouse Club premiered on Monday April 24, 1989. Production concluded in October 1994 and the last episode was broadcast in 1995. The show continued in reruns through 1996.

There were theme days for *The All New Mickey Mouse Club.* Music Day was on Mondays for seasons 1–5, then Tuesdays for season six. Guest Day was on Tuesdays for seasons one to five and on Monday for season six. Anything Can Happen Day was on Wednesdays during seasons one to five, Party Day ran on Thursdays for seasons one to four and six and on Fridays in season five. Hall of Fame Day happened on Fridays for seasons one to four.

Produced at Walt Disney World in Orlando, Florida, the show was conceived as a variety-comedy show and more. Some typed it as "Carol Burnett meets *American Idol*." The kids were schooled in academics daily and studied with dance teachers, choreographers, and vocal coaches. Acting ability was essential. The Mouseketeers collaborated with writers and directors on comedy sketches. Sketches could be silly, such as a commercial for a mouth spray that gave the user bad breath for situations where one wanted to turn someone off, like a young persistent male trying to date a group of girls. The content of the skits varied; the Mouseketeers did parodies of well-known movies, musicals, and cartoons. Also in the repertoire were life-lesson sketches that taught the home viewers how to handle everyday situations.

Music was a big part of the entertainment. There were concerts performed by the Mouseketeers, and music videos were taped in front of a live audience. The singing and dancing was highly professional and done with passion for the craft.

Well-produced packages were aired to profile the individual Mouseketeers. Britney Spears was shown back home in Louisiana, riding a go-cart, watching a local baseball game, and playing basketball, before going to her grandmother's deli where she works readying crayfish for consumption and works the room.

Early on the producers on the show understood they had major singing talent in the class of 1994, but in no time, they realized that they had young superstars in Justin Timberlake, Christina Aguilera, and Britney Spears. In addition to dancing and the ability to whip a live audience into a frenzy, they all had strong voices, especially Aguilera. All three grew up to be celebrated talents. The three performed in all combinations and were highlights of the show, backed by musicians, dancers, and backup singers.

The evolution of *The Mickey Mouse Club* from the 1950s to the 1990s progressed from an iconic show embraced by kids and teens to a mega-production comedy-variety show where future superstars were seen as they grew in talent, professionalism, and popularity as they captured the hearts and minds of America's youth.

See also: *Vol. 1, The 1950s–1960s:* Disney, Walt; *The Mickey Mouse Club.*

Further Resources

Berk, Sheryl. 2007. *True Brit: The Story of Singing Sensation Britney Spears.* New York: Ballantine Publishing Group.

Schwartz, Heather E. 2015. *Justin Timberlake: From Mouseketeer to Megastar.* Minneapolis, MN: Learner Publications.

Amazing Stories (NBC, 1985–1987)

Amazing Stories was an anthology program with stories touching on director/executive producer Steven Spielberg's (1946–) favorite genres: science fiction, fantasy, subjects about kids, and American history. The show was named after a comic book Spielberg's father read as a young man, and described as a cross between *The Twilight Zone* and *Alfred Hitchcock Presents.* Despite Spielberg's prominence in the mid-1980s, the show enjoyed little success.

In the mid-1980s film director Spielberg's films were popular and high grossing. He had directed, by this point, *Jaws* (1975), *Close Encounters of the Third Kind* (1977), *Raiders of the Lost Ark* (1981), *E.T. The Extra-terrestrial* (1982), and *The Color Purple* (1985). NBC and the other networks were more than anxious to entice the wunderkind into development of a television series.

NBC signed Spielberg to an unprecedented deal. The network gave Spielberg a two-year commitment, promising to broadcast 44 episodes regardless of ratings. Network standards and practices were relaxed and the director/executive producer was given total creative freedom. The common budget for each half-hour episode was one million dollars, which was the current amount for a one-hour dramatic series episode. The shows were shot in between six and eight days. Spielberg lined up a strong stable of directors including himself and protégés Joe Dante, Phil Joanou, Kevin Reynolds, and Lisli Linka Glatter, and big names such as Martin Scorsese, Clint Eastwood, Robert Zemeckis, and Irvin Kershner.

The reviews, even those generated by avid Spielberg supporters, were disastrous. After the first complete season viewers also rejected the show and it landed in the basement at 35 in the ratings. Brandon Tartikoff, president of NBC Entertainment, found *Amazing Stories* childish, which led Spielberg to make the second season less immature, but the ratings continued to plummet until the end of the two-year run.

Despite all the talent in front of and behind the camera, Steven Spielberg couldn't achieve the success his idols Rod Serling and Alfred Hitchcock had enjoyed. The stories and the delivery just weren't good enough and Spielberg's platinum name in the movie theaters, even with all the fanfare, failed to keep viewers on their couches and in their comfy chairs.

Film and television makers inherently know that storytelling is the key to their craft. The opening episode of *Amazing Stories* began with an Indian shaman telling a story to his tribe sitting around a campfire. There are a series of rapidly moving images: playing cards, a ghost, and books flying to the soaring music of John Williams (1941–). On an anthology series such as *The Twilight Zone* there is a high percentage of memorable episodes, a feat Steven Spielberg just couldn't achieve on the small screen.

See also: *Vol. 1, The 1950s–1960s: Alfred Hitchcock Presents/The Alfred Hitchcock Hour; The Twilight Zone.*

Further Resources

Lamson, Laurie. 2014. *Now Write! Science Fiction, Fantasy and Horror: Speculative Genre Exercises from Today's Best Writers and Teachers.* New York: Jeremy Tarcher/Penguin.

Schickel, Richard, and Steven Spielberg. 2012. *Steven Spielberg: A Retrospective.* New York: Sterling Publishing.

America's Most Wanted (Fox, 1988–2012)

Following the kidnapping and murder of his son, Florida hotel manager John Walsh (1945–) was able to secure a deal with the Fox Network to create the show *America's Most Wanted,* launched February 7, 1988. Walsh was already a nationally known figure because of the tragic, brutal murder of his son Adam and Walsh's well-publicized actions to find missing children and to

Host John Walsh on the set of *America's Most Wanted*. This interactive program asked the viewers' help in catching criminals on the loose and was very successful in aiding in their capture. (Yann Gamblin/Paris Match via Getty Images)

After the death of Adam Walsh, a law was signed by President George W. Bush creating the Adam Walsh Child Protection and Safety Act. The act organizes sex offenders into three tiers with varying requirements. The most serious tier, Tier 3, requires offenders to submit to lifetime registration and update their location every three months. It also created a national database for DNA evidence collection, created a child abuse/neglect registry, increased funding for law enforcement, and increased penalties for sex trafficking, child prostitution, and kidnapping.

Many stores, amusement parks, hospitals, museums, and federal office buildings participate in the Code Adam program. These companies display a blue-and-white "Code Adam" sticker at the front entrance of the building. If a child is reported missing and Code Adam is invoked, all exterior doors are immediately locked and monitored, all employees begin looking for the child, and law enforcement is called.

help those who were exploited. It became Fox's highest running crime reality show in the network's history. Walsh turned his personal nightmare into a media system that actually solved crimes and caught criminals. By 2011 over 1,000 fugitives had been captured and incarcerated because of the efforts on *America's Most Wanted*.

During the summer of 1981 John Walsh was a partner in a hotel management company situated in Hollywood, Florida. On July 27, 1981 John's wife Revé was shopping in a Sears store with their six-year-old son Adam, (1974–). She left her son in the toy department while she looked for a lamp and returned several minutes later to find Adam missing. Police records released in 1996 documented that a 17-year-old security guard instructed four boys to leave the store. An intense search for Adam Walsh lasted 16 days and ended when the boy's severed head was found in a drainage canal 120 miles from his home.

Turning Tragedy into Positive Action

In 1983 an NBC television movie, *Adam,* dramatized the days before his murder. Daniel J. Travanti (1940–) portrayed John Walsh and Jo Beth Williams (1948–) played Revé Walsh. The real Walsh couple appeared at the end of the film to display photographs of missing children. In 1986 a sequel was broadcast, also on NBC, titled *Adam: His Song Continues* with both actors reprising their roles as the Walshes.

A few years later, Fox launched *America's Most Wanted*, with Walsh as its host. The format and concept were clean, specific, and integrated the public as a tool to inform law enforcement about the whereabouts of criminals, many of whom had been hiding in plain sight in society for years. In 1992 *America's Most Wanted* was expanded to one hour.

Walsh was the host of the weekly half-hour show—a good-looking, no-nonsense sort of man with a single focus: to honor his dead son by hunting down predators who preyed on children and committed heinous crimes against adults.

The show's basic set was a call center where phones were manned and information and tips were gathered and processed. The show often began here; other times it was broadcast from remote exterior locations all over the United States. While Walsh explained the cases to be explored on the evening's episode, the background action showed his dogged staff.

There was a toll-free number available for watchers who had any information on the profiled criminals. This network of citizens was able to identify and locate criminals they had seen on the show and notify the police. Some shows resulted in as many as four captures, criminal arrests based on a tip from the show. Walsh would remind the audience about the dirty deeds of these criminals and then end with a graphic over their face that said "Captured."

Each week several new cases were presented, first by Walsh in a detailed introduction and then through a high-production-value package that recreated the particular crime using actors. The emphasis was always on the seriousness of catching the person under discussion. During the piece John Walsh would do voice-over to progress the story. To bring veracity to the recreation, there were talking head interviews by individuals involved in the case. They were shown on-camera and were also used as voice-overs. These segments were never slick, but compelling in their gravitas. As the show progressed, Walsh would continue to repeat the names, the crimes, and the all-important toll-free telephone number. All information phoned in was confidential; the callers could be anonymous.

The most shocking and challenging case of the 1980s profiled on *America's Most Wanted* actually began in 1971 when suspicious police in Westfield, New York, entered the home of John E. List (1925–2008), a 46-year-old failed New Jersey accountant. The officers found the body of List's wife Helen, 46; his daughter Patricia, 16; sons John, 15, and Frederick, 13; and his 85-year-old mother, Alma. John List had shot and killed all these family members. Police were not able to locate and arrest List. As to his motive, List left a letter with his pastor saying the world was too evil and he had ended the lives of his loved ones to save their souls.

After years of a manhunt that stretched from the United States to overseas, the Union County, New Jersey prosecutor's office in 1989 asked the producers of *America's Most Wanted* for assistance in finding List and bringing him to justice. The show enlisted the talents of Frank Bender, a forensic sculptor, and Richard Walter, a criminal psychologist. Bender studied pictures of List in his forties and set about forming a bust that reflected how he would have aged since 1971. Walter added that List would still be wearing horn-rimmed glasses so he would appear successful.

The episode of *America's Most Wanted* on John List aired on May 21, 1989. An estimated 22 million people heard about his heinous crime and saw Frank Bender's remarkable sculpture picturing an aged John List as he probably would look. A woman watching the show from Richmond, Virginia, thought the bust looked like her neighbor, Robert Clark, a churchgoing accountant who wore horn-rimmed glasses. Police confronted his stunned wife and she cooperated fully about facts from his past that would identify him. The wife knew nothing about the murders. On June 1, List was arrested at his office; he denied everything but fingerprints matched up. List was tried for five counts of murder in the first degree and on April 12, 1990 he was sentenced to five consecutive life terms. In 2008, at age 82, he died in a prison hospital in New Jersey.

The logo for *America's Most Wanted* looks official, even sporting an eagle. *America's Most Wanted* is not part of any law enforcement agency, but it interfaces with many of them. This is a reality show with meaning, purpose, and results that make America a little bit safer.

Further Resources

Breslin, Jack. 1990. *America's Most Wanted: How Television Catches Crooks*. New York: HarperCollins.

Walsh, John, and Susan Schindehette. 2008. *Tears of Rage: From Grieving Father to Crusader for Justice: The Untold Story of the Adam Walsh Case*. New York: Pocket Books.

The Arsenio Hall Show (Syndication, 1989–1994)

In 1989 Arsenio Hall (1956–), who was born in Cleveland, Ohio, became the first African American to host a late night talk show with *The Arsenio Hall Show*, which followed Hall's hosting of *The Late Show* and the cult following that he obtained.

As a child, Hall performed magic, and later pursued a career as a stand-up comic, clocking in several appearances on *Soul Train*. For Hall this was a lifelong dream; he performed monologues and interviewed imaginary guests as a teenager in his bedroom. During the 1980s Arsenio Hall was a regular on several short-lived variety and talk shows: *The ½ Hour Comedy Hour* (1983), *Motown Review* (1985), and *Thicke of the Night* (1983–1984). In 1987 Hall became the regular host of

Basketball great Earvin "Magic" Johnson (left) talks with host Arsenio Hall in 1992. *The Arsenio Hall Show* offered a youthful alternative to the traditional late-night fare of *The Tonight Show with Johhny Carson*. (AP Photo/Kevork Djansezian)

> One of the most memorable moments from the Arsenio Hall Show was presidential candidate Bill Clinton's visit in 1992. Clinton, then governor of Arkansas, appeared in sunglasses playing "Heartbreak Hotel" on his saxophone. While many pundits thought this was undignified, embarrassing, or coarse, the appearance struck a new chord with many voters and opened up the late-night world to politicians.

The Late Show (1986–1987) on Fox, when Joan Rivers left after relations between Fox executives and Rivers deteriorated. *The Late Show with Joan Rivers* was renamed *The Late Show.* Several hosts had a try at the show. Hall did so well that he developed a cult following. The ratings were improving, but Fox programming put an end to the show and replaced it with *The Wilton North Report*, a comedy/newsmagazine hybrid that only ran for 21 episodes. Sensing he was onto something fresh and new, Paramount gave Arsenio Hall a contract to host a syndicated late night talk show—*The Arsenio Hall Show*.

The King of Late Night Dethroned

In 1989 there were two late night talk shows going up against the undisputed king of the form, Johnny Carson. In addition to *The Arsenio Hall Show* CBS put forth *The Pat Sajak Show,* hosted by the popular host of the game show *Wheel of Fortune*. Hall had something new to offer late night audiences: he was young, black, and hip. For younger viewers who felt *The Tonight Show with Johnny Carson* was old-fashioned and represented their parents' generation, *The Arsenio Hall Show* fit the bill. Sajak aimed at Carson's audience but didn't have the experience, name recognition, or abilities for late night. His show lasted less than a year at 298 episodes.

Arsenio Hall did not have a traditional sidekick on the show, but he did have an announcer, Burton Richardson (1949–). Each night before the star made his entrance, Richardson belted out in a strong voice "Arseniooooooooooooooo" (he would hold the "o" for at least 10 seconds). Then Hall would take the stage and, using the same breath, Richardson would announce "HALL!" The whole event lasted as long as 20 seconds and fired up the audience. While being introduced Arsenio Hall would stand with his head down, and his hands together, with legs apart to form the letter "A" for Arsenio.

The row of audience members behind and near the band were identified as the "Dog Pound." These special audience members would interact passionately with Hall, often standing up and fist pumping while howling, "WUFF, WUFF, WUFF."

The Dog Pound was often the butt of Hall's jokes. He would point to the section and say, "Those are people who . . . " One variation was the phrase keyed into the shot, "People who are currently in a witness protection program." The camera then revealed a shot of the Dog Pound members digitally pixilated to hide their identity.

The Arsenio Hall show targeted an urban audience, African Americans, Latinos, and young Caucasians. In addition, consistent with the new, young, and hip format, *The Arsenio Hall Show* did not book old staples of Hollywood and television. The lineup included a fresh crop of vibrant guests like Eddie Murphy, Paula Abdul, George Lopez, Andrew "Dice" Clay, Jim Henson, and Jason Vourhees (the main character from the *Friday the 13th* films). Sports figures included new wave wrestlers Hulk Hogan, Ravishing Rick Rude, Randy Savage, and the Ultimate Warrior, and a variety of basketball and other sports stars.

A Revolution in Nighttime Music

Johnny Carson had Doc Severinsen (1927–) and *The Tonight Show Band.* Hall called his house band the Posse. Severinsen had jazz men who specialized in standards. Leader Michael Wolff (1952–) and the Posse were rock and rollers who were loud, fast, cutting-edge musicians.

Although modern rap music began around 1978, it was building in popularity among young people throughout the 1980s. Mainstream variety shows including those of Carson and Pat Sajak were not booking this music. The presentation of polished rap acts by *The Arsenio Hall Show* was an important contribution that satisfied and increased his young demographic. Just some of the many rappers appearing on the show included M. C. Hammer, Queen Latifah, Naughty by Nature, Ol' Dirty Bastard, Wu-Tang Clan,

YoYo, Ice-T, Dr. Dre, 2Pac, Snoop Dogg, LL Cool J, Jazzy Jeff and Fresh Prince, Heavy D., 2 Live Crew, and NWA.

Hall often shouted out to his off-camera director when he wanted something to happen. His signature line was "Kick it, Sandi!" Sandi Fullerton was a female TV director known also for her work on *Rock Concert, The Soul Train Awards, The MTV Music Awards,* and as director of music videos for Sting, David Bowie, Whitney Houston, and Michael Jackson. When she died on May 18, 2014 her career had spanned over 30 years.

The Arsenio Hall Show held strong ratings, but in 1993 problems with the numbers appeared and worsened due to competition from a newly launched late night show. By 1994 the innovative, breakthrough show was cancelled. After a long break from the late night circuit, Arsenio Hall made a comeback in 2013. The show was simply named *Arsenio*. A dispute with his executive producer, Neal Kendeall, led to a walkout and a transition period when the show was in reruns. Ratings tumbled and by 2014 *Arsenio* left the airwaves.

Arsenio Hall's contribution to late night television was to break the mold of *The Tonight Show* and prove there was a new audience who wanted their own show after the 11 o'clock news. This audience signaled a rapidly changing American culture that needed to be reflected on television.

See also: *The Late Show Starring Joan Rivers*; *Soul Train*; *Vol. 1, The 1950s–1960s: The Tonight Show*.

Further Resources

Ferrell, Randy. 2014. *Arsenio Hall: 191 Success Facts—Everything You Need to Know about Arsenio Hall.* Emereo Publishing.

King, Norman. 1993. *Arsenio Hall.* New York: William Morrow. Amazon Digital Services.

Baywatch (NBC, 1989–1990; Syndication, 1991–2001)

On television or in motion pictures there really wasn't a genre labeled *lifeguard*. On television shows most lifeguards were male, and usually in the background, or in a quick foreground appearance for a rescue. In movies, there were the Roger Corman (1926–) beach romps starring Annette Funicello (1942–2013) and Frankie Avalon (1940–), and in those films lifeguards were there for verisimilitude. NBC was convinced that a show that centered on the lives, actions, romances, and dangers confronting lifeguards could draw an audience. The concept was close to the "jiggle TV" phenomenon where the majority of the content involves watching curvaceous young women running or moving in ways that cause parts of their bodies to be in motion. The decision to film women and also men running, usually into the camera in slow motion, pushed the standard and practices department into new categories on which to pass judgment. *Baywatch* went beyond the stereotype of the well-built male lifeguard of the sixties. These men would be muscle cut and hunky. The women were selected for their representation of different types in terms of hair color, facial beauty and a variety of shapes and sizes; everyone was extremely physically fit. The pilot of the original show was broadcast as an NBC TV Movie on April 23, 1989.

> Significant in the incredible rise and fall of *Baywatch* is its record for being the most-watched television show in the world. While clearly an American show, *Baywatch* has been wildly embraced by a worldwide audience. A few of the countries where the show gained a large audience include Belgium, Germany, Guatemala, Malaysia, Kenya, the Philippines, Israel, and Egypt. *Baywatch* is an international phenomenon.

Actor to Lifeguard

The casting of *Baywatch* evolved over 11 seasons, and, although acting skills were important, the hunkability and sexiness factors were paramount. The original cast was headed by David Hasselhoff (1952–), who achieved some stardom on the small screen with *Knight Rider,* playing a government field agent who drove an indestructible car controlled by artificial intelligence. On *Baywatch* "the Hoff," as he is known, played Mitch Buchannon, a newly promoted lieutenant, who leads a coed squad of lifeguards who protect all aspects of the beach and ocean environment. His best friend was played by Parker Stevenson (1952–), a lawyer and part-time lieutenant lifeguard. Beauty queen Shawn Weatherly (1959–) was killed by a shark in mid-season, and Billy Warlock (1961–), Erika Eleniak (1969–), and Peter Phelps (1960–) are rookies. Gregory Alan-Williams (1956–) was Sergeant Garner Ellebee. Monte Markham (1935–) played Mitch's boss, Holly Gaigner (1958–) played Gina Pomeroy, Brandon Call (1976–) appeared as Mitch's son, and John Allen Nelson (1959–) ran a beachfront rental store. Usually, the show was filmed on location at Will Rogers State Park in Southern California.

Even with beautiful locations and elements of drama and romance, *Baywatch* failed to get the ratings it needed to please NBC prime time. The show was cancelled as it was deemed unable to reach its potential for massive audiences and a cult/iconic status. The numbers were bad—*Baywatch* landed at 73 out of 103 shows in the seasonal ratings. To make matters worse, the production company GTG, which produced the show, ceased to exist. Down but not out, Hasselhoff and show creators Michael Berk, Douglas Schwartz, and Gregory J. Bonann (1952–) decided to revive *Baywatch* through syndication in 1991. Hasselhoff was given executive producer credit for his part in keeping *Baywatch* alive. Over the seasons cast members were added, and the female cast increased. The actors who joined the cast included Tom McTigue (1959–), David Charvet (1972–), Jeremy Jackson (1980–), Jaason Simmons (1970–), David Cokachi (1968–), Jose Solano (1971–), Kelly Slater (1972–), Michael Newman, Michael Bergin (1969–), who was the only real lifeguard on *Baywatch,* Charley B. Rumbly, and Jason Brooks (1966–). Actresses added to *Baywatch* over the seasons included Nicole Eggert (1972–), Alexandra Paul (1963–), Pamela Sue Anderson (1967–), Yasmine Bleeth (1968–), Gena Lee Nolin (1971–), Donna D'Errico (1968–), Traci Bingham (1968–), Nancy Valen (1965–), Carmen Electra (1972–), Angelica Bridges (1970–), Marliece Andrada, (1972–), Kelly Packard (1975–), Brook Burns (1978–), Brandy Ledford (1969–), Simmone Jade Mackinnon (1973–), Stacy Kamano (1974–), Brandi Roderick (1974–), and Krista Allen (1971–).

The One-Piece Bathing Suit

To create the iconic red one-piece bathing suit worn by the female lifeguards on *Baywatch*, the producers did not use a Hollywood costume designer. Instead Greg Boann, the show's co-creator and an actual Southern California lifeguard, went to TYR, a company in the competitive swimming business. He developed his own specs in visualizing the suits' look. Coming from the specific background, Boann knew that the perfect suit for comfort and swimming ability would not be a bikini, which didn't offer support and durability. He knew that the suit needed to be one-piece, especially since lifeguards might be rescuing a victim who is grabbing at the lifeguard out of panic. The iconic bathing suit was one of the elements that eventually catapulted *Baywatch* into a syndicated success with an international audience of more than one billion by 1994.

The suits did not have a generalized fit. Pamela Sue Anderson's bathing suit had a lower neckline and the armholes were lower while the legs were cut higher at the sides. She and a few of the more voluptuous women wore this design cut to fit. A medium pattern was cut out of red Lycra for the women who had more average body types. Alexandra Paul's suit was designed with a higher neckline for her less curvy, but sleek physique. The fine balance between eye candy and functionality was always maintained. All the male lifeguards wore red Lycra boxer suits.

Not everyone who auditioned for *Baywatch* got a part—actually some of those rejected have gone on to major careers: Teri Hatcher (1964–), Neve Campbell (1973–), and Leonardo DiCaprio (1974–).

For the final two seasons, *Baywatch* left California and was named *Baywatch Hawaii*. In the 50th state the lifeguards wore lemon yellow, so a new set of suits for the males and females were made for realism's sake.

If the location shots and beauty shots of the lifeguards are the background, the content of *Baywatch* is in the detail of the rescues, the investigation of relationships and romances, crime, illness, drama, comedy, and a healthy narrative. Some of the storylines included the suspected murder of a drowning victim, disappearance of the mother of a homeless girl, hostage taking, pursuit of criminals, assault on the environment, an *E. coli* poisoning, a deadly creature entering the Baywatch waters, gang confrontation, suicide, and rape.

Baywatch the Movie: Forbidden Paradise, a direct-to-video movie, was released in 1989. The cast included David Hasselhoff, Pamela Anderson, Yasmine Bleeth, Alexandra Paul, and David Charvet. It concerns a vacation trip to Oahu, Hawaii and the misadventures experienced by the lifeguards.

A spin-off series, *Baywatch Nights,* ran for two seasons in syndication from 1995 to 1997. It started off as a detective story and switched in the second season to the science fiction mode in the style of *The X Files*.

See also: *Charlie's Angels*.

Further Resources

Bonann, Gregory L., and Brad Alan Lewis. 2000. *Baywatch: Rescued from Prime Time*. London: New Millennium Entertainment.

Schwartz, Debbie. 1995. *"Baywatch": The Inside Story*. Harmondsworth, Middlesex, UK: Michael Joseph.

Beauty and the Beast (CBS, 1987–1990)

The deeply romantic story of Beauty and the Beast was brought to television in an updated grand style with elaborate production design and poetic dialogue, taking place in contemporary New York City. A strong cult audience quickly developed, but CBS, the network that carried *Beauty and the Beast*, was not satisfied with the numbers, which most likely shortened its run.

Linda Hamilton (1956–) portrayed Catherine Chandler, an upwardly mobile New York corporate lawyer who was badly beaten, slashed in the face with a knife, and then left for dead in Central Park by her attacker.

Ron Perlman (1950–) plays Vincent, a furry-faced, lion-like man-beast who finds Catherine and carries her to an underground city below New York—a unique environment with a high moral sensibility and a timeless sense of place.

There Vincent heals her wounds with his unusual and magical powers. Eventually Catherine goes back to her world but realizes she is in love with Vincent, who has the power to "read" her feelings. Their romance had a kiss, but their love was not physical, more psychic. When Catherine got into trouble in the above world, Vincent would leave his netherworld and rescue her. Poetry and literature were a strong form of communication between them. After the death of her father, Catherine decides to live below ground with Vincent forever.

Although *Beauty and the Beast* was an original show, well mounted and well acted, for the 1987–1988 season, it only finished 40th in the ratings. For the second season, 1988–1989, it dropped to the 55th position. In its third (incomplete) season it plunged to 93rd in the ratings.

Beauty and the Beast had a lush feature-film look. Its loyal cult audience was attracted to the sumptuous, mysterious, and atmospheric mien of the show. The literate storytelling, the poetic dialogue, and the totally convincing acting were innovative. Ron Perlman's head-to-toe "beast" makeup and the ornate and detailed costumes strongly contributed to the verisimilitude of a fairy tale that comes alive. It captured the hearts of those looking for exceptional television programming. To the larger audience the show was too fantastical. *Beauty and the Beast* was ahead of its time; there would later be a reboot of this tantalizing series.

This lush and romantic television series derives from a fairy tale written by French novelist Jeanne-Marie Leprince de Beaumont, published in 1756. Variations of the story have been known all over Europe. Over a long period of time, adaptations of the tale have appeared in literature film and television. The complex narrative centers on the beautiful daughter of a merchant who runs into an ornate castle and a hideous beast who slaves over her. He wants her to marry him, which after further complications is achieved for a "happily ever after" ending.

The most famous adaptation is *La Belle et la Bête,* released in 1946 and directed by Jean Cocteau (1889–1963). The most metaphorical application of the Beauty and the Beast legend can be found in *King Kong* (1933).

Further Resources

Gross, Edward. 2012. *Above and Below: The Unofficial 25th Anniversary Beauty and the Beast Companion*. Duncan, OK: BearManor Media.

Perlman, Ron. 2014. *Easy Street (the Hard Way): A Memoir*. New York: Da Capo Press.

Body by Jake (Syndication, 1982–1998)

Jake Steinfeld (1958–) is considered the creator of the personal training industry, acquiring the title "Trainer to the Stars." The body builder became very successful by developing workouts and making private calls to celebrities' homes, commanding up to $200 for a half-hour session. In 1982 he made a deal with Ted Turner (1938–) to eventually air 600 episodes of *Fitness Break by Jake*. In 1986 he produced and was featured on the syndicated *Body by Jake*. In 1989 Steinfeld moved that show to ESPN, which ran 200 episodes. Steinfeld eventually became an entrepreneur, expanding to exercise DVDs, books, and personalized exercise equipment.

There were successful exercise shows before *Body by Jake* but Steinfeld created a brand and a simple, fun way to exercise the entire body in a short period of time each day. His personality was really the star of the show. More like a body builder than other male physical fitness celebrities, Steinfeld stressed fun and hosted the show with a very positive attitude. He often had two women exercising with him, one a professional and the other a member of his "gang." He constantly referred to the viewers as his "gang" and used lively, simple language to explain the exercises. A favorite was calling the rear end the "buttismo." The set was a stripped-down carpeted living room. Very little equipment was needed, mainly a broom handle/stick with small rubber covers on each end. Steinfeld gave special attention to the viewer selected to exercise with him and to the invited professional. Steinfeld, the personal trainer, comes through as a gentle guide, providing encouragement and rewards with his praise.

Giveaways were staples on the show. There was a *Body by Jake* T-shirt, which fitted tightly on the body and had a solid, strong color field with an oval just above center featuring the logo "Body by Jake." For example, on one episode that featured the lower part of the body, Steinfeld repeatedly and with glee said "buttismo." Later he told "the gang" that he knew how many times he said it and that the exact number would be provided to the audience. Everyone who wrote in with that number would get a free *Body by Jake* T-shirt.

The exercises performed by Steinfeld and his partners were generally standard. His commands, number of repetitions, and the necessary speed were delivered in a likeable, comforting, and encouraging manner.

Along with his cheerful voice and solid delivery as he talked to the gang and his on-stage exercise buddies, Steinfeld had fairly short hair combed straight back, which contributed to his identity. Often the pro looked into the audience when they worked out, but the person selected from the gang only paid attention to her trainer, Steinfeld. Although men did watch the show, the core audience was female; so largely Steinfeld had young women working out with him. Pink leggings or tights were often the outfit of choice topped off with a *Body by Jake* T-shirt.

During the 1980s' physical fitness revolution when the average person was looking to be fit, trim, and in fine form, the search was on for the best workout in the shortest time. Steinfeld promised a Body by Jake in 10 minutes; that offer was hard to turn down. In 1993 Steinfeld developed a 24-hour fitness channel—FiT TV, which he sold to Rupert Murdoch in 1998.

See also: *The Richard Simmons Show*.

Further Resources

Steinfeld, Jake. 1984. *Body by Jake*. New York: Simon & Schuster.

Steinfeld, Jake. 2002. *Get Strong!: Body by Jake's Guide to Building Confidence, Muscles, and a Great Future for Teen Age Guys*. New York: Fireside.

Buffalo Bill (NBC, 1983–1984)

Going against the grain, creators Tom Patchett and Jay Tares (1939–) brought to television "Buffalo Bill" Bittinger, a talk show host in Buffalo, New York, broadcast on WBFL–TV. This unusual sitcom violated the rules strictly adhered to by all those before it—that the main character, although flawed, was clearly likeable with a value system the audience could relate to. Buffalo Bill was not likeable; he was snide, sarcastic, rude, and extremely egotistical. His value system only revolved around himself, a celebrity who looked down on his colleagues and his viewers. He had a bad temper, was a liar, and without any really good qualities.

The Right Man for the Right Job

Dabney Coleman (1932–) was perfect for the part; the actor had basically built a career playing characters like "Buffalo Bill." Coleman began his long career on an episode of *Naked City* in 1961. Some of the movies and TV shows Coleman appeared on include *Mary Hartman, Mary Hartman* (1976–1977), *9 to 5* (1980), and *Tootsie* (1982). *Buffalo Bill* was a tour-de-force for Coleman. He was the ultimate actor for "Buffalo Bill" and there really wasn't a second choice in the casting.

The supporting cast were all recognizable to the audience, and the two actresses in the cast members would be in well-known films in the near future: Joanna Cassidy (1945–) (*Blade Runner,* 1982) played Jo-Jo White, Buffalo Bill's show director; and Geena Davis (1956–) (*Tootsie,* 1982) was Wendy Killian, an inexperienced researcher with whom Bill has an affair. Max Wright (1943–) (*All That Jazz,* 1979) is Karl Shub, Bill's station manager who doesn't particularly like his host. John Fielder (1925–2005) (*Twelve Angry Men,* 1957) appears as the lightweight stage manager who actually likes "Buffalo Bill," and black actor Charles Robinson (1945–) (*King,* 1978) plays Newdell, the cantankerous makeup man.

In all, NBC aired 26 episodes of *Buffalo Bill*. The plot lines that convinced an audience to watch *Buffalo Bill* involved Bill's abominable behavior at work and in his personal life, where from time to time he suffered the consequences by comeuppances he surely deserved. In various episodes, Bill was seen insulting his interview subjects and his staff and crew while on the air. He also routinely blames his staff for the show's problems, instead of himself. Outside of work, Bill was rude and inconsiderate to people, such as refusing to give a homeless man a quarter. As a result, the man punched Bill out cold.

A memorable episode occurred on Bill's birthday. The staff held a backstage party for him but he was having trouble on stage, he was silent for a long time, then spoke too quietly and finally walked off leaving the audience. He was angry about his birthday. Jo-Jo went to his apartment to bring him the gifts he'd left behind. The phone kept ringing; he answered it and was upset. He told Jo-Jo the caller was a crazy woman who said he'd fathered her child and if she didn't marry him she'd commit suicide. The staff hunted for the woman. A woman dressed as a cleaning lady appeared in the office hall. Bill started the show and saw the woman. She was brought on the show and Bill talked to her gently and with great humanity (a new side of him). When he finished and the woman calmed down after crying a lot, he called off stage to the police, "Cuff her."

Buffalo Bill took on the kind of issues usually seen on a Norman Lear show. Racism was handled in a fever dream Bill had after an argument with Newdell. There were Zulu warriors, pushy black hookers, and a panoply of African American stereotypes all chasing Bill. The dream was scored by the Ray Charles classic "Hit the Road, Jack."

See also: Lear, Norman.

Further Resources

Television Obscurities. 2009. "Q & A: Buffalo Bill." August 10. http://www.tvobscurities.com/2009/08/q-and-a-buffalo-bill/

Wallace, David. 1983. "As TV's Macho Buffalo Bill, Dabney Coleman Finds That Sexism Breeds Success." *People*. July 11. http://www.people.com/people/archive/article/0,,20085459,00.html

Cagney & Lacey (CBS, 1982–1988)

Executive producer Barney Rosenzweig (1937–) had worked on *Charlie's Angels* (1976–1981) and didn't want to work on a superficial show like *Charlie's Angels* again. The result of his research and brainstorming became *Cagney & Lacey*, the first television crime show whose two central characters were women. It was time. The women's movement of the 1970s made an impact and made it an opportune time for a show about two female characters. Influential for Rosenzweig was the seminal 1974 nonfiction book *From Reverence to*

Cagney & Lacey featured Sharon Gless (left) as Christine Cagney and Tyne Daly as Mary Beth Lacey. Although both characters were New York City police detectives, Cagney was portrayed as a single, career-minded woman, while Lacey was a married working mother. (Pictorial Parade/ Courtesy of Getty Images)

Rape by author and film critic Molly Haskell (1939–), which studied the treatment of women in motion pictures. Another influence was *Butch Cassidy and the Sundance Kid* (1969), a New Wave Western that starred Paul Newman and Robert Redford, a seminal buddy movie. Rosenzweig transferred that relationship concept to a TV series with two female cops.

The Women's Movement Comes to Primetime Television

The basis for *Cagney & Lacey* was a TV movie that aired October 8, 1981. In it Loretta Swit (1937–) and Tyne Daly (1946–) played police officers Sgt. Christine Cagney and Mary Beth Lacey. When the project went to series Loretta Swit was unable to continue because of her commitment to *M*A*S*H* and Meg Foster (1948–) was signed to appear as Cagney for the spring 1982 episodes. When *Cagney & Lacey* was picked up for the next season, Meg Foster had been dropped from the cast. *TV Guide* reported that an unnamed CBS executive felt Foster was too tough and not feminine enough. Another network executive said audience testing revealed both Daly and Foster were too masculine. Actress Sharon Gless (1943–) came in for the second season to play Chris Cagney. Rosenzweig and Gless would marry in 1991 after the series concluded.

Gless was Rosenzweig's first choice for Cagney during the original casting, but she was tied up in a contract with Universal Studios and couldn't do it. The CBS executives who had problems with Meg Foster's look and approach to the character were hopeful that Gless could play the part with a more feminine demeanor. They attempted to persuade the producers to make Cagney someone from a wealthy family who was high-class but not snobbish. At first Rosenzweig and Barbara Corday (1944–), his co-producer and one of the show's producers, flatly rejected the suggestion and encouraged Gless to continue playing Cagney as a tough working-class woman with a good sense of humor. Eventually they moved a bit in the direction preferred by the executives and stated that Cagney may have been born to a well-to-do woman who married a working-class cop, Charles Cagney, played by Dick O'Neill (1928–1998).

Gless and Daly worked well together. Daly's Lacey was an earthy wife and mother. Gless's Cagney was single, beautiful, and spontaneous by nature. They made a great team and delighted both male and female demographics with their portrayals and abilities to advance cops and robbers action. Between the two of them, Daly and Gless won six consecutive Emmy awards for outstanding actress in a drama series. The show had a fine supporting cast including Al Waxman (1935–2001) as the team's boss, Lieutenant Bert Samuels.

The story lines for this police drama with a twist included a murder of a Latino gang member; high-end beauty parlors are robbed and the team eventually catches the robbers; Cagney is shot and Lacey temporarily has to deal with a new male partner; and an episode in which the women work on a kiddie porn case with a high-profile district attorney.

What made *Cagney & Lacey* special for its time is that the two female cops didn't just fight the bad guy criminals, but also the chauvinism they experienced from their male colleagues.

After the first season of *Cagney & Lacey* the CBS executives continued their negativity toward the show. They decided not to renew the show at the end of the 1982–1983 season, but a wave of complaints from the viewers and the network changed their mind. Seven episodes were ordered for midseason replacement and *Cagney & Lacey* returned to air in March 1984, enjoying their highest ratings that spring.

There were several made-for-TV movies in which Gless and Daly reprise their roles, including *Cagney & Lacey*: *The Return,* which aired on November 6, 1994, and *Cagney & Lacey: Together Again,* which aired May 2, 1995.

See also: *L.A. Law*.

Further Resources

Rosenzweig, Barney. 2007. *Cagney & Lacey . . . and Me: An Inside Hollywood Story OR How I Learned to Stop Worrying and Love the Blonde*. Lincoln, NE: iUniverse.

Stevens, Serita Mendelson. 1985. *Cagney & Lacey*. New York: Dell.

The prolific television producer and writer Stephen J. Cannell was responsible for many shows, including *The Rockford Files, The A-Team, The Greatest American Hero, 21 Jump Street*, and *The Commish*. (AP Photo/Frank Wiese)

Cannell, Stephen J. (1941–2010)

Stephen J. Cannell has created or co-created as many as 40 television series, many in the crime genre. By his estimate he wrote more than 450 individual episodes and produced or executive produced 1,500 episodes. Cannell became the hottest and most prolific pilot writer in Hollywood. At one point he was making $400,000 a year in pilot fees alone.

Born in Los Angeles, California, Stephen J. Cannell's father, Joseph Knapp Cannell, owned a highly successful interior decorating company. Young Stephen had difficulties with dyslexia in school, but was able to graduate from the University of Oregon in 1964 with a bachelor of science degree in journalism. Upon graduation he worked in the family business for four years. He sold his first script to the Universal TV series *It Takes a Thief* in 1968. He was hired by the company and then worked as a freelance writer for crime shows such as *Ironside* (1967–1975) and *Columbo* (1968–2003). He was asked to write a script as quickly as possible for the Jack Webb series, *Adam-12* (1968–1975), and delivered it in only one day. He was then hired as the show's story editor. In 1979 Cannell formed Stephen J. Cannell Productions where *The Greatest American Hero* (1981–1983) was his first series followed by *The A-Team* (1983–1987), *Riptide* (1984–1986), and *Hunter* (1984–1991).

In 1987, to reduce production costs, Cannell produced his new series, *Stingray* (1986–1987), in Canada, followed by *21 Jump Street* (1987–1991). When problems securing locations and studio space occurred because of competition with big studios, he built his own state-of-the-art studio. Other series included *Wiseguy* (1987–1990), *J.J. Starbuck* (1987–1988), *Booker* (1989–1990), *The Commish* (1991–1996), *The Hat Squad* (1992–1993), *Cobra* (1993–1994), *Hawkeye* (1994–1995), and a number of television films. *The A-Team* and *21 Jump Street* were translated into theatrical motion pictures.

In 1995 New World Communications acquired Cannell Entertainment. He then created the Cannell Studios. Also at this time Cannell began writing novels, 11 of which featured the character Detective Shane Scully of the Los Angeles Police Department.

Until his death on September 30, 2010 from complications of melanoma, Cannell wrote his scripts on an IBM Selectric typewriter and only used the computer for research.

Because Cannell wrote so quickly, often a full script in one day, the signature closing of his shows pictures him typing furiously. When he is finished, he whips the page out of the typewriter and it flies into the air, transforming into an animated logo.

See also: *The A-Team*; *Columbo*; *21 Jump Street*; *Wiseguy*; *Vol. 3, The 1990s–Present: The Commish*.

Further Resources

Abbott, Jon. 2009. *Stephen J. Cannell Television Productions: A History of All Series and Plots*. Jefferson, NC: McFarland.

Thompson, Robert. 1990. *Adventures in Prime Time: The Television Programs of Stephen J. Cannell*. New York: Praeger.

Cheers (NBC, 1982–1993)

A bar named Cheers located on Beacon Street in downtown Boston is the location for the show of the same name. It was based on the Bull and Finch Pub in the area. It had three steps down to a brick-walled room with diamond glass windows, Tiffany lamps, and wooden benches. The producers knew immediately this was the right atmosphere for their show and an exact replica of the original was built on a Hollywood sound stage. This half-hour sitcom captured the hearts of a large audience. The tavern was owned by Sam "Mayday" Malone, a former Red Sox baseball player who was a reformed alcoholic and an active womanizer, portrayed by Ted Danson (1947–). From 1982 to 1987 Shelley Long (1949–) played Diane Chambers, a highly educated intellectual who took the waitress job at Cheers only on a "temporary" basis and eventually became romantically involved with Sam. From 1982 to 1985 Nicholas Colassanto (1924–1985), who died of a heart attack while the show was still running, played "Coach" Ernie Pantusso, the stubborn bartender who was a former Red Sox manager. Rhea Perlman (1948–) played waitress Carla Tortelli, known for her sharp tongue. George Wendt (1948–) played Norm Peterson, a stocky beer-guzzling regular. Cliff Clavin, another regular, is a postal employee. As the series moved on other characters were brought in including: Dr. Frasier Crane, played by Kelsey Grammer from 1984 to 1993, a snobbish psychiatrist who dated Diane for a period of time. From 1985–1993 Woody Harrelson (1961–) played Woody Boyd, the replacement bartender after Nicholas Colassanto passed away. From 1986 to 1992 Bebe Neuwirth (1958–) played a cold psychiatrist, Dr. Lilith Sternin, who dated and later married Dr. Crane.

Things changed in the *Cheers* narrative in 1987. Diane left the bar and Sam to pursue a writing career. Sam sold the bar to a conglomerate and set out to sail around the world, but the boat sank and Sam returned to *Cheers,* this time as the bartender. Kirstie Alley (1951–) came on as the new manager, Rebecca Howe, and she and Sam began a romantic relationship.

New characters and new subplots continued to develop. By 1990 Sam again owned Cheers, and Rebecca became his employee. In 1992 Ted Danson announced he would leave the show after that season. The producers decided not to replace him or to continue the show without him.

The last episode of *Cheers* was a 90-minute special that made history, drawing a massive viewing audience, placing it all-time second best in the Nielsen ratings for an episodic television program. Sam and Diane come back together and after a series of backs and forths decide to marry and move to sunny California. With the clock running down Sam decided he must stay in Boston and at Cheers to really live the rest of his life. The final scene of *Cheers* has Diane and the regulars now gone. Then a customer walks up to the bar's door but Sam sends him away by saying "Sorry, we're closed."

The theme song "Where Everybody Knows Your Name" by Judy Hart Angelo and Gary Portnoy and sung by Gary Portnoy reflected the warm mood of the Cheers bar.

Sitcoms are driven by story and especially dialogue. *Cheers* was known for its great characters, terrific one-liners, and witty, sometimes sarcastic dialogue. To drive a half-hour show on dialogue most often in the same location was a challenge for the creators, Glen Charles (1947–), James Burrows (1940–), and Les Charles (1943–). The trio lived up to and surpassed the test. Over the years *Cheers* received 28 Emmy awards and a record 111 nominations.

See also: *Vol. 3, The 1990s–Present: Frasier.*

Further Resources

Bjorklund, Dennis. 2012. *Cheers TV Show: A Comprehensive Reference*. Praetorian Publishing.

Bjorklund, Dennis. 2014. *Cheers Trivia: It's a Little Known Fact . . .* Maizeland Books.

China Beach (ABC, 1988–1991)

China Beach was a show set during the Vietnam War (1954–1975) in the 1960s, focused on American women who served during this conflict. The result was a stirring drama and an emotional point of view about women and war seldom portrayed on television.

China Beach took place at a U.S. Air Force hospital and recreational facility at Da Nang in Vietnam. Dana Delany (1956–) played Nurse Lieutenant Colleen McMurphy. Her character was loosely based on Lynda Van Devanter (1947–2002), who wrote the book *Home Before Morning* (1984). Nancy Giles (1960–) played Armed Forces Radio DJ Frankie Bunsen, Concetta Tomei (1945–) portrayed Major Lila Garreau, and Marg Helgenberger (1958–) won the Emmy for outstanding actress in a dramatic series in 1990 for portraying Karen Charlene "K.C." Koloski, a drug-addicted prostitute. Chloe Webb (1956–) played USO entertainer Laurette Barber, Nan Woods (1966–) played Red Cross volunteer Cherry Vaughn, and Ricki Lake (1968–) played Red Cross volunteer Holly Pellegrino.

There was a strong male cast as well who interacted with the women, but this was a women's movement genre, and the supreme and wide-ranging performances made *China Beach* a distinctive show that provided an exceptional look at a significant aspect of American history.

The music for the show took a different approach, relying on rock and pop songs of the era for the soundtrack. The theme song was "Reflections" by the Supremes, and Nancy Sinatra (1940–) actually appeared on the show singing "These Boots Are Made for Walking." Some of the many songs from the soundtrack of *China Beach* included "Hang On Sloopy" by the McCoys, Big Brother and the Holding Company backing vocalist Janis Joplin in "Piece of My Heart," and Katrina and the Waves covering "We Got to Get Out of This Place," originally recorded by the Animals.

A memorable episode aired on March 15, 1989. Actual Vietnam veterans appeared on the show to reminisce about their experiences during the war. These moments of reality were intercut with dramatic scenes played by the actors. The final episode of *China Beach* was set at a 1988 reunion of the characters and involved a visit to the Vietnam Veterans Memorial in Washington, D.C.

China Beach did for the Vietnam War what *M*A*S*H* did for the Korean War (1950–1953): it deconstructed the conflict to show the physical and mental toll on the participants. The show was highly and favorably recognized by the critics, but it was constantly in a ratings struggle.

China Beach was nominated for numerous Emmys and won many times in a wide range of categories. Dana Delany won for outstanding actress in a drama series in 1989 and 1992.

See also: *M*A*S*H*; *Vietnam: A Television History*.

Further Resources

Rushton, Patricia. 2004. *Vietnam War Nurses: Personal Accounts of 18 Americans*. Jefferson, NC: McFarland.

Van Devanter, Lynda. 1984. *Home before Morning: The Story of an Army Nurse in Vietnam.* New York: Warner Books.

CNN (Cable News Network, 1980–)

The Cable News Network (CNN) is a 24-hour cable television news network that is a subsidiary of the Turner Broadcasting System (TBS). The network was the brainchild of TBS founder Ted Turner, who wanted to establish a network that would be able to broadcast breaking news immediately and around the clock. In 1996, TBS was purchased by Time Warner, which was purchased by America Online in 2000, making CNN part of a vast array of entertainment and Internet interests.

Turner founded CNN in 1980 as an alternative to the television news establishment of ABC, NBC, and CBS. From the beginning, CNN was different. Instead of establishing headquarters in Manhattan, CNN was based in Atlanta; it had a news budget of $25 million for 24 hours of programming; the news itself was treated as a star rather than the anchors and correspondents; and its on-air reporters were typically less attractive than those hired by the major networks. CNN's lack of glamour contributed to its reputation for straight, balanced journalism, and by the late 1980s, the network was expanding, establishing bureaus around the United States.

In 1990, Turner hired Tom Johnson, a former *Los Angeles Times* publisher, to run CNN. Johnson arrived at the network on the eve of the Persian Gulf War, which proved a turning point for the company. To many people, CNN was the true victor of the war. Its correspondents stayed in Baghdad after being warned by the government to leave, setting up a transmission line that gave it a link even when power and phone lines went down. Correspondents like Peter Arnett, Bernard Shaw, and Wolf Blitzer became stars, and CNN's ratings occasionally beat the major networks. By the end of the Gulf War, CNN had established itself as a trusted news source, one that could be turned to at any hour of the day.

After the war, however, CNN's ratings fell off, hampered by the establishment of such other 24-hour news channels as MSNBC, the Fox News Channel, and CNBC. Turner sold CNN's parent company, TBS, to Time Warner in 1996 for $7.5 billion and became the vice chairman of Time Warner. He also began looking for ways to boost CNN's ratings and in 1997 hired news showman Rick Kaplan away from ABC with hopes of acquiring some of the stylishness of the big networks. Kaplan's goal was to establish prime-time programming that viewers would turn to when there was no breaking news, and he quickly created *NewsStand,* three series linked to the Time Warner magazines *Time, Fortune,* and *Entertainment Weekly.* Prior to *NewsStand,* CNN had one big show in prime time—*Larry King Live,* a so-called appointment program, or one that viewers watch regularly. With *NewsStand* and similar programs, CNN hoped to go to the next level in news broadcasting, combining live broadcasts with regular nightly programs. Time Warner's purchase by America Online in early 2000 paved the way for CNN to move onto the Internet as well.

CNN offers its viewers news updates on domestic and international events, business, weather, and sports. It also provides analysis by experts and investigative reporting. Programs are transmitted by satellite to cable systems throughout the United States and to Africa, Asia, the Middle East, Latin America, and Europe as CNN International. In early 1997, CNN became the first—and only—U.S. news organization in almost 30 years to establish a bureau in communist Cuba.

CNN, Inc. consists of four networks: CNN, Headline News, CNN Radio, and CNN International. Headline News operates under a separate CNN executive vice president, and the corporation also has separate sports and financial divisions.

ABC-CLIO

See also: *Crossfire*; *The Larry King Show (Larry King Live).*

Further Resources

Boyer, Peter J. 1998. "The People's Network." *New Yorker,* August 3.

Flournoy, Don M. 1997. *CNN: Making News in the Global Market.* Essex, UK: University of Luton Press.

Smith, Perry M. 1991. *How CNN Fought the War: A View from the Inside.* Secaucus, NJ: Carol Publishing Group.

Whittemore, Hank. 1990. *CNN, the Inside Story.* Boston: Little, Brown.

The Cosby Show (NBC, 1984–1992)

Bill Cosby's most notable accomplishment on television to date was *The Cosby Show,* which ran from 1984 to 1992. Instead of the more common approach to family sitcoms with dysfunctional parents and mischievous children, the show featured an upwardly mobile set of happily married, well-educated professional African American parents and a houseful of normal, well-adjusted kids and their everyday issues. The Huxtables embraced black culture and were aware of

The Cosby Show was a landmark situation comedy that focused on the household of an affluent African American family, a perspective that was new to network television at the time. Shown here are Bill Cosby (center) as Dr. Heathcliff "Cliff" Huxtable, and, on the phone, Phylicia Rashad as his wife, Clair Huxtable; between them is Clarice Taylor as Anna Huxtable. Next to Cosby are (left to right) Earle Hyman as Russel Huxtable, Raven-Symone as Olivia, Keisha Knight Pulliam as Rudy, and Malcolm Jamal Warner as Theo. (AP Photo)

events in black history, discussing issues like ending apartheid. With the Huxtables, Bill Cosby continued his tradition of presenting imperfect but likeable people dealing with realistic, current everyday situations.

Bill Cosby (1937–) played Heathcliff "Cliff" Huxtable, a beloved obstetrician. His wife Clair, a lawyer, was portrayed by Phylicia Rashad (1948–). They had five children ranging in age from preschool to a college graduate. In the first season the lineup was Sondra (Sabrina LeBeauf), Denise (Lisa Bonet), Theo (Malcolm-Jamal Warner), Vanessa (Tempest Bledsoe), and Rudy (Keisha Knight Pulliam). Later Olivia Denise's stepdaughter played by Raven-Symone was added. Although the show centered on an African American family, race was not made a predominant issue.

It was well known that Bill Cosby was a rabid fan of blues and jazz music. Some of the show's musical celebrity cameos included Sammy Davis Jr., Dizzy Gillespie, B.B. King, Lena Horne, and Stevie Wonder. Other cameos were by his *I Spy* partner Robert Culp, and several of the Muppets including Gonzo also appeared on the show. Many of the Huxtables' characteristics were applicable to any family, like the running gag that Cliff always tried to fix broken things in the house but almost never succeeded. The children grew up over the years in a color-blind environment with the comedy coming from their growing up foibles. Interaction between Cliff and his kids, Clair and her kids, Clair and Cliff's involvement with the kids, and the Huxtable marriage was the major focus of the show.

Cosby had a firm hand in every aspect of the show, reflected in the credits: "Bill Cosby in *The Cosby* Show. Created by Ed Weinberger & Michael Leeson and William Cosby, Jr., Ed.D." "Theme by Stu

Gardner & Bill Cosby, Executive Consultant: William H. Cosby, Jr." "A Carsey Werner production in association with Bill Cosby."

Cosby's color-blind philosophy moved through his career. He managed to embrace his African American heritage while creating comedy that satisfied a big tent.

See also: *Fat Albert and the Cosby Kids*; *The Jeffersons*; *Vol. 1, The 1950s–1960s: The Bill Cosby Show*; *I Spy*.

Further Resources

Cosby, Bill, and George Booth. 2011. *I Didn't Ask to Be Born (But I'm Glad I Was)*. New York: Hachette Group.

Whitaker, Mark. 2014. *Cosby: His Life and Times*. New York: Simon & Schuster.

Crime Story (NBC, 1986–1987)

Crime Story was a period-piece crime drama set in Chicago in 1963. Created by film director and producer Michael Mann (1943–), *Crime Story* ran for only two seasons, but during its run it established itself as ahead of its time for its genre. Dennis Farina (1944–2013), a former real-life Chicago police officer, played Lieutenant Mike Torello who had a vendetta against mobster Ray Luca, portrayed by Anthony Denison (1949–). Torello headed the Major Crime Unit of the police department, which included Sergeant Danny Krychek played by Bill Smitrovich (1947–), Detective Nate Grossman portrayed by Steve Ryan (1947–2007), Joey Indelli played by Bill Campbell (1959–), and Detective Walter Clemmons portrayed by Paul Butler (1942–2010). Stephen Lang (1952–) played prosecutor David Abrams, Ray Luca's loyal, but limited henchman, and mobster Paulie Taglia was portrayed by John Santucci (1940–), who in the past was a real-life criminal. Using authentic locales from Chicago to Las Vegas, executive producer Michael Mann established a signature look, sparing no expense on production that was his stamp in other endeavors such as *Miami Vice.* There were guest mobsters from time to time including Joseph Wiseman (1918–2009) as Manny Goldman, Jon Polito (1959–) as Phil Bartoli, and controversial comedian Andrew Dice Clay (1957–) as another wise-guy.

In the series' midseason Luca and Taglia moved their mob operations out of Chicago to Las Vegas. Torello and his men followed their target and became agents of a federal strike force. To escape the strike force, Taglia drove Luca to a safe house, but it turned out to be the site of a nuclear bomb test location. Later Luca escaped to a Latin American country, but he was eventually tracked down by Torello.

For Mann, *Crime Story* was a serial with built-in cliffhangers. Unlike other crime shows, this was a continuing story about the good guys chasing the bad guys in which characters could be developed as the story moved to major locations and the narrative unfolded. Mann considered *Crime Story* a novel specifically covering 1963 to 1964.

The shooting schedule was practically unheard of in television. Two episodes were completed every three weeks. Shooting took up to 12 hours a day, seven days a week. In the second season, an average episode cost between $1.3 and $1.4 million, approximately the same as *Miami Vice,* which was a solid ratings hit. The show was shot on location. Because it took place in the 1960s, the production design, props, and costumes had to be totally accurate in order to establish authenticity that would be believable to the viewers. The large cast also contributed to the massive budget.

Musician and record producer Todd Rundgren (1948–) was the first musical director for *Crime Story.* Later rock legend Al Kooper (1944–) followed and allowed songs from the years after 1963 to play on the soundtrack. Del Shannon (1934–1990) rewrote and updated the lyrics to his 1961 classic "Runaway" and it was used as *Crime Story*'s theme song.

The list of actors and celebrities who made appearances on *Crime Story* is long and storied. They include Michael J. Pollard, Dexter Gordon, Miles Davis, Deborah Harry, Ving Rhames, Kevin Spacey, and a young Christian Slater.

Although this cop and crime show embraced large themes and deep emotional profiles, it never really caught on with the public, perhaps because its intensity was too strenuous for the viewing audience. It had a short two-season run. Admirably, NBC believed in *Crime Story* and allowed the show to stay on the air for two full seasons. Regrettably, the show never achieved the ratings that were necessary to maintain its continued place in the lineup.

See also: *Miami Vice*; *Police Story*; *Vol. 1, The 1950s–1960s: Hawaii Five-0.*

Further Resources

Feeney, F. X., and Paul Duncan. 2006. *Michael Mann.* Cologne, Germany: Taschen.

Sanders, Steven, and R. Barton Palmer. 2014. *Michael Mann Cinema and Television: Interviews, 1980–2012.* Edinburgh: Edinburgh University Press.

Crossfire (CNN, 1982–2005, 2013–2014)

Crossfire was a half-hour news-related program that began on radio and aired on television's CNN Monday through Friday, featuring two hosts with opposing political views engaging in a lively debate on the topics of the day. At the start Patrick Buchanan (1938–), who had been a presidential adviser to Richard Nixon, Gerald Ford, and Ronald Reagan, represented the conservative view and Tom Braden (1917–2009), a journalist who wrote the book on which *Eight Is Enough* (1977–1981) was based, defended the liberal view until 1989.

The content on *Crossfire* was strong as were the points of view of the two politically opposing hosts. Topics included American neo-Nazis, AIDS, free speech, and a packed schedule of national and global current events.

The precedent for the verbal jousting on *Crossfire* was a segment on *60 Minutes* in the 1970s called "Point/Counterpoint" with liberal Shana Alexander arguing with the more conservative James J. Kilpatrick. The verbiage did get into a bit of an attack mode, but never as much as in the *Saturday Night Live* takeoff with Jane Curtin and Dan Aykroyd impersonating their roles.

From 1989 to 1995 the liberal position was filled by political journalist and commentator Michael Kinsey (1951–). Syndicated columnist and television personality Robert Novak (1931– 2009) took over the conservative spot in 1987 when Buchanan was the White House director of communications. Novak was succeeded by former White House chief of staff John Sununu (1939–) in 1991. Other participants on *Crossfire* included Bill Press (1940–), a liberal political commentator who appeared from 1996 to 2002; Republican political consultant Mary Matalin (1953–), who was on the show from 1999 to 2001; James Carville (1944–), presidential strategist and Democratic commentator who was on *Crossfire* from 2002 to 2005; Paul Begala (1961–), Democratic consultant and commentator whose run was from 2002 to 2005; and Tucker Carlson (1969–), conservative pundit and founder and editor-in-chief of *The Daily Caller,* whose stint was from 2003 to 2005.

In 2005 CNN had a new CEO, Jonathan Klein, who did not renew Tucker Carlson's contract and wanted to change the tone of the programming. Thus, *Crossfire* was not on the viewing schedule. In 2013 *Crossfire* returned to CNN with Newt Gingrich, S. E. Cupp, Stefanie Cutter, and Van Jones in rotation. The show was preempted for breaking news, particularly the disappearance of Malaysia Airlines Flight 370, and by 2014 the show was cancelled.

See also: CNN (Cable News Network); *The McLaughlin Group*; *Vol. 1, The 1950s–1960s: 60 Minutes*; *Vol. 3, The 1990s–Present: Hardball with Chris Matthews.*

Further Resources

Buchanan, Patrick J. 2002. *The Death of the West: How Dying Populations and Immigrant Invasions Imperil Our Country and Civilization.* New York: St. Martin's Press.

Gingrich, Newt. 2013. *Breakout: Pioneers of the Future, Prison Guards of the Past, and the Epic Battles That Will Decide America's Fate.* Washington, D.C. Regency.

A Current Affair (Syndication, 1986–2005)

A Current Affair was a television newsmagazine, a genre first created for CBS's *60 Minutes* (1968–), but it was more down-market than the high journalistic standards set on the CBS program. It ran nightly for a half-hour and was syndicated. *A Current Affair* was produced at 20th Century Fox and based at Fox's flagship station, WNYW, in New York. From the mid- to late 1980s the host was Maury Povich (1939–), who later would host his own show, *The Maury Povich Show* (1991–), later renamed *Maury*.

At first *A Current Affair* was a New York broadcast with an attitude that distinguished it. As it expanded, the producers gave the show a specific mission—to report on stories across America that were overlooked or ignored by the big three networks.

The logo of the show became part of pop culture. The visual was a pyramid that flies in from the back and lands center front. The show title flies in first as gold particles form the appropriate letters, but it is the sound that captured the most attention. At a key moment a low-pitched twanging sound plays loudly, getting everyone's attention. The sound effect has been labeled as "Ka-Chung." The pyramid and the connected sound effect open the show and are used between stories whenever the director wants an emphasis. The set has two major components—a wall and a desk. There is a double screen panel which allows Povich and a guest to be seen simultaneously.

Occasionally *A Current Affair* would run a special that covered the entire show. One example was a whole show devoted to Elvis Presley, which focused on negative aspects of the performer's career such as his drug use and violent tendencies.

A typical show had a variety of subjects and a strong tabloid point of view. Some of the personalities featured were G. Gordon Liddy, Brian Wilson, and Don Imus, all of whom were controversial figures. Povich began with a preview of the night's segment to entice the viewer. One episode featured a lead-in segment about a boy who was abducted on the street by a masked gunman while two other boys watched. There were interviews with the parents, home movies, and other footage. Reporter David Lee Miller narrates when necessary and closes the piece sadly because the boy was never found.

A second story was about actress Jill Ireland (1936–1990) who was dying of breast cancer. The story included a touching interview with Ireland, who was married to actor Charles Bronson (1921–2003). The final segment was on Zsa Zsa Gabor (1917–2016), who at the time might have faced jail time for slapping a police officer who stopped her for speeding. The segment was mainly comprised of an old Hollywood documentary of Gabor preparing to go to a premiere of *Dr. Zhivago* (1965). Then Povich visited Gabor at her home and interviewed her. Back in the studio Povich simply displayed his disgust with the actress as he looked directly into the camera, an action suited to a gossip tabloid show. His closing tag line was, "Until next time, America."

In 2005 *A Current Affair* was revived after a nine-year hiatus, and with Tim Green as its new anchor it had a short-lived reappearance. However, when Roger Ailes became the news head at Fox, he eliminated the show from the lineup.

See also: *Hard Copy*; *Inside Edition*; *20/20*; *Vol. 1, The 1950s–1960s: 60 Minutes*.

Further Resources

Povich, Maury, with Ken Gross. 1991. *Current Affairs—A Life on the Edge*. New York: Putnam.

Stones, Rob. 2015. *Why Current Affairs Needs Social Theory*. London: Bloomsbury.

Doogie Howser, M.D. (ABC, 1989–1993)

There have been many television medical shows over the decades but none of the doctors were 16-year-olds like Doogie Howser, played by young Neil Patrick Harris (1973–). Howser spent only nine weeks in high school and graduated from Princeton University at age 10. Then his life normalized. It took him the standard four years to finish medical school and two years to be in his second year of residency.

Doogie Howser, M.D., created by Steven Bochco (1943–) and David E. Kelly (1956–), had a cast that included James B. Sikking (1934–) as Doogie's father, Dr. David Howser; Belinda Montgomery (1950–) as his mother, Katherine; Max Casella (1967–) as Doogie's friend Vinnie Delpino; Lawrence Pressman (1939–) as chief of staff Dr. Canfield; Mitchell Anderson (1965–) as Dr. Jack McGuire; Kathryn Laying (1960–) as nurse Curly Spaulding; Lisa Dean Ryan (1972–) who portrayed Doogie's girlfriend Wanda Plenn; and Lucy Boryer (1966–), who played Vinnie's girlfriend Janine.

The major theme on *Doogie Howser, M.D.* was acceptance. The 16-year-old wanted to be understood in both aspects of his life, medical and personal. Because he was an adolescent, it was important for him to be part of the youth culture. At the hospital, he sought to have the doctors, nurses, and staff treat him as an equal.

The show was a dramedy. The comedy primarily came from his exploits with Vinnie and his relationship with his girlfriend. The serious side explored many issues confronting the medical community and society at large. These included AIDS, racism, homophobia, sexism, gang violence, access to quality medical care, and personal issues such as Doogie's virginity, body issues, and friendship.

Steven Bochco planned to end *Doogie Howser, M.D.* with a season-long story arc in which Doogie becomes dissatisfied with the medical profession and leaves the hospital to become a writer, but ABC abruptly cancelled the show after four seasons because of low ratings. Thus, Bochco and his writers were not able to accomplish this concept with the exception of showing Howser's resignation and his departure to Europe in the final episode.

Although *Doogie Howser, M.D.* wasn't always accepted as a serious show because of the child prodigy premise, it managed to bring issues about health and well-being to a new generation in the same way serious shows in this genre like *Ben Casey* (1961–1966) had done in the past.

See also: *Vol. 1, The 1950s–1960s: Ben Casey*; *Vol. 3, The 1990s–Present: ER*; *Grey's Anatomy*; *House*; *How I Met Your Mother*.

Further Resources

Harris, Neil Patrick. 2015. *Neil Patrick Harris: Choose Your Own Autobiography*. New York: Three Rivers Press.

Entertainment Tonight (Syndication, 1981–)

Entertainment Tonight was one of the first programs to feed its syndicated show from Los Angeles to local stations around the country by earth-orbiting satellites. This allowed the local stations to tape the feed and air the program at the time slot of their choice. The show was designed to be a newscast for the entertainment world: movies, television, music, and other areas of media and show business. The show carried stories that reflected the week in entertainment; there was gossip, some meaningful stories and others less so, upcoming movies, profiles of actors and actresses, and a seemingly endless flow of material that filled a half-hour slot, five days a week, and concluded with a weekend wrap-up show. The hosts were on camera, in voice-over during story footage, and were also featured in on-camera personal interviews.

The original hosts were former soap opera actor Tom Hallick (1941–), actress Marjorie Wallace (1954–), and Ron Hendren (1945–), a former San Francisco television critic who also had been a regular contributor on the *Today Show*. Hallick and Wallace were quickly terminated and Hendren became co-host with Dixie Whatley in November 1981. Then in August 1982 Whatley was replaced by Mary Hart (1950–). Hendren left the show in September 1984 and was succeeded by co-host Robb Weller (1949–), who in turn was replaced by John Tesh (1952–) in the fall of 1986. Then a new set was designed and built to minimize the height difference between Tesh and Hart and included a glass desk to feature Hart's legs, which had been insured by Lloyds of London for one million dollars.

Each half-hour was segmented with stories and special features such as film reviews presented by film historian Leonard Maltin (1950–). Other specialists included gossip columnist Rona Barrett (1936–), Bill Harris, who was alternately a gossip reporter and a film critic, and entertainment reporter Jeanne Wolf. The show ended with a birthday segment in quiz form that is resolved after the final commercial of the program episode.

The show became known as "E.T." and the theme song, written by Michael Mark, is one of the most famous in all of nonfiction television. It begins with a fanfare and then leads with six distinctive notes that are easily recognizable to the public. Because of the longevity of *Entertainment Tonight,* the show has become a staple for anyone looking to see what is happening at the moment in show business.

See also: *A Current Affair*; *Hard Copy*; *20/20*.

Further Resources

Gibbons, Leeza. 2013. *Take 2: Your Guide to Creating Happy Endings and New Beginnings.* Carlsbad, CA. Hay House.

Maltin, Leonard. 2015. *Turner Classic Movies Presents Classic Movie Guide: From the Silent Era through 1965*, 3rd ed.

Faerie Tale Theatre (Showtime, 1982–1987)

Faerie Tale Theatre was a live-action anthology series for children conceived by actress Shelley Duvall (1949–). Because of her own celebrity and cult style, Duvall was able to attract top stars and directors to *Faerie Tale Theatre* even though she was working with a low budget and only had a slate of 27 episodes. The show aired on Showtime and featured interpretive adaptations of classic children's fairy tales in a one-hour format.

Shelley Duvall introduced each episode with a synopsis. The shows had inventive production design, interpretations, and costumes. Film director Tim Burton (1958–) directed an episode. Burton was a perfect match for the show, which seemed to echo Burton's quirky fantasy film vision. Some of the shows were inspired by specific artists and children's book illustrators such as Maxfield Parrish (1870–1966), Norman Rockwell (1894–1977), Aubrey Beardsley (1872–1898), and Gustav Klimt (1862–1918).

The show was not a traditional children's show in that adults enjoyed it also because of the offbeat, sometimes dark retelling of classic fairy tales. The shows were artfully produced, well acted, and laced with just the right amount of comedy to balance the elements of fairy tales that historically frightened children.

The series was recognized for its inventive and intriguing casts. Some of the fairy tales broadcast included "The Tale of the Frog Prince" with Robin Williams and Teri Garr; "Pinocchio" with Pee-Wee Herman; "Rip Van Winkle" with Harry Dean Stanton, directed by Francis Ford Coppola; "Rapunzel" with Jeff Bridges, Shelley Duvall, and Gena Rowlands, narrated by Roddy McDowall; "Sleeping Beauty" featuring Christopher Reeve and Bernadette Peters; "Goldilocks and the Three Bears" with Tatum O'Neal and John Lithgow; "Beauty and the Beast" featuring Susan Sarandon and Klaus Kinski, directed by Roger Vadim; and "The Three Little Pigs" featuring Billy Crystal, Jeff Goldblum, and Valerie Perrine.

Shelley Duvall was discovered by American maverick filmmaker Robert Altman (1925–2006). When she became executive producer of *Faerie Tale Theatre*, she had already appeared as an actress in Altman's feature films *Brewster McCloud* (1970), *McCabe & Mrs. Miller* (1971), *Thieves Like Us* (1974), *Nashville* (1975), *Buffalo Bill and the Indians, or Sitting Bull's History Lesson* (1976), and in *Annie Hall* (1977) directed by Woody Allen and *The Shining* (1980) directed by Stanley Kubrick.

This wasn't the first attempt to bring fairy tales to television. From 1958 to 1961 on NBC *Shirley Temple's Storybook* retold classic fairy tales with celebrity actors in a conventional style in contrast to *Faerie Tale Theatre*.

See also: *Amazing Stories*; Showtime; *Vol. 1, The 1950s–1960s: Playhouse 90.*

Further Resources

Duvall, Shelley, and Bridget Terry. 2008. *Shelley Duvall's Faerie Tale Theatre Collector's Storybook: 26 Ways to Live Happily Ever After.* Beverly Hills, CA. Platypus Productions.

Ludwig, Coy. 2007. *Maxfield Parrish.* Atlen, PA. Schiffer Publishing.

Family Ties (NBC, 1982–1989)

Family Ties was a popular family sitcom of the 1980s created by Gary David Goldberg (1944–2013). The original concept highlighted liberal parents, still embracing their 1960s ideology, confronting the generation gap between them and their kids. Network research revealed that audiences were more interested in the kids, launching one of them, Michael J. Fox (1961–), into superstardom.

The Keatons lived in Columbus, Ohio. Meredith Baxter Birney (1947–) played Elyse Keaton, wife/mother who was an architect. Michael Gross (1947–) was the husband/father, Steven, who was the manager of WKS-TV, the local public television station. Alex, the eldest child played by Michael J. Fox, was an ardent admirer of President Richard Nixon (1913–1994) and William F. Buckley Jr. (1925–2008) and read the *Wall Street Journal* religiously. Justine Bateman (1966–) was the older daughter, Mallory, who was better at shopping than doing schoolwork, and Tina Yothers (1973–) played the youngest daughter, Jennifer. On January 31, 1985 Elyse gave birth to baby Andrew, played by Tyler and Grant Merriman and Brian Bonsall (1981–), who took over the role in 1986. Andrew grew to worship his older brother Alex.

Many Hollywood stars appeared on *Family Ties* before they were famous. Tom Hanks (1956–) played Elyse's alcoholic brother; River Phoenix (1970–1993) played Alex's genius math tutor who develops a crush on Jennifer; Geena Davis (1956–) played a housekeeper; Joseph Gordon-Levitt (1981–) played Andrew's kindergarten friend; and Christina Applegate (1971–) played Kitten, a member of Jennifer's band.

Although a comedy, *Family Ties* had its serious moments such as a three-part episode when Steven had a heart attack, and an emotional one-man episode featuring Michael J. Fox as Alex coming to grips with the death of a friend who was killed in an automobile accident. Possibly because Steven worked for a local public television station, PBS on October 15, 1988 paid tribute to *Family Ties,* broadcasting a one-hour special detailing the preparation of a single episode of the show.

From 1984 to 1987 *Family Ties* followed the immensely popular *The Cosby Show* (1984–1992) on Thursday nights and benefited from the time slot in the ratings race. In fall 1987 the network moved the show to Sunday nights opposite *Murder, She Wrote* (1984–1996), whose popularity negatively affected the ratings for *Family Ties*. The last episode aired on May 14, 1989 during which Alex leaves home.

Using comedy and one American family, Gary Goldberg and *Family Ties* examined the country in the 1980s. The country was moving from the liberal 1960s to a more conservative culture. The conflict between the two generations on *Family Ties,* while funny, also focused on how families dealt with American society in flux. Michael J. Fox won Emmy awards for outstanding lead actor in a comedy series in 1986, 1987, and 1988.

See also: *All in the Family*; *The Cosby Show*; *The Partridge Family*.

Further Resources

Fox, Michael J. 2003. *Lucky Man: A Memoir*. New York: Hyperion.

Goldberg, Gary David. 2009. *Sit, Ubu, Sit: How I Went from Brooklyn to Hollywood with the Same Woman, the Same Dog and a Lot Less Hair*. New York: Rivers Press.

Fox Broadcasting Company (1988–)

The Fox Broadcasting Company is a U.S. subsidiary of the international News Corporation Ltd. (News Corp), which is owned by Australian media magnate Rupert Murdoch.

News Corp bought into 20th Century Fox Film Corporation in 1983, later making it a wholly owned subsidiary. Murdoch purchased the six television stations belonging to Metromedia in 1985 and, in October of that year, announced plans to combine Fox with the television stations. The company was named Fox Television Network and was headed by Barry Diller, who had become the head of 20th Century Fox when Murdoch's firm took it over. The six original stations covered 22 percent of the nation.

In 1988, Murdoch started the Fox Broadcasting Company as a new network designed to challenge the big three networks (ABC, CBS, and NBC). It started out slowly, airing a lot of reruns and broadcasting only two evenings a week to begin with. In the 1993–1994 television season, Fox broadcast 20 shows over seven nights.

In December 1993, the network completed a stunning coup, winning the right to broadcast games from the National Football Conference of the National Football League over CBS. One month later, Fox signed the top football broadcasters from CBS, John Madden and Pat Summerall. Fox also secured a contract to air the 1996 Major League Baseball World Series, which it again broadcast in 1998. After a move back to NBC for 1999, the World Series again moved to Fox in 2000, where it has remained since. The network's contract to broadcast the World Series is slated to continue through the 2021 Series.

Later in 1994, Fox agreed to purchase a part interest in New World Communications, a move that would eventually give the network new or stronger affiliates in at least 12 cities nationwide, converting some stations from CBS, ABC, and NBC affiliates. From that point on, Fox gained ground on the "Big Three" networks, taking much of their share with younger audiences, thanks to such memorable programs as *Married . . . with Children, Melrose Place, The Simpsons,* and the *American Idol* competitions.

In the mid-1990s, the company was the focus of controversy because 99 percent of the firm belongs to News Corp. and because Federal Communications Commission (FCC) rules stipulate that television companies can only be 25 percent foreign-owned. Fox noted that News Corp is owned by Murdoch, who became an American citizen just after Fox began buying television stations, and the FCC ultimately ruled in favor of Murdoch.

ABC-CLIO

See also: *Alien Nation*; *America's Most Wanted*; *The Late Show Starring Joan Rivers*; *Married . . . with Children*; *The Simpsons*; *The Tracey Ullman Show*; *21 Jump Street*; *Vol. 1, The 1950s–1960s:* The World Series; *Vol. 3, The 1990s–Present: American Idol.*

Further Resources

Barnouw, Erik. 1990. *Tube of Plenty: The Evolution of American Television.* New York: Oxford University Press.

McNeil, Alex 1996. *Total Television: The Comprehensive Guide to Programming from 1948 to the Present.* New York: Penguin Books

Fridays (ABC, 1980–1982)

Fridays was a comedy-variety series that aired in a late night slot and ran a peculiar 70 minutes. It was perceived by audiences and critics as an attempt to create a knock-off of the mega-successful *Saturday Night Live* (1975–) airing on Friday nights. When *Saturday Night Live* premiered, the cast was largely unknown, but countless cast members became stars after appearing on SNL. *Fridays* had the same potential, but only a few would go on to recognition: Larry David (1947–), Michael Richards (1949–), and Rich Hall (1954–). The *Fridays* troupe had worked the comedy club circuit and other venues. The show featured notable guest stars: George Carlin (1937–2008), Billy Crystal (1948–), Andy Kaufman (1949–1984), Henny Youngman (1906–1998), Don Novello (1943–), and Victoria Principal (1950–). Musical guests included the Beach Boys, Heart, Devo, Chubby Checker, Kiss, and many others.

Most of the elements of *Fridays* were cribbed from *Saturday Night Live*. There was a celebrity host each week who also participated in the sketches, which were the mainstay of both shows; *Fridays* even copied the "Weekend Update" fake news segment. The major difference between the two shows was that while *Saturday Night Live* aimed to be edgy to attract young viewers, *Fridays* went so far over the top that some of the affiliates wouldn't run the offensive sketches. These included "Dinner of the Living Dead" in which the characters ate human flesh, and "Women Who Spit." They did become more sophisticated with a 17-minute musical comedy sketch that was a satire of *The Rocky Horror Show* called "The Ronny Horror Show" starring a mock Ronald Reagan. There were regular characters: John Roarke portrayed Reagan, Mark Blankfield played a speed-freak pharmacist, Larry David played a rabbi, Bruce Mahler portrayed a Spanish announcer, and Darrow Igus, the only African American in the cast, played the Rasta chef.

Andy Kaufman, known for his risky stunts and as a comedian/performance artist, could spontaneously surprise and shock an audience. In February 1981 he hosted *Fridays* and was in a restaurant sketch broadcast live. The diners were discussing smoking marijuana when Kaufman went off the cue cards saying that he felt stupid and he wouldn't say what was written. Michael Richards, also in the sketch, became irritated with Kaufman's antics, grabbed the cue cards, and threw them into Kaufman's lap. Then he got up and the two men got into what seemed to be a real fist fight. The director abruptly cut to a commercial. When the show was transferred to DVD decades later, co-creator John Moffitt revealed that the incident was totally planned and members of the cast including Richards were in on the scam.

Where *Saturday Night Live* succeeded, *Fridays* failed. It's in the nature of the television industry that producers and networks try to get on board when a new genre or style can be developed. Whether one show is better than another does not necessarily determine audience acceptance. Factors such as time slot, sketch material, the cast ensemble, and other variables seem to have contributed to *Fridays'* demise.

See also: *Saturday Night Live.*

Further Resources

Dolman, Paul Samuels. 2014. *Hitchhiking with Larry David: An Accidental Tourist's Summer of Self-Discovery in Martha's Vineyard.* New York: Gotham Books.

Perrin, Dennis. 2012. *Fridays: The SNL Rip-off That Nearly Surpassed the Original.* January 31. http://splitsider.com/2012/01/fridays-the-snl-ripoff-that-nearly-surpassed-the-original

Frontline (PBS, 1983–)

Frontline is a nonfiction news/public affairs program that produces and broadcasts detailed documentaries covering a wide range of subjects. It was produced at WGBH-TV in Boston, Massachusetts, and distributed through the Public Broadcasting Service (PBS). This critically acclaimed series also features the work of independent filmmakers.

Frontline's debut in 1983 was hosted by NBC anchorwoman Jessica Savitch (1947–1986), who was tragically killed in a car accident at age 36 in the show's first season. Judy Woodruff (1946–) of *The MacNeil/Lehrer NewsHour* took over as the anchor in 1984 and was the host for five years. In addition, since 1988 *Frontline* has aired "The Choice," a series of special editions aired before the presidential elections focusing on the candidates.

Since 1983 when *Frontline* premiered, Will Lyman (1948–) and his distinctive voice narrated most of the installments of the series. Some reports have been narrated by David Ogden Stiers (1942–) and Peter Berkrot (1959–).

Frontline focused its reporting on political, social, and criminal justice issues. A significant number of films were produced on the criminal justice system in the United States. The issues range from postconviction DNA testing to the use of drug snitches and mandatory minimum sentencing laws, the plea system, and the use of eyewitness testimony. As activist media, *Frontline* has helped in the release of 13 people from prison.

The average episode of *Frontline* runs an hour, but some shows can be 90 minutes, two hours, or longer. *Frontline* also produces and airs occasional specials such as *From Jesus to Christ, The Farmer's Wife,* and *Country Boys.*

Frontline has covered a wide range of other subjects: the history of the NFL, the power of the Pentagon as a business and economic force, a journey to Russia to look at the Kremlin and Moscow in the 21st-century capitalist era, a Vietnamese man's journey home to Vietnam 30 years after the war, three girls caught in an economic crisis in the United States, the assault on affirmative action in public higher education, the war in Nicaragua, apartheid, Mark David Chapman, the man who shot John Lennon, and the real life of Ronald Reagan.

See also: PBS (Public Broadcasting Service); *Vol. 1, The 1950s–1960s: 60 Minutes.*

Further Resources

Nash, Alanna. 1996. *Golden Girl: The Story of Jessica Savitch.* New York: HarperCollins.

Woodruff, Judy. 1982. *This Is Judy Woodruff at the White House.* Boston: Addison-Wesley.

The Frugal Gourmet (PBS, 1983–1997)

The man known as the Frugal Gourmet was Jeff Smith (1929–2004). *The Frugal Gourmet* was a popular television cooking show that began in Tacoma, Washington in 1973, and later moved to WTTW in Chicago where it aired nationally on PBS. Smith was a skilled television chef. He could film a show straight through without pausing, doing reshoots, or stopping to correct mistakes. His wife Patricia thought up the name "Frugal Gourmet," as it defined Smith's commitment to the economy of home cooking and delivering high-quality gourmet cuisine at low prices.

Smith's style was chatty and very animated with large moving gestures. He embraced the food cultures of countries all over the globe and brought foods from all nations to Americans at a time when they were unknown and exotic. Jeff Smith's tag line at the end of each episode was to say "I bid you peace." He was always excited about food and cooking and spread his enthusiasm to viewers.

On a particular episode Smith talked about soul food and black cooks before slavery. Every episode was filled with as much food history as he could incorporate. He would prepare a number of dishes in a show. He started with spreading them out on a table, then he would offer details about some of them, do some cooking, and explain the recipe.

Smith was an ordained minister and served as chaplain at the University of Puget Sound where he opened the Chaplain's Pantry, a deli and kitchen supply store in Tacoma, Washington where he offered cooking classes to the public. Smith also had degrees in philosophy and sociology.

Like other television chefs he published many cookbooks that include *The Frugal Gourmet* (1984), *The Frugal Gourmet Cooks with Wine* (1986), and *The Frugal Gourmet Cooks Three Ancient Cuisines: China, Greece and Rome*.

Smith had supporters and detractors. Some found him generous and knowledgeable. Others claimed his recipes simply didn't work and criticized him for being paid to promote products and kitchenware. Many viewers watched him and bought his books. They found him more accessible as a cook than other TV chefs. Many related to the wide range of dishes cross-cutting American regional cooking and global cuisines.

After all of Smith's success, the bottom dropped out. In 1997 seven men filed a civil lawsuit against Smith charging sexual abuse in the 1970s while he was working at his Tacoma food establishment. One claimed he was assaulted by Smith when he was 14 and they were hitchhiking. Smith denied the allegations and no criminal charges were filed, but he and his insurers settled the cases for undisclosed amounts in 1998. The scandal ended Jeff Smith's television career. He did continue writing and doing charitable work along with traveling and researching a book on biblical foods.

See also: PBS (Public Broadcasting Service); *Vol. 1, The 1950s–1960s*: Child, Julia; *Vol. 3, The 1990s–Present:* Food Network.

Further Resources

Smith, Jeff, and Chris Cart. 1987. *The Frugal Gourmet Cooks American*. New York: William Morrow.

Smith, Jeff, and Gary Jacobsen. 1987. *The Frugal Gourmet*. Boston: G. K. Hall.

Full House (ABC, 1987–1995)

Full House was a 30-minute sitcom that aired on ABC for eight seasons, concerning a widowed San Francisco sportscaster, Danny Tanner, played by Bob Saget (1956–), who convinces his best friend, stand-up comic Joey Gladstone, portrayed by Dave Coulier (1959–), and his brother–in-law, exterminator and part-time rocker Jesse Katsopolous, played by John Stamos (1963–), to move in and help him raise his kids.

Danny's oldest daughter, Donna Jo, known as D.J., was played by Candace Cameron (1976–). Jodie Sweetin (1982–) played the middle daughter, Stephanie; twins Mary Kate and Ashley Fuller Olsen (1989–) played baby Michelle. Other characters appeared as the show moved into the 1990s. The show's comical plot lines worked through the myriad difficulties between the adults as they confront their differences, the challenges between the kids and the adults, and issues between the adults and the kids. Ultimately the characters all bonded and became one big happy family. The positive extended family unit made this show a crowd pleaser.

A cottage industry for books based on *Full House* grew out of the series. The demographic was between ages 8 and 14. There were at least four different series. "Full House Stephanie"—33 books written from the point of view of the middle daughter. "Full House Michelle" —41 stories told from Michelle's point of view. "Full House Sisters"—14 books focused on

Michelle and Stephanie's friendship; and "Full House: Dear Michelle"—four books that are written by Michelle in the fourth grade when she authors an advice column for her school newspaper.

Much of the human story that is the thread throughout *Full House* involves Danny learning to be a single father without his beloved, deceased wife. The humor is family-oriented and there are plenty of characters who become involved in the controlled mayhem.

Some of the themes and narratives on *Full House* included: D.J wins two tickets to a Beach Boys Concert. She doesn't know whom to take without offending others. The group drops by before their concert and invites everyone to come along. Stephanie is invited to a mother/daughter slumber party; due to a car breakdown she has to phone Joey and the games designed for females don't work out for him.

In 2016 a sequel arrived on the streaming service Netflix, called *Fuller House*, which has several of the original actors reprising their roles. A second season of the sequel series was released in December 2016.

See also: *All in the Family*; *The Cosby Show*; *Family Ties*; *Vol. 3, The 1990s–Present: The Fresh Prince of Bel Air*; *Modern Family*.

Further Resources

Olsen, Mary Kate and Ashley. 2008. *Influence*. New York: Razorbill.

Saget, Bob. 2014. *Dirty Daddy: The Chronicles of a Family Man Turned Filthy Comedian*. New York: Harper Luxe.

The George Michael Sports Machine (Syndication, 1984–2007)

This unique sports show started in Washington, D.C. as a local show then called *George Michael Sports Final*. What made this show different from most Sunday-night sports wrap-ups is that Michael covered a wide range of sporting events beyond baseball, basketball, hockey, and football. As the eventual title intimated, there was a large machine with lights and sound effects that the audience believed was presenting the images and clips they saw on the show. At the dawn of the computer revolution this "sports machine" was offered as a large computer with several monitors attached to a videotape reel-to-reel unit that played the clips—but all of this equipment was fake. The clips were broadcast in the traditional manner. The producers rightly felt that viewers would be attracted to the high-technology aspect of the show.

Host George Michael (1939–2009) was a sports reporter for the NBC station WRC–TV. The show was fast-paced and irreverent with an extensive use of video highlights from the week's games. Player profiles, bloopers, and footage of nontraditional sports such as rodeos and wrestling were also part of the format. High school sports footage was played at times, as well as NASCAR races and equestrian events. The show was mainly broadcast by NBC affiliates across the country.

Unlike other sport shows of the time, *The George Michael Sports Machine* did not offer commentary or criticism; it kept the focus on the video clips. Michael, who had a vibrant personality, ended each show by telling the viewers, "Thank you for letting us be a part of your weekend." *The George Michael Sports Machine* was a groundbreaking show whose legacy can be seen on ESPN and other modern sports channels.

See also: ESPN; *Vol. 1, The 1950s–1960s:* Boxing; The World Series.

Further Resources

Deninger, Dennis. 2012. *Sports on Television. The How and Why Behind What You See*. New York: Routledge.

Michaels, Al, and Jon Wertheim. 2013. *You Can't Make This Up: Miracles, Memories, and the Perfect Marriage of Sports and Television*. New York: HarperCollins.

Geraldo (Syndication, 1987–1998)

Geraldo Rivera (1943–) was an ABC news correspondent in the early 1980s for *20/20* and *Nightline*. In 1987 he began a daily syndicated talk show simply called *Geraldo,* signaling his popularity, but for the last two seasons the title was *The Geraldo Rivera*

Show. It was in a one-hour time slot, had an in-studio audience, and each day presented a single topic.

Although some in the media called *Geraldo* "Trash TV," Geraldo Rivera did have many legitimate guests on this talk show along with those who had a tabloid bent. The daytime talk show aired in the daytime on CBS and in syndication. Rivera liked to deal with provocative subjects and subject matter. An episode on November 3, 1988 has a notorious legacy and is a legend in talk TV. It was a show on white supremacists, racist and skinheads, black activists and Jewish activists. One of the supremacists goaded Roy Innis (1934–), who was the national chairman of the Congress of Racial Equality (CORE), by calling him an "Uncle Tom." Innis was infuriated, got up from his chair, and grabbed the young man by the neck with significant force. A full brawl broke out with chairs and punches thrown. The audience got involved as did stagehands and Geraldo Rivera himself. Rivera got hit in the face with a chair and suffered a broken nose that bled on camera.

The show had the reputation of being more controversial and edgy than its competition. One episode was taped at a topless donut shop in Colorado. By January 1990 Rivera told *TV Guide* that he was embarrassed by some of his shows and promised to show better judgment in topic selection. The pledge didn't stick; during May 1995 he aired "Girls Who Will Commit Crimes for Their Men," "Family of Prostitutes," "Bisexuality," "Ménages à Trois," and "Couples Who Detest Each Other."

The show did have more conventional guests but they usually had some personal or professional story that was titillating. These included Dionne Warwick, Lindsay Wagner, Tonya Harding, Todd Bridges, Dana Plato, Howard Stern, and Margaux Hemingway. Talk show host Jerry Springer (1944–) and others were influenced by Rivera's kind of television, and a clear link to reality television can be made.

See also: *The Phil Donahue Show*; *The Oprah Winfrey Show*; *Sally Jessy Raphael*; *Vol. 3, The 1990s–Present: Geraldo at Large*.

Further Resources

Rivera, Geraldo. 2009. *His Panic: Why Americans Fear Hispanics in the U.S.* New York: Penguin Books.

Rivera, Geraldo. 2009. *The Great Progression: How Hispanics Will Lead America to a New Era of Prosperity.* New York: Celebra.

The Golden Girls (NBC, 1985–1992)

Golden Girls was the first successful modern sitcom in which all of the stars were women. Further, the actresses were all more than 50 years old. The setup was that four mature women were living together in Miami, Florida. Bea Arthur (1922–2009) was teacher Dorothy Zbornak, a divorcée; Betty White (1922–) played a naïve grief counselor, Rose Nylund; Rue McClanahan (1934–2010) played the sex-obsessed museum worker Blanche Devereaux, who owned the house where all the ladies lived. The cast also included Dorothy's sharp-tongued mother, Sophia Petrillo, portrayed by Estelle Getty (1923–2008), who moved in with the other women after her retirement facility burned down. They all kept young at heart looking for romance and maintaining their interest in sex.

The Golden Girls was created by Susan Harris (1940–) and was produced by Paul Junger Witt (1943–) and Tony Thomas (1948–). The theme song spoke to the bond between the women, "Thank You for Being a Friend" written by Andrew Gold (1951–2011).

The show was popular because audiences enjoyed the women's antics. *Golden Girls* won many awards and was in the top 10 for ratings six out of seven seasons. In 2013 *TV Guide* ranked the show number 54 on its list of 60 greatest shows of all time. In 2014 the Writer's Guild of America placed *The Golden Girls* number 69 on their list of the 101 best-written TV series of all time.

Although principally a comedy, *The Golden Girls* did tackle serious topics such as coming out (sexual orientation), same-sex marriage, elder care, homelessness, AIDS and HIV discrimination, U.S. immigration policy, death, and assisted suicide.

On the final episode Dorothy married Blanche's Uncle Lucas, played by Leslie Nielsen (1926–2010). The other three ladies carried on with another series, *The Golden Palace* (1992–1993).

The Golden Girls was a popular sitcom that followed the exploits of four older women who share a home in South Florida. Pictured (left to right) are Estelle Getty, Rue McClanahan, Bea Arthur, and Betty White. (AP Photo/Nick Ut)

Further Resources

Craig, Michael D. 2013. *Thank You for Being a Friend: A Golden Girls Trivia Book*. Five Apples Press.

White, Betty. 2012. *If You Ask Me (And of Course You Won't)*. New York: Berkley.

Hard Copy (Syndication, 1989–1999)

One of several tabloid TV series of the late 1980s and 1990s, *Hard Copy* was a 30-minute investigative series hosted by Allan Frio and Terry Murphy, who previously had been a news anchor at WLS–TV in Chicago, KCBS–TV, and KABC–TV. A weekend edition of the show known as HCTV, focused on showbiz subjects, was hosted by Diane Diamond (1952–).

This magazine-style, 30-minute syndicated show consisted mostly of celebrity interviews and revelations and investigative reports covering sensational stories of the day. In its first season *Hard Copy* provided viewers with a 900 telephone number to call in and comment on stories that aired. The producers chose the comments that were broadcast over the closing credits. *Hard Copy* was based out of Los Angeles. In fall 1990 senior correspondent Barry Nolan (1947–), who previously was a presenter on Comcast's cable channel CN8, started appearing semiregularly as a New York–based host. Alan Frio left the show the following fall and Nolan moved to Los Angeles to take over as full-time co-host with Terry Murphy. In fall 1997 Doug Bruckner, the show's New York correspondent, was made the third host of *Hard Copy* and

Jerry Penacoli (1956–) took over as the weekend edition host.

The show was given a major overhaul at the start of the 1998–1999 season. The new host was Kyle Kraska, the former KFMB sports director, and the weekend show was cancelled. Penacoli was made a correspondent and the producers made a pledge to the viewers that the show would carry more in-depth, longer stories than in earlier seasons.

Tough Stories

Some of the *Hard Copy* stories included shows on competitive modeling agencies, Madonna, a tourist's girlfriend who was killed so he could get the insurance money, sex tips, Marilyn Monroe and the mob, and the mother of a porn star trying to get her daughter out of the business. In the fall of 1994 the producers of *Hard Copy* sensed the celebrity crime of the century in the O. J. Simpson (1947–) murder case. The story was covered by as many as 30 reporters.

Hard Copy was not without its own controversy. In 1992 Elton John threatened to sue the show, alleging that a reporter tried to blackmail him into giving an interview by falsely claiming the popular entertainer had AIDS. *Hard Copy* claimed John moved to an area because it had an AIDS clinic. The lawsuit charged extortion, slander, invasion of privacy, and reckless endangerment. The day after the filing *Hard Copy* ran a positive story praising John for all the good work he'd done for those afflicted with AIDS. This was the show's method for sidestepping John's lawsuit, and his attorney suggested that the show had changed its point of view based on John's threat to sue.

In 1996 George Clooney began a boycott of *Hard Copy* and *Entertainment Tonight* after *Hard Copy* violated a six-month agreement not to broadcast anything on the debonair actor. The show aired footage of Clooney and his then girlfriend Celine Balitran on a film set. Many celebrities supported Clooney in his efforts. Paramount, the studio behind *Hard Copy* and *Entertainment Tonight,* agreed to modify the way that both shows gathered information for their stories. They also agreed not to air unauthorized footage of celebrities or footage that was known to have been illegally obtained.

Hard Copy searched for an opening logo to equal or top the iconic opening for *A Current Affair.* The title itself reflected news or a newsroom and news that was hard and tough. The graphic is the two words of the title moving forward backed by the slamming sound of a one-two punch similar to a high-tech typewriter.

See also: *A Current Affair*; *Entertainment Tonight*; *20/20*.

Further Resources

Biressi, Anita, and Heather Nunn. 2007. *The Tabloid Culture Reader*. Shoppenhangers Road: Open University Press.

Glynn, Kevin. 2000. *Tabloid Culture: Trash Taste, Popular Power, and the Transformation of American Television*. Durham, NC: Duke University Press.

Highway to Heaven (NBC, 1984–1988)

In *Highway to Heaven*, Michael Landon (1936–1991) played Jonathan Smith, an angel who came down to earth to help people. The character was Landon's brainchild, who struggled to sell the concept. NBC eventually bought the show and it was a Nielsen ratings winner.

Prior to *Highway*, Landon was a very successful man. He was an actor, teleplay writer, producer, and director. In addition to other work in television, he had been involved in three very successful series, all family shows that were extremely popular. He played one of the sons, Little Joe, in *Bonanza* (1959–1973); the husband and father in another landmark family show, *Little House on the Prairie* (1974–1982); and his most challenging role would be *Highway to Heaven*.

Victor French (1934–1989), who worked with Michael Landon on *Little House on the Prairie*, played Jonathan's sidekick, ex-cop Mark Gordon, who had been depressed and feeling helpless until he was uplifted by Jonathan Smith.

Jonathan was not a full-fledged angel; he was on probation. His mission was to seek people who needed help. Love and understanding were his main tools.

Although he had angelic powers, he rarely utilized them. Rather, he applied comforting persuasion and a guiding example to aid those in need. Jonathan believed peace and love could lighten someone's load and transform them from a state of pain to release. Some of the people he encountered were a mother whose child was dying of cancer, an African American boxer who was pressured to throw a fight, and a Vietnamese child who faced prejudice in her new American hometown. Jonathan roamed the country as an itinerant laborer. The tone of *Highway to Heaven* was to project the value of kindness. Tenderness was woven through these emotional stories.

This was Michael Landon's show; he was involved in every part of production including directing. As an actor, Landon turned in another fine performance and his kind smile functioned as one of his greatest strengths in helping humankind.

An iconic image on *Highway to Heaven* was the road Jonathan found himself on as he walked to find those in need. The blacktop well suited the show's title and was a multifaceted metaphor for the spiritual journey of life.

Further Resources

Greenland, David R., and Cindy Landon. 2015. *Michael Landon: The Career and Artistry of a Television Genius*. Albany, GA: BearManor Media.

Ito, Tom. 1992. *Conversations with Michael Landon*. Contemporary Books.

Hill Street Blues (NBC, 1981–1987)

Hill Street Blues was a groundbreaking show that brought comedy and tragedy to the cop genre. The cast was large and full of interesting, well-drawn characters. The show aired in prime time on NBC and took place in one police precinct on Hill Street in a fictional large city. The show's production values were innovative and the story lines were for mature audiences, delving into the private lives of the police officers and detectives.

In 1980 Fred Silverman (1937–), who at the time was president of NBC, approached two producers from MTM (Mary Tyler Moore) Enterprises, Michael Kozoll and Steven Bochco (1943–), and pitched a cop show whose emphasis was on the personal lives and relationships of the characters. The two producers liked and agreed to the proposal, but only on the condition that they'd have absolute total control. Silverman said yes. Bochco and Kozoll started casting actors who were experienced but not necessarily known to general TV audiences. The producers also agreed that not all cases or crimes would be solved within an episode and, as in life, some would never be solved at all.

Urban But Unspecific

The police precinct was set in a crumbling ghetto in a large American city that was never identified. Despite the squalor and serious criminal activity, humor would unexpectedly break through.

Hill Street Blues had a realistic look and atmosphere. Interiors were often underlit, pictorial compositions were crowded for realism, and the episodes were shot with a camera technique considered controversial in television. Historically cameramen and directors working with the actors play camera movements that are motivated by the action. *Hill Street Blues* introduced the unmotivated camera in which the lens would move around the frame in its own artistic interpretation, usually not related to what was going on in the story or with the characters or action. There were rapid cuts between scenes, lots of close-ups, and extensive use of overheard and off-screen dialogue. The program dealt with real-life issues and more than ever before used commonly spoken language and slang.

One of the great television theme songs was written for *Hill Street Blues* by Mike Post (1944–). It begins with a clean series of notes played on a piano, then a series of rhythmic chords are backed by a synthesizer, strings, and other instruments. It is uplifting and ironically doesn't seem to speak to the crime genre, rather to the spirit of the men and women who fight crime. Post became a household name to television aficionados and has a long list of winning themes for TV shows including *The Rockford Files* (1974–1980), *L.A. Law* (1986–1994), and *Law and Order* (1990–2010).

The ensemble cast, one of the largest in television at the time, included Daniel J. Travanti (1940–) as

Captain Frank Furillo, the dedicated commanding officer of the Hill Street Station. Veronica Hamel (1943–) was a no-nonsense professional public defender. Sergeant Phil Esterhaus, played by Michael Conrad (1925–1983), conducted the daily roll call and ended with the show's signature line, "Let's be careful out there!" Sadly, Conrad died at age 58 in November 1983. Bruce Weitz (1943–) played the scruffy and disheveled detective Mike Belker, who sometime resorted to biting criminals he had arrested. James B. Sikking (1934–) portrayed the conservative Lieutenant Howard Hunter, head of the precinct's SWAT team. Joe Spano (1946–) played the compassionate detective Henry Goldblume. Betty Thomas (1948–) played Officer Lucy Bates. Robert Prosky (1930–2008) played Sergeant Stan Jablonski, who picked up the roll call after Bates.

Almost 70 fine actors from film and television did guest shots on *Hill Street Blues*. They included Don Cheadle, James Cromwell, Lindsay Crouse, Timothy Daly, Jill Eikenberry, Laurence Fishburne, Andy Garcia, Cuba Gooding Jr., Danny Glover, Linda Hamilton, Chazz Palminteri, Edward James Olmos, Christopher David Noth, CCH Pounder, Michael Richards, Tim Robbins, Mimi Rogers, Helen Shaver, Ally Sheedy, Lawrence Tierney, Jennifer Tilly, Meg Tilly, Michael Tucker, Forest Whitaker, and Alfre Woodard.

Hill Street Blues premiered to rave reviews but unimpressive ratings. Their time slot was changed more than once but ratings did not improve much. NBC decided to renew the show for the 1982–1983 season. The show won eight Emmy awards, a record for a single season, and a Peabody Award. The audience was now larger, although not by industry standards, but fans were loyal and enthusiastic. They continued on, achieving a respectable seven-season run.

See also: *L.A. Law*; *21 Jump Street*; *Vol. 3, The 1990s–Present: Law & Order*.

Further Resources

"Series: Hill Street Blues." *TV Tropes*. http://tvtropes.org/pmwiki/pmwiki.php/Series/HillStreetBlues

Thompson, Robert. 1997. *Television's Second Golden Age: From Hill Street Blues to ER*. Syracuse, NY: Syracuse University Press.

Hour Magazine (Syndication, 1980–1988)

Hour Magazine, a show in the tradition of the television magazine format, was co-hosted by Gary Collins (1938–2012) and Pat Mitchell (1943–) for the first two seasons, then by Collins and Bonnie Strauss until 1985, and then by Collins and celebrity guest hosts. Collins saw *Hour Magazine* as an alternative to the confrontational, hard-edged, tabloid shows. He once described himself as "inquisitive, sensitive, caring, likable, and *non-confrontational*" (Michaelson 1989).

There were resident specialists on *Hour Magazine*, including cardiologist Dr. Isadore Rosenfeld, beauty expert Jose Eber, and sex and relationship psychologist Dr. Karen Shanor. Other features were celebrity interviews and visits to intriguing places in the United States. Episodes were balanced with a range of segments such as a look at teenage alcoholism, a visit to a family farm in Georgia, a talk with Dick Clark about his health and vitality secrets, the trauma of wives whose husbands were POWs in Vietnam, a segment with a gay couple, actor Richard Thomas on the joys of fatherhood, a look at current plastic surgery, the rock group Black Russian, an interview with Shelley Winters, and a visit to a specialty store for cats.

Transsexuals were presented on the show in a caring, nonexploitive manner. Annette Funicello (1942–1913) talked about her three children and her years on *The Mickey Mouse Club* (1955–1959). The cast of *The Adventures of Superman* (1952–1958) were on *Hour Magazine*. They were interviewed and a clip from the show was shown. Watching this televised magazine was instructive, entertaining, and easy to "read."

See also: *Inside Edition*; *Vol. 1, The 1950s–1960s: 60 Minutes*.

Further Resources

Michaelson, Judith. 1989. "TV Talk Shows Going . . . and Coming . . . : The Impact of Tabloid TV Ends Gary Collins' Daytime 'Hour'." *Los Angeles Times*. January 2. http://articles.latimes.com/1989-01-02/entertainment/ca-180_1_gary-collins. Accessed March 8, 2017.

Mittell, Jason. 2009. *Television and American Culture*. Oxford: Oxford University Press.

Ponce de Leon, L. 2015. *That's the Way It Is: A History of Television News in America*. Chicago: University of Chicago Press.

Inside Edition (Syndication, 1989–)

Inside Edition is a 30-minute syndicated magazine format show. Originally the stories were mainly tabloid crime stories, investigations, and celebrity gossip. *Inside Edition* was one of many tabloid and news shows that began in the 1980s. The original host was David Frost (1939–2013). Also hosting in 1989 was Bill O'Reilly (1949–), who would much later become a Fox News superstar with his own brand and a library of books. Deborah Norville (1958–), who became the *Inside Edition* host, was hired by *The Today Show* supposedly because the NBC brass felt she was younger and prettier than the co-anchor, Jane Pauley (1950–). She began to host in 1995 and is still the host of the show. Steve Kramer has been the announcer since the premiere of the show.

Correspondents and former on-air staff include Lisa Guerrero (1964–), who was a chief investigative correspondent; Jim Moret (1956–), Los Angeles–based correspondent; Rudy Giuliani (1944–), chief legal analyst; Nancy Glass (1957–), weekend anchor/senior correspondent; and Star Jones (1962–), chief legal analyst following Giuliani.

Some of the varied but often exploitive stories aired on *Inside Edition* included the high living of TV preachers, a flu shot that destroyed a child's motor skills, dental abuse, the winning price revealed too soon by a model on *The Price Is Right*, how cheap fish can make one sick, holiday commercials for a porn website, a beauty queen revealing seven cosmetic surgeries, and a woman who forgives her best friend who accidentally ran over the woman's toddler.

For the 1992–1993 season a spin-off *Inside Edition Extra* was broadcast. It was a co-production between King World and Boston television station WHDH. It didn't achieve high ratings and was cancelled.

See also: *A Current Affair*; *Hard Copy*; *20/20*.

Further Resources

Hegarty, Neil. 2015. *Frost: That Was the Life That Was: The Authorized Biography*. Amazon Digital Services. Virgin Digital.

O'Reilly, Bill. 2013. *Keep It Pithy: Useful Observations in a Tough World*. New York: Crown Publishing Group.

It's Garry Shandling's Show (Showtime, 1986–1990)

It's Garry Shandling's Show was created by stand-up comic Garry Shandling (1949–2016) and former *Saturday Night Live* writer Alan Zweibel (1950–). It borrowed from the early innovations of *The George Burns and Gracie Allen Show* (1950–1958), with the principal concept that the star directly addressed the camera. This has been identified as breaking the "fourth wall." As he did in the earlier show, Shandling played himself, a stand-up comic, at his home. He would use the direct address technique when he wanted to comment on the plot, update the story, or make a joke. He was the star of his own TV show broadcast from his fictional condominium in Sherman Oaks, California. Originally Shandling was in a sketch on NBC's *Michael Nesmith in Television Parts* (1985) in which he was on a date with Miss Maryland and he narrated the event to the camera. The series was pitched to the major networks but all rejected it. Shandling had done two well-received comedy specials for Showtime, which picked up the series in late 1986. The Fox network began airing the Showtime series in 1988. By 1990 Fox dropped the show and Showtime continued to run new episodes after Fox cancelled. In all, 72 episodes were produced.

Also in the show was Shandling's friend and neighbor Nancy Bancroft, played by Molly Cheek (1950–); Michael Tucci (1946–) as his neighbor Pete Schumaker; Bernadette Birkett (1946–) as Pete's wife Jackie; and Scott Nemes (1974–) as their son, Grant. Leonard Smith, the condo manager, was portrayed by Paul Willson (1945–), and Barbara Cason (1928–1990) played Garry's mother, Ruth. All these characters knew they were on television and complained at times on camera that they weren't featured in a particular episode. At times, an eclectic selection of guest stars was also on the show. They included Red Buttons, Zsa Zsa Gabor, Tom Petty, and Gilda Radner.

In fall 1989 Shandling had a regular girlfriend, Phoebe Bass, played by Jessica Harper (1949–). They were married on the show in early 1990 with witnesses Connie Stevens, Bert Convy, and Ned Beatty in attendance.

At times Shandling walked into the studio audience and asked them their personal reactions to what was going on in the show. The theme song, "This Is the Theme to Garry's Show," mocked others on TV and at times his neighbor would come by to complain it was too loud. If Shandling (the character) didn't like the way things were going on the show, he would change the outcome. Some episodes involved the studio audience; others were a parody of television shows such as *Lassie* and *The Fugitive*. One show was broadcast live. It was an election special with *Soul Train*'s Don Cornelius (1936–2012) as a guest political analyst.

Decades had passed since George Burns shook up the sitcom form. Shandling was inspired by it and transformed it into a contemporary 1980s/1990s program. What had been old (and highly innovated) was now new to a new audience.

See also: *Michael Nesmith in Television Parts*; Showtime; *Vol. 1, The 1950s–1960s:* Burns, George.

Further Resources

Domino, Matt. 2013. "It's 'Garry Shandling's Show': Just as Influential as You Probably Don't Remember It." February 8. *Split Sider*. http://splitsider.com/2013/02/its-garry-shandlings-show-just-as-influential-as-you-probably-dont-remember/

Shandling, Garry, and David Rensin. 1998. *Confessions of a Late Night Talk Show Host: The Autobiography of Larry Sanders*. New York: Simon & Schuster.

Joseph Campbell and the Power of Myth (PBS, 1988)

Joseph Campbell and the Power of Myth aired on PBS in six one-hour segments and featured Bill Moyers (1934–) talking to scholar, professor, and mythologist Joseph Campbell (1904–1987) about the relevance of mythology in modern society. Campbell's books, which included *The Hero with a Thousand Faces* and *The Masks of God*, caught the attention of Moyers, a journalist and political commentator who had been White House press secretary for President Lyndon Johnson.

In 1986 Moyers and his wife Judith Davidson Moyers formed Public Affairs Television. One of their first projects was *Joseph Campbell and the Power of Myth.* The massive, complex, and detailed documentary covered Campbell's exploration of the monomyth and the hero cycle. What made this scholarly material so enticing to viewers was that Campbell's work was evidenced in George Lucas's *Star Wars* film (1977). Campbell's and Moyers's discussions explored the connection between Campbell's work and the creative achievements of George Lucas (1949–). Lucas had read Campbell's *The Hero with a Thousand Faces* in college. In 1975 George Lucas had written two drafts of the *Star Wars* script and Campbell's "hero's journey," as he named this aspect of his studies, became the blueprint for the filmmaker to bring his sprawling imaginary universe into a single story.

Campbell saw Obi-Wan Kenobi, played by Alec Guinness (1914–2000), as an adviser and a Japanese sword master—the theme of the hero aided by a stranger. He most liked that the film communicated to young people.

Campbell discussed some of his major theories with Moyers. He talked about the whole of the human race seen as making the world "transparent to transcendence" and about an eternal source pouring its energies into this world of time, suffering, and eventually death.

The monomyth story is broken down into masks. The basic story is classified by the stages of a hero's adventure through the story: the call to adventure, receiving supernatural aid, meeting with the goddess, and atonement with the father.

In premodern society, myth was a proto-science offering explanations for physical phenomena such as change of seasons and the life cycle of animals and plants. There were also many complex thoughts and manners of explaining the universe, the natural world, and the spiritual world.

Bill Moyers had superb interviewing skills and was especially effective with Joseph Campbell, asking for explanations, definitions, and how to understand the totality of the function of myth in everything for life itself and in *Star Wars.*

PBS was the ideal venue for these sweeping discussions. The regular viewer looked for something new, different, and intellectually stimulating. PBS did a service for television by bringing the thoughts and fertile mind of an unconventional scholar to those thirsty for knowledge and understanding.

See also: PBS (Public Broadcasting Service).

Further Resources

Campbell, Joseph, with Bill Moyers. 1991. *The Power of Myth*. New York: Anchor Books.

Campbell, Joseph, with Dianne K. Osbon. 1995. *Reflections on the Art of Living: A Joseph Campbell Companion*. New York: HarperCollins.

The Joy of Painting (PBS, 1983–1995)

Painter Robert "Bob" Ross (1942–1995) hosted the half-hour program *The Joy of Painting,* instructing viewers on how to render landscapes using oil painting techniques. The show was taped at WIPB–TV in Muncie, Indiana. Viewers were brought into this instructional show by Ross's soothing manner, in addition to his considerable ability to create a complete original oil painting in less than 30 minutes during the show.

When Ross was in Alaska working as a part-time bartender, he fell upon a television show called *The Magic of Oil Painting* hosted by German painter William Alexander (1915–1997). Ross studied painting with Alexander and learned he could make more money selling his paintings than from his current position, which was in the Air Force. Before launching *The Joy of Painting*, Ross tried to promote his painting techniques, but attracted little interest. To save money, Ross decided to get his hair permed; once on television it became a significant aspect of his brand.

During an episode Ross taught the viewers a quick-study technique in oil painting that employed a limited palette and a deconstruction of the painting process into simple steps. Ross's manner was gentle, with a soft voice and manner. He encouraged the audience using clear and understandable actions. The set for the show was simple; basically, Ross was standing in front of a canvas mounted on an easel with virtually nothing else in the frame except his paints and brushes. As he explained how to paint the picture, Ross would talk about the content, the water, the trees and mountains that made up the scene of the day.

Ross built a $15 million business selling art supplies, how-to books, and painting classes by instructors trained in the "Bob Ross Method," which was a wet-on-wet technique, so there was no wait for layers of paint to dry. Ross used one- and two-inch brushes and painting knives to paint trees, clouds, mountains, and water in a matter of seconds. Ross would begin a painting with simple strokes that looked like smudges and as he added more strokes, the blotches would transform into intricate landscapes.

The landscapes Ross painted, mountains, lakes, snow, and log cabins, were influenced by the years he lived in Alaska. He constantly told his audience that everyone had inherent artistic talent and that dedication was the key to success. He also estimated that in his lifetime he had created as many as 30,000 paintings. Being happy and making others happy was very important to him. Ross donated all the paintings he generated on the show to PBS stations as charitable contributions.

Bob Ross died of cancer at age 52 on July 4, 1995. In the end, the art of Bob Ross took second place to his generous personality and ability to inspire and encourage. His gentleness and natural smile charmed many viewers who felt his show brought them to a peaceful place.

See also: PBS (Public Broadcasting Service).

Further Resources

Ross, Bob. 1984. *The Joy of Painting*. Sterling, VA: Bob Ross Publications.

Ross, Bob. 1995. *Best of the Joy of Painting*. William Morrow Paperbacks.

The Krypton Factor (ABC, 1981; Syndication 1990–1991)

Dick Clark (1929–2012) hosted *The Krypton Factor*, a summertime nighttime game show unlike any other show in television history at the time. Each week four contestants competed in a series of matches: arithmetical exercises, an obstacle course, a memory test, and finally, a general knowledge quiz. The winner earned $5,000 and the four weekly winners went up against each other in the show's finale for a grand prize of $50,000. The significance of the title was that a contestant's score was referred to as their "Krypton Factor."

The specific competitive categories on *The Krypton Factor* made it a highly unusual game show. The players' reflexes were tested by requiring them to navigate a difficult video or computer game such as Atari 2600, Dodge 'Em, Outlaw, and Space Invaders. The obstacle course was not on foot but run in speedboats, dune buggies, or motorcycles; mental agility was measured by giving the contestants difficult brain teaser situations.

This ABC show that went into syndication began in England and the American version was modeled on it. Sixteen contestants competed in the five-week series. Viewers were flabbergasted by the movie round in which a scene from a film was screened for the contestants. When the lights came up Dick Clark explained that in the scene that was screened there was a waiter in the background. Then Clark brought out a lineup of men dressed the way the waiter was dressed in the scene. The contestant had to find the right waiter purely by sight recognition. There were some contestants who actually got it right.

At times game show hosts can be overly enthusiastic and bombastic. What gave *The Krypton Factor* an almost surreal quality was Dick Clark's classic youthful look and even-handed delivery during this somewhat outlandish summer replacement game show.

See also: *Vol. 1, The 1950s–1960s:* ABC (American Broadcasting Company); Clark, Dick.

Further Resources

Graham, Jefferson. 1988. *Come On Down: The TV Game Show Book*. New York: Abbeville Press.

The Krypton Factor Team. 1984. *The Krypton Factor*. London: Arrow Books.

L.A. Law (NBC, 1986–1994)

Steven Bochco and Terry Louise Fisher (1946–) created the series *L.A. Law* about a Los Angeles law firm. Bochco had been involved in *Hill Street Blues* and Fisher was an attorney who produced *Cagney & Lacey*. This popular NBC show that aired for eight seasons had the trademark elements of a Bochco series—more than one story line running simultaneously, a large ensemble cast, a dry sense of humor interspersed in the teleplays, and romantic relationships that complicated the workplace atmosphere. The practice focused on many hot-button issues of the day such as capital punishment, sexual harassment, and gay rights. The high-powered attorneys enjoyed the visibility these matters brought to the firm that distinguished them from others in their profession. Still, there was a typical pecking order between the partners and the support staff that was no different from standard law practices.

Genesis

Television and its audience have always had a passion for the legal drama. Just some before and after *L.A Law* include *Eli Stone, Petrocelli, Paper Chase, Judd for the Defense, Law & Order: Special Victims Unit, Reasonable Doubts, Matlock, Murder One, Law & Order: Criminal Intent, Harvey Birdman, Attorney at Law, Civil Wars, Shark, Jag, Owen Marshall: Counselor at Law, Judging Amy, Damages, Boston Legal, Rumpole of the Bailey, Ally McBeal, The Practice, Law & Order, The Defenders,* and *Perry Mason.*

L.A. Law borrowed a bit from *Hill Street Blues*: There was an ensemble cast, a standard opening scene similar to the squad room in the opening for *Hill Street Blues,* which took place in a conference room; the theme and score were by Mike Post; and there were multiple story lines, many of which were carried over from week to week. The firm's cases ranged from the serious to the trivial. Unlike most legal shows the lawyers on *L.A. Law* occasionally lost a case. The large cast included Richard Dysart (1929–2015) as Leland McKenzie, the senior partner of McKenzie, Brackman, Chaney & Kuzak; Alan Rachins (1942–) as a managing partner, Douglas Brackman Jr., whose father founded the firm with McKenzie; Harry Hamlin (1951–) as lawyer Michael Kuzak; Corbin Bernsen (1954–), who portrayed a divorce lawyer Arnie Becker; Jill Eikenberry (1947–) as lawyer and partner Ann Kelsey; Michael Tucker (1945–) as a tax partner, Stuart Makowitz;

Jimmy Smits (1955–), who played associate Victor Sifuentes, the firm's sole Hispanic attorney; Michelle Greene (1962–), who played associate Abby Perkins; Susan Dey (1952–), who played assistant district attorney Grace Van Owen; and Susan Rattan (1948–), who played Becker's secretary Roxanne Melman. The fourth partner, Chaney, was discovered dead over a law book in the opening scene of the first episode.

There were changes in 1987. Blair Underwood (1964–) appeared as associate Jonathan Rollins, the firm's first black lawyer. Larry Drake (1950–) also joined the show as Benny Stulwicz, the firm's mentally challenged office boy.

There were guest stars who were not necessarily well known when they appeared on *L.A. Law* but later gained stardom. They included Kevin Spacey, Jeffrey Tambor, Bryan Cranston, Don Cheadle, Kathy Bates, David Schwimmer, Christian Slater, William Macy, C.C.H. Pounder, and Lucy Liu. The show also featured celebrities in cameo roles appearing as themselves: Buddy Hackett, Mamie Van Doren, and Vanna White.

L.A. Law was successful in presenting the legal process in a realistic way and not compressing every case into one episode. Some of the issues dealt with on the show were adultery, vices, AIDS, computer hacking, divorce settlements, the outing of prominent homosexuals, dwarf tossing, antidiscrimination in Japanese firms, sexual harassment, domestic violence, capital punishment, abortion, and a case concerning a man with Tourette's syndrome, which caused him to shout obscenities at inappropriate moments.

A shocking episode occurred in 1989 when Rosalind Shays, played by Diana Muldaur (1938–), a hyper-successful but disagreeable lawyer, was brought in to increase the firm's sagging finances. Eventually she was forced out after almost destroying the firm. She sued the office and won $2.1 million, but in March 1991 she stepped into an empty elevator shaft and fell to her death.

Other controversies on the show included a scene in the episode "He's a Crowd" in which Abby Perkins has a romantic kiss with C.J. Lamb, another lawyer who is bisexual, played by Amanda Donohue (1964–).

Throughout its run, *L.A. Law* won 15 Emmy awards. The critics lauded it and loyal audiences enjoyed it.

See also: *Cagney & Lacey*; *Hill Street Blues*; *Vol. 1, The 1950s–1960s: The Defenders*; NBC (National Broadcasting Company); *Perry Mason*; *Vol. 3, The 1990s–Present*: *Boston Legal*; *Law & Order*.

Further Resources

Asimov, Michael. 2009. *Lawyers in Your Living Room! Law on Television*. American Bar Association.

Hamlin, Harry. 2014. *Full Frontal Nudity: The Making of an Accidental Actor*. New York: Scribner.

The Larry King Show (*Larry King Live*) (CNN, 1985–2010)

The *Larry King Show* (known as *Larry King Live!* from 1985 to 2010) was a syndicated talk show, a staple of nighttime television where dedicated viewers

Larry King of the *Larry King Show* during an interview at the CNN studios in Washington, D.C. A keen interviewer that guests felt they could trust, King welcomed politicians, celebrities, and other newsmakers on his show, and often had them on for the full hour. (AP Photo/Dennis Cook)

could see actors, celebrities, newsmakers, sports figures, authors, government figures, and practically anyone else and hear them talk in a more intimate way than on other shows. Guests were comfortable and more open because they trusted the host and interviewer, Larry King (1933–). The majority of the shows were produced in a studio. There was a large desk with King on one side and guests across from him. In the background was a series of colorful light shapes.

King had an all-radio talk show that was nationally syndicated. When he made the move to television, at first the results were tepid. The show's first incarnation was a 90-minute broadcast live on Sunday nights from Washington, D.C. It featured a link so viewers could call in and talk directly to Larry King and his guests. A second attempt was more successful. It was renamed *Larry King Live!* and premiered on CNN on June 3, 1985. King was then on weeknights for an hour a night.

The show became so successful that it became CNN's most watched and longest running program. It accumulated 6,120 episodes. King would book one or two guests per night so he could conduct as comprehensive an interview as possible. Critics and others accused King of asking "softball" questions rather than the tougher ones seen on some other shows. King shook off this criticism. His method was to be direct and honest, but to make each guest feel comfortable, which is why potential guests lined up to be on the show. King never put the focus on himself. Actually, if guests asked him a question, he would shift the focus back to them. Surprisingly, Larry King did almost no research for the interviews. His method was to be sincere and earnest. He wore a shirt, pants, and suspenders, which became his trademark. He never attacked his guests but always followed up a question with another to get deeper into the subject. King was known to say to his guest "let's touch a few more bases" when he wanted to let them know he intended to expand the interview into other areas.

When one of his celebrity guests died he would put together a tribute show and play parts of an earlier interview with them. King had a vintage RCA mike on a stand on his side of the table; it was there symbolically because lapel microphones were used on the show.

When King was not on the show a series of other hosts appeared including Geraldo Rivera, Ryan Seacrest, Nany Grace, Wolf Blitzer, Bob Costas, Kathie Lee Gifford, Dr. Phil, Star Jones, Glenn Beck, Tavis Smiley, and Donald Trump. After 25 years, in 2010 Larry King retired. His show was replaced by *Piers Morgan Tonight* on January 17, 2011.

See also: CNN (Cable News Network); *Vol. 3, The 1990s–Present: Eye to Eye with Connie Chung*; *Hardball with Chris Matthews*.

Further Resources

King, Larry, and Bill Gilbert. 1995. *How to Talk to Anyone, Anytime, Anywhere: The Secrets of Good Communication*. New York: Three Rivers Press.

King, Larry. 2009. *My Remarkable Journey*. New York: Weinstein Books.

The Late Show Starring Joan Rivers (Fox, 1986–1987)

Joan Rivers (1933–2014) was the first female comic to become a permanent substitute host on *The Tonight Show with Johnny Carson*. Earlier in 1965 she came to prominence due to her guest shots on *The Tonight Show*. Carson liked Rivers and found her new and original. She also became Carson's handpicked choice to succeed him. The king of late night was a mentor to Joan Rivers. When she started her career, it was unusual for women to be stand-up comics and from the beginning Rivers had an edgy style in content and delivery. In 1986, Rivers signed with Fox Network to host the first nighttime talk show they would air, called *The Late Show with Joan Rivers*. The creation of a new show, instead of Rivers succeeding Carson, reportedly damaged the relationship between the two stars.

Rivers's husband Edgar Rosenberg (1925–1987) and Bill Sammeth (1951–) were the executive producers of the show. A $2 million 420-seat studio was built to Rivers's specification. There was an attempt to bring in a younger audience than Carson's demographic. The first night, October 9, 1986 was broadcast to 95 stations. Booked for the premiere were Cher, Elton John, David Lee Roth, and Pee-Wee Herman.

Broadcast from the Fox Television Center in Hollywood, Rivers came out to a torrent of applause and cheers, so much so that it took an effort to calm the audience, including kissing members in the front row. There was a desk with a stand-up mike on it, a chair, and a couch. After the audience quieted down she told them she was skipping the monologue and after all she had been through to get the show on the air, she just wanted to thank them. After a break she was at her desk with a window revealing a cityscape behind her. She made a series of jokes referencing that a TV station in Boston banned her and that another was broadcasting audio only on the radio. She handled guests well, bringing out a cupcake with a candle to commemorate David Lee Roth's birthday, and receiving a bunch of gag gifts from Pee-Wee Herman.

Over the run of the show many notables were booked including Sam Donaldson, Chris Rock, Howie Mandel, George Carlin, Jimmy Breslin, Betty Ford, Reba McEntire, Ray Charles, and Kool and the Gang.

The Late Show Starring Joan Rivers was not particularly groundbreaking in terms of content and format except that a woman was the host. The band was the Party Boys and the Tramp led by Mark Hudson of the Hudson Brothers.

Initial ratings were good, but by the end of October they had dropped sharply. Fox had promised advertisers a rating of 5 but the show was then averaging less than half that. This meant Fox would have to offer "make goods" or subsequent free spots to its sponsors.

Rivers's staff and the Fox executives became tense; then the situation worsened. In February 1987 Fox took over control of the show and Rosenberg felt unwanted. Ratings stayed low and in April 1987 Fox announced it was pulling support for *The Late Show Starring Joan Rivers.* The last show aired on May 15, 1987 followed by four nights of reruns. Fox first decided to have a different celebrity host the show each night, but that was not possible. Then various celebrities took a longer tenure on the show, including Arsenio Hall (1956–), who would go on to host his own very popular late night show.

See also: *The Arsenio Hall Show*; *Vol. 1, The 1950s–1960s: The Tonight Show.*

Further Resources

Rivers, Joan. 2015. *Diary of a Mad Diva*. New York: Berkley Books.

Rivers, Melissa. 2015. *The Book of Joan. Tales of Mirth, Mischief and Manipulation*. New York: Crown Publishers.

The Life and Adventures of Nicholas Nickleby (1983)

The stage production that brought Charles Dickens's (1812–1870) epic work *The Life and Adventures of Nicholas Nickleby* to such prominence was a large-scale production by playwright David Edgar (1948–). It premiered in 1980 in London's West End by the Royal Shakespeare Company. The play ran eight and a half hours from beginning to end. Figuring intermissions and a dinner break, the audience was actually there for 10 hours. This production was acclaimed by critics and audiences alike. There are an enormous number of characters, so the actors played multiple roles except for Roger Rees (1944–2015), who played Nicholas Nickleby, and David Threlfall (1953–), who portrayed Smike. The play moved to Broadway in 1981 to equal acclaim.

In 1982 the Royal Shakespeare Company recorded the show as three two-hour episodes and one three-hour episode for Channel 4 in England. It became the channel's first dramatic presentation.

In 1983 it was broadcast in America and won an Emmy award for best miniseries. It was shown in four parts that totaled nine hours. The project was produced by the Mobil Showcase Network. This television version was written by David Edgar and directed by Trevor Nunn and John Caird (1948–). It was based directly on the 1980 stage version mounted by the Royal Shakespeare Company. The massive production involved 150 roles by an ensemble of actors.

The Royal Shakespeare Company's production included highly trained actors, well versed in the plays of William Shakespeare and his contemporaries. Their skill and precision brought theatricality and elegance to the performance of original Dickens characters. Bringing culture to television was an ongoing process but productions like *The Life and Adventures of Nicholas Nickleby* elevated television watchers, proving there was more out there than commercial fare.

The focus of the story was Dickens's depiction of the Yorkshire School run by Wackford Squeers. It takes place in London, Portsmouth, Yorkshire, and Devon. Squeers is an evil man who tricks parents with children with physical and mental disabilities and puts the money in his own pocket rather than use it as he promised for the health and well-being of the kids.

The History of Dickens's Novel

There have been as many as seven adaptations of *Nicholas Nickleby* over the decades, a testament to the timeless quality of the story, the memorable characters, and the themes that define humanity.

In 1977 the BBC produced a production of the novel and also produced the work in 2002. In 2002 an American film arrived directed by Douglas McGrath, with a cast that included Nathan Lane, Christopher Plummer, Alan Cumming, Anne Hathaway, and Jim Broadbent. In 2012 the BBC presented a modern-day version of *Nicholas Nickleby* that required changes to the plot and characters. It was aired in five parts, each running 45 minutes.

Further Resources

Dickens, Charles. 1999 [1839]. *Nicholas Nickleby*. London: Penguin.

Tomalin, Claire. 2012. *Charles Dickens: A Life*. New York: Penguin.

Lifestyles of the Rich and Famous (Syndication, 1984–1995)

Television shows that visit the homes of celebrities were an established genre with *Person to Person* in 1950s and *Here's Hollywood* in the early 1960s. In the 1980s Robin Leach (1941–), a former reporter on *Entertainment Tonight,* planned to take the genre to new heights. He hosted *Lifestyles of the Rich and Famous*, which was syndicated for 11 years and profiled celebrities' homes and activities in a voyeuristic way.

An *Entertainment Tonight* producer told Robin Leach he wanted the show to go deeper into the personalities of Hollywood celebrities. Leach told him that wasn't the way to go, that the audience wanted to see celebrities in exotic places, in hot tubs and pools. Leach was told his idea would never work, so he moved forward independently.

Colorful Englishman Robin Leach in 1990, sipping champagne as the host of *Lifestyles of the Rich and Famous*. Each week he would visit the home of a celebrity to bring their opulent way of living to the home viewing audience. (Maureen Donaldson/Getty Images)

The celebrity homes chosen for *Lifestyles of the Rich and Famous* were large and ostentatious and viewers were drawn to the glitz; but the show's real attraction was Robin Leach himself with his pronounced English accent and loud voice. His language was beyond purple prose and seemed to be an endless stream of superlatives. The show began in syndication in 1984 and did so well that it was run on ABC during 1986 in both a daytime and a nighttime slot. The show glorified wealth. Leach seemed to know that regular folks would watch the show to dream of what life could be.

The secret to the show's success was the variety of the profiles. A viewer would expect to see Liberace

(1919–1987) on a show called *Lifestyles of the Rich and Famous* with his luxurious penthouse, many homes, flashy and glitzy clothes, and ornate décor, but Leach was interested in investigating celebrities who might not be connected to an elegant or exotic lifestyle, such as Mike Love (1941–), who had homes in Lake Tahoe and vacationed in Maui, Hawaii. Leach was also interested in the personal aspects of their lifestyles, showing the Beach Boys meditating and talking about spiritual matters. At times, it seemed that Leach was going overboard with this celebrity profile, constructing and executing his voice-over, using every Beach Boy song title imaginable. But this grandiosity became the Leach trademark.

A segment on Raquel Welch (1940–) dealt less with her Hollywood celebrity and more with her dedication to good health and the cottage industry she created with exercise programs and books. The show could often be exploitive, inserting a shot of a blonde in a bikini, or a close panning highlighting Welch's well-toned body in a tight exercise outfit.

Leach is expert and smooth at dropping the names of all the rich and famous people he counts as friends. Other subjects profiled on the show are Sylvester Stallone playing polo, Luciano Pavarotti, Princess Diana, and Sophia Loren.

Watching an episode of *Lifestyles of the Rich and Famous* made viewers feel that the extravagant lifestyle, where the champagne constantly flowed, was almost within reach. Television viewers like being voyeurs. These visits made the audience feel as if they owned the celebrities who were profiled. *Lifestyles of the Rich and Famous* went beyond the studio for an intimate glimpse of exotic ways of life.

See also: *Entertainment Tonight*; *Vol. 3, The 1990s–Present: Access Hollywood*; *E! True Hollywood Story*; *VH1 Storytellers*.

Further Resources

Leach, Robin, with Judith Rich. 1986. *Lifestyles of the Rich and Famous*. New York: Doubleday.

Leach, Robin. 1992. *The Lifestyle of the Rich and Famous Cookbook: Recipes and Entertaining Secrets from the Most Fabulous People in the World*. New York: Penguin USA.

Live! with Regis and Kathie Lee (Syndication, 1988–2000)

A number of previous programs led to the extremely popular, nationally syndicated daytime talk show *Live! with Regis and Kathie Lee*. From 1971 to 1991 *A.M. Los Angeles* was a local show on KABC-TV. In 1975 when it went national, the title was changed to *A.M. America*. Regis Philbin (1931–) co-hosted this news and talk show paired with various female partners. In 1978 Cyndy Garvey (1949–) joined Philbin and they were co-hosts until 1981.

On April 4, 1983 *The Morning Show* premiered on the local station WABC-TV in New York, co-hosted by Philbin and Garvey. In 1984 Garvey left the show and Philbin hired Ann Abernathy with whom he had worked compatibly at KABC. When she married and returned to California, Kathie Lee Johnson (1953–), who later became Kathie Lee Gifford when she married legendary football player and sports commentator Frank Gifford, joined Philbin on June 24, 1985. Their chemistry brought the show to number 1 in its market, according to Nielsen research, and on September 5, 1988, it debuted in national syndication with a new title: *Live! with Regis and Kathie Lee.*

The Pair America Wanted to Watch

The one-hour daily broadcast began with what they called "host chat." Regis and Kathie Lee would sit in front of the cameras and talk about how they had spent the previous evening. It seemed like small talk, but what captured the viewer's attention was the so-called sexual tension between two people who couldn't be more different in their lifestyles, thoughts on religion, and frequent lack of interest in one another. There was more than a 20-year age difference between the two who took turns carrying on about one thing or another and detailing the previous night's restaurant meal and other trifles. These conversations could last as long as 15 or 20 minutes, then a viewer call-in trivia segment commenced with the hosts responding to the callers and the live audience reacting. After a commercial a celebrity guest would be introduced and interviewed, usually to promote an upcoming project. At times, there was more than one guest.

This morning talk show first featured Regis Philbin and Kathie Lee Gifford, then later Regis with Kelly Ripa, and was a ritual for millions of viewers, once the local version of the show expanded its reach to a national audience. The hosts would begin the show with a brief chat about their personal lives before moving on to interviews and other segments. (AP Photo/Gerald Herbert)

Regis Philbin had an operatic, hysterical personality and often provoked and kidded with executive producer Michael Gelman (1961–), who was the perfect foil. Kathie Lee would follow suit. Another executive producer of the show, Art Moore, dressed in loud clothes and laughed as Regis hurled insults at him. Kathie Lee reacted to some of Regis's lines by smirking and slowly closing one eye. Regis was almost always excited, animated, and extremely self-centered.

There were also backup co-hosts. When Kathie Lee couldn't be on the show, such as during maternity leave with her two children, Cody and Cassidy, Regis's wife Joy Philbin (1941–) often took over. Kathie Lee's husband Frank Gifford (1930–2015) would occupy the co-host chair when Regis was sick, on vacation, or not available.

Live! with Regis and Kathie Lee was nominated for numerous Daytime Emmy awards for Outstanding Talk/Entertainment Show. On July 28, 2000, Kathie Lee left *Live! with Regis and Kathie Lee* in an emotional farewell with Philbin seemingly very moved about the departure. Gifford planned to pursue her singing and acting career.

A search commenced for a new female co-host. Gelman and Philbin held auditions with a wide selection of pairings including Rosie O'Donnell, Joy Philbin, Jan Carl, Whoopi Goldberg, Gloria Estefan, and Caroline Rhea. On November 1, 2000 Kelly Ripa (1970–) auditioned and secured the job. She was quick-witted and fun-loving. Her position as the permanent replacement was made official on February 5, 2001 and the show became *Live! with Regis and Kelly.*

In 2011 Regis Philbin retired at age 80. After a major search, New York Giants football player and sports analyst Michael Strahan (1971–) became the next co-host and the show became *Live with Kelly and Michael.* On April 29, 2016, ABC announced Strahan would be leaving the show in September 2016.

See also: *Good Morning America*; *Vol. 1, The 1950s–1960s: The Today Show*.

Further Resources

Gifford, Kathie Lee. 2010. *Just When I Thought I Dropped My Last Egg: Life and Other Calamities.* New York: Ballantine Books.

Philbin, Regis. 2011. *How I Got This Way.* New York: HarperCollins.

MacGyver (ABC, 1985–1992)

MacGyver was a one-hour action/adventure television series that aired on the ABC network for seven seasons. Richard Dean Anderson (1950–) played Angus MacGyver, a versatile secret agent who worked for the fictitious Phoenix Foundation. MacGyver took on covert missions for an invented U.S. government agency. Viewers were attracted to the clever and intricate techniques his character employed to solve problems on the spot. MacGyver didn't carry any weapons, instead preferring to use his intellect and encyclopedic scientific knowledge to meet challenges in a nonviolent manner.

Dana Elcar (1927–2005) appeared as his boss and close friend, Peter Thornton. Bruce McGill (1959–) played Jack Dalton, a fellow agent who provided some comic relief on the show, and Elyssa Davalos (1959–) was lawyer Nikki Carpenter. The series was created by actor Henry Winkler (1945–) of *Happy Days* fame, who had completed 11 seasons on that show and wanted to branch out as a producer. He partnered with director and producer John Rich (1925–2012) and they formed a production company. The show was initially filmed in Los Angeles. In fall 1987 the production moved from Hollywood to Canada.

In the pilot MacGyver was referred to as "Stace" and Bud by his grandfather, but after the pilot the creators decided against any reference to the character's first name or nicknames until 1991, when Angus was finally revealed as his first name during a dream sequence.

MacGyver applied scientific and engineering principles to help him during his missions. He also was a master of jerry-rigging, putting diverse elements together to make something work effectively. He always carried a Swiss Army knife as a basic tool. *MacGyver* was a fun show for action lovers. Richard Dean Anderson had real charisma, boyish good looks, and the ability to act in physical scenes, often doing his own stunts.

MacGyver episodes often began with a mission already in progress. Frequently in voice-over, MacGyver tells a story concerning his childhood. He resolved the situation concerning the mission quickly, then the open credits rolled. This was known on *MacGyver* as an "opening gambit" and was written and directed by a different team than those who wrote the body of the show. After the credits there was an opening scene, which usually didn't concern MacGyver but was used for character development. Up to this point nothing was shown that had anything to do with the night's episode.

MacGyver's adventures were worthy of any action hero. In Burma he retrieved a container with a deadly poison from a plane crash. He was confronted with modern-day pirates who used a captain's log to locate a sunken treasure fleet. Romance was involved when a Soviet dissenter whom MacGyver once loved appeared and begged for his help, but KGB agents kidnapped her and demanded a priceless national treasure from China for her ransom. Terrorism became part of MacGyver's world when terrorists became intent on wiping out a nearby city. MacGyver's life was in danger when he was blamed for an assassination attempt against a world leader during negotiations at a private girls' school. One of the girls became his only hope against further bloodshed.

MacGyver was popular in the overseas market. After the series finished its run, two TV movies were made and aired on ABC in 1994: *MacGyver: Lost Treasure of Atlantis* on May 14 and *MacGyver: Trail to Doomsday* on November 24, 1994. In 2016, a new version of *MacGyver* was developed and aired on

CBS. The reboot was produced by Henry Winkler. Lucas Till (1990–) was cast in the lead role.

See also: *The A-Team*; *Vol. 1, The 1950s–1960s: Mission Impossible*.

Further Resources

Peterson, Jack. 2014. *Richard Dean Anderson: 122 Success Facts: Everything You Need to Know.* Emereo Publishing. http://emereo.net/index.php/contacts/

Winkler, Henry. 2011. *I Never Met an Idiot on the River: Reflections on Family, Photography and Fly-Fishing.* San Rafael, CA: Insight Editions.

Married . . . with Children (Fox, 1987–1997)

In 1987 the fledging Fox network told creators Ron Leavitt (1947–2008) and Michael Moye (1954–) to develop a sitcom unlike the network fare airing on CBS, NBC, and ABC. Fox picked the right creative team because Leavitt and Moye had a strong dislike for the average polite sitcom. The result was the funny and raunchy *Married . . . with Children,* which struck a chord with viewers. The off-color sitcom ran for 11 seasons and was a popular series despite sustaining less than stellar ratings due to Fox's limited affiliate base and a weak supporting lineup. As a Sunday night show, it also had stiff competition from the perennial favorite *Murder, She Wrote*.

Married . . . with Children starred Ed O'Neill (1946–) as Al Bundy and Katey Sagal (1954–) as his wife, Peg Bundy. The name Bundy was chosen after the creators' favorite pro wrestler, King Kong Bundy (1957–). Al Bundy was a hapless shoe salesman in Chicago who had bad hygiene, obvious to anyone around him. Peg Bundy hated housework and cooking. She had teased hair and generally wore spandex outfits. The Bundy marriage was portrayed through wisecracks and one-liners with dialogue that commented on their anemic sex life. Christina Applegate (1971–) played their oversexed teenaged daughter Kelly, who was shown as an airhead. David Faustino (1974–) played their intelligent, girl-crazy teenage son Bud, who was inept with the opposite sex. The Bundys were constantly bickering about money and their semi-delinquent children, who fought with each other incessantly.

Even though Sunday-night viewing of *Married . . . with Children* grew season upon season, there was friction at Fox about airing certain episodes. One instance was "A Period Piece" in which the Bundys and their neighbors go camping and all three women simultaneously begin their menstrual periods, a story line that Fox executives found offensive. After many modifications in the writers' room, the episode did air at a later date and in a later time slot. The title was changed to "The Camping Show." Another problematic episode involved Al and Peg being videotaped having sex in a sleazy motel. This show never aired.

Another outrageous episode has Al going to his favorite nude bar and defending it by creating the anti-feminist group NO MA'AM (National Organization of Men Against Amazonian Masterhood), which preserved the right to drink excessively, act like a slob, and lust over sexually explicit material. The crude subject matter on *Married . . . with Children* caused viewer outrage in some quarters. In some cases, groups and individuals attempted to boycott the show for what they considered offensive material about sex, language, and suggestive images in the show.

In fall 1991 Peg was pregnant and actress Katey Sagal was pregnant in real life as well. Sadly, Sagal had a miscarriage late in the pregnancy. The producer turned the plot line into a dream sequence so the actress could avoid having to deal with an already terrible circumstance.

By 1994, in its ninth season, *Married . . . with Children* was the longest running sitcom on network TV. In February 1995 the show celebrated its 200th episode. The show had an opening theme song, Frank Sinatra singing "Love and Marriage" written by Sammy Cahn and Jim Van Heusen and recorded in 1953. This lighthearted ditty instantly sent the message that this was going to be an irreverent program.

Married . . . with Children took the idea of a dysfunctional nuclear family and turned it into a mockery of all the family sitcoms that had preceded it. It pushed the boundaries of marriage and parenting and brought frank sex talk into the homes of viewers who had been watching unrealistic family units on sitcoms for years. This satire and insight into the lower depths of the

American family rattled some, but, in the main, most television viewers enjoyed the edginess and laughed uproariously.

See also: Fox Broadcasting Company; *Roseanne*; *The Simpsons*.

Further Resources

Kalyn, Nick. 2012. *Christina Applegate: Beauty, Comedy and More*. Amazon Digital Services.

Married With Children Bundyology. http://www.bundyology.com/

Masada (ABC, 1981)

Masada was a four-part, eight-hour miniseries aired on ABC. The epic presentation retold the story of the siege of Masada by the Roman 10th Legion in 72–73 CE. The television event was billed as an "ABC Novel for Television." The episodes were shown on consecutive nights on April 5, 1981 through April 8, 1981.

The cast of this marathon television event included major television stars and also featured a star-studded cast from the film world. Peter Strauss (1947–) played the pivotal role of Eleazar ben Yair, leader of the Jewish Zealots who ultimately convinces his compatriots to commit mass suicide rather than face capture. Famed actor Peter O'Toole (1932–2013) played Eleazar's adversary Cornelius Flavius Silva, the commander of the Roman legions; David Opatoshu (1918–1996) played Shimon, a rabbi; Denis Quilley (1927–2003) played Quadratus; Anthony Quayle (1913–1989) portrayed Gallus; Barbara Carrera (1945–) was Sheva, Silva's concubine; Giulia Pagno (1949–) played Miriam; David Warner (1941–) portrayed Falco; and Timothy West (1934–) was the Roman emperor Vespasian.

Background for a Television Miniseries

Masada was based on the novel *The Antagonists* by Ernest K. Gann (1910–1991), who was an aviator in World War II and an environmentalist and conservationist before becoming a novelist. Among his novels was *The High and the Mighty,* which was made into a successful film. The teleplay was written by Joel Oliansky (1935–2002), who was best known for *The Law* (1974), *The Competition* (1980), and *Bird* (1988). The epic miniseries was directed by Boris Sagal (1923–1981), who directed episodes of *The Twilight Zone, Columbo*, and *The Man from U.N.C.L.E.* and brought his credentials on miniseries having directed the highly successful *Rich Man, Poor Man.*

In history, Masada was an ancient fortification in the southern district of Israel on the top of a rock plateau next to a mesa on the eastern edge of the Judean Desert overlooking the Dead Sea. *The Antagonists: A Novel about Masada* is a historical novel about the siege of Masada. The novel explores the themes of patriotism and leadership by contrasting the protagonists and antagonists in the narrative. Very little of a historical nature has survived, so the account was largely fictionalized.

Masada was one of several substantial undertakings in the era of miniseries in the late 1970s and 1980s. The major successes of *Roots* (also on ABC) and *Shōgun,* which were both historical narratives, encouraged the networks to produce this type of entertainment. ABC was concerned about whether the viewing audience would be familiar with the ancient era depicted in *Masada.* To educate its audience, the network commissioned a 30-minute documentary, which it distributed to its affiliates to air weeks before the premiere of *Masada*. It featured Peter O'Toole and explained the history of the Jewish revolt against Rome.

The network edited *Masada* to feature length for theatrical release in other countries under the title *The Antagonists*. This version eventually was made available as a home video release. The production of *Masada* cost $25 million. Hundreds of extras were employed in the old Hollywood tradition of "a cast of thousands." The production design was opulent as befitted the subject. Nino Navarese (1907–1983), technical adviser and costume designer, devised an opulent and detailed look he brought to such films as *Spartacus, Cleopatra,* and *The Agony and the Ecstasy*. The sweeping, dramatic music was in part composed by Jerry Goldsmith (1929–2004), who scored *Planet of the Apes*, *Papillon*, and *Chinatown*. For verisimilitude, virtually the entire production was filmed in Israel, a key reason for the large budget.

When it originally aired *Masada* drew in good ratings, but in reruns its numbers were the lowest in modern television history indicating that this miniseries, unlike others, didn't have lasting power. New audiences were not attracted to seeing it, suggesting the possibility of negative word of mouth after the original broadcasts.

See also: *North and South*; *Shōgun*.

Further Resources

Quayle, Anthony. 1990. *A Time to Speak*. London: Barrie & Jenkins.

Sellers, Robert. 2015. *Peter O'Toole: The Definitive Biography*. London: Sedgwick & Jackson.

Max Headroom (ABC, 1987–1988)

Way ahead of its time, the science fiction satire *Max Headroom* presented outrageous imagery that looked digital with variated sound and wacky plots. Produced in England and based on the British pilot *Max Headroom. 20 Minutes into the Future* that originally appeared on Britain's Channel 4, the American version aired on ABC for a total of 14 episodes. It was considered one of the most innovative television shows of the era.

The title character was played by American-Canadian actor Matt Frewer (1958–). Through the use of makeup and elaborate production techniques, Max Headroom appeared on screen as a computer-generated image. The character, who was originally created to host a music video show on English television, at times interrupted the video clips with irreverent comments. By 1985 Max Headroom began to interview celebrities. There was so much interest in the character of Max Headroom that a one-hour special, *Rebus: The Max Headroom Story,* was produced. The documentary served as inspiration for the series, which at one point was airing simultaneously with the Channel 4 series.

Cinemax aired *Rebus: The Max Headroom Story* in 1985 and picked up the British series in fall 1986. The 1987 version of the talk show was produced in New York and titled *Original Max Headroom* to differentiate it from the English show.

A second imaginary sci-fi series titled *Max Headroom* was set in an undisclosed time in the future, in a world where television sets could not be turned off, where there was fierce competition among a slate of networks. Matt Frewer played Edison Carter, a reporter for network 23 who barely escaped death in a motorcycle accident. The network's young research chief Bryce Lynch, played by Chris Young (1971–), created Carter's computerized alter ego—Max Headroom—named for the last words Carter saw on a warning sign before his accident. Carter recovered and scoured the postmodern city investigating stories. He came upon a secret plan by the networks to compress commercials into ultra-short spots known as "blipverts." Max was able to materialize on a TV screen whenever he wanted, and he used this power to insult viewers.

Other regular members of the cast included Amanda Pays (1959–) as Theora Jones, Carter's assistant, Jeffrey Tambor (1944–) as Murray the news producer, George Coe (1929–2015) as Ben Cheviot, president of network 23, and William Sheppard (1932–) as the heavily earringed Blank Reg, who ran an underground TV channel.

Max Headroom was a barrage of sounds and images. Voices are heard via walkie-talkie; visually there were views from cameras, video phones, computer graphics, a television control room, and through electrical charges; cameras were everywhere, and there was extensive camera movement and slow motion.

Max Headroom was not a hit in the United States. It ran two seasons and produced only 14 episodes, but its significance was enormous. It represented a roadway to the cyberpunk movement and introduced state-of-the-art television techniques to the masses. It satirized television networks, suggesting their eventual control over humankind. In the end *Max Headroom* foretold a future of television that has yet to arrive.

Further Resources

Hansen, David, and Paul Owen. 1986. *Max Headroom's Guide to Life*. New York: Bantam.

Roberts, Steve. 1986. *Max Headroom: 20min F.* New York: Vintage.

The McLaughlin Group (PBS, 1982–)

The McLaughlin Group was a lively half–hour weekly news analysis program from a decidedly conservative viewpoint. John McLaughlin (1927–2016) created and produced this syndicated public broadcasting show and was responsible for its format. McLaughlin was host and moderator from its initial airing in 1982 until his death in 2016. McLaughlin never missed a broadcast. John McLaughlin was an ordained priest who left the priesthood in 1975. His early political affiliation was Democratic, but he became a Republican and through his friendship with Pat Buchanan was a speechwriter for President Richard Nixon.

The show's format consisted of a panel of four permanent news analysts who discussed current events, tightly moderated by McLaughlin, who introduced the topics and asked questions, calling on each panelist. The principal players with long tenures were Robert Novak (1931–2009), a conservative syndicated columnist, journalist, and television personality who hosted the *Capital Gang* on CNN; Patrick Buchanan (1938–), senior adviser to Presidents Richard Nixon, Gerald Ford, and Ronald Reagan, who was the original host of CNN's *Crossfire* and unsuccessfully sought the Republican presidential nomination in 1992 and 1996; Morton Kondracke (1939–), political commentator and journalist and executive editor and columnist for the nonpartisan Capitol Hill newspaper, *Roll Call*, who frequently appeared on television news-based programs; Jack Germond (1928–2013), sharp-witted journalist, syndicated columnist, and author (who abruptly resigned from the show after 15 years); Fred Barnes (1943–), editor of *The Weekly Standard*; Eleanor Clift (1940–), liberal political reporter and author; Clarence Page (1947–), journalist, syndicated columnist, and senior member of *The Chicago Tribune* editorial board; and Mort Zuckerman (1937–), owner and publisher of the *New York Daily News*.

The participants sat at a roundtable. McLaughlin, who had a loud, powerful, bellowing voice, started the show by pronouncing "Issue One," then presenting the topic, a pressing news or political item, and continued by designating one of the panel members to give their view. When the panelist finished, he would call on another group member, then another, until everyone had spoken. There was some back and forth, not enough to call it a discussion, but some individual commentary from the news and political analysts who shared their observations and possible outcomes about the issues at hand. When necessary McLaughlin reminded the analysts that he was the boss. If he wanted to end a particular discussion he would announce "Exit Question," communicating that it was time for a wrap-up. A last question was posed. After the issues were explored, McLaughlin moved the discussion to calls for predictions. He would summarize these predictions alternately in the form of realistic political forecasting or by making outlandish statements. McLaughlin's persona was dour and serious; he was perceived as a unique character not recognizable on other news or current affairs programs at that time. *The McLaughlin Group* was entertaining and sometimes informative, but it was criticized for its lack of decorum, its simplification of serious issues, and McLaughlin's exaggerations. The personalities of the participants were vibrant and their viewpoints were usually strong.

The character of the program was so distinctive that it was the subject of parody on *Saturday Night Live*. Over the course of the program the longest lasting sponsor was General Electric (GE).

The topics discussed centered on current affairs that were of interest to the general public and the participants. These included the presidential administration in power, global issues, individuals in the news, constitutional matters, and Supreme Court decisions. When McLaughlin died on August 16, 2016 an outpouring of sorrow was expressed by the show's participants, whose public tributes mourned his passing.

See also: *Crossfire*; *Vol. 1, The 1950s–1960s: Meet the Press*.

Further Resources

Clift, Eleanor. 2003. *Founding Sisters and the Nineteenth Amendment*. Hoboken, NJ: John Wiley & Sons.

Stanley, Timothy. 2012. *The Crusader: The Life and Tumultuous Times of Pat Buchanan*. New York: St. Martin's Press.

Miami Vice (NBC, 1984–1989)

Miami Vice, an NBC crime series, captured the look and attitude of the 1980s perhaps more than any other contemporaneous show in its genre. On the surface it was typical cop show fare with two good guys, one white and one black, who chased the bad guys. But its attraction was its effect on the senses induced by Miami locations, which were promoted and brought to the forefront by the use of color, fashion, and contemporary music.

Miami Vice was developed when Brandon Tartikoff (1949–1997), the president of NBC Entertainment, jotted two words on a pad, "MTV Cops." Anthony Yerkovich who had written for and produced *Hill Street Blues* (1981–1987), wrote the pilot. Film director Michael Mann (1943–), who among other accomplishments had directed the TV movie *The Jericho Mile* (1979), was brought on as executive producer.

At first the producers considered placing the show in New York, but decided instead to produce the show on location in Miami, Florida. Initially, there was local resistance as officials worried the city would be portrayed in a less than flattering manner. When the show aired their worries were set aside. The popularity of *Miami Vice* contributed positively to the city's image. Like the legendary opening from the earlier cop series *Hawaii Five-0*, the title sequence alone was a boon to tourism.

There had been shows set in Miami before: *Miami Undercover* (1961), *Surfside 6* (1960–1962), *Michael Shayne* (1960–1961), and *Caribe* (1975), but *Miami Vice* was the first to make Miami itself a critical part of its concept. To cast the show the producers stayed away from big names. They wanted to create a distinctive stamp by seeking relative unknowns. Don Johnson (1949–) was chosen to play Detective James "Sonny" Crockett, an urbane, slick undercover cop and high roller who drove a Ferrari and lived on a boat with his pet alligator, Elvis. Paul Michael Thomas (1947–) played his cool partner Detective Ricardo Tubbs, a New Yorker who drove a vintage Cadillac. Tubbs wore double-breasted jackets, ties, and silk shirts; Crockett wore a European jacket thrown over a T-shirt and loose-fitting baggy pants without a belt or socks. For the first season, Crockett was unshaven, but the stubble look didn't catch on with male viewers. Edward James Olmos (1947–) was Lieutenant Martin Castillo, the dour and laconic head of the Organized Crime Bureau. Saundra Santiago (1957–) appeared as Detective Gina Calabrese and Olivia Brown (1960–) played Detective Trudy Joplin. The female detectives often went undercover as prostitutes. Michael Talbott (1955–) was Detective Stanley Switek and John Diehl (1950–) was his partner.

The architectural style of Miami was thoroughly investigated on camera. The production team was meticulous in choosing exterior locations and buildings. Because *Miami Vice* had a specific color palette of pastel colors, the rule was to find places that accentuated the warm hues and tones. Another link between *Miami Vice* and *Hawaii 5-0* was a dynamic theme song. It was written by Jan Hammer (1945–), who had solid rock and roll and jazz credentials. The theme was a powerful, driving rock melody with a precise instrumental background that featured synthesizers and electronic drums. The opening imagery had fewer shots than the *Hawaii 5-0* credit sequence, but it achieved the same purpose—placing the viewer directly in the Miami environment.

The undercover vice cops solved crimes that focused on narcotics and firearms trafficking, prostitution, and organized crime. There were also plot lines about the personal stories of the lead characters. Crockett had been separated and divorced. In fall 1987 singer Sheena Easton (1959–) played rocker Caitlin Davies, who married Crockett on November 20, 1987. It was the first episode to top the CBS show *Dallas* in the same time slot. Caitlin was killed off later in the season. Tubbs had a personal vendetta against a Miami crime family responsible for killing his brother; it was the primary reason for his relocation from New York, and so there were episodes featuring almost vigilante behavior with the Calderone mob.

Miami Vice redefined the role of guest stars by choosing people who were rarely seen on a dramatic television series. Many were from the contemporary music scene and their works contributed to the series' pulsating aural element. Rocker Phil Collins's (1951–) "In the Air Tonight" was the basis for a driving scene featuring the cops. It was presented as if it were a standalone music video. Other guests were Ted Nugent (1948–) and Meatloaf (1947–); Glenn Frey (1948–2016) recorded "Smuggler's Blues" and "You Belong to the City" for the show; and jazz great Miles Davis (1926–1991) and singer-poet Leonard Cohen (1934–2016) appeared on *Miami Vice*. In addition, Watergate figure G. Gordon Liddy (1930–), boxer Roberto Durán (1951–), socialite Bianca Jagger (1945–), auto magnate Lee Iacocca (1924–), and theater revolutionary Julian Beck (1925–1985) also did spots.

Miami Vice was originally scheduled on Friday at 10 p.m. and it landed in ninth position in the ratings by the second season. In June 1986 it was moved back an hour to compete with *Dallas* (1978–1991). The look of *Miami Vice* evolved to deeper tones as the story lines reflected darker issues. In this time slot the show dropped to 23 in the ratings and audience response was negative. By its last two seasons the stories and visuals began to suggest a neo-noir quality.

Miami Vice costume design influenced modern culture and seeped into the mainstream as men were seen wearing unconstructed jackets like Sonny Crockett and shiny pastel colors. A *Miami Vice* clothing line was available in major department stores. The series was also considered a contributing factor in the preservation of much of Miami's architectural history, which had been in jeopardy.

At the end of the fourth season music producer Jan Hammer left the show. For the fifth season Michael Mann passed the executive producer's baton to Dick Wolf (1946–), who became a highly influential showrunner in the crime story genre. Mann decided to end the show after its fifth season for financial reasons. The show had constantly gone over budget and he needed to syndicate it so Universal Studios could recoup its investment. The show was moved back to 10 o'clock for the final season, but it finished in 53rd place in the ratings. The two-hour finale in which Crockett and Tubbs both quit the force was broadcast on May 21, 1989. *Miami Vice* was then sold to the USA Cable Network. The package included the episode "Too Much Too Late," which never ran on NBC because the network found the episode objectionable. It concerned a mother who sells her daughter for sex to feed her cocaine habit. Ultimately, both Don Johnson and Paul Michael Thomas were anxious to expand into film, which Johnson did with considerable success.

See also: *Vol. 1, The 1950s–1960s: Hawaii Five-0.*

Further Resources

MacGregor, Trish, and Rob MacGregor. 2012. *The Making of Miami Vice*. Discover Crossroads Press. Amazon Digital Press.

Munshower, Suzanne. 1986. *Don Johnson: An Unauthorized Biography*. New York: Signet.

Michael Nesmith in Television Parts (NBC, 1985)

In 1968 *The Monkees* television show was cancelled shortly after the breakup of the group often referred to as the American Beatles. Michael Nesmith (1942–) who was the most mature and intellectual of the group, stayed active in music as a songwriter and solo artist. At the end of the 1970s Nesmith began producing music videos for himself and other artists. In 1982 his experimental "Elephant Parts" was the first music video to win a Grammy. On March 7, 1985 Michael Nesmith hosted a comedy special on NBC. Three months later his series, *Michael Nesmith in Television Parts*, was given a brief run. The half-hour show was a range of videos and comedy skits with Nesmith as the host. Featured guests were Martin Mull, Garry Shandling, Jay Leno, Bobcat Goldthwait, Ed Begley Jr., Jerry Seinfeld, Jimmy Buffett, and Rosanne Cash. Four of the seven programs were televised in prime time on Fridays, the remaining three were combined as a late-night Saturday special

The structure of the shows was unpredictable. Some of the musical numbers were performed in a conventional manner; some were presented as absurdist satire. The comedy was unlike any seen on television up to that time—there were surrealistic special effects and bits of comedy not comprehensible to the audience. There were guest comedians and musicians. It was left up to Nesmith to provide continuity as host when he wasn't wandering off the set, and as a participant. John Hobbs, the musical director, was also on-screen each week reworking two familiar songs into a new song.

This and the whole show were confusing and hard to comprehend for most of the viewing audience.

The sketches were not like those in *Saturday Night Live,* although they did imitate the fake news with a woman as the anchor. One sketch took place in a posh restaurant and was shot in color. A guy and his date sit at a table. When he asks her about college she goes into a long rant backed up by a black-and-white movie that comes back and forth as background and foreground. It is about why the woman didn't go to college because of Sorority Girls from Hell. She tells the story louder and louder, disturbing the whole restaurant, and eventually it turns into a knife murder. At one point the woman or a Sorority Girl from Hell is sitting in the chair where the woman was and the story continues. It has been a horror movie all the while.

In another sketch, Whoopi Goldberg (1955–) is on a beach surrounded by pretty girls in bikinis and handsome guys doing a Valley Girl routine. The ideas seemed hatched out of illogical, crazy concepts and produced a devil-may-care attitude.

The genesis of *Michael Nesmith in Television Parts* comes from the "Elephant Parts" music video, the movie *Head* (1968), avant-garde video art, and a twisted view of sketch comedy and variety shows on television.

See also: *Max Headroom*; MTV.

Further Resources

Massingill, Randi I. 2005. *Total Control: The Monkees Michael Nesmith Story*. Carlsbad, CA: FLEXquarters Publishing.

Railton, Diane, and Paul Watson. 2011. *Music Video and the Politics of Representation*. Edinburgh: Edinburgh University Press.

Monitor (First Camera) (NBC, 1983–1984)

On September 26, 1980, NBC launched *NBC Magazine with David Brinkley*, an early attempt to successfully achieve a *60 Minutes*–style show, but it was up against the wildly popular *Dallas* (1979–1991). After its first year David Brinkley (1920–2003) left NBC, which had been his home for 38 years, and joined ABC. With Brinkley gone, the show's title was changed to *NBC Magazine*, but the show failed to attract an audience and was cancelled. *Monitor* appeared approximately seven months after *NBC Magazine*'s cancellation. The title *Monitor* was lifted from NBCs long-running weekend radio service. The one-hour news show first aired in March 1983, surprisingly in one of NBC's weakest time slots, Saturday at 10:00 a.m., the same spot that produced poor results for the Brinkley magazine show. It received praise from the critics, but at the end of the season was at the bottom of the ratings heap. It was hosted by Lloyd Dobyns (1936–), Steve Delaney, and Rebecca Sobel.

The stories investigated for *Monitor* included "Children Don't Do That" concerning child suicide; "Your Land Is My Land" about the dispute between Arabs and Jews over who had the right to live on the West Bank in Israel; "King Pong," a profile of the inventor of Atari; and "The Survival of Peter O'Toole."

Not willing to give up, NBC revamped the program in fall 1983 with a sharp new title, *First Camera.* There was a new set, new music, and a new reporter, Mark Nykanen. The time slot was finally changed with a make-or-break attitude to Sunday night at 7:00 p.m. when the iconic *60 Minutes* aired on CBS. The affiliates saw this as attempted suicide and 9 percent of NBC stations declined to carry the show. NBC again found itself in a low ratings situation, this time for *First Camera.* After a few months *First Camera* left the air.

See also: *This Week with David Brinkley*; *Vol. 1, The 1950s–1960s: 60 Minutes.*

Further Resources

Hilmes, Michelle. 2007. *NBC: America's Network.* Berkeley and Los Angeles: University of California Press.

Robinson, Marc. 2002. *Brought to You in Living Color: 75 Years of Great Moments in Television and Radio from NBC.* Encino, CA: Top Down Productions.

Moonlighting (ABC, 1985–1989)

Writer, director, and producer Glenn Gordon Caron (1954–) convinced ABC to buy the series *Moonlighting* that focused on a former fashion model whose business manager embezzled her fortune. Left with only one asset, a detective agency run by a fast-talking male private eye, she is persuaded to keep the business as a joint venture. Caron's inspiration for this clever, fast-paced, one-hour detective show was the 1940 film *His Gal Friday* featuring a tough-talking female character personified by actress Rosalind Russell and inspired by William Shakespeare's *The Taming of the Shrew*. Cybill Shepherd (1950–), a model-turned-actress best known for her role in *The Last Picture Show,* played the double-crossed Maddie Hayes. Bruce Willis (1955–), then an unknown, was cast in the role of P.I. David Addison. Forced into partnership, they dubbed their venture the Blue Moon Detective Agency. The chemistry between them was perfect for the show. Maddie was icy and skillful at avoiding David's amorous advances. David was quick-witted and resembled a man from a different era, a kind of disheveled 1940s version of a private eye.

The writing was adroit, with nimble dialogue, banter, in-jokes, and double entendres that suggested a sexual undercurrent. The program combined comedy, drama, and romance and was one of the first examples of what became known as dramedy. The show enjoyed strong ratings and popularity, but was not without significant difficulties. At the helm, Glenn Gordon Caron was a perfectionist and his approach was to treat the series as if was a film production. Caron encouraged spontaneity and unorthodox techniques such as the characters talking directly into the camera, sometimes self-referentially. One production problem was extensive dialogue written for the main characters. A *Moonlighting* teleplay was appreciably longer than most other one-hour shows. Cybill Shepherd was dissatisfied with many of the scripts. She was concerned that her character was portrayed as "bitchy" and had too many screaming moments. As the series progressed, friction increased between Shepherd and Caron.

A 1985 episode was created to be broadcast in black-and-white. Another episode was a full dress production spoofing Shakespeare's *The Taming of the Shrew* that was a reference to the creator's concept for the program. These elaborate productions caused delays and cost overruns. For the 1985–1986 season the production ran out of time and was two episodes short. One episode didn't reach the required 48-minute length. The producers resolved it by having Shepherd or Willis in character talking to the camera. Some shows were delivered a day or two before airtime, thereby making it impossible for the network to promote the episodes. Sometimes reruns had to be substituted at the last minute.

In 1987 after more than two years of teasing and verbal foreplay, Maddie and David finally consummated their relationship. But the show mishandled the romantic angle. At the end of season three, Maddie had a romance with another man, Sam Crawford, played by Mark Harmon (1951–). Impulsively, she married yet another man she met on a train, although the marriage was later annulled. She also suffered a miscarriage. After experiencing Maddie's persona for over two years, viewers were not happy with the arc of Maddie's character—her promiscuity and life choices.

Then real life intervened. In February 1987 Shepherd announced she was pregnant with twins. When she was ready to shoot new episodes in June 1987, Bruce Willis was not available—he was shooting a movie. When Willis returned Shepherd was not available for medical reasons. Shepherd returned to the set in January 1988 but was displeased with all the apology lines the writers had written for Maddie because she'd been absent. The 1987–1988 season was chaotic and only 14 episodes were produced—few featured Maddie and David together. By season four, 20 percent of the viewing audience had been lost.

The 1988–1989 season was filled with tension. A power struggle developed between Caron and Shepherd. Caron left the show and two key writers left with him. Ultimately, ABC made the decision to cancel the show. When the last episode aired, *Moonlighting* had dropped to 41st place in the ratings.

Further Resources

Parker, John. 1997. *Bruce Willis: The Unauthorized Biography*. London: Virgin Publishers.

Shepherd, Cybill, and Aimee Lee Ball. 2009. *Cybill Disobedience*. New York: HarperCollins.

The Morton Downey Jr. Show (WWOR, 1987–1988; Syndication, 1988–1989)

The Morton Downey Jr. Show was a raucous, profane, and rebel-rousing show with roots in the confrontational talk shows pioneered by Joe Pyne (1924–1970) and Alan Burke (1922–1992) during the late 1960s. Morton Downey Jr. (1932–2001) was the son of Morton Downey, a mellow tenor who had been an early television star. Morton Downey Jr. was a radio call-in show host who made the transition to television.

The Morton Downey Jr. Show was first broadcast on October 12, 1987 as a live evening talk show on the New York/New Jersey station WWOR. A professed patriot and a chain smoker, Downey rapidly gathered a cult following, especially among young males who embraced his need to insult guests in a loud, abrasive style. Downey seemed angry about everything, such as heavy metal music and any issue he saw as a threat to the country. Profanity spewed from his mouth and although it was bleeped by the station, the viewers knew what he said. In January 1988, Downey wrapped himself in an American flag and told an Iranian guest to "kiss it." By 1988 *The Morton Downey Jr. Show* was syndicated nationally and for a time enjoyed strong popularity despite a decidedly mixed critical reaction.

The show began in a hallway with Downey striding onto the stage to fervent audience cheers. Two podiums were set up called "Loudmouth 1" and "Loudmouth 2" so audience members could ask questions and hurl insults at guests. There were many controversial shows. One involved black activist Roy Innis (1934–) and Reverend Al Sharpton (1954–), whose heated discussion deteriorated into a fist fight. In 1989 a punched and bruised Downey claimed on live television that he had been attacked and beaten by skinheads in the San Francisco airport. No evidence was uncovered to prove this assertion, suggesting that Downey might have fabricated the story. Audiences began to reject the constant barrage of anger and agitation on the show, and 14 months after its national premiere, it was gone from the airways.

In 1989 Downey appeared on the CNBC cable network as a co-host of *Showdown*, an interview show. In 1990 he came back with a new *Morton Downey Jr. Show*. He seemed to be the same outrageous character, but was considered to be tamped-down on cable TV.

See also: *Vol. 3, The 1990s–Present: Politically Incorrect.*

Further Resources

Downey, Morton, Jr., with William Hoffner. 1989. *Mort! Mort! Mort!* New York: Dell.

Grindstaff, Laura. 2002. *The Money Shot: Trash, Class, and the Making of TV Talk Shows*. Chicago: University of Chicago Press.

MTV (1981–)

MTV (originally an initialism of Music Television) launched on August 1, 1981, as a cable network entirely devoted to broadcasting music videos. The programming was originally guided by "video jockeys" or VJs, and over time, MTV expanded to maintain its prominent place on television, with original programs, reality shows, and award programs for music, movies, and more. MTV is owned by Viacom Media Networks, headquartered in New York City.

A Hard Day's Night (1964), the Beatles' first movie, shot in black-and-white and directed by Richard Lester (1932–), an American filmmaker based in England, is commonly considered the genesis of the music video. The Beatles songs in the movie have fast-moving imagery that expresses the feeling and content of the song.

Throughout the mid-1960s and into the 1970s major record companies paid for promotional films for many of their artists. The films depicted the performers singing and playing their songs in a youth-oriented and visually expressive style. These rock films were mainly shown at music conventions and venues other than television. Before this period, Hollywood made short films that featured singers and orchestras. They were not shot and cut in a straight forward manner, although they were music films, and the usual intent was to memorialize a performance.

In 1977 Warner Cable launched the first two-way interactive cable television system, QUBE in Columbus, Ohio. It offered many specialized channels. One was called Sight and Sound, a music channel that presented concerts and music-oriented television programs. An interactive service was also available so viewers could vote for their favorite artists and songs.

In the late 1970s Michael Nesmith (1942–) formerly of *The Monkees* (1966–1968), had become deeply involved in video music. He created a television series called *Pop Clips,* which was inspired by a New Zealand program.

Music Television Comes of Age

The format that became MTV was devised by media executive Robert W. Pittman (1953–), who became its CEO. Pittman, who oversaw the creation and rapid growth of the music television channel, became a radio announcer at age 15 to earn money for flying lessons. He was an announcer in many cities and then by age 23 was successfully programmed on radio stations in Chicago, Pittsburgh, and eventually at the NBC flagship station WNBC–AM in New York City. He also produced and co-hosted a music video and news show that ran on NBC's O&O television stations. He has been a pilot for 40 years, flying airplanes and helicopters. To be sure MTV would work, Pittman tested the MTV format by producing and hosting a 15-minute show, *Album Tracks,* on WNBC in New York in the late 1970s.

John Lack announced MTV's launch with the words "Ladies and gentlemen, rock and roll," played over footage of the *Columbia* space shuttle launch and also *Apollo 11* (the 1969 moon landing would become a famous image in the network's history). Then an original MTV video was aired in the hard rock style. The *Apollo* moon landing flag is seen with the MTV logo and rapidly changing colors and patterns. The footage was in the public domain. Neil Armstrong's "one step" quote was requested, but the copyright was in the legendary astronaut's name and he refused to allow its use on MTV. This clip was shown every hour in various forms since that first airing. It was pulled in early 1986 after the *Challenger* disaster. Other promotional elements were notable rock stars saying "I want my MTV," such as the Police, Pat Benatar, Pete Townsend, Cyndi Lauper, Billy Idol, David Bowie, and Boy George.

The first video was chosen carefully to send a message that a new age in music was upon us, by running "Video Killed the Radio Star" by the Buggles (1980). At the end of the video, identifying credits appeared at the bottom of the frame. Others tried to create competition. HBO introduced a 30-minute show called *Video Jukebox.* Cinemax, Showtime, and the Movie Channel would occasionally play a video or two in between their movies, and both cable and network outlets embraced the new form and tried to capitalize on it. Having created the concept, MTV was by far the dominant force. Part of the package was to run videos 24 hours a day, seven days a week.

There were VJs who came on between videos to do outros and intros, much like a disk jockey. The original five VJs were Martha Quinn (1959–), Nina Blackwood (1955–), Mark Goodman (1952–), Alan Hunter (1957–), and J.J. Jackson (1941–2004). The MTV motto was "You'll never look at music the same way again."

Early videos were also shot on film. They were short films, the length of a single record. The aesthetic for music videos was rapidly developing. Some had simple narratives that complemented the song, others had an alternate story. Humor and sex were a big part of the attraction. Particular artists seemed to take to the new form more than others. Eighties videos included "Sussuido" with Phil Collins appearing in a small club performing his song. ZZ Top came up with a cute and funny way of interpreting their song "Leg" in which a young woman is harassed by men and women everywhere until some hip girls drive into town and turn her into a hip chick. Taking place in a room, "You Can Call Me Al" featured Paul Simon who was singing with comedian Chevy Chase lip syncing the song and leaving the backup singing to a sort of glum-looking Simon. Instrumental musicians came in and out; sometimes they'd do fancy steps as they played, some were funny and fit the song. Michael Jackson's "Billy Jean" was a huge hit for Jackson, who danced on an urban street, demonstrating great moves and framed by various clips of split-screen manipulation. "Love Stinks" was a huge hit for the J. Giles Band, which was seen playing the song, intercut with images of a marriage, the band partying, and a man playing two trumpets. The Australian band Men at Work had a video for "Down Under" with the band acting out the song in a lighthearted and silly manner. Others who had videos on MTV during this period included Madonna: "Borderline"; the Cars: "Drive"; the B-52s: "Love Shack"; and the Bangles: "Walk Like an Egyptian."

MTV had a wide scope of popular music on the channel: new wave, heavy metal, and classic rock. The artist playlist was enormous so it was able to satisfy the around-the-clock mission.

In 1984 MTV initiated the first MTV Music Awards. In 1986 they began spring break coverage at Daytona Beach, Florida. On July 13, 1985 MTV broadcast the Live Aid concerts held in London and Philadelphia with fundraising for famine relief in Ethiopia. *Dial MTV*, a top 10 video show where viewers could call in to vote for their favorite video, premiered in 1986. Also in 1986 *120 Minutes* came on the channel, which played alternate rock and underground videos. In 1987 *Headbangers Ball* featured heavy metal music and news. In 1988 *Yo! MTV Raps* started on the channel. In 1989 MTV started music-based specials like *MTV Unplugged.*

As music videos continued evolving, many well-known film directors such as Martin Scorsese became involved in collaborating with current artists. Scorsese directed "Bad" by Michael Jackson in 1987, and Spike Lee directed Public Enemy's "Fight the Power" in 1989.

In the 1990s, MTV premiered reality programs unrelated to music, such as *The Real World* and *Road Rules*, the former becoming one of the most successful reality programs on television. They also experimented with reality programs such as *Jackass*, where individuals performed dangerous practical jokes in public.

The network's original programming expanded in the early 2000s with other reality shows that followed celebrities, such as *The Osbournes* (2002–2005) about rock and roll legend and Black Sabbath front man Ozzy Osbourne and his family. Also launched was the program *Newlyweds: Nick and Jessica* (2003–2005), which followed the lives of the pop-singer couple Nick Lachey and Jessica Simpson. Other reality programs that have aired include *Jersey Shore* (2009–2012), *16 and Pregnant* (2009–2014), and *Teen Mom* (2015–).

Scripted programs over the years have included teen soap opera *Undressed* (1999–2002) and the horror show *Scream* (2015–), which was a spin-off from the successful Wes Craven film franchise of the same name.

See also: *Michael Nesmith in Television Parts*; *Vol. 3, The 1990s–Present: Jackass*; *The Osbournes*; *Punk'd*.

Further Resources

Anson, Robert Sam. 2000. "Birth of an MTV Nation." *Vanity Fair.* November. http://www.vanityfair.com/news/2000/11/mtv200011

Blackwood, Nina, and Mark Goodman, Alan Hunter, and Martha Quinn with Gavin Edwards. 2013. *V.J: The Unplugged Adventures of MTV's First Wave*. New York: Atria Books.

Tannenbaum, Rob, and Craig Marks. 2012. *I Want My MTV: The Uncensored Story of the Music Video Revolution.* New York: Plume.

Murder, She Wrote (CBS, 1984–1996)

Murder, She Wrote was a very successful and popular crime-mystery show on CBS featuring a woman as the sole lead character. It was created by Richard Levinson (1934–1987), William Link (1933–), and Peter S. Fischer and was related in tone to other series they created, such as *Columbo* (1968–2003) and *Ellery Queen* (1975–1976). Angela Lansbury (1925–) played Jessica Fletcher, a middle-aged widow who was a mystery writer living in Cabot Cove, Maine, who at times is called upon to solve a real crime. The cast included Tom Bosley (1927–2010) as Sheriff Amos Tupper, William Windom (1923–2012) as Dr. Seth Hazlitt, Michael Horton as Jessica's nephew, accountant Grady Fletcher, and Ron Masak (1936–) as the new sheriff, Mort Metzger, a former New York cop. The fan favorite ran for 12 seasons.

A Great Actress and a Great TV Role

Angela Lansbury came to the series as a very accomplished actress. At only 17 she appeared in *Gaslight* (1944), directed by George Cukor. In 1948 she appeared in *The Three Musketeers* and in the same year, *State of the Union*. Also in 1948 Lansbury performed in a radio production of *Of Human Bondage* for the NBC University Theatre. Among many other films she appeared in the contemporary classic *The Manchurian Candidate* (1962) in the prime role of a maniacal mother. In 1966 she dominated the Broadway stage

Beginning in the 1980s, CBS aired the long-running mystery series *Murder She Wrote.* Pictured is Angela Lansbury who played Jessica Fletcher, a best-selling mystery writer who was also was an amateur sleuth. (AP Photo)

with her lead performance in the play *Mame.* She did Shakespeare's *Macbeth* and wowed Broadway again when she was featured in *Sweeney Todd: The Demon Barber of Fleet Street.* At this point her career was filled with a first-class resume of movies and plays. She won four Tony awards, was nominated for Oscars, and was an international star, but global fame came to Angela Lansbury when she played Jessica Fletcher in *Murder, She Wrote.*

Because of her many commitments, by the 1989–1990 season Lansbury's role was reduced so much that she was no longer the star in each episode. On several shows she appeared only at the beginning to introduce the evening's "Guest Sleuth." In fall 1991 Lansbury returned to the show full-time as Jessica and split her time between Cabot Cove and New York, where she had taken a teaching job. In subsequent seasons Fletcher spent even less time in Cabot Cove, traveling all over the country and the world to solve crimes. By 1994 *Murder, She Wrote* was the longest currently running drama on network television and had consistently placed in the top 10 of the annual Nielsen ratings.

The success of *Murder, She Wrote* was in the plotting and especially each story's twists. Jessica really knew how to read a clue, no matter how complicated or obtuse. She stayed with each case, examining evidence, engaging with good and bad guys, trying to figure out who was who. Angela Lansbury inhabited Jessica Fletcher. She totally convinced the viewer that she was a bestselling writer on the subject of fictional murder and she applied those skills to the real-life murder cases that she got involved in often, situations that occurred in front of her. The dialogue was sharply written and the ensemble casts each week created the right atmosphere.

The crime/murder genre needs many elements to succeed week after week and season after season, but it was the character and the star that drew in the audience. Viewers found it intriguing that a middle-aged woman who was a writer could take the lead in solving a complicated mystery. *Murder, She Wrote* was that rare show that kept the viewer guessing and playing along with the lively goings-on until the very end.

See also: *Columbo*; *Vol. 3, The 1990s–Present: Diagnosis Murder*.

Further Resources

Fletcher, Jessica, and Donald Bain. 2015. *Murder, She Wrote: Death of a Blue Blood.* New York: Berkley.

Gottfried, Martin. 1999. *Balancing Act: The Authorized Biography of Angela Lansbury.* New York: Little, Brown.

Murphy Brown (CBS, 1988–1998)

Murphy Brown was a half-hour sitcom located in Washington, D.C. in the offices of *F.Y.I.,* a fictitious television magazine show. It was created by Diane English (1948–) and Joel Shukovsky. The title role, played by Candice Bergen (1946–), was a high-strung reporter who gave up alcohol and cigarettes after a stay at the Betty Ford Clinic. Grant Shaud (1961–) played her new 25-year-old producer, Miles Silverberg. Faith Ford (1964–) portrayed Corky Sherwood,

This CBS sitcom *Murphy Brown* ran for almost ten years, beginning in 1988. Candice Bergen played the title character, an investigative journalist for *FYI*, a fictional CBS news magazine. Pictured (from left) are Joe Regalbuto as Frank Fontana, Candice Bergen, Faith Ford as Corky Sherwood, Grant Shaud as Miles Silverberg, and Charles Kimbrough as Jim Dial. (CBS via Getty Images)

a not-so-bright reporter and former Miss America. Joe Regalbuto (1949–) played the intense reporter Frank Fontana. Charles Kimbrough (1936–) was the nose-in-the air anchor, Jim Dial. Pat Corley (1930–2006) portrayed Phil, the owner of Phil's, the local bar, and Robert Pastorelli (1954–2004) was Eldin Bernecky, the world's slowest painter, hired by Murphy to redo her apartment.

Over the seasons many actors appeared as continuing characters including Colleen Dewhurst (1924–1991) as Murphy's mother Avery Brown, Scott Bakula (1954–) as reporter Peter Hunt, Garry Marshall (1934–2016) as network executive Mitchell Baldwin, and Paul Reubens (1952–) as the nerdy Andrew Lansing who becomes a network executive.

One of the running gags on *Murphy Brown* was that she couldn't find a suitable secretary. In almost every episode a new candidate would arrive and would be quickly sent packing by Murphy. Her 93rd and last secretary was played by Bette Midler (1945–). Murphy also liked Motown music so titles or lyrics from that catalogue were related to the story line.

Romantically Murphy had a relationship with Jerry Gold, played by Jay Thomas (1948–), and a brief fling with ex-husband Jake Lowenstein, played by Robin Thomas (1949–). She later realized she was pregnant with Jake's baby. She made the decision to have the baby and raise the child herself. The baby was born on the final episode of the fourth season. This plot line pretty much went unnoticed until Vice President Dan Quayle (1947–) made a speech in May 1992 focusing on the "poverty of values" in America and actually criticized a fictional character, Murphy Brown, for having a child out of wedlock. This became a cause célèbre all summer and in fall 1992 when *Murphy Brown* had its season premiere, it had been propelled to the top of the ratings. The baby was named Avery, but there was no mention of the controversy until later episodes. Diane English was outspoken in her rage about the vice president's remarks. Others defended him. Then an hour-long episode made fun of the way Dan Quayle misspelled the word potato.

Many real-life news personalities did cameos on *Murphy Brown*, including Linda Ellerbee (1944–), Connie Chung (1946–), Walter Cronkite (1916–2009), Larry King (1933–), and Paula Zahn (1956–).

In October 1997 Murphy Brown was diagnosed with breast cancer. Her reaction to the situation and the surgery and treatment afterward played out over the course of the season. At one point when doctors were checking for a recurrence of the cancer, she was under anesthesia and imagined she was in heaven having a contentious conversation with God (Alan King, 1927–2004), who told her not to retire but to continue with her work. When she came out of the anesthesia the doctor told her it was just a cyst. Murphy stayed with the show.

Ratings were generally excellent for the show. For four out of nine seasons, the show was in the single digits according to the Nielsen ratings. Until the 10th and last season, the show never placed below 36 in the ratings. Tenth-season ratings were at 86, suggesting the show had run its course. *Murphy Brown* won a Peabody Award and Candice Bergen won five Emmy awards for her efforts.

Further Resources

Bergen, Candice. 2014. *Knock Wood*. New York: Simon & Schuster.

Bergen, Candice. 2015. *A Fine Romance*. New York: Simon & Schuster.

Mystery Science Theater 3000 (1989–1999)

Station KTMA in Minneapolis, Minnesota first aired *Mystery Science Theater 3000*, an original series that had little precedent in television. Premiering in November 1988, the concept was that a janitor and two robots were shot into space by mad scientist Dr. Clayton Forrester and landed on the Satellite of Love. Their purpose was to watch bad movies forever as an experiment about the effect bad movies had on the human race.

There have been local programs whose premise was to screen an inferior science fiction or horror film, at times interrupted by the host and sometimes friends, usually in costume, to make a silly joke or comment. Silent films have been altered so characters speak funny and usually moronic dialogue. On *Mystery Science Theater* the inferior and usually unintentionally funny science fiction movie was shown in a movie theater setting. Our three heroes sat in the theater shown in silhouette and watched the entire film along with the home audience. They made nonstop jokes that were very funny and commented on the movie, how bad it was, and other issues. The movies were rarely seen science fiction and horror films that were beyond bad. They included *Godzilla vs. Magdalen* (1973), *Girls Town* (1959), *Invasion U.S.A* (1952), *The Brain That Wouldn't Die* (1962), *Teenage Strangler* (1964), *Alien from L.A.* (1988), *Kitten with a Whip* (1964), and *The Slime People* (1963).

The creator of *Mystery Science Theater 3000* was Joel Hodgson (1960–) a former stand-up comedian who sold the idea to the local television station in Minneapolis in 1988; a year later it was picked up by the fledging Comedy Channel, which merged with Ha! and became Comedy Central in 1991. Hodgson played Joel Robinson, the janitor, and series writers Kevin Murphy (1956–) and Trace Beaulieu (1958–) voiced the two robots, Tom Servo who looked like a light bulb and Crow who was bug-like. The show quickly achieved cult status. The bad movie aesthetic attracted an audience that especially appreciated the hundreds of pop-culture references that whizzed by as the movie unfolded. In 1993 *Mystery Science Theater 3000* won a Peabody Award.

In the later years of *Mystery Science Theater 3000*, the show took a blow from movie executives who owned the films featured on the show; they claimed they didn't want their films demeaned by all the wisecracks made while the films were running.

In 1996 Comedy Central cancelled *Mystery Science Theater 3000* due to low ratings. The viewers made it known they wanted their show back and the Sci-Fi Channel picked it up. The show narrowed its focus to old, bad science fiction films. By 1996 the show was available in more than 50 percent of American homes.

Further Resources

Beaulieu, Trace, and Paul Chaplin. 1996. *The Mystery Science Theater 3000 Amazing Colossal Episode Guide.* New York: Bantam Books.

Morgan, Chris. 2015. *The Comic Galaxy of Mystery Science Theater 3000: Twelve Classic Episodes and the Movies They Lampoon.* Jefferson, NC: McFarland.

Newhart (CBS, 1982–1990)

After only four years since his previous successful series, Bob Newhart (1929–) came back to network television on CBS with *Newhart* on which he portrayed Dick Loudon, a New York writer of "how-to" books such as *Enjoy Your Tubing* and *Get to Know Your Harley*, who decided to change his and his wife's life by buying an inn in Vermont. Eventually he became a local TV celebrity as the host of *Vermont Today*. The musical theme was composed by Henry Mancini. The opening montage consisted of overhead shots traveling to the rustic area where the Stratford Inn is located. The show's working premise was that the guests and locals were all very quirky characters and Loudon had to be nice and comforting to them regardless of their behavior. The excellent supporting cast was Dick's wife Joanna played by Mary Frann (1943–1998); Tom Poston (1921–2007) as George Utley, the handyman; Peter Scolari as Michael Harris, Dick's yuppie television producer, who was married to the maid; and Stephanie, played by Julia Duffy. Three brothers, two of whom were named Darryl and the third, Larry, ran the Minuteman Café. William Sanderson played Larry, while Tony Papenfuss and John Voldstad played the two Darryls. Neither Darryl brother spoke until the show's final episode. Kirk Devane, played by Steven Kampmann, was the previous owner of the Minuteman Café, who departed the show after two seasons.

The series finale of *Newhart* is one of the most memorable and surprising in television history. A Japanese mogul has bought the whole town to turn it into a resort and massive golf club. Dick and Joanna are the only owners who won't leave. Others receive large payouts. Five years pass; the inn is in the middle of the golf course. The townspeople are now rich and even quirkier than before the Loudons came to the inn. The two silent Darryl brothers speak for the first time, shouting "quiet" in a threesome. Dick is agitated and yells at everyone and at that moment he is hit with a golf ball and knocked cold. The final scene is in a bedroom, the one from Newhart's second series. Dr. Bob wakes up and so does his wife, played by Suzanne Pleshette. He explains his weird dream, which is in effect his existence at the inn from the third series. For Bob Newhart fans, water cooler chatter focused on this clever, crazy surprise for some time, while Bob Newhart was headed for another show.

As always, from his stand-up material through two sitcoms, Bob Newhart was one of the television medium's great reactors. Both shows had terrific writing and great casts, all of which allowed Bob Newhart to give a great comic take with subtlety and slight changes from situation to situation.

See also: *The Bob Newhart Show*; *Vol. 3, The 1990s–Present: Bob*.

Further Resources

Newhart, Bob. 2007. *I Shouldn't Even Be Doing This: And Other Things That Strike Me as Funny*. New York: Hachette Books.

Sorenson, Jeff. 1988. *Bob Newhart*. New York: St. Martin's Press.

Night Court (NBC, 1984–1992)

This clever oddball half-hour comedic series featured an ensemble cast of legal and paralegal professionals working the graveyard shift in a rundown New York City municipal courtroom. The show began as a midseason replacement and immediately benefited from its time slot, which followed the enormously popular *Cheers* (1982–1993).

Night Court featured a constant flow of defendants, litigants, and lawyers, and as it developed episode by episode on NBC, *Night Court* became a rather quirky and droll show as the narratives were more and more about the regular characters, the majority of whom were not married and each of whom had eccentric and conspicuous personality traits. This show was created by comedy writer Reinhold Weege (1949–2012), who had worked as a writer on *Barney Miller,* and the earlier seasons of *Night Court* somewhat resembled *Barney Miller* in style and because it also took place in a dingy Manhattan environment. The original cast included Harry Anderson (1952–), who played Judge Harry T. Stone, a young judge with unorthodox methods who was also an amateur magician, and who sat in the night sessions in Manhattan's district court. Harry T. Stone was only 34 and claimed to have been assigned as a judge in the waning hours of the outgoing New York City mayor's term when the mayor had difficulty filling open judicial assignments. Karen Austin (1955–) portrayed Stone's clerk, Lana Wagner, and Paula Kelly (1943–) portrayed the public defender, Liz Williams. John Larroquette (1947–) played the sexed-up, lecherous prosecutor Dan Fielding, who became a fan favorite as the series progressed; Richard Moll (1943–) was the tall and thick-headed court officer Bull Shannon; and Selma Diamond (1920–1985) was the diminutive and acid-tongued court officer Selma Hacker. In the third season Markie Post (1950–) joined the regular cast as attractive and earnest public defender, Christine Sullivan, who became Stone's love interest.

Over its eight-season run, more than most shows, the cast went through personnel changes. In addition to the main cast there were occasional courtroom regulars who included Terry Kiser (1939–) as reporter Al Craven, William Utay (1947–) as Phil the derelict, Bumper Robinson (1974–) as Leon the runaway, Mike Finnegan as Art the courthouse's hapless janitor, Denice Kumagai as Quon Le, Mac's wife, John Astin (1930–) as Harry's flaky father, Buddy Ryan, and Jolene Lutz as Lisette Hocheiser, the court reporter. Harry Anderson was good friends with singer and actor Mel Tormé (1925–1999), so he appeared in a few episodes as himself.

Night Court mocked the judicial system by demonstrating how it handled the denizens of the night in one of the biggest cities in the country. The humor came from the characters and how the judge used a cockeyed logic to apply justice to them. The show was well received throughout its run and several cast members were nominated and won awards for their performances. John Larroquette won four consecutive Emmys for Outstanding Supporting Actor in a Comedy Series from 1985 to 1988.

Further Resources

Anderson, Harry. 1991. *Harry Anderson's Games You Can't Lose: Guide for Suckers.* New York: Pocket Books.

Caveney, Mike. 1993. *Harry Anderson: Wise Guy from the Street to the Screen.* Magical Publications.

North and South (ABC, 1985–1986)

At a time when novels for television were in their prime, *North and South,* which aired on ABC, was the top-rated miniseries of the season. It was adapted from the novel by John Jakes (1932–) and was structured into six parts with a total running time of 12 hours and a budget total of $25 million. The executive producer was David L. Wolper (1928–2010).

The story chronicles the tensions leading up to the Civil War seen through the eyes of two families—the Mains of South Carolina (South) and the Hazards of Pennsylvania (North). Orry and James, the two sons of the families, become close friends as cadets at West Point. After their time as students during the pre–Civil War period, their lives and the lives of their families are intertwined. The cast included Patrick Swayze (1952–2009) as Orry Main; James Read (1953–) as George Hazard; Lesley-Anne Down (1954–) as Madeline; Robert Guillaume (1927–2017) as Frederick Douglass; Inga Swenson (1932–) as Maude Hazard; Jonathan Frakes (1952–) as Stanley Hazard; David Carradine (1936–2009) as Justin LaMotte; Jean Simmons (1929–2010) as Clarissa Main; Genie Francis (1962–) as Brett Main; Terri Garber (1960–) as Ashton Main; Kirstie Alley (1951–) as Virgilia; and Elizabeth Taylor (1932–2011) as Madame Conti.

Book I (1985) and Book II (1986) of the series take place over more than 20 years beginning in 1842 and concluding at the end of the Civil War (1861–1865). The continuing stories chronicle the marriages, births, deaths, personal bonds, and conflicts of the Main and Hazard families who symbolize the massive gulf between North and South and the differences of a torn nation. On the one side are Southerners defending the concept of slavery and on the other side are Northerners supporting individual freedom and a seismic change in American society. Over the course of a generation, individual sagas of love and loss unfold, told in a hyper-dramatic soap opera style involving intrigues that include adultery, rape, illegal abortion, drug use, family secrets, sibling rivalry, and suicide and murder.

The re-creation of the Civil War was impressive in its presentation of period detail. The acting style was less nuanced and more mannered, less subtle. The dialogue is on the nose and precise. The pageantry and the horror of the war were both displayed. Many guest stars appeared in the miniseries adding color and prestige to the epic. Historical figures such as Abraham Lincoln, Frederick Douglass, Ulysses S. Grant, and John Brown enhanced the production to attract those viewers interested in the historical aspects of the story.

Both *North and South Book I* and its sequel *North and South Book II* were equally successful, but when the producers and network tried to make it a trilogy with *Heaven and Hell: North and South Book III* taking place during the postwar period when the South was experiencing severe problems, the 1994 airing did poorly in the ratings.

See also: *Masada*; *Shōgun.*

Further Resources

Foote, Shelby. 1986. *Civil War Volumes 1–3* Box Set. New York: Vintage.

Jakes, John. 2013. *The North and South Trilogy: North and South, Love and War, and Heaven and Hell.* New York: Integrated Media.

The Oprah Winfrey Show (Syndication, 1986–2011)

Over the years Oprah Winfrey (1954–) has become a major brand, commanding her own empire that includes television, movies, radio, business ventures, magazines, and seemingly endless enterprises. She rose to prominence in 1986 when she became the first black woman to host a successful daytime talk show. Her career began when she became a local news anchor in Nashville. Later she co-hosted a local talk show in Baltimore and moved to Chicago. In early 1984 Oprah became the host of another local talk show titled *A.M. Chicago.* In two months the show beat the popular *Phil Donahue Show* (1970–1996) in the local ratings

The Beginning of an Era

In fall 1986 *The Oprah Winfrey* show was syndicated and enjoyed great popularity. In 1986 Winfrey arranged to obtain ownership of her program and purchased her own production studio in Chicago. *The Oprah Winfrey* show concentrated on one topic a day and was taped before a live studio audience, which

A dominant force in daytime talk shows, Oprah Winfrey's program frequently focused on weight loss. Pictured here on *The Oprah Winfrey Show* on November 15, 1988, is the host showing off her new figure, which was some 67 pounds lighter after a regime of exercise and a liquid diet. (AP Photo/Charles Bennett)

was encouraged to participate and ask questions. Depending on the topic, the show could be very emotional. Winfrey was known to hug her guests, and she and the guests frequently cried on camera. Oprah was exceptionally candid with her studio and home audiences, frequently talking about her own life and even revealing that as a child she was sexually abused. She struggled with her weight and on one show brought out a wagon piled with 67 pounds of animal fat signifying the amount of weight she had lost. Winfrey continuously struggled with her weight, and at one point went on the Optifast diet on which she went from 212 pounds to 145 pounds. She showed off her weight loss in size 10 Calvin Klein jeans. Oprah didn't shy away from volatile subjects. She even admitted past drug use.

In 1987 when the show had only been on the air for five months, Winfrey left the studio and filmed a segment about racial prejudice. It was taped in virtually all-white Forsyth County, Georgia, where there had been anti-integration rallies. Oprah Winfrey used her show for education and inspiration. She created a book club in which she would select a title and encourage her viewers to read it. Bookstores benefited from her endorsement. A special sticker was put on the chosen book, and copies were sold all over the country. She had inspirational speakers as guests and put a lot of emphasis on fitness.

There were plenty of celebrities on *The Oprah Winfrey Show* including Elizabeth Taylor and Michael Jackson. On May 23, 2005 Tom Cruise was on the show acting strangely, jumping around the room and then onto a couch and finally onto one knee to profess his love for actress Katie Holmes. This moment was ridiculed and spoofed repeatedly in other venues.

Oprah also had guests who had experienced pain and tragedy; a boy who killed his friend when the boy used his father's gun, a mother who was dying of cancer trying to cope with the fact that her daughter would have to grow up without her.

Oprah introduced several experts who spun off to their own shows. Among these were psychologist Dr. Phil McGraw who aided people in matters of the mind and heart; Suze Orman, a guru on financial matters; and Dr. Mehmet Oz who addressed health and medical concerns. She was also known for the giveaways as part of her show. Once she gave every member of the audience a new car.

There were controversies on air as when Winfrey made derogatory statements about meat after a major outbreak of mad cow disease. Texas cattle ranchers launched a lawsuit against her; eventually Oprah was found to be not liable. During the 2008 presidential campaign Oprah refused to have vice presidential nominee Sarah Palin (1964–) on the show until after she lost the election.

In 2011 Oprah announced that the show's 25th season would be the last. It was considered the end of an era for millions of people who had watched the daily show religiously.

See also: *The Phil Donahue Show*.

Further Resources

Winfrey, Oprah. 2014. *What I Know for Sure*. New York: Flatiron Books.

Winfrey, Oprah. 2015. *Oprah: 40 Inspirational Life Lessons and Powerful Wisdom from Oprah Winfrey*. Entrepreneurr Publishing.

P.O.V. (PBS, 1988–)

P.O.V. is a film term meaning point of view, either the filmmaker's approach to the material or a shot that represents what a particular character sees. This is the title of a Public Broadcasting Service (PBS) series that presents independent documentaries. Taking the wider definition, it represents as many different ways of presenting content as possible, and a myriad of explorations of a subject. As many as 16 programs were broadcast each year and the series has exposed 400 films to American audiences since 1988. Each one has a social issue focus. Many important directors have aired their work on *P.O.V.*: Michael Moore (1954–), Jonathan Demme (1944–), Errol Morris (1948–), Albert Maysles (1926–2015) and David Maysles (1931–1987), Frederick Wiseman (1930–), and Ross McElwee (1947–).

Whether it is labeled nonfiction television or documentary filmmaking, the genre is the same. The intention is to document an aspect of reality in an authentic fashion. The primary purpose is to teach, instruct, or establish for the historical record an aspect of the content that is the subject of the documentary. Originally these films were all shot on film, which was expensive because it was most often necessary to shoot a high ratio of material. This is because it took multiple takes to get what was necessary for the documentation process and have enough material to obtain a good result in the editing room. A strong point of view (POV) helps focus the movie; a lack of POV may muddle the content and be less successful in communicating to the viewer.

Over its long history, this show has been highly acclaimed. *P.O.V.* has received 33 Emmy awards and 18 Peabody awards. Some of the films aired as part of this series include *American Tongues* (1988), which takes a whimsical look at the way people speak around the United States; *Living with AIDS* (1988), in which a community takes care of a 22-year-old man suffering with AIDS; *The Good Fight* (1988), an in-depth examination of the Spanish Civil War; *Best Boy* (1988), the story of a 53-year-old mentally disabled man who is adapting to an independent life; *No Applause, Just Throw Money* (1989), a look at the musicians and entertainers who work the streets and subways of New York; *Lost Angeles* (1989), depicting the lives and struggles of the homeless in Los Angeles; and *Girl Talk* (1989), a portrait of three runaway girls who have been neglected and abused.

Documentaries are not often booked into first-run movie theaters. *P.O.V* created a vital opportunity to expose viewers to films that explore every area of life with a strong and clear voice.

Further Resources

Barnouw, Eric. 1993. *Documentary: A History of the Non-Fiction Film.* Oxford: Oxford University Press.

Zinnes, Andrew, and Genevieve Jolliffe. 2012. *The Documentary Filmmaker's Handbook: The Ultimate Guide to Documentary Filmmaking,* 2nd ed. New York: Bloomsbury Academic.

Pee-Wee's Playhouse (CBS, 1986–1990)

In 1986 the CBS entertainment division responded to the film success of *Pee-Wee Herman's Big Adventure* (1985), starring Paul Reubens (1952–), and signed him to act, produce, and direct a live-action children's show. Reubens was given a budget of $350,000 per episode, equal to a prime-time sitcom, but unheard of for a children's show. Although Pee-Wee was an original character created by Paul Reubens, his love for children's shows from his own childhood had an influence. Two major ones are Pinky Lee and Soupy Sales. From Pinky Lee, Reubens got the silly behavior and the idea of a uniform; Pee-Wee had a short haircut with a curve of hair in the front, and sported a white dress shirt and red bow tie with a light-colored sports jacket. Also Pee-Wee had that high voice and laugh. The character was like a man-child. From Soupy Sales he was inspired by the interior set with the half-opening door and a flow of interruptions. Sales pushed the standards of good taste on a children's show with jokes and routines more suitable for adults that went over the heads of the kids who were watching. The visualization of the Playhouse was complex, imaginative, and colorful. It was just past a grouping of trees and monkeys and other animals, which were accomplished with clay animation. Instrumental music leads to the theme song sung by Bette Midler (1945–). Inside was a mélange of talking furniture, a talking genie with only his head showing, a talking globe, an outside pool, a sphinx, a slide, a neon sign, a talking computer, flowers, an animated dragon family, talking fish in a tank, go-go dancers, a female cab driver, and an ice cream soup snack. The overall impression was that this just wasn't an ordinary set for a kids show but that Reubens was a performance artist and his background was a surreal house in which he and his friends played.

> As a child Paul Reubens often frequented the Ringling Bros. and Barnum & Bailey Circus. The circus atmosphere intrigued him and influenced his later work. He also loved to watch reruns of *I Love Lucy,* which motivated him to want to make people laugh. Later, he made four appearances on *The Gong Show* as part of a boy-girl act he developed with Charlotte McGinnis called "The Hilarious Bettie and Eddie." He has worked as a waiter and a Fuller Brush salesman. He became friends with Phil Hartman, later of *Saturday Night Live* when the two were in *The Groundlings,* often writing and working on material together. In 1980 he had the part of a waiter in *The Blues Brothers.*

In the 1980s, Paul Reubens created a children's program in the spirit of the 1950s program *The Pinky Lee Show*, called *Pee Wee's Playhouse*. Pictured here is Paul Reubens (right) as Pee-Wee, with Laurence Fishburne as series regular Cowboy Curtis. (John D. Kisch/Separate Cinema Archive/Getty Images)

Pee-Wee's Playhouse was peopled with an eclectic group including Lynne Stewart (1946–) as Miss Yvonne, Johann Carlo (1957–) as Dixie, Gilbert Lewis (1941–) and William Marshall (1924–2003) as King Cartoon, Gregory Harrison as Conky the Robot, S. Epatha Merkerson (1952–), John Paragon (1954–) as the disembodied Genie, Shaun Weiss (1979–) as Elvis, Diane Yang as Cher, Natasha Lyonne (1979–) as Opal. Other actors that appeared or lent their voice to the show include a young Laurence Fishburne (1961–).

Pee-Wee wore pajamas around the playhouse at times, there was a talking window, jump cuts were used to accentuate Pee-Wee's hyper activity, there was a hole in the wall that led to the Dinosaur family's home, one door was made of padded red leather, there was a picture phone, sort of a pre-Skype technology, old vintage cartoons were shown during the program, and the projector that delivered them was displayed.

The show balanced being a show for kids with the occasional joke or routine that was blatantly sexual or touched on other adult themes. Miss Yvonne was a large lady who wore a dress that fanned out at the bottom and was low cut on the top, revealing her cleavage. Some of the characters were aware of this and tried to get into angles so they could see more; at one point Pee-Wee held a mirror under her dress so he could see further up. There were a lot of sexual innuendoes, especially concerning men with big feet as an inference about their private parts.

There is a notion that sometimes children's programming is not strictly for the young or very young.

This theory derives from the reality that often adults are in the room watching a kid's show with a young person. Thus, creators of children's shows bear this in mind and build in material that will "go over the heads" of the young audience and "speak" to the older folks in the room. In some cases the show may be watched more by adults than kids.

Before his television career, Paul Reubens was a comedian in a comedy group named the Groundlings. In 1978 during an improvisational exercise, Reubens created the character Pee-Wee Herman, a silly little man who jumps all over a room and speaks with a high-pitched voice, often punctuated by a laugh that sounds like a short burst from a machine gun.

Reubens created a stage show, *The Pee-Wee Herman Show,* which ran for five straight sold-out months. HBO learned of its triumph and produced a successful special that focused on it. Pee-Wee Herman became an iconic cult figure, combining silly with hip and avant-garde with retro.

With this burgeoning success, Warner Brothers hired Reubens to write a feature-length script. At first Reubens wanted to do a remake of his favorite movie of all time, *Pollyanna* (1960). Well into the writing process, Reubens noticed that everyone on the Warner Brothers lot rode a bicycle. This observation inspired him to write a different script working with actor-comedian Phil Hartman (1948–1998). When Reubens and his producers saw short films directed by Tim Burton (1958–), the iconic filmmaker was hired to direct *Pee-Wee's Big Adventure* (1985), the story of Pee-Wee as he goes on a nationwide search for his stolen bicycle. The film earned over $40 million with a budget of $7 million, therefore reaping almost six times its original cost.

In July 1991 the career of Paul Rubens came crashing down when he was arrested for indecent exposure and a lewd act during a screening in an adult theater. *Pee-Wee's Playhouse* was in syndication and because of the arrest CBS cancelled reruns. Although the playhouse was finished, after some time Reubens appeared in many movies and television shows.

See also: *Vol. 1, 1950s–1960s: Captain Kangaroo*; *Mister Rogers' Neighborhood*; *Sesame Street.*

Further Resources

Gaines, Caseem. 2011. *Inside Pee-Wee's Playhouse: The Untold, Unauthorized, and Unpredictable Story of a Pop Phenomenon.* Toronto, Ontario, Canada: FCW Press.

Paul Reubens: Biography, Actor, Comedian (1952–). Bio. http://www.biography.com/people/paul-reubens-222297

The People's Court (Syndication, 1981–1993)

Courtroom shows have had a long tradition in television. They present drama, interesting individuals, and generally involve low production costs. There were many courtroom programs in the 1950s: *They Stand Accused* (1949–1954), *Famous Jury Trials* (1949–1952), and *Traffic Court* (1957–1959). In the 1980s *People's Court* brought back the genre, but with a twist. It was an early version of reality television. On this half-hour syndicated show, real-life small claims cases were litigated by the actual plaintiffs before a real judge, Joseph A. Wapner (1919–2017), a retired judge of the California Superior Court, who became a star because of his wit, wisdom, and snappy style in getting to the bottom of a case. The show was created by John Masterson (1912–1995), who had created other early reality-based shows such as *Queen for a Day* (1956–1964).

All parties appearing on the show agreed to be bound by Judge Wapner's rulings. A successful plaintiff could recover up to $1,500 and the defendant $25,000. A successful defendant would split $500 with the plaintiff. The show's staff looked for out-of-the-norm cases like that of a strip-tease artist who failed to disrobe completely, or the case of a babysitter who was not paid, and a woman who sued her hairdresser for giving her a bad haircut. The host was Doug Llewelyn (1938–), who interviewed the litigants after the verdicts were announced. The bailiff was Rusty Burrell (1925–2000).

The set looked like a courtroom. The judge sat behind his bench and there were spectators in the gallery. The musical theme for the show was a series of staccato low notes followed by bongo drums. The effect was a hyper-dramatic mood. The show opened with the announcer speaking and introducing everyone in the case, what the situation was, and the amount of money involved in the suit. Most often there was more than one case per show. The cases had snappy titles like "The Case of the Ticked-Off Tenant."

The narrator also explained to the viewing audience: "What are you about to see is real, the participants are not actors. They are the actual people who have all read either a filed suit or have agreed to dismiss their court cases and have their disputes settled here in our forum. . . . The People's Court."

Judge Wapner was quick in everything he did; he read the complaint before coming out to the group. He questioned both sides as a lawyer would. When he'd heard enough of the required answer from the plaintiff or defendant, he cut them off abruptly. He got testy quickly.

The legal consultant for the show was Harvey Levin (1950–). At the show's conclusion Doug Llewelyn looked into the camera and said to the public: "Remember, when you get mad, don't take the law into your own hands—take 'em to court."

See also: *Vol. 3, 1990s–Present*: Court TV.

Further Resources

Levin, Harvey. 1984. *The People's Court: How to Tell It to the Judge*. New York: William Morrow.

Wapner, Judge Joseph. 1987. *A View from the Bench*. New York: Simon & Schuster.

Police Squad! (ABC, 1982)

From the inception of television, police dramas of every stripe were an essential part of programming. Those decades of shows were satirized, skewered, and ridiculed by a half-hour series called *Police Squad!* The ABC show was appreciated but short-lived. It aired for only six episodes. Then-ABC entertainment president Tony Thomopoulos, in announcing its cancellation, somewhat whimsically said *Police Squad!* was cancelled because "the viewer had to watch it in order to appreciate it." Although the show was a failure, it spawned the enormously successful film series *The Naked Gun*. *TV Guide* ranked it seventh on the list of television shows that were cancelled too soon.

The police squad was an elite unit of a big-city police force. Leslie Nielsen (1926–2010) was Frank Drebin, whose rank floated between sergeant and lieutenant. Alan North (1920–2000) was his boss, Captain Ed Hocken. Ed Williams was a demented lab man, Peter Lupus (1932–) was Norberg, and William Duell (1923–2011) was Johnny the shoeshine boy. The show was filled with a constant barrage of sight gags for the viewers. The show was more of a flow of jokes than a comedy narrative. One of the things that may have overwhelmed the audience was that each episode had two titles. One title was spoken by the announcer and a different title appeared on screen at the same time, so episode one was seen on the screen as "A Substantial Gift" but the announcer said "The Broken Promise." This was intended as part of the show's humor.

The creators of the popular and successful movie *Airplane!* (1980), David Zucker (1947–) and Jerry Zucker (1950–), brought their at times adolescent humor to *Police Squad!* Frank Drebin played it straight down the line while crazy visuals and non sequiturs were all around him. A typical day would include Frank and his team arriving at a murder scene to find the body of the victim outlined in chalk written in Egyptian hieroglyphics. A policeman takes a picture, another policeman poses next to the corpse with a big grin. A witness is questioned but has trouble speaking through her braces. Outside is a police car with "Police Car" written in big letters on the hood.

Police scientist Ted Olson would assist on a case, but not always with accuracy. He was given a ransom tape and identified the background sounds as a foghorn and a bell buoy. Drebin drove to the waterfront with an army of policemen. He stopped for gas and noticed that the "bell buoy" sound had a similarity to the bell on the gas pump. The foghorn was really a tuba, so they drove off to find a tuba next to a gas station. The immature humor didn't play well.

The show's humor did better on the big screen when Nielsen starred in a series of feature films based on the series: *Naked Gun from the Files of Police Squad* (1988), *The Naked Gun 2½: The Smell of Fear* (1991), and *Naked Gun 33 1/3: The Final Insult* (1994).

See also: *Vol. 1, The 1950s–1060s: Dragnet*; *Vol. 3, The 1990s–Present: Police Academy: The Series*.

Further Resources

Nielsen, Leslie, and David Fischer. 1993. *Leslie Nielsen: The Naked Truth*. New York: Pocket Books.

Sabin, Robert, with Ronald Wilson, Linda Speidel, Brian Faucette, and Ben Bethell. 2015. *Cop Shows: A Critical History of Police Dramas on Television*. Jefferson, NC: McFarland.

Quantum Leap (NBC, 1989–1993)

This one-hour science fiction fantasy series, which aired on NBC, starred Scott Bakula (1954–) as Sam Beckett, a quantum physicist who became involved in a time travel experiment that went bust, thereby making it impossible for him to return to present time. What Beckett could do was time travel back around 30 years, and he could assume the identities of other people, male or female, young or old. This was an unusual premise for a science fiction series that usually focused on space, spaceships, and aliens. It explored what it was like to be someone else and to understand other personalities and emotions.

There were particular rules to this inhabitation. He traveled only within his own lifespan, roughly from the mid-1950s through the 1980s. He could only minimally change a past event. The course of ordinary people's lives could be altered for positive change, but historical events such as the assassination of President John F. Kennedy could not be changed at all. To the viewers, Beckett appeared as himself no matter what body he inhabited, but the characters around him saw Beckett as that person.

The people whom Sam Beckett "leaped" into were a diverse group: a gorgeous secretary subjected to sexual harassment, an elderly black man in the Jim Crow South, a blind concert pianist, a nerdy teenage hot-rodder, and a young girl about to give birth.

Dean Stockwell (1936–) co-starred as Sam's holographic adviser, known first as the Observer, then later as Al. He was only visible to Sam. Al provided Sam with some details of his new identity and gave him advice about the people around him whose lives could be affected by his presence. Al never seemed to provide all the information Sam needed, which forced the time traveler to improvise with every new identity. Once Sam arrived inside someone, he often found the improvisation difficult. For example, inside the body of a trapeze artist, the stunts were challenging to manage. In addition to Al, there was a small computer named Ziggy to help Sam.

Even with its wacky concept, *Quantum Leap* managed to investigate important social issues including racism, prejudice against the mentally disabled, Vietnam, and problems of single parents. The major theme was seeing the world through someone else's eyes.

Quantum Leap ended its run on April 20, 1993 when Sam leaped into the body of a young and unknown Elvis Presley. The final episode was broadcast as a special depicting Sam leaping into his own body in a 1953 mining town tavern where a mysterious bartender seems to hold the answers about his fate. Other leapers appear as well as ghosts from his life and the Quantum Leap project itself. Sam desperately wanted to go home. When confronted with the decision, he couldn't do it and leaped ahead to the Vietnam War at the same time that Al's wife was about to leave him. He saved her from ruining his friend's life. In the end, viewers were told that Sam never returned home.

See also: *Battlestar Galactica*; *Star Trek: The Next Generation*; *Starman*; *Vol. 1, The 1950s–1960s: Star Trek*.

Further Resources

Barrett, Julie. 1995. *Quantum Leap: A to Z*. New York: Berkeley Boulevard.

Robitaille, Julie. 1994. *Quantum Leap: The Ghost and the Gumshoe*. London: Boxtree.

The Ray Bradbury Theater (HBO, 1985–1986; USA, 1988–1992)

Many of the adaptations that appeared on *The Ray Bradbury Theater* were based on works by the master himself, Ray Bradbury (1920–2010), who also hosted the show. Bradbury was a literary writer who was credited with bringing science fiction into the modern era. He reconceived some of his work for the anthology series that aired on HBO three times a year in 1985 and 1986. Many of the episodes were based on a single Bradbury work, but occasionally the writer would include material from other works, taking a character from one story and integrating it into a different story. An opening sequence from one story might be placed in another. Sometimes characters were renamed and, at times, elements were added to original works to bring the episode up to the allotted time of 23–28 minutes. Some changes were made so the stories would work more effectively in the medium of television. From 1988 to 1992 the USA Network showed the majority of the 65 episodes that were created.

Each episode began in Bradbury's office where the writer was surrounded by memorabilia of his life, which he used to inspire story ideas. Anthology shows encourage guest stars. Among those who appeared on *The Ray Bradbury Theater* were Peter O'Toole, Drew Barrymore, Eddie Albert, David Carradine, Jean Stapleton, and Shelley Duvall.

Some of the stories that were included in the series were "The Lonely One," which referred to the name of a serial killer. "The Happiness Machine" is about a small-town inventor who learned that his effort to create a machine to make people happy was a difficult endeavor. "Tomorrow's Child" was a tale that involved an experimental childbirth procedure that resulted in a child being born in another dimension.

Although Bradbury's writing style and content reflected interest in Americana and American life rather than spaceships and aliens, he still is placed in the company of other giants in the science fiction field: Robert Heinlein (1907–1988), Arthur C. Clarke (1917–2008), and Isaac Asimov (1920–1992). His work influenced countless young writers who were attracted to his subject matter.

Ray Bradbury wrote the landmark novel *Fahrenheit 451* published in 1953 about a time in the future where books were burned by men called "firemen." The novel *Something Wicked This Way Comes* was written in 1962. He was a prolific short story writer and his collections include *The Martian Chronicles* (1950) and *The Illustrated Man* (1951).

All of the 65 episodes were written by Bradbury and many were based on his novels and short stories including "A Sound of Thunder" (1953), "Marionettes Inc." (1949), and "The Toybee Convector" (1984). These episodes later appeared in reruns telecast on the Sci-Fi Channel.

What separated *The Ray Bradbury Theater* from other similar anthology shows such as *The Twilight Zone* (1959–1964) and *The Outer Limits* (1963–1965) was that Ray Bradbury was the mind behind all of the stories. His highly original work made for uniquely inventive narratives.

See also: HBO (Home Box Office); *Vol. 1, The 1950s–1960s: The Twilight Zone*; *The Outer Limits*.

Further Resources

Bradbury, Ray. 2013. *Bradbury Stories: 100 of his Most Celebrated Tales*. New York: William Morrow.

Weller, Sam. 2006. *The Bradbury Chronicles: The Life of Ray Bradbury*. New York: William Morrow.

The Richard Simmons Show (Syndication, 1980–1984)

The Richard Simmons Show was an Emmy award-winning program featuring Richard Simmons (1948–) that focused on health, fitness, exercise, and healthy cooking. The show was enormously popular, drawing a large audience. The hyper Richard Simmons was the host of this syndicated popular half-hour physical fitness and talk show. Simmons was inspirational to the viewing public because he managed to reduce his weight from 268 pounds to 137 pounds. During the show he led his viewers through exercises and presented recipes for nutritious and low-calorie dishes. At times he would focus on specialized areas of health and fitness. One show might be dedicated to yoga, the positions and exercises, its philosophy, and proper eating, cooking a brown rice casserole as a suggested meal.

In the 1970s Simmons opened his own exercise studio originally called the Anatomy Asylum, which stressed eating the right food in the proper portions and offered enjoyable exercises in a supportive atmosphere. Because of the club's success Simmons gained media attention. It began with *Real People* (1979–1984), a reality show where Simmons was shown at his job. Because of his bubbly personality he did guest shots on *Battlestars* (1981), *Body Language* (1984), *Super Password* (1984–1989), *Win, Lose or Draw* (1987), and Nickelodeon's *Figure It Out* (1997).

Positive reaction to Simmons led to a role as himself on *General Hospital* (1963–). His fame grew further when he toured U.S. malls and conducted exercise classes, spreading his brand of fun. In the early 1980s Simmons also hosted *Slim Cookin'* in which he made low-calorie dishes and gourmet delicacies.

Richard Simmons was unique in the world of TV exercise shows. He was funny, motivational, always moving or talking or both, and a man who was on a mission to make people more healthy.

See also: *Body by Jake.*

Further Resources

Simmons, Richard. 1985. *Richard Simmons' Better Body Book*. New York: Warner Books.

Simmons, Richard. 1999. *Still Hungry After All These Years: My Story*. GT Publishing.

Ripley's Believe It or Not (ABC, 1982–1986)

Robert L. Ripley (1890–1949) was an American cartoonist, entrepreneur, and amateur anthropologist who created the "Ripley's Believe It or Not" newspaper panel series (begun in 1918), and a radio and television show that presented and highlighted odd and unusual facts from all over the world. There were several incarnations of this documentary-reality show on television. In 1982 actor Jack Palance (1919–2006), known for his deep, gravelly voice and indelible presence, hosted a version on ABC that ran for four seasons. It was one hour long and was classified as a reality show. Each week startling, amazing, and incredible but true facts were depicted, usually on film. Palance's first co-host was the Canadian actress Catherine Shirriff. In early 1983 she was replaced by Holly Palance (1950–) the host's daughter. Marie Osmond (1959–) of the storied Osmond family was the show's co-host for the fourth and final season.

The show had the complete cooperation of the Ripley estate and they also looked for new material. They traveled to remote areas of the world as Palance relished hunting among the ruins they found. He liked to add an ominous tone to the narration of some of the stories, like finding the skeleton of the queen of Portugal, secret weapons of World War II, and strange rituals. Other narratives included the Texas millionaire who had it stipulated in her will that she would be buried in her Ferrari wearing her sexiest nightgown; the first showing of a long-lost film production number with Judy Garland, Ray Bolger, and Jack Haley from the 1939 classic *The Wizard of Oz*; and life aboard the Skylab space station.

The first *Believe It or Not* television series was broadcast live and hosted by Ripley himself. It premiered on NBC March 1, 1949. Ripley sat in a living room that was decorated with Oriental antiques and mementos of his worldwide travels. Ripley would tell the viewers strange and odd stories often using exhibits or dramatizations. At times the show had a carnival freak show quality. Guests included Kuda Bux, the Indian fakir with "X-ray vision," a man who could thread a needle with one hand while balancing his body parallel to the floor with the other, and a four-eyed Mongolian. Also there were individuals who had triumphed over great adversity and went on to live normal or extraordinary lives.

On May 27, 1949 shortly after 13 broadcasts, Ripley died of a heart attack. To continue the series, several of his friends took turns as host including Doug Storer, the future president of *Ripley's Believe It or Not*. Robert St. John (1902–2003) was the host from the second season until the series ended on October 5, 1950. In 1956 ABC Films Syndication had John Gibbs and Meridian Pictures prepare a *Ripley's Believe It or Not* pilot.

On November 26, 1993, TBS aired a two-hour documentary, *The Incredible Life and Times of Robert Ripley, Believe It or Not*. For a short time in July 1999, the Fox Family Channel ran a daytime cartoon, *Ripley's Believe It or Not,* which followed the adventures of Robert Ripley as a teenager.

In January 2000 *Ripley's Believe It or Not* came back in its original format on TBS hosted by Dean Cain (1966–). In the fall of 2001 the WB network ran reruns previously aired on TBS.

See also: *That's Incredible!*

Further Resources

Anderson, Kirsten, and Tim Foley. 2015. *Who Was Robert Ripley?* New York: Penguin.

Ripley's Special Edition 2016. 2015. New York: Scholastic.

Roseanne (ABC, 1988–1997)

Roseanne was a working-class sitcom created by housewife turned stand-up comedian Roseanne Barr (1952–). In the early 1970s Barr was married and had three kids, and then a fourth child who was put up for adoption. She worked as a waitress while writing comedy for her act and playing local comedy clubs. In 1985 Barr appeared on *The Tonight Show* for the first time, chewing gum and calling herself a "domestic goddess." In 1987 Roseanne Barr had her own comedy special that aired on HBO. In 1988 Roseanne signed with ABC to star in a sitcom with Marcy Carsey and Tom Werner, the highly successful producers behind *The Cosby Show* (1984–1992) and *A Different World* (1987–1993). The series was to be called *Life and Stuff* and it had not been specifically created for Roseanne Barr, but Roseanne with strong comic sensibilities made it her own. It was set in Lanford, Illinois and starred Roseanne Barr (a name she was still known by) playing Roseanne Conner, a wife and mother of three who worked in a plastics factory. John Goodman (1952–) played her husband Dan, a contractor. The show differed from typical family sitcoms by its portrayal of an average working-class family. Neither actor fit the stereotypical skinny body image of Hollywood actors and both were more representative of average Americans. As parents they didn't always know all the answers. Lecy Goranson (1974–) played their older daughter, Becky; Sara Gilbert (1974–), who became executive producer and co-host of *The Talk* (2010), played the younger daughter, Darlene; Michael Fishman (1981–) was their son, D.J.; and Laurie Metcalf (1955–) played Roseanne's unhappy sister, Jackie Harris, a police officer. Natalie West (1956–) was Roseanne's thrice married co-worker, Crystal Anderson, and George Clooney (1961–) played supervisor Booker Brooks from 1988 to 1989.

Roseanne was a bona fide hit, consistently placing in the highest echelon of the Nielsen ratings; in 1990 it reached number one. Almost immediately, Roseanne began to clash with the producers and writers. She was a powerful force who didn't give up until she got what she wanted. The series' creator Matt Williams (1964–) and director Ellen Falcon (1948–) left the show in the middle of the first season. Carsey and Werner stayed away from the studio stage. In 1990 Barr married stand-up comic Tom Arnold (1959–), who occasionally appeared on the show as Arnie Thomas, Dan's pal.

Staying true to working-class life and concerns, Roseanne lost her job and then worked in a coffee shop at a mall. These situations brought on new characters, situations, and plot lines. In 1991 Dan opened his own motorcycle business. Darlene became more and more morose and stayed in her room most of the time. By 1992 Dan's motorcycle enterprise went bust and the family was thrown into a financial crisis. Eventually, Dan managed to get a municipal job and Roseanne raised money to open the Lanford Lunch Box.

The plots, action, narratives, and situations were significant to the success of the sitcom. By and large, they dealt with family and domestic situations emblematic of the middle class but also universal. Just some of the stories developed on *Roseanne* included Roseanne and Dan talking to Becky about birth control, dealing with Darlene caught making out on the couch, the girls watching a slasher/horror movie, and a sleep-deprived Roseanne coping with Darlene's recurring nightmares until they understand the insomnia is actually caused by Darlene's puberty. In one episode, a tornado barrels through Lanford and threatens the family's safety.

In 1990 a Saturday-morning cartoon show based on a younger version of Roseanne's character was created. Roseanne Barr was a lightning rod for controversy and made major headlines in 1991 when she came forth and claimed she had been a victim of incest and sexual abuse. Also in that year she became known professionally as Roseanne Arnold.

At the end of 1992 Roseanne and Tom Arnold launched *The Jackie Thomas Show* on ABC, piggybacking on *Roseanne*'s time slot. The show was a sitcom featuring Tom Arnold; many viewers and critics perceived it as a fictionalized version of the Arnolds' relationship. The ratings were good but the show ran 18 episodes and was not renewed. Roseanne threatened to take her series off the air, but nothing really materialized. In the spring of 1994 Roseanne filed for divorce against Tom Arnold. In 1994 the seventh season premiered and Roseanne was identified only as Roseanne. In the closing credits all the cast and crew were identified only by their first name.

Roseanne's success paved the way for a spate of successful sitcoms fronted by stand-up comedians such as *Seinfeld* (1989–1998), *Home Improvement* (1991–1999), *Grace under Fire* (1993–1998), and *Ellen* (1994–1998). By 1995 Roseanne had become the most powerful woman in television, earning an estimated one million dollars per episode; she also negotiated deals to produce four new television series for ABC.

See also: *Married . . . with Children*; *The Simpsons*; *Seinfeld*; *Vol. 3, The 1990s–Present: Ellen*; *Home Improvement*.

Further Resources

Barr, Roseanne. 1989. *Rosanne: My Life as a Woman*. New York: Harper & Row.

Barr, Roseanne. 2012. *Roseannnearcy: Dispatches from the Nut Farm*. New York: Gallery Books.

St. Elsewhere (NBC, 1982–1988)

This one-hour medical dramedy took place at St. Eligius, a decrepit city-run hospital in Boston. It got its negative nickname "St. Elsewhere" because of its reputation as a dumping ground for patients other hospitals didn't want. In addition to medical story lines, the show was considered a black comedy. It was also labeled *Hill Street Blues* in a hospital. Both shows were part of the MTM (Mary Tyler Moore) Enterprises production company, and both aired on NBC and had large casts and continuing narratives. *St. Elsewhere* received high praise from the critics but low ratings during its inaugural season in 1982. Somehow it was renewed for a second season even though it landed 86th out of 98 prime-time series. In six seasons it never reached above the 49th position in the Nielsen ratings, but it had a loyal viewership and a young, affluent demographic, a market that was of great importance to the networks in the wake of cable television. The series received many Emmy nominations and awards during the course of its six-season run.

The doctors were skilled and caring but unlike other medical shows there were no miracles. Patients survived and got better sometimes, patients also died and, as in real life, they weren't always courageous. The neighborhood surrounding St. Eligius was very down-market and not always safe. A doctor could get mugged in the emergency room, mentally ill patients wandered off, and a drug addict attempted to rob the hospital pharmacy.

A Heavily Peopled Cast of Characters

The large cast of *St. Elsewhere* included Ed Flanders (1934–1995), who played Dr. Donald Westphall, the caring and well-respected chief of staff. Westphall was a widower who lived with his teenage daughter and autistic son. William Daniels (1927–) played Dr. Mark Craig, an abrasive but highly capable chief of surgery, and Norman Lloyd (1914–) was hospital administrator Dr. Daniel Auschlander, a liver specialist who battled his own liver cancer. These physicians were the teaching staff who guided the interns and residents. As with most serial dramas that ran for many seasons, there were cast changes over the course of the series. The large medical team included Ed Begley Jr. (1949–) as Dr. Victor Ehrlich, the clumsy resident who worshiped Dr. Craig. David Morse (1953–) played long-suffering Dr. Jack Morrison, who was put through as much travail as the writers could devise; Howie Mandel (1955–) played Dr. Wayne Fiscus, specialist in emergency medicine. Christina Pickles (1935–) was the often married nurse Helen Rosenthal. Denzel Washington (1954–) played Dr. Philip Chandler, David Birney (1939–) was libidinous surgeon Dr. Ben Samuels, G. W. Bailey (1944–) was psychiatrist Dr. Hugh Beale, Kavi Raz was anesthesiologist Dr. V. J. Kochar, Cynthia Sykes (1954–) was Dr. Annie Cavanero, and Alfre Woodard (1952–) was obstetrician-gynecologist Dr. Roxanne Turner. There was also an impressive roster of guest stars.

The series went beyond the boundaries of a medical genre. Other TV shows and movies were often referenced, and the name of an NBC executive was ascribed to a cadaver. Rock videos were introduced in a dream sequence where Dr. Fiscus goes to heaven with a flashback to the origins of St. Eligius 50 years earlier, revealing many of the older regulars playing younger versions of themselves. Plots could focus on the hospital personnel who despite their talents and abilities were depicted as vulnerable and imperfect.

In fall 1987 St. Eligius was sold to a private health care corporation determined to run the hospital at a profit. Ronny Cox (1938–) was the new administrator, Dr. John Gideon, who immediately was at odds with Drs. Auschlander and Westphall. Ed Flanders left the show after the first three episodes of the season; his character, Dr. Westphall, dropped his pants and mooned Gideon. He returned for the series' concluding episode, "The Last One," broadcast May 25, 1988. In that final scene Tommy, Westphall's autistic son, is at home playing with a snow globe that is a miniature of St. Eligius. The viewers saw Donald Westphall, not as a doctor, take the globe from his son's hands, thus making the assumption that the entire series had been a figment of the imagination.

From the beginning of television, genres have had landmark shows that redefined the category. *St. Elsewhere* accomplished that redefinition for the hospital drama by affording a unique perspective, dark humor, and sense of humanity.

See also: *Hill Street Blues*; *Vol. 3, The 1990s–Present: ER*; *Grey's Anatomy*; *House*; *Scrubs*.

Further Resources

Lloyd, Norman. 2004. *Stages of Life in Theatre, Film, and Television*. New York: Limelight Editions.

Nickson, Chris. 1996. *Denzel Washington*. New York: St. Martin's Paperbacks.

Sally Jessy Raphael (Syndication, 1983–2002)

The 1980s were a hotbed of daytime talk shows, many of which looked for controversy and topics that had been taboo on television. These types of talk shows anchored by distinctive personalities were typically named after the host. Sally Jessy Raphael (1935–) began as a call-in radio show host and made the transition to TV in 1983 with a syndicated talk show. Like most programs of this genre, there was a studio audience and they were encouraged to ask questions and to react to statements made by the guests. The show, initially called *Sally Jessy Raphael* and eventually shortened to *Sally*, featured many titillating subjects, with sexual topics high on the list. Raphael was popular and her program aired for almost two decades. In 1989 she won a Daytime Emmy award for Outstanding Talk Show Host against stiff competition, notably Phil Donahue and Oprah Winfrey.

Running a daytime talk show presented some distinct challenges. It was sometimes difficult for the host to maintain decorum, control off-color language, prevent fights, and avoid outrageous situations. The public wasn't really aware that some of the guests were not who they said they were—they were impostors

Sally Jessy Raphael was the host of *The Sally Jessy Raphael Show* which was on the air from 1983 to 2002 in a very competitive daytime talk show market. Her distinctive looks and aggressive interviewing style made her popular among viewers. (AP Photo/Ed Bailey)

and, awkwardly, there were instances when the same person appeared in more than one venue. One man claiming to be an impotent husband on Sally Jessy Raphael's show also appeared as an unmarried virgin on *Geraldo* (1987–1998). A woman masquerading as a surrogate sex partner had been a wife who hated sex on *The Oprah Winfrey Show* (1986–2011).

Some of the topics discussed on *The Sally Jessy Raphael Show* included overweight people's fashion blunders, female teenage bullies, girls embarrassed by their mother's sexy styles, videotaped indiscretions, and teens who flaunted their sexuality.

Raphael's trademark was a pair of wide-frame bright red glasses, which matched her red hair. The glasses were not by design. One day Raphael was having a hard time reading the teleprompter, so she went out to buy a pair of glasses. She didn't have much time, so she made a purchase in the first store she found. The red glasses were the only choice, so she bought them. Her bosses didn't like the fashion accessory, but the audience loved her iconic look, which separated her from her mostly male competitors.

See also: *Geraldo*; *The Oprah Winfrey Show*; *The Phil Donahue Show*.

Further Resources

Raphael, Sally Jessy. 1984. *Finding Love: Practical Advice for Men and Women*. Gettysburg, PA: Arbor House.

Raphael, Sally Jessy. 1990. *Sally*. New York: Morrow.

Saved by the Bell (NBC, 1989–1993)

This NBC Saturday-morning show for kids and young people was not animated like most of the lineup. It was more like programming of the 1960s in that it was a live-action production. The show took place at Bayside High School in Palisades, California.

Saved by the Bell was a retooling of the Disney Channel series *Good Morning, Miss Bliss* that ran for 13 episodes. Both shows were created by playwright Sam Bobrick (1932–), who began his career writing for *Captain Kangaroo* (1955–1984). The new show followed a group of friends and their principal. It mainly focused on lighthearted comedic situations but on occasion delved into serious social issues like substance abuse, driving under the influence, homelessness, divorce, remarriage, death, women's rights, and environmental issues. *Saved by the Bell* predated the enforcement of the 1990 Children's Television Act and has since been classified as educational and informational programming. To build an audience the series was given two prime-time spots before settling on the NBC Saturday-morning schedule in September 1989. Brandon Tartikoff (1949–1997), then president of NBC entertainment, was responsible for renaming the show. The theme song for *Saved by the Bell* reached back to the 1950s and early 1960s music loved by the retro group Sha Na Na.

The regular cast was led by Mark Paul Gosselaar (1974–) as Zack Morris, a girl-crazy teenager known for his schemes who harkened back to *Dobie Gillis* in the 1960s and, at times, addressed the camera directly and called "Time out!" which froze the action, allowing Zack to address the audience. Mario Lopez (1973–) portrayed his pal A.C. Slater, an army brat and the jock of the group who transferred to Bayside. Tiffani-Amber Thiessen (1974–) played Kelly Kapowski, a cheerleader who was considered the most popular girl in school and was a love interest for Zack. Elizabeth Berkley (1972–) portrayed Jessie Spano, who was a feminist and activist, especially about the environment. Jessie was extremely bright and academically driven. She had a brush with addiction when she took caffeine pills to stay awake to study. She wanted to be class valedictorian and was just slightly behind their nerdy friend Screech, who wanted to let her take the place. In the end she realized friendship was more important than the top spot. Screech, whose real name was Samuel Powers, was portrayed by Dustin Diamond (1977–) and was considered a nerd. He and Zack had been friends since elementary school. He often did Zack's homework. He had an unrequited love for Lisa Turtle, played by Lark Voorhies (1974–), who was gossipy and fashion conscious from a wealthy family. Although she didn't respond to Screech, out of kindness they went to the Senior Prom together. The school's principal, Richard Belding, played by Dennis Haskins (1950–), was the authority figure on the show and genuinely cared for his students and helped them mature and learn about life. Preteens and teenagers related to *Saved by the Bell,* which taught them life lessons in a fun manner.

Two prime-time specials aired on the network during the 1992–1993 season, *Saved by the Bell—Hawaiian Style* and *Saved by the Bell Goes to College*. This last special led to a shift of the series to prime time in the fall of 1993, which was called *Saved by the Bell: The College Years*. A new cast was put together for the Saturday-morning show to continue, now named *Saved by the Bell: The New Cast*. The show was a huge hit and is often cited as one of the best high school television shows of all time. *Rolling Stone* placed *Saved by the Bell* 20th on its top 20 list in 2014 (Collins 2014).

See also: *21 Jump Street*; *Welcome Back Kotter*; *The Wonder Years*; *Vol. 3, The 1990s–Present: Beverly Hills 90210*; *Buffy the Vampire Slayer*; *Glee*.

Further Resources

Collins, Sean T. 2014. "Class Acts: 20 Best School TV Shows." *Rolling Stone.* September 3. http://www.rollingstone.com/tv/lists/20-best-school-tv-shows-20140903

Cruise, Beth. 1995. *Surf's Up! (Saved by the Bell)*. New York: Aladdin Paperbacks.

Running Press. 2011. *Saved by the Bell Guide to Life*. Philadelphia: Running Press.

Seinfeld (NBC, 1989–1998)

Identified as the show about nothing, *Seinfeld* was an NBC sitcom that captured a diverse and massive audience for a more than impressive nine seasons yielding 180 episodes, which in syndication may run late at night forever. The show was co-created by Jerry Seinfeld (1954–) and Larry David (1947–), known later for *Curb Your Enthusiasm* (2000–2011) and for his dead-on imitation of presidential hopeful Senator Bernie Sanders (1941–) during the 2016 elections.

Seinfeld was a stand-up comic whose act contained a unique perspective about everyday life. This perspective translated in large part to the content of the show. David had been a stand-up comic and used some of his experiences and people he had known to contribute to the concept of *Seinfeld*. On the show Jerry Seinfeld played himself, a stand-up comic who lived in an Upper West Side apartment. When not home or in other haunts he was briefly seen on stage doing portions of his routines. Atypical of the sitcom form, the other characters were not co–workers or related to Jerry in any way.

One of many unique facets of this show was that Jerry Seinfeld literally brought his whole stand-up act to the show. This was in opposition to the more common practice of casting the comic as a character, as was the case with Bob Newhart or Lucille Ball. Many issues that Seinfeld dealt with were described during his stage act and then were intercut as scenes or episodes played out with the show's characters.

The Cast

Seinfeld's cast included Jason Alexander (1959–) as the bumbling and hapless George Costanza, who was a realtor at the beginning of the show and then had several jobs including working for the New York Yankees baseball team. Julia Louis-Dreyfus (1961–) played Elaine Benes, Jerry's ex-girlfriend who worked for a publisher, and Michael Richards (1949–) was Kramer, whose first name eventually was revealed as Cosmo, and who was Jerry's very oddball neighbor. There were long story arcs such as George's engagement, which ended to his all too obvious relief when his fiancée died after licking out of date cheap envelopes for their wedding invitations.

There were recurring characters including Jerry's parents, Helen Seinfeld played by Liz Sheridan (1929–) and Morty Seinfeld played by Barney Martin (1923–2005), and George's parents, Estelle Costanza played by Estelle Harris (1928–) and Frank Costanza played by Jerry Stiller (1927–).

Jerry and his immediate friends hung out at Monk's Diner, the exterior of which was actually shot at Tom's Diner in Morningside Heights in Manhattan. The interior was a set.

Some memorable episodes were built around mundane topics such as Elaine showing too much of her breast on a Christmas card, Jerry wearing a silly puffy pirate shirt on *The Today Show*, and eating soup made by the infamous "Soup Nazi." There was a black-and-white episode where scenes were shown in reverse order, first the final scene, a wedding in India, then all the scenes that led up to it going back 13 years before the ceremony.

Insignificant snippets were the focus of scenes or whole half–hour episodes. The scripts were carefully constructed to emulate a stand-up comedian's routine: forgetting a date's name, looking for a parking spot, and the etiquette of double-dipping—putting a chip back in the dip after taking a bite. Bodily functions might also be part of a story line. "The Contest" includes Jerry, Elaine, Kramer, and George attempting to see who could last the longest without masturbating. The episode actually won an Emmy for the script.

The writers based many episodes on real-life experiences. George's story line "The Revenge" is based on Larry David's experience at *Saturday Night Live.* "The Smelly Car" is based on a lawyer friend's troubles with not being able to get a bad smell out of his car. Another writer made up his own holiday called "Festivus." "The Chinese Restaurant" is an entire episode with three of the characters waiting for a table. Many catchphrases now in popular culture originated on *Seinfeld*. One of the most famous is "Yada, yada, yada."

The signature theme music was written by Jonathan Wolff. It consists of sampled bass synthesizer notes played on a Korg M1 synthesizer, which opened the show and was used to transition scenes.

Seinfeld was not an immediate hit. It was introduced in a four-week trial run in 1989. A pilot of sorts named *The Seinfeld Chronicles* aired on NBC on July 5, 1989. *Seinfeld* was strictly a cult show until early in 1993 when it moved from Wednesday nights to Thursdays following *Cheers.* In fall 1993 it replaced *Cheers* as NBC's Thursday night anchor show and was third in the seasonal Nielsen ratings, and then topped the ratings the following season. In 1992 it won a Peabody Award.

The End

The finale of *Seinfeld* was, if not one of the best, certainly one of the oddest episodes. It took the show's loyal viewers by surprise. In December 1997 Jerry Seinfeld announced he was ending the *Seinfeld* series the following spring. Like Johnny Carson and *The Tonight Show* he wanted to leave while he was on top. *Seinfeld* had been the number one or two rated show for the last four years of its run. The last show, which aired on May 14, 1998, was heavily hyped. In the finale NBC was again focused on developing a pilot (for a fictitious show) based on an idea established in an earlier episode. The network loaned Jerry and his friends a plane and they were on their way to Paris for a holiday when the plane was forced to make an emergency landing in Latham, Massachusetts. While waiting for the plane to be fixed they witnessed a car-jacking and they began making jokes about it, resulting in their arrest under the Good Samaritan law because they made no attempt at stopping a crime. The incident quickly escalated with Geraldo Rivera (1943–) reporting live from the scene. Characters from the past eight seasons who had been slighted by the foursome were delighted to testify against them. In the end they were convicted and sentenced to a year in jail. Jerry immediately began doing his stand-up routines for the inmates, who were less than interested. George, Jerry, Kramer, and Elaine had gotten their comeuppance for being so self-centered and obnoxious to everyone.

Seinfeld is a legendary show. Its legacy is simple: sitcoms over the decades have always been about something, staking their success on a concept that may or may not click. Then *Seinfeld* emerged as a show with no central theme and proved that a show about nothing could be a substantial attraction and that the so-called insignificant aspects of life could be compelling.

See also: *Vol. 3, The 1990s–Present: Curb Your Enthusiasm*; *Louie*.

Further Resources

Bjorklund, Dennis. 2013. *Seinfeld Secrets: An Insider's Scoop about the Show*. Praetorian Publishing.

Seinfeld, Jerry. 1994. *Seinlanguage*. New York: Bantam Books.

Shōgun **(NBC, 1980)**

This NBC miniseries was structured in five parts and ran for 12 hours. The cast included Richard Chamberlain (1934–) as John Blackthorne, the English pilot of a Dutch ship that was wrecked off the Japanese coast; Toshiro Mifune (1920–1997) as Toranaga, a powerful warlord with whom Blackthorne united; and Yoko Shimada (1953–) as Lady Mariko, the interpreter with whom Blackthorne fell in love. Also featured were John Rhys-Davies (1944–) as Rodrigues, a Portuguese emissary; Damien Thomas (1942–) as Father Alvito, a Portuguese missionary; Frankie Sabai as Yabu; Nobuo Kaneko (1923–1995) as Ishido, Toranaga's enemy; and Alan Badel (1923–1982) as Dell' Aqua.

Shōgun's author, James Clavell (1921–1994), fought and was wounded in World War II and was interned in a Japanese prisoner of war camp. After the war he became a prolific screenwriter and novelist. His intense interest in Japan led him to write the novel *Shōgun* (1975), the first book of Clavell's Asian Trilogy. The story took place in feudal Japan in the early 1600s. Clavell executive produced the miniseries.

The series was written for television and produced by Eric Bercovici (1933–2014) and was directed by Jerry London (1947–), who directed more than 40 television movies. The miniseries was filmed on location and made extensive use of the Japanese language, which was captioned in English. When *Shōgun* was rerun in 1983 additional narration was spoken by Orson Welles (1915–1985) to clarify the Japanese dialogue.

By sharing his fascination with Japanese history and Japanese culture, especially the way life was lived there centuries ago, Clavell struck a chord with American viewers. So the miniseries managed to put across a strong dramatic story while simultaneously offering a history lesson. The story is loosely based on an Eng-

Shōgun, based on the bestselling historical novel by James Clavell, was a popular 1980 miniseries about life in feudal Japan as experienced by English sailor John Blackthorne. Pictured here are Toshiro Mifune (left) as Yoshi Toranaga and Richard Chamberlain as John Blackthorne. (Silver Screen Collection/Getty Images)

lish navigator, William Adams, who traveled to Japan in 1600 and rose high in the service of the shōgun, who was viewed as the real ruler of the country until feudalism was abolished in 1867.

The story line begins when Pilot-Major John Blackthorne is blown ashore on the east coast of Japan after a violent storm and is imprisoned by samurai warriors. When he is released he needs to adapt to the Japanese culture in order to survive. There are religious differences as Blackthorne is Protestant and the Catholic presence in Japan is strong. However, not all Japanese are responding to the introduction of Catholicism and Blackthorne comes to the attention of Lord Toranaga, who is competing with other samurai for the powerful position of shōgun. Over time, Blackthorne is taught Japanese by the beautiful Lady Mariko with whom he is infatuated but who is married. Blackthorne saves Toranaga's life when he is threatened by an enemy. In gratitude Toranaga makes him a samurai and a *hatamoto,* a personal retainer. Blackthorne works to rebuild his ship so he can leave Japan, but Toranaga recognizes that the karma that brought Blackthorne to Japan will keep him there as a trusted samurai. In an epilogue the viewers learn that the emperor of Japan offers Toranaga the title of shōgun.

See also: *Masada*; *North and South.*

Further Resources

Clavell, James. 1986. *Shōgun.* New York: Dell Reissue edition.

Ryder, Jeffrey. 1988. *Richard Chamberlain.* New York: Dell.

The Simpsons (Fox, 1989–)

Now the most successful and longest-running animated program in the history of American prime-time television, *The Simpsons* immediately struck a chord with viewers across the country when it first appeared as a series of 48 brief cartoon segments on *The Tracey Ullman Show* from 1987 to 1989. With its subversive humor and wit, *The Simpsons* has made an indelible impression on American pop culture, and the characters have become television icons.

The Simpsons is the brainchild of cartoonist Matt Groening, also the creative force behind the weekly comic strip *Life in Hell.* In the mid-1980s, Groening's strip was brought to the attention of Hollywood producer James L. Brooks, who invited the writer to develop a series of short, animated skits to run as "bumpers" into and out of commercials on Ullman's program. Skeptical about surrendering creative control of his *Life in Hell* characters, Groening decided to create something new. The result was *The Simpsons*, featuring Homer and Marge and their three children, Bart, Lisa, and Maggie. The initial characters were named for Groening's family members, with "Bart," an anagram of "brat," substituted for "Matt." *The Simpsons* is a Gracie Films production in association with 20th Century Fox Television. James L. Brooks, Groening, and Al Jean are the executive producers. Film Roman, a Starz Media company, is the animation house and Mike B. Anderson is supervising animation director.

The Simpsons' run on *The Tracey Ullman Show* was followed by a 1989 Christmas special, after which the show was awarded its own weekly prime-time slot. It debuted on the Fox network on December 17, 1989. The Simpson family has become as prominent a part of American culture as any TV family that went before, including the Nelsons, the Cleavers, the Jeffersons, the Huxtables—or the Flintstones, to whom episodes of *The Simpsons* often pay homage.

Diverging from previous family sitcoms, *The Simpsons* turned the genre into something much more modern and cutting-edge. From the beginning, the show has satirized American suburban life, providing wry, pointed commentary on American popular culture and concerns of the day, from energy, to pollution, corporate corruption, politics, gun control, and violence on television. *The Simpsons* themselves have become beloved figures, symbolic of all that is good—and bad—about American life. Although the family is portrayed as wittily dysfunctional, many episodes examine their relationships and bonds with each other. The Simpsons rush home to share a couch and watch television, but they do so together, remaining a close-knit unit, despite seeming to drive each other crazy.

The Simpson family lives at 742 Evergreen Terrace in a town called Springfield in an unidentified state. Homer, the father, who is voiced by actor Dan Castellaneta, works as a safety inspector at the Springfield Nuclear Power Plant. A caricature of the American working-class husband and father, he is crude, overweight, incompetent, clumsy, lazy, and ignorant, yet fiercely devoted to his family. He loves his wife and kids almost as much as he loves beer and doughnuts. Homer is the son of Abraham, also voiced by Castellaneta, and Mona Simpson and has a half-brother, Herb Powell.

Homer's wife, Marge Simpson, voiced by Julie Kavner, is a stereotypical suburban housewife and mother who is patient, moral, and forever trying to maintain order in her household, as generations of TV moms have before her. Her most distinguishing feature is her tall, blue beehive hairdo. Marge's parents are Clancy and Jacqueline Bouvier. She has two sisters, Patty and Selma, also voiced by Kavner.

Homer and Marge are the proud parents of Bart, Lisa, and Maggie. Ten-year-old Bart is voiced by Nancy Cartwright, who also plays several of the other Springfield children. He is a troublemaker and proud underachiever, known for catchphrases such as "Eat my shorts," "Ay, caramba!" and "Don't have a cow, man!" Lisa (Yeardley Smith) is a precocious eight-year-old activist and the brains of the family. Maggie, the year-old baby, rarely speaks, but communicates by sucking on a pacifier. Maggie is also, paradoxically, a crack shot.

The family owns a dog, named Santa's Little Helper, and a cat, Snowball V, renamed Snowball II in an episode of the program. Both pets have had starring roles. Despite the celebration of holidays and birthdays, the Simpsons do not physically age and still appear just as they did at the end of the 1980s.

In addition, *The Simpsons* features a number of recurring secondary characters. Besides Homer and Abraham, Castellaneta voices Groundskeeper Willie; Bart's TV hero, Krusty the Clown; and "Diamond" Joe Quimby, the modestly corrupt mayor of Springfield. Hank Azaria supplies the voices of the Kwik-E-Mart clerk Apu, bartender Moe Szyslak, and Police Chief Wiggum. Harry Shearer voices Homer's boss, C. Montgomery Burns, as well as Burns's toadying personal assistant Waylon Smithers, neighbor Ned Flanders, local news anchor Kent Brockman, the Reverend Lovejoy, and the much-embattled Principal Skinner.

Numerous guest actors have voiced characters for the show over the years, among them Phil Hartman, Joe Mantegna, Kelsey Grammer, Mel Brooks, Bob Hope, Paul Newman, Richard Gere, Ian McKellen, Brooke Shields, Mel Gibson, James Woods, Pierce Brosnan, and Jon Lovitz. Appearances by figures from the world of popular music have also been a frequent feature. Three of the Beatles have appeared, as have Mick Jagger and Keith Richards of the Rolling Stones. Little Richard, Lenny Kravitz, Elvis Costello, Elton John, Sting, Tom Jones, Linda Ronstadt, Tony Bennett, and James Brown have also appeared, as have such groups as U2, R.E.M., Smashing Pumpkins, the Red Hot Chili Peppers, and Aerosmith.

The Simpsons has also featured appearances by talk-show and game-show hosts, including *Jeopardy*'s Alex Trebek, Johnny Carson, Jay Leno, Steve Allen, Larry King, Charlie Rose, and Conan O'Brien, who was a writer for the program before becoming the host of *Late Night with Conan O'Brien*.

A parody of TV and movies, as well as of American life, episodes of *The Simpsons* have drawn from a broad range of other creative efforts, including *The X-Files* and films as divergent as *The Right Stuff* and *Mr. Smith Goes to Washington*. Since its inception, *The Simpsons* has been heavily influenced by stories and characters from science fiction and fantasy. The annual "Treehouse of Horror" episode, for example, is a direct tribute to the classic TV series *The Twilight Zone*. *The Simpsons* constantly pokes fun at Fox, its sponsoring network.

The show received five Emmy nominations for the 2008–2009 season. The series has won 24 Emmy awards over its two-decade-long run: 12 for outstanding voice-over performance, 10 for outstanding animated program, and two for outstanding original main title theme music. In 2010, *The Simpsons* received two Emmys, one for outstanding voice-over performance and another for outstanding individual achievement in animation.

A show that makes viewers laugh even as it makes them think, *The Simpsons* has become an integral part of the cultural landscape of contemporary America, as well as a significant force in television itself. The explosive popularity of *The Simpsons* helped to trigger a renaissance in prime-time television animation, while the show's irreverent satire paved the way for more outrageous programs, such as *South Park*.

On February 19, 2012, *The Simpsons* hit the 500th episode milestone. This accomplishment has only been achieved by two other long-running television series: *Gunsmoke* (1955) and *Lassie* (1954).

Barbara Lencheck

See also: Fox Broadcasting Company; *Vol. 3, The 1990s–Present: Family Guy*; *South Park.*

Further Resources

Booker, M. Keith. 2006. *Drawn to Television: Prime Time Television from the Flintstones to Family Guy*. Westport, CT: Praeger.

Gimple, Scott M., ed. 1999. *The Simpsons Forever!* New York: HarperCollins.

Westfahl, Gary. 2005. *The Greenwood Encyclopedia of Science Fiction and Fantasy*. Volume 3. Westport, CT: Greenwood Press.

Skag (NBC, 1980)

Writer Abby Mann (1927–2008), best known for the television drama *Judgment at Nuremberg*, created *Skag*, a drama about a blue-collar family in crisis. *Skag* was a one-hour show on NBC that began as a three-hour television movie on January 6, 1980. It had a stellar cast led by Academy Award–winning actor Karl Malden (1912–2009) as Pete "Skag" Skagska, a foreman at a Pittsburgh steel mill, and Piper Laurie (1932–) as Skag's second wife, Jo. Craig Wasson (1954–) was their son David, Peter Gallagher (1955–) was their son John, Leslie Ackerman (1956–) portrayed their daughter Barbara, and Kitty Holcomb was their other daughter Patricia.

Skagska suffered a crippling stroke, which forced him to stay home temporarily to recuperate and try to pull his life together. He is agitated about his second wife, the only Jewish member in a staunchly Serbian Orthodox Catholic household, who was 12 years his junior. His relationship with his children was strained. David, his oldest son, worked with his father at the mill but wanted to break away from factory life. John, who was 24, was in medical school and more interested in making money than about his family. Patricia was 18, shy and insecure, and 15-year-old Barbara was having promiscuous sex to make herself popular despite her obesity. Skag's elderly father Peter, played by George Voskovec (1905–1981), was unable to speak and was partially incapacitated by a major stroke; he lived in the Skagska household. Whalen, played by Powers Boothe (1948–), was a young steelworker who took over Skag's job while he recovered and coveted the job on a regular basis. Skag was a traditionalist and a fiercely stubborn man trying to adjust to a rapidly changing world whose values he didn't understand.

The themes on *Skag* were heavy going even for a nighttime drama: impotence, senility, prostitution, labor conflicts, jealousy, family discord, and the generational struggles caused by changing mores. Critics gave *Skag* high marks for its realism and its pull-no-punches approach to life's adversity. It was highly publicized and at first was well received, but when it moved to its regular Thursday night slot, it slid down dramatically in the ratings. It may have been perceived as too depressing. A full-page nationwide newspaper campaign was launched urging viewers to save the show, but *Skag* didn't catch on, and after only five regular episodes it was cancelled for lack of viewing interest.

Further Resources

Laurie, Piper. 2011. *Learning to Live Out Loud: A Memoir*. New York: Random House.

Malden, Karl, with Carla Malden. 1997. *When Do I Start?* New York: Limelight.

Solid Gold (Syndication, 1980–1988)

This one-hour syndicated variety show put a spotlight on the week's top records with personal appearances or video clips of the featured recording artists. The Solid Gold Dancers, a high-energy dance troupe with skimpy and sexy costumes, were also part of the countdown production.

For the first season Dionne Warwick (1940–) was the show's host. Each week she was joined by a guest host. For the 1981–1982 season the co-hosts were Andy Gibb (1958–1988), youngest brother of the Bee Gees brothers, and Marilyn McCoo (1943–), formerly of the Fifth Dimension. In fall 1982 Rex Smith (1955–) succeeded Gibb as co-host with McCoo. For the 1983–1984 season, McCoo was the sole host. In fall 1984 disc jockey Rick Dees (1950–), who became infamous to some, famous to others with his big hit record "Disco Duck," became the sole host of the show. He did the job for a season and then in the fall of 1985 he was replaced by Dionne Warwick; in another change McCoo replaced Warwick in the fall of 1986. In the fall of 1987 the show underwent a title change to *Solid Gold in Concert* to let audiences know that most of the performers were playing and singing live during the broadcast.

Some of the many performers and acts who appeared on *Solid Gold* included Chuck Berry, Michael Bolton, Marie Osmond, Bachman-Turner Overdrive, Captain and Tennille, Fat Boys, Glenn Campbell, the Byrds, Peter Frampton, Tiffany, and Grace Jones. Wayland Flowers (1939–1988) and his hand puppet Madame were regulars on the show. Madame had a very salty mouth, which was kept within television guidelines.

Later two new segments were added to *Solid Gold*. One involved an interview in which disc jockey Nina Blackwood (1955–) talked to leading rock and pop stars. The other was called "Flashback" in which rock stars from the 1950s, 1960s, and 1970s recreated their big hits from the past.

In June 1984 a second version of the series aired briefly with the title *Solid Gold Hits*. It aired daily in a half-hour format. The host was Grant Goodeve (1952–), an actor who appeared on *Eight Is Enough*.

See also: *Vol. 1, 1950s–960s: Hullabaloo.*

Further Resources

Davis, Billy, and Marilyn McCoo with Mike Yorkey. 2004. *Up, Up, and Away*. Chicago: Northfield Publishing.

Warwick, Dionne, and David Freeman Wooley. 2010. *My Life, as I See It: An Autobiography*. New York: Atria Books.

Star Search (CBS, Syndication, 1983–1995)

Ed McMahon (1923–2009) was the host of this syndicated talent competition for singers, dancers, actors, and comics. Originally the competition was divided into eight categories: male actor, female actor, female spokesperson, male vocalist, female vocalist, vocal group, comic, and dancer. Each week seven pairs of contestants competed in those categories. The acting competition was conducted with the contestant playing a scene with actors like Tony Geary and Joan Collins. The spokesmodel posed for glamour shots taken by a fashion photographer and also read the rules of the competition. A panel of judges comprised of producers and talent agents determined the winners, who returned the next week to face a new challenger in their category. The longest reigning champions in each category returned in the spring for a final competition to determine who was the best new star of the year and won up to $100,000.

There had been talent competitions on television before, but *Star Search* was slick and well produced. It was created by Alfred Masini (1930–2010), who won more than 35 Emmy awards and also conceived *Entertainment Tonight. Star Search* produced a long list of winners who went on to professional acclaim. They included the country music band Sawyer Brown, Tiffany, Britney Spears, Christina Aguilera, Brian Bloom, Sinbad, Amy Stock, Dennis Miller, Rosie O'Donnell, Drew Carey, Martin Lawrence, and Chris Rock.

In fall 1992 a daily version of *Star Search* premiered, but lasted only a few months, while the weekly show continued. In fall 1994 the show was renamed *Ed McMahon's Star Search* and a male spokesmodel category was added. Former MTV VJ Martha Quinn (1959–) emceed the vocal competition segments.

See also: *Vol. 1, The 1950s–1960s: Ted Mack and the Original Amateur Hour*; *Vol. 3, The 1990s–Present: America's Got Talent*; *American Idol*.

Further Resources

Lane, Chris. 2015. *How to Create an Amateur Show Without Killing Anyone: A Complete Guide for Directors and Producers Planning an Amateur Stage Show*. Amazon Digital Services.

McMahon, Ed. 2001. *For Laughing Out Loud: My Life and Good Times*. New York: Warner Books.

Star Trek: The Next Generation (Syndication, 1987–1994)

The original NBC *Star Trek* (1966–1969) television series was not a success in its premiere run, but it became a bonanza in continual reruns. The first five *Star Trek* movies were all box office hits, so it was logical that another *Star Trek* TV series might be well received, but it took 18 years to test the theory. The creator of the original series, Gene Roddenberry (1921–1991), was the executive producer of *Star Trek: The Next Generation*, which was syndicated and aired for seven seasons. This show took place in the early 24th century around 80 years after the original series. It featured a new and larger starship *Enterprise*. The crew numbered more than 2,000 and this time there were children aboard. The new cast included Patrick Stewart (1940–) as Captain Jean-Luc Picard. Johnathan Frakes (1952–) played Commander William Riker. LeVar Burton (1957–) was Lieutenant Geordi La-Forge, the blind flight controller and later chief engineer who wore a special sensor enabling him to see. This character was named to honor a real-life "trekker," George La Forge, a disabled fan who died in 1975. Denise Crosby (1957–) was security chief Tasha Yar, Gates McFadden (1949–) was medical officer Dr. Beverly Crusher, Marina Sirtis (1955–) was half–alien Starfleet counselor Denna Troi, and Brent Spiner (1949–) portrayed Lieutenant Commander Data, an android. Michael Dorn (1952–) was Worf, a Klingon. Wil Wheaton (1972–) was Beverly's son Wesley, who became a crew member in the second season.

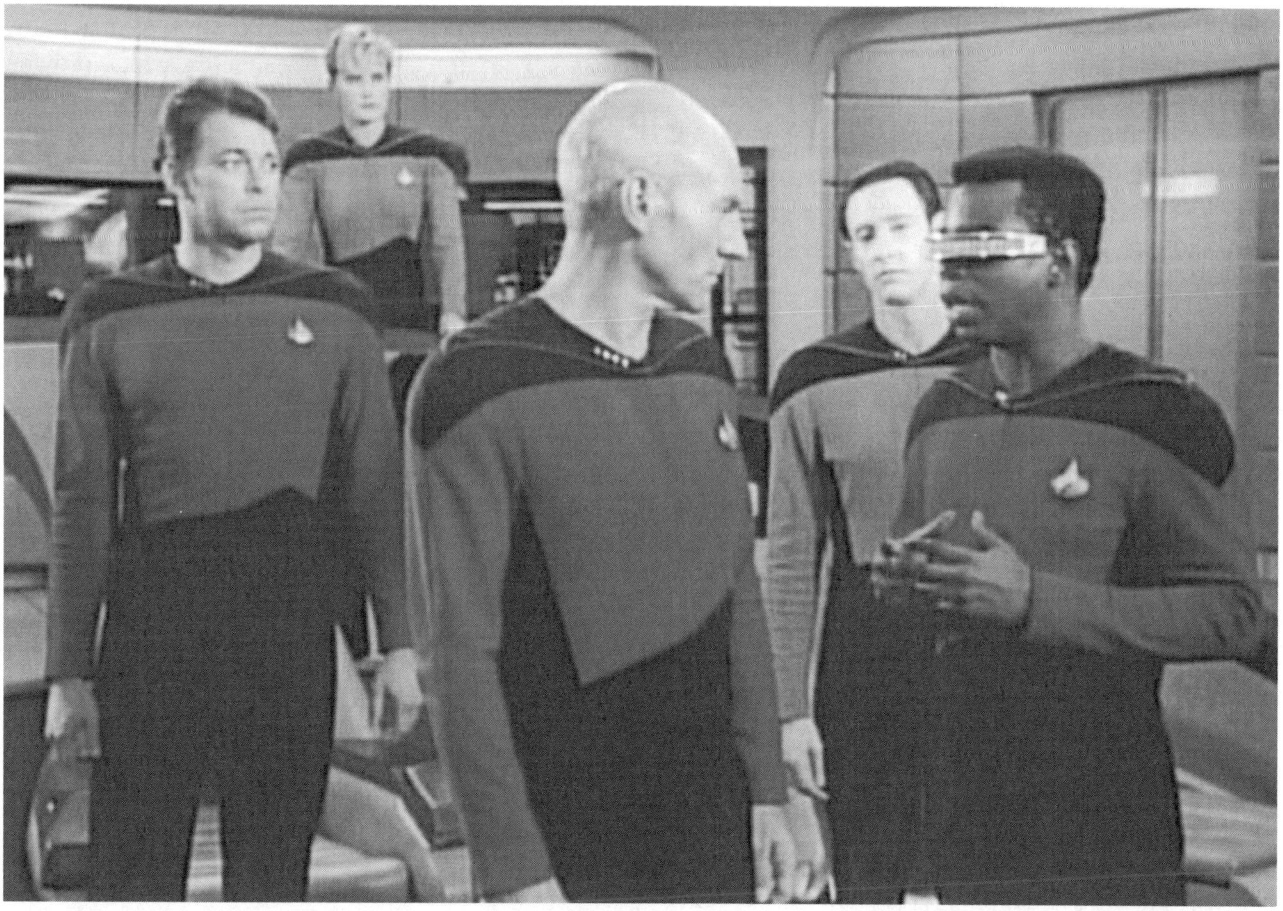

The gradual success of the original *Star Trek* eventually spawned a reboot in the late 1980s. *Star Trek: The Next Generation* featured (from left) Jonathan Frakes as William Riker, Denise Crosby as Tasha Yar, Patrick Stewart as Jean-Luc Picard, Brent Spiner as Data, and LeVar Burton as Geordi La Forge. (CBS Photo Archive/Getty Images)

Colm Meaney (1953–) was transportation chief Miles O'Brien, Diana Muldaur (1938–) played medical officer Dr. Kate Pulaski, and Whoopi Goldberg (1955–) appeared occasionally as Guinan, hostess of the *Enterprise*'s lounge.

Gene Roddenberry made sure that the new series featured stories that had a strong moral sense and social conscience. Without Roddenberry *Star Trek: The Next Generation* would not have been a worthy successor to *Star Trek*. He was able to figure out how space life would develop in 80 years. It was its authenticity and believability and Roddenberry's respect for the original that contributed to the *Star Trek* legacy.

Star Trek: The Next Generation was an excellent example of how *Star Trek* constructs would be presented in the future. The quality of the 1980s–1990s output took advantage of the leap in television production since *Star Trek* was first on the air. The visual effects were more sophisticated as were the sets and costumes. There were other actors and characters who appeared periodically, most notably Leonard Nimoy (1931–2015), who did a guest spot as Spock in a two-part 1991 episode. As a sequel series *Star Trek: The Next Generation* was more popular than the original *Star Trek* in its first run. It also spawned a spin-off series, *Star Trek: Deep Space Nine* (1993–1999), and a successor series, *Star Trek: Voyager* (1991–2001). The two-hour finale for *Star Trek: The Next Generation* broadcast in May 1994 and was the highest rated syndicated program of the season. In 1994 a feature film, *Star Trek Generation,* was released. It included most of the cast of *Star Trek: The Next Generation* and William Shatner (1931–) as Captain James T. Kirk.

See also: *Battlestar Galactica*; *Vol. 1, The 1950s–1960s: Star Trek*; *Vol. 3, The 1990s–Present: Stargate SG-1*; *Star Trek: Deep Space Nine*.

Further Resources

Block, Paula, and Terry Erdmann. 2012. *Star Trek: The Next Generation 365*. New York: Harry N. Abrams.

McMahan, Mike. 2015. *Warped: An Engaging Guide to the Never-Aired 8th Season (Star Trek: The Next Generation)*. New York: Pocket Books.

Starman (ABC, 1986–1987)

Usually television adapts a motion picture as a series sourcing material available from the original script; then story lines are devised based on it. *Starman* is unusual in that this ABC TV series began 15 years after the feature film's narrative ends. The movie *Starman* was released in 1984. It was the eighth motion picture directed by John Carpenter (1948–). He is best known as a director of horror films and rose to prominence with *Halloween* (1978).

The movie *Starman* is classified as a science fiction romance film. The story concerns a Starman played by Jeff Bridges (1949–), who visits Earth after getting a message that the planet welcomes aliens. In spite of that the Starman is shot down and crashes into a bay in Wisconsin. He finds the home of the recently widowed Jenny Hayden, played by Karen Allen (1951–). The Starman takes a lock of hair from her deceased husband and uses it to create a human body. He has with him seven silver spheres, which provide energy to make miracles.

At first Jenny is frightened by the Starman but she helps him to reach a crater in Arizona where he must be or he will die. The authorities find out about the Starman and chase him and Jenny across the country. They crash the car and continue by hitchhiking. While stowing away on a train they make love and he tells her, "I gave you a baby tonight." He tells her the baby will be the son of her late husband but will have all of the Starman's knowledge. National security agencies learn about the Starman and plan an intervention even though the government had invited aliens in peace. Another government official helps the now dying Starman to escape. A space vehicle arrives and the Starman is restored to full health. Although Jenny wants to go with him, he tells her she couldn't live on his planet. Before his departure, he gives her the last silver sphere and tells her their son will know what to do with it.

The television series *Starman* is more science fiction and less romance than the movie. Robert Hays (1947–) was the Starman and Jenny was played by Erin Gray (1950–).The son, Scott Hayden, was portrayed by C. B. Barnes (1972–). The Starman returned to earth to find his now-orphaned son whose foster parents died and to look for the boy's mother, Jenny.

The Starman assumed the identity of photographer Paul Forrester, who was killed in a helicopter crash. The boy helped his father learn about the ways of Earth and humans. Michael Cavanaugh (1942–) played George Fox of the Federal Security Agency who hunted the fugitive father and son who are considered threats to human society. The Starman and the boy eventually are reunited with Jenny in Arizona.

Starman the television series didn't do as well as the movie. It only ran one season, but the concept of starting a TV version where the film ended seemed a novel idea worthy of consideration.

Further Resources

Fulton, Roger, and Roger Betancourt. 1998. *The Sci-Fi Channel Encyclopedia of TV Science Fiction.* Austin, TX: Aspect.

Telotte, J. P. 2014. *Science Fiction TV*. New York: Routledge.

Super Dave (Showtime, 1987–1991)

The character Super Dave Osborne, a parody of uber-stunt performer Evel Knievel (Robert Craig, 1938–2007), was first introduced on *Bizarre,* a Canadian sketch program that aired from 1980 to 1986, hosted by John Byner and produced by CTV, and on Showtime in the United States. Super Dave Osborne was the creation of comedian Bob Einstein (1942–). This offbeat sketch comedy and variety show ran five seasons.

Stunts That Outdo Other Stunts

Super Dave is constantly setting up and performing death-defying stunts that go wrong. He is a man who acts as if he is at the top of his game, performing never-done-before feats. He lords over an empire built on the enormous fees obtained from television stations and networks, but he is really a bumbling stuntman. Einstein looks the part, a big man always dressed in a white jumpsuit with red and blue trimmings, connoting a blend of Evel Knievel and Elvis Presley.

The centerpiece of the show was a big stunt performed by Super Dave. The humor existed both in Dave's verbiage and from others in his entourage. There was also the onsite television announcer Michael Walden who gave overblown introductions and interviewed Dave. Walden was most likely to be unhelpful when things went wrong and Dave needed help when Walden signed off as the credits rolled. The stunts were comedic gems: Super Dave was on top of an endlessly tall building. He planned to jump from the top but the wind was too strong and he canceled the feat, concerned he wouldn't survive the attempt. A reporter talked with him and then left, closing the door, giving Dave a shove into the air where he fell rapidly. Dave landed in the parking lot. An ambulance arrived and rode right over him. The laugh track is timed perfectly to emphasize the absurdity of the proceedings.

Musical guests and variety acts appeared on the show including Ray Charles, Celine Dion, k.d. lang, Jerry Lee Lewis, Bobby McFerrin, Kenny Rogers, and Sonny Bono. On the variety side ventriloquists Ronn Lucas and Jeff Dunham, comedian and raconteur Steve Allen, talk show host Regis Philbin, and the Smothers Brothers were guests. Einstein got his start writing for their comedy variety show.

Dave talked up a stunt he was going to do concerning a large roller coaster. He went into long detail about the background of the stunt and exactly how he planned it. Finally, he got into the front car of the roller coaster; piling in were nuns and other folks and a boy who sits next to him. He is even asked for his ticket. The gag is that Super Dave is afraid of roller coasters and he yelled to stop it and then was sick during the ride. All along the customers are laughing and having a good time.

With the assistance of Dave's stunt coordinator, Fuji Hakayito, played by Art Irizawa in a manner where he is just on the threshold of being understood, Dave attempted a chair ride to death. He is on a chair welded to a pair of skis. He is attached to a truck with rocket speed. He asks to come back a bit for some slack, then says he's ready and the truck rockets back, running over Super Dave Osborne. Asking for help he goes into fast forward and is dragged all over the track.

An archery stunt in which Dave is strapped to an oversized target and spun quickly goes very wrong when the archer hits Dave in all parts of his body with the arrows. There is an ongoing bit with Dave and Michael Walden. Walden's sartorial style made fun of old-school sports announcers who wore patterned jackets and odd color combinations. Dave often jabbed Michael with an insult line about his appearance.

What made *Super Dave* work so well was that the parody and satiric aspects were so close to the truth. Coming up with crazy stunts week after week was part of the fun of the show. Bob Einstein stretched the realm of comedy by playing Super Dave Osborne and showing how absurd epic stunts could be.

From 1992 through 1993 the Fox Network aired *Super Dave,* an animated version of the live-action comedy series. It also featured live-action wraparounds by Bob Einstein. After a special premiere it settled into a Saturday-morning slot.

Further Resources

"A Blast from the Past: 10 Hilarious Super Dave Osborne Stunts." 2010. *Unreality Magazine*. http://unrealitymag.com/television/a-blast-from-the-past-10-hilarious-super-dave-osborne-stunts/

Wayne, Jesse. 2013. *Confessions of a Hollywood Stunt Man (or It Seemed Like a Good Idea at the Time!)*. Amazon Digital Services.

T.J. Hooker (ABC, 1982–1985; CBS, 1986–1987)

William Shatner (1931–) played Sergeant T.J. Hooker, a hard–nosed veteran police officer, in this one-hour police drama. When the show began as a mid-season replacement in 1982 on ABC, Hooker was mainly assigned to train new recruits at the police academy. The cast included Adrian Zmed (1954–) as Office Vince Romano, a trainee assigned to Hooker; April Clough (1953–) as Vicki, a recruit; Richard Herd (1932–) as Captain Sheridan, Hooker's by-the-book superior; and Lee Bryant (1945–) as Fran, Hooker's ex-wife.

As an instructor Hooker taught the recruits street work, the rights and wrongs of policing. He was a man who believed in traditional values; he was impacted by the death of his partner, killed in the line of duty, and a marriage that ended in divorce.

When the show returned in fall 1982 Hooker had more responsibilities and Clough and Bryant had been dropped. Heather Locklear (1961–) came on the force as Stacey Sheridan, the captain's daughter, a new officer. In 1983 James Darren (1936–) came on regularly as Officer Jim Corrigan, Stacy's partner. ABC dropped *T.J. Hooker* from their prime-time schedule in fall 1985 and it was picked up by CBS for a weekly late-night slot. Seventeen new episodes were produced during the 1985–1986 season with Shatner, Darren, and Locklear. Adrian Zmed quit the show because he was unwilling to take a pay cut. CBS picked up the series during the 1986–1987 season and developed 90-minute segments shown late at night as part of the network's "Crime Time after Prime Time" programming.

T.J. Hooker stood alone in the police drama genre. The production values were realistic and the cops were as close to authentic as possible. None of the flash from other shows in the genre got in the way of the main theme, which was to focus on how police officers work, how dangerous it could be, and how mundane. The temperament and training of an officer was examined in detail. It was not stylized like *Dragnet*, but contained that show's spirit—no glamour or glitz, just the facts.

See also: *Hill Street Blues*; *Police Story*; *Vol. 1, The 1950s–1960s: Dragnet*; *Vol. 3, The 1990s–Present: Law & Order*.

Further Resources

Sabin, Roger, with Ronald Wilson, Linda Speidel, Brian Fauchette, and Ben Bethell. 2015. *Cop Shows: A Critical History of Police Dramas on Television*. Jefferson, NC: McFarland.

Shatner, William, and David Fisher. 2008. *Up Till Now: The Autobiography*. New York: St. Martin's Press.

Tales from the Crypt (HBO, 1989–1996)

Tales from the Crypt was a horror comic book anthology series published by EC Comics from 1950 to 1955. The editor of EC Comics was William Gaines (1922–1992). In the late 1940s and early 1950s comic books came under attack from parents, clergymen, and schoolteachers who objected to their graphic content. Psychiatrist Fredric Wertham (1895–1981) wrote *Seduction of the Innocent*, published in 1954, about the harmful effects of the material. In that same year there

Tales from the Crypt was inspired by a number of horror comic books, notably *The Crypt of Terror, The Haunt of Fear, Vault of Horror, Crime Suspense Stories*, and *Two-Fisted Fear*. Horror comics grew from the genre due to the popularity of literary works such as Edgar Allan Poe's, Bram Stoker's *Dracula* (1897), and Mary Shelley's *Frankenstein* (1818). The macabre and supernatural are themes found in the genre, which can also overlap with fantasy, supernatural fiction, and thriller genres.

was a Senate Subcommittee on Juvenile Delinquency that targeted violent comics. Eventually, the industry engaged in self-censorship. Gaines was under great pressure and believed his horror comics were being singled out and blamed for polluting the minds of young people. He decided to cease publication of *Tales from the Crypt. Tales from the Crypt* was resurrected as a television anthology series that appeared on HBO in June, 1989 and ran for seven seasons producing 93 episodes.

The Crypt Keeper was the principal host of the *Tales from the Crypt* comic stories. He was a scary presence, a decrepit hermit sitting framed in the lightless crypt's half-open door, his face all but hidden by his long stringy white hair. Eventually the character injected macabre humor into his introductions to the horror stories.

From Comic Book to Television Screen

Early episodes were directed by noted Hollywood directors: Walter Hill (1942–) (*The Warriors,* 1979; *48 Hrs*, 1982; *Deadwood*, 2004), Richard Donner (1930–) (*Superman* 1978; *Lethal Weapon*, 1987; *The Goonies*, 1985), and Robert Zemeckis (1952–) (*Back to the Future*, 1985; *Who Framed Roger Rabbit*, 1988; *Forrest Gump*, 1994). Other notable directors who helmed episodes included John Frankenheimer, William Friedkin, Tobe Hooper, and Mary Lambert.

Many of the most popular actors of the period were guest stars on *Tales from the Crypt*. They included John Lithgow, Isabella Rossellini, Demi Moore, Teri Garr, Margot Kidder, Joe Pesci, Martin Sheen, Priscilla Presley, Christopher Reeve, Beau Bridges, Donald O'Connor, Harry Anderson, Katey Sagal, Tim Roth, Kirk Douglas, and Malcom McDowell.

The Crypt Keeper was voiced by John Kassir (2006–). He came across as a talking skeleton with a wicked and irreverent sense of humor about the proceedings, which were horrific. In effect, the Crypt Keeper was an animated puppet and a crew was assigned to make him move appropriately. The stories on *Tales from the Crypt* covered a wide range of gruesome elements and often had surprise endings. There was considerable violence, blood, nudity, gore, profane language, and sexual situations. The producers were able to get away with this kind of material because *Tales from the Crypt* was not on network television and cable outlets had radically different standards.

Actually, few of the stories were based on stories from the *Tales from the Crypt* comics. Many were based on stories from other EC titles like *The Haunt of Fear*, *Shock Suspense Stories*, and *The Vault of Horror*. The generic opening had the camera approaching a haunted house and then going inside. The scary yet ironic music was by film composer Danny Elfman (1953–). It ends with the Crypt Keeper uttering a high-pitched cackle/laugh and the title of the show is revealed in garish colors.

One episode told the story of an executioner who relishes his job as the master of the electric chair in a prison's death row. The state votes to revoke the death penalty and the man loses his job. When a criminal gets off on a legal technicality, the executioner hunts him down with a portable electric shock unit that kills him. He continues to go to the courtroom seeking people who have gotten away with murder, and then extracts his own form of justice as he electrocutes them himself. The twist is that the police have been following his actions; they arrest him and he is tried for murder and given the death penalty. When he was the executioner he made fun of prisoners about to get the electric chair, especially that they believed the phone would ring and the governor would stay the execution. Placed in the same circumstance, he acts the same way, thrashing around in a panic as the episode ends.

Another episode involved a young pretty woman who is a prostitute working the streets of a big city. She gets into an argument with a pimp, shooting and killing him. She goes into a strange curio shop to sell jewelry she has taken from the pimp. The owner won't give her any money because he tells her the wares are all stolen. There is a lot of talk about beauty and the woman is constantly looking in the mirror to admire herself. The shop owner offers her $10,000 to make a plaster cast of her face, which she does. We find out that the man's wife was very beautiful but is now in a decorated casket and is a skeleton. The woman steals a rich man from his girlfriend and becomes "the girl of his dreams." They live the high life. The shop owner has made his deceased wife beautiful again using the cast. The woman is turning ugly and her skin is rapidly aging. She goes to the shop and steala the plaster cast. As she runs in the street she crashes into one of her former prostitute pals. She collapses in agony on the street as the camera pulls back and she gets lost in the crowd.

Tales from the Crypt was *The Twilight Zone* on steroids. It dealt with social themes, but from the dark side. The stories were well crafted, the episodes well produced, and the content was in the same mode of bad taste as the comic books that spawned it.

See also: HBO (Home Box Office); *Tales from the Darkside*; *Vol. 1, The 1950s–1960s: The Outer Limits*; *The Twilight Zone.*

Further Resources

Geissman, Grant. 2005. *Foul Play!: The Art and Artists of the Notorious 1950s E.C. Comics!* New York: Harper Design.

Various. 2015. *The EC Archives: Tales from the Crypt*, Vol. 1. Milwaukee, OR: Dark Horse Books.

Tales from the Darkside (Syndication, 1984–1987)

A half-hour syndicated horror anthology series produced by George A. Romero (1940–), which began its television run in 1983. In the late 1960s Romero reinvented both the independent film and the zombie film with *Night of the Living Dead* (1969), which revitalized horror and zombie characters still prevalent on television in modern times. Romero mixed dark humor and vivid inhuman characters in well-written stories, modestly produced and well acted. The stories tended toward the macabre and only let up for a twist ending, which usually was grimmer than the rest of the episode.

The cast in the shows included mainly character actors: Arnold Stang, Connie Stevens, Keenan Wynn, Fritz Weaver, Justine Bateman, Eddie Bracken, Peggy Cass, Harry Anderson, Jean Marsh, Bill Macy, Darren McGavin, and Phyllis Diller. In 1982 Romero in collaboration with Stephen King (1947–) created *Creepshow*, a horror anthology feature film that was successful at the box office and increased interest in the horror genre.

There were discussions and inquiries about adapting *Creepshow* into a television series. Warner Bros. owned aspects of *Creepshow* so Laurel Entertainment, co-founded by Romero and Richard P. Rubinstein (1947–), decided to take their developing project into a similar but decidedly different direction. They changed the name to *Tales from the Darkside*. Because of Stephen King's participation the production was able to attract a stellar group of writers. They would either write original episodes or contribute previously published stories that were just right for the show. The writers included Frederick Pohl, Harlan Ellison, Clive Barker, Michael Bishop, Robert Bloch, John Cheever, Michael McDowell, and Frederic Brown. Stephen King also contributed many stories to the show. The show's overall look was low budget with a concentration on story. Each episode found its own way to scare or frighten the audience. The series remained in first-run syndication for four seasons, airing a pilot and 89 episodes.

A story line typifying the elements of the anthology entitled "Inside the Closet" involves a college anthropology professor who has a large house and rents a room that had been his daughter's to a female graduate student. Some doors won't open, some open by themselves. The professor was sardonic and very strict and instructed her never to open the closet in the room. When the girl reports a rat in her room, he makes fun of her. The student disobeys the professor's instruction and gets the always-locked door open, where she finds clothes for a little girl and dolls. Ultimately, the student is attracted to and then murdered by the creature under the bed who is revealed as the professor's daughter.

Another typical episode called "I'll Give You a Million" featured two men, Williams played by Keenan

Wynn (1916–1986) and Blaine played by George Petrie (1912–1997), who like to make wagers about trivial things. Williams suggests a contractual bargain for Blaine's soul and Blaine accepts. Then Blaine finds out he is dying of cancer and tries to buy back the contract, but Williams, who is cruel and tickled that the other had almost no time left to live, refuses. There is arguing about the contract. Blaine dies and comes back from the dead looking mangled and ghoulish. When he sees him Williams has a heart attack and dies. His chest is on fire and when the smoke clears the words "Paid in Full" are burned into his chest.

Some audiences enjoy anthology shows because each week there is a different story set in a different place. Others don't like this format because they are used to the consistency of a story that develops with the same characters each week. The audiences for horror anthology shows are loyal and wait to see what next week will bring.

See also: *Tales from the Crypt*; *Vol. 1, The 1950s–1960s: The Outer Limits*; *The Twilight Zone*.

Further Resources

Gagne, Paul R., and Tom Allen. 1987. *The Zombies That Ate Pittsburgh: The Films of George A. Romero*. New York: Dodd, Mead.

Williams, Tony, ed. 2011. *George A. Romero: Interviews*. Jackson: University Press of Mississippi.

Tanner '88 (HBO, 1988)

Robert Altman (1925–2006) was one of the most accomplished and prolific film directors of his time. Before he began directing motion pictures, Altman had a lengthy resume in television and was considered one of the significant powers behind *Combat!* (1962–1967), the landmark World War II series. In 1988 he collaborated with popular comic creator Garry Trudeau (1948–) of "Doonesbury" fame to take a satirical look at an American presidential campaign; the series was called *Tanner '88*. Michael Murphy (1938–) played a hopeful Democratic nominee, Jack Tanner. Others in the cast include Cynthia Nixon (1966–) as Alex Tanner, and Pamela Reed (1949–) as T.J. Cavanaugh. The 12-part series for HBO also gained the involvement of real political figures who did cameos including Bruce Babbitt, Bob Dole, Gary Hart, Jesse Jackson, Pat Robertson, and Kitty Dukakis.

Tanner '88 was a mockumentary, a fictional film based on real events and produced to look like a documentary. It was broadcast during the months leading up to the 1988 presidential election. The story shows the behind-the-scenes machinations of a former Michigan representative, Tanner, who strives to gain the Democratic Party nomination.

Each episode covers the campaign as it moves from place to place. Viewers are provided different points of view. The weekend before the New Hampshire primary, Tanner and his daughter talk to voters, and a campaign commercial is examined. His slogan is "For Real." There is an assassination attempt, which affords him Secret Service protection. Tanner talks to an old friend from the civil rights movement on how to attract black voters. There is a fascination in watching the faux campaign; it offers the viewer an opportunity to observe the inevitable hypocrisy of the candidates and a seemingly realistic view of how the electoral process works.

Altman described the manner in which the series was made. It was two-thirds scripted and one-third found art/improvisation. *Tanner '88* fitted neatly into Altman's filmography. It worked well for a director who embraced the talent of actors and used the camera in his version of run-and-gun. Altman won a Primetime Emmy Award for Outstanding Directing in a Drama Series for the episode "The Boiler Room."

See also: HBO (Home Box Office).

Further Resources

Trudeau, Gary. 2010. *40: A Doonesbury Retrospective*. Kansas City, MO: Andrews McMeel Publishing.

Zuckoff, Mitchell. 2009. *Robert Altman: The Oral Biography*. New York: Vintage Books.

That's Incredible! (ABC, 1980–1989)

The 1980s solidified a new genre—the reality show. It had existed before in different forms but the first sustained wave began in the eighties. Actually, in the last year of the 1970s, NBC rolled out *Real People* (1979–1984). The team of hosts introduced real people who had odd or strange occupations or hobbies. In 1982–1986 the unusual one-panel comic strip "Ripley's Believe It or Not" came to the small screen. In 1980 ABC wanted to get in on the trend and *That's Incredible!* was created. The show had elements of both prior shows, but was somewhat controversial because of claims that may have been fraudulent and manipulated by the production.

Incredible but True?

The show aired in prime time and was hosted by John Davidson (1941–), Cathy Lee Crosby (1944–), and former football star Fran Tarkenton (1940–). Many of the incredible events were staged specifically for the show. Some proved too dangerous for those who attempted them. Stan Krumi was badly burned as he ran through a "tunnel of fire"—his fireproof gloves melted in the 1,800-degree heat. Some events were bogus, such as an inventor who claimed he found an easy way to make hydrogen fuel by utilizing mass-produced solar cells. He was later convicted on 10 counts of fraud. Other segments were silly, like a Frenchman who ate a10-speed bike.

To keep the viewers engaged *That's Incredible!* and its three hosts presented the oddest feats they could: a dentist who cures pain with clothespins, a man who catches arrows with his bare hands, an acrobat who leaps over cars speeding at him at 60 mph, a dog that catches sharks, a skydiver who jumps over an airplane while handcuffed and straightjacketed, a man who catches a bullet in his mouth, a yogi who is sandwiched between two slabs of nails sealed with a sledgehammer, a band of karate specialists who take down a barn.

Time magazine in 1980 gave ABC's *That's Incredible!* its dubious achievement award for "Most Sadistic Show." There was a push for higher ratings and not everything went well; one man nearly lost a foot, another burned his fingers to the stumps, and another received fractures and a ruptured aorta.

A 1982 issue of *TV Guide*, the television bible, revealed that several of the stunts were rigged or complete frauds; nevertheless the producers pressed on. There were informative segments on medical breakthroughs and profiles on individuals who overcame difficult disabilities.

It seemed that the audience wanted to see the death-defying stunts more than anything. There was a man who juggled roaring chainsaws while a caption said "Don't try this yourself!" The hosts moved within the studio audience and took turns speaking and presenting the feats. When a film clip was run one of the hosts did the voice-over. An expert on carnivorous plants explained how they function. A car stopped in neutral on a section of road pointed toward an upward stretch was able to drive by itself. This was debunked by the town's mayor who explained it as an optical illusion. In 1980 another incredible feat was highlighted when five-year-old Tiger Woods was introduced and profiled. He was in the studio, then seen on the greens. His father explained how his son became a champion by age three.

Four years after *That's Incredible!* was taken off the ABC schedule, it came back for an additional season, now called *Incredible Sunday*. Everything was basically the same. John Davidson was again the host with model Christina Ferrare (1950–) and early in 1989 teen actress Tracey Gold (1969–).

For the first episode the show presented an African woman who became the surrogate mother for her own daughter, implanted with her daughter's fertilized eggs—she gave birth to her own grandchildren.

See also: *Ripley's Believe It or Not*; *Those Amazing Animals*.

Further Resources

Crosby, Cathy Lee. 1998. *Let the Magic Begin*. New York: Dell.

Tarkenton, Fran, and Jim Bruton. 2009. *Every Day Is Game Day*. Chicago: Triumph Books.

thirtysomething (ABC, 1987–1991)

In the early 1980s the term *yuppie* was coined. After the 1960s some in the baby boomer generation continued to live the hippie ideal in spirit and in dress. Others strove to get great jobs, live in posh neighborhoods, and be very much into themselves and their families.

The one-hour drama *thirtysomething* was about the baby boomers as they worked, created families, and struggled with issues. It was created by two baby boomers, Ed Zwick (1952–) and Marshall Herskovitz (1952–), who had been writers on *Family* (1976–1980). Asked by MGM/UA to develop a series, they drew on their own experiences as husbands and fathers and developed a series like *Family* that explored everyday life in a contemporary domestic setting.

They experimented with the original structure of *Family* and made the series about the interwoven lives of seven adults, all in their 30s and living in Philadelphia (where both writers were originally from). All seven were longtime friends, two of the couples were married as the show began, and three of them were single.

The fine ensemble cast included Mel Harris (1956–), who played Hope Murdoch, a wife and mother who placed her career as a freelance writer on hold to raise a child, and Ken Olin (1954–), who was her husband Michael Steadman, an advertising executive. Another couple was played by Timothy Busfield (1957–), who was Elliot Weston, Mike's business partner, and Patricia Wettig (1951–) (who was married to Ken Olin in real life) as Elliot's wife, Nancy. Polly Draper (1955–) played Hope's best friend, Ellyn Warren, an administrator at City Hall. Melanie Mayron (1952–) was Michael's cousin Melissa Steadman, a photographer. Peter Horton (1953–) played Gary Shepard, a college teacher. Jade Mortimer and Brittany and Lacey Craven portrayed Jane, Hope and Michael's young daughter. Luke Rossi was Ethan, Elliot and Nancy's son, and Jordana "Bink" Shapiro and Leslie Riddell played Brittany, Elliot and Nancy's daughter. Hope and Michael had a second child, Leo, in 1990.

The narratives presented through the *thirtysomething* episodes reveal their daily lives: Gary is up for tenure and Ellyn is thinking of buying her co-op apartment; the women face some past demons on a camping trip while the men call a truce to keep the home fires burning; in his fight over a campaign with the creative directors, Michael creates a strategy from a similar incident in his adolescent years; Ellyn gives Michael and Elliot a tough account as she considered a romantic relationship with her boss.

Thirtysomething won a Peabody award and was generally well received by the critics. Audiences had a strong reaction both ways as far as the characters being highly emotional and analytical at times. Some episodes dealt with serious issues such as cancer, divorce, and death. There were moments of humor, including one episode with a black-and-white recreation of *The Dick Van Dyke Show* (1961–1966).

See also: *Cheers*; *Family*; *Vol. 3, The 1990s–Present*: *Friends*.

Further Resources

Gencarelli, Thom, Ph.D., and Brian Cogan. 2010. *Baby Boomers and Popular Culture: An Inquiry into America's Most Powerful Generation.* Santa Barbara, CA: Praeger.

Holst, Sanford. 2015. *Baby Boomers: 76 Reasons Why It's Great to Be a Boomer*. Los Angeles, CA: Santorini Books.

This Week with David Brinkley (ABC, 1981–1996)

David Brinkley (1920–2003) began reporting on NBC from Washington, D.C. in 1952. He became a household name in 1956 when he was paired with Chet Huntley for the network's *Huntley-Brinkley Report*. His dry delivery and equally dry sense of humor built a large fan base. He was at NBC for 38 years, then left for rival ABC where he was given his own hour-long news magazine show, *This Week with David Brinkley*, scheduled on Sunday morning, which replaced *Issues and Answers* (1960–1981). Just some of the commentators regularly featured included George Will (1941–), Ben Bradlee (1921–2014), Karen Elliot House (1947–), Hodding Carter (1907–1972), James Wooten, and ABC correspondents Sam Donaldson (1934–), Brit Hume (1943–), and Cokie Roberts (1943–).

The centerpiece of *This Week with David Brinkley* was a roundtable discussion that included Donaldson, Roberts, and George Will as well as a guest, who all discussed the major issues of the week. The body of the show featured guests and news from Washington, D.C. and the world. This was serious news and expanded coverage compared to the nightly news on the networks.

Sunday morning became the time for viewers to understand in depth what was behind the news of the week. *This Week with David Brinkley* was lively, intelligent, filled with concurrence and lack of agreement. The discussion was moderated by Mr. Brinkley with panache, style, and an occasional flippant remark.

Guests displayed a range of political thought from all political parties, and included journalists with a spectrum of knowledge, points of view, and insights into our government and global issues.

After David Brinkley retired in 1996 the show was co-hosted by Sam Donaldson and Cokie Roberts, then in 2002 George Stephanopoulos (1961–), from a co-host job on *Good Morning America,* took over the position. From March to July 2010 ABC News senior White House correspondent Jake Tapper (1969–) was interim anchor of the program. In August 2010 Christiane Amanpour (1958–), the longtime world affairs correspondent on CNN, became the host, but the ratings were poor and she stepped down after two months. George Stephanopoulos returned to the show as host and remained there as of 2016.

See also: *A Current Affair*; *Hour Magazine*; *Monitor (First Camera)*; *20/20*; *Vol. 1, The 1950s–1960s: 60 Minutes*; *Vol. 3, The 1990s–Present*: *Eye to Eye with Connie Chung*.

Further Resources

Brinkley, David. 1995. *David Brinkley*. New York: Knopf.
Brinkley, David. 1996. *Everyone Is Entitled to My Opinion*. New York: Ballantine Books.

The Thorn Birds (ABC, 1983)

The Thorn Birds was a best-selling novel published in 1977 and written by the Australian author Colleen McCullough. It is set primarily on Drogheda, a fictional sheep station in the Australian outback, named after Drogheda, Ireland. The story focuses on the Cleary family and spans the years 1915–1969.

Adapted into a miniseries, *The Thorn Birds* ran as a four-night 10-hour event on ABC. Enormously popular, it was ranked the second highest rated miniseries ever broadcast, only behind *Roots* (1977). *The Thorn Birds* took place in Australia between 1915 and 1969. The cast was filled with A-list actors including Richard Chamberlain (1934–), who starred as Ralph de Bricassart, a Roman Catholic priest torn between his desire for advancement within the priesthood and his love for a woman, Rachael Ward (1957–), who co-starred as his love Meggie Cleary. Barbara Stanwyck (1907–1990) played Meggie's strong-willed grandmother, Mary Carson. Jean Simmons (1929–2010) was Fee Cleary, Richard Kiley (1922–1999) played Paddy Cleary, Christopher Plummer (1929–) was Archbishop Contini-Verchese, Bryan Brown (1947–) was Luke O'Neill, and Mare Winningham (1959–) was Meggie's daughter, Justine.

This epic story begins in New Zealand in the early 20th century focusing on Meggie Cleary as a beautiful little girl from a poor family of all brothers. Her father, Paddy, is poor but has a rich sister, Mary Carson, in Australia who offers to relocate his family to her large sheep farm. In Drogheda, Ralph de Bricassart, a Roman Catholic priest, has been assigned to this undesirable post because he insulted a bishop. De Bricassart is handsome and ambitious and tries to build a relationship with Mary Carson as he sees her wealth as a possible way to improve his standing in the church. He cares for all the Clearys and especially treasures Meggie, who sees Ralph as the center of her life.

When Meggie is 17 her aunt dies and bequeaths her entire fortune to Ralph, who parlays it to become a powerful figure in the Catholic Church. Before Ralph leaves Drogheda, Meggie confesses her love for him. After three years Meggie marries, but she has made a poor choice and is indentured to a family with all her earnings going to her husband. She bears a child and while she is in labor Ralph comes to say goodbye as he is leaving Australia for Rome. On a return trip to Australia, Ralph seeks out Meggie and their long-smoldering love is consummated. Unbeknownst to Ralph, Meggie bears his son, Dane. Now a cardinal, when Ralph meets Dane he is drawn to him and eventually, despite Meggie's objections, Dane decides to become a priest, mentored by Ralph. While Dane is vacationing in Greece he drowns trying to save two women caught in a riptide. Meggie tells Ralph that Dane is his son and Ralph dies in Meggie's arms. The allusion to a thorn bird in the story's title refers to a bird that searches for thorn trees from the day it is hatched. When it finds the perfect thorn, it impales itself, and it sings the most beautiful song ever heard as it dies.

The Thorn Birds was produced by the highly regarded David L. Wolper who had produced *Roots* (1977). Many of the actors in the production received Prime Time Emmys for their performances including Richard Chamberlain, Barbara Stanwyck, Richard Kiley, and Jean Simmons.

See also: *Roots*.

Further Resources

McCullough, Colleen. 1979. *The Thorn Birds*. New York. HarperCollins.

Plummer, Christopher. 2012. *In Spite of My Self*. New York: Vintage.

Those Amazing Animals (ABC, 1980–1981)

Those Amazing Animals aired on Sunday evenings at 7 p.m. on ABC. The one-hour reality show targeted a family demographic. The animals appeared on stage and in filmed segments. The show used experts to familiarize the audience with the characteristics and nature of different animals and also to show enjoyable vignettes in which the animals behaved in interesting and sometimes unexpected ways. The hosts were Burgess Meredith (1907–1997), Priscilla Presley (1945–), and Jim Stafford (1944–). Others who appeared regularly included Joan Embry (1952–), a naturalist at the San Diego Zoo, oceanographer Jacques-Yves Cousteau (1910–1997), and underwater photographers Ron Taylor (1934–2012) and Valerie Taylor (1935–).

Those Amazing Animals was a spin-off from the animal segments presented on *That's Incredible!* Unlike animal shows before it such as *Wild Kingdom* (1963–1988) shot on location, *Those Amazing Animals*, in addition to film segments in the wild, had a magazine format and invited a live audience to see the animals that were brought into the studio. There also was a focus on the sensational aspects of the animal world: a horse that could count, an elephant walking on Jim Stafford, a reptile expert who could hypnotize alligators, a 121-pound dog that could bite sideview mirrors off passing cars, but most of the reports were educational and instructive especially when given by the house experts.

Those Amazing Animals went well beyond the simple presentation of various species of different groups of animals into the deeper connections between humans and the animal world. Some of the segments were offbeat and peculiar.

One gentleman claimed that horses had ESP and could read the mind of humans. A series of tests were set up to see if this was true. In every one of the tests, the horse was asked a simple mathematical problem, but the man was told by the producer to think of another answer that was not the right one, and each time the horse would tap or scratch out the man's answer. A sea lion was injured and was pulled out of the ocean—it took nine days to rescue. Finally the sea lion was operated on—but after the operation it still came across to the handlers and viewers, who judged the sea lion in human terms, as unfazed and a bit cranky. Once back in the ocean it came alive again, happy and swimming joyously. A long-haired black cat rides on the headlight of a motorcycle and goes with the speed and the turns and angles of the bike without falling. A doctor working in a mental ward for dangerous individuals got the idea that if playing with his dog calmed him, it might make a significant difference with these mental patients. The ward had a terrible record of suicides and the men were depressed and not in real communication with anyone. The doctor called the ward "The Open Mind" and received permission to conduct experiments with the men. They were murderers, some who had spent most of their lives in prison, unhappy and withdrawn. Each was given a bird, a rabbit, or a guinea pig, and each became less self-centered and more involved with caring for the animals and becoming normalized in their emotions. The doctor's experiment proved that the companionship of an animal could have a positive effect even on those who had been considered lost causes. The power of animals and their closeness to humans was a steady theme on *Those Amazing Animals*.

See also: *That's Incredible!*; *Vol. 1, The 1950s–1960s: Mutual of Omaha's Wild Kingdom*; *Vol. 3, The 1990s–Present:* Animal Planet.

Further Resources

Spelman, Lucy. 2012. *National Geographic Animal Encyclopedia: 2,500 Animals with Photos, Maps and More!* Washington, D.C. National Geographic.

Stuart, Tracey, and Lisel Ashlock. 2015. *Do Unto Animals: A Friendly Guide to How Animals Live and How We Can Make Their Lives Better*. Artisan.

The Tracey Ullman Show (Fox, 1987–1990)

The Tracey Ullman Show was one of the first programs on the Fox network. It was a sketch comedy program featuring the amazing and versatile actor/comedienne Tracey Ullman (1959–) who hailed from England. Tracey Ullman could act, sing, dance, and be very funny. Before her show she was not well known in the United States; she had been in a few films and had a top 10 record, "They Don't Know," in 1984. Her series was produced by James L. Brooks (1940–), who had written for *The Mary Tyler More Show* (1970–1977). Ullman's show consisted of two to three sketches; not all were comedic and many incorporated a rock and roll musical number. Paula Abdul (1962–) and funk master George Clinton (1941–) composed the show's theme music. There were guest stars, but most of the sketches involved Julie Kavner (1950–), Dan Castellaneta (1957–), Joe Malone, and Sam McMurray (1952–). Tracey Ullman's gifts extended to a shockingly wide group of characters she could create—men and women seemingly with any kind of accent. Some of her recurring characters included Kay the boring secretary, materialistic yuppie Sara Downey, anthropologist Ceci Beckwith, divorcée Francesca, the teenager being raised by her gay father and his lover, South African golf pro Kiki Howard S. Smith, and Tina the New York postal worker.

At the end of each show Tracey Ullman came on stage without makeup in her housecoat to talk briefly to the studio audience—her last words were always "go home."

Between the sketches were short animated films created by Matt Groening (1954–), author of the *Life in Hell* comics. Groening then created *The Simpsons,* which in 1990 was given its own series. In 1988 Tracey Ullman won the first Emmy for the Fox Network.

See also: Fox Broadcasting Company.

Further Resources

Ullman, Tracey. 1983. *Tracey Ullman: You Broke My Heart in 17 Places*. RCA.

Ullman, Tracey. 1998. *Tracey Takes On*. New York: Hyperion.

Training Dogs the Woodhouse Way (Syndication, 1980)

Training a dog would hardly seem to make riveting television but when *Training Dogs the Woodhouse Way* first appeared in England, it flew to the top of the ratings. It was produced by the BBC. Later in the United States the show was wildly popular. The production was low budget and hosted by dog trainer Barbara Woodhouse (1910–1988) and was filmed at Campions, her Hertfordshire home, in 10 episodes. Each week she turned her skills on another group of incorrigible dogs and their baffled owners. She spent as much time instructing the humans as she did the dogs. She was often heard to say, "The main thing is to get the owner right for the dog."

Two of Woodhouse's favorite expressions on the show are "Sit" and "Walkies." Woodhouse with her high-toned voice and her proper methods were highly parodied in England and the United States. "Sit" was parodied in the James Bond movie *Octopussy* released in 1983 in which James Bond does a Barbara Woodhouse imitation. He puts his hand up in a command posture, repeats Woodhouse's words to a tiger, and the animal responds by obeying.

The 10-part series was syndicated on more than 100 stations in the United States. In Britain it was so popular it was run twice. The series made Barbara Woodhouse famous among dog owners everywhere. She continued to state that there were no bad dogs, only bad owners who did not assert their position in the pecking order of dog society. Even with her success and popularity, her advocacy for better designed and more humane cages for dog transportation was slow to gain widespread acceptance. During the series she would issue abrupt commands to the owners, offering her on-air criticism of their behavior. Often the owners looked more terrified than the dogs.

Further Resources

Woodhouse, Barbara. 1983. *Walkies: Dog Training and Care the Woodhouse Way*. New York: Simon & Schuster.

Woodhouse, Barbara, 1984. *No Bad Dogs: The Woodhouse Way*. New York: Fireside.

21 Jump Street (Fox, 1987–1991)

An updated version of *The Mod Squad* (1968–1973), *21 Jump Street* was part of the Fox Network's scheme to appeal to younger viewers. It concerned a young group of big-city cops who could pass as high school students or college students. The cast included teen heartthrob Johnny Depp (1963–) as Tommy Hanson, Holly Robinson Peete (1964–) as Judy Hoffs, Dustin Nguyen (1962–) as H.T. (for Harry Truman) Ioki, Peter DeLuise (1966–) as Doug Denall, Frederic Forrest (1936–) as the boss, Captain Jenko, and Steven Williams (1949–) as the new boss, Captain Adam Fuller.

The young cops formed a special unit of the Los Angeles Police Department that fought crime in the schools, dealing with drug trafficking, extortion, school gangs, teenage prostitution, and murders. The unit was housed at an abandoned chapel at 21 Jump Street, the link to the show's title. Most episodes ended with a PSA featuring one of the cast members listing agencies that were helpful in addressing a problem covered on that week's program.

21 Jump Street was not an average cop or even an average undercover cop show. The focus on teenage crime prompted intense investigation into that subculture. How the young cops passed for students while they functioned as cops produced tension and made the audience worry for their heroes every week. *The Mod Squad* was formed in the late sixties when youth culture was changing. By the 1980s youth culture had spread, evolved, and changed, so *21 Jump Street* had cultural significance. Fox aired a spin-off series, *Booker*, for one season in 1989–1990, featuring the *21 Jump Street* character Dennis Booker, played by Richard Greico (1965–).

Along with the feature film *Nightmare on Elm Street* (1984), *21 Jump Street* helped launch the acting career of Depp, who was a teen idol in the 1980s and went on to become a highly versatile and successful actor in film, earning three Academy Award nominations.

The popularity and success of *21 Jump Street* propelled it through pop culture into the present day. In 2012, a comedy film based on the show of the same title starred Jonah Hill and Channing Tatum in the roles of the undercover officers attending a local high school. Ice Cube played their hard-nosed superior officer, Captain Dickson. In the film's climax, a surprise reveal featured Depp and DeLuise as their original *21 Jump Street* characters, albeit as undercover Drug Enforcement Agency (DEA) agents, far grown up from the days of their high school undercover operation. The film's success earned it a sequel, entitled *22 Jump Street*, in 2014, which again featured Hill, Tatum, and Ice Cube, except this time, the officers went undercover during college spring break.

Solidifying its spot in the late 1980s and early 1990s pop culture, *21 Jump Street* was named the 19th-best school television show of all time by *Rolling Stone* in 2014 (Collins 2014).

See also: Fox Broadcasting Company; *Saved by the Bell*; *Vol. 1, The 1950s–1960s: The Mod Squad*.

Further Resources

Collins, Sean T. 2014. "A Class Act: 20 Best School TV Shows." *Rolling Stone*. September 3. http://www.rollingstone.com/tv/lists/20-best-school-tv-shows-20140903/saved-by-the-bell-20140903

Doyle, Wanda. 2014. *21 Jump Street: 201 Success Secrets—201 Most Asked Questions on 21 Jump Street—What You Need to Know*. http://emereo.net/index.php/contacts/. Emereo Publishing.

White, Danny. 2011. *Johnny Depp: The Unauthorized Biography*. London: Michael O'Mara.

United States (NBC, 1980)

United States was a landmark show in the archives of television history, which presented a contemporary and honest look at an American marriage, airing on NBC for two months. However, the show experienced disastrous ratings, ranking 102nd of 105 television series in 1980.

Larry Gelbart (1926–2009) based this show on his own marriage and those of his friends. It began when the NBC brass approached Gelbart, co-creator of *M.A.S.H.*, to develop a half-hour comedy about contemporary marriage. Beau Bridges (1941–) and Helen Shaver (1951–) played Libby and Richard Chapin, with Rossie Harris (1969–) and Justin Dana (1970–) as their children Dylan and Nicky. The show was taped without a laugh track, had no theme music, and had handwritten credits. The network gave *United States* a big sendoff with the publicity machine of NBC singing its praises, but the show was apparently too far ahead of its time and audiences either dropped out early or never tuned in. It was dropped by the network after just seven weeks.

In 1980 a show was basically a comedy or a drama. Some did add a hint of the other, but the two distinct tones were kept separate. Larry Gelbart had a vision for *United States* as a show that would explore the joys and problems of marriage through both a comedic and dramatic prism. This concept now known as a dramedy made Gelbart's *United States* a touchstone in the design of a domestic television series.

The Chapins were young and middle-class. Most of the episodes took place in their home. Discussions about family and marriage were direct and frank. They discussed death and dying, drinking and debt. Libby met with an old family friend who had molested her at age eight. Richard and Libby had mixed feelings about being parents. They had differing attitudes toward their sexual relationship and were open to each other about infidelities each had experienced. Hostilities between the two were not guarded, but were open and raw. Most shows presented resolutions; this one did not. It was difficult for the couple to achieve "united states" at a time when they truly wanted to function as a couple.

The bravest aspect of *United States* was Larry Gelbart's view that marriage could be tedious, boring, and didactic. He presented this as part of the experience and it defied previous rules of television drama and comedy. Gelbart broke new ground with *United States* and paid a price for it.

See also: *thirtysomething*.

Further Resources

Gelbart, Larry. 1998. *Laughing Matters: On Writing M*A*S*H, Tootsie, Oh, God! and a Few Other Funny Things*. New York: Random House.

Gottman, John, PhD, and Nan Silver. 2015. *The Seven Principles for Making Marriage Work: A Practical Guide from the Country's Foremost Relationship Expert*. New York: Harmony Books.

Unsolved Mysteries (NBC, 1987–1997)

Unsolved Mysteries began as a single special that aired on NBC on January 20, 1987. Raymond Burr (1917–1993) was the host and he looked at four real-life mysteries: a Wyoming man found dead under strange circumstances three years after he disappeared from his home; a 72-year-old Detroit woman who claimed to be the Siamese twin of a member of the Dodge auto family, separated at birth and put up for adoption and now heir to the family fortune; the professional murder of a Tulsa executive of a country club; and two especially dangerous bank robbers who were then at large.

This special was so popular that six more were produced during 1987 and 1988. The first two were hosted by Karl Malden (1912–2009). Then this one-hour nonfiction television series was hosted by Robert Stack (1919–2003) and focused mainly on the topics of missing persons, unsolved murders, and unclaimed estates. The format included interviews with persons who had knowledge of the situation, and law enforcement officials. It featured dramatic recreations of the actual events. Some of the mysteries presented on the show were solved. In spring 1988 Jerry Strickland, wanted for homicide, was apprehended the day after the episode featuring his story was broadcast. Strickland had seen the program and had agreed to tape an interview for a future episode. He told producers of *Unsolved Mysteries* it was still his favorite TV show.

Persistent legends and UFO sightings were also explored. In one episode the producers did an elaborate recreation of the famous 1962 escape attempt from Alcatraz prison to determine if the escapees who were never found might have survived the chilly waters of San Francisco Bay.

Within a segment *Unsolved Mysteries* did a professional and thorough job of presenting missing persons and other unsolved situations. The shows were well directed. Good interviews appeared on camera and there was a good use of the voice track from an off-camera interview that showed still photographs or footage. Everyone and everything was well researched, produced, and structured. The stories were gathered from many sources and woven into a coherent narrative, which was as up to date as possible. Everyone available and willing to talk participated, on the theory that the more facts presented, the better chance someone would be found or that a mystery would be solved.

An 800 number was provided for viewers to call in clues. By the end of the show's eighth season, *Unsolved Mysteries* claimed to have been responsible for 87 reunions, the capture of 140 fugitives, and the solving of 250 cases.

See also: *America's Most Wanted.*

Further Resources

Aron, Paul. 2001. *Unsolved Mysteries of History: An Eye-Opening Investigation into the Most Baffling Events of All Time*. New York: John Wiley & Sons.

Editors of *Life*. 2009. *LIFE: The Greatest Unsolved Mysteries of All Time: 50 Baffling Cases from the Files*. New York: LIFE Books.

V (NBC, 1983)

V which stood for the Visitors, was a two-part science fiction miniseries on NBC that followed the story of the Visitors, lizard-like aliens from another planet who arrived on Earth in an assumed human form. The Visitors hid the fact that they were on Earth to take over the planet. They were eventually stopped by a Los Angeles group of resistance fighters. There was a conscious decision by the show's creators to make an analogy between the Visitors' invasion and the Nazi takeover of Europe during World War II.

The Visitors arrived in 15 motherships. At first the Visitors claimed they could solve all of Earth's problems and just wanted some needed minerals. Through a skillful use of the media and a gullible Earth population, they manage to overthrow the humans. After the show's run in October 1984, it was rerun in May 1985, and a weekly series followed a year after that.

The cast included Jane Badler (1953–), leader of the Visitors, who was kidnapped by an American industrialist on the eve of her trial for crimes against humanity. Marc Singer (1948–) played resistance leader Mike Donovan, a television newscaster. Faye Grant (1957–) was a resistance scientist, Julie Parish. Lane Smith (1936–2005) was Nathan Bates, Diana's kidnapper and collaborator; Jeff Yagher (1961–) portrayed Nathan's son Kyle, who sided with the resistance. Blair Tefkin (1959–) was Robert Maxwell, who had an affair with an alien, and Jenny Beck (1974–) and Jennifer Cooke (1964–) were Robert's half–human, half-alien daughter Elizabeth. Robert Englund (1947–) played Willie, a Visitor who defected to the resistance, and June Chadwick (1951–) was Lydia, a Visitor who was Diana's chief rival. Duncan Regehr played Charles, a Visitor who forced Diana to marry him and died shortly thereafter. Nicky Katt (1970–) played Mike's young son Sam Donovan. Howard K. Smith (1914–2002) appeared as himself, a newscaster who tried to negotiate a lasting peace.

It seemed unlikely that a science fiction two-night miniseries would appeal to the general public. It was a genre usually confined to B movies. But with *V* it became clear that the science fiction genre could be used to reflect history, politics, and current events. The miniseries was a hit because its subject and subtext were more sophisticated than what it appeared to be on the surface. In 2009 *V* was remade as a series that ran on ABC for three seasons until 2011.

See also: *Alien Nation*; *War of the Worlds*; *Vol. 3, The 1990s–Present: The X-Files.*

Further Resources

Crispin, A. C., and Kenneth Johnson. 1984. *V.* Wisconsin: Pinnacle Books.

Stanley, Joel. 2014. *Life Beyond Earth: Do Aliens Exist? Do UFOs Exist? What Else Is Out There?* Amazon Digital Services.

Vietnam: A Television History (PBS, 1983)

The Vietnam War (1955–1975) was a subject of contention before, during, and after the conflict. PBS, in its tradition of presenting educational and well-researched nonfiction programming, made a commitment to telling the story of the Vietnam War in 13 separate parts. The focus was on American participation and involvement in the war and on earlier participation by the French. For a war that generated so many points of view and divisiveness, *Vietnam: A Television History* was objective and fact based. The structure employed extensive use of news footage and contemporary interviews with as many of the surviving principals, both American and Vietnamese, as possible. Surprisingly, only two men declined to be interviewed for the program. These were former defense secretary Robert McNamara and former South Vietnamese president Nguyen Van Thieu. The narrator was Will Lyman (1948–), and two members of the rock band the Grateful Dead, Mickey Hart (1943–) and Billy Kreutzmann (1946–), composed the music.

The gestation of *Vietnam: A Television History* began in 1977 when filmmaker Richard Ellison and foreign correspondent Stanley Karnow (1925–2013) began to discuss the project. Karnow had been a journalist in Vietnam since 1959. His 1983 bestseller *Vietnam: A History* was a tie-in to the documentary.

The documentary received strong positive reviews. It was called a landmark in television journalism. Even-handed and objective, it came to some conclusions that went against popular opinion and made historic observations. Most important of these was that the peace movement did nothing to change the course of the war and that by attacking presidential candidate Hubert Humphrey, the movement helped to elect Richard Nixon as president.

The series titles covered the events in the following manner. Part 1: "Roots of a War" (1945–1953), Part 2: The First Vietnam War (1946–1954), Part 3: "America's Mandarin" (1954–1963), Part 4: "LBJ Goes to War" (1964–1965), Part 5: "America Takes Charge" (1965–1967), Part 6: "America's Enemy" (1954–1967), Part 7: "Tet 1968," Part 8: "Vietnamizing the War" (1968–1973), Part 9: "Cambodia and Laos," Part 10: "Peace Is at Hand" (1968–1973), Part 11: "Homefront USA," Part 12: "The End of the Tunnel" (1973–1975), Part 13: "Legacies."

The importance of *Vietnam: A Television History* is as a vital reference, a detailed historic narrative for those born after the war and for the baby boomers and their surviving parents it is a way of cutting through the rhetoric of the era. Most important, whether Republican or Democrat, liberal or conservative, it filled in the wide gaps left by the divisive nature of the war and provided benefits from the research that can only be secured many years after the event.

See also: PBS (Public Broadcasting Service); *Vol. 1, The 1950s–1960s: The Twentieth Century*; *Victory at Sea*.

Further Resources

Karnow, Stanley. 1984. *Vietnam: A History. The First Complete Account of Vietnam at War.* New York: Viking.

Turse, Nick. 2013. *Kill Anything That Moves: The Real American War in Vietnam.* New York: Picador.

War and Remembrance (ABC, 1988–1989)

Herman Wouk (1915–) is a Pulitzer Prize–winning author and bestselling writer whose work has been translated into popular motion pictures including *The Caine Mutiny* (1954), *Marjorie Morningstar* (1958), and *Youngblood Hawke* (1964), which was a drama about the rise and fall of a writer modeled on Thomas Wolfe (1900–1938).

Wouk's earlier World War II experiences influenced the monumental novel *The Winds of War*, which was published in 1971 to great critical acclaim and book sales. Wouk adapted his own novel for the screen, broadcast as a miniseries on the ABC Network. It was presented from February 6, 1983 through February 13, 1983.

The sequel to *The Winds of War* novel became *War and Remembrance*, published in October 1978. It was also a bestseller. Like the first book, it was adapted into a miniseries. It aired on ABC November 13–23, 1988 and May 7–14, 1989, and ran 30 hours. This time the screenplay was written by Herman Wouk, Dan Curtis, and Earl W. Wallace. The formidable Curtis, who earlier was best known as the creator of the vampire soap opera *Dark Shadows,* was also the executive producer and director of *War and Remembrance.*

Filmmaking took place in 10 countries employing 757 sets. Some of the concentration camps were filmed on location in Poland at the infamous Auschwitz death camp. The November section of *War and Remembrance* was shown in seven episodes and covered the period from 1941 to 1943. The May broadcasts continued from 1943 and moved to the end of World War II in 1945, then beyond into 1954.

Complex Casting

The reception to *War and Remembrance* was not positive. The casting may have contributed to the lack of rating success. Some television critics and TV historians blamed the show's failure on the sense that the public was tired of the long form miniseries, which decidedly was a factor. However, from the first episode in part one of *War and Remembrance* the sizable audience that had watched *The Winds of War* was distracted and confused about which actors played what parts. Although many of the regular actors reprised their roles and as was standard practice new characters and actors were introduced to freshen the narrative and provide new connections, important characters from the first miniseries were played by different actors than those who had played them originally. ABC was believed to have lost at least $20 million on the production.

John Houseman (1902–1988) was too frail to reprise Aaron Jastrow and was replaced by John Gielgud (1904–2000). Ali MacGraw (1939–) was considered too old to play Natalie Henry at the time of the sequel, so she was replaced by Jane Seymour (1951–). Jan-Michael Vincent (1944–), who played Byron Henry in *The Winds of War,* was busy shooting the action lead on the television series *Airwolf* (1984–1987), but information also pointed to his excessive drinking making him difficult on the set. Vincent was replaced by Hart Bochner (1956–). Other major replacements for various reasons include: Sharon Stone (1958–) as Janice replacing Deborah Winters (1953–), Leslie Hope (1965–) as Madeline replacing Lisa Eilbacher (1955–), Michael Woods as Warren replacing Ben Murphy (1942–), Robert Morley (1908–1992) as Alistair Tudsbury replacing Michael Logan, Barry Bostwick (1945–) as Aster replacing Joseph Hacker, and Steven Berkoff (1937–) portraying Adolf Hitler replacing Günter Meisner (1926–1994).

Not only did the audience have to remind themselves about the current actor and character, they were sometimes led in different directions by the new actor's portrayal of a character they thought they knew well.

War and Remembrance seems to be accurate about the timeline of the war. Graphics spelled out the time and place periodically. The production values were strong. Those interested in a straight historical account were pulled in by many romantic plot lines. These subplots humanized the great catastrophe that was World War II and also added a dramatic feel reminiscent of a nighttime soap opera. Still compelling, epic, and massive with beautifully staged battle scenes and the size and space of an epic, *War and Remembrance* helped mark the end of an era, a great experiment called long form television—the miniseries.

See also: *The Winds of War*; *Vol. 1, The 1950s–1960s: The Twentieth Century*; *Victory at Sea*; *Vol. 3, The 1990s–Present:* The History Channel.

Further Resources

Wouk, Herman. 1978. *War and Remembrance*. New York: Little, Brown.

Wouk, Herman. 2016. *Sailor and Fiddler: Reflections of a 100-Year-Old Author*. New York: Simon & Schuster.

War of the Worlds (Syndication, 1988–1990)

This first-run syndicated television series based on the H. G. Wells novel takes place in present time (the series premiered in 1988) as a sequel 35 years after Paramount Pictures released a motion picture adaptation of the Wells classic. The one-hour series ran for two seasons and totaled 43 episodes.

The iconic science fiction novel *War of the Worlds* was written by H. G. Wells and published in 1898. The story concerned aliens who come in an armada to take over the Earth. The 1953 film was produced by George Pal (1908–1980) with the director Byron Haskin (1899–1984), and it starred Gene Barry (1919–2009) and Ann Robinson (1929–). The picture won the Oscar for Best Visual Effects and had a strong influence on science fiction films that followed. At the conclusion of that film the alien invaders had been neutralized by bacteria. At the opening of the television series it was learned that the aliens had not been killed but had been dormant in a state of amnesia and had been reawakened from their underground disposal sites by a terrorist group, the People's Liberation Party. Now they had a new power, the ability to take over a human body. The government forms a group to battle the new alien threat. The war was waged by Dr. Harrison Blackwood, played by Jared Martin (1941–); computer scientist Norton Drake, portrayed by Philip Akin (1950–); microbiologist Suzanne McCullough, played by Lynda Mason Green; and Lieutenant Colonel Paul Ironhorse, portrayed by Richard Chaves (1951–).

During season one there is an effort to eradicate the aliens and the methods the government team employs are very violent and gory. The dead bodies of the aliens and their host bodies melt in a gruesome puddle. The aliens, known as Mor-Taxans from the planet Mor-Tax, have no problem torturing humans, especially by gouging out eyes using their third arm that bursts out of their chest. The leaders of the aliens, known as the Advocacy, want to colonize on Earth before their planet dies. In the first season, all the episodes had biblical titles such as "The Walls of Jericho" and "Among the Philistines."

For the second season another group of aliens known as the Morthrens landed on earth to make matters even worse. The show title had been changed to *War of the Worlds—the Second Invasion*. The Morthrens found a way to transmute into human bodies, but the bodies are easily damaged. The government team has begun to deteriorate with members missing or in conflict with each other. The original theme of war between two races has fallen by the wayside and the main story line shows humans living in a desolate world. The show was cancelled after 14 episodes in season two, but the producers were about to complete six more episodes and craft a kind of conclusion to the series. The last episode, "The Obelisk," is bleak and portends the release of a spore that will destroy all organisms on Earth.

See also: *V*.

Further Resources

Sherebourne, Michael, and Christopher Priest. 2012. *H.G. Wells: Another Kind of Life*. London: Peter Owen.

Wells, H. G. 2015. *War of the Worlds*. Mockingbird Classics Publishing.

Webster (ABC, 1983–1987)

In this half-hour ABC family-oriented sitcom an undersized African American boy recently orphaned came under the guardianship of a white couple. The boy's parents were both killed in car accident.

Alex Karras (1935–2012) was a professional football player turned actor who played George Papadopoulos, an ex–football player turned sportscaster who had promised a black teammate that if necessary he would look after his young son. Susan Clark (1940–2012), who in real life was married to Alex Karras, played George's wife Katherine Calder-Young, an ombudsperson for the city of Chicago. Emmanuel Lewis (1971–) was the orphaned seven-year-old Webster Long. The young actor was actually 12 years old but stood only three feet four inches. Henry Silver (1945–2013) played Jerry Silver, Katherine's secretary.

The series was born when ABC programming chief Lew Erlicht saw Emmanuel Lewis featured in a Burger King commercial. He wanted to build a television series around him. Concurrently producer Stu Silver wanted to create a sitcom based on the characters played by Spencer Tracy and Katharine Hepburn in *Woman of the Year* (1942). *Webster* was a hit and the chemistry between Karras and Clark was solid. America loved little Webster. Emmanuel Lewis was not just cute, he had real comic gifts and played his part to the hilt.

The content of *Webster* was largely light with kids' issues such as Webster being unable to sleep without his teddy bear. However, there were some serious themes such as teaching Webster about mentally challenged children and for George and Katherine to explain to Webster that his parents were not just "away" but had passed on and were not coming back.

There was a struggle on the set between Karras and Clark and the creators. The couple wanted the show to be more about the recently married twosome. ABC saw Emmanuel Lewis as a money maker because of his cuteness factor. Karras and Clark won most of these creative arguments, but Lewis was given production credit alongside the company.

In the end professionalism and real joy for the human premise of *Webster* won, although the reality was that viewers largely tuned in to watch Webster.

See also: *The Cosby Show*; *Diff'rent Strokes*; *Fat Albert and the Cosby Kids*; *The Jeffersons.*

Further Resources

Hall, Jane. 1984. "Emmanuel Lewis Got a Boost from Michael Jackson but as Webster He Stands on His Own." April 9. *People* Magazine. http://www.people.com/people/archive/article/0,,20087551,00.html

Karras, Alex. 1978. *Even Big Guys Cry*. New York: Signet.

West 57th (CBS, 1985–1989)

This was a prime-time newsmagazine show representative of a new administration at CBS News. It was designed to appeal to a younger demographic and be hipper and faster paced than CBS's long-running *60 Minutes,* which had veteran reporters on camera. For *West 57th* the reporters were all under 35 years old. There was a feeling that *60 Minutes* in its 17th season would start to wane, so *West 57th* was considered by the new executives both as competition to *60 Minutes* and its eventual replacement.

West 57th was given a trial run in late summer 1985. The support staff came from the ranks of CBS and others were hired away from MTV and *Entertainment Tonight.* The name of the show came from the Manhattan street where the offices of CBS news were located.

The rapid-fire opening of the show pictured the four correspondents, John Ferrugia (1951–), Bob Sirott (1949–), Meredith Vieira (1953–), and Jane Wallace (1956–), walking the halls, grabbing coffee, talking on the phone, and meeting each other to the accompaniment of a musical score. The format was similar to that of other magazine shows, but *West 57th* presented five stories each week, two more than *60 Minutes.* Show business figures and rock and roll stars were regularly profiled; there were quite a few investigative reports, including reports on drugs, right-to-lifers, and the Nicaraguan contras. Even though they were young, three of the four correspondents had network news experience. Sirott was the exception; he was a lifestyle and entertainment editor at a Chicago station.

Other stories covered included a story on Albert Goldman's scathing biography on the late John Lennon, the bad conditions in a meat-packing factory, and a profile on the lives and jobs of Major League Baseball umpires.

CBS News staffers past and present disliked the show. *The Christian Science Monitor* and *The New York Times* gave it bad reviews. It did return in the summer of 1986 and in April 1987. Don Hewitt (1922–2009), the executive producer, hired Meredith Vieira and Steve Kroft (who had joined *West 57th* in 1987) in the fall of 1989 to replace Diane Sawyer (1945–), who left for ABC and her own series, *PrimeTime Live.* The show did not fulfill its intended goal of replacing the iconic *60 Minutes.*

See also: *Entertainment Tonight*; *Vol. 1, The 1950s–1960s: 60 Minutes.*

Further Resources

Beattie, Keith. 2004. *Documentary Screens: Non-Fiction Film and Television*. Houndsmills, Basingstoke, UK.

Rapping, Elayne. 1986. *The Looking Glass World of Non-Fiction Television*. New York: South End Press.

Westheimer, Dr. Ruth (1928–)

Dr. Ruth is an icon who revolutionized the presentation of frank, honest, and detailed talk about sex in general and sexual relations between men, women, and other possibilities. Born Karola Ruth Siegel in Wiesenfeld (Karlstadt) Germany, her parents were Orthodox Jews. In January 1939 Ruth Westheimer was sent

Dr. Ruth Westheimer brought frank discussion concerning sex to television. Her jocular style helped to make serious issues more palatable to the public. (AP Photo/Scott Stewart)

to Switzerland by her mother and grandmother as part of the *Kindertransport* after her father had been captured by the Nazis. She came of age in an orphanage and in September 1941 she abruptly stopped receiving letters from both her parents. In 1945 she was told her parents had been murdered during the Holocaust, possibly at the Auschwitz concentration camp. Westheimer immigrated to the British Mandate of Palestine where her 17th birthday passed. In Jerusalem she joined the Jewish paramilitary organization Haganah, and because she was only 4' 7" she was trained as a scout and sniper. Westheimer was seriously injured in action during the Israeli War of Independence in 1948 and could not walk for several months.

In 1950 she relocated to France and studied and later taught psychology at the University of Paris. In 1956 Westheimer immigrated to the United States, settling in the Washington Heights section of New York City. In 1959 she earned an MA in sociology from the New School for Social Research and an EdD degree from Teacher's College, Columbia University in 1970. She completed postdoctoral work in human sexuality at New York–Presbyterian Hospital, training with pioneering sex therapist Helen Singer Kaplan.

Dr. Ruth is constantly in demand on the lecture circuit and she has spoken at societies, schools, and a wide range of organizations. In addition to her own television shows Dr. Ruth has been a guest on a panoply of programs including *The Today Show, The David Letterman Show, The View, Star Talk,* and *The Arsenio Hall Show*. Westheimer played herself in episode 87 of *Quantum Leap*. She also has appeared in commercials, including one for Signal mouthwash and for the Honda Prelude.

Her career on the airwaves first began in 1980. NBC Radio's New York City adult contemporary station WYNY-NY was struggling, so new talk shows were being developed. The community affairs manager heard Westheimer speak at a radio function and suggested she work for the station. The show *Sexually Speaking* was given a 15-minute slot beginning at midnight on Sunday. Dr. Ruth thought it would be effective to have guests covering urology, neurology, gynecology, and other such topics. Alternatively, it was suggested there be no guests and that the doctor answer questions from the listeners. NBC was reluctant to allow the Q&A format. The problem was resolved by getting letters from the public so the network could control the way Westheimer answered them on the air.

The show quickly became known as *Dr. Ruth* and caught on in almost every sector. After two months the program was expanded to one hour and was broadcast live. Now Westheimer could directly answer callers' questions. NBC put in a 7-second delay to protect itself against any obscenity or controversial language. Dr. Ruth was candid, informational, funny, and respectful. She was unafraid of going into any area—her tag line was "Get some."

Dr. Ruth became a national celebrity and a household name, broadcast on radio across the country. In 1982 she became an electronic sexual pioneer with a television show that first aired in 1982 as a 15-minute taped program on Lifetime Cable (1984–). It continued to grow in popularity and was nationally syndicated.

Dr. Ruth Westheimer has written several books on human sexuality including *Dr. Ruth's Encyclopedia of Sex* (2000) and *Sex for Dummies* (2001). Some of the topics discussed on *Dr. Ruth's* TV show included group sex, penile implants, vaginal orgasm, clitoral orgasms, anal sex, kinky sex, pornography, foreplay, talking dirty during sex. She had high-profile guests who talked sex and joked with the doctor. They included Réne Taylor, Abe Vigoda, Sarah Bernhardt, Jerry Seinfeld, Erica Jong, and many others.

The brand that is Dr. Ruth is made up of more than her mind and expertise; she also has the gift to talk to people about sex. She always wears a colorful dress with pearls or a necklace and has a full mane of hair fashioned in a high-layered old-style hairdo, and an infectious laugh, which is really a cackle, that is loved by all.

Further Resources

Westheimer, Ruth. 1986. *Dr. Ruth's Guide to Good Sex.* New York: Grand Central Publishing.

Westheimer, Dr. Ruth K., and Pierre A. Lehu. 2015. *The Doctor Is In: Dr. Ruth on Love, Life and Joie de Vivre.* New York: Amazon Publishing.

Who's the Boss? (ABC, 1984–1992)

This ABC sitcom involved a widower who left New York City with his young daughter to become the housekeeper for a divorced woman and her young son in Connecticut. As time goes by the adult relationship moved toward love. The cast included Tony Danza (1951–) playing Tony Micelli; Judith Light (1949–) as Angela Bower; Alyssa Milano (1972–) as Tony's daughter, Samantha; Danny Pintauro (1976–) as Angela's son, Jonathan; Katherine Helmond (1929–) as Angela's mother, Mona Robinson; and Jonathan Halyalkar as Billy, a five-year-old taken in by Tony when his grandmother became too ill to care for him.

Tony was a former second baseman for the St. Louis Cardinals. He was fed up with the hustle and bustle of Brooklyn and wanted to relocate to a more suburban area to provide a better quality of life for his daughter. He became a domestic for Angela Bower, who was a high-powered but disorganized president of the Wallace and McQuade advertising agency.

Although Angela always worried about her career, she was fired in 1986, which prompted her to open her own agency. Romance walked into her life when she met handsome Geoffrey Wells, played by Robin Thomas (1949–), and this caused her to recognize her growing fondness for Tony. By 1991, a full seven years after Tony and Angela first met, they admitted they were in love.

The reversal of roles was very important for television and the culture. *Charles in Charge* (1984–1990) and *Who's the Boss?* demonstrated that men could do the same domestic work as women, acknowledging the idea that masculinity wasn't defined by what you do. Tony Danza was perfect for the role, energetic, a guy's guy, and a good father. The humorous show was popular for those reasons. The producers were tempted by the idea of having Tony and Angela marry, but when the show ended there had been no wedding; however, Tony earned a college degree. The program won a prime-time Emmy and maintained consistently good ratings throughout its tenure.

See also: *Taxi*.

Further Resources

Danza, Tony. 2013. *I'd Like to Apologize to Every Teacher I Ever Had: My Year as a Rookie Teacher at Northeast High*. New York: Random House.

Milano, Alyssa. 2010. *Safe at Home: Confessions of a Baseball Fanatic*.

The Winds of War (ABC, 1983)

Herman Wouk's (1915–) World War II experiences influenced his monumental novel *The Winds of War,* published in 1971 to great critical acclaim and book sales. Wouk won the Pulitzer Prize for his bestselling 1951 novel *The Caine Mutiny,* which like his next book, *Marjorie Morningstar,* was turned into a popular movie, as well as his 1960 novel *Youngblood Hawke,* a drama about the rise and fall of a writer modeled on Thomas Wolfe (1900–1938). Wouk adapted *The Winds of War* for the screen and it was broadcast as a miniseries on the ABC Network, which had a fine record for long form television. It was presented February 6–13, 1983. The series' budget was $40,000,000, the script was 962 pages, and there were 1,785 scenes filmed in six countries over 14 months. The action started in the earliest years of World War II from the Nazi Blitzkrieg of Poland in 1939 and the Japanese attack on Pearl Harbor in 1941.

The Characters

The central character was Victor "Pug" Henry, an American naval officer played by the notorious and legendary Hollywood movie star Robert Mitchum (1917–1997), whose assignments during those years took him all over the world.

The epic cast included Polly Bergen (1930–2014) as his wife, Rhoda Henry; Ben Murphy (1942–) as their older son, Warren; Jan-Michael Vincent (1944–) as their younger son, Byron; and Lisa Eilbacher (1956–) as their daughter, Madeline. Ali MacGraw (1939–) portrayed Nathalie Jastrow, who eventually married Bryon. David Dukes (1925–2000) played an American diplomatic officer, Leslie Slote. Peter Graves (1926–2010) played Palmer Kirby, Ralph Bellamy (1904–1991) portrayed President Franklin Delano Roosevelt, Howard Lang (1911–1989) portrayed Winston Churchill, Gunter Meisner (1926–1994) portrayed Adolf Hitler, and Jeremy Kemp (1935–) played the German general Von Roon.

Dan Curtis, who was responsible for *Dark Shadows,* the vampire soap opera, produced the series and was a director on it as well. *Winds of War* was so successful that in mid-1984 plans for a sequel, *War and Remembrance,* were announced.

To increase the realism factor for *The Winds of War,* documentary footage from the war was integrated into the scenes. A period-sounding announcer used voice-over in many places throughout the story. William Woodson (1917–) lent his considerable talents to this effort.

The music had sweeping memorable themes composed and conducted by Robert Cobert (1924–). *The Winds of War* garnered 10 Emmy nominations and won for Outstanding Cinematography for a Limited Series or a Special and Outstanding Individual Achievement—Costumers and Outstanding Individual Achievement—Special Effects.

The popularity of *The Winds of War* was in the power and accuracy with which it depicted political and war situations. The characters are not just pawns but living, breathing people with desires and ambition. There is quite a bit of romance in this miniseries to heighten the drama and to build as big a viewer base as possible. There were more female characters than usual in this type of narrative and plenty of action for everyone. There are considerable graphics spelling out time and place, especially as the assault on Poland moves ever closer. The imagery of the weapons of war—the bombs and tanks rolling—is overwhelming, and the old technology of matte painting was utilized to create vivid backgrounds.

An epic of its time, *The Winds of War* would be difficult to mount in the 21st century because production costs would be prohibitive. It stands as a monument to television at a time when the networks took risks and producers like Dan Curtis were convinced they could accurately depict World War II on the television screen.

See also: *War and Remembrance*.

Further Resources

Beichman, Arnold. 1984. *Herman Wouk: The Novelist as Social Historian*. New Jersey: Transaction Publishers.

Wouk, Herman. 1972. *The Winds of War*. New York: Little, Brown.

Wiseguy (CBS, 1987–1990)

Stephen J. Cannell (1941–2010) Productions offered this one-hour crime show on CBS, which starred Ken Wahl (1957–) as Vinnie Terranova, an undercover agent for the Federal Organized Crime Bureau. Jonathan Banks (1947–) played his high-pressure boss, Frank McPike, and Jim Byrnes (1948–) played Lifeguard, the communications expert who provided Vinnie's sole link to the O.C.B. when on assignment. In order to prove to the mob he was one of them, he served 18 months in prison.

The show was structured in story arcs. Each story spanned from five to 10 episodes. This was a clear break from the traditional crime show where there was one crime and one crook per week. For the 1987–1988 season there were two stories. The first featured Ray Sharkey (1952–1993) as Sonny Steelgrave, an Atlantic City mobster. The second starred Kevin Spacey (1959–) and Joan Severance (1958–) playing a deranged brother/sister duo, Mel and Susan Profitt, with William Russ (1950–) as fellow wiseguy Roger Locco. In the second season Vinnie's brother Peter died and Vinnie investigated a white supremacist group and the garment industry. Vinnie also investigated the record business, which allowed the producer to cast some known rockers such as Deborah Harry (1945–).

Wiseguy was a crime show, a genre widely represented throughout the history of television. *The Untouchables* (1959–1963) showed law enforcement fighting the mob. *Wiseguy* was unique because of Vinnie's underground position as an outsider who was really an insider. This perspective allowed audiences to see mob activity and the investigation process in a manner they were not used to but found fascinating.

Further Resources

Abadinsky, Howard. 2012. *Organized Crime*. Belmont, CA: Wadsworth Cengage Learning.

Tamblyn, Robin. 2010. *Looking Closer: Kevin Spacey, the First Fifty Years*. New York: iUniverse.

The Wonder Years (ABC, 1988–1993)

This critically acclaimed and popular half-hour ABC comedy/drama was the lead character's 20-year backward look to 1968. Fred Savage (1976–) played the central character,12-year-old Kevin Arnold, who was just about to start school at John F. Kennedy Junior High. Daniel Stern (1957–) provided the voice of the adult Kevin and was the narrator for each episode. Jason Hervey (1972–) played Kevin's older brother, Wayne, who delighted in teasing him. Olivia d'Abo (1969–) played his hippie older sister, Karen. Dan Lauria (1947–) played his gruff father, Jack; Alley Mills (1951–) was his mother, Norma; and Dancia McKellar (1975–) was his neighbor and sometimes girlfriend, Gwendolyn (Winnie) Cooper. Josh Saviano (1976–) was his nerdy friend, Paul Pfeiffer; Ben Stein (1944–) portrayed his science teacher, Mr. Cantwell; and Robert Picardo (1953–) was the fearsome gym teacher, Coach Ed Cutlip.

The Wonder Years had a special preview in January 1988 immediately following ABC's telecast of the Super Bowl. In the spring it surfaced for a limited run and then went into full production in the fall. In fall 1991 Kevin and his pals left junior high school and entered McKinley High School.

Like *Happy Days* (1974–1984) and *Laverne and Shirley* (1976–1983), *The Wonder Years* looked back with a gentler eye and concentrated on relationships and family. It covered a time of great upheaval in the United States, but audiences enjoyed its focus on growing up and home life. Nostalgia was still very much in demand with a desire to push back the bad and remember the good. There was plenty of television dealing with reality, history or otherwise. *The Wonder Years* made viewers remember what it was like dealing with those growing-up issues with humor and innocence.

See also: *Happy Days*; *Laverne and Shirley*.

Further Resources

Anderson, Terry H. 2011. *The Sixties*. Boston: Pearson.

Arnow, Fred. 2015. *Baby Boomer Reflections: Eighteen Special Years between 1946 and 1964*. CreateSpace Independent Publishing Platform.

Essays

The Decline of Family Sitcoms and the Rise of More Urban and Social Issue–Oriented Programs

As the family sitcoms of the 1950s and 1960s such as *Father Knows Best* (1954–1963), *Leave It to Beaver* (1957–1963), and *The Adventures of Ozzie and Harriet* (1952–1966), which portrayed the traditional family unit as it reflected American home life, began to fade out, a new kind of family sitcom was on the rise, one that more closely mirrored life in the United States.

The Eisenhower 1950s were largely a time of peace and prosperity. The Kennedy and Johnson era of the 1960s brought violence, war, a counterculture, a renaissance of the arts, and a cultural revolution for women, African Americans, and gay pride. However, as the decade of change ended, the joy of Woodstock turned to death at a Rolling Stones concert at the Altamont Speedway and on December 6, 1969, the dawning of Aquarius was all over before New Year's Eve could ring the official bell bringing in the 1970s. Financial and psychological depression, unemployment, and a presidential scandal of epic proportions turned the country largely away from the light to the dark. Television provided some illumination with humor and a looking glass into the myriad cultures and issues facing the nation.

No show of the 1970s better reflected culture, class, and bigotry than the Norman Lear (1922–) production *All in the Family* (1971–1979). The show's high ratings reflected a high viewership in the upper, lower, and middle classes in America. The draw was the head of a middle-class family, the Bunkers. Archie Bunker, played by Carroll O'Connor (1924–2001), sat in a revered chair in the center of the lower floor of the home as if it were a throne. His wife Edith (Jean Stapleton, 1923–2013) was called "Dingbat" by her husband and demeaned by him as someone who is ditzy and not too smart. The reality was that Edith was smarter and not bigoted and prejudiced like Archie. Sally Struthers (1947–) was the Bunker's long blonde haired hippie daughter Gloria, who shared Aquarian views with her equally counterculture and hippie-haired husband, Michael, played by Rob Reiner (1947–).

The focus of practically every episode of *All in the Family* was Archie Bunker spewing his views on race, the current state of affairs, religion, and the stupidity of his son-in-law, who was of Polish descent. Norman Lear had it all, a hit sitcom and a show that jabbed back at the early clean-cut, white bread sitcoms of the 1950s and 1960s and broke new ground by presenting bigoted ideas and speech through the vessel of Archie Bunker. Archie's marriage with Edith represented the stereotypical gender roles, where the man of the house ruled everything and the woman tended the home, while Mike and Gloria were the 1960s flower children trying to set their elders straight. The arguments and colorful dialogue and situations made *All in the Family* a classic of New Wave television.

Divorce statistics were on the rise in the 1970s, whereas the greatest generation believed in staying together despite negative issues. Baby Boomers lived less moral lives, there was a sexual revolution during the 1960s, they married young, and during the seventies they were breaking marriage bonds in record numbers.

This was represented on 1970s television in *One Day at a Time* (1975–1984). Bonnie Franklin

(1944–2013) played Ann Romano, a single mom of two teenage girls, the older, Julie, played by Mackenzie Phillips (1959–) and the younger, Barbara, played by Valerie Bertinelli (1960–). The action centered on Ann's struggles with taking care of her family on child support and trying to find a job, as well as bringing up the girls and confronting subjects such as virginity, sex, birth control, alcohol, and drugs. This show did all this with a direct and forthright tone and still managed to keep viewers laughing.

Coming a long way from *Amos 'n' Andy* and *Beulah,* the 1970s exploded with African American comedies that stayed away or reversed prior stereotypes; many were very popular across the country. They included *Sanford and Son* (1972–1977), *Good Times* (1974–1979), *The Jeffersons* (1975–1985), *What's Happening* (1976–1979), and *Diff'rent Strokes* (1978–1986).

The Jeffersons was a spin-off from *All in the Family* and portrayed George Jefferson (Sherman Hemsley, 1938–2012) and his wife Louise (Isabel Sanford, 1917–2004). They were once neighbors of the Bunkers in Queens, New York, then moved to Manhattan and became rich from George's string of dry-cleaning stores. *The Jeffersons* was a landmark show for shattering African American stereotypes on TV by leaping from the image of butlers and maids and working for whites to ownership and having the whites pay him for services rendered. Also George Jefferson had plenty of confidence in himself and his business; he was blustery and cocky at times but always proud that he had made it.

Good Times (1974–1979) was a spin-off of *Maude* (1972–1978) and took place in a high-rise project in Chicago. Struggling to survive was the theme here. The principal cast comprised John Amos (1939–) as James Evans and Esther Rolle as his wife Florida (1920–1998). They had three children but it was J.J., played by Jimmie Walker (1947–), who stole the show with his outrageous antics and constantly yelling "Dyno-mite!" which caught on as a catchphrase across the country and was included in lists of great television phrases. *Good Times* presented a strong black family trying to get out of the lower classes as well as the parental relationship, the parent-child dynamic, and the interplay of siblings. It also reflected racial issues from the inside and their effects.

Raunchy stand-up comedian Red Foxx (1922–1991) cleaned himself up of curse words only to exchange them for bigoted language toward almost anyone white as the cantankerous Fred Sanford in *Sanford and Son,* in which his son Lamont was played by Demond Wilson (1946–). Norman Lear (1922–) was behind this NBC series, which he hoped would be an answer to *All in the Family,* which was running at CBS. Fred Sanford was a widower who made his living as a junkman. He constantly spewed racial humor and bigotry, and was a schemer in the get-rich-quick school like *The Honeymooners*' (1955–1956) Ralph Kramden. His relationship with his son Lamont mirrored that of Archie Bunker with his son-in-law Mike Stivic. Again it was the young trying to lead the elder. Lamont lectured his father about his old school ways, which made Fred let loose with the worst he had.

The Hispanic voice came through on *Chico and the Man* (1974–1978) in the form of Chico Rodriguez, a Mexican American automobile mechanic played by Freddie Prinze (1954–1977) and the Man being the cranky owner of the shop, Ed Brown, played by Jack Albertson (1907–1981). Ed Brown was a nonstop human insult machine. Chico always saw the bright side and was proud of his heritage. His boss, although situated in an east L.A. ghetto, spent much time attacking Hispanics and taunting his good-natured mechanic. Brown was not too nice to his customers as well.

The gay community was rarely depicted on screen, and when it was, it was often in the most negative terms. Also a landmark show, *Soap* (1977–1981), which was a nighttime parody of daytime soap operas, followed the wild exploits of two sisters and their families. The show was in a serial format like a soap opera and had a very large cast. A range of strange topics tackled on *Soap* included alien abduction, demonic possession, murder, and kidnapping. At the time viewers thought that one of the characters, Jodie Dallas played by Billy Crystal (1948–), was the first openly gay male character on television in a major part, but that distinction belongs to Vincent Schiavelli (1948–2005), who played Peter Panama in the short-lived series *The Corner Bar* (1972–1973). However, Crystal did play an openly gay man among a torrent of controversy from the religious right, which was deeply offended by the character. Although Jodie maintained his homosexuality through the run, he fathered a child during a one-night stand with a woman, and it was known to the regular audience that Jodie had other relationships with women. Whatever the reason and motivation, Jodie was a prominent gay character on screen, and Crystal was brilliant and brave to take on such a controversial role.

"Jiggle TV" was a genre of the 1970s created by remarks made by NBC executive Paul Klein criticizing a programming trend on the ABC network of shows in which the body of an actress was known to move in a manner considered seductive or salacious. This genre includes such 1970s shows as *Charlie's Angels* (1976–1981), *Love Boat* (1977–1986), and *Fantasy Island* (1978–1984)—all shows under the Aaron Spelling (1923–2006) banner. *Three's Company* (1977–1984), which was not produced by Spelling, was a popular example of "jiggle TV" especially in the character Chrissy Snow played by the blonde Suzanne Somers (1946–). This show was principally known for another variation on the family sitcom. Three single roommates, Chrissy Snow, Janet Wood (Joyce DeWitt, 1949–), and Jack Tripper (John Ritter, 1948–2003), lived together in an apartment. They were not involved in a relationship with each other in any way. This was a new kind of nuclear family, one that reflected the growing trend of men and women living together as roommates for convenience and economics. Keeping up with the rent generated some of the humor as well as story lines concerning relationships they were having on the outside, continual misunderstandings, financial struggles, and private lives of the trio. Chrissy did wind up being a stereotypical dumb blonde, proving some viewers didn't want total changes in television programming.

The 1970s progressive sitcom owes a lot to *The Dick Van Dyke Show* (1961–1966), featuring an upwardly mobile nuclear family consisting of a husband, Rob Petrie, his wife, Laura, and their son, Ritchie; as well as having a second family at work with two other comedy writers, one female, one male; and their boss, the host of the comedy show they write for, and his dour right-hand man.

Television tends to reflect the world as it is in any decade in America. These sitcoms used what was happening in the country as a frame, but they still were meant for entertainment. Using comedy to address family issues and relationships showed the humor in the human condition. The sitcoms of the 1970s shunned the all-white perfect families of past decades and presented diversity in all its glory. This liberated writers and performers as well as the audience, who could now directly relate to TV sitcoms because they had their own representation, regardless of race and gender. Although the 1970s seemed to many to be a come-down from the highest of the 1960s in terms of economics and politics, the seventh decade of the 20th century was an era that saw a new kind of cinema, a new kind of music, literature, art, and especially a time in television when many doors were opened and windows shattered.

Further Resources

Berman, A. S. 2013. *Soap! The Inside Story of the Sitcom That Broke All the Rules.* Albany, GA: BearManor Media.

Dalton, Mary M. 2016. *The Sitcom Reader,* 2nd Edition: *America Reviewed, Still Skewed.* New York: State University of New York.

Lear, Norman. 2015. *Even This I Get to Experience.* New York: Penguin Books.

McCrohan, Donna. 1988. *Archie & Edith, Mike & Gloria: The Tumultuous History of All in the Family.* New York: Workman Press.

Waldron, Vince. 2011. *The Official Dick Van Dyke Show Book: The Definitive History of Television's Most Enduring Comedy.* New York: Applause Theatre Books.

Wilson, Demond. 2009. *Second Banana: The Bitter Sweet Memoirs of the Sanford & Sons Years.* Demond Wilson Enterprises. http://www.demondwilson.org/

The Evangelical Electric Church: High-Powered Religion Comes to 1970s Television

Religion has always been a major part of the fabric of American society, with many Americans attending their houses of worship in many faiths and denominations. Americans also have followed media trends, so the invention of the radio gave birth to a new kind of preaching that later in the 1980s would be called televangelism. One of the first ministers to broadcast his interpretation of the scriptures was S. Parkes Cadman

(1864–1936), reaching millions of parishioners who didn't have to leave their homes to receive the gospel from this powerful orator. As 1928 came Cadman was now on weekly, broadcasting on NBC on Sunday afternoons. Many other radio preachers followed: Aimee Semple McPherson (1890–1944); the notorious anticommunist, antisemitic Father Charles Coughlin (1891–1979); Bishop Fulton J. Sheen (1895–1979); and many others into the 1930s and 1940s, plying their pastoral duties inside the electric church.

On February 12, 1952 on the DuMont Network, Bishop Fulton Sheen (1895–1979) became one of, if not the first televangelist with a weekly program: *Life Is Worth Living,* which ran to April 26, 1955, then shifted to ABC until 1957. The bishop would later have similar programs. He often addressed his home audience directly, dressed in his bishop's robes. His face was strong, as was his voice. Bishop Sheen's oratory skills were superb, achieving a connection with his parishioners outside of the actual church. On *Life Is Worth Living*, Bishop Sheen's one-on-one rapport caused a deeply religious experience for home viewers. He was not paid for his television appearances and spoke without a script or cue cards; occasionally he would demonstrate a thought on a chalkboard. Although he often spoke to a live audience, which made the viewers feel they were part of a crowd, at the same time he communicated with home viewers in their homes, which became a church. Everyone felt that Bishop Fulton J. Sheen was there for them individually.

Another major early televangelist, Billy Graham (1918–), was the pastor to presidents and millions of people all over the world as well as holding a strong base in the United States. The Reverend brought a new kind of religious programming to Americans. He created what he called a Crusade—a mammoth gathering of believers at which he would preach the word of the gospels and his views on society. The auditoriums, stadiums, and other venues would act as an off-site church and he would stand as if in a pulpit. These Crusades were broadcast across America (and across the globe) and were very highly publicized. Billy Graham was not only a spiritual adviser to every president of his time, but he became a spiritual leader to many Americans.

Oral Roberts (1918–2009) is an example of a preacher who made claims that got to the edge of believability even for the faithful. The controversial Roberts, who preached for over six decades, widely told the story in 1977 that a 900-foot-tall Jesus Christ told him to build City of Faith Medical and Research Center. *The Oral Roberts Show,* which began in 1954 and went beyond the late 1960s, contained passages from the gospel and singing in a plain setting. Roberts also conducted crusades and presented specials.

Pat Robertson (1930–) is best known for his participation in *The 700 Club*. In 1962, when a local TV station in Portsmouth, Virginia was struggling and about to close its doors, a telethon was launched. Robertson suggested a goal of getting 700 members who would each contribute ten dollars—a sum that would keep the station financially afloat. He called them the 700 Club. In 1966 the *700 Club* evangelical television show began and into the 1970s and beyond it became a bully pulpit for the political and social views of Robertson, the son of a U.S. senator with his own political ambitions. As of December 2016 *The 700 Club* was still on the air. Robertson made controversial remarks and presented extremely controversial views. He also considered himself a man who could predict the future, often making dire statements about where humanity was headed. Among the many comments he made on *The 700 Club,* Robertson displayed his negativity toward Muslims and his homophobic views, and compared people who get plastic surgery as looking like Asians, pulling the corners of his eyes to demonstrate.

Robert Schuller (1926–2015) was best known for his pastoring work on *Hour of Power* (1970–), which at first was hosted by his father as a church service at the Garden Grove Community Church (California). The son hosted the show from 2006 to 2008. In 2008 his son-in-law Jim Coleman took over. Schuller announced that he wanted to take the ministry in a different direction and used guest speakers while his son resigned from his role as senior pastor. At his height Schuller had a television audience of over 20 million viewers worldwide. It was at the time the most watched religious show and he was the number one orator. It was a place on the dial where viewers could not just go to church but could hear a fiery speaker who believed in faith and people.

The Trinity Broadcasting Network, which began in 1973, now owns and operates six broadcast networks, including Hillsong Channel, Smile of a Child TV, TBN Enlace, TBN Salsa, and JUCE TV. It owns over 35 full-power television stations and 252 low-power stations. TBN provides a wide range of Christian broadcasting such as gospel music concerts, live coverage of Christian events, talk shows, health and fitness programs, children's shows, Christian music videos, marriage enrichment series, holiday shows, Christian dramas, and full-length family-oriented movies. TBN shows the growth from a simple one-pastor show to a major corporation of religious broadcasting.

PTL Club (1974–1989) was created by Tammy Faye Bakker (1942–2007) and her husband Jim Bakker (1940–), who built a worldwide Christian satellite cable show that resembled *The Tonight Show*. Featured were well-known ministers and Christian recording artists. They even had an announcer and a sidekick. Later the production was moved from the Bakkers' Heritage Village to South Carolina where they had 2,500 acres and a family theme park at newly built studios. The combination of religion and entertainment made the Bakkers famous and wealthy. A complex scandal involving Bakker and a woman who was part of the ministry destroyed his marriage and lost him his ministry.

Jimmy Swaggart (1935–) began his television ministry in 1975 with a half-hour program; as he built its popularity it was expanded to one hour. Later he began a daily weekday broadcast featuring music and Bible study. On the weekend his show included a service from his church, Family Worship Center, or an on-location crusade in a major city. Scandal nearly destroyed him. It was uncovered that the pastor had been in the company of prostitutes. He used the television camera to beg for forgiveness and called himself a sinner, crying uncontrollably. That moment has been often played and is a seminal image in televangelism.

Jerry Falwell (1933–2007) dominated religious broadcasting in the 1970s. He became synonymous with televangelism and was an unstoppable force in spiritual, political, personal, and cultural matters. Falwell's background didn't bode well for a man of such enormous reach, power, and influence in the religious world. His father had been a bootlegger and was agnostic. His grandfather was a dedicated atheist. On April 12, 1958 Falwell married the former Macel Pate (1933–2015). They were both born and raised in Lynchburg, Virginia. Macel reported later that God spoke to her and Jerry and told them to create a ministry. Falwell founded what has become known as Liberty Christian Academy. During the 1950s and 1960s Falwell spoke harshly against the Reverend Martin Luther King Jr. and racial desegregation. In 1971 he co-founded Moral Majority, which was the centerpiece of Christian fundamentalism and took strong conservative views on the media, abortion, and the Equal Rights Amendment.

The Old-Time Gospel Hour (1956–) was hosted by Falwell and often taped at one of his revival meetings. Falwell, who was a Baptist, preached in the old tradition. He was well groomed and spoke in a controlled manner with great conviction about the Bible and his views concerning the direction of the country during the 1970s. He made viewers a part of his churchly home, calling it a ministry, telling the viewers they were part of a congregation at their neighborhood house of worship. Falwell empowered broadcast television to bridge the link between the pastor and those who were part of his ministry. There was plenty of gospel music to move the brethren. Jerry Falwell believed he influenced his viewers by telling them that God loved them and Jesus Christ loved them. He was a preacher just like the one people heard in a physical church on Sunday. Bible study was an essential segment of *The Old-Time Gospel Hour*. The complex holy book was used to support Falwell and his church's belief. Jerry Falwell liked to tell stories about viewers he met in his travels, one who claimed he was going to commit suicide until he heard the Reverend talk about getting a personal relationship with God, which was the way he ended most shows. Falwell preached eternity and salvation as well. Until the end of his days Jerry Falwell grew his brand, visiting talk shows and embroiling himself with denouncing people in the public eye like Ellen DeGeneres and Larry Flint. He also engaged with political figures to spread his conservative philosophy and apply his religion to the morals and actions of life in America. The legacy of Jerry Falwell is the power of Christian conservatism, religion as a powerful force, and strong inspiration to the next generation, like Joel Osteen (1963–). The television religious figures of the 1970s grew the idea of praying at home and studying the scriptures at home by sitting in front of one's television. The movement would grow beyond the dreams of the men who helped grow it.

At present there are numerous religious channels, enough to keep people in this electronic church 24 hours a day. Television is an entertainment, news, sports, and other areas medium. Since the beginning of television actors, newsmakers, advertisers, and many others have used it to get a message across. Religion is a big part of the lives of many Americans. In the 1970s, the rise of televangelism allowed viewers looking for spiritual guidance and grace to pray and worship at home. Once they could only go to the outside church; now, not only is the church on TV, but viewers no longer have just one priest, minister, or pastor but many with various views to expand the spirituality of those watching.

Further Resources

Falwell, Macel. 2008. *Jerry Falwell: His Life and Legacy*. New York: Simon & Schuster.

Graham, Billy. 2015. *Where Am I: Heaven, Eternity and Our Life Beyond*. New York: Thomas Nelson.

Roberts, Oral. 2005. *When You See the Invisible, You Can Do the Impossible*. Shippensburg, PA: Destiny Image.

Robertson, Pat, and Jamie Buckingham. 1976. *Shout It from the Housetops (The Autobiography of Pat Robertson)*. Plainfield, NJ: Logos International.

Schuller, Robert. 1986. *Move Ahead with Possibility Thinking*. New York: Jove.

Swaggart, Jimmy, 2013. *The Message of the Cross*. Baton Rouge, LA: Jimmy Swaggart Ministries.

Martial Arts and Blaxploitation Television in the 1970s

From the birth of the motion picture, the movies have created and presented genres that reflect their time. After World War II crime films, later labeled film noir by French and global critics, gave an interpretation of the despair, anger, and deep frustration felt by servicemen who survived that bloody war. In these movies, men often turned to crime and the look of the productions was physically dark. The films also featured a woman, known as the femme fatale, responsible for tormenting, if not killing, the doomed male protagonist. Largely in the 1970s two genres became interesting to, if not a wide audience, certainly a niche one—martial arts and blaxploitation. Each had its following; each has its big hits.

Martial arts, the use of the body itself to engage in combat, began around 2879 BCE. When trade increased between the United States and China and Japan at the conclusion of the 19th century, American interest in martial arts began to grow. Soldiers engaged in World War II and then the Korean War (1950–1953) were exposed to jujitsu, karate, and judo.

On television *The Green Hornet* (1966–1967), starring Van Williams (1934–2016) in the title role and Bruce Lee (1940–1973) as Kato, his valet, was a precursor to martial arts on TV in the 1970s. The Green Hornet was, like Batman's Bruce Wayne, very rich and fought crime at night or whenever he could. Kato used his great martial arts skills to assist the Hornet in their missions. Some say Bruce Lee was the greatest martial artist ever in television or film. Lee was the star of many movies, including those responsible for the martial arts movie craze. His work on celluloid includes *The Chinese Connection* (1972), *The Way of the Dragon* (1973), and most famously, *Enter the Dragon* (1973).

The great success of these films, especially *Enter the Dragon,* led to a torrent of martial arts films of all kinds including *A Touch of Zen* (1971), *Five Fingers of Death* (1972), *Lady Snowblood* (1973), *Lone Wolf and Cub: Baby Cart in the Land of Demons* (1974), *The Streetfighter* (1974), *Master of the Flying Guillotine* (1976), *Karate for Life* (1977), *Heroes of the East* (1978), *The 36th Chamber of Shaolin* (1978), and *Five Deadly Venoms* (1978).

Local TV stations across the nation ran a martial arts film on a Saturday or Sunday afternoon. Two of the shows that featured kung fu films were *Kung Fu Theatre* and *Black Belt Theatre*. Some of the films programmed included *The Big Boss* (1971), *Drunken Master* (1978), and *Fatal Needles vs. Fatal Fists* (1978). This practice was very popular among viewers who either had seen the films before or had never seen them because they were foreign. Now they were dubbed in English, usually poorly, with over-the-top sound effects of kicks and bones all over the body being violently broken. This practice continued to the 1980s. The names of the programs usually were combinations of the words of the arts such as Kung Fu, Karate, and an Asian-sounding name or phrase.

In the early days of television stations found it necessary to run motion pictures that had already played on the theater circuit. Usually they were old movies and by the 1950s and 1960s local stations had movie programs like *Million Dollar Movie* that featured films the young audience had not been able to see in their original time; older viewers remembered these films and enjoyed repeat viewing. One of the main differences was that the original screenings were uninterrupted; the television broadcasts were often edited for time and structured with regular intervals of television commercials hawking products. As the decades moved on a new crop of previously released motion pictures came into play, and when blaxploitation and martial arts films came around, local television stations put them into the rotation.

There was one major original martial arts TV series that captured the imagination of more than a niche audience: *Kung Fu* (1972–1975), broadcast on ABC. It was a breakthrough television program that starred David Carradine (1936–2009) as Kwai Chang Caine, a peaceful Shaolin monk. Caine moved through the old American West, searching for his half-brother, Danny Caine. His only training and preparation for this quest was spiritual training and skill in the martial arts. The interest in the show was partly in Caine's Asian spirituality as religions like Zen Buddhism were thriving during the 1970s. Viewers also enjoyed the action aspects of the show. Caine detested injustice and put himself in the position of punishing the perpetrators whenever it arose by applying his deadly martial arts skills, often shot in slow motion to emphasize each blow to the bad guys.

The setting in the West made the show partly a Western but the Asian character and influence turned *Kung Fu* into an East/West affair. The Western genre showed the difficulty of life in America's early days—the Eastern aspect brought Zen-like philosophy, and the martial artist skills bestowed on Caine merged peace with violence for the cause of justice and righteousness.

Kung Fu was literally a new television genre in itself. Although it had a decent run it was not imitated. Maybe it was because of a Bruce Lee lawsuit claiming he was once considered for the role or maybe a martial arts television series was too complex to produce. *Kung Fu* was a unique show in its visualization and content and had a unique star, one who was not Asian but was associated with higher thought.

In the 1970s the idea was hatched that African Americans needed a black James Bond and other action characters. Blaxploitation was born in the early 1970s, a term possibly created by a National Association for the Advancement of Colored People (NAACP) official who named the genre by merging *black* with *exploitation*. This type of film and television show continues to be controversial because of two issues. Blaxploitation's positive aspects are that these action films are peopled with African American actors, showing strong main characters, usually male but also female, who fought for their rights, are good looking, and are sexy. They featured excellent evocative music that also came to be associated with the genre. Negative aspects were that they exploited and glorified stereotypes of African Americans as being involved in drugs, crime, guns, violence, and casual sex. Some of these films include *Cotton Comes to Harlem* (1970), *Sweet Sweetback's Baadasssss Song* (1971), *Shaft* (1971), *Across 110th Street* (1972), *Superfly* (1972), *Black Caesar* (1973), *Black Sampson* (1974), *Mandingo* (1975), and *Brotherhood of Death* (1976).

One of the most successful blaxploitation films was *Shaft,* released in 1971. It featured Richard Roundtree (1942–) as John Shaft, a private investigator who was rebellious against the police and worked his own way to solve cases in the black community. It was directed by renowned photographer and filmmaker Gordon Parks (1912–2006). The low-budget film grossed $13 million, an astonishing figure for the time. There were two sequels made: *Shaft's Big Score* in 1972 and *Shaft in Africa* in 1973. In 2000 another *Shaft* film was released, but this time Samuel L. Jackson (1948–) played John Shaft II and was the nephew of the original character.

Shaft was also a television series that was created as made-for-television movies that were programmed with two other shows, running once every three weeks.

It premiered on CBS in 1973. Richard Roundtree reprised his role and in fact is the only actor to have appeared in all three movies as well as the TV series. In the television series Shaft worked with, not against, the police, because studio executives were nervous about the reaction TV audiences would have if Shaft was against the police as he was in the movies. Urban themes were accepted and drugs were part of the landscape. The production values were weak, including very long takes to avoid moving the camera; the sets looked like sets, the lighting was unimaginative, and the pace was slow for an action show. Roundtree made it very clear in the press that he was displeased with the show. One of the shows in the rotation was *Hawkins* (1973–1974), starring legendary Hollywood superstar James Stewart (1908–1997), which was geared to an older demographic than for *Shaft*. Executives felt that audiences would be confused as to who watched what show, so after seven episodes *Shaft* was cancelled. It still has the legacy of being only one of two blaxploitation shows to be on TV.

Get Christie Love! (1974–1975) starred Teresa Graves (1946–2002) in the title role. Christie Love was an unassuming young woman who just happened to be a highly skilled undercover cop for the Los Angeles Police Department. The creation of this show was solely to bring blaxploitation to the small screen. Rather than present the show as a cop drama, the intention was to have it look and sound like the films that were so dominant in the 1970s. There also were at least two featured women in blaxploitation films: Pam Grier (1949–) as *Foxy Brown* (1974) and Tamara Dobson in *Cleopatra Jones* (1973), and they were inspiration for the Christie Love character. Black women had been in their own TV shows before the 1970s—*Beulah* was a housekeeper for a Caucasian family and *Julia* was a single mom raising her young son who worked as a nurse—but neither was in a law enforcement position in a show with any action at all, let alone the aggressive nature of Christie Love.

Julia and *Get Christie Love!* were the same; both Diahann Carroll and Teresa Graves were attractive women—a television trope for lead actresses in a series. Both were smart and very skilled, but where *Julia* had one profession, nursing, Christie Love had many as part of her undercover work, including acting as a prostitute and a jewel thief among many others, to catch as many criminals, thieves, and bad guys as she could. Teresa Graves had a bit of clout on the production. It could have been more violent and salacious, at least for television standards, but she was a religious woman and vetoed many of the ideas presented that concerned sex and violence.

Westerns, cop and detective shows, variety, and sitcoms continued to be part of the network television menu during the 1970s. Throughout the history of this electronic medium the powers-that-be somehow agreed that to keep television alive, fresh ideas and new venues of narrative exploration were necessary and needed to be created. The martial arts and blaxploitation genres, although short lived, gave the viewers an opportunity to watch something at home that many craved and consumed at their local movie theater. Television always delivers, and if blaxploitation and martial arts shows were few and far between, there was always the next fall season or the next.

Further Resources

Anderson, Freddy J., Jr. 2016. *The Blaxploitation Encyclopedia*. https://www.createspace.com/ CreateSpace Independent Publishing Platform.

Howard, Josiah. 2008. *Blaxploitation Cinema*. http://www.fabpress.com/ FAB Press.

Little, John, and Linda Lee Cadwell. 2016. *The Warrior Within: The Philosophies of Bruce Lee*. New York: Chartwell Books.

Meyers, Ric. 2011. *Films of Fury: The Kung Fu Movie Book*. Guilford, CT: Emery Books.

Pilato, Herbie J. 1993. *Kung Fu Book of Caine*. North Clarendon: Tuttle.

Tidyman, Ernest. 2016. *Shaft: The Original Novel*. Mt. Laurel, NJ: Dynamite Entertainment.

From Outer Body to Inner Mind: The Evolution of the Medical Drama

The medical drama was a staple of American television through the 1950s and 1960s. The focus in this era was mainly on doctors and nurses in a hospital setting, such as *City Hospital* (1951–1953), *Dr. Kildare* (1961–1966), *Ben Casey* (1961–1966), and *The Nurses* (1965–1967). The evolution of the medical drama does not begin in the 1960s or the 1970s but in the 1950s. *Medic* (1954–1956) starred Richard Boone (1917–1981) as Konrad Styner, a doctor confronted with challenging medical maladies and illnesses.

What was so far-reaching about *Medic* was not just the medical challenges, which included mental illness, deciding which life to save in a devastating pregnancy situation, or a young man experiencing violent seizures. This groundbreaking program explored these and many other topics to the fullest and in as graphic a fashion as television would allow at this time. Although not well watched or remembered by the public, *Medic,* with its first-person point of view and narration style, had a solid impact on medical shows of the future.

There was the general family practitioner who saw patients out of their office like *Marcus Welby, M.D.* (1969–1976), who was portrayed by Robert Young (1907–1998) with a gentle bedside manner, who still managed to proceed in unorthodox ways. Ironically Dr. Welby was considerably older than his younger participant in the practice, Dr. Stephen Kiley, played by James Brolin (1940–), who was a by-the-book physician and demonstrated a conservative manner. The show was also controversial on at least one occasion when the gay community protested the program for an episode in which Dr. Welby tried to convince a young gay patient that he could be straight.

Big hospitals were still broadcast to viewers who enjoyed medical dramas. *Medical Center* (1969–1976) was an unnamed university facility that further developed the theme of the clash of cultures between those under 30 and those over 30, begun in the 1960s. An older Dr. Paul Lochner played by James Daly (1918–1978) was superior to the younger Dr. Joe Gannon portrayed by Chad Everett (1937–2012). Just some of the topics that also confronted society and were part of *Medical Center*'s repertoire included child abuse, abortion, illegal drugs, the generation gap between the two doctors as well as throughout society, as well as a possible cure for cancer.

The Bold Ones: The New Doctors (1969–1973) took place at a high-end and exclusive clinic, the David Craig Institute of New Medicine, created by the highly successful neurosurgeon David Craig, portrayed by E. G. Marshall (1914–1998). A team of forward-thinking doctors was assembled by Dr. Craig consisting of chief of surgery Dr. Ted Stuart played by John Saxon (1935–) and Dr. Paul Hunter played by the pre–*Good Morning America* David Hartman (1935–). Medical and social subjects covered included organ transplants, women with postpartum depression, rare diseases, the struggle to communicate with some patients, and those who suffer from pain disorders with psychological connections.

Also running one season from 1970 to 1971 was *The Interns.* This show took place at New North Hospital and followed Dr. Peter Goldstone, played by Broderick Crawford 1911–1986), and five medical interns. This show broke ground for the genre by presenting the racism felt by one of the African American interns, in addition to other hot topics of the day.

Dr. Simon Locke was a Canadian medical drama that was syndicated in the United States from 1971 to 1974. This show was unique in several ways; although it took place in a fictional small town, the themes were of a thriving city because topics included a typhoid epidemic, child abuse, and murder. It began with the young title character, played by Sam Groom (1938–), arriving to assist the veteran Dr. Andrew Sellers, played by the well-seasoned Jack Albertson (1907–1981), but in 1972 Albertson left the series under negative circumstances. The show then changed its title to *Police Surgeon.* Dr. Locke returned to the big city he first came from and went to work for the police department's emergency unit where he became a solver of crimes in which medical research was necessary. This sort of shifting of location and jobs was not common in the era, but it helped the show resolve a cast crisis and let it run for around two more years.

The other doctor who was different from those usually portrayed on television medical shows was *The Psychiatrist* (1971–1974) whose name was Dr. James Whitman, played by Roy Thinnes (1938–). The doctor did more than use talk therapy one on one in his office; he followed his patients out to the street at times, digging into their minds to resolve issues and bring peace of mind to his patients.

Another psychiatrist show was *Matt Lincoln* (1970–1971), which brought *Ben Casey*'s Vince Edwards (1928–1996) back to another but very different kind of medical show. This psychiatrist created a telephone hotline for troubled teens and a walk-in clinic to deal with young people's mental health. Sadly, the show was probably too far ahead of its time. It never gathered much of an audience and was cancelled in midseason.

*M*A*S*H* (1972–1983) was an adaptation of the hit film of the same name directed by Robert Altman (1925–2006) and released in 1970. Altman did not have anything to do with the TV show but a few of the actors made the transition from film to TV for the project. Standing for Mobile Army Surgical Hospital, *M*A*S*H* was unique as a medical show in that it was set back in the 1950s during the Korean War, but it really reflected the Vietnam War (1955–1975), which was still raging for the first few years of the show, through character, dialogue, and action. The show had broad appeal but a special audience among the young and the counterculture. The principal focus of the show, which was a dramedy, was to use the medical aspects, tending to the wounded and severely injured, for a forum of rapport among the sexes, among themselves, questioning authority and the ethics of war. In its time the last show of the last season set a record for sets watched. It was number 256 of the 11th season and ran on February 28, 1983 for two and a half hours. This set a precedent for ending a long-running series, network or cable, in a big and often controversial manner.

Emergency! (1972–1977) was a new kind of medical show and way ahead of its time. This Jack Webb (1920–1982) production concerned units of paramedics who were out on the street as fast as possible for any kind of medical emergency. The show also combined elements of the action and adventure genre with the medical show. The public knew about paramedics on a superficial level, but this show went into the details of their operation and their role in saving lives.

Doctor's Hospital ran one season from 1975 to 1976 even though it was created by the legendary producer James I. Moser (1921–1993), who is known for *Dragnet, Medic,* and *Ben Casey*, and starred the very handsome and very capable George Peppard (1928–1994). *Doctor's Hospital* took place in Los Angeles in the fictitious Lowell Memorial Hospital where a team of neurosurgeons performed their delicate and precise medical art. At the end of the season Peppard announced he didn't want to play his role anymore and left the show. The producers discussed recasting with Zohra Lambert (1937–), who played a resident, but they came to the conclusion that the fine actress didn't have the same name recognition as Peppard and the show closed for good. Like *Medic, Doctor's Hospital* will be remembered for its intense realism not found on the other medical shows of the time. Critics and cultural historians had credited the show with influencing medical shows to come such as *Chicago Hope* (1994–2000), *ER* (1994–2009), and *St. Elsewhere* (1982–1988).

A significant leap into exploring the medical drama on television came from two different kinds of TV doctors. *Quincy, M.E.* (1976–1983) concerned a medical examiner whose last name was Quincy but his first name was never revealed—only hinted at in one episode when a flash of a business card read Dr. R. Quincy. Jack Klugman (1922–2012) played the role with a gruff attitude and a gravelly voice that spit out words to whomever he was questioning or informing.

Quincy was more than exacting in a field that demanded precision. *Quincy* was unique in that it was a medical show. Quincy was a doctor and he did examine patients, albeit deceased ones, but *Quincy, M.E.* was also a crime drama. The cases this medical examiner worked on were murder cases. It was made clear who the murderer was but Quincy always disproved his superiors and came up with the actual killer because of his keen forensic skills.

The medical dramas of the 1970s advanced the genre, making it more current and tackling the big issues of the day as well as reflecting the working space, manner, and approach taken by the new doctor. The genre doesn't have the violence of police and detective shows or the historic sweep of the Western, but by focusing on health and illness the producers, directors, cast, and crew were able to examine the human heart and mind as well as the soul.

Further Resources

Kalisch, Philip Arthur. 1983. *Images of Nurses on Television*. New York: Springer.

Malmsheimer, Richard. 1998. *Doctor's Only: The Evolving Image of the American Physician*. New York: Praeger.

Reiss, David S. 1983. *M*A*S*H The Exclusive, Inside Story of TV's Most Popular Show*. New York: Macmillan.

Rosin, James. 2009. *Quincy M.E., the Television Series*. Duncan, OK: BearManor Media.

Rothel, David. 2000. *Richard Boone: A Knight without Armor in a Savage Land*. Dahlonega, GA: Empire Publishing.

Yokley, Richard, and Rozane Sutherland. 2012. *Emergency! Behind the Scene*. Burlington, MA: Jones & Bartlett Learning.

Rockin' Out in the Living Room: Rock and Disco Music in 1970s Television

The 1950s were the beginning of rock and roll and television was there to showcase the architects, men such as Chuck Berry (1926–2017), Jerry Lee Lewis (1935–), Little Richard (1932–2017), and "the King" himself, Elvis Presley (1935–1977), broadcasting this new genre of music into the homes of countless teenagers. Presley was problematic because of his wide-ranging hip action and ability to whip women into a frenzy. Dick Clark (1929–2012) interviewed him from Germany when Elvis was in the service but he never performed on *American Bandstand* (1950–1989). Ed Sullivan had him on *The Ed Sullivan Show* (1948–1971) and a directive was given to shoot him only from the waist up. Rock and roll was a raucous business. Sullivan was not the host of his own show the night of Elvis's first appearance there on September 9, 1956; that was renowned thespian Charles Laughton (1899–1962), who was brought in because the impresario was recovering from the effects of a car accident. Actually, although many have reported about the waist up shot, Elvis was seen in a full body composition as he rocked and rolled through "Love Me Tender," "Don't Be Cruel," "Hound Dog," and "Ready Teddy."

Elvis Presley never once appeared on *Bandstand* but teenagers danced to his records on the show. Clark had guests such as Richard, Berry, and Lewis and many, many others. They would not perform live but lip sync to their record. Clark spun rock records throughout the show as the camera focused on the dancers presenting the latest dances such as he Mashed Potato, the Monkey, and the Watusi. They worked in couples and many would come to the show day after day, selected by Clark and his staff to be featured. Clark was a DJ so he had a mellifluous voice and although conservatively dressed and coiffed he was super cool. The show was on frequently, allowing young viewers to listen, watch, and dance to rock and roll.

As a rock and roll revolution took over the country, music now categorized as classic rock created a new history of music for young people by young people. Inevitably problems would arise during the 1950s and into the 1960s when content and action was amped up by rock bands who in songs talked about sex and drugs, used profane language, and moved with sexual prowess. Censors were on their toes because rock songs were moving away from innuendo and becoming stark in language and story.

Record sales were high because new groups were coming out and putting their albums into the stores at a fast pace. The television audience who feasted on rock and roll didn't have to go to concerts or even buy records to watch and hear rock and roll in their homes. Seventies rock was harder than in the 1960s; it also spawned the punk, country rock, and many other movements. To most fans the rock concert was the best venue to hear a band, on stage, with lights, light shows, and more.

Soul! (1967–1973) was hosted by African American Ellis Haizlip (1929–1991), who at the time was strongly associated with the African American arts movement. *Soul!* featured a wide array of soul, Latin, jazz, and rock and black performers as well as controversial black speakers, all with strong views on the African American experience. The major impact of *Soul!* (which ran on Public Broadcasting [PBS] stations) on its mainly African American but also Caucasian audiences was to clearly present by example the reality of the two cultures, and conclude that each has its merits and contribution to the arts and ethos.

Creator and host Don Cornelius (1936–2012), sponsored by Afro Sheen hair products, made *Soul Train* (1971–2006) a national institution of R&B, funk, and soul music for black and white audiences as well. Cornelius was the essence of cool with his deep baritone voice, elegance, and matchless moves. The essential aspect of *Soul Train* was the "Soul Train Line." As music played two vertical lines were formed, creating a center area that was for spotlight dances. The line dancers would move to the music and watch as a couple would enter the center and do moves way ahead of their time. Couples took turns, each more flamboyant than the last. Even though it was not a contest, the dancers often seemed to outdo the others. There were musical guests, record playing, and plenty of dancing. The animated opening featured the "Soul Train," which seemed to drive the entire show. Cornelius had a memorable tagline, "Love, Peace, and Soul."

Don Kirshner (1934–2011) was a record man through and through. He knew every aspect of the recording business and performing business. At this time all the other shows that had rock acts invited them to their stage or maybe an occasional remote feed. On *Don Kirshner's Rock Concert* (1973–1981), Kirshner's concept was to present actual rock concerts to viewers around the country featuring the biggest acts of the day. The viewer was put into the middle of the concert with the band playing and the ticket holders grooving to the sound.

The Midnight Special (1973–1981) was created and produced by Burt Sugarman (1939–). It was cleverly scheduled on NBC on Friday nights after *The Tonight Show with Johnny Carson* (1962–1992). Top rock acts performed on the show, which often had guest hosts. From July 1975 to March 1976 singer Helen Reddy (1941–) was the regular host. The legendary deep and growly throated disc jockey Wolfman Jack (Robert Weston Smith, 1938–1995), who had a key role in the George Lucas film *American Graffiti* (1973), was the show's announcer and often the guest host. Other guest hosts included Chuck Berry, Joan Baez (1941–), and Elton John (1947–).

Chip Monck, born Edward Herbert Beresford "Chip" Monck (1939–), was a significant figure in 1960s and 1970s rock and roll circles as a lighting designer, and he also worked with Bill Graham at the Fillmore East and was the master of ceremonies at the iconic Woodstock music festival. In 1974 he was the host of a rock talk and music show called *Speakeasy,* which was an hour format and was short lived, not making it into 1975. *Speakeasy* was an eclectic show with hand-picked bands, not the usual fare. Monck prided himself on finding little-known bands like Zephyr with lead singer Candy Givens (1946–1984) and guitarist Tommy Bolin (1951–1976). Discussions were topical with guests and an in-studio audience. One episode on which cartoonist Al Capp (1909–1979) appeared began with an on-screen message explaining that a part of the show in which Mr. Capp engaged in an inappropriate discussion with a member of the audience had been excised. The creator of Lil' Abner was still on the program but minus the uncomfortable exchange. This made the show "dangerous" as if anything could happen at any time.

Also in the 1970s there was the birth and growth of a new kind of music, not really born out of rock, and only partially born of soul, R&B, and other black music. Rock always had dances that listeners could move to if they wished. Dances such as the Frug, the Twist, and the Jerk, among many others, took a back seat to the listening experience of rock and roll. Disco is a music with a driving counter-balance beat, both instrumental and with lyrics. There were disco groups and disco solo singers.

Disco came about as a strong reaction against rock and roll and its culture as well as an artistic attack against the counterculture that largely did not embrace the joys of dancing to music. A keystone in disco history was the release of *Saturday Night Fever* (1977), starring John Travolta (1954–) as a young man who worked at a mundane job during the day and was a disco club king at night. Travolta and *Saturday Night Fever* brought the disco craze, which swept the country in clubs and other venues, television as well.

Soul Train presented some disco dancing but it was just part of the wide swath of dance styles on the show. When disco television in the 1970s comes up, the name Deney Terrio (1950–) is front and center. He was the host of *Dance Fever* (1979–1987), created and produced by Merv Griffin (1925–2007). He also taught John Travolta his special moves for *Saturday Night Fever. Dance Fever* was an entertainment show that also was a contest. Each week four couples danced for a prize of $1,000. Each dance routine lasted two minutes while judges carefully watched every move and groove of the performance. The panel included Carmen Electra, M.C. Hammer, and Jamie King. They were scored between 70 and 100 points. The highest scorers went on to the next round. The contest continued until a $5,000 prize was available. There was plenty of other dancing on the show from Terrio flanked by two women and a good helping of guests performing, all the artists of the disco movement.

During the 1970s rock and roll continued to grow and compartmentalize into new forms, and it stayed alive on TV. It has yet to go away as *American Idol* and *The Voice* have proven in the 21st century. Television in the seventies did a great service to contemporary music fans. Without paying for a ticket a fan could watch part of a concert. Music fans knew what shows to watch and in some cases what group or singer was going to be on at a particular time. And the tradition of the dance show nurtured through the 1950s–1960s was not only alive and well but moving forward by presenting the latest steps and trends. For stations and networks the under-30 demographic was crucial as far as being consumers and watching more TV than their elders. They watched all sorts of shows but rock, disco, and other contemporary music was tailored and delivered to the masses for their personal pleasure.

Further Resources

George, Nelson. 2014. *The Hippest Trip in America: Soul Train and the Evolution of Culture and Style.* New York: HarperCollins.

Jack, Wolfman, and Byron Laursen. 1995. *Have Mercy!: Confessions of the Original Rock 'N' Animal.* New York: Warner Books.

Jackson, John. 1999. *American Bandstand: Dick Clark and the Making of a Rock 'n' Roll Empire.* Oxford: Oxford University Press.

Morgan, Johnny. 2011. *Disco: The Music, the Times, the Era.* Ontario, Canada: Sterling.

Podolsky, Rich. 2012. *Don Kirshner: The Man with the Golden Ear: How He Changed the Face of Rock and Roll.* Emeryville, CA: Hal Leonard.

Rolling Stone Magazine. 1992. *The Rolling Stone Illustrated History of Rock and Roll: The Definitive History of the Most Important Artists and Their Music.* New York: Straight Arrow.

Television Takes on the Novel—Invents Long-Form Programming and Challenges the Movie Studios on Their Own Turf

From the early days of motion pictures the literary form of the novel has been adapted and released to an audience that may or may not be familiar with the book. Some examples of this practice include *Of Human Bondage* (1934), *The Good Earth* (1937), and *Rebecca* (1940). The goal was to put a good story on the screen and to capitalize on the name recognition of a great novel. In most cases an attempt was made to be faithful to the original, but it's been estimated that even a short novel if filmed page for page would translate into a movie of at least six or seven hours in running length, so the screenwriter had to cut, trim, drop scenes, and take several characters and make them into a single composite at times.

There's no way of knowing how many audience members read a book or if those who haven't enjoy a movie based on a literary story and characters. Those who have are concerned with what the characters look like, the casting, external details like the settings, and of course are sensitive to new characters and story.

Actually in the silent film era one movie director did take a massive novel and filmed it page by page. The novel *McTeague,* written in 1899 by Frank Norris, was made into a 1924 movie directed by Erich von Stroheim, retitled *Greed.* Through a merger MGM inherited the project and the man known as the boy genius, Irving Thalberg, was put in charge of production.

Only 12 people saw the 42-reel version of the film in a screening room where it ran almost eight hours. The film was taken away from the director and without his participation it was edited down to only two hours.

During the 1970s this quest to film a novel in its entirety was satisfied by television—it was called the miniseries. A prestigious or bestselling book would be purchased, produced, and then shown usually on a consecutive series of evenings. Besides giving the viewing audience the pleasure and enjoyment of "seeing" a book, the networks were attempting to secure for a number of days or longer a guaranteed audience, dominating the time slot decided upon for the project.

Not really knowing what they were in for, audiences tuned into ABC on April 29, 1974 to watch *QVII,* based on the book by Leon Uris, the author of *Exodus.* The book was a bestseller and the author renowned. The story involved heinous acts by a doctor during World War II who tortured patients by operating on them without any kind of pain protector or relief, played by Anthony Hopkins (1937–). This is described in a book written by a man who served during the war and was a reporter, played by Ben Gazzara (1930–2002), who was in a concentration camp for a time and witnessed Nazi atrocities conducted by the doctor. Later the doctor sued the writer for libel and won the case, but the jury, understanding that the doctor was a vicious butcher, awarded him one-half penny in damages, the lowest amount possible. The story ended with the beginning of the Six-Day War and the audience learned that the writer's son had immigrated to Israel where the fighting was taking place. Members of the television audience who were familiar with the novel and its background were aware that *QVII* was based on a true story concerning the novel's author, Leon Uris. Those who had watched that series of broadcasts had witnessed television history—the birth of the miniseries—and clamored for more.

On February 1, 1976, ABC struck gold again with a miniseries based on the 1969 bestselling novel *Rich Man, Poor Man* by powerhouse author Irwin Shaw. This project aired on Monday nights mainly, in one- or two-hour installments over seven weeks. The 600-page novel told the story of two brothers, Rudy and Tom, played in the miniseries by Peter Strauss (1947–) and Nick Nolte (1941–), as their family's story is told from World War II to the early days of Vietnam. The story has an epic sweep and is full of conflict. Audiences often favor family stories because they can relate to the concept of familial dynamics. The show was a big success and a sequel was mounted.

On August 17, the miniseries was warmly embraced by the American public and ABC was growing the form, constantly looking for new books to adapt to a multi-night presentation. In 1976, African American author Alex Haley (1921–1992) published *Roots: The Saga of an American Family,* and it quickly became a major bestseller. He announced that he had traced his ancestors back to 1776 when his relative Kunta Kinte was captured by a rebellious tribe who sold him to slave traders. As the story progressed Kinte's struggle was passed down from ancestors in the late 18th century to the mid-20th century and some back and forth in between. It was a huge risk to put so much effort into a project on slavery, important but not widely accepted across the country. The key was that 1976 was America's bicentennial and Americans were very interested in every aspect of their history. So when *Roots* was announced and scheduled for the next year, ABC hoped there would be an audience for the eight-night presentation. They had no idea just how successful it would be.

The executive producer of *Roots* was David L. Wolper (1928–2010), a highly experienced man who often found creative ways to tell true stories. Some of his productions that were produced for television and the movies include *The Making of a President, 1960* (1963), *The Undersea World of Jacques Cousteau* (1967–1968), and *The Hellstrom Chronicle* (1971). Stan Margulies (1920–2001) was the producer of *Roots*, well known as the producer of two wildly successful movies: *Those Magnificent Men in Their Flying Machines: Or How I Flew from London to Paris in 11 Hours 25 Minutes* (1965) and *Willy Wonka and the Chocolate Factory* (1971).

The budget of *Roots* was $6.6 million. If the first episode didn't play well, it was doubtful viewers would tune in for the rest. The cast of *Roots* was massive. The principal role of the young Kunta Kinte was played by African American actor LeVar Burton (1957–) in his acting debut, which was a daring risk for the actor and especially ABC, which bet its huge investment in time and money on the beginning actor. If this aspect didn't work out, the whole series could have been in jeopardy.

As for the rest of the cast, ABC made another bold move by casting some of the more prominent names in roles that went against their known image on television. Of the almost 100 players in *Roots* just some include Louis Gossett Jr., Ben Vereen, Vic Morrow, John Amos, Edward Asner, Chuck Connors, Carolyn Jones, Leslie Uggams, Sandy Duncan, Lloyd Bridges, Cicely Tyson, Ralph Waite, Scatman Crothers, George Hamilton, Lorne Greene, Moses Gunn, Maya Angelou, Gary Collins, Macdonald Carey, Burl Ives, Todd Bridges, and Yvonne DeCarlo.

That first critical night the show was watched by 28.84 million households and the numbers continued to grow as the rest of the series unfolded. A 40.5 percent rating was acquired with a 61 percent share. *Roots* soared to the highest plane in many ways, artistic, social, as well as cementing the miniseries as a television genre with staying power and limitless possibility. The world stopped when an episode was being telecast. Black, white, brown, and otherwise, the show cut across the color line. It was the talk of the town every morning. When award time came around *Roots* had a bushel of treasures. For the Emmy awards alone the show received a whopping 37 nominations. *Roots* was an entertainment milestone. It also was a visual and audio television historic event and a document with which to understand the civil rights movement.

The miniseries was produced by all the networks on myriad subjects. Just some of the miniseries in the 1970s include *The Kent Chronicles* (1978), *Centennial* (1978), and *Holocaust* (1978). Television is its own medium unlike any other, so it made sense that it would make its own structures and genre. The novel for television brought literature to those who read traditional books and those who liked their reading on the television screen. Sometimes these two groups came together and sometimes they switched places. Critics and viewers have always questioned the motion picture adaptations of their favorite books, especially the classics. Some succeed, many don't. A majority of the audience for an adaptation film in a motion picture theater probably hasn't read the book and judges the film on its own merits. Those who have read the book question casting, characters, as well as the tone of the film—does it do justice to the book? The birth of the miniseries gave viewers lots of programming and a commitment to watch every night of the event. Casting issues remain the same, but the viewer is seeing all the scenes from the book and the original characters without hybrids or those created by a screenwriter to make up for what is cut out, which in most cases is around five or six hours. The miniseries is television's own. They continued after the 1970s but that decade was graced with this new television form called the miniseries.

Further Resources

Griggs, Yvonne. 2016. *The Bloomsbury Introduction to Adaption Studies: Adapting the Canon in Film, TV, Novels and Popular Culture*. London: Bloomsbury Academic.

Haley, Alex. 2016: *Roots: The Saga of an American Family*. New York. Da Capo Press.

Maril, Alvin H. 1987. *Movies Made for Television: The Telefeature and the Mini-Series: 1964–1986.* New York: New York Zoetrope.

Schmidt, Michael. 2014. *The Novel: A Biography*. Cambridge, MA: Belknap Press.

Uris, Leon. 1982. *QB VII.* New York: Bantam Books.

Wolper, David L. 2003. *Producer: A Memoir*. New York: Scribner.

The Greening of the Late Night Talk Show

In order to understand how the genre of the talk show evolved and blossomed during the 1980s, a look back to the variety show on radio is necessary. Radio was a strictly audio medium. There were announcers, hosts, singers, comedians, instrumental music, and accompaniment from the house band. Training for the talent who began in radio often were those who began in vaudeville, which was very popular in the United States and Canada from the early 1880s until the early 1930s. Vaudeville developed from concert saloons, minstrel shows, and American burlesque, which, unlike vaudeville, included women performing striptease routines. Vaudeville acts were varied and included popular and classical musicians, singers, dancers, comedians, trained animals, magicians, female and male impersonators, acrobats, illustrated songs, jugglers, one-act plays, scenes from plays, lecturing celebrities, minstrels, and movies. Before they moved on to radio and talking motion pictures and then television, former vaudeville performers such as the Marx Brothers, George Burns and Gracie Allen, Jack Benny, and W. C. Fields honed their skills in what was called the Borscht Belt located in the Catskill Mountains, where summer resorts largely attended by Jewish people from New York City thrived from 1920 to around the 1970s.

The variety show was immensely popular before television because it offered a range of acts during one program. Al Jolson (1886–), considered in his time America's all-around greatest entertainer, had his own radio musical variety show, *The Al Jolson Show,* which aired on NBC and CBS from 1932 to 1956. *The Big Show* was a 90-minute radio variety show that featured top comedians, singers, and musical talent, hosted by actress and personality Tallulah Bankhead (1902–

1968). From November 5, 1950 on NBC guests included Frankie Laine, Ethel Merman, and Jimmy Durante. *The Edgar Bergen and Charlie McCarthy* show featured the famous ventriloquist and his muse in a variety show that ran on radio from 1935 to 1955 and featured such guests as Judy Garland, Fred Allen, and Frank Sinatra.

The radio variety shows made the transition to television during the 1940s, and most if not all were very successful because the introduction of sight allowed expressions and actions to affect the viewing audience's reactions. Some of the most influential television variety shows were *The Toast of the Town,* which became *The Ed Sullivan Show* (1948–1971), which presented practically every major singer, dancer, and comedian of the time. Starting with Elvis Presley, then later the Beatles, bands of the British Invasion, and American groups of the Woodstock generation, the *Sullivan Show* could boast he had entertainment for the youngsters, oldsters, and everyone in between. *Texaco Star Theater* (1948–1955) featured Milton Berle (1908–2002), who was crowned Mr. Television by critics and the public because of his often silly cause and effect humor. Singers who performed on the show included Eddie Fisher, Rudy Vallee, and the Andrews Sisters. Guests who joined in on comedy sketches included Danny Thomas, Bert Lahr, and Zsa Zsa Gabor. These two landmark shows proved that audiences wanted audio and visual entertainment in their living room.

The next step was to bring talk and discussion into the home along with an occasional singer or comedian. The talk show would also present celebrities and other interesting people so the viewer could enjoy being part of the experience from a listening point of view. Talk is the most human of endeavors, a communication system that allows talkers to express themselves and listeners to interpret and respond. A discussion or interview is not conducted in a flat line; emotion, control of volume, and inflection cause a reactive impulse in those listening. It is these principles that drove the late night talk show and allowed the viewers to receive communications that made them think, laugh, or be emotional or angry.

The structure of the television talk show genre began with a person talking to the audience in the form of a monologue; then that host interviewed several guests. He sat behind a desk and they sat on a couch or on chairs. A full-piece band played segments on and off and backed up the singer of the night. There could be a comedy sketch or two but the focus was on the talk, which separated the genre from the variety show. The talk show borrowed singers and musical acts from the variety genre, in some cases the same person who was on radio and now television, and added the gift of conversation.

Surprisingly, the talk show genre has not changed dramatically in most ways. The basic elements are the same. The technology improved, so multiple cameras expanded the scope and choice of shots, whether the show was live, on tape, or live on tape, which is a method where the show is taped "live" and runs live until there is a technical problem or an issue with the talent. The image and sound quality were better and visual effects could be employed. What did drastically change by the 1980s was the diversity of hosts and especially the content—what could be said, what topics could be discussed, social and moral areas never before presented on a talk show in earlier decades. The discussion of sex and morality became wide open. Political figures, celebrities, and people in the news were the subject of jokes and at times outright insult. Each host had a point of view different from the others, and the whole tone of the talk shows in the 1980s was more mature, more adult, and at times more outrageous than their predecessors.

The first late night talk show was *Broadway Open House,* which aired in 1950, but it was cancelled after one year because there were not enough television sets in homes, bars, restaurants, and other establishments to support a nighttime talk show. The host was Jerry Lester (1910–1995), a vaudeville, Broadway, and radio star, and featured the statuesque blonde bombshell known as Dagmar (Virginia Ruth Egnor, 1921–2001), a model, actress, and television personality. The show was raucous and rambunctious, driven by nightclub-type humor of the era.

The first appearance of *The Tonight Show* was in 1954 on NBC and it was a resounding success. The host, Steve Allen (1921–2000), who is mostly credited as inventing the role of the late night show host and the late night show's contents, was so popular that he was given another program: *The Steve Allen Show* (1956–1964). Allen then split hosting duties with Ernie Kovacs (1919–1962). Kovacs, with his antics and visual experimentation on his own show, *The Ernie Kovacs Show* (1952–1962), also inspired future late night talk shows by expanding the medium, exploring its nature for humorous and entertainment achievements. *The Tonight Show* was the model for the late night talk show. The desk, the couch, the band, the guest, everything that is still known as what makes up a talk show was conceptualized by the genius Sylvester "Pat" Weaver (1908–2002), the president of the network in 1954, who also devised *The Today Show,* which began in 1952 and as of 2016 continues to entertain and inform its morning audience.

From October 1, 1962 through May 22, 1992 Johnny Carson (1925–2005) was emperor of the nighttime talk show. He was the third host of *The Tonight Show* but his name is synonymous with NBC's institution; first host Steve Allen (1921–2000), who was host from 1954 to 1957, and Jack Paar (1918–2004), who hosted from 1957 to 1962, had their own visions for *The Tonight Show*, but Carson turned it into an institution to which viewers could relate. He interviewed a cornucopia of those in show business, discovered comics who became superstars, talked to prestigious writers, performed in skits, and perfected the art of the monologue. Carson joked that because the show was on late and most couples watched *The Tonight Show* in the bedroom, he was providing a nightlight for romantic activities. Carson was a quick wit, good in sketches, and had a rapport with announcer Ed McMahon (1923–2009), whom he insulted while the big man laughed, and he constantly jibed his bandleader, Doc Severinsen (1927–), for his outlandish wardrobe. There were many running segments on the Carson *Tonight Show*; "Stump the Band," where audience members came up with archaic song titles and the band would say they knew it and proceed to play a gag tune, giving a prize to the winning audience member; "The Great Karnack," which was Carson in a turban holding a sealed envelope to his forehead, saying a few words, then opening the envelope and reading what was on a paper inside to make a joke connection. Art Fern, played by Carson, was a slick con man who quickly spoke hysterical patter during a break in the "Tea Time" movie segment, selling everything he could while the voluptuous blonde Carol Wayne (1942–1985) posed next to him.

The next generation of talk shows and talk show hosts came up during the 1980s and were inspired by the earlier pioneers. David Letterman (1947–) began his late night career in the daytime. In June 1980, NBC gave him a morning comedy show, *The David Letterman Show.* It started out at 90 minutes but later was reduced to one hour. Although it was a critical success and won two Emmy awards, the ratings were poor and NBC cancelled it in the same year after only 90 episodes. NBC kept Letterman under contract and tried him in a different time slot, *Late Night with David Letterman*, which premiered on February 1, 1982. The show ran Monday through Thursday at 12:30 a.m. Eastern time after *The Tonight Show with Johnny Carson.* Letterman quickly gained a reputation as an acerbic interviewer to many celebrities who were booked for the show. There were comedy segments and reoccurring characters and the show was very much influenced by Steve Allen. Regular segments included "Stupid Pet Tricks," which were very popular, and "Stupid Human Tricks" like throwing objects off a five-story building. Letterman demonstrated odd clothing like suits made of Alka-Seltzer and Velcro. A big fan favorite was a nightly Top Ten list, which had a wacky topic and a countdown of answers designed for escalating laughs. There was an audience cam, a monkey cam, and a film, "My Dog Bob," which featured Dave's dog with a camera strapped on him.

In 1992 Johnny Carson retired and it was assumed Letterman, who often hosted *The Tonight Show*, would be the new host, but NBC announced it would be Jay Leno (1950–). Letterman left NBC in 1993 and CBS brought Letterman over to their network. The *Late Show with David Letterman* debuted in 1993 with Paul Shaffer (1949–) as the rock and roll bandleader and Letterman's sidekick. This show built on the NBC show and developed its own nature. Letterman became a cult figure and many were tuning out of Leno and onto Letterman. The Top Ten was featured along with Letterman standards and new developments. In the Steve Allen tradition Letterman liked to surprise his audience and anything could happen at any time. Letterman retired on May 20, 2015 and his era in late night entertainment was over.

No one in the industry thought Johnny Carson was vulnerable, but as time moved on the show seemed geared to an older generation. There was a fear about going up against Carson. He had comedian Joan Rivers (1933–2014) on the *Tonight Show* as a guest and substitute host and promised her she would take over when he retired. The two stars had a falling out when in 1986, the Fox network offered Rivers her own late night show. *The Late Show with Joan Rivers* (1986–1987) was a one-season failure. Rivers didn't get along with the brass at Fox so she walked away, which left a train of guest hosts to sit behind the desk for the run of the show. However, Joan Rivers made television history as the first woman to host her own late night talk show.

After *The Late Show* with Joan Rivers failed with other hosts ending in 1987, Fox tried another late night show, *The Wilton North Report* (1987–1988), this time forging the newsmagazine with a talk show and variety show. The original idea was to start the show with the hard-hitting headlines of the day backed up by news footage to depict the event. Then the hosts, Phil Cowan and Paul Robins, did tough analysis with comedy laced in. By the premiere it had interviews, remote reports, some serious, some not so, comedy bits and sketches, and musical performances. The show only ran from December 11, 1987 to January 9, 1988 and it still managed to turn itself into a comedy show with no news.

Thicke of the Night starred Canadian actor and songwriter Alan Thicke (1947–2016) and was produced by MGM television and syndicated by Metromedia. It ran from 1983 to 1984. The show's regulars included Richard Belzer (1944–), Arsenio Hall (1956–), Rick Ducommun (1952–2015), Charles Fleishman (1950–), Gilbert Gottfried (1955–), Chloe Webb (1956–), and Fred Willard (1939–). The producer was the legendary Fred Silverman (1937–), who at various times ran all three major networks. This was another attempt to rival Johnny Carson. Alan Thicke was popular in Canada for hosting *The Alan Thicke Show,* a daytime show. Critics were not kind to the show. They didn't like the untraditional blend of sketch comedy, stand-up comedy, and talk show. Midseason several stations dropped the show. A retooling occurred. The house band was switched. Thicke's wife at the time, Gloria Loring (1946–), joined the cast as did controversial Los Angeles area talk show host Wally George (1931–2003) on a semi-regular basis. None of these changes could raise the bad ratings and it was cancelled at the end of the 1983–1984 season.

David Brenner (1936–2014) was a stand-up comedian who had many successful appearances on *The Tonight Show*. In 1986 King World Entertainment gave Brenner a 30-minute time slot, which was uncommon for a late night talk show. *Nightlife* was another attempt to challenge Johnny Carson. It premiered on September 8, 1986 on 102 stations. The word was spread that it was an "alternative" show. It was filmed in Manhattan and Brenner dressed in casual attire. It was that rare late night talk show that did not have a monologue but opened with a comedy sketch. On October 17, 1986 Brenner gave an extended monologue that went over two commercial breaks and until the closing credits. There were reports that none of the scheduled guests showed up, but Brenner's publicist claimed the monologue was intentional. Musician Billy Preston, who had played with the Beatles and many others, led the house band and was the first African American musical director for a national talk show. The formalistic experiments didn't work out and *Nightlife* was cancelled after just one season.

Larry King Live (1985–2010) was on CNN and ended about an hour and half before the late night shows began. Larry King (1933–) was a good interviewer, the kind of person who asked the questions the viewer at home would like to hear. Although Larry King covered all the bases and would touch on the hot-button areas of each guest, some felt his questions were too soft. Everyone, actors, actresses, singers, sports figures, and political figures, was on *Larry King Live* many more times than once over the years. King started in radio and during many of the years when he did his nightly television show he also did a radio interview show. People were pleased to be on *Larry King Live* because they knew he wasn't a shotgun interviewer but would give them a fair shake. The breadth of a Larry King interview covered enormous ground and most of the time he had one guest, so the viewer would get intimate with the subject. This was a no-frills show, a simple set, a table where King sat on one side, the guest on the other. He had a theme song and a logo. He was a character, hair slicked back, an old-school radio voice, and his signature suspenders, which he called braces, as they do in the United Kingdom. It takes a particular skill to interview a former president one night, a comedian the next, then an actor as well as a sports figure. He seemed worldly, as if he'd seen it all. He was the cornerstone of the CNN lineup. Larry King owned the 9 p.m. to 10 p.m. broadcast spot. He celebrated the art of talk.

Pat Sajak (1946–) continues as of late 2016 to be the popular host of *Wheel of Fortune* (1983–). In order to host *The Pat Sajak Show* (1989–1990) late night he had to leave the daytime edition of the game show but remain host of the syndicated nighttime version. CBS wanted to have a late night talk show ready when Johnny Carson announced his retirement from *The Tonight Show*. In an interview Sajak made it clear that he was not looking to break new ground but to steal from past nighttime talk shows. The format borrowed liberally from Carson. It began as a 90-minute show but was reduced to 60 minutes in October 1989. Jazz musician Tom Scott (1948–) was the bandleader. *The Pat Sajak Show* had a short life. It began on January 9, 1989 and finished on April 13, 1990. Sajak was not able to transfer his amiable personality from the game show to a late night talk show position.

Arsenio Hall (1956–), who was very popular as a host on *The Late Show* after Joan Rivers left, was given his own syndicated show, *The Arsenio Hall Show,* in 1989, and he became the first African American to host his own talk show. Now Carson had a worthy competitor in Hall, who was funny, a good interviewer, and booked guests and musical acts that appealed to the younger demographic the networks were looking for, especially hip-hop music groups. A new model for the late night talk show was born. The set was modern; the band was rock and roll, not a holdover from the big band era. Arsenio had catchphrases and riffs including a section of his audience called the Dog Pound who were very vocal and part of the comedy routines. He even had one of the very few female television directors, Sandy Fullerton, with whom he would be in a dialogue at times during the show, which the audience and the viewers could hear.

When Johnny Carson retired on May 22, 1992, the floodgates opened. Now that the networks, producers, and programmers understood it was an open field, the shows came and went. Few networks understood what it took to create and maintain a late night talk show. It seemed that networks and local stations found almost any celebrity a candidate to host their own talk show.

Audiences in the 1980s continued to enjoy late night talk shows because they got to see celebrities, got to laugh, and felt that they were not alone. This was an era of television talk shows that didn't talk down to the audience but brought it in for the fun and at times controlled chaos of hilarity. Talk shows had always been topical, especially in the opening monologue, but in the 1980s the topics really reflected the times and the subject matter could be raw but honest. Audiences weren't so much shocked by what they saw now but enjoyed being treated like adults. The form and structure had not changed much, but the content that drives the late night show seemed to have no boundaries. There was still censorship, but the 1980s host largely knew how to get around it with buzzwords the audience loved because it gave them a direct connection with their show. A late night talk show became a place that a viewer could count on for entertainment. After viewers turned off the television, the room may have gotten dark, but the mind continued to play the late night shows with thoughts that made them laugh, think, and marvel as they drifted off to sleep.

Further Resources

Alba, Ben. 2005. *Inventing Late Night: Steve Allen and the Original Tonight Show*. Amherst, NY: Prometheus Books.

Carter, Bill. 1995. *The Late Shift: Letterman, Leno, and the Network Battle for the Night*. New York: Hatchette Books.

Carter, Bill. 2011. *The War for Late Night: When Leno Went Early and Television Went Crazy*. New York: Plume.

King, Larry. 2010. *My Remarkable Journey*. New York: Weinstein Books.

King, Norman. 1993. *Arsenio Hall*. New York: William Morrow.

Lemon, Tim. 2013. *Late Night Wars—TV's Most Famous Rivals*. Amazon Digital Services.

Reich, A. Charles. 1971. *The Greening of America*. New York: Bantam.

How Ted Turner Challenged Network News with the Creation of CNN in the 1980s

Television news before CNN was largely a network evening news broadcast on CBS, NBC, and ABC where national and international news stories were presented. The shows ran from Monday to Friday from 6:30 to 7:00 p.m. Local news was also a half-hour at 6, then again at 11:30. Each affiliate reported the local news in their area. If there was a major national or even international story they would lead with that before returning to the local news of the day. In time there were weekend news shows and even mid-day local news shows on the three major networks, but not more than that.

Ted Turner (1938–), the general manager of Turner Advertising, bought up radio and television stations in the late 1960s. In 1976 the FCC allowed him to transmit content via satellite to local cable operators around the country. He turned WTCG into a superstation broadcasting old movies, cartoons, sports, and general fare such as *I Love Lucy* (1951–1960) and *Star Trek* (1966–1969), and eventually reached 2 million subscribers. He continued to purchase television stations like TBS, the Turner Broadcasting System, that aired movies and other content. Then Ted Turner looked at the manner in which the networks handled local and national news and envisioned a 24-hour, seven-days-a-week cable and satellite news network that he named CNN, Cable News Network. Turner took the network model of the news bureaus across the country and internationally so when something happened, no matter where it was, he and his team could cover it. The networks did have the ability to break into regular programming if a catastrophic event like the assassination of a political figure, a ruinous weather event, or a serial shooting at an outdoor venue was taking place. Turner's cable network news organization could cover events live for as long as was necessary to investigate the story intensively and thoroughly.

The major limitation of network or local news was that a story that happened early in the day had to be filmed, narrated, and then fronted by a correspondent and run many hours later. With a 24-hour news network the possibilities were endless. CNN began with a short news cycle under 30 minutes and largely repeated that package all day until something newsworthy demanded to be included. In time Turner and his programming team would add more and more anchors and give them their own shows, which could continue to cover the news of the day or become a solid unit handing off from one to another, covering a breaking news story, one the was happening as the viewer watched CNN. Upon launching CNN on June 1, 1980 at 5:00 p.m., Ted Turner gave a proclamation that defined his vision for his cable/satellite network: "We won't be signing off until the world ends. We'll be on, and we will cover the end of the world, and that will be our last event. . . . we'll play 'Nearer My God to Thee' before we sign off" (Wilkinson 2013, 90).

At first CNN was headquartered in a former country club on the outskirts of midtown Atlanta, Georgia. Then Turner purchased the Omni International Hotel, also in Atlanta, from developer Tom Cousins and relocated CNN there. The new complex was named the CNN Center. As part of the sale Turner received the Atlanta Hawks sports basketball franchise, which was part of the National Basketball Association (NBA). CNN was now in the tower that once housed the World of Sid and Marty Krofft, the world's first indoor amusement park created by television creators and puppetry pioneers, brothers Sid Krofft (1929–) and Marty Krofft (1937–), which closed after six months due to poor attendance. In addition to its role as a 24-hour news station, CNN became a force in the revival of Atlanta's downtown.

When CNN was officially launched, the broadcasting began with an introduction by Ted Turner. The first anchors of CNN were the husband and wife team of David Walker (1941–) and Lois Hart (1950–), who presided over CNN's first newscast. At the time of CNN's launch Burt Reinhardt (1920–2011) left Paramount Pictures as executive vice president of the nontheatrical and educational film division to become the executive vice president of CNN. He had the responsibility of hiring most of the network's first 200 employees. Reinhardt also hired CNN's chief news anchor, Bernard Shaw (1940–). In an era when whites dominated the anchor news desk, it was a bold choice to select an African American to help represent the new network. Shaw brought a lot of experience to the job; he had been an anchor and reporter in Chicago. He moved to Washington to be a White House correspondent for CBS, and then switched to ABC before coming to CNN.

For all his accomplishments Bernard Shaw is best known for his work during a presidential debate in 1988 when he became the story. He knew that the Democratic nominee, Michael Dukakis (1933–), was opposed to the death penalty, and Shaw asked Dukakis if he would be for the death penalty if Kitty Dukakis, the candidate's wife, was raped and murdered. Dukakis said no. After the debate there was a furor over the question from Kitty Dukakis and others who felt it was inappropriate for a presidential debate, but it further put CNN on the map because a major figure at the network shook things up with a risky question.

Ted Turner and his team recognized that you couldn't run a 24-hour news network by just putting up an anchor reading the news and showing news footage. They had to come up with shows with a news theme. *Moneyline*, a financial show hosted by Lou Dobbs (1945–) focusing on politics and economics, went on the air in 1980 and ran for 20 years. After graduating from Harvard Dobbs worked in government and banking before becoming a reporter for several media outlets. Later *Moneyline* began to head toward general news and economic and political commentary and was renamed *Moneyline with Lou Dobbs,* then *Lou Dobbs Moneyline*, and then *Lou Dobbs Tonight.* In July 2009 Dobbs was the only major news anchor to give air time to the "birther movement," those who believed that President Barack Obama wasn't a U.S. citizen, a qualification for president in the U.S. Constitution. After much pressure from within and outside the network, Lou Dobbs, who had been at CNN from the initial launch, left the network.

CNN Daybreak, an early morning news show hosted by Carol Costello (1961–), debuted on June 1, 1980, the same day CNN went on the air. It covered the news with correspondents on location or stories taped the night before. The show aired weekdays starting at 5 a.m. and ran one hour. Programming at CNN wanted to present a special show for early risers while they got ready for their day by giving an overview of current news that would be useful for viewers who wanted to be informed about their world.

The popular political discussion show *Evans and Novak* was also created in 1980. The hosts were Rowland Evans (1921–2001) and Robert Novak (1931–2009). It became CNN's most watched discussion program. A short time after its launch Al Hunt (1942–) and Mark Shields (1937–) joined the show as occasional panelists. The show's title was eventually changed to *Evans, Novak, Hunt & Shields* in 1998 when Hunt and Shields were named as permanent members of the show. The show stated a news topic of the day or an ongoing national or international issue and then the men would present opposing viewpoints. The range of thought went from very conservative to very liberal. The drama was rooted in heated arguments that would emerge from the discourse, which still remained highly intelligent and informative.

On June 1, 1980 CNN premiered a sports bulletin with baseball and North American soccer highlights. This later became *Sports Tonight*, a late night show. The co-hosts were Nick Charles (1946 2011) and Fred Hickman (1956–). One of the popular features on this show was "Play of the Day" (later known as "replay of the day"), when a highlight containing a spectacular play was shown. CNN also aired a weekend sports show called *Sports Saturday* and *Sports Sunday*. Sports news coverage on the major networks covered a narrow range of sports, but this CNN show took a wide look at sports including baseball, horse racing, football, basketball, gymnastics, wrestling, tennis, golf, and many other sports.

In 1980 CNN brought out a show with no real competition. *Style with Elsa Klensch* presented fashion and style from the United States and all over the world. It was this kind of show that separated CNN from other networks as the program was not there to sell anything, but to educate viewers about current fashion and design. Elsa Klensch (1933–) was an Austrian American journalist who often wrote on style and fashion. She would cover international designers and shows of their collections. The show was also educational about the design process and covered history by presenting leading designers. With this show Ted Turner was showing the breadth of CNN's coverage with an art that contained both glamour and craftsmanship.

In June 1982 *Crossfire,* a late night political debate program, premiered. The format was to discuss political issues from opposing viewpoints. The hosts were liberal Tom Braden (1917–2009) and conservative Pat Buchanan (1938–). The genesis of the show goes back to 1978 when the two men debated each other on radio. Their show became very popular and was moved to prime-time television on CNN. In 1985 Buchanan left the show to become the communication director for the Ronald Reagan (1911–2004) administration. He was replaced by Robert Novak, who was already on CNN. Buchanan returned to *Crossfire* in 1987 replacing Novak. In 1989 Braden was replaced by Michael Kinsley (1951–), a liberal columnist. What separated this show from *Evans and Novak* was the tone; it appeared that each man was out to get the other by every means necessary in terms of word use and phrases, as well as the timber of the voice. *Crossfire* was not so much a political discourse but a battle between right and left.

In June 1985 CNN took a leap and went after prime time—the 9 to 10 p.m. slot that the networks had had a lock on for decades. Turner put his trust in a man known as a strong and popular radio interviewer. Larry King (1933–) was very experienced in talking to celebrities, actors, sports figures, and political figures on *Larry King Live*. Often the full hour was devoted to one person. Many guests were on the show many times during its run. It was a call-in show so the viewers were involved. *Larry King Live* was the place to go if you had something to say that you wanted a big audience to hear. King's interviews were in depth, and he could ask a question within a question. Guests liked going on *Larry King Live* because they trusted him and felt safe. Even if he asked a tough question, he asked it with no malice. For the viewers, many who watched the show Monday through Friday were willing to skip the network show they normally watched at that time. Larry King, with the exception of a few nights off, did the show every night for 25 years. He became an icon and CNN not only had a star but an even stronger voice.

CNN proved what they did best was to cover live events as they occurred. On January 28, 1986 CNN was the only news outlet to cover the launch of the space shuttle *Challenger*. Seventy-three seconds into the launch the space vehicle disintegrated, instantly killing the entire crew including a schoolteacher. CNN's camera caught the terrifying explosion and the faces of those gathered to watch the launch including family members. There was also extensive reporting by experts about what might have happened and reactions from a wide range of commentators.

On October 14, 1987, an 18-month-old toddler, Jessica McClure, fell down a well in Midland, Texas. CNN was immediately on the story and was able to cover it with more depth and length than the other networks. The workers toiled for 58 hours straight to save Jessica. The image of the site and the process of the rescue were dramatic and filled with tension. So many Americans were cheering for the child's safety and were thrilled to see her come out of the dirt with her rescuer holding her tight.

Over the decade of the 1980s many other anchors and reporters appeared on CNN. John Holloman (1948–1998) was the first member of the CNN Washington News Bureau, which existed from 1980 until 1998; in 1985, Frank Sesno became a correspondent, anchor, and Washington Bureau chief and is still with the network; Christiane Amanpour (1958–) became a foreign affairs correspondent in 1983; Jeanne Moos, reporter of humorous short subjects, joined the network in 1981; Candy Crowley (1948–) was a political reporter at CNN from 1987 through 2015; Peter Arnett (1934–) was a war reporter from 1981 to 1999; Bobbie Batista (1952–) anchored news programs from 1981 to 2001; and Lou Waters, one of the original anchors, was a mainstay from 1980 until 2001.

CNN started with the concept that the news goes on for 24 hours a day so there should be a network there to cover it. Starting with the news radio concept of presenting the news in a 20- to 30-minute cycle that repeats constantly to developing sophisticated programs that presented the news in myriad ways as well as devoting time to fashion and sports, to a developed news entity with an army of reporters, anchors, crews, and informative graphics, CNN is a force in cable news. For many CNN has become a way of life. Those who were interested in the news before 1980 had limited access to what was going on in the United States, abroad, and in their town. Ted Turner understood that and created the news watchers' dream and a place for anyone to either watch a news show or watch an event unfold live on their TV when no one else was doing it.

Further Resources

Auletta, Ken. 2005. *Ted Turner's Improbable Empire*. New York: W. W. Norton.

Frank, Reuven. 1991. *Out of Thin Air: Insider's History of Network News—the Beginning and the End*. New York: Simon & Schuster.

Schroeder, Alan. 2008. *Presidential Debates: Fifty Years of High-Risk TV*. New York: Columbia University Press.

Turner, Ted, and Bill Burke. 2009. *Call Me Ted*. New York: Grand Central Publishing.

Whittemore, Tom. 1990. *CNN: The Inside Story: How a Band of Mavericks Changed the Face of Television News*. New York: Little, Brown.

Wilkinson, Todd. 2013. *Last Stand: Ted Turner's Quest to Save a Troubled Planet*. Guilford, CT: Lyons Press.

Williams, Christian. 1981. *Lead, Follow, or Get Out of the Way: The Story of Ted Turner*. New York: Times Books.

Music Television: MTV and the Video Revolution

The content of a music video in the 1980s was a visual interpretation of a pop or rock recording (other musical genres would come later) in which the band engaged along with others in interpreting the music and lyrics of a song that they performed during the video. MTV launched as a cable network that played videos as their programming in the way a disc jockey would play a record over the radio. Before MTV earlier forms of music videos were used as promotions for albums or new single records coming out. Most of this was industry based but later with MTV, singles and albums were advertised by repeatedly being played on the network, which motivated mainly young people to go out and buy the record.

A music video in the 1980s was photographed with a video camera, then edited in a video console suite or photographed with a motion picture camera, and then either edited on film or transferred and edited to video. There were performance videos where the band performed the song to the cameras much the way they would on a television show such as *The Ed Sullivan Show* (1948–1971). An interpretive music video would utilize settings, props, costumes, and other performers in addition to the band. The interpretation was specific, either directly picturing the record or putting the song in a different context. Dancers, usually females in spandex outfits, sexualized the video music experience. Eventually music video directors emerged; they were artists that did not come out of theater or film but out of this new medium. At the beginning well-known and established contemporary film directors helmed the project, bringing a film look and style to the project before the music video aesthetic emerged full blown in which continuity, matching, and traditional compositions were largely excluded. In 1984 Sam Peckinpah, best known for *The Wild Bunch* (1968), directed Julian Lennon in the 1984 music video for his song "Too Late for Goodbyes." Contemporary film master Brian De Palma directed Bruce Springsteen in the 1994 music video of his song "Dancing in the Dark." A young yet to be discovered Courtney Cox is brought on stage and dances with Springsteen before she would become a major star on *Friends* (1994–2004). John Landis, who came to fame directing *National Lampoon's Animal House* (1978), was behind the camera in 1983 for the landmark video "Thriller" starring Michael Jackson and coming in at a record (for the time) 13 minutes.

With MTV the music video revolution exploded. Kids and the teens to mid-twenties demographic grabbed this as their medium and others watched the new music video channel as close to around the clock as they could. Viewers waited for their favorite video to air and waited until it cycled around again. Video music was a new delivery system and all you had to do was put on your TV and click the remote. Music videos had an impact on musical tastes, fashion, and attitudes, but like all revolutions in the arts there was a beginning.

History of the Music Video

The prehistory of the music video began during the motion picture studio era, especially in the 1940s and 1950s. A trip to the local motion picture theater involved an A picture, a B movie, cartoons, a newsreel, and short subjects. The latter were short films that could be comedies, travelogues, nature films, or music films. Simply done with little coverage or editing, a big band either with a singer or not would be brought into a studio with basically no set and facing the camera play either an instrumental of a popular song of the day or back up the singer. There is a long artistic road to travel from basically a long take of a big band playing on a movie screen to an intricate short video shot with many camera positions and machine-gun editing. The Beatles, Jimi Hendrix, and other musicians in the mid to late 1960s had promotional films made; financed by the record companies, they were only seen in limited presentations and were shown at meetings, conventions, and other events. Decades after the Beatles movie *A Hard Day's Night* was released in 1964, followed by *Help* (which was in color, not black–and-white like the first film) in 1965, on June 26, 1999 MTV honored director Richard Lester (1932–) for "basically inventing the music video."

Mason Williams (1938–), the head writer on the always controversial *Smothers Brothers Comedy Hour* (1967–1969), pitched an idea to CBS for a TV show that featured "video-radio" on which disc jockeys would play avant-garde pieces set to music on the air, but CBS cancelled the idea. In 1968 the Smothers Brothers ran promotional videos of the Beatles singing "Hey Jude" and "Revolution" and performances of the Bee Gees, and this format would eventually become the music video. They also had musical performances by leading rock bands such as the Jefferson Airplane, Cream, Buffalo Springfield, and the Who, a band known for their theatricality and destruction. At the end of their performance the bass drum exploded and guitars were smashed to bits. This and all of the many music youth acts on *The Smothers Brothers Comedy Hour* had many camera angles and complex sets, producing a step toward the music video.

In 1970 Philadelphia-based disc jockey Bob Whitney was the creator of *The Now Explosion,* a TV series filmed in Atlanta, Georgia that was broadcast to local television stations across the United States. *The Now Explosion* featured video clips from musical artists of the day. The distributor of the show cancelled it in 1971. Whitney made the connection from radio Top 40 music to music-driven videos. By the mid-1970s stations began airing video clips when it was difficult to get a particular artist to perform live in their studio.

In 1974 the vice president of Televak Corporation introduced an idea to distribute a music video channel to record stores across America and promoted it to distributors and retailers in a May 1974 issue of *Billboard* magazine. The channel featured disc jockeys who had signed a deal with US Cable, a provider with a large subscription base in 12 states in 1978, to expand their audience from retail to cable television. Soon MTV would be born and their service was no longer available.

Launch of MTV

The journey to get MTV on the air began in 1977. Warner Cable launched the first two-way interactive television system, QUBE, in Columbus, Ohio. This system offered many channels, and one was *Sight and Sound,* a channel that featured concert footage and music-oriented TV programs. This channel was interactive so viewers could vote for their favorite artists and songs.

The original format for MTV was created by Robert Pittman (1953–), who became president and CEO of MTV Networks. He knew the concept would work as he had produced and hosted a 15-minute show, *Album Tracks,* on WNBC, a local New York City television station in the late 1970s. The show did not present music videos but short concert clips. The importance of *Album Tracks* was that it was a music news show with still pictures and other imagery about current rock artists. It also gave information about the pop charts and background on singers and bands. This proved to Pittman that there was a market for music TV. He was ready to take the next step.

John Lack, Pittman's boss, was behind *PopClips* a television series created by Michael Nesmith (1942–), a former member of the Monkees, and a music pioneer and avant-garde television pioneer in his own right. The idea for *PopClips* came from a show on TVNZ (a television station in New Zealand), *Radio with Pictures,* which had premiered in 1976. Their concept had been in the works since 1966 when major record labels supplied the New Zealand Broadcasting Corporation with promotional music clips to play at no charge because it was difficult to get artists to come to New Zealand to perform live.

On Saturday, August 1, 1981 at 12:00 a.m. Eastern time, MTV launched. The first sounds and images were the voice of John Lack heralding "Ladies and gentlemen, rock and roll!" over footage of the first space shuttle launch countdown that had taken place earlier in the year and of the launch of *Apollo* 11 from 1969. Then the original MTV theme song was played, best described as high-octane rock and roll guitar and drum driven, then the planting of the American flag on the moon. On the flag, however, is not the red, white, and blue but the MTV logo rapidly changing colors and textures.

The first music video broadcast on MTV was carefully and cleverly chosen: "Video Killed the Radio Star" by the Buggles. This proto–music video released in 1977 has many of the elements that would define the music video: images turned from color to black-and-white and doubled, a roaming camera, band members and other performers working together to illustrate the song, and flashing colors. The song was written by Trevor Horn, Geoff Downes, and Bruce Willey. The group Camera Club had the first recording but it is this cover by the Buggles that is forever connected with the birth of MTV. Ironically, the lyrics are nostalgic and sad about losing radio as a form of communication, but ambivalent and at the same time accepting as fact that video killed the radio star. There are prop radios and television sets in a pile. The chorus, which is the title repeated, often has the quality of a jingle. The musicians are very modern with electronic instruments. In the end the choice of first song was brilliant and the anthem resonated across the country.

The original concept was that MTV would play music videos 24 hours a day, seven days a week. MTV's earliest format was modeled after AOR (Album-Oriented Rock) radio where sides of record albums would be played at a time but they would eventually transition to a top 40 station in 1984, which was singles-oriented with selections based on a music magazine chart. MTV didn't employ disc jockeys, but called their on-camera people VJs, or video jocks, who would introduce the videos, do an outro, report music news, conduct interviews, and provide concert dates and promotions. The original group of VJs were Nina Blackwood (1955–), Mark Goodman (1952–), Alan Hunter (1957–), J.J. Jackson (1941–2004), and Martha Quinn (1959–). The videos were on cassette tape cartridges; when an MTV staff member changed the tape there would be a temporary moment of black on the screen.

The music of the 1980s presented a wide range of expression. Some of the movements and styles during the decade include pop, hard rock, alternative rock, punk, R&B, hip-hop, electronic music, and country music. MTV played new wave music, pop, hard rock, and heavy metal because of what they at first determined as their target audience. They were also selective as to what artists to play in each genre and were limited to song choice but also what was available in video. Because MTV played so many videos to feed their around-the-clock format, many, many bands and singers recorded videos, especially during the 1980s. These included Adam Ant, Blondie, Eurythmics, Culture Club, Mötley Crüe, Prince, Duran Duran, Van Halen, Bon Jovi, the Police, the Cars, David Bowie, Dire Straits, Journey, Rush, Linda Ronstadt, Genesis, Aerosmith, the Rolling Stones, the Moody Blues, John Mellencamp, Billy Joel, Rod Stewart, the Who, ZZ Top, and Kiss.

The first film to have clips run from it on MTV was *Flashdance* (1983). Musical segments were excerpted by the producers and MTV put them into their regular rotation. As the music video revolution grew more and more popular, artists got involved with the form. From the more primitive videos viewers saw the art become more like short films. They featured dynamic and lush cinematography, higher budgets, greater and more accomplished sets and costumes, and lavish choreography.

In 1981 MTV ran into a racial issue. All the videos that had been playing featured Caucasian performers. Rick James, an African American musical artist (1948–2004), submitted a video for his "Super Freak" record and it was rejected as part of the playlist. A black woman, Carolyn B. Baker, who at the time was head of acquisition and talent, made the decision to reject James's video. She said it was of bad quality and had a lot of half-naked women in it (Tannenbaum and Marks 2012, 167–168). Others said that MTV had a particular rock and roll focus, and it was hard to find African Americans who were in that category. Ultimately it was Michael Jackson (1958–2009) with a series of major hit productions that broke the color barrier while setting a new standard in the art of music videos. In addition to "Thriller" he created videos for "Billie Jean" (1982), "Beat It" (1982), "Bad" (1987), and others. Rap music and hip-hop was emerging during the 1980s. MTV put them into the rotation with artists including Run–DMC, the Fat Boys, Whodini, L.L. Cool J, and the Beastie Boys.

Eventually, MTV began to expand beyond broadcasting only music videos. The network soon created more programs, some of which maintained their connection to music and music videos. The very first MTV Video Music Awards debuted in 1984. It also featured a performance of "Like a Virgin" by Madonna (Madonna Louise Ciccone, 1958–), who would go on to take the music video into erotic, religious, and verboten areas. The award statuettes are the image of the MTV Moon Man, an astronaut like the one in the original opening. Known as the VMAs, the award show was created as an alternate to the Grammy awards. Award categories in the 1980s included Best Overall Performance in a Video, Most Experimental Video, Best Concept Video, Best Post-Modern Video, and Special Recognition Award.

Three major stars emerged as video artists in the vanguard of the field. Phil Collins (1951–), former drummer and singer of the band Genesis, moved into a long and successful solo career. His videos "In the Air Tonight" (1981), "Against All Odds" (1984), and "Another Day in Paradise" are part of a body of diverse work that merges the emotion and mood of the song with stunning visuals. Peter Gabriel (1950–), the original front man of Genesis, also left the group for a solo career. Just one of his music videos, "Sledgehammer" (1987), won a then record nine MTV Music Awards for its technique of flashing color and innovative rhythmic camerawork. Michael Jackson was an innovator in employing state-of-the-art dance and movement with distinctive vocals and seductive narratives. He performed in almost 50 music videos. "Beat It" (1982) puts the film version of *West Side Story* (1961) into a new context when two opposing gangs fight by dancing out their anger toward each other. "Billie Jean" (1981) uses split screen and altering frame sizes to expand Jackson's abilities in dance. "Thriller" (1982) is a fun horror show that made the music video form into a major production.

In 1985 MTV covered the Live Aid concerts held in London and Philadelphia. Sixteen hours of the benefit event were broadcast. In 1986 MTV launched *Dial MTV,* a daily top 10 music video countdown where viewers could call in via telephone. Also in 1986 *120 Minutes* was introduced, featuring low–rotation alternative rock and other underground videos. In 1987 the late night *Headbanger's Ball* was put on the schedule. It featured heavy metal music and news. In 1988 MTV premiered *Yo! MTV Raps,* which featured hip-hop and rap music. In 1989 MTV started to introduce music-based specials such as *MTV Unplugged,* an acoustic performance show.

In 1986 MTV ran its Spring Break program held in Daytona Beach, Florida for a week in March, broadcasting it eight hours a day. MTV felt this was part of the youth culture that was their demographic. Starship and the Beastie Boys performed to a beach packed with young men and women in bathing suits. There is a real spring break every year in various locations and many who were never able to go heard all the tall tales. MTV Spring Break brought the beach into the living room of all those who couldn't be at the real thing. The event and crowd looked natural, and for the most part it was, but it was also controlled for TV.

MTV was a developmental step in the evolution of television. Networks and producers were always looking to tap more deeply into the youth market, and rock and roll had been strong through the decades. During the 1980s MTV turned the television into a video jukebox, but it was more than the music. MTV became part of the culture and gave young people someplace to stay on the television map. MTV became synonymous with youth. Young people loved to listen to their music and now with MTV they could see it.

Further Resources

Blackwood, Nina, and Marc Goodman. 2013. *VJ: The Unplugged Adventures of MTV's First Wave.* New York: Simon & Schuster.

Kennedy. 2013. *The Kennedy Chronicles: The Golden Age of MTV Through Rose Colored Glasses.* New York: St. Martin's Press.

McGrath, Tom. 1996. *MTV: The Making of a Revolution.* Philadelphia: Running Press.

Rettenmund, Matthew. 1996. *Totally Awesome 80s: A Lexicon of the Music, Videos, Movies TV Shows, Stars and Trends of the Decadent Decade.* New York: St. Martin's Press.

Schwartz, Lara M. 2007. *Making Music Videos: Everything You Need to Know from the Best in the Business.* New York: Billboard Books.

Tannenbaum, Rob, and Craig Marks. 2012. *I Want My MTV: The Uncensored Story of the Music Video Revolution.* New York: Plume.

The Answer Is . . . : Game Show Hosts during the 1980s

When the game show genre began in the 1940s, the only trait needed for a host was a good voice in terms of tone, elocution, pace, and an engaging vocal personality. Producers recognized that a game couldn't run itself so a person was put in that position to interact with the contestants, govern the rules of the game, and keep the audience pleasantly occupied. The personality traits and skills required are many. As for a host's looks, it is critical to understand that hosts in the 1980s were more often than not male. This kind of sexism is consistent from decade to decade. They had to be a skilled speaker, similar to radio hosts. They should talk to the eyes of the studio audience and, more importantly, play into the camera to connect with the home audience. The host needed to be comfortable, thereby making the audience comfortable and in a state of excitement. Also, hosts could have their own specific personality or style, as many hosts were laid back, or smooth, or elicited high energy. The physical looks of a game show host ranged from very handsome to average guy-next-door. They must wear clothes well. Talk show hosts do not wear their own outfits during the game. A specific designer or fashion house provided the host with clothes for every show. These designers may even had suggested what sartorial item may go with another. A host needed to get the attention of contestants, the studio audience, and the home viewers with phrases like "Now look," "Do you get the picture?" "Let me show you," or "See what I mean?" They must be more than a talking head but a physical being. Television game show hosts were really playing themselves—great hosts were playing themselves at the very best they could be.

Early game show technology was mechanical. The host may call for something to happen on the game show board or physically do it himself. The former was executed by a stagehand behind the board pushing the indicated area so it changed from one number, word, or symbol to another. The latter involved the game show host physically touching the area with his finger or hand and the backstage stagehand guiding the successful change from one message on the board to another. During the 1980s game show sets and boards were electronic and hand-operated sets became obsolete. Every aspect was wired so it could move when indicated by someone backstage or offstage using a controller that could target any area on the board. Some of the legendary hosts of the 1980s and the games they presided over are varied and individualistic.

Bob Barker (1923–) was the country's foremost game show host, having spent 50 years in television. His amazing career covered a number of shows: the classic *Truth or Consequences* (1956–1974), *End of the Rainbow* (1957–1958), *The Family Game* (1967), *Simon Says* (1971), *That's My Line* (1980–1981), and the all-star classic *The Price Is Right* (1972–2007). Barker won 19 Emmy awards, 14 for outstanding game show host and four as executive producer of *The Price Is Right*, and also a lifetime achievement award for daytime television. He became an animal rights activist and even ended his show with a signature message about the care of animals. Unfortunately Barker has had legal problems including claims of sexual harassment from several of the women who were models who helped display the prizes on *The Price Is Right.*

The Price Is Right was first hosted from 1956 to 1965 by Bill Cullen (1927–1990). The game was revamped and from 1972 to 1977 Dennis James (1917–1977) was the host; and from 1985 to 1986 Tom Kennedy (1927–) hosted the nighttime version of the show. From 1972 to 2007 Bob Barker made his long run as the host of *The Price Is Right,* choosing to retire after 35 years on the job. As of October 2016, Drew Carey (1958–) is the host following Barker in 2007.

Bob Barker is a tall, elegant man, well dressed and always in command on camera. His hair transitioned from jet black in the early years to stone white in the later years. The show involved dealing with a row of contestants who bid on items introduced by Barker with the winner coming on stage to play a pricing game for cash. At the end of the show the two winners with the highest amounts get to see two extravagant showcases and the one who comes closest with a bid without going over wins the day's big prize. Barker worked the audience and conducted the original bidding, then he played one of the pricing games with the winner of that round and later had to oversee the presentation of the showcases and the bidding process as well as determining the winner. His voice was very calm amidst some of the chaos of the show. During the pricing game he was at his best, now one-on-one with a contestant being kind, helpful, inserting a little joke here and there for the audience in the studio and the one at home, which he made contact with at times. From the first sound of his voice to the last image of him giving his goodbyes, Bob Barker was smooth.

Dick Clark (1929–2012) was a media mogul, music and dance show host, game show host, game and award show producer, reinventor of the televised New Year's Eve show, and much, much more. Dick Clark was the CEO of Dick Clark Productions but in the end he loved hosting. He was first up on *The $10,000 Pyramid* with a stint from 1977 to 1988, and audiences daily were convinced they were seeing the real Dick Clark. His image was a man with a strong radio/television voice, one who could explain anything and have it make sense. He was helpful guiding the game along with finesse, but it was when a contestant and their celebrity helper would go for the big money that Clark showed the depth of his intelligence and humanity. He was the contestant's biggest cheerleader. If they weren't doing well he would bend down just a bit and talk to the unsuccessful contestant and make a string of intelligent suggestions that may have worked. Not like a know-it-all but like a helpful teacher.

Dick Clark also hosted what may be the strangest game show up to this point in American game show history. *The Krypton Factor* (1981) was a summer show that ran one season. This was a mental and physical test to find perfect human specimens. One of the rounds involved the contestants watching a clip from a movie. A couple talked at their dinner table. When it was over the contestants were told that there was a waiter walking in the very back of the shot. Then a line of men dressed the same as in the waiter in the clip came out and the correct one had to be identified correctly for points to add to the quotient.

Dick Clark was a man who never seemed to change—certainly not by the 1980s. He appeared youthful in mind, body, and spirit. Always helpful, always ready to speak or move to another space on the set without apparent forethought, Clark proved that with all the changes from the 1950s through the 1980s, being timeless made the audience feel calm and without the fear that anything would go wrong.

Englishman Richard Dawson (1932–2012) was another game show host who worked on a major hit, *Family Feud*, which Dawson hosted from 1976 to 1985. Dawson hosted other game shows, but he created the mold for a popular one and added to the profile of a game show host with his individualistic ways. He was the original host of *Family Feud.* He personalized the show to the extent that he was the real star of the show and most viewers tuned in to see and hear his antics. One player from each team races to determine which team goes first by naming something that is on the survey topic board. When the player slams the buzzer and says their guess, Dawson shouts at the top of his lungs, "The survey says!" and either the board stayed still (due to a wrong answer) or a panel with the right guess opened up, confirming the right answer. Nobody told Dawson to yell those words. Whether it was to be gallant, romantic, respectful, or for some other reason, Dawson would kiss every woman on both teams on the cheek. Some found it quaint, others were offended by it, but the women didn't seem to mind; they seemed to know it was innocent. It garnered him the nickname "The Kissing Bandit." Network executives tried but failed to stop Dawson's cheek-pecking. Dawson asked viewers to write in on the matter and the vote was 704 against and 14,600 in favor. Then there were complaints about Dawson kissing nonwhite women. He answered that it was important that he kissed all women, making a statement against the racism that was implied by the complainers. Dawson said the kisses came from his mother, who when he was a child told him a kiss was for love and luck.

When he went down the row of family members to talk to them and receive their guesses for the main part of the game, he was funny with the men and a bit flirty with the women. Dawson sprinted around the set, moving from a team on one side to the other team on the opposite side. A bonus round was held at the end of the show. Dawson would stand close to the contestants chosen for it by the families. He almost always put his arm around the back of the female contestants. Those on the show and those at home knew it was all in good fun. Dawson was a good-time guy, the type of fellow you may chat with in a bar or pub. During the 1980s he brought fun to the game show.

Family Feud was home to another personable game show host of the era, Ray Combs (1956–1996), who was a stand-up comedian in the early 1980s. He appeared on *The Tonight Show*, and in 1987, he was a celebrity panelist on *Hollywood Squares* hosted by John Davidson (1941–). In 1988 Combs signed a seven-year contract for a new version of *Family Feud.* This extremely popular game, which still airs as of October 2016, was hosted by a string of men including Louie Anderson, John O'Hurley, and Steve Harvey. Combs, who had an even and steady manner, would introduce a topic on a big board, then go down the line of each family asking them for something that would match. Combs's greatest skill as host on the show was going from family member to family member and chatting with them about wherever he wanted to take them, and then ask for their answer. Viewers enjoyed the banter that was totally improvised on both sides. He was very popular because of his friendly manner and ability to draw in the audience as well as the contestants, but didn't draw enough rating points to keep the network happy. Combs was dismissed from *Family Feud* on March 26, 1993, and although he made some appearances on television they were never as an active host of a game show. In June 1996 after experiencing a severe psychiatric episode he committed suicide.

During the 1960s Bob Eubanks (1938–) produced concerts for major acts such as the Beatles and the Rolling Stones. In Los Angeles he produced Barry Manilow, the Supremes, Dolly Parton, Bob Dylan, and Elton John. In 1966 Chuck Barris (1929–2017), the Mad Hatter of television game shows, asked Eubanks to host a brand-new game show, *The Newlywed Game*, which premiered on ABC. The show was a big success—audiences enjoyed the naughty answers and provocative questions. In between tapings of the show Eubanks managed many country music stars. In 1988 he left *The Newlywed Game* and continued hosting *Card Sharks* (1979–1989), which he had been taping while doing *The Newlywed Game*. Other game shows Eubanks hosted include *Dream House* (1983–1984) and *Trivia Trap* (1984–1985). He has also worked as a television producer for game and variety shows.

As a game show host Bob Eubanks is best known for his work on *The Newlywed Game* on which four couples were asked questions about their spouses and wrote their answers on cards so the other half could guess what answer was given. Points were given for right answers. He was young when he started on the show and youthful as the years moved by. His Ricky Nelson/Fabian 1950s/1960s rock and roll hairstyle, which is combed back with a dip created in the middle, and his casual attire often topped by a collegiate sweater gave him a hip, suave appearance. His mellifluous voice sounded as if it came out of a top 40 FM rock radio station. The viewers never knew if he was married or had a girlfriend. He acted aloof and as if he was above the newly married couples on the show. The questions and answers from the contestants were playful at times and bordered on being censored. The pro ducers decided that instead of saying "making love" Eubanks should intone "making whoopee." Eubanks teased and at times made fun of the contestants. He was the ideal host for this show. As of 2016 Eubanks no longer hosts game shows but he makes numerous television appearances, has hosted a beauty pageant, written a book, and kept his hand in the industry.

Ken Ober (1957–2009) broke into show business in 1984 when he was a contestant on *Star Search* where he did stand-up comedy. He was best known as the host for the MTV game show *Remote Control,* which he did three seasons from 1987 to 1990, which then ran in reruns for two more years. This show was geared to a young demographic and to those who watched TV and MTV incessantly. The set was open; the back of flats could be seen as well as the cameramen. It was a den in which to watch TV. The three contestants each sat in a high-backed leather chair. A back wall had framed pictures of famous talk show hosts. Ken Ober as the host was next to a large TV monitor. The contestants chose TV-oriented topics and were asked questions. At times a clip to be identified appeared on the TV, manipulated by remote control. The contestant with the most points won. There was a loud, boisterous live audience. This was a trivia game strictly geared to TV and what can be seen on it. It was the MTV generation joyfully exploring the medium they spent so much time watching. Ken Ober also hosted *Make Me Laugh* (1997), and *Smush* (2001) with Lisa Dergan. Ober's career ended when he died of a sudden illness at age 52.

Pat Sajak (1946–) was a radio man and a television weatherman when in 1981 Merv Griffin asked him if he would take over for Chuck Woolery in hosting *Wheel of Fortune*, another classic game show that as of 2016 is still running and with Sajak as the host. The game couldn't be simpler. A contestant spins a wheel to get letters that fit as part of a word puzzle on the wall. Solve the puzzle and the contestant wins money. Female models have been part of game shows since their inception, but they usually stood around next to a prize and pointed. On *Wheel of Fortune* Vanna White (1957–), who became a star because of her participation on the show, was there to turn the tiles when someone guessed a letter correctly. She was different. She and Sajak would have exchanges during the show, often a light remark, and with Sajak constantly referring to her by her first name. She became a solid part of the game and is still with the show as of 2016. So a simple game is made fun and engaging because of a host and his assistant/collaborator. Maybe in the age of digital technology just spinning a mechanical wheel as if it were a carney's wheel is just as exciting.

Marc Summers (1951–) began as a disc jockey and stand-up comedian. He had various television production jobs but received his big break when in 2000 Nickelodeon hired him as the host of *Double Dare.* The show was syndicated in two years and had a brief network run in prime time as *Nickelodeon Family Double Dare* in 1988. The show was very popular, leading to more work for Summers. He then hosted the syndicated show *Couch Potatoes* in 1989 and Nickelodeon's *What Would You Do?* In 1991 Game Show Network (GSN) hired him to host its original game show *Win Tuition.* Later Summers transitioned to the Food Network where he hosted and produced shows.

Marc Summers had a warm, friendly style. His disc jockey voice produced a smooth communication style. *Double Dare* was a physical game for young people. It featured an obstacle course that has contestants climbing, diving, and running from one roadblock to another, getting over them until they reach the finish line. The emphasis was on fun and Summers was a cheerleader for their success. It was loud, fun, and very messy. *Couch Potato* (1989) was a syndicated show that was a takeoff on *Remote Control.* This time there were two teams, three boys on one side, three girls on another. TV trivia was the theme. Questions about TV past and present were asked and answered or missed. Musical themes were played, television clips were shown. The winners got a prize. Summers was amiable with both groups and kidded lightly. He moved things along and at times commented on how hard a question was.

Peter Tomarken (1942–2006) made his entrance into show business by playing a reporter in the popular motion picture *Heaven Can Wait* (1978). He later started his own advertising company, which gave him the opportunity to be behind and in front of the camera during production of commercials during the late 1970s. His agent convinced him to try hosting a game show because of the easy schedules and six-figure salaries. He made two pilots and both failed, *Rodeo Drive* for NBC in October 1980 (later picked up by Lifetime) and *Duel in the Daytime* in August 1981. Tomarken landed his first network hosting job as the host of *Hit Man* for NBC, but it only lasted 13 weeks from January 3 to April 1, 1983. He also briefly co-anchored on Playboy TV. He was then offered *Press Your Luck,* which he hosted for three seasons on CBS from 1983 to 1986. Next he hosted the very short-lived *Bargain Hunters* (1987) for ABC. After a year he hosted and produced *Wipeout* (1988–1989), which ran in syndication. After the 1980s Peter Tomarken was on GSN where he served as host for their evening interactive phone games, *Prime Games.* For Fox Family Channel he hosted the game show *Paranoia.* Sadly on the morning of March 13, 2006 he and his wife Kathleen were killed in a plane crash. Peter Tomarken was a professional talk show host more in the tradition of those who came before him. He was a modern man in the 1980s working in a profession he was good at and loved.

Hit Man did not catch on with the game show viewing public. It also was focused on television trivia. The questions were asked in *Jeopardy* style; the answer was given first, then the contestant needed to provide the question. Before each round a video package was shown that concerned an aspect of television, as in shows that had the sponsor's name on screen while the program was running. Many clips providing much information was in the package with a voiceover by Tomarken. All of this would be the base of the questions the three contestants would take on. Memory and connection was as important as general knowledge. The information, both verbal and visual, moved at a quick steady pace. Tomarken was ebullient and enjoyed the proceedings. *Press Your Luck* was a raucous game show with a huge lit-up board with markers for money and prizes. When a question was answered correctly by one of the three contestants, they got a spin at the board, a light flashed quickly around the square filled with goodies, and when the player yelled "Stop" the light halted, usually on a prize, but there were also several "Whammies" in play and if they were hit, the winnings were wiped clean. Peter Tomarken was sharply dressed, usually in a three-piece suit, often in stagey colors like shades of pink. *Bargain Hunters* was also short lived; the game involved contestants trying to determine if an item they are shown with a price is a bargain or not. *Wipeout* was a more traditional television game with a board that contained right and wrong answers to a question and the three players had to find the correct ones.

Canadian-born Alex Trebek (1940–) began his illustrious television game show hosting career in Canada on *Music Hop* in 1963. In 1966 he hosted *Reach for the Top,* a high school quiz show. From 1967 to 1970 Trebek hosted for the CBC introducing classical music programs including performances by the quirky genius, pianist Glenn Gould (1932–1982). In 1973 he came to New York and hosted a new game show for NBC, *The Wizard of Odds*. The next year he was the host of *High Rollers*. After a number of other shows he shot two pilots for a game show devised by Merv Griffin called *Jeopardy.* It was popular in an earlier incarnation hosted by Art Fleming (1924–1995), a real gentleman, but never as popular as it would be with Trebek at the helm, starting in 1984. *Jeopardy* is still running five nights a week as of 2016. Trebek struck the balance on the show where the contestant gets the answer and must give the question. He is commanding, interested in the players, strict with them at times, sarcastic yet funny, a stickler for pronunciation, and a host who makes sure there are enough questions that concern Canada, and because Trebek speaks French, the players better be letter perfect on anything in that language.

A serious man, Trebek has become more professorial looking over the many years he has been associated with *Jeopardy.* Often with a mustache and always with short hair, he dresses in a discreet suit and is always aware of the business at hand. In a career of so much accomplishment, in February 1991 Trebek was the first person ever to host three American games show at the same time—*Jeopardy, Classic Concentration*, and *To Tell the Truth*.

Chuck Woolery (1941–) was the original host for *Wheel of Fortune* from 1975 to 1981, *Love Connection* (1983 to 1994), and *Scrabble* (1984–1990). Before he became a game show host, Woolery had been a popular singer, making records and even a top 40 hit. Chuck Woolery was good-looking, very cool and laid back. *Love Connection* involved a person going on a date, then reporting on the outcome. There was back and forth between the three suitors or dates and the principal person looking for a love connection. Woolery did an in-depth interview with the person who had to choose whether to go out with one of the three candidates or to move on. The humor came out of the differing stories and how naïve the three suitors could be. The show also encouraged the viewers to react to everyone and be judgmental about the outcome. Woolery could be engaging and rise above the proceedings at the same time. He never took the contestants or himself all that seriously and could put on an emotion when it was necessary. *Scrabble* was based on the classic board game but for television it was played by two contestants on a computer-generated board. Woolery again displayed his country charm and urban wit. He seamlessly addressed the audience, then shifted to one player, then the next with smooth and friendly patter. In 1981 Woolery was in a salary dispute with the producers of *Wheel of Fortune*. The show was drawing a 44 share at the time, the percentage of an audience viewing a particular show, so Woolery asked for a raise from $65,000 a year to about $500,000 a year, which was common among other game show hosts at the time. Show creator Merv Griffin (1925–2007) offered Woolery $400,000 and NBC offered to pay the additional $100,000, but when Griffin threatened to move the show to CBS, NBC withdrew their offer and Griffin let Chuck Woolery go, allowing Pat Sajak to take over hosting duties. As of 2014 Chuck Woolery is the co-host with Mark Young of the game show podcast *Blunt Force.*

During the 1980s the game show became expansive with lots of money to give out. There was less attention to the quiet intelligence of the game and more to the exploration of bombast, speed of play, and the interaction with the studio audience. The talk show host was a professional who knew his genre and how to manage people and actions. This was easier in earlier decades when the games were tamer but being able to function during a hurricane or tornado that was the 1980s television game show took hosts that each had their own style, but were united in holding back chaos. There may be a basic blueprint for success as a talk show host. But as hosts such as Trebek, Dawson, Clark, and others proved there was something else needed—individuality—that made a host truly shine. After the 1980s the games changed. Much more money was at stake, a million or more, and the scope of the game was multifaceted and complex. It became common to hire a celebrity to manage these epic events. Producers later tapped Regis Philbin (1931–) (*Who Wants to Be a Millionaire?* 2002–2014), Howie Mandel (1955–), *Deal or No Deal* (2008–2010), and actor and comedian Bob Saget (1956–) *1 vs 100* (2006–2008), all celebrities with strong audience recognition, to host new game shows. They had plenty of personality, but the charismatic professionals of the 1980s proved that game show hosting was an art and a craft.

Further Resources

Barris, Chuck. 2002. *Confessions of a Dangerous Mind: An Unauthorized Autobiography*. New York: Hyperion.

Eubanks, Bob, and Matthew Scott Hansen. 2004. *It's in the Book, Bob!* Dallas, TX: BenBella Books.

Griffin, Merv, with Peter Barsocchini.1980. *Merv*. New York: Simon & Schuster.

Ryan, Steve, and Fred Westbrock. 2005. *The Ultimate TV Game Show Book*. Lanham, MD: Taylor Trade Publishing.

Schwartz, David, and Steve Ryan and Fred Westbrock. 1999. *The Encyclopedia of TV Game Shows*. New York: Checkmark Books.

White, Vanna, with Patricia Romanowski. 1987. *Vanna Speaks*. New York: Warner Books.

Reading Your Television: The Proliferation of Magazine Shows during the 1980s

Before the creation of the television newsmagazine in the late 1960s, news and entertainment items were handled by the networks and local stations. What they presented was short concise stories, heavy on fact whether local, national, or international news. One story followed another and they were presented by a news team, one or two anchors, reporters in the field, an entertainment specialist, and sports and the weather. The news magazine takes its presentation from the print magazine. The setting in the studio is glossy. There usually is a team of reporters who each present a story. The content line is varied from hard news to long interviews with politicians and world leaders as well as those from all aspects of entertainment. The stories, which range in subject, are lengthier than those on the evening news but still light and breezy. The segments run 15 to 20 minutes and are presented by the reporter who researched the story. They do an introduction and often have a graphic behind them with an image and title of the story. It is as if a viewer were home reading a print magazine and the reporter of a particular story is in their living room to introduce it, make comments, and wrap it up at the end.

When network news divisions began, which came first from radio and moved to television, the principle was to deliver the news, stories of the day, and ongoing events such as war, but the coverage had its roots in the newsreels, film compilations of current events shown in movie theaters as part of a double bill package that rapidly moved from one subject to another. The companies who created and supplied newsreels like *Fox Movietone News* began to crumble when television news began to rise to prominence in the 1950s. TV news in general hurt that industry further with newsreel-style programs on CBS, NBC, and ABC in the late 1940s, early 1950s.

News items on television were short and arranged in a particular order based on importance as well as for keeping the viewer from turning the dial by quickly promoting what was coming up after the commercial breaks. Primarily because of Edward R. Murrow (1908–1965) and the team of reporters utilized at CBS, it was long considered the most important and trustworthy network for news. Anchorman Walter Cronkite (1916–2009) was considered to be the most trusted man in America. These men exuded integrity, accuracy, and fairness. CBS, known as the Tiffany Network, was ranked especially high by critics and viewers as the most accurate, dependable, and trustworthy television news.

The model of the television newsmagazine, and also considered the first, is *60 Minutes* (1968–). Americans saw a new kind of television when watching *60 Minutes* for the first time. The program was not the news broadcast viewers were used to, but one where a reporter followed a story and put it into a longer documentary form (although not as long as a traditional documentary film). This type of programming was like a long form magazine story except with film and video. Don Hewitt (1922–2009), who directed the 1960 John F. Kennedy and Richard Nixon debates and was executive producer of the *CBS Evening News with Walter Cronkite* (1962–1981), is credited with creating *60 Minutes*. There are at least two precedents, both from Canada, *This Hour Has Seven Days* (1964–1966) and *W5* (1966–).These two news magazine programs contain the format DNA that *60 Minutes* would make famous. Both featured hosts and reporters and stories of interest, interviews, and reports structured in a mix of features.

60 Minutes had reporters, researchers, and a production team that crafted stories on various political, entertainment, and social topics, and each week they would run a small number of them, usually between three or four. The reporter would sit in front of a large billboard card that had an illustration that went with the story and had text information concerning its topic and the reporters' bylines. In time they added segments: *Point/Counterpoint,* which ran for most of the 1970s and featured conservative James J. Kilpatrick and liberal Shana Alexander in debate. A topic was selected and the two had a very lively debate. *A Few Minutes* with Andy Rooney ran for 34 years. Rooney would be at his desk addressing the camera and each week at the end of the show he would ponder with a humorous view everyday objects or situations. It often involved him purchasing a wide number of items and commenting and comparing them. He was a curmudgeon and the viewers loved him for it.

As of October 2016 *60 Minutes* is still on the air, same night (Sunday), same time (7 p.m. to 8 p.m.) and it is a tradition many Americans participate in watching. The reporters have changed over the years but not the basic essence of the show. Even in the 1980s they continued to practice "gotcha" journalism where by any means necessary the interviewer was able to extract an answer that appeared to show the subject was lying or admitting something that was suspected. Often this was done with editing. A technique that became a signature of the show was to ask a highly inflammatory question to a subject, then cut to them making a clear declaration, then cut to another interview where another subject says that the first is lying, then back to a reaction shot of the main person looking guilty and back-wheeling on his statement. This technique made the subject look bad and the reporter heroic.

20/20 was created by ABC News and Sports innovative genius Roone Arledge (1931–2002). The show debuted on June 6, 1978 with anchors Harold Hayes (1926–1989), the highly respected editor of *Esquire* magazine, and famed art critic and historian, then working for *Time*, Robert Hughes (1938–2012). Arledge designed the show to resemble CBS's *60 Minutes* with in-depth story packages. The difference was *20/20* would focus more on human interest than social and political issues. The title referred to perfect visual acuity of *20/20* vision. The program is now a renowned television magazine show and as of 2016 is still on the air.

The reviews for the first show were scathing, insulting, and without anything good to say. The *New York Times* called *20/20* "dizzyingly absurd" and *The Washington Post* trashed it by saying it was "the trashiest stab at candy cane journalism yet" (Archive of American Television). The hosts, although learned men, were more suited to print than television. Arledge was appalled to learn there was a Claymation puppet segment with President Jimmy Carter singing "Georgia on My Mind." They even used a clip of Walter

Cronkite of CBS News saying his iconic closing line, "That's the way it was," to close their ABC magazine show. The producer and the two hosts were immediately fired. The semi-retired Hugh Downs (1921–) was asked to solo host *20/20* for the next week.

Barbara Walters (1929–) joined *20/20* in a role less than co-anchor in 1979. She soon became a regular special contributor in the fall of 1981, and in 1984 she and Downs reunited as a team after having worked together on *The Today Show* from 1961 to 1971. Downs and Walters would be the *20/20* hosts for the next 15 years. The anchors, reporters, contributors, and solid human interest stories made the show that was almost cancelled in a week last for decades. As of 2016, *20/20* still airs every Friday night at 10 p.m.

Reporters from *20/20* covered the 1980s music scene with a hip-hop special, cultural interests like Nintendo and video games, interviews with musicians Blondie, Pat Benetar, Michael Jackson, and Billy Joel, as well as people and issues in the news, such as Andy Warhol, and the early years of Howard Stern. The team of Downs and Walters had just the right chemistry to reach the widest audience. They were solid journalists who presided over *20/20*'s investigation of the 1980s without looking down on the changing culture.

CBS News Sunday Morning premiered on January 28, 1979 and as of 2016 continues to run. It was co-created by Robert Northshield (1922–2000) and the original host Charles Kuralt (1934–1997) was famous for his "On the Road" segments on *The CBS Evening News with Walter Cronkite*. Kuralt maintained the position of host on *CBS News Sunday Morning* for 15 years. The concept here was for the show to be a broadcast version of a Sunday newspaper magazine supplement like the one put out every week by the *New York Times*. The format was devised to be the Sunday equivalent of *The CBS Morning News.* Following the debut of the Sunday show they retitled the rest of the week *Monday Morning, Tuesday Morning,* and so on. The weekday shows concentrated on hard news as opposed to the Sunday show's focus on feature stories, and often on the fine and performing arts not covered on network news: architecture, painting, ballet, opera, and classical music. The original correspondents were Faith Daniels (1957–); film, book, and drama critic John Leonard (1939–2008); Russ Mitchell (1960–); Ron Powers (1941–); film, book, and drama critic Terrence Powers; jazz and modern music correspondent Billy Taylor (1921–2010); Roger Welsch (1936–); Tim Sample (1951–); and classical music correspondent Eugenia Zuckerman (1944–). The appeal of *CBS News Sunday Morning* is that it offered a pleasant alternative to the contentious issues of the day by presenting peaceful artistic stories. Kuralt was folksy and a fine storyteller. There were peaceful images of the wilderness with natural sound and no narrator. It was a show that informed and entertained in the spirit of those lazy Sunday mornings some remember in the past.

During the 1980s, *CBS News Sunday Morning* presented an eclectic range of stories to reflect on that decade. There was a review of the events of 1980 including the presidency of Jimmy Carter. The explosion of Art Deco from the 1920s alive in the 1980s was covered, and endangered rivers highlighted the dangers facing our natural resources.

Just like print magazines, the newsmagazine television program had competitors who were very close in style and content. When a new genre like the newsmagazine entered the television market and was successful like *60 Minutes*, other broadcasting companies from local stations to networks were eager to cash in. While *60 Minutes* may have been the prototype, other tele-creators saw the form and collaborated until they came up with something that was similar to the newsmagazine show but distinct.

Airing a good part of the decade, *Hour Magazine* (1980–1989) developed a format that the public liked. The producers seemed to have their finger on the pulse of the daytime American viewer. It was the least political of the magazine shows of the era and projected to the audience that they were there to inform them and make their life better. The hosts were Gary Collins (1938–2012) and Pat Mitchell (1943–). The show had a team of specialists to render advice; some of these areas included cardiology, beauty, and sex and relationships. Celebrities were on the show and profiled. There were visits to intriguing places in the United States. They interviewed Annette Funicello (1942–2013), who talked about life on *The Mickey Mouse Club* (1955–1959). The cast of the original *Superman* (1952–1958) TV show were on. Richard Thomas

(1951–) of *The Waltons* (1972–1981) talked about fatherhood. Serious topics examined included transsexuals and the lives of the wives of Vietnam prisoners of war.

West 57th, which aired from August 13, 1985 to September 9, 1989, took its name from the street where the CBS broadcasting facility rested—West 57th Street in New York City. There was talk among young reporters that there was an under-30 demographic not being catered to by *60 Minutes*. The stories were geared to an older demographic, the reporters were of an older generation, and the set and presentation was old. So a team of reporters set out to make a hip *60 Minutes.* While the idea was good, the show only lasted from 1985 to 1989. However, it did create one superstar—Meredith Vieira (1953–), who went on to be the moderator on *The View* from 1997 to 2006, host of *Who Wants to Be a Millionaire* from 2001 to 2013, and host of her own daytime talk show, *The Meredith Vieira Show* (2014–), but maybe the research or their approach was wrong. *60 Minutes* as of 2016 seems as if it will run forever because it keeps current but has never radically changed its style. *West 57th* existed in the second half of the 1980s and it tried to reflect the culture of the times. The fast-paced opening of the one-hour show pictured the four correspondents, John Ferrugia (1951–), Bob Sirott (1949–), Vieira, and Jane Wallace walking the halls, grabbing coffee, talking on the phone, and meeting with each other, to a musical score. The format was similar to other magazine shows but *West 57th* presented five stories each week, two more than *60 Minutes.* Show business figures and rock and roll stars were regularly profiled, and there were quite a few investigative reports including reports on drugs, right-to-lifers, and the Nicaraguan contras. Even though they were young, three out of the four correspondents had network news experience. Sirott was the exception; he had been a lifestyle and entertainment editor at a Chicago station. Stories covered included an examination of Albert Goldman's scathing biography of the late John Lennon, the bad conditions in a meat-packing factory, and a profile on the lives and jobs of Major League Baseball umpires. CBS News staffers past and present disliked the show. *The Christian Science Monitor* called it "a ditzy disco-beat docu-mag for viewers with a short attention span" (Unger 1985), and *The New York Times* stated that the show "isn't really television, and it certainly isn't journalism, it's video, and it's a mess. Nothing works well except the synthesizer music. It's as if news and entertainment fell into combat and neither side won" (Corry 1985). It was a bold experiment but favored one generation over another, cutting its viewership potential.

Americans have enjoyed gossip about celebrities going back to the heyday of the gossip columnist. Women like Hedda Hopper and Louella Parsons, and men like Walter Winchell kept readers glued to their respective papers for the latest developments in Hollywood gossip. In the 1980s gossip became a driving force in at least two different television magazine platforms. *A Current Affair,* which premiered on January 18, 1988, was first an irreverent late night New York City broadcast. Then it expanded to cover stories across America that were overlooked and ignored by the network news departments. One of the lead contributors to the show was Steve Dunleavy, a reporter for the tabloid *New York Post* newspaper. They did present some hard news but primarily focused on entertainment, gossip, scandals, and exploitive tabloid journalism. The distinctive logo was a pyramid with a loud sound effect that came to be known as the "ka–chung."

Inside Edition started out as a highbrow newsmagazine that debuted on January 9, 1989. The ratings were poor so the host, David Frost (1939–2013), was demoted to a correspondent and replaced by the now nonfiction television superstar Bill O'Reilly (1949–). The content shifted to celebrity gossip, crime, and investigations. Journalistically *Hard Copy* was the bottom of the barrel, constantly going after questionable material and gratuitous violence. The show was sued by Elton John (1947–) and in another case George Clooney (1961–). A story on spring break on Daytona Beach was lighthearted but exploitive by lensing every girl in a bikini they could. A flashy piece on computer graphics presented the state-of-the-art in the field. A profile of former Olympic gymnast Nadia Comaneci concentrated on her exit from Romania. The politics and news were light, focusing on the evils of communism.

During the 1980s the television newsmagazine matured and became multifaceted. New features were added and detail was embraced for projecting content. Longevity was indicated by the number of viewers for the various shows whether entertainment or news. The television newsmagazine was now part of the television horizon. What was once a new way of presenting the news in the late 1960s and 1970s was now a genre, a standard item in television programming. Newsmagazines continue to expand, grow, and in many cases prosper. In the 21st century people still read newspapers and magazines, search the Web, and watch TV to get the news and learn something about their world—the television newsmagazine has become a staple of the information highway.

Further Resources

Archive of American Television. "20/20." emmytvlegends.org/interviews/shows/2020

Coffey, Frank. 1993. *60 Minutes: 25 Years of Television's Finest Hour*. General Publishing.

Corry, John. 1985. "TV Review: 'West 57th,' on CBS: Magazine Has Its Debut." *The New York Times*. August 13. http://www.nytimes.com/1985/08/13/arts/tv-review-west-57th-on-cbs-magazine-has-its-debut.html

Hegarty, Neil. 2016. *Frost: That Was the Life That Was*. London: Ebury Press.

Hewitt, Don. 2002. *Tell Me a Story: Fifty Years and Sixty Minutes on Television*. Cambridge, MA: PublicAffairs Books.

Kuralt, Charles. 1996. *Charles Kuralt's America*. New York: Anchor Books.

O'Reilly, Bill. 2013. *Keep It Pithy*. New York: Crown.

Rooney, Andy. 2007. *Out of My Mind*. New York: Perseus.

Unger, Arthur. 1985. "What's Yupdoc? Find Out on 'West 57th,' CBS's Slick New Newsmagazine." *The Christian Science Monitor.* August 12. http://www.csmonitor.com/1985/0812/l57.html

Walters, Barbara. 2009. *Audition: A Memoir*. New York: Vintage Books.

Saturday Morning Cartoons in the 1980s

In the 1950s, 1960s, and 1970s children and teenagers spent early morning to early afternoon every Saturday on the living room couch in front of the television. There were three networks then and only so many scheduling slots available, some a half-hour, others one hour in duration. Usually children watched the same shows they liked in the same grid every week. When a youngster "lost a show" they "found" a new one, and that became a favorite on the new grid. Saturday was the big day for cartoon watching on television because school was out.

Back in the 1950s, 1960s, and 1970s some of the cartoons came from studio vaults and were once shown in movie theaters during double bills, when everyone cheered if Bugs Bunny popped up on the screen about to begin one of his hilarious antics. Superhero cartoons of the time were not humans, but anthropomorphic animals. *Mighty Mouse* (1955–1957) was a super-powered mouse, *Quick Draw McGraw* (1959–1962) was a talking horse who was a sheriff in the Old West involved in comic antics, and *Magilla Gorilla* (1963–1973) was a talking gorilla and a ne'er-do-well who hung around a pet shop and was a drain against the business because of his frolicking. There were many live-action shows including *Sky King* (1951–1959). who had a private plane and helped law enforcement catch the bad guys; *Watch Mr. Wizard* (1951–1972), in which science whiz Don Herbert (1917–2007) taught children the wonders of science by producing experiments, which he conducted with a boy or girl assistant; and *The Lone Ranger* (1949–1957), a Western featuring a masked man who sought justice again the villains among the plains, mountains, and towns. The cartoons that were created just for television were executed in the tradition of animated films with lush renderings and full movement.

By the 1980s, the technology changed as did the sophistication of material, although these were not educational cartoons but pop culture. Limited animation was in fashion, the characters and backgrounds didn't move all the time, there would be moments where the head was animated but the body wasn't. The surrounding areas were simply drawn and painted, not detailed and complex as before. Color was also limited to a palette of few colors. Also, 1980s cartoons presented more variety, with a lot of superheroes and space operas. Programs were combined; one half-hour would lead to another so the billboard would bring in more young viewers, such as *The Tarzan/Lone Ranger Hour* (1980–1982). Cartoons made up a typical 1980s Saturday morning bill and live action, which was more expensive to produce, largely disappeared.

The 1980s was a stark contrast to the decades before, especially the 1960s and 1970s when real people played out stories for kids in dramatic narratives like *Sky King* and *The Lone Ranger*. The cartoons with the exception of Disney's were simply done and there were entertainment shows where kids were involved in fun activities. The 1980s were more hard-edged, the animation sophisticated and fast moving, and the day of live action was exchanged for a cartoon marathon. Animated Saturday morning shows in the 1980s had two major attributes: the content could come from a toy product or a movie or a TV show. Science fiction and war dominated the subjects, although some shows appealed to the kinder and gentler side of children.

Mr. T, the popular character from *The A-Team* (1983–), was given his own show aptly named *Mr. T* (1983–1984). In it his character played a gymnastic coach who traveled the world with several of his students and solved mysteries. Each episode began with the live-action Mr. T addressing the kids on camera looking just the way he did on *The A–Team,* bare chest, gold medallions, a lot of muscles, and a Mohawk haircut. He and his team rode through cities and town to their next meet and invariably ran into bad guys whom Mr. T defeated with brains and brawn as his team adapted their gymnastic moves and techniques to escape from trouble and team up to capture the villains. This show was violent but too breezy to be taken seriously. Mr. T tried to put his philosophy on life into the show through his long dialogue passages, but they were not much different from the live action Mr. T did as part of the *A-Team.*

Rubik: The Amazing Cube (1983–1984) focused on four kids who discovered that their Rubik's cube had amazing powers and they decided the best use of its powers was to solve mysteries. This three-dimensional puzzle took the country and the world by storm during the 1980s. It seemed the younger you were, the better chance you had of solving it. Cartoon makers were always looking for brands or well-known persons or shows that would immediately attract an audience because of recognition. This at times didn't work. The main character on *Rubik: The Amazing Cube* was a Rubik's cube with a little blue man in the middle of it who could fly and do other wondrous feats along with the gang of kids that followed him.

It's Punky Brewster (1985–1986) was the animated version of the live-action TV series that ran on NBC from 1984 to 1986 and in first-run syndication from 1987 to 1988. The plot lines revolved around a little girl being raised by a foster parent. For the cartoon all of the original actors were brought back to voice their now animated characters. This was a warmhearted show about getting by and adapting to life's curveballs. The animation was seamless and this spinoff allowed fans of the live-action show to see the characters from a different spectrum, one that softened the show yet maintained realism because the viewers were looking at cartoon versions of the characters that were accurate and listening to the same voices they knew from the show, which was comforting.

The 1984 smash film *Ghostbusters* sported a brilliant idea and the comic horror/fantasy instantly became a hit and contained a song with the word "Ghostbusters" belted out throughout the tune that had everyone singing. *The Real Ghostbusters* (1986–1991), an animated version of the film, ran for five years, proving people could not get enough of those ghost hunters. The cartoon series took what was in the movie and continued the adventures of the spook hunters who hunted down ghosts and slimed them out of existence when they caught up with them. The characters, the ghost creatures, and the narrative drove this show, which had very limited animation and was far from state of the art, proving viewers were less interested in aesthetics than the adventures of the paranormal investigators who were always on the job hunting down ghosts.

Chuck Norris: *Karate Kommandos* (1986) featured well-known martial arts master and actor Chuck Norris (1940–) starring in this show in which he (in animated form) was an operative for the U.S. government. Producers extended the brand of Chuck Norris, already internationally known in movies and on television in live-action adventures, by putting his name above the title on this animated action show with plenty of testosterone. Norris and his diversified crew included Asian fighting masters, a young boy, women who are as adroit with the martial arts as anyone, and a super specimen that is all purple. The show featured arch villains and their terror gangs. Good guys versus the bad guys was clear in every episode; there were no moral gray areas. Young people were deep into martial arts at the time, many taking classes, so the show although violent at times was a classroom for karate and other styles of fighting. In many cases technology was seen as evil and destructive. Norris and his team used their human skills to thwart attacks triggered by computers and other electronic devices.

Teen Wolf (1986–1987) was another movie adaptation, this time of the 1985 movie *Teen Wolf* that starred Michael J. Fox (1961–) as a high school student who changed into a werewolf. The animated program used the young man's experience as a coming-of-age situation. He never hurt anyone when transitioned into a wolf but the theme here was dealing with isolation and being different. The lead character was voiced by Townsend Coleman.

Garfield and Friends (1988–1994) concerned the adventures of Garfield the Cat, Odie the Dog, and the messes they get into. Garfield was a cat who was featured in his own comic strip created by Jim Davis and first published in 1978. He was perfect for animation because the viewer could hear his thoughts. Garfield was mischievous and caused constant trouble for the man whose house he lived in. Voiceover was used to project Garfield's voice. The animation was colorful and bright. His friends who lived on a farm included a rooster, a pig, and a duck, all of whom could talk. Garfield was constantly nosing in on his owner's business. His friends love him for who he is. The show perfectly pictured Garfield and captured his personality perfectly. Most of the success of the comic strip came from Garfield being a curmudgeon. Readers and viewers found that lovable and the show was light entertainment.

Shows featuring the theme of war included *Thundar the Barbarian* (1980–1982), *Ulysses 31* (1981–1982), and *He-Man and the Masters of the Universe* (1983–1985). *Thundar the Barbarian* was set in 3994 in a postapocalyptic setting that was divided into kingdoms or territories ruled by wizards. In 1994 there was a crash in space that caused the destruction of all humanity on planet Earth. This show joined the science fiction genre with the barbarian genre. Savagery, super-science, and sorcery combine with battles over good and evil to save the world.

Ulysses 31 featured the main character Ulysses's attempts to get back home and heal his cursed crew. He was a great space hero and his child companions must find the kingdom of Hades fighting all evil opposition. This was an update of the Greek mythology saga of Odysseus, which later became Ulysses. The main character was the captain of the spaceship *Odyssey*. The animation was extremely limited. Much of the story took place in space, making this science fiction with a Greek mythology construction. The ship was controlled by a computer with a female voice. Ulysses was always defending his ship and its members from evil forces, good versus evil being the most common theme of 1980s Saturday morning cartoons.

As the most powerful man in the universe *He-Man* battled the evil force of Skeletor to save planet Eternia and to protect the secrets of Castle Grayskull in *He-Man and the Masters of the Universe*. This was one of the most popular children's shows of the 1980s. It was also based on action figures. Magic, myth, and fantasy drove this show as Prince Adam battled evil forces. There was a transformational character, a sorceress who transformed herself from a beautiful woman to a bird who could communicate through mind waves with the forces of good. The animation featured many special effects for narrative aspects like disappearing and transportation. The show was lively and very imaginative, which contributed to its popularity.

Science fiction genre animated shows included *Inspector Gadget*, *Kidd Video*, *Thundercats*, *Galaxy High*, and several that crossed multiple genres, such as *G.I. Joe*, *Transformers*, and *Teenage Mutant Ninja Turtles*. *Inspector Gadget* (1983–1986) was a bumbling bionic police inspector stumbling about on his cases while his niece and dog secretively did the real investigative work. Gadget wore a hat and trench coat, resembling actor Peter Sellers in a Pink Panther movie as Inspector Jacques Clouseau. There were also connections to the live-action television series *Get Smart* (1965–1970), especially Gadget's voice spoken by Don Adams, who played a spy in that earlier comedy. Gadget's boss, also called Chief, sent him on missions to stop the bad guys. Gadget could call for any tool with the line "Go, go, gadget," and the tools often sprang out of his body, like telescopic binoculars and extensions for his arms. *Inspector Gadget* fell into the tradition of those bumbling spies who preceded him.

Kidd Video (1984–1985) was a half-hour animated program with a great premise. A rock band was abducted to a cartoon fantasy world where music was the key to defeating their enemies and finding their way back home. This show had several aspects that appealed to kids. It was filled with music because the stars were young members of a rock band. In addition to the main theme song members of this group would burst into song at times, and there were keyboards and other instruments on the ship on which they were being transported. Synthesizers, which were very popular in the 1980s, could be heard on the underscore. The show was also very high-tech with one of the band coming up with a technical solution for a problem they had to solve. Having "video" in the title was a good idea because this medium was becoming a major influence on movies and music.

Thundercats (1985–1989) concerned a team of humanoid cats who fought evil in their adopted home world. Each cat was colorful and a powerful fighter, looking as if they all came from a different species. A sword was the force of all their power. Each can use its body as a weapon. In the science fiction fantasy vein this show, if not highly original, was well done and appealed to fans that were attracted to other worlds and the fight of good against evil.

Galaxy High (1986) featured two high school students from Earth chosen to attend a school in outer space. This was a Japanese/American project. On Earth the good-looking and popular Doyle was on a school scholarship for sports and taunted Aimee, the smarter student in the school, who was pretty but not popular because she was not cool. While teasing Aimee, Doyle grabbed what seemed to be a Frisbee but it was a saucer from outer space, and the two of them were taken to Galaxy High floating just past Saturn. No one at Galaxy High looked like anyone on Earth; the class president had six arms, another student had three eyes, a teacher looked like a horse with a human style. The lesson here was diversity; everyone was different and got along with each other. The lives of the two humans experienced a reversal. Aimee was embraced for her high intelligence and was given a scholarship, a vehicle, and the adoration of the student body. Doyle was told he had to get a job at a pizza place to pay for his scholarship while he had one back home. He was given a space skateboard to get around on and was shunned by his fellow students. The animation was not very sophisticated and the limitations were clear to the viewer. In content this was *The Jetsons* (1962–1963) taken farther into the future.

The legendary toy soldier G.I Joe had his own animated TV show, which spanned multiple genres common in the 1980s, the show based on a popular toy, with themes of war and good vs. evil. *G.I. Joe* (1983–1986) featured an elite special mission force against Cobra, a terrorist force. To boys and teenagers in the 1980s the G.I. Joe action figure was their equivalent of Barbie. The plastic toy soldiers of the 1950s and 1960s gave way to this sophisticated doll that a boy could use to play fantasy battles and wars. The show had G.I. Joe in a rogue special mission group fighting Cobra Commander, whose objective was to take over the world. The show was action packed with explosions, military fighting, and the constant pursuit of the enemy. The show was very patriotic with flags and the effort to protect America. The animation was strong on line. The color was adequate but the line drawing technique gave it the appearance of a comic book come to life.

In *The Transformers* (1984–1987) two opposing factions of transforming alien robots battled for the fate of the world. This was another show that spanned multiple genres, being based on a popular toy line, and having science fiction and war themes. They began as a popular Japanese, then American toy by Hasbro, who put out the robot figure with interchangeable parts. The concept was that the robots were built to fight. The TV series has two armies, the heroic Autobots and Decepticons. the villains. Lots of animated effects and weaponry are featured, which lead to firefights. The bots were huge and each part of their body was connected separately to the other. Science fiction and war merge together for this popular figure. Usually the movie comes first but here it was the TV series followed later by the motion picture *Transformers* (2007), which grew into a franchise of five films all directed by superstar movie director Michael Bay.

An animated series that embraced the war and magic/fantasy themes was *She-Ra: Princess of Power* (1985–1987), which followed the adventures of Adora, who led a group of freedom fighters to free Etheria from the tyrannical rule of Hordak and the Evil Horde.

This was a girl-power show where the lead character held command and strength, possessing good and fighting evil. The animation was very limited but the characters and backgrounds were very colorful. The magic theme of the show brought on many special effects to depict out-of-body visits from the bad guys, tremendous bolts of lightning and lighting effects to give the princess an aura. There was a magic sword and a dark blue and orange lair for the evil forces. The drawn and painted costumes were elaborate and included an eagle head piece for the princess. The networks were always looking for shows to appeal to girls, and this one had a lot of action to pull in boys as well.

Teenage Mutant Ninja Turtles (1987–1996) were four little turtles that came into contact with toxic ooze, turning them into anthropomorphic turtles. An anthropomorphic rat named Splinter trained the turtles to be ninja fighters and the group went after the evil Shredder, who was trying to take over the world with his Foot Clan. While not based on a toy line, these characters came from a very successful comic book series and a popular motion picture, *Teenage Mutant Ninja Turtles* (1987), which spawned multiple sequels and then a rebooted franchise: *Teenage Mutant Ninja Turtles II: The Scent of the Ooze* (1991), *Teenage Mutant Ninja Turtles* (1990), *Teenage Mutant Ninja Turtles* (2014), and *Teenage Mutant Ninja Turtles: Out of the Shadows* (2016). As a result of the comic book, film, and cartoon's popularity, the turtles continue to be pop culture icons in the United States.

Some shows were less hard-edged and were for younger audiences, with cute and funny characters. *The Kwicky Koala Show* (1981) featured the titular koala, *Kwicky*, who moved so fast he disappeared when Wilford Wolf was about to catch him. This was one of the last projects by legendary cartoon director Tex Avery (1909–1980), who died during production of this show. Although it was created in the 1980s, Avery's experience of working with the likes of Porky Pig, Bugs Bunny, and other animated stars brought the golden years of cartoon sensibility to this new show. Kwicky Koala ran as fast as Speedy Gonzales or the Roadrunner, and Wilford Wolf, who always tried to grab Kwicky, failed every time, just like Wile E. Coyote did no matter what he did to catch the Roadrunner. The animation was limited, not full like Avery's early works, due to budget constraints, but the flow of the action and characters covered that up. Also on the show were the Bungle Brothers, the biggest little act in show business, Dirty Dawg and his sidekick Ratzo, and Crazy Claws with a sharp wit and the claws to match. The death of Tex Avery put an end to what could have been a running tribute to cartoons' best days.

The Wuzzles (1985) were a variety of creatures made of at least two different animals. They all lived in the land of Wuz in this Disney animated show. There was a voice-over to set the scene before the Wuzzles spoke. Although each was a combination, they appeared to be a lion, elephant, hippo, bear, and monkey. They were strange in a funny way because they didn't look like traditional animals with the added parts. Action took place in the woods in a land we've never seen before, the narration intones. The animation was of a high quality in the Disney tradition and the show was also gentle and kind. Intended or not, the theme appeared to be that people are all made of different parts, such as ethnicity, and who we are came from more places than one.

Dink: The Little Dinosaur (1989–1990) was a small Apatosaurus and he and his pals learned important life lessons through their adventures. During the 1980s grammar school children studied dinosaurs, so that interest motivated the concept of this series, which showed mostly the kind and human sides of these early creatures. The animation was lusher and deeply saturated, more than most cartoon shows of the time. The environment, the forest, rivers, mountains, and trees were rendered in great detail and movement all around was increased. The young dinosaurs were happy and playful. There were lessons in race because different groups were different colors and shapes and got along well. Accepting the very young and very good was prevalent. Although there were specific and defined families, all the dinosaurs in the area were part of a community—a big family. The underscore was the kind of music heard in earlier animated films, played by a full orchestra and accentuating the emotions of the story.

Technology speeded up the animation process but the advent of limited animation was a setback when this decade is compared with cartoons from Warner Brothers and Disney in the 1950s and 1960s. Economics played a part. Animation had become very expensive by the 1980s even with digital technology, so to keep the budget down the amount of movement and detail in the characters and background suffered. The less movement, the faster and cheaper the process became. Some producers would even get by with a close-up on a character where absolutely nothing was moving except the lips because the character was speaking. Ironically 1980s cartoons on Saturday morning were becoming like graphic novels, which appeared in full in the very late 1970s. As long as there are children there will be cartoon shows. The style and content are always dictated by the times. The cartoon show was prevalent during the 1980s motivating future animators, studios, directors, and creators to evolve the art from there.

Further Resources

Erikson, Hal. 2016. *Television Cartoon Shows: An Illustrated Encyclopedia 1949–2003*. Jefferson, NC: McFarland.

Laybourne, Kit. 1998. *The Animation Book: A Complete Guide to Animated Filmmaking—From Flip–Books to Sound Cartoons*. New York: Three Rivers Press.

Lenberg, Jeff. 2006. *Who's Who in Animated Cartoons: An International Guide to Film and Television's Award-Winning and Legendary Animators*. New York: Applause Theater and Cinema Books.

Maltin, Leonard, and Jerry Beck. 1987. *Of Mice and Magic: A History of American Animated Cartoons,* Revised and Updated Edition. New York: Plume.

McCray, Mark. 2015. *The Best Saturdays of Our Lives*. Bloomington, IN: iUniverse.

Woolery, George W. 1991. *Children's Television: The First Thirty–Five Years, 1946–1981. Part 1: Animated Cartoon Series*. Lanham, MD: Scarecrow Press.

Stretch! Exercise Television Programs and Videotapes in the 1980s

In the 1980s the country was exercise and gym crazy and there was a workout explosion. The unisex gym became the new bar, club, or disco where you could meet a guy or a gal. Aerobics were usually performed to rousing music and weightlifting was performed by both genders. Step class training was also introduced. Those exercising walked up and down a hard plastic step, adding units for greater resistance. Fashion involved sweatbands to keep the hair back and perspiration out of one's eyes. Women's exercise outfits were made of spandex, a tight clinging material that revealed every curve and line on the body. Leg warmers were fashioned out of various materials and worn from the ankle upward to keep warm. Prior to the 1980s exercise programs were limited and sparse. Jane Fonda wouldn't make her first exercise video that was sold in the marketplace until 1982. The revolution in exercise in the gym, on the street, and in the home during the 1980s would have its roots on television where a man or woman, or a group could work out while watching the instructor on the screen via videotape or during a broadcast from the shows that were on at the time offering exercise routines and instruction. The genre improved over time with artistic development and breakthroughs in equipment and technique.

Gyms or gymnasiums date back over 3,000 years to ancient Persia. Friedrich Jahn and the Turners, a 19th-century political and gymnastic movement, built gyms in the United States for keeping the population fit. In the 1920s schools were built with gyms to provide exercise for the youth. By the 1960s Gold's Gyms founded in Venice, California by Joe Gold in 1965 became a mecca for body-builders. In the 1970s weight training became popular not just to keep fit but to build muscle mass.

The person most responsible for getting Americans to get up and work out was the remarkable Jack LaLanne (1914–2011), who lived to 96 because he believed in total fitness for the mind and body. His influential and inspirational television program *The Jack LaLanne Show* was televised from 1951–1985. His spirit, expertise, and athletic abilities had people all over the country following his every move and feeling good about themselves.

Until the 1980s LaLanne's program was bare minimum. The set was a floor and walls and he had an occasional chair to demonstrate a leg lift or other exercise. The show was in color and began with stills of the man at various stages of his career, then a full screen shot in the water with LaLanne on his 70th birthday swimming in front of a boat filled with people. He was rigged to the front so he was actually pulling hundreds of pounds with his body. There were video squares moving in and out with clips of LaLanne exercising with machines, free weights, and traditional exercises. After this opening of the show, now called *Jack LaLanne and You* instead of the earlier *The Jack LaLanne Show*, he appeared standing, fit in a purple jumpsuit zipped down to mid-chest, ready for another workout with his beloved audience.

The exercise craze of the 1980s had a huge impact on television. Networks and local channels couldn't find enough material to put on the air concerning fitness programs. Instructors male and female were approached by producers to star in TV shows or workout videotapes. This was interactive television as viewers watched and joined with the instructor and their group in working out during the program.

TV was changing. The invention of the videocassette meant that consumers could buy exercise videos, insert them into their home player, and watch the tape on their television. This could be done from top to bottom like a broadcast show or the tape could be rewound any number of times to check a move or repeat an exercise or the whole routine. Control was in the hands of the person with direct access to the remote control of the VCR. Television shows and exercise videos tended to create a star or a superstar out of the exercise guru.

Richard Simmons (1948–) also had an exercise show on television. Simmons was probably the liveliest, most excitable of all the exercise gurus. What people ate and how much they weighed were very important to him because he once was vastly overweight and by eating properly and exercising he got down to a healthy size and shape. Simmons put out many exercise tapes and was beloved by mostly everyone. A bit of a clown, Richard had a loud high-pitched voice and laughed a lot. It was his spirit more than his technique that took the pounds off his worshipers. He allowed people to tell their stories to the camera and cried, often out of empathy.

On *The Richard Simmons Show* (1980–1984) Simmons worked in a large room where the walls were constructed out of slatted light wood. Centered at the head of the space was a raised platform with a beige-colored run which is where Simmons would oversee the group. He would call for music to begin and he started giving instructions, counting, keeping track of reps (the groupings of exercise), and shouting out joyfully so everyone could hear as the music continued to play below his voice. Simmons was short and had long puffy hair like a 1980s rock star. Simmons is best known for a franchise that began with *Sweating with the Oldies*, a series of tapes that feature old rock and roll as Simmons and his group of exercisers work out. The nostalgia for the music and the attraction of younger exercisers who love classic rock made this series a mega hit.

In 1983 the *20 Minute Workout* appeared. The concept of this show was to have at least three pretty women in skin-tight exercise outfits working out while a number of camera angles including overhead shots captured their routines. The women were experts in executing each exercise on their own. Having more than one expert on the screen at a time was extremely useful in understanding the intricacies of each move and exercise. Instruction was communicated either by voice-over or by one of the three women demonstrators. Already in the early 1980s people were looking to shorten their daily exercise time and this innovative program provided this.

In 1982 Jake Steinfeld (1958–) went on the air with *Body by Jake*. A big man considered to be the creator of personal training of celebrities, show biz types, and the wealthy, he later made video and television deals with Ted Turner (1938–) and ESPN. Steinfeld worked "Body by Jake" into a brand selling DVDs, books, and personalized exercise equipment. He was popular because of his energetic personality and friendly communication. He dressed in a tight T-shirt with the show's logo on it and exercise pants. The set looked like a living room with long windows, wood encasing, a soft chair, a table with a small lamp, and a beige rug. Exercise bikes were placed strategically around the room. He referred to his loyal viewers as the gang and would invite a woman, who was a home viewer, to be exercising on camera next to him. On the other side of Jake was a female pro instructor or someone who was aspiring to be one and they would all work out together with Jake leading everyone with instruction, encouragement, and compliments. One of the challenges of the TV exercise show or video is what the instructor is to call particular body parts. Jake did this in the spirit of fun. If an exercise was going to exercise the abdominals, muscles in the lower stomach region, he called them "Abadabras." For the buttocks it was a bit tricky to say something that would indicate the area but not be offensive. This he called "The Buttisimo." It became his signature phrase. In fact at times he would tell the viewers at home if they could come up with the correct number of times he said that word in a specific period of time he would send them a *Body by Jake* T-shirt.

Exercise videotapes were a huge market in the 1980s. Some exercisers would buy one that they liked and would stick with it; others had a drawer full of different trainers and would mix and match them. The most famous actress to have gotten involved in exercising is Academy Award–winner Jane Fonda (1937–). She originally used the money generated from her Workout Studio and books and tapes and from her acting work for her then husband Tom Hayden (1939–2016), who at the time was running for political office. Her workout sessions were considered by most to be the definitive workout programs of the 1980s. The tapes were beautifully produced and Fonda led a basic, but perfect workout. The team of exercisers with her was well chosen and included men and women. Her video output in the exercising field includes *Jane Fonda's Original Workout*, *Jane Fonda's Low Impact Workout* (1992), *Jane Fonda's Easy Going Workout* (1984), *Jane Fonda: Firm & Burn* and *Jane Fonda's Complete Workout*.

Fonda and her group worked out in an exercise room built all in wood with long windows on the back wall. Music was played and she shouted out the instructions from the front center. The mood was lively and everyone seemed to enjoy exercising. The name recognition and the expertise were attractive to a large audience. The exercises were easy to do and were created for the average person, not a body builder.

Kathy Smith (1951–) has sold a staggering 16 million of her exercise videos, which include *Build Muscle Shrink Fat*, *Tummy Trimmers*, *Total Body Toning*, *Step Aerobics Workout*, and *Staying Strong*. Her tapes are set in pleasant indoor surroundings with many small groups working out with her. Smith began, like Jake Steinfeld, as a personal trainer, so her one-on-one experience is strongly felt by listening to her strong and specific instructions. A technical master, Smith was a role model of the 1980s projecting hard work, skill, and a wide range of techniques for every part of the body.

Denise Austin (1957–) produced over 30 exercise videos including *Non–Aerobic Trim & Tone Workout*, *Hit the Spot—Abs*, *The Complete Workout*, *Stretch & Flex*, *Ultimate Fat Burner*. Her sister-in-law is tennis champion Tracy Austin. She is college trained in her field with a bachelor's degree in physical education and a minor in exercise physiology from California State University, Long Beach. Denise Austin has girl-next-door looks and works out with a cheerful attitude. Her educational background shows in how precise yet comfortable everything she does looks. Her neighborly appearance was nonthreatening and made owners of her tapes feel that they knew her.

Celebrities and actors need to be in good physical shape because they are seen by millions of viewers on TV and by large audiences at the movies. Many have personal trainers, a full working gym in their home, and consultants of all types concerning health and fitness. Over the years many have taken what they have learned or developed their own exercises and techniques and put them in a book, then a videotape or both.

Actress Suzanne Somers (1946–) is best known for playing Chrissy Snow on *Three's Company* (1977–1984). She is also associated with the Thighmaster, a mechanical device that she has promoted, demonstrated, and written books and shot videotapes about. The Thighmaster is used by placing it between the knees and pushing in and out, causing the muscles in that area to develop. Somers received a lot of publicity from being associated with the Thighmaster and some ridicule as well, which she took in good stride.

On a tape demonstrating the Thighmaster, Somers does an introduction to inform the viewer what is to come. The set looks like a void, white with a few light slashes of purple. This is most likely achieved with seamless paper, the kind used by still photographers. As she's demonstrating the equipment, Somers's instructions are presented in voice-over, allowing the viewer and Somers to concentrate on the exercise.

Raquel Welch (1940–) is the glamourous star of many films and TV events including *Fantastic Voyage*

(1966), *The Three Musketeers* (1973), and *The Wild Party* (1975). The actress has always believed in a full fitness approach as demonstrated in her videotapes, which include *A Week with Raquel: 7 Day Wake-Up and Shape-Up Program 15 Minutes a Day*; *Raquel: Total Beauty and Fitness*; *Raquel: Lose Ten Pounds in Three Weeks, Body and Mind.*

The setting for a Raquel Welch exercise videotape appears to take place in an exercise studio or living room, but this is a glamorous movie star so the image is of an exclusive Hollywood spa, more ornate with a sitting room and couch, chandeliers, and more space. When many other shows were set in less well appointed spaces, it was as if Raquel Welch wanted to bring the lavish settings of Hollywood into the homes of the video exercisers. Welch is serious about fitness and teaching others and it shows by her command and understanding of each move. She talks as the leader and at times we hear her voice-over giving short encouraging comments on every move.

Another icon of the 1980s fitness revolution was singer Olivia Newton John (1948–), who had a monster hit record with "Physical" released in 1981. Although she is dressed and coiffed in exercise fashion of the time and the music video is set in a sort of a gym, it contains not only a depiction of common 1980s workout culture, but also a sexual double entendre. John plays a fitness instructor with all male students. "Physical" may take place in a gym but is also interpreted to be about sex. John sings some suggestive lyrics, makes sexual gestures, touches some of the men, and mentions the word "horizontal." Throughout the decades this video is constantly held up as an icon of the 1980s workout era but sex is the major theme. Despite the sexuality layered within the lyrics and the music video's content, "Physical" and Newton John are remembered as the prime example of the 1980s workout culture.

Other icons of the 1980s fitness revolution include two major male superstars who proudly displayed their bodies on screen: Arnold Schwarzenegger (1947–) and Sylvester Stallone (1946–), and the entire cast of *Baywatch.*

The fitness craze of the 1980s could have grown out of President John F. Kennedy's efforts toward promoting a healthy America, especially his efforts with the President's Council on Youth Fitness in the early 1960s. Once the fitness craze started in the 1980s, it expanded rapidly in myriad areas, including sneakers, exercise equipment, and books. Television and videotape in the 1980s made it possible for almost everyone to exercise. The tapes usually showed groups of people exercising together, which makes the home exerciser feel part of a movement. Americans continued to exercise after the 1980s concluded, but for one special decade when the country watched every workout show they could and bought every exercise tape they could afford, everyone got "physical" in the true sense of the word.

Further Resources

Austin, Denise. 2002. *Pilates for Every Body: Strengthen, Lengthen, and Tone—With This Complete 3-Week Body Makeover.* Emmaus, PA: Rodale.

Fonda, Jane. 1981. *Jane Fonda's Workout Book.* New York: Simon & Schuster.

Schwarzenegger, Arnold, and Bill Dobbins. 1999. *The New Encyclopedia of Modern Bodybuilding: The Bible of Bodybuilding, Fully Updated and Revised.* New York: Fireside.

Simmons, Richard. 1999. *Still Hungry After All These Years: My Story.* Vancouver, BC: GT Publishing.

Smith, Kathy. 2001. *Lift Weights to Lose Weight.* New York: Time Warner.

Somers, Suzanne. 2009. *Breakthrough: Eight Steps to Wellness.* New York: Crown.

Steinfeld, Jake. 1984. *Body by Jake.* New York: Simon & Schuster.

Welch, Raquel. *Raquel: The Raquel Welch Total Beauty and Fitness Program.* New York: Holt, Rinehart & Winston.

You Don't Just Watch TV on It Anymore

During the 1940s and 1950s the purchase of a television set for the home was to watch whatever local or network programming was available. There were a number of brands, models, and screen sizes, and it may have been considered by some a piece of furniture. By the 1980s, television had changed, some companies folded, many more new ones came on the scene, and most importantly, the size of the screen increased. Resourceful inventors and engineers began to think of how the TV set could be used and most radically how the content that was at times pasteurized by network brass, censors, and community groups could be presented. Aesthetics would be reinvented, partially borrowed from all kinds of motion pictures, and partially borrowed from inventive television programming from here and abroad.

A television set can also be used as a monitor, a way of looking at something captured by a camera and an electronic signal. When the first major television control rooms were built, the big three networks, ABC, CBS, and NBC, installed small television sets that came to be called monitors so the director of a live show or a producer of a recorded one could establish exactly what was going over the air or on the videotape at any particular time. For live TV the monitors were labeled and coordinated with the cameras on the floor so the director could make a decision of how to cut to the next shot by commands heard over headsets. He or she would look at the monitors, see what they wanted and call for camera two to come online with the shot that followed the previous one.

The establishment of the monitor opened up a lot of possibilities of using a television set. Many companies, organizations, and schools found a wide variety of uses for the now widely available video camera. Schools bought video equipment and used it for educational purposes. They recorded an event or a class, whatever was necessary, and then played it back on a VCR (videocassette recorder), which fed it to a monitor so the teachers and students could see the images. The football coach taped practices and the game and used it to analyze plays. The technology allowed forward and reverse action, the ability to pause an image and to play either direction in high or slow speed.

Plays performed at a school, at semi-professional and professional venues were taped on stage for posterity. They could be played back on a monitor on-site or at home on a standard television. Corporations began to tape meetings and archive them for further examination. Training videos were made for companies and other businesses. Quality ranged widely because the video could be made by an amateur to save money or be part of the burgeoning industry of companies who made professional-quality videos. Weddings and other family affairs were once captured on 8mm, then Super 8mm film, or 16mm film, captured by a family member with a knack and the equipment, or on video in the same manner. Companies specializing in wedding videos became popular and charged a substantial fee for their work. Casting units for TV, film, and theater taped auditions for later review by the director and producer. Security systems in homes, businesses, and on streets recorded what they saw and kept it for later review. All of these applications were played back on a television or a monitor.

Since the 1940s many households, especially those of middle-class families, purchased an 8mm movie camera and a projector that matched. Kodak largely sold the film. Those with more funds bought 16mm cameras and projectors for better quality. The typical content included birthdays, picnics, parties, trips, and gatherings of all sorts. Then another sort of revolution occurred during the late 1960s into the 1970s. Young people wanted to make movies with their own vision. Using their camera and an editing block, consumers made movies, and some of them went on to an official film school. Of the notable filmmakers in this manner are George Lucas (1944–) and Martin Scorsese (1942–).

Another revolution came about when 8mm and Super 8mm film cameras became obsolete. Kodak closed its home movie operation; but other companies were able to turn the large studio TV camera into a much smaller version, making it available to homes across the country. Using VHS tapes, every consumer could shoot for longer lengths of time without being tied to 50 feet of film. These works were shown on the home television set or if it could be afforded, a small monitor. Companies usually working out of a photography shop were able, for a price, to transfer 8mm film to videotape to avoid the breaking and tearing of splices while running the film through the transfer equipment. These tapes could hold family material or for the budding filmmaker copies of their finished work. When no agent or studio executive had an 8mm camera to view this work they popped in the cassette and a star could be born.

Videocassette rental was a strong business with customers picking out a movie or two or three to watch at home. Where many thought the early tapes in addition to Hollywood releases would be "How-To" tapes (cooking, how to fix your car, and so on), the number one area of tape rentals was the lowest common denominator—adult films. This spread to home use when couples realized they could set up the video camera in the bedroom and record their amorous escapades. But the "How-To" tape as envisioned did arrive later, with travelogues, stand-up routines, and musical performances of all kind, and all shown through a VCR and seen on a television set. The viewer was liberated from the limits of broadcast and cable television.

A new form of entertainment grew out of the old arcade games of the 1940s and 1950s and was revolutionized by the home television set—the video game. Instead of watching TV a person could play any number of video games after buying a unit and a cartridge. The game was shown again on the home TV or a monitor off-site. Throughout the 1980s the console units grew and expanded. The amount of bits that controlled the detail overall kept growing. Two-dimensional graphics kept improving.

Nintendo was synonymous with video gaming. Sega was a leading company as well. Atari was an early entry. The field was very competitive and cartridges were valuable, holding popular games like Space Invaders II and Pac Man. Those who were there still talk about the "Video Game Crash of 1983." Many companies went bankrupt. Some said video games were a passing fad, others blamed the ultra-poor sales behind the video game version of Steven Spielberg's film *E.T.* (1982). Rumor even had it that unsold cartridges of this title were buried in the deserts of Mexico. The industry did come back. The 1980s saw many video game franchises thrive. Some include Centipede (1981), Donkey Kong (1981), Dragon's Lair (1983), Frogger (1981), Pac-Man (1980), Pole-Position (1982), Final Fantasy (1987), John Madden Football (1988), Q*Bert (1982), Tron (1982), Street Fighter (1987), and of course Super Mario Brothers (1985).

Parents who were concerned about their children watching too much television and bought their kid a video game unit and a couple of cartridges were aghast to see that there was a hypnotic effect playing the game and their child was glued to the game screen for hours on end. Also the content was growing more and more violent.

Artists are always on the lookout for new mediums—television became one in the 1960s. By the 1980s the undisputed master of video art Nam June Paik (1932–2006) was expanding his artistic horizons. *Merce* (1987) is a single-channel video sculpture with vintage television units stacked on an angle imagining a sort of robot man who is walking forward and appears to be in flight. In 1989 he completed *Fin de Siecle II*—a four-channel video installation with 201 monitors featuring faces pointing in several directions. To offset the large monitors there are rows of small faces, flowers, and many colors. On either side are an entrance and an exit. The 1989 version of *Vramid* is a pyramid of televisions stacked up to the ceiling of the workspace, in color, with pipes holding up the structure. *One Candle* (1988) is made up of a candle and six video projectors. In 1981 Paik created *TV Scan Lines Graphite on Paper*.

Paik was dealing with a very expensive medium so he was constantly searching for old and new televisions. He was an artist who was also part scientist. Early on Paik realized the nature of television and the possibilities way beyond what was broadcast by the networks and watched in living rooms when he realized viewers should come to the museum or the gallery to watch the true art of television.

Video art became a wide-ranging art form with artists producing tapes, creating installations, and accepting commissions. Vito Acconci (1940–) made tapes exploring his ability to make contact with another human being. Andy Warhol (1928–1987) made a long series of screen tests attempting to reinvent old Hollywood. Charlotte Moorman (1933–1991) was a cellist who performed with a bra made of television monitors. Bill Viola (1951–) explored time, memory, and the human spirit with video images of indigenous people. Woody Vauskla (1937–) developed processing techniques to get a vibrating or pointillist effect on images such as the atomic bomb and the horrors of war.

The original inventors, engineers, and practitioners of early television couldn't have envisioned the massive scope of what television is and can be. Once the television interfaced with other applications such as the VCR and was taken out of the living room to educational facilities and the corporate world, the industry and the public began to understand the myriad uses of the medium. For decades television was looked at as a commercial medium and it is that, but when artists realized that video was the oil paint of the 1980s, they found content and aesthetic approaches that were once exclusive to the painter, but the electronic soon to be digital age made television into a medium for the ages.

Further Resources

Hall, Doug, and Sally Jo Fifer. 2005. *Illuminating Video: An Essential Guide to Video Art.* Reading, PA: Aperture.

Hanhardt, John. 1982. *Nam June Paik.* New York: W. W. Norton.

Hanhardt, John., ed. 1987. *Video Culture: A Critical Investigation.* New York: Video Studies Workshop.

Horrocks, Chris. 2017. *Joy of Sets: A Short History of the Television.* London: Reaktion Books.

Merrill, John. 1993. *Camcorder Video: Shooting and Editing Techniques.* New Jersey: Prentice Hall.

Newman, Michael Z. 2014. *Video Revolutions: On the History of a Medium.* New York: Columbia University Press.

Rush, Michael. 2003. *Video Art.* New York: Thames & Hudson.

Schwartz, Lara M. 2007. *Making Music Videos: Everything You Need to Know from the Best in the Business.* New York: Billboard Books.

Glossary

affiliate: Major television networks often have affiliates, local stations that carry some if not all of their programs.

air date: An exact time, month, day, hour that a television program is scheduled to run.

analog television: Before digital television became the norm, an analog signal varied signal voltage and radio frequencies.

aspect ratio: The proportional relationship between the width and height of a moving image. Early television's aspect ratio was 1.25:1. Traditional television's is 1.33.1. The common U.S. standard for widescreen in the cinema is 1.85.1.

bandwidth: The rate at which a frequency cuts off from its highest point to its lowest point.

basic cable: Anyone connected to a cable system receives basic channels. Premium channels like HBO are subscriber driven; the user pays a fee to get this channel or buys premium packages that also come with a fee and involve a grouping of channels.

BBC: The British Broadcasting Corporation, a British public service broadcaster.

billboard: A short on-screen announcement to identify a sponsor at the beginning or end of a production element.

breaking news: In the early days of television a bulletin card would suddenly appear to alert viewers to something catastrophic like an assassination, plane crash, or earthquake. Either a newsman would talk over the card or he would come on screen in a newsroom to explain what had happened. In current usage a graphic with the words "Breaking News" backed up with dramatic music comes up and then the newsroom takes over the story. It could be very serious or an event in an ongoing situation or almost anything newsworthy. It's part of the way contemporary news is presented.

bumper: A still image or short video marking the transition between a program and a commercial break. Commonly used in television until 2010.

call letters: Letters assigned to broadcast stations by the FCC by which stations identify themselves. In general call letters for stations east of the Mississippi begin with W; stations west of the Mississippi have call letters beginning with K.

channel: A frequency band assigned to a television station, usually referred to by their call letters.

Chyron: A television graphic that occupies the lower area of the screen, usually text-based video graphics mainly used by television news broadcasts. The Chyron Corporation develops and manufactures on-screen graphics for the television industry.

closed captioning: A process that displays text on a television or video screen to display additional or interpretive information.

cold open: A scene or sequence that immediately begins a show, followed by the opening credits sequence. A cold open is used to pull in viewers and gain their attention to the program to follow.

color bars: SMPTE color bars is a television test pattern where the NTSC video standard is utilized.

commercial: A television commercial is a short span of television programming that conveys a message produced and paid for by an organization, typically to market a product or service.

counter programming: The practice of offering television programming to attract an audience away from another television station airing a show believed to gain more ratings. Also the airing of a special event such as the Super Bowl, the Oscars, or the Olympic Games.

dead air: When a television image suddenly goes black or blank or in the case of digital television, a freeze frame and becomes silent due to technical issues.

decibel: A unit used to express the ratio of two values of a physical quantity, often power or intensity.

dedicated channel: An interactive cable television system, such as a one-way system in which a majority of subscribers are simultaneously provided with multi-informational television and regular television programming independently selectable and directly receivable by the individual subscriber on the television receiver channels of a conventional multichannel television receiver.

editing bay: A television editing room, a place where videotape and digital material is edited. The same as an editing room, a place where film was once edited by operating mechanical editing equipment and now digital platforms like AVID or Final Cut Pro.

encryption: When a cable channel electronically scrambles a signal so it cannot be watched until the user subscribes to the channel and pays for the service or pays a fee for a pay per view event that has been encrypted.

ENG: Electronic News Gathering is the broadcast news industry of television producers, reporters, and editors using electronic video and audio techniques for gathering and presenting news. The term was used widely in the 1980s and 1990s, less so afterwards because of advancements in technology.

FCC: Federal Communications Commission, a U.S. government agency that regulates interstate communications by television, radio, wire, satellite, and cable. Their six areas of regulation are broadband, competition, the spectrum, the media, public safety, and Homeland Security.

gain: The ratio between the magnitude of output and input signals.

HDTV: High-Definition Television. A television system providing an image resolution that is substantially higher than that of standard definition television. For example, analog TV could be in the range of 30 lines of resolution, whereas HDTV can produce 1,125 lines of resolution for a much sharper picture quality.

HUT: Households Using Television. The percentage of all television homes in a household survey area with one or more television sets during a specific time period.

kinescope recording: The recording of a television program on motion picture film. This was an early way of recording TV and was widely used until videotape dominated the field, then videocassettes and DVD.

laugh track: Prerecorded sounds of an audience laughing and clapping added to a sitcom to liven it and give viewers a cue that what they are watching is funny. Also called sweetening. CBS sound engineer Charley Douglass in the 1950s noticed this technique had inconsistencies, so he built a laugh machine with which he could map out a show for the specific kind of laugh or amount of clapping required.

letterbox: The practice of transferring film shot in a widescreen aspect ratio to standard-width video, which preserves the film's original aspect ratio. The results are two black bars, one on top of the image, the second on the bottom of the image.

live-on-tape: When a program is shot live without interruption unless a technical or content error occurs; then the production team resets and continues live and on tape from where they left off. Any interscene editing is done in the control booth when the director cuts from one of the multiple cameras to another. This process continues until the show is over. The long pieces are put together and the show is aired on a later date appearing to be live.

local station: Usually a small television station that covers and supplies a specific area in a state. They often are connected to one of the major networks or can be privately owned. They often broadcast network shows and also shows that are locally produced and respond to that community. Movies, animation, news, and other sorts of programs can also be part of the schedule.

local station cut-in: A commercial on a local station substituted in whole or in part for a network commercial shown during a nationally televised program. Cut-ins are used for test marketing copy or products and for local dealer identification.

lower-third: A graphic overlay placed in the title safe lower area of the screen, often used to present text.

miniseries: A long form television event usually based on a substantial novel that usually runs every night in prime time for one to two hours for many days or longer. It is a novel for television and often takes a high rank in the ratings as the audience follows the usually epic story from night to night in a continuous narrative form.

network: A telecommunication network for the distribution of television program content. A central operation that provides programming to many television stations or pay television providers. Major networks include ABC, CBS, NBC, and Fox.

news ticker: A horizontal text displayed in the form of a graphic that reads in the lower third of the screen, giving information in letters that move from right to left. This is television's version of the moving electronic banners that spell out the news on the top of high buildings.

Nielsen ratings: An audience measuring system supplied by the Nielsen Company to determine the size and composition of television programming in the United States.

NTSC: The National Television System Committee is the analogue system that was utilized in most of the Americas. It is a standard of technical aspects of television that are maintained by all broadcasters.

pay per view: Providers who offer special events, sporting events, adult entertainment, and concerts for a fee. Customers order via telephone or using their remote control. Once payment is received, viewers go to a specific channel on a specific day and time, and when the program starts, it will become active on their set.

pilot: A sample of a television series to sell to a network. This special episode, the first of a series, usually contains a lot of information about the characters and story to entice viewers. Many pilots are made and sold but far fewer are bought with a commitment for an order of a particular number of episodes to air on the station or network.

prime time access rule: A regulation enacted by the FCC in 1970 to restrict the amount of programming a local television station either owned and operated or affiliated with a television network can air during prime time—repealed in 1996.

simulcast: When a radio station and a television station broadcast a particular program in synch. The early simulcasts in the 1960s broadcast music and maybe narration and dialogue in stereo. These experiments were moving toward stereo television and later surround sound systems for the home.

split-screen: When the television image is split into two or more structural shapes to communicate to the viewer what is happening in two or more places.

spot: A television commercial.

superstation: An independent broadcast station whose signal is picked up and redistributed by satellite to local cable television stations.

syndicated program: A program offered by an independent organization or producer, sold to a local station for local sponsorship.

teaser: Also called a cold opening. A short scene designed to get viewers curious and interested to see the show that follows. Teasers often end with a murder or some suspenseful event.

test pattern: An image with precise patterns to be used by engineers to perfect the broadcast image.

It also was a sign that there was no programming available at the moment and when it was taken off the screen a show would begin.

UHF: Ultra High Frequency. These channels are usually given higher numbers on the dial or remote.

VHS: Video Home System. A standard for consumer-level analog video recording on videocassettes.

voice-over (VO): A narrator or a character in a show speaking to the viewer without being seen. Used in news broadcasts as well.

Index

About the Author

Vincent LoBrutto is a film instructor in the Department of Film, Video, and Animation at the School of Visual Arts in Manhattan. He is the author of numerous books on filmmaking, including *Stanley Kubrick: A Biography* (Penguin, 1999), *Martin Scorsese: A Biography* (Praeger, 2007), and *Gus Van Sant: His Own Private Cinema* (Praeger, 2010). In 2010 Vincent LoBrutto received the Robert Wise Award for Journalistic Illumination of the Art of Editing from the American Cinema Editors Society.